SECOND EDITION
CRIME
AND
CRIMINOLOGY

JAY LIVINGSTON
MONTCLAIR STATE UNIVERSITY

PRENTICE HALL
UPPER SADDLE RIVER, NJ 07458

Library of Congress Cataloging-in-Publication Data

Livingston, Jay.
    Crime and criminology/Jay Livingston.—2nd ed.
      p. cm.
    Includes bibliographical references and indexes.
    ISBN 0-13-328006-3
    1. Criminology. 2. Crime—United States. I. Title.
  HV6025.L537 1996
  364—dc20   95-36406
                                    CIP

Editor-in-chief: Nancy Roberts
Associate editor: Sharon Chambliss
Cover art: Kathy Willens © 1991/AP/Wide World Photos
Editorial/production supervision
  and electronic page makeup: Rob DeGeorge
Copy editor: Barbara Conner
Cover and interior design: Maria Lange
Buyer: Mary Ann Gloriande
Editorial assistant: Pat Naturale

 © 1996, 1992 by Prentice-Hall, Inc.
Simon & Schuster/A Viacom Company
Upper Saddle River, New Jersey 07458

Printed in the United States of America

10 9 8 7 6 5 4 3 2 1

ISBN 0-13-328006-3

Prentice-Hall International (UK) Limited, *London*
Prentice-Hall of Australia Pty. Limited, *Sydney*
Prentice-Hall Canada Inc., *Toronto*
Prentice-Hall Hispanoamericana, S.A., *Mexico*
Prentice-Hall of India Private Limited, *New Delhi*
Prentice-Hall of Japan, Inc., *Tokyo*
Simon & Schuster Asia Pte. Ltd., *Singapore*
Editora Prentice-Hall do Brasil, Ltda., *Rio de Janeiro*

CONTENTS

CHAPTER THREE   50

THE NUMBERS GAME: COUNTING CRIME

PART TWO: CRIMES AND CRIMINALS

CHAPTER SIX   182

VIOLENT CRIMES, PART II: WOMEN AND CHILDREN

CHAPTER NINE   282

WHITE-COLLAR CRIME

PART THREE: THEORIES OF CRIME

CHAPTER TEN   305

BIOLOGICAL AND PSYCHOLOGICAL THEORIES

CHAPTER ELEVEN   338

SOCIOLOGICAL THEORY TO 1960: OPPORTUNITIES AND ASSOCIATES

CHAPTER FOURTEEN 436

COURTS AND RIGHTS

CHAPTER FIFTEEN 473

REHABILITATION

CHAPTER SIXTEEN   498

DETERRENCE

CHAPTER SEVENTEEN   527

INCAPACITATION

PREFACE

Criminology textbooks are not like a box of chocolates. For the most part, you know what you're going to find: the chapters on crime statistics, on theory, on typologies of crime, on the criminal justice system, and so on. At least for the moment, there seems to be substantial agreement among criminologists on the important topics, the noteworthy theories, and the sources of data. With the exception of a few books dedicated to a single theoretical orientation, we are all singing the same song. What distinguishes one book from another is the arrangement—the style of presentation and the relative emphasis given to different topics.

While books overlap considerably in the topics they cover, they vary in the weight they assign to those topics. One of the reasons I began writing a textbook over a decade ago was that I was dismayed at the timid way that the available textbooks skipped quickly over questions of race and social class. Admittedly, the topics are controversial and the evidence is sometimes ambiguous. But these are crucial subjects both for the public and for criminologists.

I had three main goals when I wrote this book: first, to address questions that students might ask, while prodding them to see the relevance of other questions that might not have occurred to them; second, to answer these questions with systematic evidence from actual research; and third, to present this material in a way that keeps it interesting without oversimplifying what are often complicated issues. (One reviewer of the first edition, a professor at a community college, feared that the prose was *too* accessible, so much so that students might not realize it contained important and sophisticated ideas.)

These goals remain the core of the book, and accordingly this second edition has incorporated some notable changes. Wherever possible, I have provided the latest data, though to many students reading this, at the earliest, in 1996, crime statistics from 1993 may seem more like history than like late-breaking news. I have also tried to present more data in the form of graphs, converting abstract numbers into concrete visual figures. This edition also has far more boxes, organized into three main categories. I especially like the "On Campus" boxes, for although colleges hardly qualify as criminal hot spots, they can provide examples of more general concepts and issues in criminology. Boxes labeled "About Crime & Criminology" offer brief summaries of exemplary pieces of research. The "In the News" boxes are intended to show that the concrete facts in a news item are better understood and appreciated when placed in the context of the broader and more abstract ideas of criminology.

While I have revised, updated, re-researched, occasionally deleted, and in some cases rethought the material in the first edition, the format of the book remains the same:

PART ONE   The introductory chapter departs from standard criminology textbook protocol; it does not offer legal definitions of crime or an elaborate discussion of various methods of criminological research. Instead, it merely tries to defend empirical social science and evidence-based thinking. Its message is that in explanations of human behavior (as opposed to the "hard" sciences), what separates science from everyday talk is the systematic quality of the evidence. Using systematic evidence for assessing empirical questions seems like a stunningly obvious notion. But in an era when multibillion dollar policies are sold to the public on the basis of a slogan and a sound bite, social science must justify its principles all the more clearly.

Chapter Two starts with a seemingly naive question: Why is crime a problem? That is, what's bad about crime? Answering this question leads to consideration of popular images of crime, the costs of various types of crime, and some paradoxical evidence on the relation between fear and victimization. The latter half of the chapter explores crime as a political issue and represents my attempt to explain how over the last thirty years, the politics of crime has become the politics of race. Chapter Three begins with an evaluation of the Uniform Crime Reports and National Crime Victimization Survey as measures of crime, then compares the pictures they present of crime rates since 1973. The second part of the chapter outlines the conservative and liberal explanations for two well-documented changes in crime in the United States—the decrease in crime in the decades following the Civil War and the increase in crime in the 1960s. Chapter Four focuses on four demographic dimensions—age, sex, race, and social class—and asks three basic questions: What are the differences within each variable? How can we explain those differences? And why do different measures of crime give different profiles on these dimensions?

PART TWO   The first three chapters of this section examine in detail the "Index crimes," following the FBI's violent/property categories, although rape and family violence are subdivided into a separate category. The chapters present a mix of quantitative and qualitative evidence—data on incidence and prevalence, as well as trends and correlations, along with quotations from typical criminals. The next two chapters take a similar approach to organized crime and white-collar crime, two topics where, unfortunately, criminology must usually make do with case studies, courtroom evidence, and journalistic accounts rather than quantitative data.

PART THREE   After brief discussions of the idea of theory and the development of classical theory, this section has one chapter devoted to biological and psychological explanations of crime and two chapters on sociological explanations. Although these chapters group theories into major categories, the overall presentation follows a more or less chronological path.

PART FOUR These chapters on the criminal justice system generally emphasize the impact the police, courts, and corrections have on crime. The chapter on police also offers a historical outline—from the prepolice institutions of earlier centuries to today's community policing approach—and a discussion of police misconduct (brutality and corruption). The chapter on courts presents the historical and constitutional bases of legal "technicalities," including a discussion of a few landmark cases and an assessment of their impact on crime and the criminal justice system. The last three chapters, rather than discussing the internal, administrative, and legal problems involved in corrections (issues more relevant for criminal justice textbooks), are devoted almost entirely to the effect prisons have on crime—through rehabilitation, deterrence, or incapacitation.

SUPPLEMENTS

INSTRUCTOR'S MANUAL WITH TRANSPARENCY MASTERS (0-13-375114-7) This unique manual includes chapter summaries, lecture notes, class activities, discussion questions, term paper topics, a complete audio-visual listing correlated to each chapter, and key terms defined in the context of their meaning to the chapter. Also included are over one hundred transparency masters. All are designed to provide the professor with tools for an orderly and innovative presentation of textual materials.

TEST ITEM FILE (0-13-375122-8) The Test Bank consists of over eight hundred multiple-choice, true/false, and essay questions. All questions are page-referenced to the text.

PRENTICE HALL CUSTOM TEST This state-of-the-art electronic classroom management system offers testing options on all platforms (DOS, Windows, and Macintosh).

 ABC NEWS/PRENTICE HALL VIDEO LIBRARY: CRIMINOLOGY, SERIES I (0-13-375163-5) Selected video segments from award-winning ABC News programs such as *Nightline*, *ABC World News Tonight/American Agenda*, and *20/20* offer a resource for feature and documentary-style videos related to the chapters in *Crime and Criminology, Second Edition*. The programs have extremely high production quality, present substantial content, and are hosted by well-versed, well-known anchors.

Prentice Hall and its authors and editors provide the benefit of having selected videos and topics that work well with this course and text.

ACKNOWLEDGMENTS

I have discovered and developed the ideas and information in this book over several years of teaching criminology. To all those people, though they are far too numerous to list here by name—students, colleagues, and friends who asked questions, offered ideas, or just listened as I tried to sort out my thoughts—I owe the largest debt of gratitude. I have also benefited from the advice of the following reviewers who offered valuable comments and critiques:

Bruce J. Arneklev (University of Oklahoma), Christopher Birkbeck (University of New Mexico), Sarah L. Boggs (University of Missouri–St. Louis), Mitchell Chamlin (University of Oklahoma), Russell Craig (Ashland University), Tim Garner (Franklin College), Richard J. Lundman (Ohio State University), Lawrence Rosen (Temple University), Richard Vandiver (University of Montana). For comments on various sections of the manuscript and discussion of specific issues, I wish to thank Candace Clark, David Dodd, Sylvia J. Ginnot, Jennifer Hunt, Roger Lane, Amy Srebnick, S. A. Livingston, Peter Reuter, B. T. Bear, and Wesley Skogan.

Thanks also to Sharon Chambliss and Rob DeGeorge and the rest of the editorial and production staff at Prentice Hall.

Finally, a very special thanks to my wife, Joan Tedeschi, for her love and support throughout the years of this book's existence, and to Max Livingston, a source of much joy during the years I have been writing this edition.

CHAPTER ONE

COMMON SENSE AND SOCIAL SCIENCE

AN INTRODUCTION

CHAPTER OUTLINE

ON SCIENTIFIC THINKING AND OTHER MATTERS, OR WHAT DO I KNOW THAT A 16-YEAR-OLD DOESN'T?

One evening, on the way from the elevator to my apartment, I fell into a conversation with my neighbor's son, a bright boy of 15 or 16. He asked me what I was teaching, and when I said, "criminology," he asked what that was about. By this time, we were at the doors of our respective apartments and I wanted to say something quick yet impressive.

"Well, we try to figure out the reasons for the increase in crime," I said.

"That's easy," he said, and suddenly I found myself wondering what I had missed. How could questions I had been puzzling about for the last several years have an easy answer—an answer that had eluded me but was obvious to this teenager?

"It is?" I asked.

"Sure," he said, "the decline in morality."

At the time, I was uncertain how to respond. I couldn't tell him that he was wrong, for he might well have been right. Still, I knew that there was something wrong with his answer—but what? I was thankful that my key was

A picture may be worth a thousand words, but most likely they are words of anecdotal evidence. What general conclusions can we draw from this news photo? That most crime involves rioting? That most crime is angry and emotional rather than profit-oriented? Can we draw general conclusions about crime based solely on anecdotal evidence?

already in the lock and that I could avoid answering by merely stepping into my apartment, which is exactly what I did.

I had a similar experience one semester when I began my criminology course by asking students to compose questions for the final exam: "Ask the kinds of questions that you would like to be able to answer after taking a course in criminology." The most popular question, in various wordings, was "Why is there so much crime?" I then asked students to answer the question. At first they balked—after all, answering questions was the teacher's job—but when I insisted, they came up with answers. Among other factors they mentioned were poverty, unemployment, drugs, peer pressure, the breakdown of the family, the leniency of the courts, and the decline in morality.

At this point I realized that the students' answers were strikingly similar to the leading theories in criminology. I was facing the same problem my neighbor had raised, only worse, for this time I could not avoid it: If everybody already knows the answer to "What are the reasons for crime?" then what do I have left to teach them for the rest of the semester?

EVIDENCE

Only much later did I realize what the real problem was. It was not in people's answers to questions about crime; it was in my definition of the subject I teach. Criminology is not really about figuring out the reasons for crime. Most people, it turns out, offer answers very similar to those offered by criminologists who devote their working lives to these matters. Instead, what criminology is all about is finding out what we know about the questions that are raised and the answers that are given. That is, what is the evidence, and how can we refine our ideas to make them more consistent with it? The evidence is important because it allows us to test ideas to see to what extent they are true or false. Most of the time, of course, the evidence is not so conclusive as to prove that an idea is absolutely true or absolutely false. Instead, social scientists usually speak in terms of whether the evidence *supports* the idea.

In other words, what differentiates criminology (or any social science) from everyday conversation is that science tries to anticipate one question: What if people disagree? Suppose I had said to my neighbor, "You say that the cause of crime is the decline in morality. My other neighbor says that morality has nothing to do with it. How can I know that you're right and he's wrong?"

LOGIC AND COMMON SENSE

"It's obvious," my neighbor might have said. "Everybody knows that the level of morality has been going down. And if people are less moral, they're going to commit more crime."

At first this argument sounds persuasive. It certainly seems to me that morality is at a lower point than it was when I was younger. My neighbor's second statement about the morality-crime connection is also perfectly logical. The only problem is that he has not provided any evidence. He has offered common sense or common knowledge, and he has offered logic. But he has not offered any evidence. In everyday discussions, common sense, common knowledge, and logical deductions provide most of the support for people's arguments. But social science requires evidence to make sure that common sense and logic are actually right; sometimes, what is logical, or what everybody "knows," turns out to be wrong.

THE FIRE SERMON   Each semester, after the introductory class, I begin my criminology course with a quiz. Since it's only the second day of class, I don't expect anyone to know the answers, but I do ask students to make their best guesses. One of the first questions is this:

- Which of the following accounts for more deaths in the United States each year?
    - a. fires
    - b. drownings
    - c. neither—they are about the same

Nearly everyone selects fires. Nobody actually knows, although most people are very sure of their choice. Then I ask for the reasons for this answer. Some students have trouble coming up with a reason. It just seemed obvious, like common sense. After a moment for further thought, usually someone will say that you see more fires on the news. Other students reason that everybody lives in a building and is therefore at risk for fires, but only those who spend time on the water can die by drowning. Along the same lines, some students reason that we live in buildings all year round but spend only the summer months near the water. Still others say that a single fire can kill several people at once, but drowning is more an individual matter.

Another question I might ask is this:

- Who suffers a higher rate of death on the job?
    - a. police officers
    - b. agricultural workers

Most of us would answer *a*. If a police officer is killed on the job, it's usually front-page news, often for days, and in fictional television and movies, cops are shot every evening. But although these killings make good stories, police officers suffer less death on the job than do agricultural workers, who die in accidents. Moreover, as many officers are killed by accidents as by intentional homicide, though of course news of accidental deaths, even for the police, makes less of an impression.

EVIDENCE—SYSTEMATIC AND ANECDOTAL

These are all good reasons, often good enough to convince the few people who originally selected the other choices. But these reasons, for the most part, are not evidence. Evidence refers not to what logically *should be* but to what actually *is*. To give another example, many people believe that instituting capital punishment in their state will reduce crime. "If you stood to lose your life," they reason, "wouldn't you be less likely to kill someone?" This again is logic, not evidence. The evidence on what actually happens when states pass death penalty laws does little to confirm this logic.

But now suppose that during our death penalty discussion someone says, "I heard about this guy in some state where they'd just passed a death penalty for cop killers. He had a gun when he was arrested and was going to shoot, but he didn't. He said later that he could see going to prison for ten years for a robbery, but he wasn't going to risk losing his life for shooting a cop." Isn't this evidence that the death penalty works?

Yes, it is evidence. It refers to something that actually happened. But it is a special kind of evidence—what social scientists call **anecdotal evidence**. An anecdote is a story, usually about a single event. It provides an excellent illustration of some idea. The problem is not with the fact (the event did actually happen) but whether it represents reality in general. Is this potential cop killer typical of most other potential cop killers, or is he a rare exception? Can we go from one instance to a large generalization about cop-killer laws? (The answer is no. The death penalty for cop killing has had no general deterrent effect on the killing of police officers.)[1] Does the ratio of fires to drownings that you see on the news represent their true proportion in the real world?

Anecdotal evidence is useful for illustrating a point, but for providing information that would allow us to generalize, it is usually inadequate. Anecdotal evidence, like the preceding story, may be interesting. But if you are thinking scientifically, you should not find it very convincing. Suppose, for example, that I said that the crime rate was going down, and when you asked me for evidence, I said, "Well, I have a friend who was mugged last year, but he wasn't mugged this year." Would you find this to be convincing or adequate evidence for a decline in the crime rate? Probably not. Instead, you would want more **systematic evidence**. By systematic, I mean evidence that is gathered according to fairly regular procedures so that anybody who used those procedures would arrive at similar results. Anecdotal data usually fail this test. If you, too, asked a friend about victimization this year and last year, both of us would be using the same procedure—asking a friend about victimization—but we would probably get different results.

The most obvious type of systematic evidence comes to us in the form of statistics, or **quantitative data**—numbers that tell us how much of something there is. But nonstatistical, **qualitative data** from intensive interviews or participant observation may also be systematic. Some of the best and most durable studies in social science have been qualitative studies based on systematic observation. These studies usually describe how something works—a town government, a criminal gang, a marriage, a mental hospital. The choice of evidence—quantitative or qualitative—depends on the question being asked. If we want to know how much, we need quantitative data; if we want

ABOUT CRIME & CRIMINOLOGY

The problem with anecdotal evidence is that it may not be representative. But as a psychology experiment shows, anecdotal evidence influences people's opinions even when they are told that the evidence is unusual and in no way representative.

Subjects were asked to watch a videotaped interview with a prison guard (in reality a confederate of the experimenter) who acted in one of two ways, either a cold, inhumane person, or as a warm, caring individual. Half the subjects were told that this individual was highly representative of prisons guards; the other half were told he was atypical and unrepresentative. After watching the interview, subjects were asked to give their impressions of prison guards in general (not the individual they had seen being interviewed). The information regarding the representativeness of the guard being interviewed should have been critical to subjects. In fact, they were influenced only by the behavior of the specific individual in the interview. Those who had seen a brutal guard thought that most prison officers were inhumane; those who saw a warm individual believed that most guards were of a similar disposition.

Source: Julian V. Roberts, "Public Opinion, Crime, and Criminal Justice," in Michael Tonry, ed., *Crime and Justice: A Review of Research*, vol. 16 (Chicago: University of Chicago Press, 1992), pp. 121–122. Original research by Ruth Hamill, Timothy Wilson, and Richard Nisbett, "Insensitivity to Sample Bias: Generalizing from Atypical Cases," *Journal of Personality and Social Psychology*, vol. 39 (1980), 578–589.

to know how something works, we need qualitative data. In either case, we must be sure the evidence has been gathered systematically.

Of course, to rely on anecdotal evidence (telling stories) is much easier—easier to do and easier to understand. Some people even dismiss systematic quantitative evidence: "Oh, you can prove anything with statistics." In fact, the reverse is true. If you accept anecdotal evidence as proof, you can prove anything, for no matter how implausible the proposition, you can find at least one story that supports it: "Smoking cigarettes makes you live longer. My grandfather smoked two packs a day and he lived to be 96."

DEATH BY WATER   Let's return from this digression to our question about fires and drownings. In class, much of the logical reasoning and most of the anecdotal evidence (stories that students have heard) point to fire as the cause of more deaths. But the systematic evidence, gathered by various agencies and presented as quantitative data, gives a different answer (see Table 1–1). Each year, drowning accounts for about 25 percent *more* deaths than do fires, a fact that surprises nearly everyone.

VARIABLES

Obtaining systematic evidence to test ideas about crime is much more complicated. Let's take my neighbor's idea that a decline in morality is responsible for the increase in crime. The task for the social scientist is to make this

TABLE 1-1 •
ACCIDENTAL DEATHS IN THE U.S.

YEAR	FIRES	DROWNING
1970	6,700	7,900
1975	6,100	8,200
1980	5,800	7,500
1985	4,900	5,500
1986	4,800	5,900
1987	4,700	5,400
1988	5,000	5,300
1989	4,700	4,900
1990	4,200	4,900
1991	4,100	4,800

Source: Based on U.S. Bureau of the Census, *Statistical Abstract of the United States: 1983, 1986, 1989, 1992, 1993* (Washington, DC).

idea testable, that is, to state it so that we can get evidence to support or contradict it. To put the idea to any kind of scientific, systematic analysis, we have to separate it into its components. My neighbor was really making three assertions: (1) that morality has in fact declined, (2) that crime has in fact increased, and (3) that the decline in morality caused the increase in crime.

We have now translated the idea into a statement about the relationship between two **variables**. A variable is just what its name implies—something that can vary, that can have more than one category. Age is a commonly used variable. We can divide it into two categories (e.g., under 21, and 21 and up), or we can divide it into many categories (age 1, 2, 3, 4, etc.). Age need not always be a variable. For example, if we study only one age group—say, "people in their 30s"—without bothering to compare older 30s with younger 30s, age in this study is not a *variable* since we have only one category. In my neighbor's theory, the two variables are morality and crime.

DEFINING AND MEASURING VARIABLES

Our first task is to find out whether morality has decreased. But you can quickly see that a term like *morality* is subject to many different definitions. My idea of morality may be different from yours. But the principal problem is vagueness. To make the statement scientifically testable, we have to define morality so specifically that it can be measured. To say that morality has declined means that whatever morality is, there is less of it than there used to be. Whether the variable is something as vague as morality or as specific as a cause of death, as soon as we use concepts like more and less, we are talking about quantity. And if we are saying that there are different quantities of some-

ABOUT CRIME & CRIMINOLOGY

The theories of people who get paid for their ideas often resemble those of ordinary people. Irving Kristol, who writes frequently about social policy and edits a journal devoted to policy analysis, makes the argument that some of our current social problems are a result of the general decline in culture, a theory much like the one offered by my 16-year-old neighbor (who, however, might not have agreed with Kristol that teenagers having sex constitute a "plague").

If there is a connection between our popular culture and the plague of criminal violence we are suffering from, then is it not reasonable to think that there may also be such a connection between our popular culture and the plagues of sexual promiscuity among teenagers, teenage illegitimacy, and, yes, the increasing number of rapes committed by

teenagers? Here again, *we don't really need social science to confirm what common sense and common observations tell us to be the case.* [emphasis added]

Can anyone really believe that soft porn in our Hollywood movies, hard porn in our cable movies, and violent porn in our "rap" music is without effect?[*]

The problem, of course, is evidence. It may indeed be that watching movies makes teenagers more likely to have sex, to shun contraception and marriage, and to carry the baby to term rather than to get an abortion. It may be that it is but a short step from rap to rape. But in these as in other matters, common sense is not evidence. Common sense and common observations also tell us that fires kill several times more peo-

thing, we ought to have some way of measuring them. Of course, it takes some thought and ingenuity to figure out a way to define morality so that it is countable. But unless we do so, we have little hope of getting adequate evidence.

Social scientists, criminologists included, have spent much time trying to devise ways of turning abstract concepts like social class, opportunity, peer pressure, anomie, sociopathy, or social attachment into measurable variables. Often the measurement depends on people's responses to a questionnaire. Some questions try to assess people's ideas—their **attitudes** or **beliefs**. For example, to measure morality, we might ask people how strongly they agree or disagree with a series of statements such as "Sometimes telling a lie is unavoidable" or "With government the way it is today, you really can't blame people for cheating a little on their income taxes." Other questions ask about actual **behavior**. Our morality questionnaire might ask students whether during exams they have looked at the papers of others seated near them and, if so, how regularly. It is far beyond the scope of this book to go into all the complexities of constructing a scale or index of morality. I certainly hope I never have to construct such a scale, for no matter which items I included and how I phrased the questions or counted the behavior, many people would object that I had left out something important—and they would probably be right. Still, although even the best-constructed scale is subject to criticism, these measures do provide evidence for the purposes of testing ideas.

In criminology, the second part of our task is usually the definition and measurement of crime. Although crime is a less elusive variable than morality, ple than do drownings and that the police are at greater risk of death on the job than agricultural workers. And as we have seen, both these plausible ideas are contradicted by the evidence.

When someone—even a policy expert or a social scientist—says that we don't need evidence, it usually means that the supporting scientific evidence doesn't exist. Another strategy is to say that evidence is inferior to less scientific ways of knowing—as in the following example:

> The best evidence that the death penalty has a uniquely deterrent impact ... is not based on statistics but is rather based on common sense and experience. Death is an awesome and awful penalty, qualitatively different from a prison term.... Common sense can sufficiently verify that the prospect of punishment by death does exert a restraining effect on some criminals who would otherwise commit a capital crime.[†]

Calling common sense evidence does not make it evidence. As it happens, social science has amassed quite a bit of systematic evidence on the deterrent effect of the death penalty. Nearly all of these systematic studies conclude that the death penalty does *not* have a uniquely deterrent impact. It is no more effective than ordinary punishments like prison in deterring murder.

[*]Irving Kristol, "Sex, Violence and Videotape," *Wall Street Journal,* May 31, 1994, p. A16.
[†]Charles E. Rice, *The New American,* June 8, 1987.

it still raises questions—questions about which crimes to count and where to find statistics about them. The first half of Chapter Three explores these problems in much more detail, so for now I will say only that any measure of crime, like any measure of morality, will have its imperfections. In fact, an important question for criminologists is "How do we know how much crime there really is?" Or, put somewhat differently, "How good are our measures of crime?" To noncriminologists, defining and measuring variables may seem "merely technical" and therefore of little interest. But that's the difference between criminology and everyday discussions of crime. Criminology is concerned with *evidence*, and criminologists want to know how good that evidence is.

SOCIAL SCIENCE GENERALIZATIONS

The third part of the task—showing that a change in one variable causes a change in the other—is usually the most difficult part of social science. Even if the data show that thirty years ago morality was higher and crime was lower than they are today, that would not necessarily mean that one caused the other. Establishing a *causal* relationship between two variables is difficult, and it often involves sophisticated mathematical techniques. In some sections of this book, while discussing some actual research, I will try to describe some of the problems and methods of establishing a connection between variables.

The difficulties are such that often social scientists do not even use the word *cause*. Even when they can show that the two variables are related, they will instead say, for example, that lower morality "is associated with" higher levels of crime.

Most of the conclusions and evidence in criminology (certainly most of those you will find in this book) concern groups, not individuals. Suppose that we constructed some measure of morality and found that indeed morality was higher thirty years ago than it is now. This statement is a generalization about the difference between two groups—Americans of thirty years ago and Americans today. (Keep in mind that I am not presenting any real evidence of such a change; this example is entirely hypothetical.) But this does not mean that *every* American in the 1960s was more moral than *every* American in the 1990s. In all generalizations, even ones we are fairly certain of (e.g., men are taller than women), there will be many exceptions, so we must be careful about using a fact about group differences to make predictions about individuals.

In applying generalizations to individual cases, social science uses the language of **probability**. We cannot say with certainty that if you smoke, you will develop lung or heart disease. We can say only that if you smoke, you will increase your probability of getting these diseases. Even if smoking increased that probability to 90 percent, you might still be among the 10 percent who remain healthy. Yet just as one anecdote does not prove a generalization, the negative example of the healthy smoker does not disprove the generalization. In this case, we know that 10 cases out of 100 will be just such negative examples.

As you read this book, and more important, when you see news items about crime, I hope you will remember these distinctions and try to ask the right questions about the evidence and the generalizations.

WHAT YOU WILL NOT FIND IN THIS BOOK

Because so much of criminology revolves around these generalizations about group differences and about probability, it often ignores the individual case, especially if that case is highly unusual. Everyday discussions of crime, on the other hand, often focus precisely on the highly unusual case—the one that is in the headlines today, the one that gives rise to best-selling books and TV miniseries. But as I explain in the next chapter, criminology is not television. In this book, there will be no lengthy probing of unusually depraved, ingenious, or unexpected crimes.

Nor will this book have much to say about the solution of particular crimes. It will contain very little about criminalistics or police science—dogged investigation, high-tech tests of bullets or blood, and Sherlock Holmes–like deductions—though these are precisely the elements that make for a good story on the screen or in novels. In fact, the image of crime we get from television, movies, and fiction is one of ingenious (or psychotic) criminals eventually caught by even more ingenious and heroic police officers (mixed in with much gunfire and tire screeching). Certainly such cases exist, but most crimes involve fairly ordinary techniques on the part of both the criminal and the police.

This book lacks something else as well—an answer to the crime problem. You may find the absence of answers frustrating, but a moment's thought should rid you of such expectations. If there were an answer, certainly somebody would have discovered it by now and the problem would have been long since solved. (Also, if by some chance I were the only person with the answer, I could probably find other outlets for my unique knowledge, outlets more socially beneficial and more financially rewarding than writing a college textbook.)

In fact, perhaps it is misleading to talk about crime in terms of problems and answers, as if a complicated social issue were like one of those algebra problems whose answer could be found in the back of the book. To be sure, there are answers—ensure that every criminal is punished, eliminate poverty, provide opportunity, strengthen the family, improve education—but to translate an answer into a policy raises further questions, questions of economics, law, morality, and politics. So although this book may not have *the* answer, it does offer in the next chapter some questions and some evidence about the crime problem.

CRITICAL THINKING QUESTIONS

1. How is criminology different from everyday discussions about crime?
2. Why is evidence so important, and what kinds of evidence are there?
3. Why do criminologists look more at differences between groups than at differences between individuals?

KEY TERMS

anecdotal evidence	beliefs	quantitative data
attitudes	probability	systematic evidence
behavior	qualitative data	variables

CHAPTER TWO

THE CRIME PROBLEM

CHAPTER OUTLINE

FEAR OF CRIME

Why is crime a problem?

Every year, the opinion polls ask people to name the most important problems facing the country. You can imagine some of the choices: inflation, unemployment, peace, the environment, AIDS, education, drugs, crime, abortion, and others. Every year, I ask my students the same question, and usually several select crime as one of the top three. My next question—the one that opens this chapter—sounds rather stupid, especially coming from someone who teaches criminology. But it's my job to ask questions whose answers seem to be obvious. Often students will say that crime is a problem because there's so much of it. But "so much" of something is a problem only if that something is bad.

"Why is crime bad?" I ask. "What's wrong with crime?" This question sounds even more stupid, but I ask students to humor me and try to answer it. Often the first thing someone will say is "People get hurt." True enough. Criminals sometimes injure or even kill their victims. But more than twice as

Nearly 40 percent of Americans say they fear crime, and the proportion is greater in high-crime neighborhoods. The fear is probably more a response to visible disorder than to actual levels of predatory crime.

many people are killed by automobile accidents than by murder. Faulty consumer products and home accidents injure more people than do crimes like assault and robbery. Accidents at work and job-related diseases cause more deaths and physical harm than do murders, rapes, robberies, and other street crimes. For example, in 1992, about 3,300 people were murdered by strangers. Even adding the 9,300 murder victims whose relationship to the murderer was unknown, this number is still less than the more than 22,000 people who died in accidents at home or at work or the 40,000 who died on the highways.[1] People risk death, disease, and injury at work, at home, or on the road every day; yet not very many people would identify highway safety or dangerous working conditions as one of the nation's most important problems.

What about the costs of crime? Yes, crime costs money. But the crimes that cost the most money (and do the most physical harm) are *not* "the crime problem," which most people think of as murder, rape, robbery, burglary, and theft. The cost of these crimes, though, pales in comparison with the cost of the crimes they are not thinking of: white-collar crimes. Ways of defining and measuring the cost of white-collar crime vary. A quarter century ago, a congressional committee estimated the cost at $44 billion;[2] a Senate subcommittee on antitrust "estimated that faulty goods, monopolistic practices, and other violations annually cost consumers between $174 and $231 billion."[3] It is unlikely that the cost of white-collar crime has decreased since then. The outright fraud involved in the savings-and-loan collapse of the late 1980s is estimated at $20 billion, and the bank failures resulting from that fraud may cost the country as much as $150 billion. Tax cheating by individuals and corporations costs $100 billion each year.[4] In any case, even the lowest of these estimates far exceeds the $16 billion lost to street crime in 1992 (and of that $16 billion, more than $5 billion was eventually recovered).[5] Even if we leave out the crimes of businesses and corporations and look only at those done by individuals, the people who commit the truly costly crimes hardly fit the image of the hardened criminal. Banks, stores, and other businesses lose far more to their own employees through theft and embezzlement than they lose to shoplifters and robbers.[6] Also, the cost of responding to crime—money that goes for police, courts, prisons, parole, and so on—is currently about $60 billion, far higher than the amounts of money lost to street crime.

Why, then, when people talk about the crime problem do they mean street crime and not white-collar crime or employee theft? For one thing, street crime seems to have a greater psychological impact on its victims. Victims of rape and robbery may suffer psychological effects—depression, anxiety, phobias—even years after the crime occurred, and unfortunately the criminal justice process often does little to ease their suffering. The same can be true for the relatives of murder victims. Even victims of nonviolent crimes like burglary may feel violated. The important difference between street crime and white-collar crime is that with street crime, the victimization is sudden and direct. With white-collar crime, by contrast, the victimization is indirect; the criminal is a few steps removed from those who wind up paying the price.

In shoplifting and employee theft, the real victim is the consumer, since the store or the corporation can cover its losses by charging higher prices. Because the company spreads the cost over a large number of people, no one person's loss is very noticeable. Other businesses also can pass along the cost of their victimization in a nearly invisible way that does not arouse public outrage. Few people know just what portion of their insurance premiums goes to cover insurance fraud or how much higher the interest on their savings accounts might be were it not for embezzlement; few people filling a prescription know the excess profit the drug company may be taking through illegal monopolistic practices. Yet even if people were aware of these extra costs, it is unlikely that they would see them as a grave social problem. Our response when we read about bribes, embezzlement, kickbacks, and price-fixing may range from indifference to anger to admiration. But we probably do not rank these crimes as threats to society.

Even for crimes that cause physical harm, the more indirect the link between cause and effect, between criminal and victim, the weaker will be the public reaction. If air or water pollution from a chemical plant doubles cancer rates in a region, the cause-effect link is almost invisible—especially since it may be decades before the diseases appear. The same gradual victimization occurs in occupational diseases like black lung among coal miners, brown lung among cotton workers, or asbestosis among asbestos workers (and their families). These diseases may cause higher rates of disability, death, and financial loss than do crimes like robbery, burglary, and assault.[7] Companies in these industries might even have prevented much of this suffering; but instead, in the interest of making profits, they avoided spending money for safety measures. In some cases they may have suppressed evidence of the dangers of their products.[8] Yet when people think of the crime problem, they think of street crime, not corporate crime.

Spending by private individuals and businesses can serve as a rough indicator of people's sense of the risk of victimization. It also is part of the indirect cost of crime.

- In 1977, spending on private security began to exceed public spending.

- By 1990, when governments spent $30 billion for law enforcement, private expenditures totaled $52 billion. Public law enforcement (mostly police) employed about 600,000 people. Private security employed 1.5 million, two and one-half times as many.

- In the early 1980s, 2 to 5 percent of American residences had burglar alarms. By 1990, the proportion had doubled to 10 percent, and may double again by the end of the decade. (Ninety-five to ninety-nine percent of all burglar alarm calls are false alarms.)[9]

Clearly, street crime can be psychologically damaging for some—though certainly not all—of its victims. But the victims of accidents at work or on the roads may also suffer aftereffects and become fearful in situations that recall the accident. The **fear of crime**, however, has come to affect nonvictims as well. It seems to have become pervasive in U.S. society. When so many people are afraid, the problem goes beyond individual fear. It changes the nature of social life for everyone. "Fear of crime," the authors of one study said, exaggerating perhaps a bit, "is slowly paralyzing American society."[10] Studies like this suggest a contrast between a low-crime society, where people walk about at night, gather in public places, and feel little fear and much goodwill toward others they meet, and a society where people sit armed behind locked doors and barred windows, suspicious and fearful of others. In the words of Charles Silberman, "Crime ... undermines the social order itself by destroying the assumptions on which it is based."[11] The crime problem, then, is not a matter of money or physical harm; many things that we do not think of as serious problems (job-related risks, car accidents, white-collar crime) cause more physical harm and financial loss. What makes crime a problem is the damage it causes to social life because of fear. According to this view, America has undergone a transformation from an open society to a fearful one, and crime—street crime—has been the cause.

HOW IMPORTANT IS FEAR OF CRIME?

This idea about crime and fear sounds logical, but the matter may not be quite so simple. We must reduce this general idea to a few questions that can then be tested against the available evidence. Has fear of crime been increasing? Has fear of crime changed American society? What is fear of crime? Is crime the cause of this fear? At first, some of the answers seem so obvious that asking the questions sounds at best naive, perhaps even stupid. But as we look more closely, we may find that what is obvious and logical may be difficult to prove and may even be wrong.

Measuring fear of crime is not so simple as it might sound. Different studies produce different results. One study in 1980 found that 40 percent of Americans were "highly fearful" of becoming victims of violent crime and that half of all households kept a gun for protection. These numbers are probably too high. True, about half the households in the country own guns, but most of them are for hunting or sport. As for fear, look at Figure 2–1, based on data from a 1989 survey.

Only 12 percent said that they were very fearful of becoming a victim of violent crime during an entire decade, and the rest of the population was equally divided between those who felt some degree of fear and those who felt none at all.[12]

There is little doubt that fear of crime has increased. For over a quarter century, polls have asked, "Are there any places within a mile of where you live where you'd be afraid to walk alone at night?" In 1967, about 31 percent of the population answered yes; by 1982, that figure had risen to 48 percent, though in the last decade, fear has declined somewhat.[13] More concretely, increased sales of guns, private guard services, burglar alarms, and other protection devices attest to increases in fear. The U.S. crime rate, as measured by the Uniform Crime Reports Index of Serious Crime, was about the same in 1993 as it was in 1981. Similar, too, were levels of fear (as measured by the Gallup poll's question about being "afraid to walk alone at night." Yet compared with people in 1981, far more people in 1993 said that they had taken self-protective measures.[14] (See Figure 2–2, p. 18.)

There is also ample anecdotal evidence in people's reminiscences about less fearful times when they could safely walk anywhere, day or night; sleep

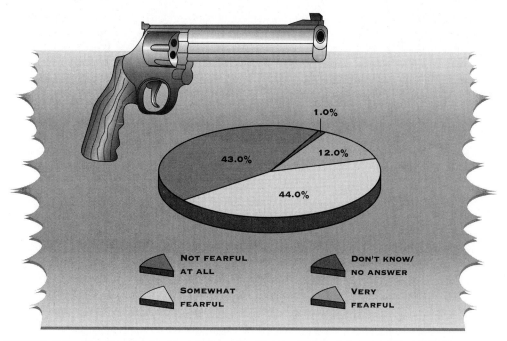

FIGURE 2–1   How Fearful Are You of Being the Victim of Violent Crime in the 1990s?

Sources: Research & Forecasts, Inc., with Andy Friedberg, *America Afraid: How Fear of Crime Changes the Way We Live (The Figgie Report)* (New York: New American Library, 1983). Frank A. Bennack, Jr., *The American Public's Hopes and Fears for the Decade of the 1990s* (New York: Hearst Corporation, 1989).

on fire escapes or in city parks; leave doors unlocked; and so on. Their routine behavior was different. In other words, fear is not just a feeling that people express in opinion polls; it changes the way they behave. Those who say they are more afraid are more likely to say that they have limited their behavior because of crime. Still, even among the most fearful people, one in three reported no such limitation of their activities.[15] These statistics suggest that while fear of crime has brought about some changes in American life, it has not "paralyzed American society."

WHO'S AFRAID?

Whatever the consequences of fear of crime, we must still ask, "What *causes* fear of crime?" The obvious answer is that crime causes fear of crime. Fear has increased because crime has increased; when crime rates go down, fear will go down. This sounds like a logical idea, and some very general evidence supports it. The changes in fear of crime follow a pattern remarkably similar to the changes in the overall crime rate in the United States, as shown in Figure 2–3. When the crime rate rose or fell, levels of fear (as measured by the "afraid to walk alone at night" question) followed in the same direction a year or two

FIGURE 2–2 Measures of Self-protection, 1981, 1993 (percent saying they do or have done)

Source: Gallup poll data reprinted in Flanagan and McLeod, *Sourcebook—1982* and Maguire and Pastore, *Sourcebook—1993*.

later. We also know that people in high-crime neighborhoods are more likely to say that they feel unsafe than are people in low-crime neighborhoods. Where there's more crime, there's more fear.

However, the connection between crime and fear may not be quite so direct or clear. Attempts to link fear specifically with crime often turn up puzzling results. One early study on crime and fear, carried out in the mid-1960s as part of a presidential commission report on crime, surveyed people in Washington, D.C., using the measure "exposure to crime," which included being a victim of a crime, a witness to a crime, or a close friend or relative of a victim. If crime creates fear, those who had been exposed should have been more fearful than others. But the two groups showed no differences in levels of fear. It turned out that people who had been exposed to crime were no more fearful than those who had not been so exposed.[16] Does this mean that exposure to crime does not create fear of crime? Not quite.

When the evidence fails to support a logical idea, we may need to change or refine or even throw out that idea. But first, we ought to check the way in which we defined and measured our variables. Measuring fear by asking people if there are places within a mile of home where they would be afraid to walk alone at night probably tells us more about neighborhoods than about individual fear. The questions about exposure to crime might also have been off-target since many of the crimes people said they were exposed to might not have been very frightening. If you return to the parking lot this afternoon to find that someone has broken into your car and taken the radio and some books and tapes, you will probably be angry, and you may be more careful

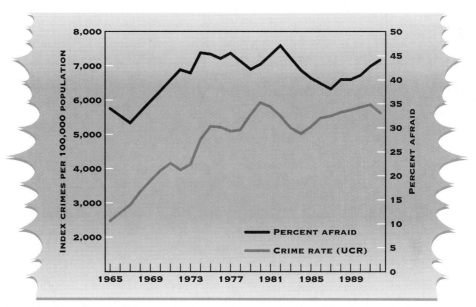

FIGURE 2–3   Fear and Crime, 1965–1992 (percent afraid and total crime rate)

Source: UCR, Gallup poll, and Roper pole data. Reprinted in Maguire and Pastore, *Sourcebook—1993*.

about where you park. But it is unlikely that you will feel generally more fearful or be more afraid to walk alone at night even in that parking lot.

Converting concepts like fear and crime into measurable variables is only one methodological problem; good research must also isolate its variables from everything else that may be affecting them. As later research showed, being victimized does in fact make a person more fearful. But this connection was hidden behind several other causes of fear that made it more difficult to distinguish the effects of victimization alone.

To see how the connections between variables can be hidden and uncovered, consider the following results from a later survey on the same question. Researchers asked a sample of people how safe they generally felt, a wording that was probably an improvement over the "places within a mile" question. People were offered four choices: very safe, moderately safe, moderately unsafe, or very unsafe. To simplify matters, Tables 2–1 through 2–4 reduce the four possible responses to two categories—safe and unsafe, regardless of degree. The people also were asked whether they had experienced a "personal victimization" (rape, robbery, assault, or larceny with contact between offender and victim). Unlike the earlier exposure-to-crime questions, this question asks only for the kinds of crime most likely to cause fear. The researchers made a further distinction, dividing the sample into three groups: people who had no such victimization, people who had been victimized only once, and people who had been victimized twice or more. The survey polled 10,000 households in eight cities; the numbers in columns B and C are estimates (in thousands) for the entire population of these cities projected from this sample.

TABLE 2-1 •
FEAR AND VICTIMIZATION[a]

A NUMBER OF VICTIMIZATIONS	B NUMBER IN CATEGORY (1000s)	C NUMBER WHO FELT UNSAFE (1000s)	D PERCENT WHO FELT UNSAFE
NONE	2977	1329	45%
1	180	90	50%
2 OR MORE	33	15	45%

[a]Derived from James Garofalo, "Victimization and the Fear of Crime," *Journal of Research in Crime and Delinquency*, vol. 16, no. 1 (1979), 80–97.

Table 2–1 shows no consistent effect of victimization. Among those who had been most victimized and those who had not been victimized at all, the proportion of people who felt unsafe was the same (45 percent—columns A and D), and those who had been victimized once were only slightly more likely than the others to feel unsafe. How can this be? How can crime—direct, personal crime—have no consistent effect on fear? One possibility is that in this research, as in life, one of the things that often complicates matters is sex. To eliminate these complications we have to separate the men from the women, as shown in Tables 2–2 and 2–3.

Looking at men and women separately, we find what we expected: The more victimizations, the greater the percentage of people who say they felt unsafe. The victimized groups have an additional 10 percent (roughly) who say they felt afraid. What confused the issue in the unseparated data was the fact that women are both more likely to feel unsafe and *less* likely to have been victimized. Of the estimated 1,777,000 women, 95,000 (84,000 and 11,000) had been victimized—5.3 percent. Of the men, 118,000 of 1,413,000—or 8.3 per-

TABLE 2-2 •
MALES ONLY

A NUMBER OF VICTIMIZATIONS	B NUMBER IN CATEGORY (1000s)	C NUMBER WHO FELT UNSAFE (1000s)	D PERCENT WHO FELT UNSAFE
NONE	1295	321	25%
1	96	32	34%
2 OR MORE	22	8	36%
TOTAL	1413	361	

TABLE 2-3 •

FEMALES ONLY

A NUMBER OF VICTIMIZATIONS	B NUMBER IN CATEGORY (1000s)	C NUMBER WHO FELT UNSAFE (1000s)	D PERCENT WHO FELT UNSAFE
NONE	1682	1008	60%
1	84	58	69%
2 OR MORE	11	7	67%
TOTAL	1777	1073	

cent—had been victimized. Yet as you can see by comparing column D in both tables, much smaller percentages of men were fearful of crime.

Fear, then, depends not just on victimization but also on sex. Therefore, to eliminate sex as a source of confusion we have done what is called **controlling for a variable**, in this case sex. We control for a variable by holding it constant—that is, not letting it vary. When we looked only at men, sex ceased to be a variable. When we do look at sex as a variable, we see that it is quite an important one. To see this effect of sex, we control for victimization. We do this by looking at each level of victimization separately and comparing men with women at each level. For example, among those with no victimizations, 25 percent of the men but 60 percent of the women said they felt afraid. For people with one victimization, 34 percent of the men and 69 percent of the women were afraid. In both cases, women were more than twice as likely to say they were afraid.

There is still another factor in fear that we need to control for—age. Older people are less likely to be victims of crime but are more likely to feel unsafe. In Table 2–4, we have controlled for both sex and age. The percentage in each category represents the percentage feeling unsafe; the number in parentheses represents the total number in that category. For instance, in the category of men thirty-five or older who had not been victimized, there were an estimated 742,920 such persons, and of those 32 percent said they felt unsafe. Table 2–4 is re-created from the original research report.

By comparing across different categories, we can at last see that in all sex and age groups, victimization increased levels of fear, something that was not at all evident before we separated the data according to these categories.

Besides showing that victimization increased fear, these data tell us other interesting things. First, victimization was fairly rare. Only 5.7 percent of the total sample (and only 12.2 percent of the most victimized group—young males) had experienced a personal victimization. (Of the total, only 1.7 percent had been injured seriously enough to require medical attention.) Usually, the more serious the crime, the more unsafe it makes the victim feel—though not always. One study of women victims found that a purse snatching increased fear nearly as much as did a rape.[17] The results also show

TABLE 2-4 •

FEAR OF CRIME (PROPORTION RESPONDING "SOMEWHAT UNSAFE" OR "VERY UNSAFE") BY TOTAL NUMBER OF PERSONAL VICTIMIZATIONS DURING THE TWELVE MONTHS PRECEDING THE INTERVIEW, BY SEX AND AGE: EIGHT IMPACT CITIES AGGREGATE, 1975

MALES		FEMALES	
LESS THAN 35	35 OR OLDER	LESS THAN 35	35 OR OLDER
15%	32%	54%	64%
(551,974)	(742,920)	(661,380)	(1,001,074)
22%	54%	63%	77%
(61,404)	(34,753)	(48,183)	(35,887)
26%	56%	64%	56%
(15,930)	(6,181)	(8,196)	(3,021)

that there is more to fear than just crime itself. Less than 6 percent of the people had actually been victimized by any of the crimes, yet nearly half said they felt unsafe because of crime. Clearly, they were not basing their fears on their own experience with crime.

FEAR AND FAMILIARITY

All this research means, first, that our original idea that fear of crime is caused by crime was not wrong; it was just a bit oversimplified. Second, we might better think of fear not just as reaction to a crime but as a person's feeling about the immediate environment. That is, the factors that affect fear lie in three distinct areas: the person, the environment, and the relationship between the two. So far, we have seen how personal characteristics—such as having been a victim of a crime, being a woman, and being older—can contribute to feelings of vulnerability and fear. A person's relationship to the environment also may increase apprehension. Something as simple as unfamiliarity can create fear. The presidential commission found, not surprisingly, that people felt safest in their own neighborhoods. But this was true even for people who lived in high-crime areas; despite the high crime rates close to home, most people still felt safer there than in other neighborhoods with less crime.[18]

It is not just the unfamiliarity of an environment that causes fear. Remember, between 40 and 50 percent of the population say they feel unsafe at night in or close to their own neighborhoods. What is it about a neighborhood that makes people more afraid? The obvious answer, of course, is crime: The more crime in a neighborhood, the more fear. Here again is the idea of a

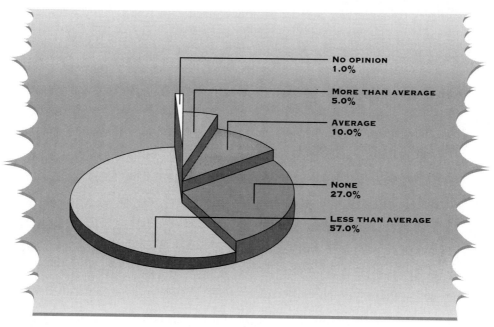

FIGURE 2–4   How Much Violent Crime Does Your Neighborhood Have?

Source: Based on *The Gallup Poll Monthly*, December 1993.

direct connection between crime and fear, only instead of looking at individual victimization and fear, we are looking at the neighborhood—its rate of crime and its level of fear. And as before, there is some evidence to support this idea: Surveys generally find that in areas of high crime, more people say they are afraid. But the question we must ask is whether it is the crime rate itself that makes people afraid.

As with research on individuals, research on fear and crime in neighborhoods is complicated by other variables. Areas that have a lot of crime are different from lower-crime areas in other ways as well. They usually have less money, more unemployment, and more single-parent families. And perhaps more important, high-crime neighborhoods often look different. Because all these characteristics tend to go together, it's hard to know which of them—the socioeconomic condition of the people, the high crime rate, or the appearance of the neighborhood—is most important in raising the level of fear.

If you think about it for a moment, the logical idea that crime itself is causing fear of crime might not seem so logical after all. For example, when you walk in a neighborhood—even your own—do you know the crime rate there? Do you really know whether it has been increasing or decreasing? Probably not. Even social scientists do not rely on statistical information in all their daily decisions. From time to time, I read newspaper items detailing local crime statistics; I usually clip and save these articles. But most of the time, as I walk down my street, I cannot recall whether my precinct reported increases or decreases, and I certainly cannot recall how many crimes there were or whether my precinct's statistics were higher or lower than those of other neighborhoods.

READING THE SIGNS OF CRIME[19]

If we don't know how much crime a neighborhood has, how do we arrive at our sense of safety or fear? Some interesting evidence on this topic comes from a 1977 study of four neighborhoods in Chicago.[20] All four had crime rates higher than the Chicago average. The researchers (Dan Lewis and Michael Maxfield) wanted to know about people's perceptions of typical predatory crimes—burglary, robbery, rape, and assault. They asked, "Where are the dangerous areas around here?" "How big a problem is each type of crime?" "How likely is it that you will be a victim?"

On the question of dangerous places, people generally had "a remarkably accurate picture of the crime problem they face" since they could identify the dangerous sections of their neighborhoods. But on the other questions, neighborhoods differed in some interesting ways. People in a section called Wicker Park were the most likely to rate crime as a big problem; they also gave relatively high estimates of their own personal risk. However, the official crime rate in Wicker Park was lower than that of two of the three other neighborhoods. Another neighborhood, Woodlawn, was much the reverse, with the highest incidence of crime (its rate of robbery was nearly double that of Wicker Park) yet lower levels of fear and concern. "Why," ask Lewis and Maxfield, "were the residents of Woodlawn seemingly unconcerned about the extraordinarily high rate of crime in their neighborhood? Why did the people in Wicker Park seem to live in fear when the rate of serious crime … was below that in Woodlawn?"

It might have been that Wicker Park had an older population since we know that older people tend to be more fearful yet less victimized. But no, it was just the opposite. In Woodlawn more than twice the proportion of the population was over 60 (22 percent vs. 8 percent in Wicker Park). Even with fewer older people and a crime rate 25 percent lower than that of Woodlawn, Wicker Park residents were more fearful. Why? A clue comes from some other questions the researchers asked—questions about problems in the neighborhood: teenagers hanging out in the street, vandalism, abandoned buildings, and drug use. The researchers grouped these **signs of crime** under the heading of **incivility**. This study was done before the cocaine and crack boom of the late 1980s. Most of the drugs involved were marijuana; heroin; and to a lesser extent, amphetamines. The study also predated the homeless—another feature of urban life that became more visible in the 1980s and would fall into the category of incivility. These are not **predatory crimes**, but they are, as other studies also have found, the kinds of things that make people feel uncomfortable and even afraid. More important, they are visible. Predatory crime rates are merely numbers on file in some government agency; even predatory criminals, who presumably make some effort to be inconspicuous, are less visible than abandoned buildings and other signs of disorder. Imagine yourself walking through a city neighborhood where several buildings are boarded up and covered with graffiti; where groups of teenagers are lounging around the streets, some of them offering you a variety of drugs as you pass. Would you feel much safer knowing that the local precinct recorded 25 percent less crime than the more pleasant-looking neighborhood you had walked through a few blocks back?

Not only were Wicker Park residents more afraid of crime, they were also more concerned about incivility. Wicker Park had both a large number of abandoned buildings (thanks to a recent wave of arson, allegedly for profit) and the highest proportion of teenagers in the four neighborhoods, more than twice that of Woodlawn. Other studies have discovered this link between incivility and the perception of danger. In a Baltimore housing project, when residents were asked what was the most dangerous place, "they mentioned a place where young persons gathered to drink and play music, despite the fact that not a single crime had occurred there."[21] Vandalism, even when minor (and in some cases artistic), may have a similar effect. An observer of New York subways noted, "The first perception of subway crime came with the appearance of widespread graffiti in 1970. It was then that passengers took fright, and ridership ... dropped rapidly. Passengers felt threatened."[22]

When we see graffiti, boarded-up buildings, abandoned and stripped cars, or loitering teenagers, we assume that less visible but more serious crimes must also be lurking. Incivility, for most people, serves as a sign of crime, and most of the time the signs are accurate. Neighborhoods with higher crime rates also have greater amounts of **disorder**, a connection that makes it harder to figure out which of the two—crime or disorder—is the real cause of fear. It is only where the two factors do not coincide, as in the Chicago study, that we can see that it is disorder rather than predatory crime that has the greatest impact on fear.

A Newark, New Jersey, experiment originally intended as a test of new police tactics provides further evidence of the links among crime, disorder, and fear. In a test of what came to be called "community policing," the city of Newark decided to put more police back on foot patrol instead of cruising in cars. The purpose of the foot patrols was to maintain order, and officers were given fairly wide discretion in deciding what "order" meant in their particular area. In one case, it might mean controlling drunks and addicts by not letting them lie down on the sidewalks (sitting was allowed) or drink on the main streets (side streets were permitted) or bother people waiting for buses. Rowdy groups of teenagers might be dispersed, prostitutes kept to certain areas. Police enforced the rules with occasional street "sweeps," arresting all those who had not heeded the loudspeaker command to "break it up." In addition, the police tried to form closer ties to the residents. They opened a storefront office where people could come with questions and problems. Officers even went door to door, distributing a crime-prevention newsletter, asking residents about problems that might need police attention, and encouraging people to join neighborhood-watch groups.[23]

In one sense, the experiment worked: People felt safer and thought crime had been reduced; they also felt better about the police. However, actual crime rates did not go down. So although people felt safer from predatory crime, they were in fact no safer than they had been before.[24] Obviously, people were taking their cues about crime from the orderliness of the neighborhood. Were they just fooling themselves?

Some social scientists argue that the people's instinctive reactions are right—that incivility or disorder does lead to real crime. For example, in an article called "Broken Windows," prominent criminologist James Q. Wilson and coauthor George Kelling cite the Newark study and conclude that "disorder and crime are usually inextricably linked, in a kind of developmental sequence." They envision a scenario in which a stable neighborhood

> can change, in a few years or even a few months, to an inhospitable and frightening jungle. A piece of property is abandoned, weeds grow up, a window is smashed. Adults stop scolding rowdy children; the children, emboldened, become more rowdy. Families move out, unattached adults move in. Teenagers gather in front of the corner store. The merchant asks them to move; they refuse. Fights occur. Litter accumulates. People start drinking in front of the grocery; in time, an inebriate slumps to the sidewalk and is allowed to sleep it off. Pedestrians are approached by panhandlers.
>
> ... Many residents will think that crime, especially violent crime, is on the rise.... They will use the streets less often....
>
> Such an area is vulnerable to criminal invasion. Though it is not inevitable, it is more likely that ... cars will be stripped, drunks will be robbed ... prostitutes' customers will be robbed ... perhaps violently.... Muggings will occur.[25]

Wilson and Kelling's logical scenario of disorder leading to serious crime is now well known; criminologists even refer to the **broken windows** syndrome. But it suffers from one major flaw: It runs afoul of the evidence of the Newark study they are discussing. Over the course of nearly a year, community policing had stemmed and reversed the tide of disorder; good citizens had come back to the streets rather than staying home behind locked doors. Yet rates of predatory crime had "not gone down—in fact may have gone up." Contrary to expectation, changes in "signs of crime" had no effect on actual predatory crime.[26]

What seems logical is not always the way the world is. Although crime is usually most prevalent in neighborhoods of much incivility and disorder, changing the level of disorder may have little effect on crime. Of course, we should distinguish among the various types of disorder. As precursors of crime, unmended broken windows are not the same as a gang of teens, and the loitering of teenagers or winos is different from the presence of drugs. Even with drugs, the connection between disorder and crime may depend on the nature of the drug. Apparently, the traffic in marijuana, heroin, and other precrack drugs was far less devastating to neighborhoods than was the crack trade that began to flourish in the late 1980s.[27] In any case, it is visible disorder and incivility, rather than the volume of crime, that make people feel unsafe.[28]

The picture of fear in relation to crime and disorder should now be a little clearer. The three are interrelated; where we find one, we usually find the other two. But which is causing which? We have gone from the simple idea that crime causes fear of crime (model A in Figure 2–5) to the realization that both disorder and crime cause fear (model B), with disorder probably being the more important. There is also Wilson's idea that disorder eventually causes crime, and both cause fear (model C).

Although the differences were not large, Woodlawn had both a higher rate of crime and a lower level of fear than did Wicker Park. Also note that in

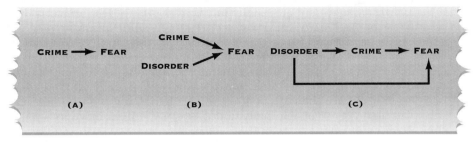

FIGURE 2–5   Models of Crime, Disorder, and Fear of Crime

all neighborhoods, people expressed more concern about incivility than they did about predatory crime.

One other neighborhood studied, Lincoln Park, had a fairly low rate of concern about crime despite having the second highest crime rate of the four areas. The low fear again demonstrates that crime is only one factor—perhaps not even the most important—in determining levels of fear. Lincoln Park was the most yuppie-like of the areas studied, with a large proportion of young, employed adults. It had the highest percentage in the 21 to 40 age group, and it was the most affluent of the four neighborhoods—the only one with income levels higher than the Chicago average. From these facts and the relative low concern with incivility, we can guess that of the four neighborhoods it was probably also the most orderly in appearance. In addition, most of the crimes committed there were residential burglaries committed during the day when nobody was at home. Lincoln Park's burglary rate was more than triple that of the city of Chicago as a whole, but its rates of violent crime were about the same as the city average.

CRIME, FEAR, AND COMMUNITY

Wilson's scenario, whatever its relevance to the Newark study, does suggest an important factor that has been missing in our discussion so far: the general quality of the neighborhood, which provides the context for crime, disorder, and fear. Our images of "bad" and "good" neighborhoods include not only the physical environment but also the social one. At one extreme is the neighborhood people leave as soon as they can: Many buildings are abandoned and vandalized; drug users and winos are in the streets; people do not know many of their neighbors; both crime rates and fear are high. At the other extreme is the kind of neighborhood where people know one another, have lived in the same place for many years, and take an active part in community life. They come to one another's aid, intervene or at least notify someone when they see someone or something suspicious, and feel safe in the streets and in their homes. Where crime and disorder are more frequent, residents also feel less attached to the community, more isolated, and more fearful.

Fear, in this picture, becomes a part of the relationship between the person and the general community, not merely an individual response to crime.

The tighter integration of people in their communities probably helps to reduce fear and also may reduce disorder and crime. Unfortunately, Americans have frequently chosen to deal with the problem of neighborhood crime through individual rather than community efforts—usually by moving to a more pleasant area. This preference for individual solutions does little to improve community conditions. On the contrary, it may worsen them. Not only does it ensure that the poorest will be left in the high-crime areas, but also the high rate of people moving out—even if others move in—makes stable attachments hard to maintain. As in Wilson's scenario of deterioration, when people are less involved, disorder may flourish; and the more disorder people see, the more they will want to move away. Once started, this cycle of deterioration is difficult to stop.

Crime is part of the general deterioration of a neighborhood already vulnerable because of its weak social integration. Strong community ties, however, may help a neighborhood resist urban decay. For example, the South Bronx section of New York City has suffered from deterioration that became the focus of national attention, with visits by presidential candidates and coverage by national TV news. Yet in the midst of the South Bronx, an area called Belmont has remained stable and low in crime. Belmont is by no means an affluent neighborhood; it could be called working class or lower middle class. But Belmont's residents have not moved out. People there know their neighbors more than do those in many wealthier urban areas. There is more of an active public life. People use the streets as a place to meet and talk. They are also more willing to take action when they see something suspicious. For example, an experiment in a busy Manhattan neighborhood showed that a person could break into a car in broad daylight on a busy street, and seldom would anybody do anything to intervene. In Belmont, such an act would draw more attention and action. Criminals are more likely to be noticed, and if noticed, are more likely to be pursued. Thus the strong sense of community, besides making Belmont a pleasant place to live, also serves to prevent crime.[29]

The tightly knit, watchful community may deter crime, but it can also have a less attractive side: brutal vigilantism tinged with racism. Three years after Belmont received attention as the nation's lowest-crime urban neighborhood, it was in the newspapers again. Belmont's population consists mostly of Italian-Americans and other "white ethnics," such as Albanians and Yugoslavians. In July 1986, two Puerto Ricans passing through the neighborhood "were attacked by eight white youths using a baseball bat and their teeth."[30]

The experience of Sally Merry, an anthropologist doing research on crime and fear, nicely illustrates the theme of this chapter.[31] Initially, when she moved into a housing project in the high-crime neighborhood that was the setting for her research, she felt afraid—nervous and tense—especially when walking alone at night. She also felt uneasy about the local drunks, who would lounge around the streets and sometimes fight with one another. However, "After several months, I learned that they … did not pose a threat to my person, only to my sense of order and propriety." As she got to know the neighborhood and its people, her fear decreased to sensible caution: "After I became aware of the frequency of purse-snatching, I stopped carrying a purse."

Citizen patrols, like this one in a New York City housing project, can give volunteers a sense that they are doing something about crime. The evidence on their effectiveness as crime stoppers is less reassuring. Some programs reduce crime; many others do not.

Eventually, she became friendly with a group of black youths that some residents thought were responsible for much of the crime in the area. Once she got to know them, she writes, "I suddenly found that I did not consider the project dangerous at all, even at night, and resumed carrying a purse." The laundromat, which had before seemed like a dangerous place where kids hung out, now "seemed like a familiar, safe place."

After two and one-half years, she was robbed one night at the entrance to her house by "a young man, his hand held inside his jacket, either holding a gun or pretending to." Merry says that she was "shaken but not frightened" by the robbery and that afterward she was only more cautious, not more afraid.

But what is the moral of this story? On the one hand, it is optimistic. It shows that in Merry's words, "Familiarity with people and places overcame an initial sense of danger, and even the experience of victimization did not lead to a resurgence of fear."[32] On the other hand, her story may be so unusual as to be cause for pessimism. After all, Merry was an educated, middle-class person whose daily work as an anthropologist was to get to know the residents. But for people with fewer resources, people with other problems to occupy their time, creating familiarity and social integration may be a nearly impossible task.

THE MEDIA AND FEAR OF CRIME

For humans, as for all animals, the cues of the immediate environment may trigger a fear reaction. But unlike other animals, humans are affected by more distant and abstract kinds of information. In estimating danger, we use not only the firsthand information of our own senses and experiences but also our general knowledge. This knowledge comes to us from other people and from less personal sources, such as newspapers, television, and the other mass media.* Tens of millions of Americans watch a single national evening news show; together the three major networks broadcast the news to as many as 100 million people. A single daily newspaper may reach a large percentage of a city's population. This central position gives the media tremendous potential power. If people form their ideas on the basis of what they know, and if people get that knowledge mostly from the mass media, the people who control the media have a great influence over those ideas. Consequently, a handful of editors may determine what millions of people will know about the world. This influence may be especially strong because people tend to believe what they learn from the media—especially television. Television, much more than newspapers, serves as the chief source of news information for most Americans. And while some polls have found Americans distrustful toward the media (with barely half believing that TV news is mostly telling the truth, and only 22 percent believing the daily papers), other polls find the public much more accepting of media news. In all these polls, however, people generally rate television as more believable than the press.[33] For some years, the news source Americans found most credible was Walter Cronkite, a man who read the news each evening on television; and Cronkite maintained this ranking even four years after his retirement.[34]

For some kinds of news, the media necessarily have a monopoly as our source of information. How else could we know about space shuttles or wars in distant countries or the general condition of the economy? Yet even closer to home, we may have to look to the media for our information. In large cities, people may be ignorant of a newsworthy event that took place in their own building unless or until they see it on the news.

CRIME WAVES—IN THE STREETS AND IN THE MEDIA

Most studies suggest that fear of crime in general or of some specific crime can increase when the media influence the public's perception about crime. Could it be that a "crime wave" that grips a city with fear is nothing more than a sudden spurt of stories in the media?

■ *The word *media* is the plural of *medium*—something that mediates or comes between (literally, in the middle); in this case, the medium comes between an event and a person's experience of that event. Newspapers, radio, movies, television, and so on are *mass* media: The same program or paper reaches a mass of people.

IN THE NEWS

In the early 1990s, as in earlier media crime waves that amplified fear, news reports of a new crime, "carjacking," raised new fears.

FOR THE CRIME-WEARY, SECURITY THROUGH THE MIST: IN A RISING CLIMATE OF FEAR, MACE AND SIMILAR SUBSTANCES FIND INCREASING POPULARITY

by Evelyn Nieves

Clifton NJ, Jan 23.—Unnerved by a spate of violent carjackings two months ago, Sandra Martinez bought some protection: a can of Mace on a key ring. A week later, she picked up another can to keep in her glove compartment. And another, to clip on her waist

when she jogs. On Thursday, she returned here to the Rowe-Manse emporium, a department store that displays Mace at every counter, and bought a fourth can of the "pepper-fortified" tear gas spray—to tape on the back of her front door.

"I know it sounds crazy," said Ms. Martinez, a 27-year-old personal fitness trainer..."but it's a lot safer than a gun."

Confronting Fear in the Suburbs

Even in the suburbs where the police blotter is a mish-mash of traffic infractions, news reports of carjackings and other random crimes in seemingly safe places like the local shopping mall have prompted a surge in sales of the pocket-sized sprays that temporarily blind, choke and hobble an attacker with a squirt or two. MSI, the ... manufacturer of Mace ... sold 10 times as much of the product in December 1992 as it did the year before.

"I've never seen anything like it," said Michael Dallett, president of the National Association of Defensive Spray Manufacturers.... He added that his company ... has been selling sprays ("Punch," "Freeze," and "Freeze Plus") for close to 20 years and saw his sales jump by 50 percent in December, even with 42 new defensive spray products on the market.

False Sense of Security

Police officials ... say they are worried that a woman or man carrying self-defense sprays may develop a false sense of security. The crimes that people carrying the sprays are trying to protect against—rape and muggings mostly—occur so suddenly that most people are caught in the middle of a situation before they can react.

Source: New York Times, January 24, 1993, pp. 25, 28.

Consider the following incident: A politician walking near his office is accosted by two men; one hits him on the head and grabs him around the neck while the other takes his valuables. It is a classic strong-arm robbery, what today is called a mugging. This incident, however, occurred in London in 1862, and the term used was *garroting*. The case of Hugh Pilkington, M.P., made the newspapers as one more event in a crime wave. For several months, this crime wave—the garroting panic of 1862—held the middle and upper classes of London in fear. As one newspaper put it, "The statistics on garroting in recent years would present a very frightful catalogue of outrages." In fact, the police statistics on "robberies with violence" (i.e., garroting) showed no such increase. They remained steady at about 2.5 per month. However, *after* the panic began, statistics showed a fivefold increase, caused not by an actual increase in gar-roting but chiefly by the heightened sensitivities of the police and courts. Under pressure to do something about this crime, the police and courts treated as garroting what before might have passed for a drunken fight or simple theft, and several "persons of bad character" and "ticket-of-leave" men (the equiva-lent of parolees) were arrested and tried for garroting.[35] Thus, although there was no real increase in garroting, a wave of crime stories in the media caused an increase both in public fear and in crime statistics.

Somewhat more recently, a team of researchers headed by Mary Baker happened upon a similar **media crime wave**. They had originally set out to measure the effects, if any, of a new style of policing in Phoenix, Arizona. Consequently, in September 1979 and again in July 1980, they asked Phoenix citizens about their victimization experiences, their attitudes toward the police, and their feelings of safety. In the ten months between the two surveys, how-ever, something much more noticeable than police changes took place. The offi-cial crime rate in Phoenix went up dramatically, and the media made this increase big news. The newspapers carried more stories on crime statistics and more editorials on crime. Some papers ran headlines like "Crime Pays ..." and began to keep running accounts of crime statistics ("35th armed robbery this month"). In short, Phoenix was experiencing a crime wave.

Or was it? Baker's victimization survey—although the sample was too small to be conclusive—showed no increase in crime, and in retrospect our best guess is that in fact no such increase occurred. Why then had crime sta-tistics gone up? For one thing, three police chiefs had resigned and the new administration changed the departmental rules for recording crime. Crimes previously classified as less than serious might now be counted as serious crimes, or perhaps previously the police chose to ignore some of the crime reports phoned in to them. (For more on the official definitions of serious crime, see Chapter Three.) In any case, the increase in crime took place on paper, not in the streets.

At the same time that the police chiefs were stepping down, the major newspapers, probably by coincidence, had assigned new reporters to the police and crime beat, and they may have been more enthusiastic about find-ing and filing crime stories. Equally relevant, 1980 was an election year, and both papers were supporting a $40 million bond issue for new jails. This polit-ical position may have influenced the editor's selection of news stories. After all, an editor who wants people to vote for money for jails may want to con-vince them that crime is on a dangerous upswing.

The criminals of Phoenix in 1980, like the garroters of London in 1862, were no more active or numerous than they had been the year before, yet a chance combination of other forces created a "crime wave": First, a change in the police department created an increase in officially recorded crimes; second, eager new reporters filed more crime stories than their predecessors; and third, the news-papers played up the crime wave as an argument for the jail bond issue.

The crime wave had a predictable effect on the public's perception. More people thought crime was increasing in Phoenix generally and even in their own neighborhoods. And the more people perceived an increase in crime, the more afraid they felt. Thus the media had—independently of actual crime—increased the fear of crime.[36]

MAKING WAVES

Baker and her colleagues did not monitor the local TV news, but another study of a crime wave in New York City found that crime news in one medium soon gets picked up by the others. The New York crime wave, rather than starting as an increase in overall statistics, concerned a very specific kind of criminal act—crimes against the elderly. In mid-October 1976, the *New York Daily News* gave prominent coverage to a couple of particularly grisly murders of elderly people. By the next week, both the *New York Post* and a local TV station had also increased the number of news items devoted to crimes against the elderly. The heightened media coverage continued for a few weeks. The mayor and the police chief made statements about the problem and their actions to combat it, and by mid-December, the number of these news items had returned to the previous level. As you might expect, most New Yorkers thought that crime against the elderly had gone up, and according to surveys, half the people over age 50 felt more fearful of crime than they had the year before.

In this case, police statistics did show that crimes against the elderly had increased, but in most cases the increase was no more than that of any other sort of crime, and murders of elderly people had actually decreased by nearly 20 percent. In other words, the statistics did not square with the image spread by the media that vicious criminals had suddenly decided to start victimizing old people. Here was another crime wave that happened in the news, not in the streets. Consequently, when criminologist Mark Fishman decided to study this crime wave, he and his assistants went not to the streets or to the police but to the offices of the newspapers and a local TV station.[37]

How did murder and other crimes against the elderly become so newsworthy when there was no substantial increase in their occurrence? To answer this question, Fishman first had to learn how any event becomes news. Let us take a hypothetical example: A man aged 72 and his wife, 70, are walking near their apartment building. Two young men approach. One grabs the man from behind; the other holds the woman by the arm and threatens her with a knife. They demand the couple's money and take the man's wallet and the woman's pocketbook—a total of eighty-five dollars in cash. Then they run off.

Is this news? Will it be in the papers or on television? The answer is, it depends. If the crime occurred in a small town, where the local weekly prints the entire police blotter including traffic tickets, it certainly will be in the paper. Or if one of the victims happened to be a senator or another important person, it will be news. But what if we are in a large city where such incidents occur each day? Will it be news?

The answer again is, it depends. It depends ultimately on a person who is neither victim nor criminal nor police officer nor criminologist. It depends on the news editor. Remember, the news stories we see in the media represent a very small number of events selected from a very large number of events. When the announcer says at the end of the news program, "And that's the news today," we may think we have seen "what happened." But millions of things happen. Which of them is important? To understand how a crime (or any event, for that matter) becomes news, it is more useful to think of the forty-five minutes of local news (sixty minutes minus the commercials, titles, and credits) not as what happened but as the outcome of decisions—decisions made by news editors about what is and is not news.

How does a TV news editor decide whether our hypothetical crime is worth presenting? Fishman, in his months of research, discovered one thing you might guess just by watching your local news: Editors like to have the news tell a story. Rather than presenting the news as a display of unrelated items, the editor will try to arrange the show so that the items fit into larger categories, or what Fishman calls "themes." Two fires in different parts of the city and having nothing in common will appear on the news one right after the other since both fit into the theme of fire. If a theme already exists, the editor tries to find items that fit into it. In the fall of 1976, even before the crime wave, the TV station had on hand a continuing series of stories on a special unit of the police department that had been set up to deal with crimes against the elderly. An item like our hypothetical robbery would have provided the perfect lead-in to one of these feature stories. However, if the station had been running a feature on drugs or auto theft, the editors might well have ignored our elderly victims. The same event that was not news last month might be the first item on the news today.

A crime theme, however, is not a crime wave. For the theme of crime against the elderly to become a crime wave, several currents had to flow together. All the media—at least the two newspapers and one TV station under study—began to stress this theme. There was no conspiracy, no design, but news editors do pay attention to other media. The TV editor fed on the news. On arriving at work, he read the papers, watched the wire services, and listened to an all-news radio station. So when the *Daily News* began to run front-page stories about elderly murder victims, the TV editor sensed that similar items were now newsworthy. In other words, like you and me, the news editor found out what was news by looking at the media. Presumably, the editors at the *Daily News* and the *Post* also watched television, and perhaps when they in turn saw crime against the elderly on the TV news, they concluded that these crimes were important enough for continued emphasis. Before long, the TV and newspaper editors had unwittingly bounced the theme back and forth, each time amplifying it, until the number of such stories in the media was six times the number of only a month before. It had become a crime wave.

Besides the interest of the various media, two other important elements were crucial to the creation of a crime wave: criminals and police. The media do not make news out of nothing. There must be actual incidents—no matter how rare—to report. In the case of crimes against the elderly, in a region of nearly 10 million people, there will be more than enough such incidents each day. Not all crimes are so common. For instance, while he was doing his research, Fishman noticed the beginnings of a "wave" of Mafia killings in the media. But the gangsters apparently did not provide more murders, and the "gangland war" theme died from lack of incidents.

At another time, New York City subway crime seemed to be drawing media attention. This theme, too, fizzled, though not for lack of incidents. Certainly enough subway crimes occur each day to fill a newscast. Why did the media lose interest? In part because the police department did not want the publicity: The transit police chief told the *Daily News* that there was no crime wave. Who was a reporter to contradict such an official statement?

Just as the police department can dampen media crime waves, it can also sustain or even create them. In the fall of 1976, the Senior Citizens Robbery Unit had been most cooperative with the TV station in creating their features on crimes against the elderly. In a more general way, the police department provides the media with their crime stories, whatever the topic. Newspapers may have reporters covering the police beat, which usually means the press room at police headquarters, but the media rely on the police wire for most of their stories. This is a wire service over which the department sends basic information on the two dozen or so stories it thinks will most interest the media. The police department, too, is making decisions about what crimes are news, selecting some items and rejecting others. According to Fishman, the police try to provide what the media want. If the media seem interested in crime against the elderly, the police wire will send out more of these stories. Television, newspapers, and police, then, all pay close attention to one another, and through this tangle of mutual influence they can create in the public mind the impression of a real crime wave, even when the statistics show otherwise.

Nobody involved necessarily wishes to raise the level of public fear. The media want to inform readers or viewers, but they must also compete with one another for the largest share of this audience. They certainly do not want to miss out on a hot story. The police want to help the media and perhaps to direct public attention to certain crime problems. In 1976 in New York City, this intertwining of cooperation and competition produced a crime wave that had little basis in reality. Nevertheless, the media changed the people's perception about crime and lowered their sense of security.

PRIME-TIME CRIME

Only some of the crimes you see on television occur on the news shows. After the news is over, prime time begins. If the news distorts the picture of crime, stressing particularly unusual or lurid crimes, at least it is constrained by the available facts. Prime-time fictional shows can give free rein to the imagination, and that imagination frequently turns to crime—an average of ten crimes a night, with a heavy overrepresentation of murder and other violent crimes.[38]

Many people think that fictional violence in the media increases the amount of violence in society. Researchers have done thousands of studies on this topic, and their results frequently contradict one another. Even when studies find that violent behavior and violent TV shows do go together, seldom can they determine which causes the other. Such a result might mean only that violent people enjoy watching violent television, not that their favorite shows make them more violent as people. Even when studies can isolate televised violence as one cause of aggressive behavior, the behavior measured is rarely serious enough to be called crime.[39]

Measuring the influence of television on people's perceptions also poses many problems, though there have been several empirical studies of this question. Generally, people who watch a lot of television also picture the real

ON CAMPUS

CAMPUS PATROLS

In the 1980s, neighborhood-watch and neighborhood-patrol programs sprang up in many places, including college campuses. The story of the rise and decline of one such program—at Drake University, a school of about 5,000 students in Des Moines, Iowa—illustrates several points about the media, public perceptions of crime, and the problems involved in organized community patrols.

Around 1980, the campus experienced an increase in the fear of crime and the perception of crime as a problem. The actual amount of crime, however, both on campus and in the bordering areas had, if anything, decreased slightly, and most of the on-campus crime was vandalism. What probably triggered the fear was a single crime—a rape that occurred in a classroom building—and a 100 percent increase of crime news in the campus newspaper.

As in other media crime waves, the amount of crime news at Drake seems to have depended much more on the editor than on criminals. The big increase in crime stories coincided with the arrival of a new editor, a student who had once worked as a police reporter. "She liked those kinds of stories," said one news staffer.

Campus politicians, too, contributed to the atmosphere of fear. After the rape on campus, the student body president took out a full-page advertisement in the newspaper entitled "Are You Safe? A Message on Crime in the Drake Community."

The heightened concern with crime led students to form a campus patrol, complete with bright yellow jackets, flashlights,

world as being like the TV programs; that is, they overestimate levels of violent crime, killings by strangers, numbers of police officers, and their own risk of victimization. Of course, television is only one of many influences on these perceptions; several other factors—socioeconomic status, sex, and education—play an important part.[40]

Assessment of TV shows as a cause of fear is complicated by a nearly insurmountable chicken-and-egg problem. Which comes first—watching television or being fearful? It is true that heavy television viewers express more fear of crime than do infrequent viewers. We cannot conclude, though, that television watching causes fear. In the first place, other factors may be at work. For example, women watch more television than do men; they also, as we know, are more fearful of crime. But it is unlikely that their television watching is making them more fearful. There is similar interference from variables like social class, race, and age. When we control for these variables, the television–fear link decreases or even disappears. Even when we find a correlation between the two, we cannot be certain which is causing which. The correlation might mean that fear causes television viewing, not that television viewing causes fear. People who are afraid to go out will stay home and watch television.

and two-way radios. Students joined for a variety of reasons, not all having to do with crime: to help the image of their fraternities, to pad out their résumés, and to meet people. Nearly 13 percent joined solely to complete the community-service requirement for a biology course. However, patrol turned out to be fairly unglamorous—escorting students (almost always female), helping to fix flat tires, or giving directions to visitors. Few students came across crimes or even suspicious persons. In addition, the typical reaction of other students was not appreciation but indifference and occasionally hostility.

The boredom and lack of any visible success eventually took their toll on the membership, until by the end of the fourth year only six students were actually patrolling. As one leader put it, "After a while, walking around for an hour, people [come] to the conclusion of 'Why am I doing this?' Because people are always conditioned that they want to see results and that's what makes people achieve. But in this, your best result is that nothing happens."

The atmosphere on campus had also changed. The campus paper no longer emphasized crime—some semesters it ran fewer than ten crime stories—nor did crime figure as an issue in student government elections. The crime problem had run its course, expanding and diminishing with little real change in the actual number of crimes.

Source: Adapted from Ronald L. Troyer, "The Urban Anti-Crime Patrol Phenomenon: A Case Study of a Student Effort," *Justice Quarterly*, vol. 5, no. 3, (1988), pp. 397–419.

Of course, specific stories in the media can raise specific fears. News of a series of rapes or murders in a particular area, with the criminal still at large, can make people reasonably more cautious. But on the whole, the currently available evidence suggests that the media usually have little direct, lasting effect on fear. Even with media crime waves, the media have a built-in corrective tendency: Their continual need for new themes may lead them to seize on certain stories and create—in the media and in the public mind—a crime wave. But the same need for something new will eventually force such a crime wave to fizzle out. After two or three weeks, yet another robbery of an elderly person is no longer interesting news; unless there is something unusual about it, it will not sell papers or attract viewers. Thus, media crime waves seem to go through a natural life cycle: a few dramatic incidents, continued reporting of similar crimes, a well-publicized response by officials that something is being done, and finally a waning of media interest.

Compared with other sources of fear—personal vulnerability and victimization and environmental cues—the media probably don't make much difference in the long run. In the short run, a media crime wave about crimes against the elderly or carjacking or some other type of crime may make more people afraid, but both the news interest and the heightened fears are short-lived. If local television and newspapers reduced their crime levels by 50 percent or 75 percent, would people feel much safer in the streets? I doubt it.

CRIME, RACE, AND POLITICS

In the last thirty years, crime has become an important public issue. It has figured in political campaigns at every level of government, and the debate at times has seemed to appeal more to emotions than to reason.

The death penalty, as far as any research can show, does not affect the murder rate. Yet effective politics and effective policy are two different things, so capital punishment is good politics. For example, in 1992, Bill Clinton, campaigning for the presidency, went so far as to make a point of returning to his home state as governor for the execution of a man so brain-damaged he did not fully understand what was happening to him.

The politics of crime, which often dominates elections these days, has its origins in the 1960s, and the debate then probably was no more or less cogent than it is today. For example, Richard Nixon, in his acceptance speech at the Republican convention in 1968, drew the most applause for his promise to appoint a new attorney general.[41] Of course, every newly elected president appoints a new attorney general (as he appoints new secretaries of defense, state, and all other cabinet positions). What Nixon meant was that he was going to get tough on crime. Again, there was less to the issue than met the eye, for crime control is largely a matter for city police and state courts. Presidential policies have little direct effect on street crime. Like the death penalty, the crime issue was more symbolic than real, for crime had become an important symbol. The only question is, what was it a symbol of?

WHAT CRIME MEANS

In the first part of this chapter, I went to great lengths to show that in surveys about the fear of crime, people are responding to something much larger than crime itself. Fear of crime includes a general feeling of vulnerability that arises from personal characteristics and personal experience. The fear people associate with crime may also be triggered by a sense of unfamiliarity and differentness. As the presidential commission concluded in 1967, "Fear of crimes of violence is ... at bottom a fear of strangers."[42] People who look different, behave differently, and perhaps speak a different language make the world seem less predictable, less familiar, and therefore more dangerous, regardless of the real risk of crime.

The blending of fear of strangers and fear of crime has important consequences, for often those strangers are "strange" primarily because of the color of their skin. In the United States, the crime problem has become almost inextricably intertwined with the issue of race. In another chapter, I will take up the question of racial differences in committing crime. In this chapter, I want to look at people's personal and political reactions to crime, reactions that frequently involve feelings about race.

The best-known recent example of the complex relationship among politics, race, and crime is the Rodney King case. On March 4, 1992, Channel 5 (KTLA) in Los Angeles played a videotape of four police officers beating Rodney King, an African-American man they had stopped for speeding after a high-speed chase. In all, the four officers hit King fifty-six times, while another two dozen officers stood by. During the next few days, the ninety-second tape was played over newscasts throughout the country and the world. Even President Bush announced publicly that what he had seen on the video was "revolting." Two months later, however, a jury drawn from a nearly all-white suburban county acquitted the officers of all criminal charges.

The jury apparently believed the police officers' defense that they were dealing in the approved way with a suspect of apparently extraordinary strength who was not complying with their commands. We cannot be certain about what went through the jurors' minds. Certainly they weighed the material presented in the trial, but they filtered these facts and arguments through a set of background ideas and images that they brought to the case. As the only Hispanic on the jury said of the others, "It's like they saw what they wanted to see, like they already had made up their minds."[43] My guess is that the jurors' basic assumptions were those that many Americans share: that the police are basically good guys protecting people like us from people like them—"us" being the predominantly suburban, white, and middle class; "them" the urban, dark, poor, and criminal. The four officers were later tried on federal charges of violating King's civil rights. A jury drawn from the more multicultural Los Angeles population convicted two of the officers.

Rodney King, in fact, was an ex-convict, he was speeding, and he did speed away when the police tried to stop him. But even when black or Hispanic victims of white violence have been completely innocent of anything except walking or driving in a white neighborhood, the incidents often evoke similarly tolerant reactions, reactions based on this same set of perceptions and assumptions about protecting "us" against "them."

THE POLITICS OF LAW AND ORDER

Almost as soon as the King verdict was announced, south-central Los Angeles erupted in one of the worst riots of the century. Within a few days the rioting had caused more than fifty deaths and over a half billion dollars in property damage. The riot only sharpened perceptions about the social divisions in American society. People who lived miles away in affluent neighborhoods were buying guns, fearful that rioters would march out of the inner city to attack the homes of the wealthy.

Unfortunately, little of this was new to American society or politics. In 1965, a riot had destroyed much of the Watts district of south-central Los Angeles, and in subsequent years, riots broke out in black neighborhoods in

ABOUT CRIME & CRIMINOLOGY

Perhaps the best example of the law-and-order politicians of the 1960s and 1970s was Frank Rizzo, who died in 1991. The following are excerpts from an obituary in the New York Times.

A "HERO" AND "VILLAIN"

by Dennis Hevesi

Frank L. Rizzo, who died of a heart attack yesterday in the midst of his second comeback campaign for mayor of Philadelphia, had been one of those seemingly larger-than-life figures, destined to be a hero to some and a villain to others.

One view was that the former Police Commissioner and two-term Mayor was the last bastion against threats to middle-class residents of the city's row-house neighborhoods.

The other view was that Mr. Rizzo was a barely educated former police officer who used a hard line on crime and tactics bordering on the dictatorial to suppress opposition and keep blacks out of middle-class neighborhoods.

Several times during his career, he was charged with beating suspects in his custody with a blackjack. The charges were always dismissed.

Rising through the ranks, Mr. Rizzo became commissioner in 1967. His supporters point out that during his five-year tenure, Philadelphia had the lowest crime rate of the 10 largest cities in the nation.

dozens of other American cities. It was during this period that U.S. politics saw the rise of **law-and-order** politicians, candidates who promised to fight "crime in the streets." It may seem odd that "law and order" and "crime in the streets" could become controversial political issues. After all, nobody was against law and order, and nobody was for crime in the streets. So what was the real issue?

LIBERAL AND CONSERVATIVE

To understand the reactions to the riots and street crime of the 1960s or the 1990s, we need to go beyond the issue of race, for these reactions illustrate a fundamental difference in political views—the split between **liberal** and **conservative**. Phrases like "crime in the streets" and "law and order" carry connotations far beyond their literal meaning. They symbolize a broad set of largely conservative ideas and attitudes. Sometimes these ideas are conservative in the literal sense of conserving things as they are (or were) and rejecting what is new. In the politics of crime, conservatism also means a more punitive approach. Conservatives talk about "getting tough" on crime and favor more severe punishment as a way to reduce it. Liberals, in contrast, are more likely to favor rehabilitation for those criminals who are caught. As for solutions, liberals often talk about getting at the "root causes" of crime, caus-

His detractors believe the price for that order was intolerable. Mr. Rizzo personally led Saturday night round-ups of homosexuals and staged a series of raids on coffee houses and cafes—saying they were drug dens. No indictments resulted from the raids.

In 1972, shortly before he resigned to run for Mayor, police officers deeply embittered Philadelphia's black community by raiding the headquarters of the Black Panthers, herding them into the street and stripping them naked.

Mr. Rizzo's iron hand in running the 7,000-member department and his highly-publicized and questionable tactics in policing the city brought him a national reputation as an advocate of "law and order." He counted on that reputation when, in 1971, while still commissioner, he announced his mayoral candidacy from Police Headquarters.

[Rizzo served two four-year terms as mayor.]

Mr. Rizzo very much wanted to stay on as Mayor, but the City charter barred anyone from serving three successive terms.

Four years later, when Mr. Rizzo sought to regain his old job, he was easily defeated in the Democratic primary by W. Wilson Goode, who received virtually all of the city's black votes as well as strong support from while liberals and moderates. Mr. Goode went on to be elected Philadelphia's first black mayor.

Source: *New York Times*, July 17, 1991, p. B5.

es found not in the individual but in the environment. In the liberal view, people commit crimes because of social or economic pressures, and the way to reduce crime is to reduce those pressures. Changing these root causes is beyond the power of any individual, so liberals look to the government to play an active role in improving schools, alleviating poverty, reducing social and economic inequality, and creating more jobs—all as ways to reduce crime. The conservative view of the cause of crime is much simpler: It downplays the environment, especially the economy, and focuses on the individual. For example, shortly after the Los Angeles riots that followed the Rodney King verdict, Vice President Dan Quayle (who was at that time one of the most prominent conservative voices) went to California to give his much noted "Murphy Brown" speech. Quayle downplayed race relations as a problem ("All of us can be proud of our progress") and said that the problems of inner-city Los Angeles were not primarily a matter of money or jobs or economic poverty. Instead, too many of the residents suffered from "a poverty of values,"[44] that is, a poverty that individuals can indeed control. Values are matters of individual choice. To reduce crime, therefore, conservatives emphasize punishment. After all, if people choose to commit crime largely because they can get away with it, the only way to alter that choice is to increase the penalty for it.

The politics of law and order, goes beyond differences in ideas about how to reduce crime. Some people claim that the real issue—both in the 1960s and the 1990s—was race. Law-and-order candidates were, in the view of their critics, using anticrime slogans as acceptable code words for antiblack feelings.

The riots and the increase in street crime during the late 1960s came in the wake of a decade of great change in race relations in the United States. In 1954, the Supreme Court issued its famous school desegregation decision (*Brown* v. *Board of Education*), and in the early 1960s, freedom rides, sit-ins, bus boycotts, and voter registration drives further challenged racial segregation and inequality. Segregation laws were overturned in courts, and the federal government passed major civil rights laws. At the same time, the media exposed the most blatant aspects of racism: Millions of Americans watched on television as white adults screamed insults at black children who were trying to do nothing more threatening than go to school or as the governor of Alabama personally tried to keep an African-American man from attending classes at the state university. All these highly visible efforts to overcome discrimination brought what public-opinion pollsters called a **white backlash**; many whites felt that the government in its civil rights policies had "done enough" for blacks or had "gone too far."

At the same time, the more things changed, the more they stayed the same. The changes in the courts, the legislatures, and the media (where blacks began to appear in respectable roles rather than the usual degrading stereotypes) raised expectations of real change. Yet to a great extent for most African-Americans, the quality of life—jobs, wages, unemployment, schools, housing, and public services—remained unequal to that of whites. In the view of many liberals, the riots were largely symptoms of frustration—the desperate reaction of people in desperate social conditions—and a demand for social change. For politicians to dismiss the riots as merely crime, as a matter of law and order, was just one more way to avoid the issue of inequality and to maintain a racially unjust society. Conservative politicians, in this view, were playing to the white backlash; rather than saying that they were against racial change, the conservative politicians and their supporters could say they were for law and order. Rather than saying that they were against blacks, they could say that they were against crime in the streets. Crime had become a code word for race. So even today, nearly thirty years into the politics of race and crime, when people tell pollsters they are afraid of crime or consider crime a big problem, perhaps they are using "crime" as a more acceptable way of saying racial change or, more bluntly, blacks.

Public opinion can sometimes change greatly in a short period of time. So when you see reports of public opinion surveys, try to find out whether the results are consistent with other polls taken in the past. Even so, it is often difficult to label public opinion as clearly liberal or conservative. Politicians and others often feel obligated to present an ideologically coherent viewpoint. Public opinion is under no such pressure for political consistency. On punishment issues, Americans appear conservative. At least four of five say that the courts are not harsh enough on criminals; about 70 to 85 percent of the American people support capital punishment (though when polls add the option of life without parole, the support for capital punishment drops to about 60 percent). Only one person in six is more concerned about constitutional rights than about courts letting people off too easily.

Yet on the liberal side, 63 percent disapprove of wiretapping, and 80 percent oppose warrantless searches, even for high-crime areas. When asked to choose between law enforcement on the one hand or root causes on the other,

Americans choose the liberal strategy of "attacking the social and economic problems that lead to crime" nearly two to one. For drug use, they favor treatment over punishment 57 percent to 33 percent. They are strongly for gun control. Nearly everyone favors a seven-day waiting period before a handgun purchase, and two-thirds favor an outright ban on assault rifles.[45]

This brief sketch of political views oversimplifies both conservative and liberal thought. I have intended these descriptions more as the ends of a continuum rather than as absolute categories. I do not mean that all people who favor punitive crime policies are racists or even that their views on other issues are predictably conservative. Any one person's own views will undoubtedly be a mixture of ideas. Many people who think of themselves as conservatives and want harsher penalties for crime may still acknowledge the importance of economic factors as causes of crime and may be vigorous advocates of racial equality. Nevertheless, the categories may be useful for understanding views about crime.

FEAR OF CRIME VERSUS CONCERN WITH CRIME

It is important to distinguish these political reactions to crime from the personal reaction of fear. Voting for a law and order candidate is not quite the same thing as being afraid to walk alone at night. Some years ago, Frank Furstenberg pointed out this distinction between concern with crime and fear of crime. *Concern* refers to political attitudes, ideas about what is best for society; *fear* refers to personal feelings about safety.[46] The two are different, and they have different causes. Sex and age are important factors in the fear of crime, but these variables make almost no difference in political views about crime.[47] What about victimization? As we have seen, victimization does increase the level of fear (although it does not seem as influential as sex or age). But does it also affect people's political views about crime? As an illustration, imagine that we have a roomful of people, and your task is to divide them into two groups. Your goal is to have two groups that are most different in the proportion who want courts to be harsher on criminals. Obviously, if you just divided people randomly, you would probably have the same get-tough proportion in each group, and I have already told you that separating the men from the women or the old from the young will not give you two groups that differ much in their support for harsher courts. To help you, I will let you use *one* of two other pieces of information: whether the person has been a victim of crime in the last year or whether the person favors busing to achieve racial integration in the schools. In other words, your two groups can consist either of victims and nonvictims or of probusing people and antibusing people. Which grouping will produce a bigger difference on the question of harsher courts?

Your first logical impulse probably tells you that you will do better if you use victimization: More people who have been victimized will favor harsher courts; those who have not been victimized will feel less strong about courts. But if you think about what you've read so far, you might choose the attitude on busing: Like crime, busing resonates with themes of racial fear, community homogeneity, and general conservatism. Tables 2–5 and 2–6 show the

TABLE 2-5 •

OPINION ON COURTS BY VICTIMIZATION (ROBBERY OR BURGLARY IN THE PAST YEAR)

	NONVICTIMS	VICTIMS
TOO HARSH	4.1	4.2
ABOUT RIGHT	10.2	9.7
NOT HARSH ENOUGH	85.7	86.1

Source: James Allen Davis and Tom W. Smith, *General Social Surveys, 1972–1988* (Chicago: National Opinion Research Center, 1988).

results of a national survey on these questions conducted in 1988. (The tables show the responses of whites only.)

The most obvious result is the widespread perception that courts are too soft. (In a result not shown in these tables, even among people who describe themselves as extremely liberal 75 percent favor harsher courts.) But we are interested in the differences between the two tables. In Table 2–5, nearly identical proportions of victims and nonvictims say they want harsher courts. Compare this result against the glib assertion that "a conservative is a liberal who has just been mugged," a cute phrasing for a plausible idea. But the evidence doesn't support it. Being a victim of burglary or robbery apparently makes no difference in a person's opinions on the courts. Instead, these opinions are part of a consistent and coherent view of the world, and they are unlikely to be shaken by a single experience with property crime.

While opinions on courts are unaffected by victimization, they do seem to be related to attitudes on busing. The differences are not large—a gap of about eight percentage points in the "not harsh enough" category—but they are larger than the no-difference of Table 2–5. Moreover, probusing people are more than three times as likely to say that courts are too harsh. To put the

TABLE 2-6 •

OPINION ON COURTS BY OPINION ON BUSING TO ACHIEVE SCHOOL INTEGRATION

	PROBUSING	ANTIBUSING
TOO HARSH	8.1	2.2
ABOUT RIGHT	10.3	8.4
NOT HARSH ENOUGH	81.5	89.3

Source: James Allen Davis and Tom W. Smith, *General Social Surveys, 1972–1988* (Chicago: National Opinion Research Center, 1988).

matter in the language of statistics, busing (at least for city dwellers) is a better predictor of attitudes toward courts than is victimization.[48]

The reverse of the idea that a conservative is a liberal who has just been mugged is the statement that a liberal is a conservative who has just been arrested. It would be hard to get good systematic evidence for this idea. (Anecdotally, though, Oliver North, a conservatives' conservative, apparently had no objection to the legal "technicalities" that overturned his criminal convictions.) However, these two glib definitions about liberals and conservatives do point out a major difference in their ideologies: Liberals fear the state and are reluctant to expand its powers; conservatives fear criminals, and in return for some hoped-for protection against criminals, they are willing to grant the government greater power over individuals.

The following tables offer further evidence that ideas about crime have less to do with personal experience than with political ideology. The relevant questions in the survey were

- Do you favor or oppose the death penalty for persons convicted of murder?

- During the last year, did anyone break into your home?

- If your party nominated a black for president, would you vote for him if he were qualified for the job?

Table 2–7 shows that burglary victims are no more likely than nonvictims to favor capital punishment. However, although victimization is unrelated to attitudes on the death penalty, other political views are significantly correlated with attitudes about punishment. Table 2–8 divides the sample on the issue of voting for a black for president. Although the table does not show it, a large majority— 84 percent—said they would vote for a qualified black. But the important point for purposes of this chapter is that the antiblack 16 percent were significantly more likely to favor capital punishment. (The tables show the responses of whites only.)

Not only are fear of crime and concern with crime conceptually different, but Furstenberg found in his research that they are also located in different places in

TABLE 2-7 •
CAPITAL PUNISHMENT BY BURGLED

	BURGLED	
	YES	NO
FAVOR	80.2	81.9
OPPOSE	19.8	18.1
	P = .70	

Source: General Social Surveys, 1989–90. (Chicago: National Opinion Research Center, 1993).

TABLE 2-8 •
CAPITAL PUNISHMENT BY BLACK PRESIDENT

WOULD VOTE FOR A BLACK FOR PRESIDENT		
	YES	No
FAVOR	77.3	85.2
OPPOSE	22.7	14.8
	P < .005	

Source: General Social Surveys, 1989–90 (Chicago: National Opinion Research Center, 1993).

society. Fear was more prevalent in high-crime neighborhoods than in low-crime areas, as you would expect. But people in high-crime areas were less likely to rank crime as an important political issue—that is, something the government should do something about.[49] Why should fear and concern appear in different places? If you think about who lives in high-crime and low-crime areas, you might find one important reason: People in high-crime areas are usually poor and often are black; they have many important, immediate concerns—poverty, unemployment, housing, schools, racial prejudice—that they would like the government to act on. But the difference in perception of crime between richer and poorer goes beyond mere self-interest. Like opinions on busing, these opinions on crime seem to be part of a more general political orientation, not just a projection of personal concerns. For example, poor people and black people are much more likely than middle-class people and white people to be victims of crime, but they are less likely to want harsher courts. Blacks are six times more likely than whites to be murder victims, but they are much less likely to favor capital punishment.[50]

However, in the years since Furstenberg's research, things may have changed. In recent polls, the poor are slightly more likely than the affluent to rank crime as a national problem. Still, in a 1993 poll, even among African-Americans, who have a higher rate of criminal victimization than other ethnic groups, only 7 percent selected crime as the most important issue facing the community today (45 percent chose education).[51]

SUMMARY AND CONCLUSION

The crime problem is not primarily one of physical harm or economic cost. Our bodies and lives are much more at risk from everyday hazards like working and driving than from criminals, and the crimes about which people are most concerned are not those that cost the most money. What distinguishes street crime as a problem is its effect on society. Since the sharp

ABOUT CRIME & CRIMINOLOGY

CRIME, DISORDER, FEAR, CONSERVATISM... AND MAYBE RACE

Crime was an important issue in the mayoral campaign in New York City in 1993. However, "crime" meant more than predatory crimes like robbery, auto theft, and burglary, nor did the evidence on these crimes seem to be crucial.

The incumbent, David Dinkins, the city's first African-American mayor, pointed out that during his administration, rates of all serious crimes in New York had decreased. Nevertheless, the challenger, Rudolph Giuliani, campaigned on crime. In one Giuliani TV ad, a restaurant worker recalled that his street "used to be lined with people sitting out in front of their houses in or in front of their apartments at night to cool off, and you don't see that in New York because everybody's afraid to come out at night."

A *New York Times* article ("Giuliani Zeroing in on Crime Issue") noted that the ads "coincided with an emphasis by Mr. Giuliani on what his campaign calls 'quality of life' issues ... promising a crackdown on street drug dealers, panhandlers and menacing 'squeegee men.' And last week he unveiled a policy to curtail serv-

ices drastically to some of the city's homeless by setting a 90-day limit on shelter stays."

Giuliani's chief advisor said of this strategy, "It takes the campaign to the record: Do you feel safer? Do you really believe that crime is down? Are you going to have to have a searchlight to walk in the streets and to step over the bodies of the homeless who need help?"

In a speech a few weeks later, Giuliani said, "The difference between the present Mayor and us is that he believes that crime has been reduced. Now if you believe that crime has been reduced, you are living in never-never land. We understand that it hasn't because the conditions of our streets have gotten much more dangerous."

In other words, for Giuliani and his supporters, the statistics on predatory crime were irrelevant; "crime" meant those visible acts of incivility or disorder that made people feel afraid—drug merchants, panhandlers, windshield washers, and the homeless.

As in other elections, it was difficult to sort out race from crime and conservatism. Higher-crime areas, largely black and Hispanic, voted for Dinkins. The lower-crime, mostly white areas like Staten Island turned out heavily for the anticrime candidate, Giuliani.

---

increase of crime in the 1960s, people have become more fearful, their lives more constrained. Yet actual exposure to crime seems to be only a minor cause of this fear. Among personal characteristics, sex and age are more important. The social and physical environment also contribute to fear. Abandoned buildings or teenagers hanging out on the street and other forms of disorder are not intrinsically criminal, but people see them as signs of crime and occasions for a heightened sense of apprehension. Unfamiliarity is another important source of fear. People become more apprehensive in unfamiliar surroundings and amid unfamiliar people.

Beginning in the 1960s, crime became not just a social problem but a political issue as well. Inevitably, the politics of crime became entwined with issues of race relations. The debate often went beyond any rational consideration of what the government could do about crime. Conservatives were accused of racism, of using "law and order" and "crime in the streets" as code words for race—as though the rising crime rates could be reversed by not speaking about them. Liberals, who stressed the need to improve the social and economic conditions of the poor, were criticized for being soft on crime and for showing too little concern for the victims—as though hatred of criminals and sympathy for victims were policies for reducing crime.

Clear thinking on crime requires accurate information. Unfortunately, the most available sources of information, the mass media, seldom give an accurate picture of the dimensions of crime. In extreme cases, the media, by giving more coverage to certain kinds of stories, can create the impression that a crime wave is occurring when the actual incidence of crime remains unchanged.

The trouble with crime news is not so much its volume but the style of presentation. Except for the occasional report of official crime statistics and overcrowding in prisons, the media seldom show crime from a sociological view. They present crime, in the words of James Q. Wilson, "as composed of individual events that have no systematic relationship to each other."[52] For the media, crime is an individual act, not evidence of some larger set of social forces. Poverty, unemployment, neighborhood conditions, peer influence, lenient courts—these are virtually invisible on TV crime shows. The cause of crime is usually either insanity or insatiable greed, especially on fictional shows. But even in the factual news, the more a crime resembles that of fictional TV or movies, the more coverage it gets. As I write this, one of the big crime stories in the news is the Menendez murders, a case in which the defense is based on legal insanity and the prosecution argues greed, and all the while I keep expecting that the brothers will soon get a surprise visit from Lieutenant Columbo. The sexually dangerous woman, long a staple of crime fiction (as well as highly successful movies like *Basic Instinct* and *Fatal Attraction*) turns up on the news as Amy Fisher or Lorena Bobbitt. The media—whether fiction; news; or that mixture of the two, the TV movie "based on a true story"—not only present crime as isolated, individual acts but also focus on unusual crimes rather than typical ones. The media seldom give us stories about ordinary crimes, even ordinary murders, or changes in neighborhood safety or the percentage of robbers convicted and imprisoned. Wilson suggests that the media should "cover crime the way the sports pages cover the American League," with "box scores tracking burglars or robbers through the system."[53]

Wilson's baseball analogy is a good one. The summer I wrote the first draft of this chapter, my local baseball team ran a thirty-second commercial encouraging viewers to watch the game on television or go out to the stadium. The advertisement showed our team hitting home runs, making diving catches, and sliding into third under the tag. They looked good—very good. Yet when I checked the standings at the end of the season, I found they had the second worst won–lost record in either league.

Crime news is like that advertisement. Choosing from all reported criminal events, the media fill a limited time or space with those stories that will most interest the public. From the media we learn little about the frequent, typical crimes that are more likely to affect us directly; nor do we see the everyday workings of the criminal justice system. Unfortunately, these ordinary events, although they do not make the news, do make up a large part of the crime problem in America today. In the next chapter, we will look at ways of keeping score.

Critical Thinking Questions

1. What are the physical, economic, psychological, and social costs of crime, and which is most important?
2. What makes some people more afraid of crime and some less afraid?
3. Why is a neighborhood's crime rate not the most important factor in its level of fear?
4. How accurate is the picture of crime we get from the media?
5. What makes a crime newsworthy?
6. What are the traditional conservative and liberal views of crime?
7. What is the connection between the politics of race and the politics of crime?
8. Does being a victim change a person's views on crime policy?

KEY TERMS

broken windows

concern with crime

conservative

controlling for a variable

disorder

fear of crime

incivility

law-and-order politician

liberal

media crime waves

predatory crimes

signs of crime

white backlash

CHAPTER THREE

THE NUMBERS GAME

COUNTING CRIME

CHAPTER OUTLINE

So MUCH CRIME

Sometimes I begin my course in criminology by asking students what they want to know about crime or what questions they would like to be able to answer after completing the course. Often, the first question is "Why is there so much crime?" I usually answer with another question: "How much crime is there?"

This is a puzzling question. In everyday speech, we often talk about problems like crime or air pollution or poverty as if they were things whose size was obvious and could be easily measured. But when we try to think of specific dimensions (instead of "so much"), we realize how vague our thinking is.

Sometimes when I ask, "How much crime is there?" a student will reply, "Too much." But this response raises the same kinds of questions. "How much is too much?" Or to put it another way, "How much crime would *not* be too much?" Occasionally a student will say that "any crime is too much— especially if it happens to me." This kind of answer usually gets a laugh, and the student does have a point. From the standpoint of the individual, even one crime is one too many. But would that standard hold true for a society? If one crime is too many for an entire society, we are failing to distinguish between that society and the society that has 100 million crimes. They are both in the category of "too much crime."

Numbers, whether compiled by the police or by less official sources, have political implications. Criminologists have done much research probing the origins and accuracy of various statistics.

The question "Why is there so much crime?" also assumes that there is in fact a great deal of crime. But is this assumption correct? "How do you know that there's so much crime?" I ask. Typical answers are "You always see it on the news" or "It's all around" or "My uncle's house was robbed last month." Of course, it doesn't take long for students to realize that these answers aren't very convincing. This anecdotal evidence tells only that there is *some* crime, not whether the overall amount is great or small.

Of course, the media do sometimes give the score. At least once a year, newspapers print items much like the following:

CRIME FELL BY 4 PERCENT LAST YEAR

AUG. 26—According to FBI figures released today, serious crimes in the United States decreased 4 percent from the previous year. Police reports showed a decrease in most major crimes. Violent crime, however, declined by only 1 percent....

At first glance, the story seems fairly obvious. It gives the score, and the score looks pretty good. But read the item again. Are you sure you know what all the words mean? What does the FBI have to do with these figures? What are "police reports"? And just what constitutes a "serious crime" or a "violent crime"?

Suppose that during that year, a government employee was convicted of selling secrets to a group of Iraqi terrorists. Is that a "serious crime"? Or suppose that a politician was caught for extorting $200,000 in kickbacks from companies that received city contracts. Is that a "serious crime"? Or suppose that you went to the parking lot only to discover that someone had taken a sledge hammer and reduced your new car to scrap metal. Is that a "serious crime"? Is it a "violent crime"? Or suppose that a drug dealer was arrested for selling heroin and cocaine with a street value of $500,000. Is that a "serious crime"?

The answer to all these questions is no. None of these crimes would have been counted among the "major crimes" referred to in the newspaper article. That story is based on something called the FBI *Index of Serious Crime*. The Index was devised in 1929, and for over sixty years it has been the official measure of crime in the United States. When criminologists speak of *official* crime rates, it is the Index they are referring to. Originally, the Index contained seven crimes: murder, rape, robbery, aggravated assault, burglary, larceny, and motor vehicle theft. In 1982, arson was added to the list. Local police departments report information on these crimes to the FBI. The FBI then compiles all these reports, and the final tally, along with a mountain of other information, is published each year in a volume called *Crime in the United States*, also known as the **Uniform Crime Reports (UCR)**. The hypothetical news item above, about serious crime in the United States, was referring to the UCR **Index crimes**: those eight crimes and no others—no drug deals, no vandalism, no extortion, no bribes. In some ways the UCR Index of crime is analogous to the Dow–Jones Index for the stock market. Of the thousands and thousands of stocks traded every day on the New York and other exchanges, the Dow includes only thirty. When stockbrokers say that "the market" was up 16 points, they are referring to an average based on these thirty stocks.

Constructing a Crime Index

Clearly, these omissions are serious drawbacks. Statements about "crime"—meaning this official crime rate—will necessarily be somewhat misleading. So why not count other crimes? To understand why the UCR Index leaves out what seem like some fairly serious crimes, perhaps we should start from scratch. Suppose that the country does not have any method of counting crime and that it is now our job to create one. What shall we count, and how shall we count it? Should we count every violation of every criminal statute—every drunk-and-disorderly violation, every playground or barroom shoving match, every joint of marijuana? What we want is not a count of all crimes, but some number that will indicate how much serious crime there is—that is, an *Index* (or indicator) of *serious* crime.

Besides seriousness, two other factors should influence our decision: convenience and accuracy. Fortunately, the police now keep records of citizens' reports of crimes. Let's assume for a minute that when a crime is committed, somebody calls the cops. Therefore, to count burglaries, robberies, and so on, we can go to police records to see how many people called the cops for each type of crime.

MAKING CRIME REPORTING UNIFORM

Besides the issues of seriousness and sources, we face a further problem of definition, that of uniformity. We are relying on local police departments for our information, but we want a given criminal action to be categorized the same way regardless of local laws. In one state, breaking into a car to steal something may be prosecuted as burglary; in another state, the same act may be called larceny.[1] Relying on legal definitions also creates problems in counting because several laws will apply to a single act. Suppose a man runs up to a woman, grabs her purse, pushes her away, and runs off. In one state, he can be charged with all of the following crimes: robbery, attempted robbery, assault, and larceny. Which shall we include in our count of crime in the United States? Suppose that the prosecutor, for want of credible evidence, decides not to charge the person with any crime at all. Even though the purse snatching undoubtedly occurred, statistics based only on legal categories would omit it from the tally.

Because of these difficulties, the UCR provides a set of definitions that is independent from the laws and the legal processing of the crime. The legal definition and handling of crimes may vary from one locality to another, but in reporting crime statistics all police departments use the same set of definitions. That is why the system is called Uniform Crime Reports: It is a uniform way of reporting crime.

We now have a uniform system for the police to report the serious crimes they discover, but should we still try to include *all* serious crimes? Perhaps not, for we also want our count to be accurate. But sometimes seriousness and accuracy may conflict with each other. In some serious crimes, nobody

IN THE NEWS

Is the crime described below "serious"? Should it be counted in the Index of serious crime? The fraud, which occurred over seven or eight years, involved falsified data from three tests performed on 4,390 missile parts. How many crimes should be counted?

COMPANY ADMITS IT FAKED TESTS ON MISSILE-SYSTEM PART

by Jonathan Rabinovitz

Uniondale, L.I., May 16—The Long Island manufacturer of a missile system component has admitted falsifying test results it provided the Government before the system's deployment, law-enforcement officials said today.

The component, known as the Launcher Electronic Unit, was used in Operation Desert Storm ... and was replaced after the missiles failed to fire....

Lucas [the parent company of the firm that committed the fraud] failed to conduct three required tests on some of the 4,390 units that it made between 1984 and 1991 as part of a classified Air Force contract, valued at roughly $58 million....

According to court papers, the company kept records on every unit it produced. In some instances these documents indicated that a unit had passed all three tests, even though none had been performed....
Sometimes supervisors would order test technicians to make the false entries, and on other occasions the supervisors would do it themselves....

Jonny J. Frank, a Special Assistant United States Attorney who worked on the case, said, "They did it this way to save time and to save money."

But one law-enforcement official ... remarked that there were some suspicions that the company chose not to conduct the tests because it knew the parts would not pass.

"This problem could have cost lives," the official said.

Source: New York Times, May 17, 1994, p. B4.

---

calls the police. If I sell you a kilo of heroin that you then divide and sell to other customers, we are both committing crimes that many people would consider very serious.[2] But who's going to call the police? With nonpredatory or "victimless" crimes (drug trafficking, prostitution, illegal gambling, etc.), the only readily available statistics are arrests, and unfortunately the number of arrests will reflect not the level of crime but the level of police activity. Therefore, if we want our Index to be an accurate reflection of crime, we had better leave out the kinds of crimes—even serious crimes—for which nobody calls the police.

In the interests of accuracy, we should also leave out crimes that are seldom discovered. Most white-collar crimes come to light not because a victim calls the cops but because some agency decides to investigate. These crimes may be quite serious. But should we include these crimes on our score sheet? If we do, our count will lose accuracy since many other similar crimes are also undiscovered. Even when the crime is discovered, how many crimes should we put on our Index of serious crimes (see the In the News box above).

THE FBI'S INDEX CRIMES

Here, then, are the Index crimes and their brief definitions:

CRIMES ON THE INDEX OF SERIOUS CRIMES

Murder and nonnegligent manslaughter	The willful killing of one person by another without legal justification.
Rape	The carnal knowledge of a female against her will. (Attempts are included.)
Robbery	Taking or attempting to take anything of value from a person by force or threat of force. (Purse snatching is not included.)
Aggravated assault	Inflicting serious bodily injury on a person. Attempts with a weapon are included, even if no injury occurs (e.g., a gunshot that misses).
Burglary	Unlawful entry of a structure (building) with the intent to commit a felony or theft. The use of force to gain entry is not required. (Attempts are included.)
Larceny	The unlawful taking of property other than motor vehicles, without force or threat of force to the person. (Included are pocket picking, purse snatching, bicycle theft, thefts from motor vehicles, theft of motor vehicle parts, shoplifting.)
Motor vehicle theft	Theft or attempted theft of a motor vehicle.
Arson	The intentional damaging by fire of a building, vehicle, etc. (Attempts are included. Fires ofunknown origin are excluded.)

The first four crimes listed—murder, rape, robbery, and aggravated assault—are called **violent crimes** or "crimes against the person." The latter term is probably more accurate since in these crimes the criminal confronts the victim directly. *All* robberies are classified as violent crimes, even if no actual violence occurs and even if the criminal's object is to get money, not to do violence to someone. In **property crimes**—burglary, larceny, motor vehicle theft, and arson—the property, not the person, is the object of the criminal's action. All burglaries are included, no matter how violent the burglar's method of breaking in.

COMPUTING CRIME RATES

Since we want to use crime statistics to compare different times and places, merely counting the crimes is not quite enough. For example, in 1981, according to the UCR, there were 22,520 murders in the United States; a decade later, in 1990, there were 23,440—slightly more. The change in the absolute number of murders is misleading, though, because there were more people in the United States in 1990 than in 1981. To compare the two years, we must make the number of murders relative to the number of people. That is, we must convert the number to a *rate* of murders *per* population. A rate is a fraction with a given denominator. In percentages—the most commonly used rate—the denominator is 100, but because the number of crimes is small compared to the population, percentages would be too difficult to interpret. We could say that in 1981, 0.0098 percent of the population was murdered, but that number hardly seems meaningful. Instead, the UCR uses 100,000 as its denominator. To convert the number to a rate per 100,000, we divide the number of murders by the number of people in the United States (which gives the rate per person) and then multiply by 100,000 to get the rate per 100,000 persons.

$$\frac{\text{Murders in 1981}}{\text{Population in 1981}} = \frac{22,520}{229,146,000} \times 100,000 = 9.8$$

$$\frac{\text{Murders in 1990}}{\text{Population in 1990}} = \frac{23,440}{248,709,873} \times 100,000 = 9.4$$

Although more people were murdered in 1990, the murder rate declined from 9.8 per 100,000 to 9.4 per 100,000.

The UCR uses this same general formula for all its Index **crime rates**:

$$\frac{\text{Crimes Known to the Police}}{\text{Population}} \times 100,000 = \text{Crime Rate}$$

Using the same formula, we can compare the rates of motor vehicle theft in Boston and Houston in 1993:

	BOSTON	HOUSTON
MVT KNOWN TO THE POLICE	11,932	25,519
POPULATION	553,870	1,724,327
RATE PER 100,000	2,154.3	1,505.3

Source: Federal Bureau of Investigation, *Crime in the United States, 1992: The Uniform Crime Reports* (Washington, DC, 1993).

Houston had more than twice as many thefts, but Boston's rate of motor vehicle theft was 43 percent higher.

Table 3–1 shows the UCR rates of Index crimes for 1993. (Because of technical problems, the FBI does not compute a national rate for arson and frequently omits arson from its totals.)

CRIME: WHAT TO COUNT?

No system of counting crime is perfect, and although the UCR solves some of the problems, it has some major flaws. First, there is the problem of seriousness. As we have already seen, the Index definition of serious crime leaves out many crimes that most people think are serious: white-collar crimes, embezzlement, drug crimes, kidnapping, all federal crimes (e.g., counterfeiting and

TABLE 3-1 •
INDEX CRIMES—1993

CRIME	NUMBER OF CRIMES KNOWN TO POLICE	CRIME RATE PER 100,000	PERCENT CHANGE IN RATE FROM 1992
MURDER	24,526	9.5	+2.2
RAPE	104,806	40.6	-5.1
ROBBERY	659,757	255.8	-3.0
AGGRAVATED ASSAULT	1,135,099	440.1	-0.4
BURGLARY	2,834,808	1099.2	-5.9
LARCENY	7,820,909	3,032.4	-2.3
MOTOR VEHICLE THEFT	1,561,047	605.3	-4.1
TOTAL VIOLENT CRIME	1,924,188	746.1	-1.5
TOTAL PROPERTY CRIME	12,216,764	4736.9	-3.4
TOTAL INDEX CRIME	14,140,952	5482.9	-3.1

Source: Federal Bureau of Investigation, *Crime in the United States, 1993: The Uniform Crime Reports* (Washington, DC, 1994).

skyjacking), and others. But even for the serious crimes the Index does include, it does not distinguish between levels of seriousness within each type of crime.

> Four robbers enter a store, beat the owner with their guns, and take $20,000; the victim calls the police. Score one robbery on the UCR.

> One boy threatens to punch another unless the victim gives up his lunch money. The victim calls the police. Score one robbery on the UCR.

In the first example, although both aggravated assault and robbery occurred, the UCR's rule for counting violent crimes is one victim, one crime, listed under the most serious—in this case, robbery. The UCR ranks murder the most serious, followed in order by rape, robbery, and aggravated assault.

POPULATION: WHO, OR WHAT, TO COUNT?

The numerator of the UCR crime rates tells us only the number of crimes, not how serious they are. The denominator in UCR rates can also be misleading. To take an obvious example, the rate for rape is computed by dividing the number of rapes by the population of the country, even though the UCR's definition of rape puts only women at risk. If the rate were computed as rapes per 100,000 *women*, it would be about twice the current rate in the UCR.

Another denominator problem arises when we try to compare crime rates between cities. The problem is not that some cities have large populations and others have smaller populations; the use of crime rates, with their common denominator (100,000), solves this problem. Instead, the problem lies in the way the population is counted. For example, each year when the UCR is published, one city that usually turns up with extraordinarily high crime rates is Atlantic City, New Jersey. Why? Your first impulse in answering this question is to think of the numerator—crimes committed. In the last twenty years, Atlantic City has built its economy on gambling, and no doubt this kind of economy brings crime. Gamblers with ready cash in their hotel rooms or pockets attract more burglary and larceny (pocket picking). These crimes increase the numerator. But remember, a rate is a fraction (crime divided by population), and there are two ways to raise the value of a fraction: Keep the numerator high, or keep the denominator low. Atlantic City's high crime rate is caused also by peculiarities in the denominator—the number of people in the population—that is, the resident population. If you go to Atlantic City, your pocket is picked, and you want to report it, you call the local police station. Score one in the numerator for Atlantic City larceny. But at census time, are you counted in the Atlantic City population? No. Score zero in the denominator. As with rape, the denominator does not really measure the population at risk. In other cities or states, commuters, tourists, migrant workers, and others all may contribute to the numerator as victims but not to the denominator as population—a combination that results in an inflated crime rate.

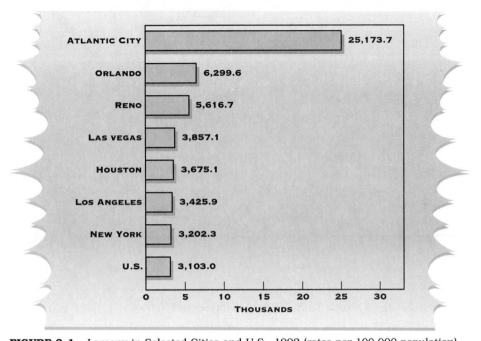

FIGURE 3–1   Larceny in Selected Cities and U.S., 1992 (rates per 100,000 population)

Source: Based on Federal Bureau of Investigation, *Crime in the United States, 1992: The Uniform Crime Reports*, (Washington, DC, 1993).

Figure 3–1 illustrates how this statistical flaw affects cities such as Orlando, Las Vegas, and Atlantic City.

The UCR crime rates, based on crimes per population, can be misleading in yet another way. In Figure 3–2, the lower line shows rates of motor vehicle theft as reported in the UCR. Between 1968 and 1978, the rate rose from about 390 to nearly 460 per 100,000 people, a 15 percent increase. In only two years out of ten did the rate decrease.

What the UCR rate tells us is the proportion of Americans whose cars were stolen. But is this the only way to measure auto theft? Why should we use the population as our denominator if what is being taken is cars? The upper line shows rates of motor vehicle theft based on the number of registered vehicles.

In each year, the rate based on registrations is higher than the UCR rate since there are fewer vehicles than people (a lower denominator gives a higher rate). But more important, the changes in rates go in opposite directions. The UCR rate shows a more or less steady increase—overall, a 15 percent increase. The per-vehicle rate shows a decrease—from nearly 760 per 100,000 vehicles to about 640 per 100,000—a 15 percent decrease. And the year-to-year changes show a decrease in seven out of ten years.

Do you find this discrepancy frustrating? Are you hoping that this paragraph will tell you which figure is "right" and whether auto theft "really" increased or "really" decreased? Sorry.

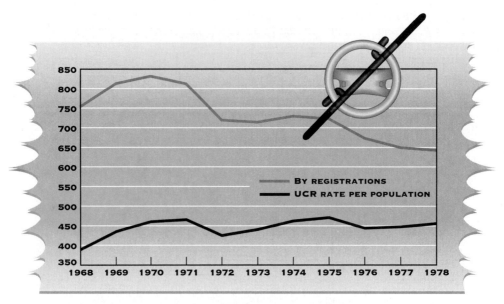

FIGURE 3–2   Motor Vehicle Theft, 1968–1978 (rates per 100,000)

Source: Data from UCR and Insurance Information Institute in Flanagan and McLeod, *Sourcebook—1982.*

WHAT CRIME RATES MEAN, AND WHAT THEY DON'T MEAN

I, too, find these statistics puzzling. But I think we are frustrated because we expect too much. We want a single statistic to tell us the entire story of auto theft. Perhaps, in some way we are not fully aware of, we even use overall crime statistics as an Index of morality. We see the UCR as a melodrama. If crime goes down, the good guys are winning; if it goes up, the bad guys are winning. We assume that if crime goes up, an increase in some other evil must be the cause—a decline in morality, the breakdown of the family, the failure of the criminal justice system, or the injustice and inequality in society.

But the two graphs tell us something more complicated: that the amount of theft depends not just on the number of "bad people" but also on the amount of stealable property. More autos were stolen because there were more of them to steal; in fact, the thieves did not quite keep up with the increase in auto sales. In the language of business, car thieves were not maintaining market share. Crime went up not just because Americans were less moral but also because they were more affluent.

The lesson on car theft may apply to other crime statistics as well. For example, during the 1970s, UCR burglary rates per 100,000 population increased by about 40 percent. But as with motor vehicle theft, factors besides the "badness" of the society can explain some of the increase. First, the number of households (like the number of motor vehicles) increased faster than did the population. In fact, while the rate of burglaries per population was increasing in the 1970s, the rate per household was decreasing slightly. Second, more of those houses were easily burglarized because nobody was home. Third, those households contained more stealable and valuable items—expensive cameras, color televisions, tape recorders, and so on.

> Fifteen years ago [i.e., around 1975] you had to do more burglaries. See, back then there wasn't a lot of merchandise like there is now. See, you wouldn't have to do three burglaries now because you have VCRs. Back then, you go in a house and get probably a TV. Maybe food. Now you can count on making much more per house for sure: a TV, VCR, microwave, watches, jewelry, and any money that's in the house.[3]

What would the statistics look like if we didn't measure burglaries per population, but instead looked at what proportion of our property was stolen? Did the increase in burglary keep up with the increase in stealable wealth? Unfortunately, there are too few statistics on this question to allow a definitive answer, although it does appear that the increase in consumer goods contributes to the increase in crime rates.[4]

Young people delaying marriage, young singles setting up their own households, women delaying first childbirth and working away from the home, more attractive consumer products bought with greater wealth—these changes are not clearly bad, yet they play an important role in crime rates. Perhaps this line of thinking does not extend to violent crimes like rape or murder. But with property crimes, which make up over 80 percent of all Index crimes, the message behind the statistics is a complicated one. In short, I am arguing that when we see crime statistics like those in the UCR, we should interpret them cautiously and narrowly rather than treating them simply as an Index of other evils.

THE UCR IN THE REAL WORLD

All of the flaws in the UCR crime rates mentioned so far are inherent in the way these statistics are computed. That is, even before it is put into operation, the UCR has several shortcomings in the way it defines and counts crime. In addition, the actual process of gathering these crime statistics has its own types of inaccuracy.

Let's take burglary as an example. In 1992, the UCR statistics showed 2,979,884 burglaries—a rate of about 1,168 per 100,000 people. Of course this does not mean that exactly 2,979,884 burglaries occurred in the United States. For a crime to appear in the UCR total, a citizen must report it to the police, and the police must record it in the figures they send to the FBI. That is why the FBI calls its UCR crime statistics "crimes known to the police." If the victim does not call the police, or if the police for some reason choose not to record it, the crime will not become part of the official statistics.

From the beginning, people interested in crime have realized that the figures in the UCR must be inaccurate. They knew that many crimes were not reported. But how many? Nobody knew; nobody even had a way of making a good guess. Criminologists refer to this unknown quantity as the **dark figure of crime**.

OTHER SOURCES OF CRIME STATISTICS

If we can't rely on information from citizens' reports, we must move back one step closer to the crime itself; we must go either to the victims or to the criminals. Accordingly, criminologists have developed two types of tools for estimating crime: the **self-report study**, in which people are asked about crimes they themselves have committed, and the **victimization survey**, in which people are interviewed about the crimes committed against them.

Self-report surveys, because of the effort and expense, have usually focused on local, captive populations—high-school students or prison inmates—rather than a national sample from the general population. These studies can be very useful for finding differences between people who commit crimes and those who do not or between the most serious criminals and the less frequent offenders. But self-report surveys are of little help in estimating overall rates of crime.

Victimization surveys, too, are costly to carry out. So it was not until the mid-1960s that the first nationwide victimization surveys were done. In 1965, the National Opinion Research Center (NORC) surveyed 10,000 households and found that of all serious crimes (all the Index crimes, except murder) only about half were reported to the police.[5] Although this study provided a better view of the dark figure of crime, it was only a one-time survey and so could not be used for assessing increases or decreases in the crime rate. However, in 1973, the U.S. Justice Department set up a regular victimization survey, known originally as the National Crime Survey (NCS) and now called the **National Crime Victimization Survey (NCVS)**.

Every six months, the NCVS conducts interviews with a national sample of 50,000 households comprising a total of about 100,000 people. Interviewers ask a variety of questions about crime, ranging from the very serious ("Were you knifed, shot at, or attacked?") to the not so serious ("Was anything stolen that is kept outside your home, such as a bicycle, a garden hose, or lawn furniture?"). Both of these would qualify as Index crimes in the UCR: The first is an aggravated assault, the second a larceny. If the person says yes, such an event occurred, the interviewer then asks a variety of follow-up questions: Was the crime reported to the police? How much loss and damage occurred? And so on. In "personal" crimes, where the victim sees the criminal, the interviewer also asks questions about the criminal (age, sex, etc.).

The NCVS sample of 50,000 households with 100,000 people constitutes .04 percent of the U.S. population. That may seem small, but in comparison with most surveys, the NCVS is very large. Surveys that estimate who voted for which candidate or how many people are watching which TV show are based on samples of between 1,000 and 2,000. The NCVS needs a large sample because the number of crime victims is so much smaller than the number of people who vote or watch television.

The NCVS, not surprisingly, turns up far more crime than the UCR. For example, the 1992 UCR shows 1,126,974 aggravated assaults known to the police. For the same crime, in the same year, the NCVS estimates 1,848,530—a figure 65 percent higher. For residential burglaries, the figures are (roughly) UCR, 2 million; NCVS, 4.7 million.

The UCR and NCVS are not directly comparable, but generally it's safe to say that the victimization survey finds two to three times as much crime as do official records. The most important reason for the difference is that victims frequently do not report the crime to the police. According to the NCVS, only about one crime in three is reported. Of course, the rate varies from crime to crime. Generally, the more serious the crime, the more likely people are to report it. When the cost of a theft is between $100 and $250, about 45 percent of victims call the police. The reporting rate on auto theft or theft of property worth $1,000 or more is nearly 70 percent. Of robbery victims who are not injured, slightly more than half report the crime to the police; among those who are injured during the robbery, the reporting rate is 67 percent. However, consider the other side of these percentages. Theft of over $1,000 and robbery with injury sound like very serious crimes, but still of every 100 victims of these crimes, 30 choose not to call the police. Perhaps you yourself did not report a victimization to the police. If so, what were your reasons? Did you report it to someone else (e.g., your landlord)? Or did you think that your loss was not great enough to bother about?

Table 3–2 shows some of the reasons victims give for not reporting their crimes. In the 1970s and 1980s, the NCVS classified the most frequent responses as "nothing could be done" and "the matter was not important enough." In recent years, the survey has refined its categories into those shown in the table. It turns out that many victims do not report the crime because they experience no property loss or recover the property themselves. Still, even with the expanded categories, it appears that victims base their decision to report a crime on some vague cost-benefit calculus involving the amount of damage, the likelihood that the police will be able to catch the criminal or recover the property, and the inconvenience of calling the police.

Similarly, when victims who do report crimes are asked for their reasons, they are most likely (45 percent) to cite the practical reasons of recovering property, collecting insurance, and preventing current or future incidents. An additional 26 percent mention catching or punishing the offender and preventing further crime. Only 8.6 percent said that they reported the crime because it was their civic duty.

With violent crimes (rape, assault, and robbery), there is another important factor—the relationship between the victim and the offender. When the offender is a stranger, victims are usually willing to go to the police. But victims who know their offenders are less likely to report the crime. Even when the crime is serious or when injury occurs—as in spousal abuse, fights between acquaintances, or marital rape—the victim may define the act as part of the relationship rather than as a criminal matter for the police and courts.

When we see statistics about crime, we probably think of them as objective, like statistics about the number of dentists or registered automobiles. But in fact, official crime statistics are the result of a filtering process that at its first stage is based on feelings. Victims of crime want, first, to deal with

TABLE 3-2 •
PERCENTAGE DISTRIBUTION OF REASONS FOR NOT REPORTING VICTIMIZATIONS TO THE POLICE, 1992, BY TYPE OF CRIME

	REPORTED TO ANOTHER OFFICIAL	PRIVATE OR PERSONAL MATTER	OBJECT RECOVERED, OFFENDER STOPPED	NOT IMPORTANT ENOUGH	NOT AWARE OF CRIME UNTIL LATER	UNABLE TO RECOVER PROPERTY	LACK OF PROOF	POLICE WOULD NOT WANT TO BE BOTHERED	POLICE INEFFICIENT OR INEFFECTIVE	TOO INCONVENIENT
ALL PERSONAL CRIMES	15.1	8.5	25.0	3.1	4.4	5.8	10.5	7.8	3.3	3.2
RAPE[a]	6.8	17.6	12.8	12.8	0.0	0.0	5.6	8.1	12.5	0.0
ROBBERY	6.0	11.2	19.0	1.6	0.0	4.1	13.2	11.2	9.7	5.0
AGGRAVATED ASSAULT	7.0	22.3	16.4	6.1	0.0	0.0	8.7	6.5	6.8	3.0
ALL HOUSEHOLD CRIMES	3.5	5.2	5.2	4.0	8.4	7.8	10.6	10.9	4.8	2.5
BURGLARY	5.6	4.9	24.3	4.4	11.3	6.6	11.0	9.3	6.3	1.9
MVT[b]	1.9	5.5	35.9	3.0	5.8	0.0	7.4	10.4	8.6	4.7

(PERCENTAGES DO NOT ADD UP TO 100 BECAUSE I HAVE OMITTED "OTHER REASONS" AND SOME OTHER INFREQUENTLY GIVEN REASONS.)

[a]The numbers of rape victims responding to this question is too small to be statistically reliable.

[b]Includes both attempted and successful auto thefts.

Source: Bureau of Justice Statistics, *Criminal Victimization in the United States, 1992* (Washington, DC: 1994).

their emotions. Often, they first turn not to the police but to a friend or relative, partly to get advice but mostly to talk about the disturbing event—just to get their feelings straight. After that, if they feel angry enough about the crime or criminal or hopeful enough about the effectiveness of the police, they will report the crime.

OFF THE RECORD—THE POLICE AND CRIME STATISTICS

The nonreporting of crime is probably the point at which most crimes are lost from official statistics, which are based on crimes known to the police. But there is another important link in the chain between the crime itself and its inclusion in the UCR tally: the police. Even if a citizen reports a crime, the police may choose to leave it out of their records.

In some cases, the reason for doing so is quite legitimate. Police standards and definitions of crime differ from those of citizens. The act that provokes a citizen to call the police may not meet the legal criteria for a crime. In other cases, the reasons for not recording the crime closely

The police will write a report when a crime is serious, when they can make an immediate arrest, and when the victim presses them to do so. Without serious loss or injury, without a suspect, and without a complainant demanding action, the incident may never become a "crime known to the police."

ON CAMPUS

Crime statistics are often not just neutral data. They can have public relations consequences for the police and perhaps other institutions as well.

Last fall marked the first reporting period of the first national law to require disclosure of crime rates on campuses. Sponsored by two Pennsylvania Republicans, Representative William Goodin and Senator Arlen Specter, the Student Right-to-Know and Campus Security Act has its origins in the 1986 death of a 19-year-old Lehigh University student who was raped, sodomized, tortured and murdered in her dorm room by a drunken fellow student. The act requires all colleges and universities receiving Federal funds to publish annually their security and crime-reporting policies, and to make public the number of on-campus inciden[t]s of murder, sexual assault, robbery, assault, burglary and motor-vehicle theft, as well as arrests for weapons possession and drug and alcohol offenses. (Larceny, arson, vandalism or disorderly conduct need not be reported.)

The Campus Security act is a consumer-information law, treating higher education not as a privilege but as a product.

But ease of public access varies. Columbia University and the University of Alaska mailed all requested information within hours. The University of Florida, four of whose students were murdered by unknown assailants in off-campus housing in 1990, dawdled two months, then sent nearly a pound of perky but largely unrelated brochures. The security office of the City University of New York said, testily, that they had never heard of the Campus Security Act. Adelphi University, on Long Island, went into frenzy: "Why do you want to know? We can't release that. Can you prove authorization from the legal department?"

According to The Chronicle of Higher Education, in the first annual crime statements submitted by more than 2,400 schools, there was a total of 30 murders, nearly 1,000 rapes, more than 1,800 robberies, 32,127 burglaries and 8,981 motor-vehicle thefts. The low figures furnished by many colleges especially on rapes make some security experts and victims' rights advocates openly skeptical. And since the Department of Education is not required to analyze campus-crime data, only collect it, a list of America's 10 Most Dangerous Campuses is not in the offing.

Source: Anne Matthews, "The Campus Crime Wave," *New York Times Magazine*, March 7, 1993, pp. 38–47.

resemble the reasons citizens have for not reporting it: It was not important enough; nothing will come of it; it was a private matter. On the basis of these criteria, the officer who arrives on the scene may decide not to write up the crime even though the victim has called the police. In addition, sometimes the complainant (the person who calls the cops) may have had a change of heart about wanting the case pursued. In that event, the police almost never write up the crime. Or if the complainant annoys the police officer, the officer may not bother to write up the crime.[6] The nonrecording of reported crime, then, is also not just the decision of the individual officer. Since crime statistics reflect on the department, the rules for recording and not recording crimes may be a matter of department policy, as well as a matter of politics. The amount of nonrecording varies from city to city according to the police department's policy and according to the political climate surrounding the department.

It is very difficult to know just how many crimes the police keep off the books. Victimization surveys can tell us about the nonreporting of crime by citizens. But nonrecording by the police is another matter. It is harder to shed light on this area of the dark figure of crime, although sometimes we can catch glimpses. For example, in 1950, New York City's rate of burglary (based on crimes known to the police) jumped by 1,300 percent. Of course, the huge increase had nothing to do with changes in the actual number of burglaries. What happened was that before 1950, most burglary reports had been removed from the records (a practice known in police lingo as "canning" or "referring the case to Detective Can"). However, the police chief, under pressure from the FBI, changed this policy; from then on, the great majority of reported burglaries went on the books.[7] In a similar scenario in the early 1980s, the FBI pressured the Chicago police for more honest statistics.[8] As a result, between 1982 and 1984, when most cities had decreasing robbery rates, Chicago's official robbery rate rose 80 percent.

The history of official crime statistics is dotted with similar tales. A national victimization survey in 1972 found that compared with other cities, Philadelphia had a high proportion of victimizations that never became official crime statistics. It is unlikely that Philadelphia victims were less willing than victims in Atlanta or Cleveland to call the police, so the crimes must have disappeared in the police precincts. But why were the Philadelphia police so reluctant to record crime? Some observers think that this policy had something to do with local politics. The former chief of police, Frank Rizzo (whose obituary appeared in the previous chapter), had just been elected mayor, campaigning on a tough anticrime platform. Low crime rates would demonstrate his effectiveness. And sure enough, one way or another, Philadelphia's crime rate remained low.[9]

A similar low crime rate occurred in Washington, D.C. shortly after the election of Richard Nixon in 1972. Nixon had campaigned strongly against crime. Given the structure of American government, the only city that a president could directly affect was Washington. (At that time the district was still controlled by the federal government.) So Washington, the demonstration city for the "war on crime," showed decreases in crime. However, the decreases occurred mostly on paper, not on the streets.[10]

The nonreporting and nonrecording of crime occur in other countries as well. The British Crime Survey found that less than half of all robbery victims reported the crime to the police, and of the robberies reported, British police recorded only 38 percent. Like police in the United States, British police in recent years have apparently become more willing to record crime. So between 1981 and 1987, while the British victimization survey estimated that robberies increased by 9 percent, officially recorded robberies increased by 62 percent.[11]

It appears that in the last two decades police departments have generally become more honest about recording crimes. To be absolutely sure of this change,

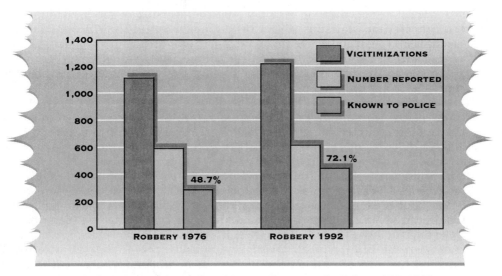

FIGURE 3–3   Victimizations Reported and Crimes Known to the Police 1976, 1992

Source: Derived from Bureau of Justice Statistics, *Criminal Victimization in the United States, 1976, 1992* (Washington, DC: 1978, 1994) and UCR, 1976, 1992.

researchers would have had to make extensive observations over a long period of time in several police departments, and nobody has done that kind of research. But we can get a rough idea by comparing police data in the UCR against the victimizations that NCVS respondents say they reported (see Figure 3–3).

In 1976, the NCVS estimated that there were 1,147,000 robberies and that 53 percent of the victims reported these robberies to the police. Thus, 53 percent of 1,147,000, or 607,910, noncommercial robberies were reported to the police. But the UCR for that year showed only about 287,000 noncommercial robberies "known to the police." That is, the number of noncommercial robberies recorded by the police was less than half of the number that NCVS interviewees said they reported.

By 1992, things had changed. The NCVS estimated 625,000 robberies reported to the police (51 percent of all victimizations). The UCR in 1992 showed that the police had recorded about 450,000 noncommercial robberies. That is, the rate of police recording had risen from 49 percent to 72 percent.[12]

HOW ACCURATE ARE VICTIMIZATION SURVEYS?

It is clear that the UCR severely undercounts crime. But how accurate is the NCVS? There are two points of view on this question. Some criminologists argue that the NCVS gives an inflated picture of crime because of the "telescoping" of memory; that is, people recall as "recent" a victimization that occurred longer ago than the six-month period. Moreover, some of the victimizations people report to NCVS interviewers might not meet the legal criteria for crime.[13]

By contrast, most criminologists think that victimization surveys give a low estimate of the amount of crime. The memory problem, they say, is not that people remember crimes too well but that they forget them. Also, some victims may not tell an interviewer about a crime for the same reasons that they don't call the police: It was a private matter, they don't want to take the time, or (in the case of rape or assault) they are embarrassed. Even when people report a crime to the police, they may still for some reason omit it later in a victimization interview.[14]

There may also be systematic differences in the way people of different social classes respond to a survey. For example, according to the NCVS figures, people with at least some college education are assaulted nearly twice as often as people who never got past fourth grade.[15] Is there really more interpersonal violence among the better educated? More likely, middle-class people remember and report many of the kinds of assault that lower-class people either forget or ignore. Thus, the NCVS rate for aggravated assault, although nearly double the official rate, still underestimates the actual amount of serious violence.

OFFICIAL DATA AND SURVEY DATA—A COMPARISON

Now that you know about the two major sources for counting crime in the United States, you may be tempted to ask, "Which one is right; which one tells us how much crime there really is?" You probably believe that the NCVS is more accurate, and perhaps you even agree with those who dismiss the UCR altogether. After all, if there are so many ways a crime can disappear before it gets into the UCR, not only is the total number wrong but also year-to-year changes will reflect changes in the behavior of victims and police, not changes in actual crime.

I think such a view is wrong. Our goal is not to select the single best measure of crime; our goal is to get as complete a picture of crime as we can. We should recognize first that both police records and the victimization survey have inaccuracies. Perhaps more important, we should remember that the two counts of crime are often measuring different things. For example, the NCVS measures only crimes against households and persons while the UCR includes commercial crime as well. Even within the same category of crime, say household burglary, the two sources of crime statistics have important differences.

The NCVS includes every violation of the law that the interviewees can recall. The UCR (at least in theory) contains only those crimes about which the victim was upset enough to call the police. The NCVS measures crimes—including attempted crimes—that happened. The UCR measures crimes that people think the police ought to do something about. The NCVS measure is objective in that it is more detached from how people feel about the crime. The UCR Index in this sense is more subjective since it depends on the feelings and behavior of the victim.

Some criminologists argue that it is precisely this subjectivity that may make the UCR the better measure of serious crime. The UCR contains crimes that are defined as serious not by some abstract, distant set of rules but by the people directly involved. There is one easy way to discover the criteria an ordinary person uses for deciding seriousness: Does he or she call the police? It turns out that most people share these same informal criteria: If a crime does not involve a loss of high value, bodily injury (or the serious threat of bodily injury), victimization by a stranger, or breaking and entering, most people do not think of it as serious. The police, too, seem to share this definition of serious crime, even though it differs from that of the official UCR Index. So while the NCVS may come closer to estimating the total amount of crime according to abstract, legal definitions, the UCR contains only those crimes that citizens thought were serious enough to report and that the police thought were serious enough to record. In this way, the UCR shows us the size of the crime problem.[16]

Of course, if the official crime rates go up, we still cannot be sure which has changed—the amount of serious crime or people's subjective judgments. This problem is especially important in comparisons between different places or times. It may be that people have become so resigned to crime that they no longer report it to the police as often as they did in the past. However, the available evidence says otherwise. The NCVS began in 1973, and since that time the percentage of victims who report crimes to the police has been remarkably stable, if anything, it has increased slightly (see Table 3–3). The

TABLE 3-3 •

PERCENTAGE OF VICTIMIZATIONS REPORTED TO THE POLICE, 1973–1992

	RAPE	ROBBERY	AGGRAVATED ASSAULT	BURGLARY	MVT
1973	46	52	52	47	68
1974	47	54	54	48	67
1975	47	53	55	49	71
1976	49	53	58	48	69
1977	46	56	51	49	68
1978	44	51	53	47	66
1979	45	55	51	48	68
1980	47	57	54	51	69
1981	47	56	52	51	67
1982	48	56	58	49	72
1983	47	53	56	49	69
1984	47	54	55	49	69
1985	48	54	58	50	72
1986	50	58	59	52	74
1987	48	55	60	52	75
1988	48	57	54	51	73
1989	45	51	53	50	76
1990	48	50	59	51	75
1991	49	55	58	50	74
1992	50	51	62	54	75

Source: NCVS, 1992.

reporting rates also tell us that police statistics on frequently reported crimes (e.g., auto theft) should be more accurate than their statistics on larceny.

REREADING THE HEADLINES—A SUMMARY

Let's return to the typical headline about an increase or decrease in the rate of serious crime. Consciously or not, people often read this statistic as a barometer that tells us how well we are doing in the fight against crime; and since it comes with the authority of the FBI, people may also tend to accept it as accurate. Of course, having read this far, you now know better. The accuracy of official crime statistics depends most on the victims and on the police. Ironically, these two groups that are so crucial to our knowledge of crime are the greatest source of error in crime statistics. Both the victim, in deciding whether to report a crime, and the police, in deciding whether to record it, have many things on their minds. Unfortunately, one of the things they are probably *not* thinking about is the accuracy of crime statistics. Victims weigh the bother of reporting against the likely benefits or, with crimes committed by acquaintances or relatives, define the act as a private matter rather than a criminal one. Police use these criteria plus the public relations value of crime rates and clearance rates.

The National Crime Survey, our other major source of information on the amount of crime, also has limitations. It omits commercial crimes; it includes many crimes that most people would regard as trivial; and it depends on the memory and cooperativeness of the victims. Nevertheless, trends in the NCVS have generally mirrored trends in official UCR rates.

Since the creation of the NCVS in 1973, the differences between it and the UCR have become steadily smaller. Figure 3–4 shows the rates of aggravated assault as measured by these two sources of national data. The NCVS shows a steady decrease, while the UCR shows a more or less steady increase.

The rise in UCR rates of aggravated assault, despite decreases in victimization rates, has two possible causes: the percentage of victims who reported the crime to the police increased, or the police recorded more of the assaults that were reported to them. Since the NCVS shows no increase in reporting rates, it seems likely that over the years the police have become more scrupulous about recording crimes they might once have kept off the books. This change is especially relevant to the crime of aggravated assault because police departments have changed their policies regarding domestic violence. A wife-battering incident that police might have once dealt with informally now requires an arrest; and if the police make an arrest, they cannot very well keep the offense out of their statistics.

Before jumping to conclusions from this year's UCR figures, there are other things we want to know. Do victimization figures from the NCVS resemble the UCR trends? Do the trends in the most accurately reported crimes (murder and auto theft) parallel those in the other crimes? Even if the answer to these questions is yes, we should be cautious about small changes in crime rates from one year to another. It is only when we look at

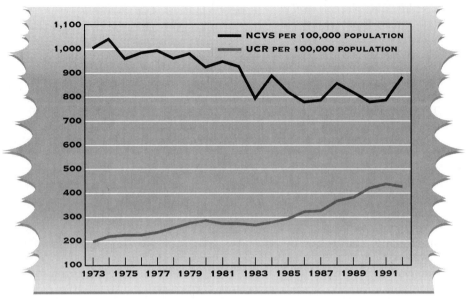

FIGURE 3–4 Aggravated Assault, 1973–1992 (rates from UCR and NCVS)

Source: Derived from Bureau of Justice Statistics, *Criminal Victimization in the United States*, 1976, 1992 (Washington, DC: 1978, 1994) and UCR, 1976, 1992.

longer trends that we can be more confident in statements about how crime is changing.

COMPARED WITH WHAT?

Let's go back to the original question: How much crime is there? Obviously, to answer this question objectively, we must count crimes, and so far, we have examined the different techniques for doing so. Each method has its own strengths and its own types of inaccuracy, and each comes up with different numbers. It's frustrating. We ask a simple question, and instead of a simple answer, we get several answers that are in some way inaccurate and are rarely in agreement.

However, even if we could arrive at a perfect, accurate count, we would still not have an answer to a more difficult and perhaps more important question. Suppose we know that last year in the United States there were exactly 24,000 murders, a rate of about 9.3 per 100,000. Is that a lot or a little?

When I ask students this question in class, they have two typical responses. Some take the absolutist position I mentioned at the beginning of this chapter: Even one murder is a lot (especially if you yourself happen to be the victim). This answer is not very useful; it does not distinguish between one murder and 24,000. Any crime is too much. Other students look at the question in relative rather than absolute terms. They answer my question with one of their own: "Compared with what?"

Excellent question. The answer is that criminologists, like anyone else, make two kinds of comparisons. Historical (or time-series) studies compare levels of crime at different times in the same place. When the newspaper headline says, "Crime in United States Down 4 percent," it is comparing the United States this year with the United States last year. Other historical studies, as we shall see, cover much longer periods of time.

Besides comparing current crime rates with those in the past, we might also want to see how the United States compares with other countries. Whether we are using crime rates as part of some Index of the quality of life, or whether we are trying to see what other factors correlate with differences in crime rates, it probably makes sense to compare ourselves with countries that are similar in many other respects. For a few specific purposes, we might compare the United States with, say, Vietnam, which is a communist, nonindustrial, and very poor country. But generally, we will want to compare the United States with countries whose society, economy, and political system resemble our own—the Western, industrialized countries. These include the countries of western Europe (e.g., Great Britain, France, Germany, Italy, and the Scandinavian countries), Canada, Australia, and Japan.

Comparisons among countries are not easy to make. All of the problems that plague crime statistics within a single country become multiplied. Countries will differ in their definitions of crime, the willingness of citizens to report crime, the diligence of the police in recording crime, and other factors that affect official crime rates. Comparisons based on victimization surveys may also be misleading. To begin with, most European crime surveys are one-shot surveys confined to one or two cities. There are few regular, nationwide surveys like our National Crime Survey. Second, the questions asked in these surveys may not always be comparable from one country to another, though a few studies have been designed explicitly for comparative purposes.

THE UNITED STATES—WE'RE NUMBER ONE

Because of all these difficulties, criminologists often look at those crimes where differences in definition and reporting will be minimal and statistics will be most accurate. The most obvious candidate is murder, especially since data on this crime come not only from the police but also from public health agencies that record cause of death. Even murder statistics must be carefully reviewed, however, for just as the UCR's definition of robbery or burglary includes attempted crimes, some countries include attempted murder in their murder statistics. Imagine what U.S. murder rates would look like were we to reclassify many of our aggravated assaults under the category of murder and attempted murder. Figure 3–5 shows the murder rates from 1984 for a few countries (including some in eastern Europe).

These figures immediately raise the question of why the U.S. murder rate is so much higher than that of other countries. The answer is complicated and

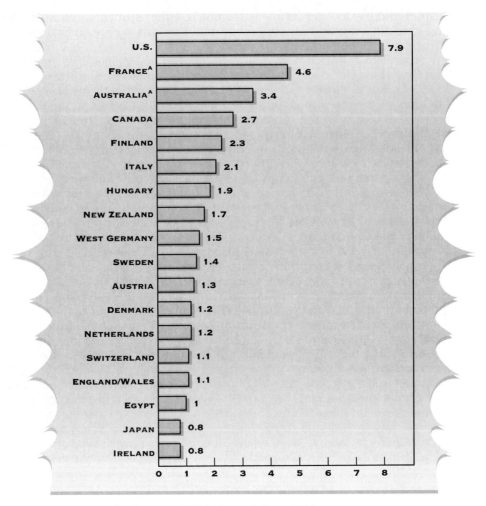

FIGURE 3–5   Murder Rates per 100,000 population, 1984

a Includes both homicide and *attempted* homicide.

Source: Carol B. Kalish, "International Crime Rates" (Washington, DC: Bureau of Justice Statistics, 1988).

a matter of some debate, which I would like to leave for another chapter. However, these murder rates raise a different question: Is the murder rate a good indicator of the overall level of crime? We know that the murder rate is the most accurate of any of the crimes we might use for comparing countries. But will a country with a high murder rate also have high rates of burglary or auto theft? There is good reason to think not. First, murder constitutes a very small part of the overall crime rate. In the United States, murder's share of the total crime Index is less than .2 percent. In addition, murder differs from most Index crimes in that it usually has no economic motive. In this way it resembles aggravated assault and perhaps rape: It shows a willingness to use

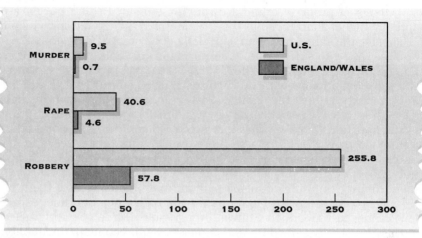

FIGURE 3–6   Violent Crimes Known to Police, 1993 (United States and England/Wales)

extreme force in interpersonal matters. But this motive probably plays a less important part in the robberies, burglaries, larcenies, and auto theft that account for nearly 90 percent of all Index crimes in the United States and an even greater proportion of comparable crime in other countries.

Therefore, while the United States clearly has more murders than other Western, industrialized countries, if we want to know about crime in general, we should look at the other crimes, even though the data will not provide as clear a conclusion. Figures 3–6 and 3–7 show crime rates in the United States and England and Wales for 1993 for rates of five Index crimes. I have omitted crimes for which the categories are not directly comparable. While the U.S. computes a rate for aggravated assault only, the roughly equivalent British category is "violence against the person," which includes mostly crimes that in the United States would be classified as simple assault.

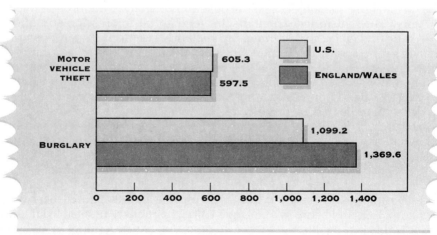

FIGURE 3–7   Property Crimes Known to Police, 1993 (United States and England/Wales)

Rates of property crime are roughly similar. British burglary rates are actually higher than those in the U.S. Motor vehicle theft, for which the rates are nearly the same, offers an especially good comparison since the statistics are least likely to suffer from differences in definition, reporting, or recording. For violent crime, however, the United States has rates several times those of Britain. Comparisons with other industrialized countries give similar results. For property crime, the United States generally has slightly higher rates (though in a few cases, slightly lower). But for violent crimes, U.S. rates are far higher than those of other industrialized countries. These statistics come from police sources, but where there are victimization surveys to make comparison possible, similar patterns turn up. Our NCVS figures, compared to a national survey in Australia, for example, show that we have 300 percent more robbery but only about 25 percent more motor vehicle theft.[17]

There are many explanations for the high rates of crime, especially violent crime, in the United States—our greater degree of ethnic heterogeneity (cultural diversity), freedom and individualism, economic inequality, and so on—too many to examine in detail and with data here. In some cases, the differences seem so great as to defy any single explanation. For example, many people attribute the high murder rate in the United States to the easy availability of guns. No doubt guns are a factor; currently handguns account for about half of all homicides. But that also means that even if we removed all handgun deaths from the total, the United States would still have a murder rate double or triple that of most European countries.

CRIME IN U.S. HISTORY

Besides comparing our crime rates with those of other countries, we also judge the current levels of crime by comparison with earlier periods in our own history. Of course, most people do not analyze the broad sweep of history. Their historical comparisons tend to be impressionistic and unsystematic and are probably limited to the fairly recent past, perhaps only as far back as personal recollection will take them. For this reason, and perhaps because we tend to remember the past as better than it actually was, it seems that many people think that crime has never been worse than it is now. There is a widespread impression that America's high crime rates are rather recent and unprecedented, a product of the most recent one or two generations. People can remember times when they felt safer, when merchants did not have to put iron grates over their store windows, when people could safely sleep in the city parks or on fire escapes in the summer.

These perceptions are reflected in more systematic kinds of evidence. Crime rates changed little during the 1950s. But in the 1960s, crime grew quite rapidly. The murder rate—our most accurate figure—nearly doubled (Figure 3–8), and between 1960 and 1971, the robbery rate tripled (Figure 3–9). Nor is this just a matter of increased reporting and recording. In 1965, the official rate of robbery of individuals (as opposed to businesses) was about 65 per

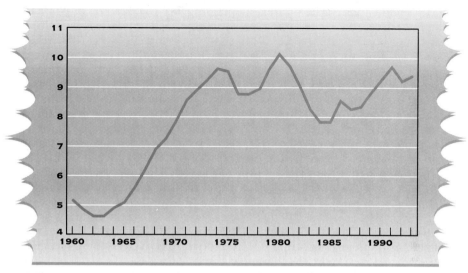

FIGURE 3–8   Murder, 1960–1993 (Rates per 100,000 population)

Source: Derived from UCR data in Maguire and Pastore, *Sourcebook—1993*.

100,000. A national victimization survey that year estimated that there were an additional 30 unreported robberies per 100,000 people. The total of all robberies—reported plus unreported—was no more than 95 to 100 per 100,000. By 1973, reported robberies alone came to 180 per 100,000, and a victimization survey estimated an additional 500 unreported robberies per 100,000.[18]

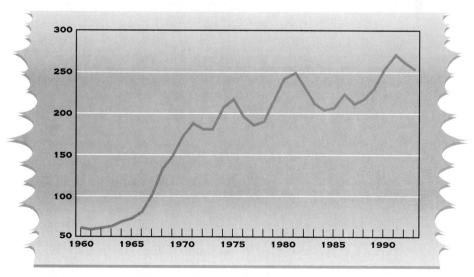

FIGURE 3–9   Robbery, 1960–1993 (Rates per 100,000 population)

Source: Derived from UCR data in Maguire and Pastore, *Sourcebook—1993*.

Since then, crime rates, depending on the source of statistics, have either increased or remained fairly stable. Police statistics (UCR) show an increase in the late 1970s, with some tapering off after 1980 (Figure 3–8). Victimization survey data (NCVS) show little overall change in robbery—if anything a slight downward trend, as Figure 3–10 shows. Burglary presents something of a puzzle (see Figure 3–11). From 1973 to 1981, official rates of burglary increased by 35 percent while rates found by the victimization survey decreased slightly, though part of the difference was caused by the choice of denominators. The UCR rate is based on the population; the NCVS rate is based on the number of households. During these years, while the population grew by about 8 percent, the number of households increased by 17 percent. That means that the denominator of the NCVS rate increased twice as fast as the denominator in the UCR rate. If the NCVS rate were based on population, the curves would look much more alike (Figure 3–12).

For motor vehicle theft, the two sources of statistics show roughly parallel trends, at least after 1978 (see Figure 3–13). This result is reassuring, for aside from murder (a crime not included in the NCVS), motor vehicle theft is the crime for which UCR figures are most accurate. (Remember that for both burglary and auto theft, the NCVS figures its rates on the basis of the number of households. One possible reason for part of the discrepancy between UCR and NCVS trends may be that the number of households was increasing more rapidly than was the population.)

Despite the discrepancies between the two major sources of data, some trends in crime over the last half century seem clear. Crime rates, which had

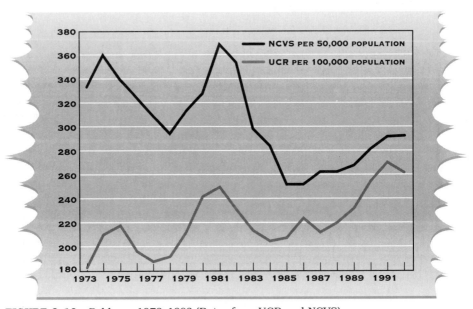

FIGURE 3–10   Robbery, 1973–1992 (Rates from UCR and NCVS)

Source: Derived from UCR and NCVS data in Maguire and Pastore, *Sourcebook—1993*.

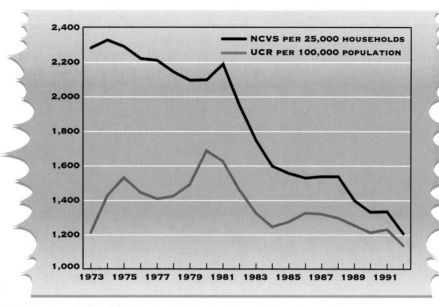

FIGURE 3–11   Burglary, 1973–1992 (Rates from UCR and NCVS)

Source: Derived from UCR and NCVS data in Maguire and Pastore, *Sourcebook—1993*.

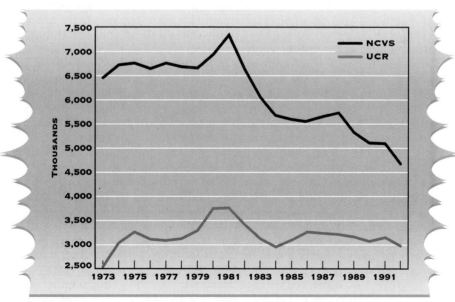

FIGURE 3–12   Burglary, 1973–1992 (Number of Crimes, UCR and NCVS)

Source: Derived from UCR and NCVS data in Maguire and Pastore, *Sourcebook—1993*.

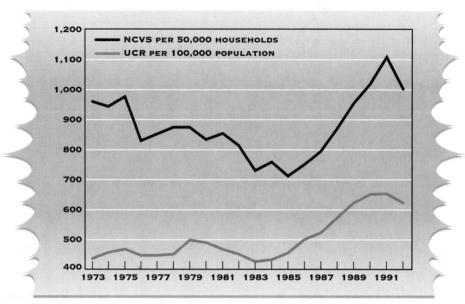

FIGURE 3–13   MVT, 1973–1992 (Rates from UCR and NCVS)

Source: Derived from UCR and NCVS data in Maguire and Pastore, *Sourcebook—1993*.

been relatively low in the 1940s and 1950s, began a sharp increase in the early 1960s. A doubling or perhaps even tripling of crime over only a twelve-year period—roughly 1963 to 1975—represents one of the sharpest increases in U.S. history, and criminologists are still trying to explain it. We are less certain of changes in crime during the 1970s, though the size of the change was relatively small. In the 1980s, crime rates decreased in the first half of the decade and rose in the second half—except for burglary, which continued to decline; and although a decrease or increase of 20 percent in a five-year period is worthy of attention, these changes were nothing compared to the increases of the 1960s. By any measure, crime rates today are much higher than those of the 1940s and 1950s. The question, though, is whether we should take crime rates from the 1940s and 1950s as our standard for comparison.

Much thinking about crime today seems to be based on the assumption that current crime rates are not only unacceptable but also unusual and unprecedented. Crime and violence have remained at high levels for over two decades now, but this persistence has done little to alter the popular notion that these rates are abnormal and downright un-American. The assumption behind this thinking is that America has always been a peaceful and law-abiding country, but that somehow things began to fall apart in the 1960s. Therefore, if only we can find the right solution, we can return to the "normal" levels of crime that characterized the 1950s.

However, some critics paint a much less flattering picture of American history. In their view, America has a long tradition of violence and crime, stretching back to colonial times. In their view, the unusual and puzzling part of this half century is not the current high rate of crime but rather the period of peace and order in the 1950s. Seen from this perspective, the rise in crime during the 1960s was just a return to America's normal high level of crime. Much of the evidence for this view concerns the more or less organized violence that has marked U.S. history: massacres of Native Americans, election riots, race riots, and labor-management battles. European countries, too, have had similar sorts of conflict—with the exception, of course, of the slaughter of Native Americans as whites extended their dominion from the Atlantic to the Pacific. But although urban riots and labor strife have occurred on both sides of the Atlantic, those in the United States have generally involved more violence.[19] To take probably the bloodiest example, the New York draft riot of 1863 lasted three days and left at least 300 dead (estimates ranged as high as 1,200). It started as an attack on draft headquarters, but the mob subsequently burned some mansions, attacked the police, and "increasingly turned its fury against blacks, burning, stomping, clubbing, hanging, shooting."[20] And that was only the first day.

Even if we acknowledge a history of collective violence, these riots and battles hardly resemble the street crime that concerns us today. It's not that this violence happened so long ago; riots like these may still occur, as demonstrated in Los Angeles in 1992. But what of the more individual kinds of crime—not the mass violence and looting but the ordinary burglaries, robberies, and murders? Are these also part of America's legacy? This is a harder question to answer since the historical record, like the evening news, usually documents only the more spectacular criminal events. Ideally, we would like some sort of statistical count of crime from previous eras, but such an Index would be hard to reconstruct. Anecdotal evidence is much easier to find.

THE WILD WEST

Some people argue that levels of violent crime in the United States today reflect the persistence of a **frontier mentality**. On the frontier, beyond the reach of the more orderly and civil ways of settled society, lawlessness came easy. Even peaceful, law-abiding folks (like Gary Cooper in *High Noon*) had to be ready to use violence in order to deal with the bad guys. America has higher crime rates than Europe, the argument goes, because while Europe's frontiers disappeared centuries ago, the closing of the American frontier, marked by the completion of the transcontinental railroad, goes back barely a hundred years. Often, the argument that violence is "as American as cherry pie" rests on historical accounts of the crime and violence that marked the frontier towns of the West—stories about cattle rustlers, famous bank robbers like Jesse James, gunfighters, and vigilantes.[21] Such evidence is more useful for making Western movies than for estimating the actual amount of crime, though the existence of vigilantism does tell us how people at the time viewed things: Apparently, they felt that crime had gotten out of hand and that the legitimate government could not control it.

Vigilantism may be a desperate expression of concern about crime. But what kind of crime were the citizens on the frontier concerned about? Did crime and justice really resemble what we see in cowboy movies? One answer

ABOUT CRIME & CRIMINOLOGY

The rioting in Los Angeles following the Rodney King verdict left fifty-four people dead and nearly a half billion dollars in property damage. Although the riot was the most destructive one of this century, it was part of a long tradition of American violence.

We are not only a nation of laws and due process. America has another way of doing politics.... Rioting and mob action have been a continuing, half-tolerated, half-hated, aspect of the national life from its beginnings.

"The Boston Mob ... Allured by Plunder ... attacked, robbed and destroyed, several Houses and amongst others, that of the Lieutenant Governor; and only spared the Governor's because his effects had been removed...."

So wrote [the] commander of the British forces in the North American colonies, of the riotous reaction to the ... Stamp Act.... Depending on who you were, the Boston Tea Party was a mob action or a heroic insurrection.

Rioting was connected with every important public issue from the ratification of the Constitution to John Jay's 1794 treaty with England.... The New York City Doctors' riot of 1788 ... involved furious public resentment against [doctors'] paying people to dig up fresh corpses for use as laboratory cadavers. The dispute ... was serious enough to require calling out the militia.

The year 1849 saw the Astor Place Opera House riot ... over who would play Macbeth ... the Englishman William Charles Macready or the American thespian Edwin Forrest.... The dispute involved nativism versus foreignism and the people versus what was then called aristocratic privilege.

By the time the night's work was done the militia had been called out and an estimated 34 people had been killed.

comes from Roger McGrath's historical study of two notoriously rough mining towns—Bodie and Aurora—that flourished briefly in the 1870s in the rugged mountains of Nevada near the California border. These were boomtowns. News of the discovery of silver or gold nearby would attract all sorts of men eager for quick fortune. A town would flourish for a few years, its population growing from a few hundred to around 5,000; then nearly as suddenly the boom would end, and the community would fade from boomtown to ghost town.

Because of this pattern, a town like Bodie at its height had all the characteristics that should make for high crime rates: The population consisted largely of single men with varying amounts of cash; no deep ties to the community; and a social life that centered around liquor, gambling, and prostitutes. Bodie even had racial minorities (Mexicans and Chinese) and hard drugs (opium). For law enforcement the town had only a constable, who doubled as jailer, and his deputies. Crime rarely resulted in arrest, much less in conviction and sentencing. Under these conditions, crime should have been widespread. But was it?

In trying to reconstruct a full picture of crime in Bodie during the five years of its heyday, McGrath read carefully through the newspapers and court documents for reports of crime. Even with a population of 5,000, Bodie was small enough that most crimes would come to light. His results appear in

The 1870s saw anti-Chinese riots in San Francisco; 70 or more blacks died in 1874 during a battle around the courthouse in Vicksburg, Miss.; 11 Italians were lynched in a New Orleans riot in 1891; in 1871 nearly 50 were slaughtered in an attempt by Irish Catholics in New York to prevent the Protestant Irish from marching to commemorate their ancestors' victory ... at the Battle of the Boyne, fought in Ireland in 1690.

Racial street violence ... claimed something in the vicinity of 50 lives in East St. Louis, Ill., in 1917, and reached a climax of sorts in 1919, when all hell broke loose. W.E.B. DuBois counted race riots in 26 cities that year.

The 20's and 30's were decades when the most deadly civil disorders revolved around labor disputes.... [In] one arising from a 1913 copper strike in Calumet, Mich . ... 72 people were killed. The next year, in Ludlow, Colo. the state militia machine gunned a strikers' tent colony, killing seven children and two women. In 1937, the Chicago police shot into a crowd of steel strikers and their families, killing 10 people and wounding many more....

In the past, rioting has been particularly intense during periods of large-scale immigration and emphasis on cultural, religious and racial difference—back at the turn of the century, in the 1840s, and now.

Putting a premium on cultural diversity instead of cultural unity doesn't mean that rioting is sure to follow. There are no known social or historical laws that people are bound to obey, but past experience does suggest that when you encourage division you increase your chances of setting loose the mob.

Source: Nicholas Von Hoffman, "The American Way of Rioting," *New York Observer*, June 8, 1992, p. 15.

Table 3–4, which gives both the absolute number of crimes known to McGrath in the years 1878 to 1882 and the rate per 100,000. For example, during this five-year period there were 21 robberies, an average of 4.2 per year. Since the population was 5,000, we multiply by 20 to get the annual rate per 100,000. For comparison, I have included more recent rates for the United States as a whole, for a small Nevada city (Sparks), and for a large western city (Denver).

Two things stand out in these figures: Compared with the United States today, Bodie had far more murder and far less of the other crimes. The robbery rate is less than half that for the United States as a whole and about one-fourth that of urban Denver (and still less than the rate of many other cities today).

Why was Bodie's crime rate, except for murder, so low? Perhaps even the criminals had a certain code of honor. Apparently, they did not victimize women. In five years, there were no known rapes. And, according to McGrath, it was not just a matter of women not reporting the crime. "For the women of Bodie, including the prostitutes of Bonanza Street, the threat of rape or robbery was virtually nonexistent."[22]

A similar code may have extended to other persons as well. For example, today most robbery victims (about two of every three) are individuals rather than businesses. But in Bodie, in half the robberies the criminals took money

TABLE 3-4 •

CRIME RATES—THE FRONTIER AND TODAY

	NUMBER OF CRIMES	BODIE, 1878–1882 RATE PER 100,000	U.S., 1993 RATE PER 100,000	SPARKS, 1993 RATE PER 100,000	DENVER, 1993 RATE PER 100,000
ROBBERY	21	84.0	255.8	172.9	373.8
BURGLARY	32	128.0	1099.2	1114.4	1831.4
RAPE	0	0.0	40.6	77.0	78.8
MURDER	31	124.0	9.5	6.8	14.8

Source: Roger McGrath, *Gunfighters, Highwaymen, and Vigilantes: Violence on the Frontier* (Berkeley: Regents of the University of California, 1984). UCR, 1993.

not from individuals but from commercial enterprises. In other words, as in the Westerns that were so long a staple of movies and television, they robbed the stagecoach, taking the strongbox and usually leaving the passengers alone.

Another factor may have been the relatively small amount of stealable property. Few of Bodie's residents owned the kind of goods taken in today's burglaries and larcenies—televisions, VCRs, jewelry, furs, and so on. They didn't have silverware; they had silver mines, which are a bit harder to steal. Ranches in the area did have cattle and individuals owned horses, but contrary to what we see in Western movies, Bodie's boom years saw only six horse thefts and no cattle rustling. In fact, the items most frequently stolen were firewood and blankets. (It gets cold up in those mountains.)

A frontier code of ethics and the lack of easily transferred property may have helped reduce Bodie's crime rate, but what about the high murder rate? In McGrath's view, the major cause of the low rates of stealing and the major cause of the high rate of murder are the same: Everyone had guns. Bodie had two banks, but nobody ever tried to rob them, perhaps because even the tellers were armed. Citizens, too, seemed willing to shoot to defend their own property. But although guns may have prevented some crimes, they also made ordinary conflicts much more deadly. Fights that erupted in the gambling halls and saloons could easily end in gunfire. True, the limited technology of the time reduced the accuracy of the weapons, and the unlimited liquor frequently reduced the accuracy of the shooters; nevertheless, bullets found their mark often enough to give Bodie a murder rate several times that of the most murderous cities in America today.

Are America's high crime rates today an inheritance from the frontier? The typical murder today certainly isn't much different from those in Bodie and Aurora. Perhaps the people in Bodie, Aurora, and other western towns passed their frontier mentality on to subsequent generations. Back then, for the towns' residents this kind of violence was an accepted fact of life, and some criminologists see this attitude, this acceptance of violence, as a cause of the high murder rate today. They speak of a "subculture of violence" flourishing in certain sectors of American society.[23]

The idea that current crime is part of our frontier legacy may sound good at first; it may even have some validity. However, violent traditions do not always survive. Australia, like the United States, also had a violent frontier in the nineteenth century—guns and livestock and cowboys. A great many of its settlers were English criminals sentenced to "transportation" and tough enough to survive the wretched conditions of both the voyage and the inhumane penal colonies. But today, Australia's levels of crime and violence are similar to those of western Europe. Even in Bodie and Aurora, the evidence should make us look more critically at the idea of a violent tradition. Bodie's low rates of nonhomicide crimes seem to argue against the frontier legacy as an explanation for crime in general. The lawlessness and violence in the Wild West—at least in Bodie and Aurora—were confined largely to personal fights.

It would be hard to trace a continuous thread linking barroom brawls and shootouts in Bodie in the 1880s to mugging or burglary in New York in the 1990s. If we are looking for historical sources for today's crime, perhaps the search should start nearer to the scene of the crime. Street crime today—the burglaries and robberies and thefts—is largely an urban and suburban problem. So we might do better to look at the history of crime in the cities rather than on the frontier. If we're looking for roots, we ought to start right under the tree rather than 2,000 miles away, out in the Sierra Nevada.

MEANWHILE, BACK IN THE EAST

While towns like Bodie changed as people came West seeking their fortunes in mines and cattle ranches, cities in the East were changing in quite a different way. These changes, too, were expected to have serious consequences for crime. History textbooks usually group them into three broad categories: industrialization, urbanization, and immigration.

In 1830, most Americans worked on farms or in small-scale enterprises that employed only a few people. The word *factory* still meant a shop run by someone who bought and sold (a *factor*). However, as the century wore on, this meaning and the way of life that went with it eventually gave way to steam-driven, mass-production factories.[24] These changes were most visible in eastern cities like Boston, where by 1870 44 percent of the population was employed in manufacturing.

Accompanying the change in work was another demographic upheaval—urbanization. What had been a nation of small towns and villages was becoming a nation of cities. In Massachusetts, the urban proportion of the population rose from 19 percent in 1835 to 79 percent by the turn of the century.[25] The cities swelled with people, many of them immigrants—from Germany and Ireland in the first part of the century, from Russia and southern Europe in the last decades. In many cities in the late nineteenth century, one-third to one-half of the population was foreign-born.[26]

People today (criminologists included) would look at changes like these as a cause for concern, as did many citizens over a century ago.

"We receive the scum of Europe," Arnold White ... declared. As Congregationalist minister Josiah Strong ... announced in the best-selling book *Our Country*, "[I]mmigration complicates our moral and political problems by swelling our dangerous classes."

Far from friends and neighbors, cut off from family and from community, and isolated from the "civilizing" influences of respectable society, immigrants fell under the influence of a vicious element or succumbed to the evils of the city.... "They go to pieces and become drunken, vagrant, criminal, diseased and suppliant."[27]

By the mid-nineteenth century, cities were already thought of as cauldrons of disorder and riot, a breeding ground for what came to be called "the dangerous classes." (Today, few people use this phrase. We are more likely to hear of "the inner-city underclass," though this term too has come to carry connotations of the threat that the urban poor pose to "respectable" people.) Many middle-class people feared that these demographic trends—**industrialization, urbanization, immigration**—would cause even further increases in crime. Many of the newcomers to the cities were young, single men who might easily turn to crime and violence. But did they?

As nearly as we can tell, urban crime did not increase during the late nineteenth century; it decreased. Of course, assembling evidence on nine-

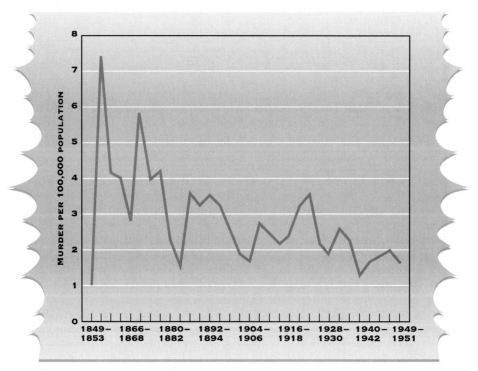

FIGURE 3–14   Murders per 100,000 Population in Boston, 1849–1951

Source: Theordore N. Ferdinand, "The Criminal Patterns of Boston since 1846," *American Journal of Sociology*, vol. 73 (1967), 84–89.

teenth-century crime rates presents historians with difficult problems. Many records from a hundred years ago may have been thrown out or destroyed by fire or water. Fortunately, one of the cities whose police records still exist is Boston, whose history should be most useful for studying the effects of social change. It was the center of the textile industry and it was a major port. Consequently, it grew rapidly, swelling with large numbers of immigrants— first the Irish in the 1840s and 1850s, then later in the century the Italians. Certainly, if any city should show the effects of industrialization, immigration, and urbanization, it is Boston.

To trace crime rates in Boston, historian Theodore Ferdinand went through police files, grouping the records of arrests into three-year periods from 1850 to 1950. He counted every arrest for crimes that correspond to today's Index crimes and converted these arrests to an annual rate per 100,000. His results for murder, robbery, burglary, and "all major crimes" appear in Figures 3–14 through 3–17.

The graph for murder is certainly the most accurate, and the graph for all major crimes, though inaccurate, gives the broadest picture. Both show a similar trend. Crime rises sharply in the 1850s, decreases during the Civil War (in the early 1860s), and rises in the period just after the war. The effect

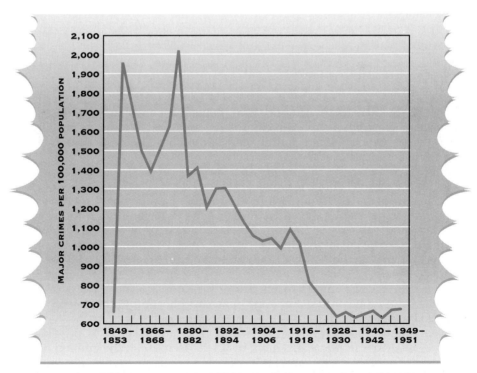

FIGURE 3–15   All Major Crimes per 100,000 Population in Boston, 1848–1951

Source: Theordore N. Ferdinand, "The Criminal Patterns of Boston since 1846," *American Journal of Sociology*, vol. 73 (1967), 84–89.

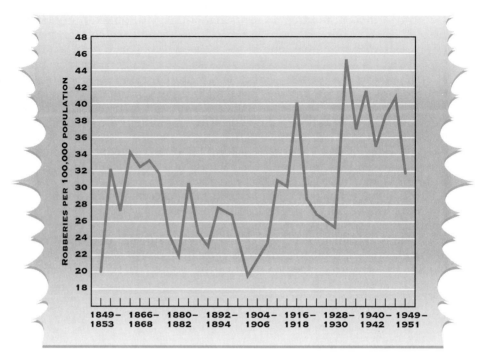

FIGURE 3–16   Robberies per 100,000 Population in Boston, 1849–1951

Source: Theordore N. Ferdinand, "The Criminal Patterns of Boston since 1846," *American Journal of Sociology*, vol. 73 (1967), 84–89.

of the Civil War is not unique. Wars deplete the number of young men in the civilian population, so during wars, crime rates—and especially murder rates—go down. "When Johnny comes marching home," crime rates go back up. In countries that fought in the two world wars, for example, postwar murder rates were generally higher than prewar rates.[28]

The graphs show no consistent increase of crime during economic crises. The panics of 1873 and 1893 do not cause great swings in crime rates. The Great Depression of the early 1930s seems to have brought increases in burglary and robbery in Boston, but nationwide crime rates showed no such changes. The most striking feature of Ferdinand's data is the overall trend across most of the 100-year period. From roughly 1875 through 1950, crime decreases.

The graphs raise two important questions: First, do they reflect a real change in crime or just a change in arrests? Second, if the downward trend is real, what caused it?

The question of accuracy is a serious one since it is possible that the decline in arrests was caused not by a real decrease in the amount of crime but by fewer citizens and police officers doing something when a crime occurred. Did Boston's residents become more tolerant of less serious offenses?

The answer appears to be no. Of course, there are no victimization surveys or other independent measures of crime. Historians can, however, make

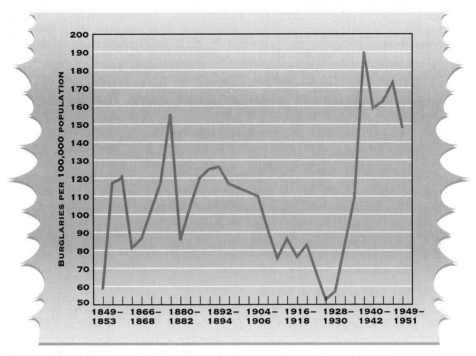

FIGURE 3–17   Burglaries per 100,000 Population in Boston, 1849–1951

Source: Theordore N. Ferdinand, "The Criminal Patterns of Boston since 1846," *American Journal of Sociology*, vol. 73 (1967), 84–89.

good guesses about changes in attitudes toward crime, and their studies point to the same conclusion. City residents in the nineteenth century were growing less tolerant of all sorts of lawbreaking. Evidence for this conclusion comes from records of arrests for less serious crimes. Although Ferdinand's graphs do not show it, at the same time that arrests for major crimes were decreasing, court cases involving disorder increased greatly.[29] That is, the criminal justice system was turning its attention to drunkenness and disturbing the peace rather than theft and burglary, probably because thieves and burglars were no longer as much of a threat. With these criminals more under control, people were calling on the police to deal with disorder—the kinds of rowdiness that people decades earlier took for granted. (Apparently a similar change took place in London earlier in the century. At the same time that many Londoners were demanding more action against disorder, they also called for less brutal punishment for major crimes.)[30] Both these changes in public opinion suggest that major predatory crimes were decreasing.

In the decades preceding the Civil War, the city was a much rougher, more riotous place. No police force existed, only a town "night watch," which served mostly to warn of fires, and it would not enter some of the more dangerous neighborhoods. Periodic mob violence was a fact of life. Between 1830 and 1860, the four largest cities in the country saw thirty-five riots.[31] Youth gangs regularly fought one another and attacked other citizens as well. Some gangs also specialized in theft and robbery. In Philadelphia, youth gangs became part of volunteer fire companies, and some of the worst battles occurred between rival fire brigades. One company might even deliberately set a fire in order to ambush the fire brigade that responded. Weapons included bricks, stones, and even guns.[32] However, by the 1870s, the city had changed substantially. A police force had been established, and people called on it to intervene in brawls, to deal with drunkenness, to prevent riots—in short, to keep order.

The city was gradually becoming less criminal, as the decrease in arrests for major crimes shows. But more than that, it also was becoming less tolerant of disorder, a trend evidenced by the increase in less serious court cases. A similar trend might occur in cities today if serious, predatory crime were to decline. In that case, we would probably see an increase in arrests and even jail terms for "quality of life" offenses that today are all but ignored.

EXPLAINING THE PAST—THE TRIUMPH OF MORALITY?

Why didn't the great social changes of the nineteenth century create greater chaos and crime? Why did crime, in fact, decrease? There are two leading explanations, both with some relevance for today's crime problem. The first one is more conservative: It emphasizes individual morality. It argues that the demographic trends of the nineteenth century did indeed create pressure toward more crime, but that these pressures were offset by other forces—in particular by people's participation in various moralistic and religious movements. The second explanation is more liberal, holding that the major sources of the change in crime rates were larger social and economic forces—forces over which the individual has very little control. This explanation argues that contrary to what most of us think, the process of industrialization itself was a force for reducing crime and making life more orderly.

In explaining the decrease in crime in the late nineteenth century, a prominent, conservative criminologist, James Q. Wilson, points to the variety of programs that flourished then—traditional churches; the Sunday school movement, which meant all-day lessons in both Bible and self-restraint; the Young Men's Christian Association (YMCA); the temperance movement—these and other growing organizations all shared "a desire to alter and strengthen human character."[33] The effects of the temperance movement were especially evident. Between 1830 and 1850, per-capita alcohol consumption declined from 7 to 10 gallons per year to about 2 gallons per year. This decrease probably contributed to the orderliness of life, though its effect on predatory crime is not clear. Still, Wilson argues, the importance of the temperance movement lay not just in its campaign for sobriety but also in its general fostering of self-restraint. It may be hard for us today to get a sense of what **temperance** meant. In this era, drinking carried a social meaning roughly similar to that of heroin today. It was the preferred drug of the disreputable and violent urban lower class (in those days, the Irish). This was also an era when neither middle-class status nor middle-class morality could be taken for granted. So temperance—abstaining from drink—was an emblem of this newly-expanding middle class.[34]

As Wilson sees it, young men who in earlier eras might have devoted their energies to the saloons and the streets instead became caught up in the trend toward self-improvement through self-restraint and social conformity, and crime rates declined. In the twentieth century, Wilson's argument continues, the morality that emphasized the community came to be replaced by one that emphasized the individual. An **ethic of self-restraint** gave way to an **ethic of self-expression**. The value placed on self-expression appeared first among intellectuals in the 1920s, and it subsequently affected the way "experts" in popular magazines advised parents on child rearing. They began to emphasize the child's happiness and personality rather than his or her moral character. "Permissive" child rearing and the new "fun morality"[35] did not take hold immediately. The hardships of the Depression and World War II delayed these changes, Wilson says. But amid the affluence and youth culture of the 1960s, they became an additional factor contributing to the steep rise in crime to levels that have persisted for over twenty years.[36]

Strictness versus permissiveness, self-restraint versus self-indulgence, temperance versus mood-altering substances, church organizations versus individual nonattendance—it all has a familiar and contemporary ring, a sort of Jerry Falwell view of crime and history. However, there are some problems with Wilson's theory. To begin with, if it were the new morality that caused crime to increase, we should expect to find the most crime among those groups that most adopted this permissive, individual-centered morality, that is, the elite and then the middle class. But they are not the ones committing most street crimes.

In addition, the timing of the changes in culture doesn't always coincide with the changes in crime. For example, religious revivalism was still strong in the 1830s and 1840s; it was also in these decades that Americans greatly reduced their alcohol consumption. From Wilson's theory, we should expect crime to decrease in this period. But contrary to what Wilson's argument would predict, these were decades of high levels of crime and violence. Also, as the temperance movement gathered strength and rolled toward its greatest triumph—Prohibition—crime and violence should have decreased. But they did not. The temperance movement began to win passage of county and state prohibition laws in the early 1900s. National Prohibition was passed in 1917. So we should expect decreasing crime roughly from the turn of the century to 1930, a few years before repeal. But if anything, crime increased during these years. Murder rates (again, our most accurate indicator) rose nationally from about 1 per 100,000 in 1900 to more than 4 per 100,000 in 1910 to nearly 9 per 100,000 in 1930, a rate similar to today's murder rate.[37]

EXPLAINING THE PAST—THE IMPACT OF THE INDUSTRIAL CITY

The other explanation for the decline of crime in the late 1800s clashes with our commonly held notions about industrialization, cities, and the causes of crime. In this view, the Industrial Revolution may have caused much hard-

IN THE NEWS

Conservative columnist George Will finds merit in Wilson's idea that the crimes of the poor have their origins in the ideas of the affluent and liberal intellectuals. As in the conservative explanation for the increase of crime in the 1960s, the villain of the crack crisis of the 1980s is an ideology of self-discovery, self-expression, and self-indulgence.

Novelist Jay McInerney knows about fashions, being a chronicler, product and shaper of them. He says drug use is going out of fashion. But the bad news is that unfashionable people are inheriting the whirlwind. This is especially so regarding crack.

James Q. Wilson writes that most of the dangerous drugs—heroin, cocaine, LSD, for example—have first been used by affluent, educated people. Drug use was promoted by people who considered themselves liberated from deadening restraints (including the law). Such people were intellectual at least in the limited sense that they possessed (or were possessed by) theories—about drugs as keys to peace, self-discovery, self-expression.

When self-discovery turned into self-destruction, these experimenters, "being affluent and educated, had access to treatment programs and support sys-

tems that gave them a good chance of finding their way back to normality." But, says Wilson, to people less advantaged, the pursuit of bliss was a one-way path to an abyss.

"What began as a clever experiment for affluent Americans quickly became a living nightmare for disadvantaged Americans. Drug use has not spread because drug pushers have forced it on us, but because the apostles of unconstrained self-expression ... celebrated the value of self-indulgence."

Source: George Will, "Inherit the Whirlwind," *New York Daily News*, January 8, 1989.

---

ship and disruption in people's lives, but in the long run it exerted a "civilizing" influence. To quote historian Roger Lane, the chief proponent of this idea, "The regularity, cooperation, and interdependence demanded by life and especially work in the city literally 'civilized' its inhabitants."[38]

If Lane is correct, violent crime should have decreased not just in America but in other countries undergoing industrialization and urbanization. And indeed, that is what happened. The decline of criminal violence in the nineteenth century was not unique to American cities. A similar pattern occurred in England, despite the absence of widespread religious revivalism, temperance, or similar social movements. In England, this process—the decline in crime and the onset of industrialization and urbanization—began a generation or two earlier than in the United States, but the pattern was the same. This historical trend to lower crime rates may seem surprising since it seems to contradict the negative image we have of the early industrial city—the crowded and huddled masses of people living in slums and shantytowns. However, although industrialization may cause much human misery, it also seems to bring a decrease in violence. Historians have found this pattern in cities as culturally and geographically diverse as Stockholm and Calcutta.[39] In our time, the cities in Third World countries have been undergoing expansion and industrialization. The trend in violence in these cities is hard to assess, especially in countries torn by war and political violence, but at the very least we can say that there is no consistent increase in murder rates as these cities grow.

Although Lane's ideas on the decline of violence may have general application, the research that inspired these ideas was quite detailed and specific—a study of causes of death in Philadelphia in the late 1800s. Lane was particularly interested in death by murder, suicide, and accident. He found, as you can already guess, that murder rates declined during this period. At the same time, death by accident also decreased, but suicide rates increased. Lane attributes all three trends to industrialization and the ways it reshaped the way people lived.

Lane contrasts the structure of earlier forms of work with work in the newer, industrialized sectors of the economy. Both factories and office bureaucracies require the coordination of many people. To accomplish this coordination, businesses imposed the kind of structures workers today often take for granted: scheduling, whistles and bells that told workers when to start and stop, and foremen or supervisors to make sure that everything ran according to schedule and plan. In contrast, the pace of agricultural work on the small farms of the nineteenth century was determined by the season—long slack periods alternating with periods that demanded long, hard working hours. One person's work was not closely linked to or dependent on another's. Factories required close coordination and synchronization among workers; farms did not. Farm workers could interrupt their work for diversion or excitement; factory workers could not.

This less restrained work style characterized not just farming but also the preindustrial production in the cities. Most enterprises employed only a few workers, and the hours and pace of work depended on how much there was to do, not on the clock. Lane's conclusion is that nonindustrial work, both rural and urban, permitted a greater amount of spontaneity, impulsiveness, and even recklessness. These qualities—at home, at work, and at play—often led to accidents and to interpersonal violence, and sometimes the accidents and violence were fatal.

As the century wore on, especially after the Civil War, factories and their regimen of discipline and control came to dominate the work life of more and more people, even children. For those children who did not work, there was the childhood equivalent of the factory: the school (which even today still emphasizes scheduling, bells, and restraint of movement). As a result of this transition to a fully industrial society, over the course of the decades deaths by recklessness and violence toward others gradually decreased; deaths by suicide (i.e., violence directed inward) increased.

None of this should blind us to the harsh conditions in which many people lived in the late nineteenth century. Especially for immigrants, the industrial city meant low-paying factories and crowded tenement housing; living and working conditions were frequently hazardous to health. But we are concerned here with crime and violence. Yes, there was urban violence; but as most historians agree, it decreased over time. More significantly, the violence tended to occur more among those not yet affected by the Industrial Revolution. Even among those violent youths with the volunteer fire companies in the 1840s and 1850s, "most came from traditional crafts, such as tailoring, shoemaking, and construction, rather than from more innovative, discipline-oriented enterprises carried on in factories."[40] Later in the century, rates of violent crime were highest among the one ethnic group excluded from the industrial economy: African-Americans. In the 1890s nearly half of Philadelphia's paid labor force worked in manufacturing and industry; but only 8 percent of blacks had that kind of job.[41] Accordingly, blacks also had higher rates of violence.

THAT WAS THEN; THIS IS NOW

What can this analysis of crime in the Industrial Revolution tell us about crime a hundred years later in today's postindustrial age? For one thing, it can tell us how we got here. From the historical perspective outlined here, the mugging, rape, and murder in today's cities are a legacy of the past. The Industrial Revolution over a century ago was not just a revolution in the organization of production; it also brought about a revolution in personality. The hard-drinking, free-swinging, and wild-shooting men, whether in the saloons of Bodie or the streets of Philadelphia, gave way to the regular nine to five employees of today's factories and offices. The transition was gradual and in many ways painful. For those who never got inside the factory gates, however, things were even worse.

The impact of the Industrial Revolution on those who were left out is most clearly visible in the case of African-Americans, if only because records of crime and death have always taken note of race and because we know that African-Americans were systematically kept out of the industrial labor force. Over the years, patterns of both work and violence changed among whites but not among blacks. In 1850 in Philadelphia, the black murder rate was high but not much higher than that of the recently arrived Irish; in the 1890s, the black murder rate was about the same as that of the Italians, who were now the newcomers to the United States. These white groups, however, eventually became integrated into industrial America and the more regulated existence it imposed. Outright discrimination prevented African-Americans from entering the industrialized sectors of the economy. Consequently, through the twentieth century the gap between black and white murder rates increased. There was a brief hopeful period in the 1940s and 1950s, when factories began to hire larger numbers of blacks. But soon, as America entered the postindustrial age, this sector of the economy began its long decline, and as it faded so did the chance for blacks to follow the path taken by white immigrant groups.

Lane ends his book rather pessimistically: "The essential problem for blacks in the modern city has been ... the lack of the kind of employment that not only sustained but *socialized* the white immigrant groups of the nineteenth and early twentieth centuries."[42] Even schools can no longer socialize youngsters to middle-class norms of restraint since it is not at all clear to students that such socialization will lead to a decent job.

The new society makes educational and technical demands unprecedented in the history of the species, leaving millions behind. Good blue-collar jobs were once open to most who would fit themselves to the discipline of industrialism, but no longer. It was never easy to get young people—especially young males—to go along with that discipline, and now that there is little room for those who do not take to purely academic achievement, it is nearly impossible. The result is that the schools and cops, the injunctions to stay clear of the prevailing drugs, no longer work because they are no longer serving their former economic function, and much of the population, suffering from structural un- or underemployment, no longer accepts the kind of social psychology that built the industrial city. In some ways ... many citizens have reverted to the free-swinging preindustrial psychology....[43]

Summary and conclusion

A news item about this year's crime rate has little meaning without some comparison. Usually, news reports confine that comparison to the last year or two. In this section, I have tried to provide a broader global and historical framework. Comparisons with other countries and with other historical periods are necessarily inexact, but the following conclusions are probably valid.

1. Rates of economic crime in the Wild West were relatively low. Rates of interpersonal violence, including deadly violence, were quite high.

2. Compared with today, the nineteenth and early twentieth centuries had higher levels of collective violence—riots, labor wars, and gang wars. These forms of violence also occurred in Europe but probably with less death and bloodshed than in the United States.

3. Cities in the first half of the nineteenth century were more disorderly and violent than they are today.

4. Starting about 1870, crime rates began a long, slow decline, except for an increase in murder during the 1920s and, perhaps, a rise in urban, economic crime during the depression of the 1930s.

5. Crime remained low through the 1940s and 1950s, rose sharply for a decade beginning in the early 1960s, and leveled off in the 1970s and 1980s.

6. Wars decrease crime, especially violent crime, to the extent that they remove young men from the civilian population. Crime rates rise when "the boys" come home.

7. Economic depressions, panics, and recessions appear to have no general, consistent effect on crime rates. Economic crises may increase crime in certain areas among certain populations.

8. Rates of crime in the United States, especially violent crime, have always been higher than those of other Western, industrialized countries.

Finally, I have sketched three general ideas that attempt to explain some of these facts about crime and relate them to current rates. First, the frontier theory sees levels of crime and violence in the United States today as a legacy of our frontier traditions. The frontier way of life emphasized independence, action, masculinity, and a disdain for the inhibiting niceties of the law. This mentality, coupled with the easy availability of guns, made for high rates of violence—both then and now.

Two other theories attempt to explain the decline in crime rates in the late nineteenth century, despite demographic changes that might have led to an increase in crime. The more conservative theory argues that self-improvement movements emphasizing moral uplift and social conformity counteracted the disruptive effects of urbanization and industrialization. The more liberal theory sees industrialization as a civilizing force that eventually imposed a more orderly, less violent way of living on those who worked in factories and large-scale organizations.

Each of these last two theories fits with a perspective on crime today. On the one hand, if crime results from a morality that emphasizes the individual over social institutions, proposals on crime should aim at establishing more respect for social institutions—not just the police and the law but also family, church, government, school, and work. On the other hand, if crime is more related to the kinds of work available, government policy should try to extend decent, respectable jobs to those people now excluded from the industrial labor market.

Of course, the national economy and individual morality are only two factors that might be connected with crime. The next chapter discusses four others—demographic variables that have traditionally been of interest to criminologists: sex, race, age, and social class.

CRITICAL THINKING QUESTIONS

1. What are the main sources of information about the amount of crime in the United States? What trends do they show in crime rates over the last twenty-five years?
2. What is serious crime? What serious crimes are not included in the FBI's count of serious crime?
3. How does a crime become a statistic, and why do some crimes not become statistics? Why do victims not always report crimes to the police, and why do the police not always record the crimes reported to them?
4. How do U.S. crime rates compare with those of other countries?
5. How have U.S. crime rates changed in the last half century?
6. Is crime part of our frontier tradition? How much crime was there in the Wild West?
7. How did urban crime rates change during the period of immigration and industrialization of the late nineteenth century?
8. What are the conservative and liberal explanations for the changes in crime rates—both in the nineteenth and twentieth centuries?

KEY TERMS

crime rates

dark figure of crime

ethic of self-expression

ethic of self-restraint

frontier mentality

immigration

Index crimes

industrialization

National Crime Victimization Survey (NCVS)

property crimes

sample

self-report study

temperance

Uniform Crime Reports (UCR)

urbanization

victimization survey

violent crimes

CHAPTER FOUR

WHO COMMITS CRIMES?

DEMOGRAPHIC CORRELATES OF CRIME

CHAPTER OUTLINE

Who commits crimes?

This is not quite the big question. That question, the one most people ask, is "*Why* do people commit crimes, and how can we get them to stop?" However, although *why* may be the most natural question to ask, it may also be the most difficult and least rewarding to answer. We probably get a better picture of crime if we ask the other reporter's questions: who, what, when, where, how? These questions provide the evidence on which to build explanations. If we can answer them, we will find that we have gone a long way toward answering *why*.

Explanations and theories of crime—the answers to *why* questions—are necessary, but first we have to discover just what facts need to be explained. It makes little sense to spin out an elaborate explanation of why poor people commit more crime if in fact it turns out that middle-class people commit just as much crime as do lower-class people. And, as we shall see, discovering the facts—finding out who commits crimes—can be a much more challenging task than coming up with explanations for those facts.

Unlike detectives, when social scientists ask *who* commits crimes, they are usually thinking about categories of people, not individuals. The categories most frequently investigated are the traditional demographic variables: sex, race, age, and social class. The results of these investigations can be quickly summarized: Crime rates are higher among males, blacks and Hispanics, younger (late teens) people, and those at the lower end of the social ladder.

However, behind these fairly simple conclusions lies a tangle of controversies and problems, and I am going to describe some of them in greater

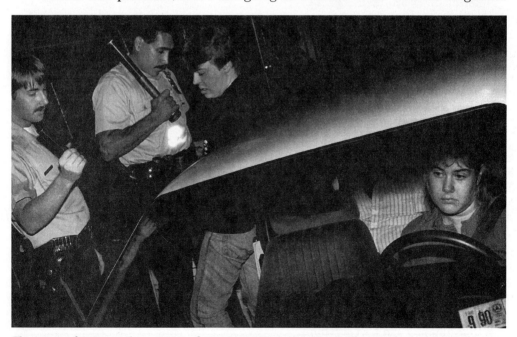

The image of crime as the province of poor, minority, inner-city youths may be exaggerated, especially for property crimes and non-Index offenses. In many areas, like Philadelphia's 25th district (shown here), the usual targets of the police are youths from the suburbs.

detail. The problems may seem merely technical, but often the way a research study is set up can greatly influence the conclusions it reaches. The more you know about the specific problems and solutions in criminology research, the better you will be able to evaluate the ideas about crime that you hear. Often, both sides of a controversy have seemingly good evidence. But this does not mean that you should shrug your shoulders and mutter in disgust that "you can prove anything with statistics." It does mean that if you read, say, that feminism has led to a "new female criminal" or that blacks have higher crime rates only because of police and court bias or that there is no connection between poverty and crime, you should be able to ask at least some basic questions about the evidence on which that statement is based.

CRIME AND SEX

IT'S A MAN'S WORLD

Of all the demographic variables, the one where there is the most agreement about basic differences is sex. Everybody knows that men commit far more crimes than women. You probably believe this, too. But how do you know? And how could you convince someone who insisted that women commit as much crime as men? You might refer to your own experience. Maybe most of the people you know who got into trouble with the law are male, and nearly all the criminals you see in the news are male. But this kind of evidence is highly selective. To be conclusive, the data should be more comprehensive and more systematic.

INFORMATION ABOUT CRIMINALS— OFFICIAL SOURCES

One of the most frequently used sources of information on criminals is the FBI's Uniform Crime Reports. Besides estimating the amount of crime (crimes known to the police), the UCR also contains information on "persons arrested for crime." As with crime-rate data, local police departments keep statistics on the people they arrest, both for Index offenses and other crimes as well. The FBI then combines these statistics to form a table such as Table 4–1. The overall male–female arrest ratio is over four to one. Among serious (Index) crimes, the ratio is about three to one for property crimes, and nearly eight to one for violent crimes. Even for larceny, the Index crime where sex differences are smallest, men still outnumber women by two to one. The only crimes for which women were arrested more frequently than men were prostitution and running away from home. (Running away is a "status offense"—an act that is against the law only if committed by someone of juvenile status. The status-

TABLE 4-1 •

TOTAL ARRESTS—DISTRIBUTION BY SEX, 1992

	TOTAL ARRESTS	MALE	FEMALE	% M	% F	RATIO M:F
MURDER	19,491	17,592	1,899	90.3	9.7	9.3:1
RAPE	33,385	32,965	420	98.7	1.3	75.9:1
ROBBERY	153,456	140,374	13,082	91.5	8.5	10.8:1
AGGRAVATED ASSAULT	434,918	370,379	64,539	85.2	14.8	5.8:1
BURGLARY	356,699	326,570	33,129	90.8	9.2	9.9:1
LARCENY	1,291,984	876,736	415,248	67.9	32.1	2.1:1
MOTOR VEHICLE THEFT	171,269	152,753	18,516	89.2	10.8	8.3:1
ARSON	16,322	14,139	2,183	86.6	13.4	6.5:1
ALL OTHER	9,412,629	7,702,301	1,710,328	81.8	18.2	4.5:1
TOTAL	11,893,153	1,931,508	549,016	81.0	19.0	4.3:1

Source: UCR, 1992.

offense category includes truancy, "incorrigibility," and drinking, among others. The only status offense tabulated by the FBI is "runaways.")

However, remember that these numbers tell us only who was *arrested*, and obviously not everyone who commits a crime gets arrested. In fact, only about one in five reported Index crimes results in an arrest. This clearance rate (the percentage of reported crimes for which an arrest is made) varies from crime to crime. For murder, it is about 65 percent; for burglary, it is only about 15 percent. Since less than half of all crimes are reported to the police, the persons arrested make up an even smaller percentage of the crime-committing population than the clearance rate leads us to believe. Therefore it is important to know whether the persons arrested accurately reflect the entire group of lawbreakers.

What if, for some reason, female criminals were more successful at avoiding arrest? It might be that the police are more "chivalrous" toward the women they arrest than toward the men. Where the police might make an official arrest of a male, they might deal with the female offender more informally, perhaps letting her off with a warning.[1]

Figure 4–1 shows the *potential* problems of relying on arrest statistics for information about who commits crime. More than ten times as many males as females are arrested for robbery, but these arrests represent only a small fraction of the total number of robberies. Many robberies of individuals are not reported to the police, and of the personal and commercial robberies reported, the police clear only 24 percent. If by some chance all of the unreported and uncleared robberies were committed by women, the profile of rob-

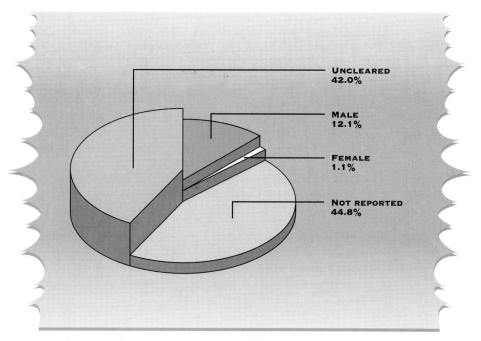

FIGURE 4–1   Robbers, Distribution by Sex, 1992

Source: Derived from UCR and NCVS data in Maguire and Pastore, *Sourcebook—1993*.

bers would show them to be overwhelmingly female. Of course, this is a ridiculous assumption. But it does show the need for other sources of data, especially for more controversial variables like race and social class.

In other words, conclusions about criminals based only on those who get arrested may present a distorted picture. Since the number of arrests is only a small fraction of the crimes committed, the question of who is *not* arrested becomes very important. For every robbery that results in an arrest, there are about seven uncleared robberies, that is, robberies for which the UCR knows nothing about the robber. For property crimes like burglary and theft, the ratio is even higher. Of course, the differences in male and female arrest rates are so large that they almost certainly reflect differences in actual behavior. Still, it would be nice if we could check by getting different sources of data on the same question.

OTHER MEASURES OF CRIME— VICTIMIZATION SURVEYS

If police arrests are at best incomplete and perhaps biased, how can we find out who commits crimes? Generally, criminologists have followed two strategies. The first of these is the victimization survey. Just as these surveys offer an alternative to police reports as a measure of the amount of crime, they can also provide information about offenders. The National Crime Victimization Survey, besides asking questions about the victims themselves, also includes questions about the offenders. Of course, victims can provide such information only for crimes where they actually see the offender. These do include the more serious crimes—assaults, robberies, rapes—but they still constitute only about 16 percent of all victimizations.

Nevertheless, for these violent crimes, the results of victimization surveys strongly resemble those based on arrests. For example, the UCR for 1992 shows that of the 153,246 people arrested for robbery, about 8.5 percent were female. The NCVS for that same year gives an estimate of victim identifications in nearly 1.3 million robberies. However, the NCVS asks only about personal robberies, not commercial robberies, a category where the male–female ratio may be even higher. According to these reports, about 7.5 percent of the robbers were female.[2] The victimization survey, which counts both unreported and unsolved crimes, obviously turns up a greater amount of robbery than police arrests, but these two completely different sources of data give very similar estimates, and in both the proportion of women robbers is quite small.

SELF-REPORT STUDIES

Victimization surveys may be useful for finding out who commits crimes against the person, but how can we determine the proportion of women committing burglary, auto theft, larceny, or other property crimes? Outside of arrest data, the most commonly used technique is the **self-report study**. This is just what the name implies: a study in which people are asked to report on the crimes they themselves have committed. Obviously, this method has its problems, though not necessarily the ones that first come to mind. That is, most people are remarkably willing to tell an interviewer about the crimes they have committed.[3]

Most of these studies conclude that although males still commit more crimes than females, the difference between the sexes is not so great as arrest data suggest. One typical study of juvenile delinquency asked boys and girls for self-reports on thirty-six delinquent acts. The results showed a male–female ratio "considerably smaller...than the official arrest ratio" and a "considerable uniformity between males and females." The ratio for self-reported robberies in this study was about 5.5 to 1, a fairly large difference but much smaller than the 11-to-1 ratio of men and women arrested for robbery.[4]

ARRESTS AS A CARNIVAL MIRROR

One explanation for the discrepancy between arrests and self-reports uses the analogy of the **carnival mirror**.[5] The logic goes as follows: Self-reports give a fairly accurate profile of the criminal population. However, the criminal justice system is biased. The statistics it produces create a distorted image, magnifying certain parts (men, blacks, the poor) and diminishing others (women, whites, the wealthy). The criminal justice system, dominated by white, middle-class males, is shot through with chivalry and paternalism, qualities based on the idea that women are the weaker sex.[6] These attitudes act at every stage of the criminal process to keep female offenders out of the system and therefore out of official counts of criminals. Chivalry, in this view, is the most important factor in determining what happens when a woman commits a crime. "Victims or observers of female violators are unwilling to take action against the offender, because she is a woman. Police are much less willing to make on-the-spot arrests or to 'book' and hold women for court action."[7]

ARRESTS AS A COARSE NET

Not all criminologists would agree with this explanation. They offer a different model of the criminal justice system, one that sees it not as a distorting carnival mirror but as a **coarse net**. The small fry swim through without being counted; only the big fish get caught. Big fish, in this case, means those who either commit crimes more frequently or commit the more serious crimes or both. Women do commit crimes, but their crimes are less serious and they commit them less frequently. Therefore, they do not appear in arrest statistics. The big fish are predominantly male. Supporters of the coarse net theory tend to accept arrest data as a fairly accurate picture of the *serious* offender.[8] They do not dismiss self-reports as hopelessly inaccurate (though inaccuracies do occur). But they do caution about the generalizations that can be made from them. The question to keep in mind about research based on self-reports is this: Whose crimes and what kinds of crimes are being investigated?

The answer, generally speaking, is that self-report studies are very useful for discovering the less serious kinds of misbehavior of young people. But for finding out about serious crime, they have severe limitations. Most self-report studies have surveyed juveniles rather than adults. It is true that juveniles (those under 18) account for a disproportionate amount of serious crime, but leaving out adults means omitting over half of the criminal population.

Typically, researchers will interview a few hundred youths, asking them about a variety of misbehavior. Some of these "delinquent acts" are serious crimes like robbery and burglary; some are less serious or nonpredatory crimes (minor theft or vandalism or drug use); some are status offenses, that is, acts that are offenses only if committed by someone of juvenile status (e.g., drinking or truancy); and some are not crimes at all (disobeying parents). Obviously, this kind of survey will produce a large amount of delinquency, especially if the youths are asked if they have ever committed the offense, even once in the last three years. Moreover, questions that seem to be asking about serious crimes—the equivalent of Index crimes—may be too ambiguous. Robbery and vandalism sound like serious crimes, and one well-known study of juvenile crime asked teenagers whether they had ever taken something from someone by force and whether they had ever deliberately destroyed property. The top category of offenders consisted of those self-reporting two or

ABOUT CRIME & CRIMINOLOGY

To see the assumptions of the carnival mirror and coarse net, imagine that we are doing some research on shoplifting in a large department store whose customers are about 50 percent male and 50 percent female. When we go to the local police department, we find that 75 percent of the people arrested for shoplifting at that store are men. Should we take this statistic at face value? We know that for an arrest to get into the police records, the person must first shoplift, then be caught by the store's security; then the store must decide to call the police. (We will assume that the police make an official arrest every time the store calls with a shoplifter in hand.)

For another perspective, we do a self-report study with a random sample of 2,000 men and 2,000 women customers. We find that exactly 100 men and 100 women report that they have shoplifted. When we ask if they have ever been caught shoplifting, 70 men and 50 women say yes. When we go to the police records, it turns out that 30 of the men but only 10 of the women have official arrests for shoplifting at the store.

	MEN	WOMEN
INTERVIEWED	2000	2000
SELF-REPORTED SHOPLIFTING	100	100
CAUGHT BY STORE SECURITY	70	50
OFFICIALLY ARRESTED	30	10

It looks as if the carnival mirror theory is right. Men and women are equally larcenous, but the store's security is much more likely to nab male shoplifters, and they are much more likely to

more such delinquent acts. Yet as Elliott Currie points out, the boy who had taken another kid's pencil and broken it in two could answer yes to both questions and wind up in the most delinquent category.

SERIOUSNESS AND SELF-REPORTS

When self-report studies do try to distinguish between levels of seriousness, they usually find what you would expect: The more serious the crime, the greater the differences between males and females. Table 4–2 shows some results from a self-report survey taken in two high schools in a city in the Midwest. For the sake of simplicity, I have left out several of the thirty-six delinquent acts that might not quite fit the pattern: drugs (where there may be some disagreement about seriousness) and offenses involving cars (which regardless of seriousness remain a masculine domain).

call the police if the shoplifter is a man (30 of 70 = 43 percent) than if it is a woman (10 of 50 = 20 percent).

Sometimes I ask students who have worked in retail stores what they did with the shoplifters they caught. Very few of them say that the gender of the shoplifter influences their decision, but most of them do say that it depends on the value of the item the person was trying to steal. So in our hypothetical research, we need to control for the value of the theft. Suppose we add a question about the value of the item: Was it worth more than $200? Our table now looks like this:

	MEN	WOMEN
INTERVIEWED	2000	2000
SELF-REPORTED SHOPLIFTING	100	100
CAUGHT BY STORE SECURITY	70	50
VALUE MORE THAN $200	30	10
OFFICIALLY ARRESTED	30	10

Now the data lend some support to the coarse net theory. It turns out that the store is basing its decision to call the police not on the sex of the offender but on the size of the theft. For big fish, they call the police, and 75 percent of the big fish are men. Of course the data still show support for the carnival mirror as well since it looks as though the store's security staff keeps a closer eye on men than on women.

Table 4–2 shows two obvious things: First, the more serious the crime, the fewer people of either sex who have committed it; second, the more serious the crime, the greater the difference between males and females. But even the largest of these differences does not come close to the comparable arrest figures. These self-reports show 4.46 times as many males as females committing burglary. The ratio of those arrested is closer to 10 to 1.

More recent self-report studies have tried to correct for some of the flaws of older studies, that is, to use a national sample, to concentrate on serious crime, and to follow people beyond their teen years. Like the earlier studies, these newer surveys find that three to four times as many males as females commit serious violent offenses. But these differences are still much smaller than the differences found in arrest data.[9]

Self-report studies, then, tell us that nearly all youths break the law, though boys do so somewhat more frequently than girls. Most of these violations, however, are relatively minor or infrequent—standard teenage misbehavior. It is useful information to have, especially in comparing the youths of

TABLE 4-2 •
PERCENT ENGAGING IN ACT ONE OR MORE TIMES

OFFENSE	MALE	FEMALE	RATIO (MALE/FEMALE)
DISTURBING THE PEACE	71.6	68.9	1.04
THEFT (UNDER $2)	66.5	58.2	1.14
THEFT ($2–$50)	33.9	26.0	1.30
THEFT (OVER $50)	12.7	4.6	2.76
BURGLARY (UNOCCUPIED)	16.5	3.7	4.46
ROBBERY	5.0	0.9	5.55

Source: Derived from Stephen A. Cernkovich and Peggy C. Giordano, "A Comparative Analysis of Male and Female Delinquency," *The Sociological Quarterly*, vol. 20, no. 1 (1979), 131–145.

different generations. But much of it is still not the sort of "real crime" people are most worried about.

FEMINISM AND THE NEW FEMALE CRIMINAL

Although women commit relatively little street crime, the subject of female crime has provoked interesting debates, both theoretical and factual. The theoretical questions concern the explanations for the low crime rate among women. Many sociological theories of crime and deviance have pointed to inequality, poverty, exclusion from legitimate opportunities for getting ahead, and other sorts of social oppression. If these theories were generally valid, women should have extraordinarily high rates of crime. It was not until 1977 that the major sociology journal carried an article pointing out that the leading theories of crime and deviance ignored half the human race and were in fact merely theories about men.[10]

As for debate over the facts, we have already looked at the amount and seriousness of female crime. However, there is one more important question left to answer: Has female crime changed over the course of recent history? After all, if the causes of crime are social, if different groups of people have different crime rates because of their position in society, when that position changes their crime rate should also change.

In the case of women, undoubtedly their role in society has changed. In the decades following World War II, more women have taken jobs and gotten college degrees. They have, on the average, been waiting longer before marrying and having children. In addition, the women's movement has probably

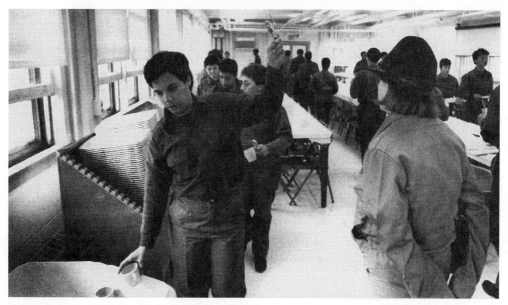

The last quarter-century has brought major changes in the social and economic position of women in the United States—and a doubling of the female proportion of the prison population. However, women still constitute only 13 percent of persons arrested for violent crime and only 6% of the total prison population.

changed the way in which many women think about themselves. I do not want to imply that we are living in the age of gender equality. Most women still marry and have children; they still face significant barriers in nontraditional roles; and although more of them are working, their salaries remain well below those of men. Nevertheless, the change is undeniable. The question is whether these changes have also brought changes in women's crime.

In the mid-1970s, the question of female crime began to receive public attention, and articles began to appear in popular magazines like *Psychology Today* and *Newsweek*. Then in 1975, the criminologist Freda Adler published a book with the title *Sisters in Crime: The Rise of the New Female Criminal*. Adler saw the social changes in women's roles not as a small and gradual improvement but as "a rising tide of female assertiveness" that "has been sweeping over the barriers which have protected male prerogatives and eroding the traditional differences which once nicely defined gender roles."[11] Part of this tidal change included a change in female crime:

> In the same way that women are demanding equal opportunity in fields of legitimate endeavor, a similar number of determined women are forcing their way into the world of major crimes.... It is this segment of women who are pushing into—and succeeding at— crimes which were formerly committed by males only. Females ... are now being found not only robbing banks single-handedly, but also committing assorted armed robberies, muggings, loansharking operations, extortion, murders, and a wide variety of other aggressive, violence-oriented crimes which previously involved only men.[12]

Was such a change actually occurring?

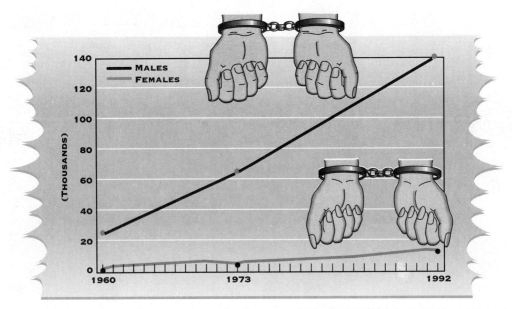

FIGURE 4–2 Males and Females, Arrests for Robbery, 1960, 1973, 1992

Source: Federal Bureau of Investigation, *Crime in the United States: The Uniform Crime Reports, 1960, 1973, 1992.*

Much of the evidence Adler used in her book was anecdotal—stories gathered from police officers and criminals. The more systematic evidence consisted of comparing the percentage increase in arrests of men and women. Consider the crime of robbery as an example: Between 1960 and 1973, arrests of men increased by 160 percent, but arrests of women increased by 287 percent. Undoubtedly, this is a big increase in arrests of women for robbery. But in what sense is it really larger than the increase in male arrests? Men's and women's rates of robbery are so different to begin with that such percentage-increase comparisons may be misleading.

The actual numbers on a graph may give a clearer picture (see Figure 4–2). In 1960, approximately 25,000 men were arrested for robbery; in 1973, the number was about 65,000—the 160 percent increase mentioned previously. For women, the corresponding numbers were roughly 1,200 robbery arrests in 1960 and 4,600 in 1973—a 287 percent increase. In Figure 4–2, I have added the data from 1992 (the most recent year for which I have data). In the period from 1973 to 1992, the percentage increase again was much larger for women than for men—roughly a 182 percent increase for women versus a 115 percent increase for men.

Two things are clear from the graph: (1) Women still make up a small fraction of robbers; and (2) in terms of absolute numbers, women have not closed the robbery gap. Since robbery by both sexes was increasing, it seems unlikely that the women's movement was the cause. More probably, the increase in robbery by women was part of a general upswing in crime and violence that occurred in the 1960s, an increase whose causes are still a matter of debate.

Some other pieces of evidence also suggest that Adler was overstating the case. First, the crimes for which sex differences narrowed were *not* crimes of violence. They were crimes like larceny, fraud, and embezzlement. As with non-predatory crimes like drug offenses and prostitution, arrest statistics for these three crimes—especially fraud—can be very misleading. Changes in arrest rates may reflect not changes in the actual occurrence of the crime but rather changes in the willingness of police officers or victims to take official action. But even if arrest figures for these crimes were accurate, the increase in embezzlement merely shows that more women were working: The more female employees there are, the more employee theft they will commit.[13] The larceny committed by females is predominantly shoplifting, which has always been women's crime of choice. It hardly suggests a change in female aggression or assertiveness.

Second, in more serious predatory crime, the women who do commit these crimes are not independent, financially successful, or in any other way "liberated." For the most part, they are drug-dependent and poor, and they turn to crime because they have been recruited by boyfriends or husbands as part of a team.[14]

These same patterns occur in other societies as well. In all types of society, from Australia to Zambia, women have much lower rates of crime and violence than men. In the more industrialized, affluent, and egalitarian societies, the female proportion of crime is higher than in societies where women have limited opportunities for education and employment and few legal rights (e.g., the right to vote, to inherit and hold property in their own name, and to seek divorce). However, the change in women's roles during the last quarter century in the industrialized countries has brought no change in the female proportion of violent crime.[15] Both in the United States and in other countries, it appears that the new female criminal is really the old female criminal.

SUMMING UP

I have gone to great lengths here to establish the unsurprising fact that women commit far less street crime than men. This sex difference occurs not just in the United States but also in every other society that keeps data on crime and violence. In some countries, male-female ratios for serious crimes may be less than in the United States. In many other countries, the ratio is even greater. Along the way to proving the obvious, I have also tried to show the strengths and weaknesses of two major sources of information on who commits crimes—arrests and self-report studies.

These two sources give somewhat different pictures of the male-female crime ratio, largely because they measure different things. Arrests give a profile of the most serious and frequent offenders; they may also reflect chivalry or paternalism on the part of the police. That is, gender as well as the crime itself may influence police officers' perceptions of how serious the criminal is and whether to make an official arrest. Self-reports usually give a picture of less serious lawbreaking, and for these lesser offenses, male-female ratios are more nearly equal. Self-report studies that focus on serious and frequent crime give a picture that resembles that of arrests.

Social class

The differences between arrest data and self-report data do not end with sex. They figure prominently in the debate over crime and **social class**, one of the enduring major controversies in criminology. At first it seems like a simple question—do people with less money commit more crime?—with an equally obvious answer: yes. For decades, many sociologists took social class as their starting point. They may have differed about exactly why social class was an important factor, but they agreed that poorer people commit more crime. However, in recent decades, some criminologists have had second thoughts.

DEFINING TERMS—SOCIAL CLASS

What is social class? What exactly do we mean when we refer to "the lower class" or "the middle class"? Most of us don't usually give the matter of social class much systematic thought. Politicians may talk a lot about the middle class, but what is it in the middle of? Logically, there should be an upper class and a lower class, but few people, especially politicians, use these terms; and almost nobody talks about class conflict, though one of the oldest concepts saw social classes as groups whose interests conflicted with those of other classes. Instead, most Americans think of themselves as middle class. They are, in President Clinton's phrase, "the people who go to work, raise the kids, and pay the bills." This may be the way most Americans think of themselves—as middle class[16]—but it is not a very useful definition for social research. Not only does it fail to distinguish between the janitor earning $20,000 a year and the lawyer making $500,000 a year, but also if everybody is middle class, class does not vary from one person to another. It is no longer a variable.

The solution to the problem that underlies much social research is to replace the concept of class with the concept of status, or more formally, **socioeconomic status (SES)**. Status is not a matter of group interests; instead it is a measure of where a person stands in relation to others in the society. Instead of two or three or six classes, status allows for an infinite number of gradations. It is also probably closer to what most Americans have in mind when they think of class. It seems to fit better with the way people see themselves and others in the society.

But now that we have a model of status, how do we measure SES to see just where everybody is? Obviously money is important. When people try to assess their own or others' social class (or SES), money is probably the most important factor.[17] In fact, it seems that for everyday purposes, the whole idea of class is being replaced with the simple idea of money. Politicians and other public speakers seem reluctant to talk about "lower-class" people. Instead, they use phrases like "lower-income groups."

Money is important in determining SES, but as the saying goes, money isn't everything. Education also counts toward a person's social standing, as does occupation—how a person earns that money (a Supreme Court justice is of higher status than a sales representative, who may make twice the justice's salary). Ideally, we would use all of these factors in determining SES, or we could use each one separately to see which made the most difference in crime. As a practical matter, however, researchers must frequently make do with less.

Like the research on sex and crime, research on social class often tries to find a correlation by measuring each individual's crime and social class. Most of this research has studied juveniles, and this focus creates a technical problem: how to measure social class. It makes little sense to measure a 15-year-old's income, education, or occupation, so researchers usually define the juvenile's SES as that of the parents. But juveniles may not always know their parents' income or education. More important the SES of the parent may not necessarily be a crucial factor in the child's social life.

Studies that look at adult criminals face a different and more theoretical problem: What is causing what? Suppose it turns out that criminals place far down on the SES scale, that they have little education or income and work only sporadically at low-paying, low-status jobs.[18] This strong correlation has two plausible explanations, one part of the liberal ideology, the other more conservative. The liberal explanation is that those who cannot get a decent education or good jobs will be more likely to turn to crime. The conservative explanation reverses this causal relationship: People who choose to commit crimes are wicked people—the kind who do not bother to stay in school, will not stick with a regular job, and prefer to commit crimes to get their money.

Which comes first, the crime or the low SES? Studying juveniles, whatever its other drawbacks, at least has the advantage of avoiding this problem since the child's delinquency is unlikely to have much impact on the parents' education or income.

MEASURING CRIME: ARRESTS   Whatever the difficulties in measuring social class or SES, they are nowhere near as controversial as the other half of the problem: measuring crime. Remember, we are trying to test the "obvious" idea that crime is more widespread among poorer people. For a long time, the evidence supporting this belief came from official figures—police records of crimes reported and persons arrested. One of the most influential and frequently cited studies of delinquency is Marvin Wolfgang's follow-up of all boys born in 1945 who lived in Philadelphia from age 10 to age 18—about 10,000 boys in all. As his measure of how much crime a boy had committed by age 18, Wolfgang went to the city's police files. As you would expect, he found that boys from the lower half of the income ladder had far more arrests than did boys from the upper half. Wolfgang could not directly measure economic status. Instead, as a measure of each boy's SES, he used the average income of the census tract (or geographical area) in which the boy lived. The differences were even greater when Wolfgang and his researchers looked not just at the number of arrests but also at the severity of the crime, based on the amount of injury and damage. On the whole, the crimes of lower-SES boys were three to four times more severe than those of higher-SES boys.[19] Many other studies in the United States and other countries have reached this same, unsurprising conclusion.[20]

But as with gender and crime, arrests represent only a fraction of those who commit crime. The carnival mirror of police bias might be distorting the true profile of the criminal population. (Jeffrey Reiman, who coined the term, devotes most of his attention to carnival mirror effects based on class rather than gender.) In Wolfgang's study, it might be possible that the middle-class boys committed as much crime as the others but merely were picked up by the police less often. Undoubtedly, police officers have a great deal of discretion in deciding whether to make an arrest, and there are many reasons they *might* discriminate against poorer people. Still, we must look for evidence that they actually *do* so. One well-known study found that youths who look or act tough in their run-ins with the police are much more likely to be arrested than are those who act properly respectful—despite the seriousness of the crime.[21] (We assume that this tough behavior and appearance will be more common among lower-class boys.) But not all research agrees that the police do in fact discriminate against poorer people. In keeping with the coarse net view of police discretion, the severity of the crime and the person's past record may play a larger part in the decision.

To sum up: The lower class is overrepresented in arrest statistics, especially in arrests for the more serious and violent crimes. The carnival mirror explanation sees this as evidence for police bias against lower-class people. However, from the available evidence, we cannot conclude definitely that police bias is, to any meaningful degree, distorting the arrest figures.

OTHER MEASURES OF CRIME—VICTIMIZATION SURVEYS   If arrest statistics are questionable, we must look to other sources of information on the connection between social class and crime. Unfortunately, victimization surveys are of little help here. Victims of a violent crime can supply some pieces of information about offenders—their race, sex, and approximate age. But NCVS interviewers cannot very well ask victims to estimate the offender's annual income, level of education, or parents' occupations.

Victimization surveys can, however, tell us the geographic and social location of the crime. These results give generally the same picture as arrests. For crimes of violence and for burglary, there is a negative relationship between income and crime: The poorer a family is, the more likely it is to be victimized. For these and some other crimes as well, the sharpest difference, at least for violent crime, seems to be between those at the very bottom of the income ladder and the next highest group (see Figures 4–3 and 4–4).

The facts about where crime occurs lead to two conclusions: first, that criminals frequently commit their crimes close to home; second, that there are greater numbers of these criminals in poor, urban neighborhoods. (The only other possible explanation is that wealthier people come to poor neighborhoods to rob and steal, a proposition that seems very unlikely.) In short, victimization surveys, like arrest data, provide some evidence that crime is related to social class.

SELF-REPORTS   In 1978, America's leading sociology journal published an article entitled "The Myth of Social Class and Criminality."[22] The authors (Charles Tittle and his colleagues) argued that although many people—social scientists included—believed that lower-class people committed more crimes, this idea was a myth. It was a convenient belief that had no basis in fact.

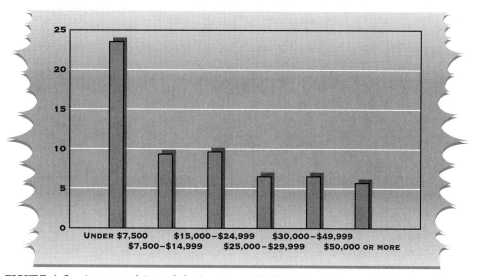

FIGURE 4–3   Aggravated Assault by Income, 1992 (Victimizations per 1,000 persons)

Source: Based on Bureau of Justice Statistics, *Criminal Victimization in the United States, 1992* (Washington, D.C.: 1994).

If the evidence from arrests and victimization surveys all pointed to a connection between social class and crime, how could the authors dismiss such a connection as a myth? First, they pointed out that most of the evidence

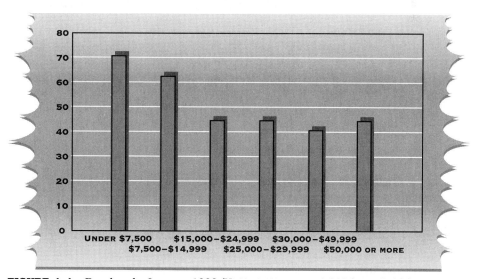

FIGURE 4–4   Burglary by Income, 1992 (Victimizations per 1,000 households)

Source: Based on Bureau of Justice Statistics, *Criminal Victimization in the United States, 1992* (Washington, D.C.: 1994).

for a class-crime connection was based on arrests and that even in these studies the differences between SES groups were not large. Second and more important, they looked at several studies that measured crime by using self-reports. In many cases, self-report studies have found that SES is not a factor in crime, at least not in juvenile crime. High-SES youths report committing as much crime as those of low SES. Even in the self-report studies that do show poorer people committing more crime, the differences between social classes are much smaller than those found in studies based on arrests.

These self-report studies, however, have their limitations. For example, most of them look only at juvenile crime, leaving out the crimes of adults. Also, as we have already seen in connection with gender and crime, self-reports and arrests are really measuring different things. Self-reports tell us who is committing the garden-variety teenage misbehavior; arrests, for the most part, tell us who is committing serious crimes or committing a variety of crimes quite frequently.

Recently, some self-report studies have tried to remedy these previous shortcomings by trying to get information on the more serious offenders and offenses. Unfortunately, the results of these recent studies are no more conclusive than the earlier ones. Some of them find no significant class differences, even among the most serious offenders.[23] For example, one national survey of youths was able to identify a small group of "serious career offenders"—the worst 3 percent of the entire sample. As we would expect, these tougher kids were more likely to come from cities than from suburbs or rural areas. However, on the average, their SES was roughly the same as that of the least criminal youths.[24] Even a study that included youths in reform schools and other detention centers found no differences in social class. Those serving time were no more likely to come from poor backgrounds than were noncriminal youths.[25]

At the same time, other surveys using the same methods have found that among the most criminal youths—those self-reporting 200 or more offenses per year or 55 or more Index offenses—more come from the lower class than from the middle class or working class.[26]

Self-report studies may find no differences in criminality among youths of different social classes because these studies do not isolate the big fish, the truly serious offenders—those who commit serious crimes and commit them frequently. One study divided youths into three levels of delinquency—no crimes, one crime, and two or more crimes—a breakdown that fails to distinguish between the youth who has shoplifted two small items from the youth who regularly mugs people in the street.

As the data in Table 4–3 show, social class does not seem to be a factor for most ordinary delinquency. Differences emerge only when we can isolate the relatively small number of youths who commit a very large number of offenses (200 or more) or who commit several violent crimes (i.e., crimes against the person).

It can be frustrating to go through so many contradictory studies without being able to find conclusive evidence for what seems like an obvious idea—that poor people commit more crime. Yet in 1990, twelve years after his "Myth" article, Tittle once again concluded, "Research published since 1978, using both official and self-reported data, suggests again ... that there is no pervasive relationship between individual SES and delinquency."[27]

TABLE 4-3 •

PERCENTAGE OF JUVENILES SELF-REPORTING DIFFERENT
LEVELS OF DELINQUENCY BY SOCIAL CLASS, 1976

NUMBER OF OFFENSES	TOTAL SELF-REPORTED DELINQUENCY		
	LOWER CLASS (%) (N = 717)	WORKING CLASS (%) (N = 509)	MIDDLE CLASS (%) (N = 494)
0–24	71.7	72.3	70.9
25–49	10.6	9.4	11.5
50–199	11.4	14.4	14.4
200+	6.3	3.9	3.2

NUMBER OF OFFENSES	CRIMES AGAINST PERSONS		
	LOWER CLASS (%)	WORKING CLASS (%)	MIDDLE CLASS (%)
0–4	77.3	80.0	84.6
5–29	18.2	16.1	13.8
30–54	1.7	2.1	0.8
55+	2.8	1.8	0.8

Source: Delbert S. Elliott and Suzanne S. Ageton, "Reconciling Race and Class Differences in Self-reported and Official Estimates of Delinquency," *American Sociological Review*, vol. 45, no. 1 (1980), 95–110.

CLASS AND UNDERCLASS

Finding systematic evidence for the expected link between social class and crime has sometimes been difficult because of the problems in defining, measuring, and categorizing crime. A similar kind of problem may lie in the definition and measurement of social class or SES. Just as we need to separate criminals who commit a handful of offenses from those who are truly criminal, we may also need a definition of social class that distinguishes different types of people who are usually lumped into the single category of lower class.[28] We need to separate those who are merely poor from those who live largely outside of the dominant institutions of society. Perhaps it is only at the very bottom of the social ladder that we find more crime.

In the 1980s, the discussion of social class turned to a relatively new term: the **underclass**. The term has no precise definition (but then neither does *middle class* or *lower class*). It refers to the lowest part of the lower class. Currently, about 25 million people in the United States have so little money that they fall beneath the government's poverty line, a rough boundary line for the category of lower class. But for many of these people, poverty is cyclical; their incomes may rise above the poverty line or fall back below it depending on a variety of factors. The difference between just getting by, on the one hand, and poverty, on the other, may be the difference between having a job and losing it, being married or getting divorced, or being in relatively good health or being ill. Although these people would be categorized as lower class, they still try to build their lives around ideals of work and family.

About 25 percent of Americans in poverty remain permanently outside the society of the employed. Some lack job skills or motivation; others are single mothers.[29] It is these people, those who seem to care little for entering the mainstream of conventional society and its institutions—work, education, conventional family—who constitute the underclass.

> Within the lower class is an underclass population, a heterogeneous grouping at the very bottom of the economic class hierarchy. This underclass population includes those lower-class workers whose income falls below the poverty level, the long-term unemployed, discouraged workers who have dropped out of the labor market, and the more or less permanent welfare recipients....
>
> The concept of "underclass" depicts a reality that is not fully captured in using the more general designation of "lower class." For example, unlike other families in the black community, the head of the household in underclass families is almost invariably a woman. The distinctive characteristics of the underclass are also reflected in the large number of unattached adult males who have no fixed address, who live mainly on the streets, and who roam from one place of shelter to another.[30]

Although the term *underclass* was coined fairly recently, the concept has appeared at various times in history to designate that segment of the poor who are not particularly attached to the dominant institutions of society. In London or Paris in the 1700s, they were the "criminal class"; in England and America of the nineteenth century, they were distinguished from the more tractable segments of the lower class by the phrase "the undeserving poor." They were the "dangerous" or sometimes the "dangerous, dependent, and delinquent" classes.

Some observers, then and now, have pointed to the labor market as the source of this class; its members are the *lumpenproletariat*, a pool of surplus labor created by the capitalist economy. More common was (and is) the view that the important causes of the dangerous class lay in its members' attitudes, which society should both repress and change. So although the language may be different, writings from the past—like Charles Loring Brace's classic *The Dangerous Classes of New York*, published in 1872—have a strangely contemporary ring: "Let but law lift its hand from them for a season, or let the civilizing influences of American life fail to reach them, and, if the opportunity afforded, we should see an explosion from this class which might leave the city in ashes and blood."

So perhaps the important distinction in terms of serious crime is not between the lower class and the middle class or working class, but between the underclass segment of the lower class and everyone else. If we revised our model of social class or SES to differentiate this underclass from the lower class, we might find the correlation that has proven so elusive. In fact, more recent self-report studies have shown that crime—especially violent crime—is most prevalent among the "disreputable poor."[31]

INDIVIDUAL AND NEIGHBORHOOD

Another possibility is that we've been approaching the problem in the wrong way. Remember, one of the reasons we intuitively think that crime and class are related is our sense that lower-class neighborhoods are more dangerous. But most of the studies we have looked at have emphasized the *individual's* social class and not that of the neighborhood (even the quotation from Tittle specifies "individual SES"). These studies that search for a correlation between an individual's SES and his or her crime seem to assume that the decision to violate the law is somehow based on where the person stands in relation to some large, vague thing called American society. Perhaps this assumption does not make much sense, especially for studying juvenile crime. After all, which is likely to have more effect on whether a teenager commits crimes—the parents' occupations or the kind of kids in the neighborhood? Common sense (and much research) tells us the answer: The peer group has more effect than the parents' social status.[32]

Some recent studies have turned away from individual-based measurements of social class. Instead of measuring the social class of each youth's family, they measure the class of the area where he or she lives. Fewer studies have taken this approach, but they give more consistent results than do the individual-based studies. Lower-class neighborhoods have more violence than do middle-class neighborhoods,[33] and youths from lower-class areas are more criminal than those from middle-class areas.[34] As sociologists have long noted, there seems to be something about the area, not just its individual members, that shapes people's behavior.

This fact lends some support to one part of the conservative view of crime. Conservatives argue that economic want is not a cause of crime. The evidence on lower-class areas and individuals suggests that these kids steal not for lack of money, and certainly not to buy necessities for their families, but rather because they live in areas where crime is more accepted, at least among youths. It's a matter of attitudes or values, not finances. Of course, what the conservative argument cannot explain is why these attitudes are more prevalent in poorer neighborhoods.

SUMMING UP

What can we conclude from all this?

1. Research confirms one bit of commonsense knowledge: Lower-class neighborhoods have more crime than middle-class neighborhoods.
2. This difference is greater for violent crime than for property crime.
3. Among individuals (as opposed to neighborhoods), lower-class people are more likely to be arrested than middle-class people, although, especially for juveniles, it is not clear to what extent arrest data reflect criminal behavior or police bias.

4. Adult criminals rate low on most indicators of SES, although it is not clear whether their low education and income cause their criminal behavior or whether these indicators are merely part of some general tendency toward crime.

5. Self-reported crime differs only slightly from one socioeconomic level to another. However, the most serious and frequent offenders are more likely to come from lower-SES backgrounds.

6. The greatest difference seems to be between those at the very bottom of the social scale and those at the next higher level.

7. For juveniles, the SES of the family is not as influential as the general social class of the neighborhood.

Many theories of crime have given economic factors and social class a central place in explaining crime. In light of this emphasis, the evidence on social class is disappointing. Some criminologists think that the correlation between crime and social class, if it exists at all, is very weak.[35] That is, differences between classes are small, and within each class there is a great deal of individual variation. Perhaps this is indeed an instance where what "everyone knows" is wrong or at least unsupported by systematic evidence. For myself, I am not so convinced, and I have tried to offer reasons why researchers often fail to find a crime–class connection. Certainly the data on victimization point to class differences, especially for violent crime. It may be that the important differences occur more for adults than for juveniles.

I have omitted here a discussion of some crucial issues. For example, this section is *not*, strictly speaking, about economics and crime. It is about social class. It does not address the economic questions of whether crime pays and whether people commit crime because it pays. These questions will be dealt with in other chapters. For the most part, I have also left out explanations for the facts on class and crime, explanations that appear in the chapters on theory. However, I hope that when you read those chapters you will keep in mind that the evidence on crime and class is far from conclusive.

RACE

Of all the demographic factors that might be associated with crime, the most controversial is race. As Charles Silberman said in 1978, "It is impossible to talk honestly about the role of race in American life without offending and angering both whites and blacks—and Hispanic browns and Native American reds as well. The truth is too terrible, on all sides."[36] The terrible truth, in his view, consists of two interrelated parts: black violent crime and white racism. On the one hand, African-Americans do in fact have higher rates of violent crime; on the other, white racism still exists and has been an important cause of black crime. Not everybody agrees with Silberman. Some people deny the existence of one point or the other, and some deny the connection between the two.

In the following pages, I will try to present the relevant ideas and evidence on this issue, much as on any other. However, I also realize that the first part of Silberman's statement is not in dispute: The topic of race is a volatile one, and some readers will doubtless take exception to what I say.

RACE AND BIOLOGY

One reason this topic causes such heated debate is the whole notion of race itself. Too often people have failed to distinguish between **race** and **culture**. Both terms imply a set of characteristics that distinguish one group from another. But while culture is learned, race is inherited. Racial characteristics are passed genetically from one generation to the next. The individual and the social environment have no power to change them. Physical characteristics—like hair texture or skin color—obviously are transmitted in this way. Nobody disputes this; it is a matter of biology. What is at issue, in part, is whether *behavioral, personality,* or *moral* characteristics also have an inherited, biological component and whether such components differ from one race to another. In other words, are some races *biologically* more predisposed to crime?

Earlier in this century, even educated people spoke of the Scots as being a "thrifty race" or the Japanese as a "clever race." This casual use of the term *race* can be misleading, even dangerous. First, identifying the Scots as racially different from the English stretches the idea of race quite a bit and raises an important question: How many different races are there, and what are the criteria for establishing some group as a race? It turns out that scientists do not agree on any single answer to these questions. In fact, because of the difficulty in defining race in a precise way, social scientists often broaden the phrase to "race and ethnicity" or "racial and ethnic groups." Second and more important, to say that the Scots are a thrifty "race" implies the biogenetic, racial transmission of what is obviously a learned cultural or personality trait (thriftiness).

Some evidence does support the idea that certain general personality tendencies like shyness may be biologically inherited, though these findings remain a focus of dispute among scientists. However, even if children may inherit some social traits from parents, a second issue is implied in the discussion of race and crime: that criminality is one such trait and that different races have a different inherited propensity to commit crime. If criminality or violence were truly a racial characteristic, criminality, like straight hair, might be greater among some races than others. By analogy, straight-haired "races" may, with much effort and expenditure on permanents and curlers, succeed in having curly hair, but their basic tendency toward straight hair will not be changed; it is inherent in their race. Similarly, if criminality were racial, the more criminal races would always need more external forces to control their crime. The implications of this idea are extremely ominous. Since crime is a moral issue, the existence of inherent biological and racial differences would mean that one race is morally superior to another.

Because of these kinds of implications, discussions of race and even scientific research on racial differences can become explosive, especially when the topic includes moral qualities like intelligence or crime. In 1985, James Q.

Wilson and Richard Herrnstein published a book suggesting that there might be a racial basis for crime differences between blacks and whites in the United States. They could not trace a direct link: "There is no evidence to suggest the existence of a 'crime gene' in the same sense that we may know there is a gene that produces red hair."[37] Instead, they say that certain inherited factors may predispose a person to crime and that races differ on these factors. One of these factors is intelligence, as measured by IQ. Wilson and Herrnstein say, first, that lower IQ makes a person more likely to be criminal and, second, that African-Americans on the average have lower IQ scores than whites. Both of these propositions touch very sensitive areas in social science. The IQ–crime connection implies that the causes of crime lie within the individual, not in society. The race–IQ connection implies that blacks are not as intelligent as whites.

The evidence on these topics is almost as controversial as the ideas themselves. In a debate too long and complex to outline here, social scientists have raised questions about the IQ tests. Are the tests biased in favor of middle-class whites? Do they measure innate intellectual capacity, or can IQ be affected by environmental factors? The evidence, for what it's worth, has shown that delinquents score, on the average, six to ten points lower on IQ tests than nondelinquents and that the mean IQ score for blacks is ten to fifteen points lower than that for whites.[38] Although Wilson and Herrnstein do not claim that these group differences are racially inherited,[39] their ideas are still extremely controversial, and it should be clear why. Remember, it was a theory of racial superiority that provided the "scientific" grounds for the horrors of nazism.

Despite Wilson and Herrnstein's tentative suggestions, I find it unlikely that the tendency toward crime or violence is a racial characteristic in the biogenetic sense. It is true that in the United States African-Americans have higher rates of violent crime than whites. But if this had something to do with their African biological, genetic heritage, we should expect to find even higher rates of violence in black African countries. Yet these countries have rates of murder, rape, and robbery well below those of American whites.[40] Even if Wilson and Herrnstein were right, genetic theories would still be useless for explaining important questions about *changes* in crime rates. For example, the alarming increase in black crime in the 1960s cannot have arisen from racially inherited factors since the genetic composition of a population does not change over such a short period.

RACE AND ETHNICITY

Although crime is probably not a racial factor in the literal, biological sense, we must still be concerned about the differences in crime rates among different racial and ethnic groups. In nearly every society with more than one racial or ethnic group, there will usually be corresponding differences in crime rates. The history of the United States, with its successive waves of immigration from various countries, provides a good example. Generally speaking, the most recent immigrant group has occupied the lowest place in the society and has had the reputation as the most criminal. Statements in mid-nineteenth century about the violence and criminality of the "Irish race" closely resemble some of the racist remarks made about African-Americans a hundred years later. When Irish railroad workers in Jersey City rioted, seeking wages owed them by the Erie Railroad, a local newspaper referred to them as "animals ... a mongrel mass of ignorance and crime."[41] Move ahead fifty years to the turn of the century, when groups from southern and eastern Europe constituted the bulk of the crime problem. In 1902, when Jewish women took to the streets to protest the price of kosher meat, some observers referred to them as a "pack of wolves"—the same kind of language used to describe African-American rioters three generations later.[42]

One function of this kind of racial remark is to focus attention on the criminals—to locate the cause within them rather than in social forces. They are of a different race, a different kind of people altogether, almost a different species—animals.

Other countries, too, have their ethnic groups. In England, people of Irish descent have long contributed in disproportionate numbers to statistics on crime and violence, though the Irish Republic from which they or their ancestors came has one of the lowest crime rates in the industrialized world.[43] In Israel, there are differences among Jewish ethnic groups. Jews of European descent have lower rates of crime and delinquency than Jews from North Africa and Asia.[44]

RACE AND CRIME IN AMERICA

In the United States, the discussion of crime and race (or ethnic groups) has had one principal focus: black street crime. Sometimes disguised by code words and sometimes out in the open, the topic has provoked bitter controversy among social scientists, politicians, and the public at large. One of the first questions to answer, then, is whether African-Americans are in fact more criminal than whites.

For a long time, most of the data showing African-Americans as overrepresented in crime came from UCR information on arrests. Table 4–4 comes from the 1993 UCR and shows the percentage of arrestees from each race. (The percentages do not quite add up to 100 because I have left out Native Americans and Asians, who account for only about 2 percent of all arrests.) The U.S. population is about 82 percent white, 12 percent black, and 5 percent Hispanic. In tables on race, such as this one, the UCR counts Hispanics as white: they account for about 12 percent of the arrests for each crime.[45]

Although African-Americans make up only 12 percent of the population, they account for one-third of all Index crime arrests. For violent crimes, the percentage is even higher, 45.7 percent, and for robbery, three out of every five people arrested were black. This is a huge difference. If we compute the robbery arrest rate for each race, we get a rate of about 27 per 100,000 among whites and over 300 per 100,000 among blacks. In other words, given an equal number of each race, twelve times as many African-Americans will have been arrested for robbery.

However, these data tell us only about criminals who were *arrested*. Remember that only about half of all crimes are reported to the police, and of the

TABLE 4-4 •
TOTAL ARRESTS—DISTRIBUTION BY RACE, 1993

	TOTAL ARRESTS	WHITE	BLACK	% WHITE	% BLACK
MURDER	20,243	8,243	11,656	40.7	57.6
RAPE	32,469	18,473	13,419	56.9	41.3
ROBBERY	153,281	55,893	95,164	36.5	62.1
AGGRAVATED ASSAULT	441,455	257,628	175,827	58.4	39.8
BURGLARY	337,810	226,857	104,473	67.2	30.9
LARCENY	1,249,303	806,511	411,705	64.6	33.0
MOTOR VEHICLE THEFT	168,591	96,328	67,938	57.1	40.3
ARSON	16,073	11,990	3,784	74.6	23.5
ALL OTHER	9,321,979	6,373,364	2,763,208	68.4	29.6
TOTAL	11,741,204	7,855,287	3,647,174	66.9	31.1

Source: Federal Bureau of Investigation, *Crime in the United States: The Uniform Crime Reports, 1993* (Washington, D.C.: 1994).

crimes reported only about one-fifth are cleared by arrest. That is, for each person arrested, there are nine crimes where the criminal (and therefore the criminal's race) is unknown. We must ask whether we would find the same racial disproportion among *all* criminals. If police are prejudiced and if their prejudice influences their decision to make an arrest, or if police departments deploy more officers in black neighborhoods, arrest statistics on race will be misleading. Some people argue that arrest data reflect police racism, not black crime.

In a study now more than twenty-five years old, Travis Hirschi asked teenage boys about their crimes and about being picked up by the police. He also looked at their records to see how many official arrests they had (see Table 4–5).

On the measure of self-reported delinquency, there was almost no difference between races. Blacks were only slightly more likely than whites to self-report two or more of the crimes Hirschi asked about, and they were only slightly more likely to say that they had been picked up by the police. But among the white boys, a police encounter wound up as an official arrest only about half the time. Eighteen percent reported one police encounter, but only 10 percent had arrests on file. Roughly 221 whites self–reported two or more police encounters (17 percent of 1,302); only about 107 (8 percent of 1,335) had two or more official arrests. However, nearly all police encounters with African-Americans became official arrests. In fact (because of rounding and the slightly larger number of youths for whom arrest data were available), the percentage with two or more arrests is *higher* than the proportion who self-report two or more police encounters.

Of course, it is still possible that the crimes for which the blacks were picked up were more serious than those of the whites—that is, that the police

TABLE 4-5 •

SELF-REPORTED DELINQUENCY, NUMBER OF TIMES PICKED UP BY POLICE AND OFFICIAL OFFENSES, BY RACE (IN PERCENT)

NUMBER OF ACTS OR POLICE CONTACTS	SELF-REPORTED DELINQUENT ACTS		SELF-REPORTED POLICE PICKUP		OFFICIAL OFFENSES	
	WHITE	AFRICAN-AMERICAN	WHITE	AFRICAN-AMERICAN	WHITE	AFRICAN-AMERICAN
NONE	56	51	65	57	81	57
ONE	25	25	18	20	10	19
TWO OR MORE	19	24	17	22	8	23
NUMBER	(1,303)	(828)	(1,302)	(833)	(1,335)	(888)

Source: Travis Hirschi, *Causes of Delinquency* (Berkeley: University of California Press, 1969), p. 76.

were basing their discretion on the seriousness of the crime and criminal rather than on race. On the face of it, though, the numbers certainly support the carnival mirror idea that arrest data reflect racial discrimination by the police.

One way of avoiding these possible statistical inaccuracies is to look at the crime of murder. A relatively high proportion of murders result in arrest (65 percent), and police officers probably do not allow prejudice to influence their decisions about homicide arrests. In 1993, 57.6 percent of all people arrested for homicide were black. This means that relative to their numbers in the population, blacks were arrested for murder more than eight times as often as whites. This overrepresentation of African-Americans in arrests for murder cannot be a mere byproduct of police racism. Even if all the uncleared murders were committed by whites, African-Americans would still account for nearly 45 percent of all murders.

For the other crimes, we should check the arrest data against information from other sources—victimization surveys and self-reports. Victimization surveys can tell us only about crimes against the person (what the UCR calls violent crime), where the victim sees the criminal. For robbery, the data from victims' reports closely resemble those from arrests. In 1992, the most recent year for which I have data from both sources, African-Americans accounted for over 60 percent of all robbery arrests. Victims interviewed by the NCVS that year also identified about 60 percent of robbers as black (56 percent of all single-offender robberies, 67 percent of all multiple-offender robberies).[46]

Self-report studies—the other source of information about who commits crimes—give less clear-cut evidence. The more recent studies generally do find blacks self-reporting more crime than whites, especially violent crime, but the differences are not as wide as those from arrest data. Of course, self-report studies have shortcomings, too: Most of them survey only juveniles, their sampling method sometimes misses the most serious criminals, and serious offenders as well as blacks are more likely to omit more of their crimes from their self-reports.[47] Still, some self-report studies—even those that include serious criminals—find little difference between whites and blacks.[48] Nevertheless, the bulk of the evidence from all three types of sources—arrests, victimization surveys, and self-reports—points to the same conclusion: African-Americans commit a disproportionate amount of crime, especially violent crime. Moreover, the more serious the category of criminal, the greater the proportion of blacks. That is, among those who commit only one or two offenses, black-white differences are small. But the population of the most serious and frequent offenders will be disproportionately black.

EXPLAINING BLACK CRIME

How can we explain this greater involvement of African-Americans in crime? Previously, I dealt with the biological explanation—the one that holds that blacks have a biogenetic tendency toward crime and violence. At present, this idea seems improbable.

A second explanation emphasizes the economic position of African-Americans in U.S. society. According to this argument, black crime is not so much a question of race as a matter of economic inequality. It only looks like a racial question because African-Americans are so disproportionately poor. Crime, so this argument goes, has its roots in poverty, unemployment, and economic inequality; since a greater percentage of African-Americans live in conditions of economic hardship than do whites, blacks have higher rates of crime.[49]

One way of testing this idea is to compare black crime rates with those of another group equally poor and equally the victim of racial discrimination. Although no group will be exactly like blacks in all ways except race, Hispanics come close. African-Americans and Hispanics have roughly the same average income (in both cases, median family income is about 40 percent lower than that of whites), and Hispanics are also the victims of racial discrimination. If discrimination and poverty are the most important factors in crime, blacks and Hispanics should have roughly equivalent rates of committing crime. But Table 4–6, adapted from a study of juvenile crime in Los Angeles, shows that these two groups have very different rates of violent crime. The proportion of black youths arrested for murder is nearly triple that of Hispanics; the robbery ratio is five times as high. Even allowing for differences in the amount of discrimination faced by the two groups, even allowing for the possible distortion of data based on arrests, these differences are too large to be dismissed.

The SES explanation may be adequate for explaining black-white differences in property crime. African-Americans make up 12 percent of the population and 30 percent of those arrested for property crimes. This degree of overrepresentation is about what we would expect just from economic factors. It is close to the crime rates of other groups (whites or Hispanics) at similar economic levels. But violent crime is another matter. Here, the differences between blacks and whites, even between blacks and Hispanics, are too large

TABLE 4-6 •
ARREST RATES (PER 100,000) OF JUVENILES IN LOS ANGELES, 1980

	WHITES	HISPANICS	BLACKS
MURDER	15	103	292
ROBBERY	250	918	5,500

Source: Peter Greenwood, *Youth Crime and Juvenile Justice in California* (Santa Monica, CA: RAND, 1983).

to fit with the SES explanation. Even controlling for other demographic variables, black rates of murder, rape, and robbery are still much higher than those of other groups.

CULTURAL EXPLANATIONS   Given the limitations of biology, economics, and social class in explaining the high rates of black violence, some criminologists have looked for an explanation in the social and cultural ways of African-Americans. The **subculture of violence** theory, for example, says that not all social groups regard violence in the same way. Some groups are more willing to accept violence as a way of dealing with interpersonal matters. Among groups that share this attitude, criminal violence will be higher. Certain white groups (e.g., some of the poorer people in the South) participate in this subculture of violence, but it is even more widespread among African-Americans.[50]

A second cultural explanation focuses on the family. Especially controversial has been the idea that black family structure contributes to crime. Since far more blacks than whites are raised in single-parent homes (nearly 65 percent for blacks—and the percentage in poor, inner-city neighborhoods is even higher—20 percent for whites),[51] perhaps single-parent families are more likely to produce violent children. Or perhaps there is something about the way black parents interact with their children that causes the increased tendency toward violence. These are very popular ideas. Many people see the family as the principal source of criminal or law-abiding behavior. But what is the evidence? To see if the family is a cause of black criminal violence, we must ask two questions: (1) Do certain family patterns (single parents, abusiveness) produce violence? (2) If so, are these patterns more widespread among blacks?

These are very important questions, and they go to the heart of a widely held, commonsense notion about crime—namely, that the breakdown of the family is responsible for high rates of crime. You would expect that by now we would have much high-quality, conclusive research on these questions. The first question, especially the broken home aspect, has provoked a great deal of research. Unfortunately, it is far from conclusive. It appears that the broken home in itself does not contribute to delinquency.[52] Even authors like Wilson and Herrnstein, who are predisposed to find a link between family and crime, must conclude that "when we look for evidence for a direct connection between broken or abusive homes and subsequent criminality, we find that it is less clear-cut than we had supposed."[53] If anything about the family affects delinquency, it is the consistency of parental supervision, not the structure of the family.[54] On the second question, that of black-white differences in child rearing, there is little systematic research. To quote Wilson and Herrnstein again, "It is astonishing how little we know about the consequences of being raised in a black family, intact or broken."[55] In other words, if there is a connection between specific black family patterns and crime, nobody has yet proven it.

THE FAMILY RECONSIDERED   We started with two important facts: First, blacks have much higher rates of illegitimacy and female-headed households; second, blacks have much higher rates of crime. How can we explain the connection between the two? So far, we have tried the commonsense explanation that the breakdown of the family is an important cause of crime; blacks have more broken homes, therefore they have more crime. Yet when we looked for evidence, we found that this idea does not go very far in explaining crime rates. Other research shows something that parents, especially parents of delinquents, often believe: Whatever the influence the family may have, it is not nearly so great as the influence of the peer group and other forces outside the home.[56]

Surely, though, the data on crime and single-parent families cannot be just coincidence. The problem is that in the search for an explanation, we have been looking in the wrong place and asking the wrong question. We have been looking inside the home and asking a psychological question: "How does the absence of a father in the home affect a child's delinquency?" Instead, we should be looking outside the home and asking a more sociological question: "How does the absence of many fathers in a *neighborhood* affect the rate of juvenile crime there?"

In any neighborhood, but especially in lower-class neighborhoods, kids get into trouble. The statistics on larceny, burglary, and auto theft are fairly clear on this point. But neighborhoods with a high percentage of working men will have less juvenile crime, and youths who do commit crime will be more likely to "age out" of crime as they enter their late teens. These patterns of juvenile and adult crime occur largely for two reasons. First, social control: There are more men around to keep young people in line. Employed men have a greater stake in their homes and their neighborhood. They will not let neighborhood youths get away with too much. Also, stronger communities make for less crime, and two-parent households can more easily form ties with formal and informal community groups. Single mothers do not have time for such luxuries.[57]

Second, alternatives to crime: Employed men provide a link to the job market. For the older teenager, a steady job at a decent wage can be an attractive alternative to an uncertain and risky income from crime. It's not a question of an employed father providing a good role model for a son; the connection between employed fathers and less criminal sons is far more concrete than this vague psychological notion. Getting jobs at this level is still largely a matter of personal contacts—knowing somebody who knows somebody. In a neighborhood where men are unemployed or employed in dead-end, low-paying, or temporary jobs, teenagers will see little reason to mature out of crime. Instead, they may turn to more profitable and more serious kinds of crime. A few may be recruited by adults and move on to dealing drugs or stealing cars for chop shops. Others will add robbery to their repertoire.[58]

This explanation, looking beyond the individual home, places the female-headed household in a secondary role. The primary factor here is male unemployment. The female-headed household does not derive from a separate, matriarchal black culture; it is a result of male unemployment.[59] Women are less willing to marry a man who brings home little money, and unemployed men find it difficult to remain in a home where they cannot fulfill their role as breadwinner.[60] So neither unemployment itself nor the female-headed household itself is the source of higher crime. Instead, the combination of these two factors—high male unemployment leading to single-parent households—creates *community* conditions for higher crime rates.

WHITE RACISM, BLACK CRIME   The previous explanation has an advantage over the other two cultural theories based on the subculture of violence or black family patterns, which ignore the social context within which a subculture or family is formed. That cultural and historical context, however, is the focus of one final type of cultural explanation—the white racism theory mentioned previously. If blacks have uniquely high rates of violence—even in comparison with other groups that have endured poverty and discrimination—in explaining that violence we must look to the unique history of blacks in the United States. Probably the best version of this theory is Charles Silberman's, "Beware the Day They Change Their Minds."[61] Silberman shows how the black experience in the United States was like that of no other ethnic group. Africans—unlike any white ethnic group—did not choose to come to this country; they were brought here as slaves, against their will. Moreover, for centuries, slavery and racism consistently kept them from moving up the social scale in the pattern followed by other ethnic groups. An Irish immigrant in the 1850s might move from less-skilled labor and unsteady employment to more highly skilled and regular jobs, and his son might even move into a white-collar position. But this kind of occupational mobility remained out of the reach of blacks. Even when African-Americans were able to get better-paying jobs—on the railroads, for example—their gains were short-lived. Another wave of white immigrants would arrive from Europe and displace them. In addition to this economic burden, blacks also bore the psychological burdens of racism—"humiliation, insult, and embarrassment as a daily diet."[62] Even into the latter half of the twentieth century, a Southern black who failed to be properly servile was literally risking his life.

Given this history, says Silberman, "what is remarkable is not how much, but how little black violence there has always been." For three centuries, blacks had developed a system of controls, mechanisms that kept anger in check or channeled it into activities that did not threaten the wider society. Some of these activities, like the dozens (a sort of rap contest based on insults), were harmless; others, like violent crime, could be deadly. But white America was willing to tolerate relatively high rates of black crime—as

ABOUT CRIME & CRIMINOLOGY

SNAPS—SAFETY VALVE OR FIGHTING WORDS

We played the dozens for recreation, like white folks play Scrabble—*H. Rap Brown, a militant black activist of the 1960s.*

In 1994, two former dozens players (Stephan Dweck, now a lawyer, and Monteria Ivey, a comedian) teamed up with a TV producer (their company's name: Two Brothers and a White Guy) to collect "snaps" (also called "toasts" or "busses") from around the United States to sell as tapes, books, and TV specials. Looking for material for a second book, Dweck and Ivey listened to some teenagers in New York City's South Bronx.

After the young men had run out of snaps, Ivey stepped up and pointed to Dweck. "When he was growing up," Ivey said, "his family was so poor, they used to go to Kentucky Fried Chicken to lick other people's fingers."

"I know his mother," Dweck said when the laughter had died down. "His mother's so fat, her blood type is Ragu."

"That might be true. But let's talk about your father. Your father's so dumb, when you were born, he looked at the umbilical cord and said, 'Look, honey, it comes with cable.'"

The dozens is often cited as an example of the

mechanisms African-Americans developed to deal with frustration, anger, and aggression. The game allows for aggression in the form of clever insults, but it also demands control of impulsive anger.

It's more egalitarian than status competitions based on money or clothes or sports ability. It takes more courage and imagination than the "Beavis and Butt-head" brand of suburban anomie. And it takes a lot more intelligence than those grand old coming-of-age rituals, fighting and killing. In the news media, young African-American men always seem to be going at one another with razors and guns, but in the real world many more prefer to use similes and metaphors.

"If you touch your opponent or get mad, you lose," Ivey explained…. "That's an important lesson for these kids. If they can learn how to be patient and take it here, it helps them stay cool when their boss gets on them. This game isn't brain surgery, but it teaches them to vent without hurting someone."

Things may be changing, however, and not for the better. Even Dweck notes that in some cities, the snaps are "very rough and raw, especially among the young guys. You can see the progression through the generations. The younger you go, the more vicious you get." And another observer in Philadelphia says, "'Busses' are either remembered as old jokes, or they take the form of 'fighting words' that often serve as the first step in chains of retributive violence."

Source: John Tierney, "The Big City: Your Father's So Dumb…" *New York Times Magazine*, May 15, 1994, pp. 28, 30. John Husemoller Nightingale, *On the Edge* (New York: Basic Books, 1993), p. 73.

long as it remained confined to the black community. The official institutions of crime control brought little pressure against black-on-black crime.

Beginning in the 1960s, things began to change. Blacks began to challenge white domination. In politics, the new black consciousness took the form of freedom rides, boycotts, voter registration, marches, and demonstrations. It was a courageous and even heroic effort. But the challenge to traditional lines of authority had a nastier underside. The 1960s was a period of general economic prosperity, but once again this prosperity largely bypassed blacks. The promise of civil rights contrasted with the realities of ghetto life, and black neighborhoods in many cities became the sites of rioting. Besides the sporadic, collective violence of riots, violent street crime became more and more a fact of life, and like the televised riots, street crime affected the wider society. Black crime began to spill over its usual boundaries, no longer a matter of young blacks victimizing young blacks. It seemed that black criminals were more often victimizing older, middle-class, and even white victims.

Black crime was breaking out because the old controls were breaking down. In part, this breakdown was caused by the large number of youths—the result of the baby boom. In part, it was a result of the new, more defiant black consciousness. And in part it was, ironically, a result of blacks' success in the battle against segregation. Middle-class blacks, kept in the inner city by segregation, provided a force for stability and control. But as laws against segregated housing were passed and enforced, middle-class and even stable working-class blacks began to leave the old neighborhoods. This increased geographic and social-class diversity among African-Americans may explain some otherwise puzzling trends in black crime: Since 1957, "for blacks, improvements in educational attainment are associated with significant *increases* in the robbery and burglary rates.... Growth in the percentage of female-headed families is accompanied by *declines* in robbery and burglary rates.... In general, median family income has a significant positive [i.e., increasing] impact on robbery and homicide rates."[63] As more blacks were able to move into the middle class and out of the ghetto, left behind were those who lacked the resources either to move or to exert much control over the burgeoning population of angry youths. The "bad nigger," long a staple of black folklore, was out of the closet.[64] Needless to say, not all social scientists agree with this theory. To quote the noted futurist, Herman Kahn, "This 'suppressed rage' idea is crap." Blacks rioted, says Kahn, because "they have no idea of what moral standards are." (Kahn's statement, by the way, echoes almost verbatim what well-established people said about Jewish, Irish, and Slavic rioters at earlier times in history.)

SUMMING UP AND A PERSONAL NOTE

In many countries around the world, the population is composed of different racial and ethnic groups, which do not always coexist in peace. Each day, it seems, the news brings us reports of regions where conflict between ethnic (or religious) groups has flared into violence and death—Bosnia, Rwanda, Northern Ireland, and India, to name a few. Conflict may be especially likely where different groups have different degrees of economic success and political power. In the United States, the most serious racial and ethnic divisions have been between blacks and whites. Although open, organized violence has been relatively rare, race remains a volatile and persistent issue. One of the most controversial parts of the issue is crime.

Our three major sources of evidence—police arrests, victimization surveys, and self-report studies—all show that in the United States blacks commit a disproportionate amount of crime, especially violent crime. African-Americans constitute about 12 percent of the U.S. population. Given their overrepresentation among the poor, we might expect them to commit twice that percentage of crime. And indeed, blacks account for roughly 25 to 30 percent of property crime. But for violent crime the proportion is more than 40 percent, and African-Americans commit 60 percent of all robberies.

There are several possible explanations for these troubling data. Biological explanations—that blacks have some biogenetic tendency toward crime and violence—seem unlikely. Even the idea that blacks have lower than average IQs and therefore higher rates of crime has come in for a great deal of criticism. In any case, these theories cannot explain short-term changes in crime, such as the rapid increase of black crime in the 1960s.

Some explanations look to family patterns as the source of crime and violence. There may be some validity to this popular notion. However, the evidence is far from clear either that specific family patterns breed crime and violence or that African-American families follow these crime-causing patterns. However the *concentration* of single-parent families and the *concentration* of unemployment in a neighborhood undermine two important forces against crime: the social control that adult men can bring to bear on misbehavior in their own neighborhoods and the link employed adults can provide to jobs.

Finally, cultural explanations look to traditions and ways of life as the principal factor in crime. Some criminologists have argued that blacks participate in a subculture of violence, which condones or even demands violent behavior. Other, more liberal cultural theories see the violence in black culture as an understandable response to the conditions that African-Americans find themselves in. For two centuries, the function of black culture was not to evoke violence but to inhibit it or channel it into behavior that did not threaten white society. Beginning in the 1960s, this control began to break down. Both types of cultural explanation are difficult to evaluate. Translating their central concepts into measurable variables seems an impossible task. It is far easier to describe subcultural norms or historical injustice than to measure them for purposes of comparison. For the moment, we should probably look on these theories as plausible but not proven.

When an issue is as politically charged as that of race and crime, most people will choose their explanations not on the basis of evidence but on the basis of their general political view. Unfortunately, discussions over explanations too often turn into arguments about who is to "blame." Conservative critics will argue that historical explanations seek to blame white racism or society and to exonerate blacks for their own crimes. Liberal critics will argue that theories based on individual deficiencies (low IQ) or family patterns (illegitimacy and father-absent homes) blame the victim and ignore the more serious problems of inequality and injustice.

Today, discussions of race often become discussions of crime. But crime is only part of the problem, and criminology by itself can offer little to resolve it. We would be kidding ourselves if we thought that the problem of black crime and violence was separate from the more general problem of the position of blacks in U.S. society. Black-white differences in crime and violence are of a piece with differences in employment, income, physical and mental health, housing, and education. Race is, as Gunnar Myrdal called it nearly a half century ago, "an American dilemma"; perhaps it is *the* American dilemma. DeToqueville, that most perceptive of observers of the American scene, predicted the dilemma in 1830, 120 years before Myrdal (and 30 years before the end of slavery). A presidential commission (the Kerner Commission) reminded us again in 1968 that "our nation is moving toward two societies, one black, one white—separate and unequal."[65] Since then, change has been slow and not entirely positive.

I wish that I could have ended this section on a more optimistic and more conclusive note. This is the area in criminology that I personally find the most distressing—not just the high levels of black violence but also the lack of convincing explanations, the tendency of discussion to degenerate into battles over blame, and the absence of workable solutions.

AGE

The principal question of this chapter is this: Who commits crimes? To answer it, criminologists try to find variables that are correlated with crime. As we have seen, it's not always easy to discover the facts. Different ways of asking questions and different ways of measuring each variable can produce different results. Even when researchers agree on the facts, they may disagree strongly on the explanations for them. Race, sex, social class and economic hardship, historical forces like urbanization—all these variables have been at the center of criminological disputes. With the variable of age, as with sex and race, many of the basic facts are by now matters of considerable agreement among criminologists. But as with the other variables, interpreting and explaining these facts are matters of some dispute.

Street crime is largely a young man's game. Look at Figure 4–5, derived from UCR information on people arrested for Index crimes in 1992. It shows the arrest rate per 100,000 for each age group. The graph makes some things obvious. First, arrest rates for property crime are far higher than arrest rates for violent crime. Second, property crime arrest rates rise sharply in the mid-teen years, then decline nearly as sharply in the late teens. Look at the property crime arrest rate for 15-, 16-, and 17-year-olds. Of every 100,000 of these mid-teenagers, more than 3,500 were arrested for property crimes. That is more than triple the rate for 25- to 29-year-olds. Third, violent crime follows a slightly different pattern: It rises more slowly, peaks at a later age (18, compared with 16 for property crime), and declines very gradually. Of course, these figures tell us only who was arrested. But most research shows that arrests underrepresent younger criminals.[66]

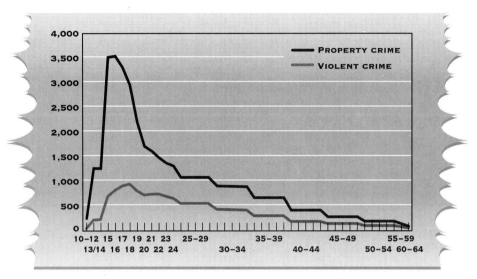

FIGURE 4–5 Age-specific Arrests Rates, 1992 (Rates per 100,000 persons)

EXPLAINING THE HIGH-CRIME YEARS

There are several reasons for this pattern of age and crime. To begin with, young children do not have much ability to commit serious crime. It is in the early teenage years that youths begin to have the capacity for serious crime. This is also the time when parental influence over children diminishes; our society expects 15-year-olds to be less dependent on their parents than are 10-year-olds, and youths at this age experience and participate in the heightening of peer pressure. To increase this pressure, the law requires that teenagers be locked up for most of the day in strictly age-segregated institutions, where, except for a relatively small adult supervisory staff, they can interact only with those who are within a year or two of their own age. Inside these peer pressure cookers (also known as schools), finding acceptance may depend on intangible qualities like personality, but teenagers may also feel pressured to have the right kinds of clothes, music (CDs, concert tickets, and sound systems), sneakers, drugs, and other items that can be bought—or stolen. Boys face an additional pressure: to establish their manhood; and some of the ways of demonstrating their masculinity—stealing, fighting, joyriding, and vandalism—may violate the law. In addition, many teenagers who break the law may have relatively little to risk. The punishment for crime is less severe for juveniles. More important, while adults risk losing jobs or families, teenagers have no such attachments.

As youths mature into their late teens—and especially as they leave school—these pressures toward crime all decrease. Males no longer have to try to prove that they are men; responsibilities like jobs and families are adequate testimony of adult status. Jobs and families also constitute investments that the person might not want to put at risk; therefore, the cost of getting caught is higher. As youths move into the adult world and out of the age-segregated world of school, peer pressure becomes less intense. Even a person's attitudes and feelings about the very act of committing a crime often change as he matures. While the youth of 16 may find crime exciting, the older man of 25 to 30 is more likely to feel worry and anxiety rather than exhilaration.

Different theories in criminology emphasize different factors—economics, peers, deterrence, feelings, and so on—but each acknowledges that young people, especially young men, are the problem and that as these youths get older, they grow out of crime. This pattern seems to be universal. If you graphed the age of persons arrested in other countries or in the United States in earlier historical periods, you would get a curve that closely resembles Figure 4–6: a sharp rise in early youth, followed by a decline. The height of the graph (i.e., the amount of crime) might be lower or higher, the peak might come at a younger or older age, but the general trend would be similar, with the highest rates occurring in the late teens and early 20s.[67]

BIRTHRATES AND CRIME RATES

In the United States, nearly half the arrests for Index crimes involve people aged 15 to 25. From this simple fact follow some obvious conclusions: The more 15- to 25-year-olds, the more crime; the greater the proportion of this age group in the population, the higher the crime rate. And since 15-year-olds do not suddenly appear full-grown, we can anticipate changes in crime by looking at the number of babies born. For this reason, the increase in crime rates in the 1960s should not have come as an unexpected shock. From only a few facts about history and demography, it was, at least in part, predictable.

World War II forced many people to postpone marriage and children. But after the war, birthrates began to rise. In 1940, the birthrate (the number of births relative to the total population) was about 19.4 per 1,000. In 1946, this rate began a sharp increase and remained high for a decade probably because of continued economic prosperity and government programs that encouraged home buying. In 1957, the rate began to decline, though it did not reach the pre–World War II level until the mid-1960s. This period of high birthrates, roughly 1947 to 1960, came to be known as the **baby boom** (see Figure 4–6).

The social effects of the baby boom should have been easy to foresee. After all, if you see a jump in the birthrate in 1947, you don't have to be too much of a genius to figure out that by the early 1950s there will be an increased demand for tricycles or that by 1957 elementary schools will be crowded unless new ones are built. Nevertheless, some of these predictable changes took many people by surprise.

You might also have predicted that in the 1960s, as an unusually large segment of the population was turning 15 and 16, crime rates would rise and that they would remain high until the last of the baby boomers began to ease into their late 20s. Had you made such a prediction, you would have been right—partly. Indeed, crime rates rose, but the increase far exceeded the rise that birthrates would have led you to expect. By 1970, the proportion of 15- to 25-year-olds in the population had increased by about 40 percent, but

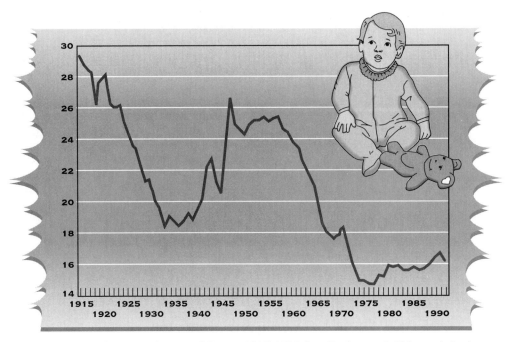

FIGURE 4–6   Birthrates in the United States, 1915–1990 (Live Births per 1,000 population)

crime rates had increased by 100 to 200 percent. Not only were there more young people, but they were committing a lot more crime.

Figure 4–7 illustrates this change by showing changes in the arrest rates of 10- to 17-year-olds for the years 1961 to 1985. By giving rates per age group, the graphs control for the size of the different **birth cohorts** (the term refers to people born during the same year). The year 1961 is the year just before the children at the leading edge of the baby boom came into the high-crime ages.

The graph of arrests of people under 18 shows that the increase in arrests per 100,000 begins in 1962, when the 1947 cohort was turning 15. In 1960, for every 100,000 teenagers, about 3,700 were arrested. By 1975, that rate had more than doubled, to nearly 8,000. Not only were there more teenagers, and not only were teenagers a larger part of the population, but as the graph shows a greater proportion were committing crimes and getting arrested.

CRIME AND THE BABY BOOM—EXPLANATIONS

Why did crime increase so steeply in the 1960s? Why were the teenagers of the baby boom so much more criminal than those of previous generations? Like other *why* questions, these have no single answer that all criminologists agree on. I cannot tell you which answer is right and which is wrong. All I can do is outline some of the more prominent explanations.

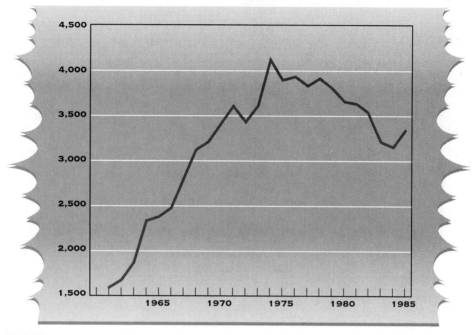

FIGURE 4–7   Arrest of Persons Under 18 Years of Age (Rates per 100,000, 1961–1985)

Source: Derived from data in Bureau of Justice Statistics, *Technical Appendix, Report to the Nation on Crime and Justice, Second Edition* (Washington, D.C.: Department of Justice, 1988).

DETERRENCE—THE VIEW FROM THE RIGHT   One explanation sees the increase in crime as one element in a set of social changes occurring in the United States in the 1960s, the period when the baby boomers were entering their teens. "It all began in about 1963. That was the year, to overdramatize a bit, that a decade began to fall apart."[68] Teenage unemployment was rising; more people were using heroin; more unwed mothers were having babies and going on welfare. And all these trends occurred most strikingly in poor, urban neighborhoods, especially black neighborhoods. It was the start of what later came to be called the underclass.

The conservative explanation for much of this decline emphasizes deterrence; it attributes the social deterioration to rational choices people made based on the attractiveness of the alternatives. Welfare payments made unemployment more attractive than working; hence the increase in the welfare rolls. Crime, too, became more attractive. Changes in the courts made it easier for people to get away with crime. Supreme Court rulings made it harder to arrest and convict criminals. A smaller percentage of crimes resulted in arrest, and of those people arrested, a smaller percentage went to prison. For juveniles, courts were even more lenient. From the conservative, deterrence perspective, these policies were "incentives to fail." Kids were committing crimes because "there was no reason not to."[69]

The most important factors in this explanation are the policies of the government and courts rather than anything specific about the baby boom itself.

Some criminologists reject the idea that the size of the baby boom generation had any direct impact on its criminality.[70] However, keep in mind one additional set of facts. The crime increase occurred not just in the United States but in most other countries involved in World War II. Countries with different systems of justice and different systems of welfare also experienced a similar pattern: a high postwar birthrate (though the increases were not as great as that in the United States) followed fifteen to twenty years later by disproportional increases in crime. For example, in England, in the twelve-year period 1948 to 1960, robbery rose by 73 percent, but in the next twelve years, it rose by 277 percent. In France, the rate of theft *decreased* in the 1950s by over 50 percent; in the 1960s, it increased by 60 percent.[71] This pattern suggests that something about high birthrates in themselves, regardless of government policy, creates pressure for crime. The notable exception is Japan, where beginning about 1950 crime rates decreased steadily for nearly three decades.

BLAME IT ON THE TUBE   Another explanation for the high crime rates of the baby boomers points the accusing finger at television. Watching television, say some social scientists, makes children violent, and the baby boomers were the first U.S. generation raised on television. The large size of the first TV generation is merely a historical accident. One exponent of this theory, Brandon Centerwall, notes that in Canada and the United States, in the period between 1947 and 1974, homicide rates nearly doubled. But in South Africa, where television was banned until 1975, homicide rates among whites during the same period actually declined slightly.[72]

Centerwall's assumptions about how television affects behavior resemble what one critic calls the "hypodermic needle" approach. It assumes that television injects its images into viewers much like a hypodermic needle. Massive injections of violence produce violent behavior in the injectees. Indeed, studies of young children show that just as they imitate things they see in real life, they also imitate what they see on television. This is a fairly simple idea and a popular one. In 1994, U.S. Attorney General Janet Reno, the highest law-enforcement official in the country, scolded the TV networks for their violent programming and issued vague threats of government action if they did not "clean up their act."

Other observers, still blaming television for crime and other social problems, take a more sophisticated view, arguing in effect that the medium is the message—that is, that television itself, regardless of the content of the programs, breeds crime. Marie Winn, author of a book called *The Plug-In Drug: Television, Children and the Family*, says that when children play with other children, the interaction teaches them to restrain their own aggressive feelings. Watching television deprives them of that experience. Television can also replace parental control, and whether it's "Power Rangers" or "Barney," television's socializing and civilizing effects are far weaker than those of real parent-child interaction.[73]

DEMOGRAPHIC OVERLOAD—BARBARIANS AT THE GATE   Two other explanations for the surge in crime during the 1960s focus on the link between birthrates and crime rates. One emphasizes social and psychological factors; the other, economic forces. Both start with the reminder that what is important is the *rate* of birth—that is, the number of babies born compared with the number of adults.

The social-psychological model views the child-adult ratio as operating much like the student-faculty ratio in a junior high school. When this ratio gets too large, things can get out of hand. Similarly, in the wider society, the important task of adults is to control children by teaching them to be good members of their society. This process is called socialization, and without it there would be chaos. Babies, after all, come into the world utterly indifferent to the rules of society. Parents may think of an individual birth as a blessed event, but to demographer Norman Ryder, it is part of a "perennial invasion of barbarians who must somehow be civilized." When the "invading army" is small relative to the "defending army" of adults, the task of socializing these children runs fairly smoothly. But when a baby boom sends in a relatively large invading army, the result is **demographic overload**, and the mechanisms of socialization break down. During the baby boom, "the increase of the magnitude of the socialization tasks in the United States ... was completely outside the bounds of previous experience."[74] Instead of adults socializing and controlling younger members of society, youths looked more to one another, to their own youth culture, for their cues for what to think and how to act.

The decade of the 1960s, during which the 15- to 24-year-old age group increased by 50 percent, marked the full flourishing of the youth culture. This culture was too broad and diverse to summarize in a single sentence, but at least in part—the part we are concerned with here—it was disdainful of "straight" behavior and tolerant of deviance. This "subterranean tradition"[75] among youths had existed in the past, but it had been kept underground by the large ratio of responsible adults. But in the 1960s, the sheer size of the young population allowed the underground, antiestablishment tradition to emerge and become a visible force in U.S. culture. Although few youths actually believed that street crime was right and good, the youth culture's generally tolerant attitude toward deviance allowed a larger place for predatory crime.

BIG COHORT, SMALL PROSPECTS Another explanation for the increased crime of the baby boom generation is fundamentally economic. In place of vague concepts like socialization and culture, this explanation emphasizes the very concrete factors of jobs and income and the very simple notion of supply and demand—in this case the supply and demand of labor. Imagine going to a job interview at a firm that has five openings. In the waiting room, you find four other people who have applied for the jobs. Now imagine going to a waiting room and finding ten other hopeful applicants. It's not hard to guess which room will produce more disappointed people.

Birth cohorts are like those waiting rooms: Some have more people than others. People born in the 1930s were members of a small birth cohort. They were lucky. As they looked toward and then entered their years in the labor market (the late 1940s and early 1950s), the economy was expanding. The demand for labor increased, but labor was in short supply. Since there were fewer young people relative to older people, young adults did not have to compete so much for jobs. Consequently, unemployment was low, wages were good, and people advanced fairly quickly up the career ladder. Of course, they were not yet making as much money as the older workers were, but their relative position was pretty good.

By contrast, people born to the large birth cohorts of the late 1940s and early 1950s faced a reversed labor market. As they reached working age, they crowded the labor market. The growth in job seekers outpaced the growth in available jobs. This discrepancy produced higher unemployment and lower wages. And since the adults of the previous generation were now occupying the higher jobs, advancement for the younger group was slower. Relative to older workers, young people in the 1960s and 1970s were doing far worse than the young people of the 1940s and 1950s.

This picture conflicts somewhat with the image of baby boomers as the successful "yuppies" of the 1980s, indulging themselves in all sorts of consumer goods. But yuppie affluence was not all that it seemed. Many baby boomers accumulated the money to spend on computers and expensive cars by delaying or foregoing entirely two much more expensive items—houses and children—that their parents in the 1950s had been able to afford while enjoying the luxury of a one-earner household.

More important, the less affluent members of the baby boom generation at the other end of the economic scale faced far less enviable decisions. For them, the choice was not between houses and BMWs; it was between unemployment and low-paying jobs. For women, it was often a question of having an illegitimate child or marrying a man with meager economic prospects. Logically, under these circumstances unemployment, divorce, and illegitimacy became reasonable economic choices, choices though that brought psychological consequences of depression, bitterness, and resentment, which in turn emerged in the form of higher rates of mental illness, suicide, and crime.[76]

This idea that the relative size of birth cohorts is of overwhelming importance is sometimes called the **Easterlin hypothesis**, after its principal exponent, Richard Easterlin. Unfortunately, although it seems very convincing in analyzing the baby boomers, it does not do so well in predicting the crime rates of other generations. For earlier and later points in history, cohort size does not seem to matter.[77]

DEMOGRAPHY ISN'T EVERYTHING

Birthrates began to decline in 1957, so the last cohorts of the baby boom were turning 25 and aging out of their high-crime years around 1982. This means that crime rates should have begun to decline early in the 1980s, and they did. Between 1981 and 1985, the murder rate decreased by 20 percent, a decrease that was demographically driven. But birthrates continued to fall during the 1960s, a demographic change that should have held out hopes for a continued drop in crime. But it didn't happen. Crimes like murder, robbery, and motor vehicle theft all rose more or less steadily after 1985. More ominously, the age curve of crime seems to be shifting lower, with more kids getting into serious crime at a younger age. In recent years, the group with the greatest increase in homicides has been boys in their mid-teens, youths who were born in the relatively small birth cohorts of the mid-1970s.

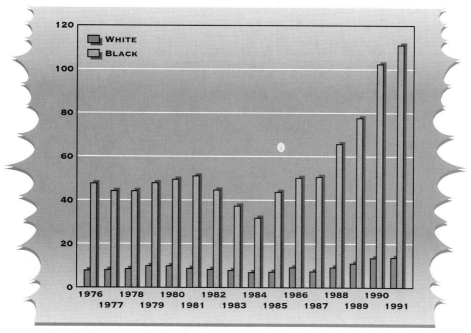

FIGURE 4–8   Homicide Rates of Males Aged 14–17 (Offenders per 100,000 population)

If the crime rate does not exactly parallel the birthrate, it may be because other factors (the economy, the criminal justice system, the weather, etc.) play a more important role.[78] It may also be that we have looked at the birthrate for the nation as a whole rather than in those areas that are likely to produce greater amounts of crime. These demographic trends in themselves are hardly good news. The baby boom produced an "echo," that is, the children of the large birth cohorts of the baby boom years. These children are now coming into their high-crime years. By the early part of the next decade, the number of 15- to 19-year-olds will increase by 23 percent, and among minorities the increase will be even greater—28 percent among African-Americans and 47 percent among Hispanics. More distressing, the teenagers in these cohorts are more violent, as Figure 4–8 shows. From the low in 1984 through 1991, homicide among white boys in their late teens nearly doubled; among blacks the rate more than tripled.[79]

SUMMARY AND CONCLUSION

I have tried in this chapter to present evidence and explanations concerning four variables—sex, race, social class, and age—and their relationship to crime. These are not the only variables that might be related to crime. The *where* and *when* questions are also important, and I have mentioned in passing, here and elsewhere in this book, differences among urban, suburban, and rural areas and among different sections of the country. Crime also varies with temperature, month of the year, day of the week, time of day, and perhaps even the phases of the moon.

However, to answer the question "Who commits crimes?" criminologists have traditionally focused their research on the demographic variables of sex, race, social class, and age. The results, though not always in agreement, show that criminals, at least street criminals (those who commit Index crimes), are usually young men, somewhat more likely to come from the lower end of the economic ladder; and in the United States, disproportionately black. These last two factors (class and race) are more strongly related to violent crime than to property crime.

Our information on crime comes from three major sources, each with its own particular strengths and inaccuracies: police arrests, self-reports, and victimization surveys. These also tell us something about the victims of crime: The demographic profile of victims closely resembles the profile of the perpetrators (with the obvious exception that the victims of rape are female). The bulk of lawbreakers commit their crimes close to home, in their own geographic and demographic areas. For crimes against the person, what the UCR calls violent crime, the similarity between criminal and victim is even more striking. Both the perpetrators and the victims of violent street crime are those people who are in the street, and young men are much more likely to be there. Often, those who commit assault and robbery have themselves been victims of these crimes.[80]

Putting together the information on these variables, we see a picture something like this: As children in all social classes grow into their early teens, many become involved in minor offenses. A smaller number, most of whom are boys, will commit more serious property offenses like burglary and auto theft. In the lower class, a small number will also commit violent crimes, including robbery. As they near age 18, most of these youths, especially those in the middle class, will give up crime. In the lower class and the working class, a minority of youths will continue to commit crimes, and an even smaller number (especially in the black lower class) will commit violent crimes as well. They will become the career criminals, those who commit a variety of crimes and commit them frequently.

Of course, this is a very general picture, and there are many variations and many exceptions. Even though most youths who get involved in crime soon go relatively straight, enough of them remain in the game to sustain high levels of violence and crime. The next chapters offer a more detailed account of these crimes.

CRITICAL THINKING QUESTIONS

1. How accurate are arrest figures for profiling criminals? What other sources of information are there on who commits crimes?
2. Did sex-role changes of the 1960s and 70s affect women's participation in crime?

3. What is social class; how many social classes are there? What does it mean to be "middle class" or "lower class"? Do middle-class people commit less crime than do poorer people?
4. Why is it so difficult to study the connection between class and crime?
5. Why is race such a controversial topic in the study of crime?
6. Are black/white differences in crime just a matter of economics?
7. Why do some kids "mature out" of crime, and why do others get more heavily involved?
8. Who are the "baby boomers" and how and why were their levels of crime so different from those of other generations?

KEY TERMS

baby boom

birth cohort

carnival mirror

coarse net

culture

demographic overload

Easterlin hypothesis

race

self-report study

social class

socioeconomic status (SES)

subculture of violence

underclass

CHAPTER FIVE

VIOLENT CRIMES, PART I

MURDER AND ROBBERY

CHAPTER OUTLINE

MURDER

Pick a crime, any crime—a crime you'd like to know more about, a crime that's interesting or important, or a crime you are afraid of. If you are like most of the people I've asked, the crime that first came to mind was murder. I am using the term *murder* here in a criminological sense, not a legal one. Laws, although they may vary from one jurisdiction to another, often make fine distinctions among different degrees of murder and manslaughter, distinctions that do not concern us here. My use of the term *murder* corresponds to the category in the Uniform Crime Reports of "murder and non-negligent manslaughter." This definition includes most willful killings; it excludes involuntary manslaughter (accidents) and "justifiable homicide."

It's easy to see why murder is the crime that most captures our attention. It is more serious than other crimes, and its effects are irreversible. Murder also

Random killings, like this one by an urban sniper, are always newsworthy but are relatively rare. Most killings occur during disputes between people who know each other or, less frequently, during botched robberies.

receives the most publicity. In the realm of fiction, few other crimes are worth bothering with. Television shows rarely depict burglaries or auto thefts, but it is virtually impossible to get through a night of prime time without seeing someone killed. And in the movies, only murder deserves serious treatment. Burglary and robbery appear, if at all, as material for comedy.

Media coverage of real crime gives a similar picture. Of all crime stories on TV news, about half are murders. Moreover, in large media markets, where TV news editors must choose from several killings each day, they choose the unusual cases that most resemble the murders of fiction. A really celebrated murder case, like the 1993 killing by the Menendez brothers in California, may give rise not just to news reports but to magazine articles, books, and made-for-television movies. Many of these "true stories" of murder probe for deep psychological twists in the mind of the murderer; other stories contain a moral about wayward youth or pathological greed or love gone wrong. The accounts

IN THE NEWS

MURDER— BODIE, NEVADA, 1880

William Page had been drinking and dancing for several hours at a dance house on King Street. About 2 a.m., he and his dance partner were bumped by Pat Keogh and his partner. Page responded by making a "threatening remark."

Keogh "made some insulting remark and used an opprobrious epithet." Page reached for his gun but was too slow. Keogh outdrew him and shot him through the temple. Page fell to the floor dead.

Source: Roger McGrath, *Gunfighters, Highwaymen and Vigilantes: Violence on the Frontier* (Berkeley: The Regents of the University of California, 1984).

MURDER—LONG ISLAND, NEW YORK, 1994

Bellmore, L.I. July 12—An argument between two brothers who had gone drinking with a third brother for the evening ended in gunfire early this morning as one shot and killed the other while the third looked on in horror.

The three Messmer brothers... began their evening like so many others, downing a few beers at the local firehouse.... Then they visited ... a neighborhood bar, to continue their drinking.

But on their way home an argument broke out between Patrick [33] and his younger brother, Sean [29]. It ended in the family's basement when ... one brother grabbed a shotgun and fired ... into the abdomen of the other as Eugene looked on.

Source: *New York Times*, July 13, 1994, p. B5.

---

create the fear that *nobody* is safe. We see the statistics from the FBI—a murder committed every twenty-five minutes. We glance at our watches, think of the murders on television, and wonder: Will we be next?

Yet despite the images in the media and perhaps in our minds, murder, relative to other crimes, is a rare event. It accounts for 0.2 percent of all crimes on the FBI's Index of serious crime. Even rarer are the kinds of homicide that make good TV stories. Instead, the more frequent, typical murders are hardly the stuff of high drama. The motives and methods in most homicides are utterly predictable and commonplace. As for fear, murder is one crime it is fairly easy to avoid. If you stay out of arguments with people who have been drinking and have weapons; if, in case you do get into such an argument, you back down before push comes to shove; and if you pursue a career in something other than drug dealing or organized crime, you will greatly reduce your chances of being murdered.

PRIMARY HOMICIDE

The two killings described in the box on this page are examples of what criminologists call **primary homicide**—deaths that result from a more or less spontaneous fight between people who know each other. Although primary homicides make much less exciting news than planned murders, they account for the largest share of murder even when other kinds of murders are on the rise as in the late 1980s and early 1990s in the United States.

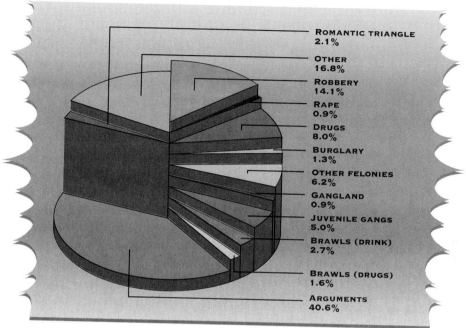

FIGURE 5–1   Murder Circumstances, 1992 (Felony and Nonfelony)

Source: Based on data from Federal Bureau of Investigation, *Crime in the United States, 1992: The Uniform Crime Reports* (Washington, D.C.: 1993).

Felony murders (the exploded section of Figure 5–1) make up slightly less than one-third of all homicides. The most frequent type of homicide is the killing that arises from an argument, which accounts for more deaths than all felony homicides. Figure 5–1 shows some other statistical realities that vary from the picture of image of murder in the media. Drunken brawls account for more killings than do drug-induced brawls, romantic triangles, rapes, or organized crime hits, although these other types of killing are more likely to be the subject of news reports or made-for-television movies.

In 1992, of all murders in which the circumstances were known, nearly half stemmed from arguments, many committed under the influence of alcohol or, less frequently, drugs. Much of this information comes from the UCR. For many crimes, these official statistics are questionable (see Chapter Three). But for murder, especially primary homicides, the accuracy of reporting and the high clearance rate (65 to 75 percent) make the data more trustworthy than those for most other crimes. The data also show a remarkable similarity between murderers and their victims. For example, 90 percent of all murders involving whites or blacks are *intra*racial (whites killing whites, and blacks killing blacks) (see Table 5–1). Also, out of 100 murders, about 89 are committed by men, 66 of these against other men (see Table 5–2). Tables 5–1 and 5–2 do not include murders where the race of either the victim or the

TABLE 5-1 •
MURDER 1992 VICTIM/OFFENDER RELATIONSHIP BY RACE
(AVERAGE PER 100 MURDERS)

RACE OF VICTIM	RACE OF OFFENDER	
	WHITE	BLACK
WHITE	42	7
BLACK	3	48

Source: UCR, 1992.

offender is "unknown" or "other" (about 4 percent of all murders) or where the sex of either the victim or the offender is unknown (about 1 percent of all cases). These statistics confirm the picture of murder as something that occurs between people who inhabit the same geographic and social space. The data on victim-offender relationships add to this view. About 12 percent of murders involve members of the same family; another 35 percent involve friends, neighbors, and acquaintances. Only 13 percent involve strangers. (In 39 percent of the cases, the police did not know the relationship between murderer and victim.)

This chapter will focus on three sociological perspectives on murder. Not all disputes turn into homicides, and the **interactionist approach** analyzes the sequence of events and contributing elements that lead to the killing. The **cultural approach** focuses not on individual incidents but on homicide rates. It sees different rates as a function of the culture of different groups—their particular values and norms. The **structural approach** explains differences in homicide rates as a function of elements of the social structure, particularly economic and social inequality.

TABLE 5-2 •
MURDER 1992 VICTIM/OFFENDER RELATIONSHIP BY SEX
(AVERAGE PER 100 MURDERS)

SEX OF VICTIM	SEX OF OFFENDER	
	MALE	FEMALE
MALE	66	9
FEMALE	23	2

Source: Derived from Federal Bureau of Investigation. *Crime in the United States, 1992: The Uniform Crime Reports* (Washington, D.C.: 1993).

THE INTERACTIONIST PERSPECTIVE: THE MURDER SCENARIO   Why do murderers kill people they know? The murderers in TV shows and movies are usually motivated either by insatiable greed or by a nearly psychotic mental warp. They plan carefully so that their crimes are unsolvable without the intervention of a heroically clever cop or private investigator. In the real world, however, homicides result from motives like anger, and they involve little or no advance planning. They occur as the culmination of an argument or fight. The deadly intent, if there is any, usually develops during the course of the interaction, and it is less crucial to the outcome of the encounter than are other elements in the situation. If the circumstances had changed—if the other person had responded differently, if the onlookers had intervened, if the weapon at hand had been less deadly—the end result would probably not have been fatal. If the people had not been drinking, the outcome might have been different, for alcohol is another element that can make conflicts more violent and more deadly. In nearly two-thirds of all murders, either the murderer or the victim or (most frequently) both had been drinking.[1] There is some debate over why alcohol is related to murder and other violent crimes. Presumably, alcohol reduces inhibitions and makes people less attentive to the long-range consequences of their behavior.

The sequence of escalation usually begins with some point of difference, which quickly leads to an argument, confrontation, and fight. Often, the victim or witnesses play an important role in the outcome. Usually the sequence begins when one person (A) does or says something that offends or upsets the other (B). Of course, murder is not B's immediate response. Instead, B needs to confirm the meaning of A's action or to give A a chance to stop. If A continues, it is one more step toward the murder. Many murders of children represent an extreme version of this pattern.

> The victim [a 5-week-old boy] ... started crying early in the morning. The offender, the boy's father, ordered [the boy] to stop crying. [The boy's] crying, however, only heightened in intensity. The ... persistent crying may have been oriented not toward challenging his father's authority, but toward acquiring food or a change of diapers. Whatever the motive for crying, *the child's father defined it as purposive and offensive.*[2]

In most cases, this vicious cycle of child abuse stops short of death. Nevertheless, about 4 percent of all murder victims are under 5 years of age, and almost all of them are killed by their parents.

Sometimes it is the victim who either starts the fight or plays a crucial part in escalating the conflict. One of the first systematic studies of homicide, published nearly forty years ago, found that about one murder in four was "victim precipitated."[3]

> During a lovers' quarrel, the male hit his mistress and threw a can of kerosene at her. She retaliated by throwing the liquid on him and then tossed a lighted match in his direction. He died from the burns.[4]

> A man, his wife, and two neighbors were sitting in the living room drinking wine. The man started calling his wife abusive names. She told him to "shut up." Nevertheless, he continued. Finally, she shouted, "I said shut up. If you don't shut up and stop it, I'm going to kill you and I mean it."[5]

Note that the latter murder took place in front of bystanders—not unusual in primary homicides. One study from a California city (population 350,000) found that 70 percent of all homicides occurred in the presence of others. In most of these cases, the "audience" actively encouraged the murderer and sometimes even supplied a weapon. In the other cases, they merely did nothing to stop the offender.[6] There were no murders in this study where bystanders tried to stop the fight. Presumably, bystanders did intervene in some fights, with the result that these incidents did not end in death. So apparently *any* intervention is sufficient to prevent an argument from turning into a murder—another bit of evidence contradicting the idea that murder begins with the murderer's unwavering intent. Even when they announce their intent ("I'm going to kill you and I mean it"), potential murderers may still be deterred by the intervention of other people.[7] (Of course, attempts at intervention may have a less happy outcome. At a criminology convention, I put this question about bystander intervention to a researcher who had just spoken about his study of murder incidents. He answered that these bystanders tended to turn up in his data in the category of victim.) On the other hand, bystanders may push the person toward murder, rather than away from it.

> The offender and his friend were sitting in a booth at a tavern drinking beer. The offender's friend told him that the offender's girlfriend was "playing" with another man at the other end of the bar. The offender looked at them and asked his friend if he thought something was going on. The friend responded, "I wouldn't let that guy fool around with [her] like that if she was mine." The offender agreed, and suggested to his friend that his girlfriend and the [man—the eventual victim] be shot for their actions. His friend said that only the [man] should be shot, not the girlfriend.[8]

This incident illustrates one other general aspect of murder (and assault), especially cases involving a lover or a spouse. Although the law would regard this shooting as a crime, the offender felt that he was acting not just out of personal anger but out of a sense of general principle. Like the woman who retaliated against her husband's verbal abuse, this man was seeking to control actions that he thought were wrong. These murders—and they are typical—occur as the last step in a sequence of attempts to control the actions of another person, to make that person behave properly. The prospective murderer interprets the other's action as a devastating and unjustified attack on the self. The murderer's response, therefore, is one of humiliation, which is then transformed into rage coupled with a sense of righteousness. The murderer feels that in order to restore the self, to right the wrongs inflicted, he or she must do something. Sometimes the enraged person sees a way out or chooses some inanimate object (like the furniture) as a target. But in other cases, the murderer takes action against the source of humiliation to remove that person forever, to "blow him away."[9] The offenders feel that their act is justified or even necessary—that they are enforcing some right or redressing some grievance. As one legal scholar puts it, "Most intentional homicide in modern society may be classified as social control, specifically as self-help, even if it is handled by legal officials as crime."[10] In the words of criminologist Jack Katz, the murder is an act of "righteous slaughter."[11]

THE CULTURAL PERSPECTIVE: ATTITUDES AND ACTIONS It is important to note that these ideas about right and wrong are not merely individual. In the barroom incident, both the offender and his friend believed that they were acting on general principles that most other people would recognize and approve of. Their actions flowed from certain parts of their society's *culture*—its *values* and *norms*. The term *values* refers to general, abstract ideas about what is right and good. *Norms* operate at a more concrete level; they are a culture's rules for everyday interaction. In the same largely unconscious and inevitable way that we come to speak our society's language, we also adopt its values and norms. Since even murderers base their behavior on these shared ideas of how to behave in particular situations, some sociologists have given culture a central place in explaining murder. Certainly in the preceding incident, the murderer and his friend felt that the circumstances justified and even required violence. But cultural theories go beyond individual incidents. They also explain something most of us know or at least suspect: Some social groups have higher murder *rates*. Cultural theories maintain that among some groups, the shared and taken-for-granted values and norms actually promote violence. These groups are more tolerant of violence and more likely to see it as a legitimate, though perhaps unfortunate, response in certain situations.

The United States has the highest murder rate of any industrialized country. Homicide rates for men aged 15 to 24 in most European countries are generally between 1 per 100,000 and 2 per 100,000. Canada's rate is about 3 per 100,000; Japan's is 0.5. But for young men in the United States the rate is 21.9 per 100,000—about fifteen times higher than European rates.[12] According to cultural theories, these differences persist because in the United States, compared with other industrialized countries, typical attitudes are more tolerant of aggression and violence, including deadly violence. Americans socialize their children into these ways of thinking and acting. "American society," to quote one typical statement, "makes relatively little collective effort to discourage physical aggression among young males."[13] The images in the media reflect the same set of attitudes. In legitimate movie theaters and on network television, while sexual images are the subject of much regulation, violence may be shown in graphic detail and great quantity.

Cultural theorists take these images in the media as reflections of American attitudes toward sex and violence—repressive toward raw sex, tolerant of raw violence. But according to cultural theory, these attitudes influence not only what happens on the screen but also what happens on the street. Where attitudes are more accepting of violence, the logic goes, violence will be more frequent and more serious. The tolerance for violence also underlies the American reluctance to limit the manufacture, importation, ownership, and sale of guns. So violence, when it does erupt, is more likely to have fatal consequences.

The theory can be used to explain not only the difference between U.S. murder rates and those of other industrialized countries but also differences among various geographic and social sectors of American society. In fact, the best known cultural theory attributed such differences to the existence of a subculture of violence within the larger U.S. society.[14] One variation of this idea (known as the Gastil-Hackney thesis, after two of its proponents) begins with the observation that U.S. murder rates are higher than those of other industrialized countries and that within the United States murder rates have always been highest in the South and in areas of the West that were settled by Southerners. It follows then that "high homicide rates in the United States today are related primarily to the persistence of Southern cultural traditions developed before the Civil War and subsequently spreading over much of the country."[15] During the last two decades, as more Northerners have migrated to the South and regional differences of all kinds have generally decreased, the murder gap between the South and other regions has narrowed.

Figure 5–2 again raises the issue of guns, for the regions with the highest rates of gun ownership, the South and the West, also have the highest rates of murder. But cultural theorists see gun ownership more as a symptom of the underlying attitude toward deadly violence than as a cause of high murder rates. Even if every murder by gun were removed from the statistics, the U.S. murder rate would still be double that of most European countries. In the same way, Southern murder rates (and gun ownership) are higher because of Southern culture and its attitudes toward guns and violence.[16] Similar arguments can be made about the social-class and racial differences

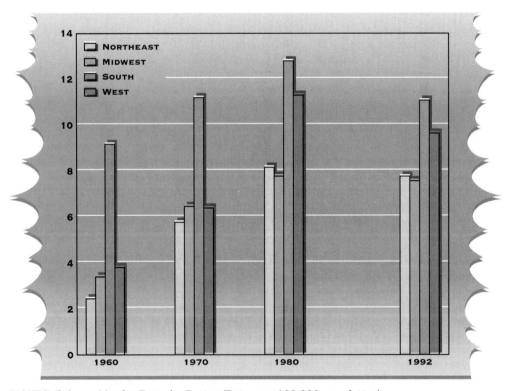

FIGURE 5–2   Murder Rates by Region (Rates per 100,000 population)

Source: Based on data from Federal Bureau of Investigation, *Crime in the United States, 1960, 1970, 1980, 1992: The Uniform Crimes Reports* (Washington, D.C.).

ABOUT CRIME & CRIMINOLOGY

DO SOUTHERN TRADITIONS INCLUDE A SUBCULTURE OF VIOLENCE?

The fierce "rough-and-tumble" fighting in the Southern backcountry that began at least as early as the mid-eighteenth century and flourished through the antebellum period offers a particularly disturbing example.... In 1774, Philip Fithian, the tutor at Robert Carter III's grand household in Tidewater Virginia, wrote in his journal:

> The cause of the battles I have not yet known; I suppose either that they are lovers, and one has in jest or reality some way supplanted the other; or has in a merry hour called him a *Lubber*, or a *thick-skull*, or a *buckskin*, or a *Scotsman*, or perhaps one has mislaid the other's hat, or knocked a peach out of his hand, or offered a dram without wiping the mouth of the bottle; all these, and ten thousand more quite as trifling and ridiculous, are thought and accepted as just causes of immediate quarrels, in which every diabolical stratagem for mastery is allowed and practiced, of bruising, kicking, scratching, pinching, biting, butting, tripping, throttling, gouging, cursing, dismembering, howling, etc.

Source: John F. Kesson, *Rudeness and Civility: Manners in Nineteenth-Century Urban America* (New York: Hill & Wang, 1990), pp. 142–143.

in homicide rates. According to the subculture-of-violence theory, the ideas and attitudes that promote violence are more prevalent in the urban lower class, especially among blacks.

Some proponents of cultural theory trace Southern violence to the origins of those who settled there. The elites who first came to the South were Cavaliers—nobles and landed gentry who took their values from medieval traditions of honor and virtue. In the later seventeenth and eighteenth century, immigrants to the South came largely from the borderlands of Scotland and Ireland, where they had been "tribal, pastoral, and warlike."[17] The pastoral part is important because pastoralists (societies whose economy is based on herding) are generally more violent than other types of society—and for good reason.

> Their livelihoods can be lost in an instant by the theft of their herds. To reduce the likelihood of this occurring, pastoralists cultivate a posture of extreme vigilance toward any act that might be perceived as threatening in any way, and respond with sufficient force to frighten the offender and the community into recognizing that they are not to be trifled with.[18]

Given this cultural heritage, Southerners were more likely to see violence as legitimate as long as the violence was defensive. Southern culture demanded that a man be ready to use violence, even lethal violence, to defend his honor, his property, and the virtue of "his" women.

The major criticism of this theory is empirical. First, as structural theorists argue, differences in homicide rates between the South and other sections of the country are not very great if we control for social and economic

ON CAMPUS

THE SOUTHERN SUBCULTURE OF VIOLENCE

Are Southerners more likely to defend their honor by using violence?

Psychologists at the University of Michigan asked out-of-state male students—some from the North, some from the South—to participate in an experiment. The experimenters rigged the setting so that each student, on his way to and from the lab, had to squeeze past another student (actually a confederate of the experimenter) working at an open filing cabinet. The confederate would appear irked at having to close the drawer and press himself against the cabinet to let the subject go by.

The second time the subject tried to squeeze past, "the confederate, who had just reopened the file drawer, slammed it shut, pushed his shoulder against the shoulder of the subject, and said, loudly enough to be clearly heard by the subject, 'Asshole.'"

When the subject returned to the psychology lab, he was asked to complete some perception and verbal tests—all designed to test for anger. He was also asked to provide endings for scenarios,

including one in which "a man's fiancee tells him that an acquaintance has made two clear passes at her during the course of the evening." Control groups—students who had not been insulted—allowed the experimenters to see not just the differences between Northern and Southern students but also those between each group's reaction to the insult.

Were Southerners more violent when honor was at stake? As it turned out, there was no difference between Southern and Northern undergraduates on some of the tests. But Southerners were far more likely to react to the "asshole" comment with anger: "For 65 percent of the Northern subjects but only 15 percent of the Southern subjects, the amusement ratings were higher than the anger ratings."

Northerners and Southerners also differed in how the insult influenced their imagination. For Northerners, the insult made no difference in the ending they created for the story. But "seventy-five percent of the insulted Southerners completed the ... scenario with events in which the protagonist physically injured, or threatened to injure, the antagonist, whereas this was true for only 25% of the Southerners who were not insulted."

Source: Derived from Richard E. Nisbett, "Violence and U.S. Regional Culture," *American Psychologist*, vol. 48, no. 4 (1993), 441–449.

variables like poverty. That is, non-Southern cities with poverty levels similar to those of Southern cities have similarly high homicide rates. Second, culture is about shared ideas—values and norms—and these may be difficult to measure accurately. If we take the actions of officials as reflections of popular sentiment, Southern culture can indeed appear violent. The South outranks the rest of the nation in state-approved violent solutions for wrongdoing—capital punishment for criminals and corporal punishment for schoolchildren. And the West and the South, the regions with the highest rates of homicide, score highest on a Legitimate Violence Index based on twelve indicators of noncriminal violence.[19] But it remains an open question whether the rules of formal institutions really tell us about the ideas that shape the everyday lives of ordinary people, especially those who commit homicides.

To measure norms and values, sociologists usually ask people to respond to multiple-choice questionnaire items. For example, in surveys asking people to rate the severity of various crimes, Southerners give lower severity scores to homicide and rape than do people from other sections of the country. Poorer, less educated, and black Southerners are especially likely to rank these crimes as less severe than their Northern or Midwestern or Western counterparts.[20] All this evidence supports the subculture of violence theory. But the research is not conclusive, and there are studies that show very little difference between Southerners and others or between blacks and whites regarding their attitudes toward violence. More interesting, these questionnaire studies also find very little difference in attitudes between men who have committed violent crimes and those who have not.[21] In fact, so many studies fail to confirm the cultural theories that some social scientists see the whole Southern violence idea as an academic form of "cracker bashing"—one more way for intellectuals to look down on the South.[22]

THE STRUCTURALIST PERSPECTIVE: MURDER AND INEQUALITY The structuralist approach seeks to explain the same data as do cultural theories—differences in murder rates among different sectors of the society. But instead of placing primary emphasis on the shared ideas within a social group, structural explanations try to link murder rates to elements of the social structure. The term *social structure* is really a metaphor; it uses the idea of a building to talk about relations among people. But the metaphor can be slippery. We know what a building looks like, and we can identify its elements—doors, stairs, rooms, levels, and so on. But what does the structure of a society look like? Usually, when social scientists use the term, they are referring to things that, like the structural elements of a building, an individual has little power to change. For example, the age structure of this society—the number of people at each age level—can have important effects on everything from the quality of the schooling you can get to your career chances and choices to your likelihood of finding someone suitable to marry. Yet although this aspect of the social structure is obviously a product of human interaction, no one person can have any real impact on it.

Criminologists interested in murder have focused on other parts of the social structure—things like poverty; population crowding; and economic and social inequality, especially between the races. From the structuralist point of view, murder rates are higher in the South not because the South has its own violence-prone culture but because Southern states have high levels of poverty and inequality.

Structuralist theories have one advantage over cultural theories: Structural variables are much easier to measure than are attitudes and values. Critics can justifiably question whether a person's responses to questionnaire choices really reflect a complex set of ideas in that person's mind.

There is far more agreement on measurements that indicate poverty—variables like low income, low education, substandard housing, and high rates of infant mortality. And all these items correlate strongly with murder rates. In the United States, the states and cities with higher levels of poverty also have higher levels of murder, regardless of geographic location.[23]

Some structural theories question whether the crucial factor in homicide rates is simply poverty. After all, some of the poorer industrialized countries in the world (e.g., Ireland) have very low murder rates. Some sociologists, therefore, prefer to look at money in relative terms. Where does this particular income (and the standard of living it buys) put a person in relation to others in this society? The issue then becomes not just poverty but also inequality. Again, the evidence is not conclusive; that is, the differences are not great and there are many exceptions. But generally the research on U.S. cities has shown that the greater the gap between rich and poor or between blacks and whites the higher the rate of murder.[24]

Though some critics have questioned the data, let us assume for the moment that the structural idea is valid—that is, that murder rates are higher where there is either more poverty or less equality or both. We must still ask why poorer or less equal people are more murderous. In the chapter on historical trends in crime, I outlined one explanation: Industrialization has a moderating effect on recklessness and violence; it imposes a more orderly way of living. Those who are left out of the industrial sector—for example, today's urban underclass—are unaffected by this process and retain higher levels of violence.[25]

A second approach resembles Robert Merton's theory of anomie. This explanation assumes, first, that much inequality is structural rather than individual; that is, people find themselves at the bottom of the social ladder not because of their individual talents but because of the narrower opportunities open to them. Second, our ideology of equality puts an added strain on those who are victims of structurally based inequality. Told continuously that in this country anyone can and should be successful, people who face every day the limitations of lower-class life—limitations they have little power to change—are likely to react with some combination of bitterness, alienation, frustration, and anger. Since race is even less changeable than the economic conditions a person is born into, these feelings will be especially acute when the inequality is based on race. Thus, the greater black-white economic differences, the greater the difference in murder rates between the races.[26]

There is another way of linking poverty or inequality with murder. Recall that murderers are often responding to what they perceive as an insult. They feel that the other person has violated some socially recognized "right." Some social scientists see important sex differences on this matter: In personal relationships men tend to think in terms of their "rights," while women think in terms of their responsibilities. Men, therefore, are more likely to kill (or get killed) defending their rights.[27] The argument may start over some trivial matter, but the minor affront becomes a matter of "honor"—a threat to the person's entire identity. How do we maintain a sense of identity or self-worth? Middle-class people may have careers, jobs, families, and houses to tell them they are "somebody." Among the poor, however, many people do not have a job; others may have a job so menial it cannot serve as a source of respect and so poorly paid it does not support a family. Poor people, therefore, may have to stake their identities entirely on their performance in interpersonal relationships. A man's self, his honor, may be all that he has. An insult or a challenge can loom as a much more serious threat, and when other people are around to remind the man of the challenge to his honor, the outcome can be deadly.[28] Ruth Horowitz writes of this process in the Chicano gang:

> In an honor-bound subculture that emphasizes manhood and defines violation of interpersonal etiquette in an adversarial manner, any action that challenges a person's right to deferential treatment in *public* can be interpreted as an insult and a potential threat to manhood. Honor demands that a man be able physically to back his claim to dominance and independence.[29]

This analysis applies to murders among youths in the inner city, where not even the status of parents can serve as an institutional source of identity, where a person's worth must be confirmed and reconfirmed in every encounter. What in other contexts might be a mere breach of etiquette becomes a sign of disrespect and therefore a challenge to a person's entire being; a person arrested for murder may explain his action with the succinct explanation, "He dissed me."

"GUNS DON'T KILL PEOPLE"—OR DO THEY? Most fights, of course, do not end in death. What, then, distinguishes the merely injurious fight from the fatal one? One obvious factor is the presence of a weapon. The deadlier the weapon, the more likely the fight will result in death. The difference between a knife and a gun may be the difference between aggravated assault and murder.

Not everyone agrees that weapons are important. You may have seen bumper stickers that say, "Guns don't kill people, people kill people." Even some criminologists maintain that "if a firearm were not immediately present ... the offender would select some other weapon to achieve the same destructive goal."[30] The evidence, though open to different interpretations, provides little support for this view. Instead, it points to the importance of guns.

The UCR provides data on the type of weapon used in homicides, as shown in Figure 5–3. Obviously, guns—three-quarters of them handguns—account for the largest number of murders. One possible conclusion you might draw from this table is that "people kill people"; that is, when people want to kill someone, they go out and get a gun. The intention comes first and determines the choice of weapons. This interpretation evokes a picture of a person bent on murder, selecting the most efficient weapon—a gun. If he can't get a gun, he settles for a knife. This picture may fit a few murders—the sniper attack or the gangland hit—but for most homicides, there is a more probable interpretation: The presence of a gun can transform an assault into a homicide. It is the weapon, not the intent, that makes the difference.

This lack of deadly intent is often clear from the scenarios of individual homicides. It also is reflected in the demographic data on murder and other violent crimes. Robbery, for example, though it is a violent crime, differs in its social and geographic location from murder. In robbery, victims and criminals are usually strangers, and rates are highest in the cities of the Northeast, lowest in the South. Patterns of murder, however, closely follow those of aggra-

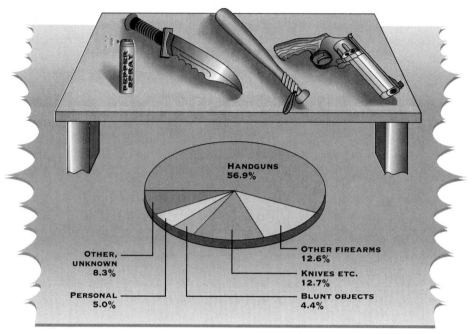

FIGURE 5–3   Murder Weapons, 1993

Source: Based on data from Federal Bureau of Investigation, *Crime in the United States, 1993: The Uniform Crime Reports* (Washington, D.C.: 1994).

vated assault. Where murder rates are high, rates of aggravated assault also are high, for to a great extent they are the same crime. The typical murder is an aggravated assault—one that becomes a bit too aggravated.

Both murder and aggravated assault begin as an attack arising from some interpersonal dispute. What determines whether that attack will become an aggravated assault or a murder? One factor—a variable rarely considered important in the murder rate—is the availability of medical help. The shooting victim who can get to an emergency room quickly has a better chance of winding up in the statistics as an aggravated assault instead of a murder. This medical factor may even account for some of the regional differences in murder rates.[31] However, a more obvious and more important factor is the choice of weapons. Assaults that involve guns are far more likely to result in death than are assaults with knives or other weapons. There may also be important differences not just between guns and other weapons but also between deadly guns and less deadly guns. When disputes between people turn violent, a knife is not nearly so deadly as even a Saturday night special, a cheap .22 caliber handgun that rose to prominence in street crime during the 1970s. In the 1980s and 1990s, the weapons of choice in the streets were even deadlier handguns—.357 Magnums and 9 millimeter weapons—and many law-enforcement officials attribute at least part of the increase in murder in the last decade to the greater availability of these weapons.

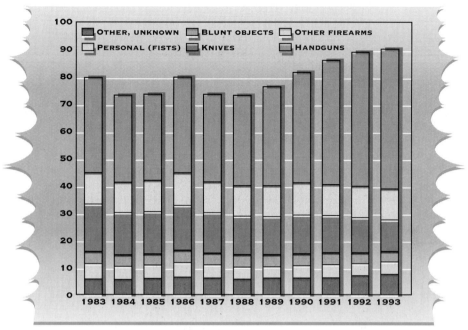

FIGURE 5–4   Murder Weapons, 1983–1992 (Homicide Rates per Million Population)

Source: Derived from UCR, 1983–1993.

Figure 5–4 shows the number of murders and nonnegligent manslaughters in which the weapon was known. Although there are other interpretations, the numbers support the idea that the increased use of handguns is responsible for the latest upsurge in murders. The increase in murder rates between 1987 and 1993 is totally attributable to handgun murders. During a six-year period when killings by other weapons decreased, the rate of handgun murders increased from thirty-two per million to fifty-one per million, an increase of more than 50 percent.

FELONY MURDERS

Most murders fall into the category of primary homicide, which in the United States comprises about two-thirds of all murders. In other industrialized societies the percentage is even higher. The remaining 20 percent of homicides are felony murders. Though far fewer in number, these murders are more likely to receive attention in the media: murders occurring in the course of another felony such as robbery or rape, mass murders and serial murders, murders between rival gangs, and planned murders meant to accomplish some rational goal (the gangland hit is a classic example). When murder rates increased dramatically in the 1960s (along with rates of other crimes), the proportion of felony murders also increased. Consequently, the clearance rate for murder dropped. In 1960, when most murders were primary homicides, police cleared 92.3 percent of all murders. By the mid-1970s, that rate had dropped to 79 percent. The proportion of felony homicides remained stable for nearly a decade but rose again in the late 1980s, and the clearance rate fell to 70 percent.[32] In 1993, the latest year for which I have data, it was 66 percent.

ROBBERY MURDER   The most frequent form of felony murder is robbery murder, a robbery in which the robber kills the victim. Of every 1,000 robberies in the United States, between 3 and 4 end in death. I have based this estimate on UCR data—robberies reported to the police. If unreported robberies were included, the proportion of murders would be slightly under 2 per 1,000 robberies. In a very few of these cases, the robbers begin the crime with the full intent of murdering the victim. The robber who robs a drug dealer of cash and inventory may think (often correctly) that unless he kills the victim, the victim will later kill him.

> Two men sat in the back seat of a car with a drug dealer and shot him and his girlfriend to death, subsequently taking money and drugs from them. One of the offenders had owed money to the male victim, and the latter, on a round of collections earlier that evening, had threatened the offender if he did not pay.[33]

Most of the time, however, as in primary homicides, the criminals do not begin the robbery with the intention of killing the victim. The factors that turn a robbery into a felony murder are the same factors that turn an argument into a primary homicide: the deadliness of the weapons, the presence of other people, and the sequence of interaction between murderer and victim.

If robbers do not intend to kill their victims, why do they still carry guns—especially since many states now have harsher penalties for crimes committed with guns? One obvious reason is that a gun is a great "equalizer." The robber who goes after a big score that is likely to be well defended needs a weapon that will overcome the resistance. In smaller robberies as well, robbers must control the actions of the victims. Usually, the mere threat of force is sufficient for this purpose, and the deadlier the weapon, the more effective the threat. Victims are more likely to resist the robber who is unarmed or has only a knife. Robberies without guns are therefore more likely to result in injury to the victim, and even in gun robberies, the gun is more frequently used to strike than to shoot. But if the victim does resist and the robber shoots, injury will be more severe, perhaps even fatal.

> The victim, a 24-year-old man, and his woman friend were walking down the street. Two men grabbed both of them, knocking the woman down and snatching her purse. The victim broke away from one man and ran toward the other, who shot him in the chest.
>
> While a holdup was in progress in a private home, a man came to the door. One of the holdup men pulled the door open all the way and told the man to "freeze." The man ran and was shot in the back of the head.[34]

Even cooperative robbery victims may be murdered. In over half of all robbery murders, victims do not resist; in some cases, they may even be tied up or otherwise immobilized before being shot.[35] However, even in these cases, the robbers often do not start with the intent to kill their victims but instead make that decision at some time during the course of the robbery. Here again, guns may make the difference between life and death since a gunshot can be deadlier than a stab wound. Moreover, the impulsive decision to kill a victim may depend on the psychological and technical ease of doing so, and it is far easier to shoot someone from a safe distance than it is to kill with weapons that require actual contact with the victim.[36]

As in primary homicides, other people involved in the robbery can play a crucial role—especially with younger, more opportunistic criminals. The highly professional minority of robbers carry guns solely for instrumental purposes—as a means toward their goal of getting the money. They prefer not to shoot and will do so only if it is necessary.[37] Even some career robbers who brutalize or kill helpless victims may nevertheless have a rational motive. There is little honor, and in fact much danger, among thieves; a robber has to worry about being robbed—or worse—by other robbers. "A reputation for violence, perhaps sustained by 'irrational' brutality against the robbery victim, could be valuable for offenders who are interested in not becoming their colleagues' secondary victims."[38]

Most robbers, however, seem to have more complicated motives, both instrumental and expressive. They want the money, though the amounts involved are often small. But they also seem to be seeking some psychological gain. Some robbers mention the sense of power and vengeance they feel during their crimes. The robber may also want to appear tough in the eyes of his fellow robbers, not afraid to use his gun. "Group members often say, 'Go ahead, shoot' to another member who has the weapon."[39] The larger the group of robbers, therefore, the more likely it is that violence will occur.[40] When the robbers have guns, especially very powerful guns, the violence is more likely to end in death.

IN COLD BLOOD: PLANNED MURDER   Some murders, including some that also involve robbery, are instrumental—performed with the express purpose of killing the victim to gain money or power. Often both victim and murderer are part of the criminal underworld. Drug dealers are especially vulnerable to robbery murder. Because they may be carrying large amounts of cash or drugs, dealers make attractive targets, and as I mentioned previously, robbers may be tempted to kill in these robberies since the drug dealer, if allowed to live, might soon take revenge on the robbers.[41]

Sometimes the murders occur in disputes between rival criminal organizations. These assassinations and executions increase when organized crime becomes somewhat *dis*organized. Disputes over territory or over control of new forms of crime may lead to a series of murders. During Prohibition in the 1920s, murder rates increased in part because of competition in a new criminal enterprise—illegal liquor. Similarly in the late 1980s, the new commerce in cocaine and crack gave rise to increases in murder in cities where rival drug-dealing organizations competed for shares of the market. (Still, the murder rate in Miami during this period, though one of the highest in the country, was only one-third of the rate in the 1920s, another period when Miami was a wide-open town.[42]) In Los Angeles in the late 1980s, the struggle between two large gang-like groups (the Crips and the Bloods) for control of the African-American sector of the drug market had a similar effect. The economic motive combined with traditional gang rivalry, the availability of Uzis and other semiautomatic military assault rifles, and the participation of younger (and therefore less prudent) gang members, have resulted in a large number of drive-by killings, including some in which nonmembers have also been killed.

Other gangland murders are intended as a way to punish someone in the organization and to deter others. These organizations may have their own members do the killing or they may hire independent contractors—hit men—to do the job. These killers are usually no strangers to violence: "As young as I was (about 16 or 17) and with sellin' drugs like I was ... I went on a couple of things with my older partners.... After they dug the nerve that I had ... they took an' offered me a couple jobs. I had been known to shoot already."[43] Like soldiers, hit men learn to distance themselves psychologically from the people they kill. Just as their employers see the murder in largely instrumental terms—a matter of practical necessity rather than anger—hit men, too, frame their action as work—very serious business, but business nevertheless.[44]

MASS MURDER   One final category of murder—mass murder—deserves mention here, not necessarily because it happens frequently but because when it occurs or is discovered it receives so much attention in the press. Mass murderers are those who kill several victims, either all at once or over a period of months or even years. Some mass murders resemble the felony murder. They occur in connection with some other crime and have some instrumental motive. Wars between criminal gangs may lead to mass murder, as in the St. Valentine's Day massacre of 1929. Other criminals commit multiple killings as a way to escape prosecution for other crimes: They kill witnesses or accomplices who might testify against them.[45]

Still, the most frequent type of mass murder is not the gangland war or the work of a psychotic gunman. It is the family killing, in which one member of a family kills several of his relatives.[46] (Nearly all mass murderers are male. Of the forty-two mass murderers Levin and Fox discovered in their research, only one was female: a woman who burned down her house with her children inside.) Often, these killings are exaggerated responses to the emotions and pressures that can occur in families. The teenage child who feels wronged takes revenge against his parents and perhaps everyone else in the house. The rejected husband, angry with his wife over the divorce, returns to kill her and her children. (In the Greek tragedy of Medea, it is the wife who kills the children as a way of gaining vengeance against the husband, who has left her for another woman. Later poets, too, have warned of "the fury of a woman scorned," an idea that, judging by the popularity of movies like *Fatal Attraction*, is still current. Such a view of the battle of the sexes does not square with statistical reality. Rejected males are far more likely to become violent, and even murderous, than are their female counterparts. The misperception by Euripides and the others is not hard to explain: They were not criminologists, and they were men.) In other cases, the dominant emotion seems to be not anger but hopelessness. A father who has suffered some setback assumes that his wife and children will share his despair; to spare them the pain of his humiliation, he kills them in what one psychiatrist has called "suicide by proxy."[47] In the end, he also may kill himself. A 1985 Iowa case, which achieved national headlines, combined elements of both revenge and suicide by proxy. A farmer whose farm was falling into bankruptcy and foreclosure took a shotgun and killed his banker, his wife, his neighbor, and himself.[48]

Finally, there are the multiple murders of strangers. Unlike the crime-related killings or family slayings, these murders involve victims chosen almost at random; they happened to be in the wrong place at the wrong time. In some cases, the murders occur all at the same time. For example, in 1984, James Huberty, despondent over losing yet another job, armed himself with a rifle, a shotgun, and a pistol; walked into a San Diego McDonald's; and opened fire. He killed twenty-one people and wounded nineteen. In a somewhat similar example in 1966 at the University of Texas, Charles Whitman, an ex-marine and A-student, turned his anger and despair into deadly violence at specific individuals and at people in general. One night, he killed his wife and his mother. The next day, he went to the campus, climbed a water tower, and opened fire on the people below, killing fourteen and wounding thirty more.[49]

Mass murderers like Huberty and Whitman do not repeat their crimes. Either they kill themselves or are killed or captured by the police. However, there is another type of murderer—the serial murderer—who kills one or two victims at a time but repeats the crime several times over a period of months or even years. Often, an obvious element of sexual sadism is involved. The killers derive sexual excitement and release by torturing and killing their victims. Serial murder seems to feed on itself. Each murder the killer gets away with makes the next one that much easier to do. The murderer will have fewer doubts and fears of getting caught. In the case of sadistic murderers, their crimes seem to grow more and more vicious, as though they needed increasingly cruel scenarios for their sexual pleasure.[50]

Serial murderers often escape detection for a relatively long period of time. Their crimes are difficult for the police to solve because either the murderer, the victims, or both move at the fringes of society. Serial murderers who drift about the country occasionally killing people are especially difficult to identify since the police in any one case will be unable to recognize a pattern. Even the serial killers who stay in one place may be hard to catch. They often choose as victims people who have few stable relationships—skid-row winos, runaway children, or prostitutes. Not many people will be able to trace the victim's whereabouts just before he or she disappeared. Moreover, since serial killers select strangers as victims, the people the police usually question—relatives, friends, underworld competitors—seldom produce any leads.

Popular analyses of murders—the kind that appear in best-selling books or on television—tend to focus on the individual crime and the way in which the police finally solved the case. The killers in these stories are of the type that is fairly rare—the middle-class family murderer or the mass murderer, people whose names live on long after they have been caught, sentenced, and in some cases executed, like Charles Manson, John Wayne Gacy, or Jeffrey Dahmer. The explanation for murder in these cases usually focuses on the tangled psychodynamics of the killer's mind.

As fascinating as these accounts may be, they seldom help us to arrive at any general statements about murder or even about mass murder, except perhaps that these murderers rarely conform to our image of the mass murderer as some sort of fiend. In their appearance and in their manner, they are usually indistinguishable from other people. Besides, even if we could find common traits, this information would have very little predictive value. Whatever those traits are (male, between the ages of 20 and 40, troubled childhood, infatuated with weapons or pornography, etc.), for every killer they described there would be millions of nonkillers who also fit the description.

Psychological concepts are even less useful in explaining the primary homicides that make up the bulk of murder statistics. People who commit murder are not easily distinguishable from those who commit other street crimes. If anything, murderers are less "criminal" than burglars or robbers. That is, they are less involved in other crimes, and when released they are less likely than other criminals to be returned to prison on a new conviction. The recidivism rate among homicide offenders is about 22 percent; for those convicted of robbery it is 35 percent, and for burglary offenders 43 percent. And when homicide offenders are returned to prison, it is usually *not* for a violent crime; instead they are returned for theft, drug possession, or parole violations.[51]

SUMMING UP

Not all murders are alike. The most frequent, accounting for up to two-thirds of all murders in the United States, is the primary homicide—a killing that evolves from an argument. Most other homicides are classified as felony murders, including rape murders and robbery murders, murders over drug deals, and mass murders.

Individual murderers—especially the rarer types like mass murderers—can make fascinating psychological studies. However, for purposes of prediction, there is no way to distinguish precisely between murderers and nonmurderers. Instead, criminologists usually ask questions not about murderers but about murder rates. Why does the United States have such a high murder rate compared with other industrialized nations? Why does the South have a higher murder rate than other sections of the country? Why do men, blacks, and poor people kill at higher rates than women, whites, and those better off?

Sociological approaches to murder fall roughly into three types: interactionist, cultural, and structural. Interactionist ideas stress the scenario of murder, particularly the ways in which the participants interpret each other's actions—interpretations that turn an ordinary dispute into a matter of life and death. These explanations focus on the sequence of interaction leading to murder. They look at contributing factors like the availability of deadly weapons, the influence of alcohol, the behavior of the victim, and the intervention of bystanders.

Cultural theories, notably that of the subculture of violence, explain murder as an exaggerated version of culturally approved behavior. In cultures that tolerate and even demand violence in certain situations, violence will be more frequent and more deadly.

Structural theories see violence, especially murder, as a product of social and economic inequality. In a society whose ideology stresses equality but whose social structure creates great inequality, the underprivileged will be frustrated and hostile. They might more rationally direct this anger into some sort of collective effort to change or overthrow the system, but they lack the resources and organization for such action. Instead, their hostility takes the form of occasional angry outbursts at the nearest available source of frustration.

WHAT, IF ANYTHING, IS TO BE DONE?   It is hard to imagine how any of these theories might lead to policies that would lower homicide rates. Certainly the government cannot legislate subcultural norms out of existence, nor can it change the ways in which people interact. As for the material factors involved (i.e., liquor, and weapons), governments have tried to control them. But restrictions on alcohol and guns, besides being controversial political issues, have not had overwhelming success in reducing murder. Government policy can, theoretically, change the economic structure. Changes in taxation and government spending could greatly reduce economic inequality and even possibly bring the urban underclass more into the mainstream of economic life. Politically, however, such changes are extremely unlikely. In fact, during the 1980s, government economic policies of one of the most popular administrations in U.S. history actually increased the gap between rich and poor. Nor does the political climate in the 1990s seem to favor vigorous government anti-poverty actions.

You may have noticed that in all this discussion of murder I have said nothing about the effects of the police or courts—and for good reason. There is little they can do to affect murder rates. They can intervene only after the fact. Punishment—even capital punishment—has no effect on murder rates. Furthermore, since most captured murderers never kill again, even after being released, locking them up for longer periods of time will not reduce the overall rate of murder.

ROBBERY

Robbery is the crime that most resembles our image of the crime problem, of street crime. It is unexpected, sudden, and sometimes terrifying. It is committed mostly by strangers, and unlike murder, it cannot be easily avoided: Robbery victims, unlike murder victims, seldom contribute to the sequence of steps that leads to the crime. Property crime rates may measure a population's dishonesty in ways of getting money. Murder rates can tell us about people's willingness to use violence to settle personal scores. But robbery rates, despite the inaccuracies of statistics, provide a measure of people's willingness to use violence against strangers in order to get money.

Robbery also conforms to our ideas about the social location of crime. While some European cities may have as much burglary as U.S. cities of similar size, U.S. cities have far higher rates of robbery. In comparisons within the United States as well, robbery fits best with popular images of crime. We often think of crime as most prevalent in the cities, especially in poorer neigh-

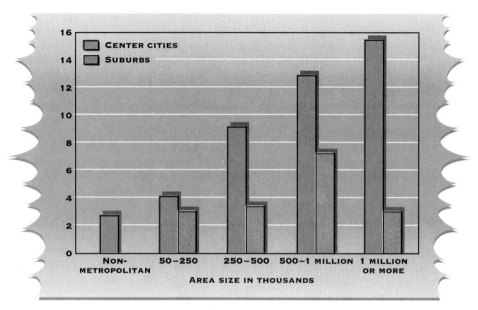

FIGURE 5–5   Personal Robbery by Area Population, 1992 (Rate per 1,000 persons)

Source: Based on data in Bureau of Justice Statistics, *Criminal Victimization in the United States, 1992* (Washington, D.C.: U.S. Department of Justice, 1994).

borhoods of the inner city. The crime that best fits this image is robbery. For larceny, burglary, and auto theft, city-suburb differences are not so great. But for robbery, cities have higher rates than suburbs; and poor, inner-city neighborhoods have the highest rates of all (see Figure 5–5).

The geographic distribution of robbery is also closer to what we would expect. Murder rates are highest in the South, and burglary and larceny rates are highest in the West. The Northeast, however, leads in robbery, with a rate nearly 30 percent above that of the nation as a whole. Of the twenty cities with the highest robbery rates, seven are northern, industrial cities like Newark and Chicago. New York City's robbery rate is more than triple the national rate.[52] Even allowing for all the inaccuracies of crime statistics, these differences are impressive.

WHAT IS ROBBERY?

Robbery means taking something from a person by force or the threat of force. This definition includes everything from sixth-graders extorting lunch money from their classmates to the multimillion-dollar heist of an armored car. What all robberies share—by definition of the word *robbery*—is that the criminal confronts the victim. That is why the FBI's UCR classi-

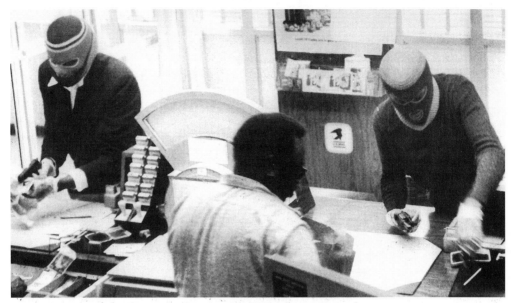

Criminals who take a more professional approach to their work, like these robbers in an Oklahoma City post office, plan their crimes for maximum payoff. Opportunistic robbers take fewer precautions and choose more convenient—if less profitable—targets, usually individuals.

fies robbery as a violent crime—a crime against the person—whether or not the criminal actually uses force. Without force or threat, it isn't a robbery. For example, purse snatchings, in the FBI's category, are larcenies, not robberies. This classification is not just a ploy to reduce the number of robberies. It follows a certain logic. The purse snatcher, unlike a robber, does not confront the victim (even though the purse snatching may involve some force). To the FBI a purse snatching is a heavy-handed version of picking a pocket.

TYPES OF ROBBERY, TYPES OF ROBBER

In 1992, the UCR counted about 627,000 robberies known to the police. The UCR broke these down by categories, as shown in Table 5–3. According to these figures, about one-third of these robberies were commercial. The other two-thirds were of individuals, either on the street or at home. (The true percentage of individual robberies is probably higher since many victims do not report the crime to the police.)

These different targets of robbery correspond very roughly to a dimension that might be called professionalism, which is based on the size of the payoff and the ease of committing the crime. At one end are the **profession-**

TABLE 5–3 •
ROBBERY, PERCENT DISTRIBUTION, 1992

	U.S. TOTAL	NORTHEAST	MIDWEST	SOUTH	WEST
STREET	55.6	62.7	60.0	50.4	51.8
RESIDENCE	10.1	10.3	9.4	12.0	7.9
COMMERCIAL HOUSE	11.9	10.3	10.1	12.0	14.5
GAS STATION	2.5	2.1	3.1	2.5	2.6
CONVENIENCE STORE	5.3	2.4	3.2	12.0	7.9
BANK	1.7	1.0	1.1	1.3	3.2
MISC.	13.1	11.4	13.2	13.3	14.4

Source: Federal Bureau of Investigation, *Crime in the United States: The Uniform Crime Reports, 1992* (Washington, D.C., 1993).

als—robbers who will overcome all sorts of difficulties if the score is large enough, and large scores usually are businesses, not individuals on the street. At the other end are the **opportunists**, who are responding to an apparently easy opportunity that crops up, even though the payoff may be very low. For these robbers, an attractive target is likely to be an individual alone, either in the street or at home. These two types of robbery—street muggings and robberies of people in their houses or apartment buildings—account for nearly two-thirds of all robberies.

The professional-opportunistic dimension comprises other factors besides payoff and convenience. The most obvious is planning. Planning and payoff logically go together since people or institutions with large amounts of money are likely to take precautions to guard it. Robbers seeking a big score must plan carefully. They must decide which target to hit and when. Among bank robbers, for instance, the opportunists do little planning and get little money. They hand a note to the teller and walk out with whatever the teller gives them—rarely more than three or four thousand dollars, often only a few hundred or even nothing. Professional bank robbers, though, are interested in more than the contents of a single till. They want to know when the bank will be holding a substantial amount of accessible cash. And they find out.

> There's quite a few mills around here, so I sat down and bought some beers for a couple of guys who work in mills, and just in conversation ... I asked them when does this group get paid.... So they told me. So I figured, well, a lot of these guys cash their cheques here [a local bank] and more do on Thursdays than on Fridays, so sure enough I went down ... the following week on Thursday.[53]

Robbers also may need to know in advance about security systems, guards, police patrol schedules, and escape routes. The plan may require special material—guns, masks or other special clothes, and a getaway car (preferably stolen so it would not be traceable to one of the robbers).

Professional robbery requires a fairly exact division of labor, and because time is an essential factor, each person must be able to carry out his task quickly and efficiently. The team may rehearse once or twice before the actual performance to make sure each player knows his part. In a bank robbery, one robber may be assigned to control the customers while another forces the bank manager to get the money; a third member will act as lookout. There may be a fourth member as a driver, though gangs now make the driver go into the bank with them. "In the old days, they used to leave the driver of a bank car outside, and most times they'd come out and the car would be gone! Now, you take the driver with you and he's the first one out."[54]

Aside from this planning, bank robbers do not much resemble the romanticized criminals of Hollywood classics like *Bonnie and Clyde*. Robbery teams today are not long-term gangs. They get together for one big job or perhaps a short series of robberies; then they split up. Nor is there necessarily honor among these thieves. The fainthearted wheelman in the preceding quotation is only one example of a general problem of loyalty. The norms of the criminal world say that the team member who is caught should not tell on his partners. But robbers today recognize that this norm is more an ideal than a reality. They know that the police and prosecutors can pressure the robber to give up his partners, so most robbers expect that if one of the gang gets caught, the others are likely to be arrested as well.[55] Worse things could happen, and do. As shown in the movie *Goodfellas*, some of the robbers who participated in the multimillion-dollar robbery of the Lufthansa Terminal at Kennedy Airport in 1978 were murdered by their greedier partners.[56]

Professional robbers may also go after smaller scores than six-figure or million-dollar targets. Supermarkets and payroll offices may yield tens of thousands of dollars, depending on the time of day, and they are usually less well defended than banks and armored cars. Below the large-score professional jobs come all the smaller commercial robberies—gas stations, liquor stores, convenience stores, and taxicabs. The more professional robbers reject such targets because the payoff is too low and the possibility of trouble too great: "I would rather walk into a bank any day with all their cameras and security officers and ... alarms.... I would rather go facing the cameras and the FBI than rob a gas station. Not only will the guy in the gas station buck on you, but he will pull a gun and shoot somebody."[57]

For most robbers, however, the danger of these smaller robberies is offset by their convenience. A single robber can do the job unassisted and without much planning: Just wait until there is nobody around, show a weapon, and demand the money—hardly the level of skill and planning implied by the word *professional*. Robbers themselves do not use the word *professional*. They are more likely to use the word *good*. A criminal would say, "He's a good stick-up man," not "He's a professional robber." Criminologists have looked for other terms to describe these stickup artists: *habitual* robbers, *career* robbers, or *experienced* robbers.[58] All these terms imply a certain level of skill, frequency of crime, and general involvement with the criminal world—something between the professional and the impulsive opportunist.

There are also "intensive" robbers—those who commit a large number of crimes in a short time span.[59] The payoff in each robbery is fairly low, so these robbers will have to commit several robberies to get enough money, and since they do not take professional precautions, such as wearing a mask or using a stolen car or a stolen license plate, they can be identified more easily. As a result, these intensive robbers soon get caught and go to prison.

The professional-opportunistic dimension clearly is useful for distinguishing types of robberies—the well-planned bank heist, the convenience store stickup, the street mugging. It also seems logical to apply these distinctions to the robbers themselves; that is, we assume that professional robberies are committed by professional robbers. In reality, however, this distinction often breaks down. Except for the most skilled professionals, criminals do not limit themselves to one type of crime. People who commit professional robberies may also commit opportunistic robberies as well as a host of other crimes—selling drugs, dealing in stolen goods, pimping, and perhaps engaging in burglary or auto theft.[60] In other words, by looking at planning, payoff, and other factors, we can easily classify robberies, but we are much less certain about classifying the robbers who have committed them. I recall interviewing a robber who described at length the planning and organization that went into one of his big scores. It was a professional job, well planned and highly profitable. Yet a few months later, this same man had been eating in a luncheonette, sitting near the cash register, when another customer paid her bill. When this "professional" robber saw all those green bills in the till, he jumped up, grabbed a knife from behind the counter, threatened the counterman, took the money, and ran. Of course, the victim ran out and hollered for the police, who easily caught the robber, which is why the setting for our interview was the state prison. John E. Conklin implies that professionals commit unplanned, impulsive robberies only when they are drunk.[61] However, since robbers are drunk quite a bit of the time, their impulsive crimes are probably not such a rarity. Laurie Taylor says of English robbers, "It isn't a case of two kinds of professional criminals—the small-time and the big-time. Only the opportunities which are available fit into these two categories. The criminals move between them."[62]

MUGGING—THE CRIME IN THE STREETS   Over half of all robberies are **muggings**—robberies of individuals in a street or other public place or in the entrance of a building. Compared with more professional robbers, muggers are usually younger, more likely to work in groups, more likely to come from the lowest social class, and more likely to be black.[63] Most muggers are at the opportunistic end of the scale. They focus on the ease of committing the crime rather than the size of the payoff, and their planning of the crime may be minimal or nonexistent: "You don't plan anything.... You're just standing there.... It's like, let's take the box [radio] or buy some herb. Some guys are still doing school-yard jobs. They take $2 or $3 from kids around the school."[64]

Muggers do not even need a weapon—just one person to grab the victim, another to take the money. These weaponless "strongarm" robberies account for about 40 percent of all muggings today.[65]

Despite their impulsiveness, muggers may make some choices in order to get the largest payoff for their efforts. They may try to judge from a potential victim's appearance how much money he or she might be carrying. Or they may follow people coming out of a store, a bank, or a check-cashing agency, on the assumption that shopping and banking indicate cash on hand. Muggers may even use moral criteria in choosing their victims. They "have predispositions for or against mugging women (generally against); for or against mugging old people (generally against); for or against mugging whites rather than blacks (generally for); and for mugging the rich rather than the poor (always the rich)."[66] But frequently, despite these preferences, they end up robbing whoever is most available and most vulnerable.

> One thing I could never do—I could never rip off a female. I could never snatch a pocketbook, even though I was a dope fiend. One day my package didn't come through; my connection didn't show. I had no choice. Went out there looking for something, and it so happens that a pocketbook was the best thing that came along.[67]

If the payoff is small, muggers may have to commit two or three muggings before they get enough cash for their immediate needs, enough to have a good time for a day or two—what they call "getting over."

MONEY   All robbers commit their crimes for the money, but obviously the financial motives of muggers differ from those of older robbers. Younger, more opportunistic robbers tend to use their money for spur-of-the-moment pleasures—clothing or music, drugs or fast food. Professional robbers tend to be older, and their needs are different. They may have regular expenses like rent or even family expenses. They also are more likely to use the money to support a drug habit (rather than just buying drugs for kicks). Professional robbers sometimes intend to use the money from a big score to get out of crime altogether—to get start-up capital for a legitimate business.[68] However, they almost never carry out these plans. Instead, they celebrate: They buy themselves a few nice things; they drink and they spend money on women; they lend money to friends. In a few days or weeks or perhaps months, the money is gone.

> Since we were spending money so fast we had to pull jobs at least once a week. We'd spend $200 a day [this was in the 1960s] buying everything we wanted. You spend money like this because in the back of your mind you know that you can always get more just by pulling another job.[69]

Even the few who say they want to leave crime usually abandon their good intentions.

> When I start out I say, "Well, man, I need about $15,000 to get on my feet." That's what I'll say.
>
> So I start out and I'll work and I'll save; I don't spend any money, I don't party, I don't do anything but steal—until I get that amount of money in my bank account, and then I quit; I throw away my tools and I just say, "Now I've forgotten how. I'll never crack another safe."
>
> I'll sit around a few days ... and I'll be ready to ... go to work, get a job.
>
> And believe me, I've had some good jobs offered to me, but I just never take them. I don't know why.
>
> So I'll get off and I'll start partying and it doesn't take me very long to spend that money.[70] (The man quoted here is obviously a burglar, not a robber. Still, his statement is typical of robbers as well.)

Robbery, by definition, combines two elements: the taking of property and the use or threat of violence. What makes robbery of special concern is the question of violence. In recent years, the "violent offender" has come to occupy a place of special attention in the media, in criminological research, and in the criminal justice system. Jurisdictions with overburdened courts and prisons may choose to focus on the violent offender by devoting valuable court time and prison space disproportionately to robbers. At the heart of this strategy is the idea that robbers are different from mere thieves.

VIOLENCE: EXPRESSIVE AND INSTRUMENTAL   Are robbers different from other criminals? Are they violent people? Some evidence suggests that the answer is yes, that robbers are the most hardened of criminals. For example, people arrested for robbery are worse bail risks than those arrested for other crimes. They are more likely to commit further crimes while on bail than murderers, rapists, or property criminals.[71] In addition, criminals themselves often regard robbery as different from other illegal ways of getting money. Nearly all career criminals do commit a variety of crimes, but most limit themselves to property crimes. On the one hand, a burglar, even a fairly skilled burglar, might also sell drugs, pass bad checks, steal cars, and shoplift, but he will draw the line at robbery. Robbers, on the other hand, commit all these crimes and robbery as well. They even commit more of the other crimes than robberies. But it is the robberies that distinguish them from other criminals.[72] Apparently, even for career criminals, it takes something special to be able to go up to somebody and forcefully demand money.

To say that robbers are violent people implies that robbers are *essentially* different, that their robbery results from some internal impulse toward violence and power. No doubt this generalization applies to some robbers. But just as robbers have different views of money—the amount needed and their motives for seeking it—the same may be true of violence. Robbers differ in their use of violence and in their motives for using it.

It is useful here to distinguish between **instrumental** violence and **expressive** violence. These two terms—*instrumental* and *expressive*—refer to the motives or purposes behind an action. Instrumental action serves to accomplish some ulterior, rational purpose like getting money. Expressive action is a goal in itself; it serves to express some inner psychological state. For example, if I am driving 90 mph in order to get my son to the emergency room, my lawbreaking is instrumental. Many others would do the same even if they did not like to speed. But if I am driving 90 mph just because I really like going fast, it is expressive. Only those with similar tastes, only similar kinds of people, would do likewise. When we speak of robbers as violent people, we are implying that their violence is expressive.

Headlines about "senseless," or "excessive," or "sadistic" violence are referring to this kind of noninstrumental violence—violence that goes beyond what is necessary to get the victim's property. Of course, any crime probably combines both expressive and instrumental motives, and it is difficult to know just how much of the violence in robbery is expressive. However, we can make some guesses. Of every 100 victims in noncommercial robberies, about 33 are injured, 5 of them seriously enough to require medical care.[73] One researcher concluded, "In a high proportion of these crimes, the attack that caused the injury was not instrumental to the robbery, but rather was a distinct act."[74] The robbers who injure their victims are good candidates for the label "violent people," and they are likely to commit other violent crimes like assault.[75] We can see expressive violence in one other fact about robbery: If the violence in robbery were purely instrumental—a means to overcome the victim's resistance—large groups of robbers would have less need to resort to the actual use of violence, and their crimes would be less likely to result in injury. But in fact, large groups of robbers are more likely to injure victims. Solo robbers or robbers working in pairs injure their victims less than one-third of the time. In contrast, nearly half the robberies committed by three, four, or more robbers result in injury to the victim[76] (see Figure 5–6). The violence seems aimed not so much toward getting the money but toward noninstrumental goals, perhaps the need to appear tough in the presence of peers.

Professional robbers, of course, look down on such unnecessary violence: "When you're out on a heist, you're out to get the dough and keep out of trouble. Halloween's the night for scaring people."[77] Professionals see the actual use of force as something they would rather avoid. That's why they carry guns; the deadlier the weapon, the more likely it is that the victim will cooperate.

There are two arguments against the idea that robbers are essentially different or that they are basically violent people. First, on the issue of violence, victims and robbers may see the same act from very different viewpoints. A violent act that to the victims may seem excessive may seem absolutely necessary to the robber. Second, the idea that robbers are violent

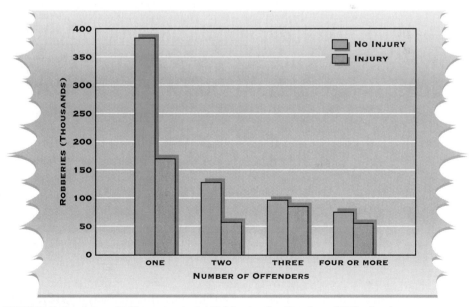

FIGURE 5–6   Injury in Noncommercial Robberies (by Number of Offenders)

Source: Derived from Bureau of Justice Statistics, *Criminal Victimization in the United States, 1992* (Washington, D.C.: 1994).

people assumes that violent motives come first, that they are part of the person's original psychological makeup and are the cause of his violent crimes. He is a violent person; therefore he commits violent crimes. But it may be the other way round: Expressive, violent motives may be the result of committing robberies rather than the cause. He commits violent crimes; therefore he develops a violent personality.

The first argument starts from the observation that the violence in robbery is essential to the job. In this one important way, the robber's job is similar to a police officer's. Both jobs involve the control of other people. Both jobs require force—actual or potential—to get people to do something they don't want to do and to do it quickly. Robbers have only a few minutes to get the money and run, and force is an excellent way to make victims comply immediately. In other words, the violence is instrumental. It is part of the job, not necessarily part of the person performing the job. To appreciate this distinction, consider professional football players. The violence in their work is instrumental; if they could not use force effectively, they would be lousy football players. We understand that the violence we see on Sunday is part of the job, not necessarily part of the person; off the field the players may be quite gentle. (The difference is most striking among those who play the more violent positions. For example, defensive tackle Merlin Olsen, as seen in old Ram game films, certainly looks violent. But compare that picture with his subsequent screen career as a gentle priest or flower salesperson. The violence, like the gentleness, is part of the role, not the person.)

Here is a professional bank robber describing the opening seconds of a bank robbery:

> Sometimes we select the strongest person—the manager especially or another teller which is very big—a six-footer, or something like that, you know. And we won't say a word, we just walk up to him and smash him right across the face, you know, and we get him down. And once he's down the people, the girls especially, they look at him and they say, "My God—big Mike, he's been smashed down like that—I'd better lay down too, and stay quiet." You know—it's sort of like psychology, to obey us immediately.[78]

To the people in the bank, the violence appears to erupt from the uncontrollable urges of a dangerous person. But in reality, the robber is deliberately creating this image. From the robber's own viewpoint, the violence is purely instrumental: "We made him know that we are brutal, subhuman bastards.... We project that image."[79] Street muggers, too, usually see their violence as instrumental:

> I didn't go with the intention of hurting him—because I figured he was smart enough to give up the money. But what he did when I had him in the hallway: He screamed. And I got uptight, you know. And me being uptight, I used the knife. And other times people I went to rob, they gave me a hard time. To get the money that I wanted to get I had to stab them.[80]

In the cases just quoted, the victims resisted. But what about the seemingly senseless use of violence when the victim does not resist? Isn't such violence purely expressive? Undoubtedly, some of it is, but not all of it. For example, sometimes muggers attack the victim after the mugging has been completed. These attacks may look senseless, but to the robber, they are quite instrumental: "You push them down hard so that they don't get right up and yell, but we're gone. We're fast."[81]

Sometimes a mugger attacks before demanding the money. Again, from the victim's viewpoint such violence is irrational ("I would have given him the money...."). But how does the mugger know this in advance? Here is a mugger whose previous attempt had been foiled when he failed to control the victim: "The second time I said, "I'm not gonna fumble up the job. And I'm not gonna let him scream either."... This time I didn't even tell him he was getting held up.... I just hit him, you know, to make sure he knew I meant business. I hit him with the pistol."[82]

VIOLENCE: PSYCHOLOGICAL TRAIT OR ACQUIRED TASTE? If what seems like expressive violence can also include instrumental motives, the reverse is also true. Instrumental violence may take on expressive qualities. The robber who sees his methods largely as instrumental may nevertheless come to enjoy them. He may get to like the power, control, and violence for themselves, not just because they are necessary tools. The taste for violence, then, is not necessarily inborn; it is acquired—perhaps too easily acquired—in the course of one's work. It is acquired by both professional robbers and opportunistic muggers (and perhaps even by legitimate users of violence like football players and police officers).

> You're a pretty big man standing there with your gun. Makes you feel oh—kinda important—big, somebody people don't mess with.[83]

> Sometimes we would get somebody and they would have nothing. And a lot of times ... we would get mad, so mad that we wanna hurt the person that has nothing. You're saying: "I'm going through all this for nothing." That's how a lot of times, you know, things happen.[84]

Does this taste for power and violence mean that the robber is a different sort of person than other criminals? This is the standard psychological view: It assumes that the robber begins with a personality that needs violence and power; he then seeks out robbery as a way of gratifying those needs. By contrast, the sociological view I am sketching here argues that the "need" or liking for violence is acquired on the job. It does not take an unusual personality type to learn to enjoy these feelings or to engage in cruel and senseless violence. For example, we are horrified at the mugger who laughs about the suffering he has inflicted on a victim:

> We were goofing around and bragging: "Eh, man, we got this guy. We kicked the s— out of him." We started goofing on the guy's head, calling him rockhead.... I don't know if he had a steel plate or something; that bottle bounced off his head like it didn't even phase him.[85]

You and I could never deliberately inflict that kind of suffering on a person, let alone find it something to enjoy and laugh about. Or could we? Many colleges have fraternities, whose members tend to be nice, middle-class youths who think of themselves as neither criminals nor sadists. These fraternities usually have what they call hazing and initiation, rituals that some-times involve inflicting extreme psychological and even physical suffering. This collegiate brutality is so common that it becomes newsworthy only in two extremes: when it kills someone or when a fraternity decides not to use it.[86] Frequently, those inflicting the torture laugh and apparently enjoy the pro-ceedings. They may still laugh about it weeks later—something like the mug-ger just quoted. Apparently, many people, given the right setting and social support, can commit sadistic acts. Muggers are no exception.

Muggers do not start out viewing crime as a way to satisfy their need for power. They enter into their first mugging with the same feeling that most peo-ple would have—fear.

Q: How did you feel about doing this?

R6: Fear. Cold-blooded fear.

R12: Only thing, I was scared. That's all. Other than that I don't know other feelings that I can remember.[87]

If left to their own devices, most muggers probably would not go through with it, but the more experienced members of the group teach them. So the novice mugger learns not only how to commit the crime but also to enjoy it—especially if he continues to be successful. In fact, the mugger acquires a set of attitudes com-pletely different from those he started with; he moves from a sense of fear in tak-ing someone else's money to a belief that once he decides to rob someone the money is rightfully his, an idea that gets reinforced with each successful mugging. Young street muggers go into the crime almost impulsively. They work in groups, where no one wants to appear unmanly in front of his colleagues, and over the course of many successful muggings they acquire a sense of entitlement. This is the formula for the excessive, senseless violence that sometimes accompanies rob-bery: "Like I tell him: 'Give it up!' He says: 'No.' He's giving me, you know, trouble. I'm gonna feel like he has a whole lot of nerve. Dig it. I'm gonna get violent. I would get extremely violent. I felt like it was my right; it was my due."[88]

One final cop-robber comparison: Police officers who engage in petty cor-ruption may acquire a similar attitude of entitlement to others' property. They may come to feel that the merchant who demands payment for merchandise has some nerve. And cops, like muggers, find ways to convince the merchant to adopt their point of view. There are two important differences: (1) Muggers threaten and use violence; cops harass by using their power of law enforce-ment. (2) The mugger's victim is victimized only once; the merchant finds that the cops keep coming back.

Even among older robbers and those who prefer commercial targets, the potential for seemingly irrational violence is always present. Although sociological accounts of robbery had long tended to emphasize the rational aspects of it, to see it as "work," criminologist Jack Katz in his 1988 book, *Seductions of Crime*, returns to the idea that the motivation for robbery lies primarily not in economics but in something more personal. Katz sees robbery as a source of identity, a par-ticular kind of identity that Katz calls the "hardman," an identity built around other forms of "action": gambling and other types of risk, illicit sex, alcohol, drugs, and especially flirtation with and control of chaos. "In countless stickups, the primary causal process is the project of being a 'badass' or 'bad nigger,' which brings on chaotic situations.... By carrying out the robbery in the face of chaos, [the robbers] imposed a transcendent control ... reconfirmed as triumphant hardmen."[89]

The robber makes a commitment to this identity even in the face of the grave risks and powerful emotions that fill each robbery—risks and emotions that the robber must conquer. Katz, therefore, sees robbery not as a matter of work and payoff but as something more cosmic. Each robbery is an enactment of the robber's self, his sense of who he is. To resist even in the slightest way is to threaten that self.

> In stickups, as in other fields in which a difficult spiritual commitment must be made, many are called but few are chosen. A large number of adolescents in low-income ghettoes try stickups, doing one or a few and then stopping; only a small percentage continue into their late 20s and 30s, becoming the relatively few heavies who commit scores or even hundreds of robberies for each year they spend out of jail....
>
> The practical constraints on making a career of stickups are such that one *cannot* simply adopt violence as an instrumental device to be enacted or dropped as situational contingencies dictate. It is practically impossible to make a career of stickups just by making a calculated show of a disposition to be "bad"; you must live the commitment to deviance. You must really mean it.
>
> The commitment according to which violence with robberies makes sense to the offenders is the commitment to be a hard man—a person whose will, once manifested, must prevail, regardless of practical calculations of physical self-interest. Fatal violence in robberies is far less often a reaction of panic or a rationally self-serving act than a commitment to the transcendence of a hard will.[90]

In this paragraph, Katz is seeking to explain fatal violence, but his analysis applies equally to nonfatal violence as well.

ROBBERY AND SOCIETY

Bank robbery and street mugging represent two obviously different forms of robbery. The robbers, too, differ from each other. Their typical profiles would show differences in age and race, in their use of violence, in how they spend their money, and probably in career paths. There is another interesting difference between these two types of crime: While street mugging has changed little over the course of the last few centuries, bank robbery has undergone a continuous and rapid evolution. The bank robber of a generation or two ago, like the family doctor who makes house calls, is almost an endangered species. I am not being frivolous in comparing doctors and robbers. The comparison can be very useful for understanding how and why crimes change. It redirects our focus from the individual practitioner to the more general sources of change. In the practice of robbery, just as in the practice of medicine, change arises not so much from individual motivations as from changes in technology and society.

THE DECLINE AND RISE OF BANK ROBBERY   Table 5–4 shows the number of bank robberies in the United States over a sixty-year period. You

TABLE 5-4 •
NUMBER OF BANK ROBBERIES IN THE U.S., 1932–1992

YEAR	NUMBER OF ROBBERIES
1932	609
1937	129
1943	24
1950	81
1963	3,346
1976	4,565
1984	6,800
1992	11,400

Source: Derived from James A. Inciardi, *Careers in Crime* (Chicago: Rand McNally, 1975), p. 97; UCR, 1984; UCR, 1992.

don't have to be a statistician to see that these numbers show some big changes—from 609 in 1932 to only 24 in 1943, and then a huge increase beginning in the 1950s.

How can we explain these changes? There is a popular and simple idea that since crime is bad, it is caused by bad people (or as one criminologist put it, "wicked people exist"). Changes in crime, therefore, reflect the number of bad people or their level of activity. This is a logical and morally reassuring idea. But the numbers given in Table 5–4 show how inadequate it is. Can the population of wicked people decrease by 94 percent or increase by 1,000 percent in the space of only a few years?

A fuller explanation would emphasize not just people but the social context as well. Yes, some people are more wicked than others, more willing to commit crimes. But the pressures and opportunities pushing and pulling them toward particular types of crime also contribute to changes in the overall number of bank robberies. Behind the numbers are some important developments—changes in banks, changes in criminal techniques, and changes in law enforcement. These changes, in turn, have transformed the number of robbers and their typical profile.

Until the 1930s, there were relatively few banks in the United States, and banking was greatly centralized. A bank would keep its money in one place, not spread out over a number of branch offices. Consequently, banks made an attractive target for professional robbers. With enough organization, planning, and weapons, they could overcome the bank's defenses. Since the take from a robbery was likely to be high, robbers could build up a nice nest egg without risking too many robberies. In addition, the only law enforcement was at the local level, and it was frequently ineffective (movies like *Bonnie and Clyde* are accurate when they show the robbers reaching safety by crossing a state line). Robbers, therefore, often worked in gangs and moved from place to place.

In the 1930s, two important changes occurred. First, the depression reduced the number of banks. Between the stock market crash of 1929 and Roosevelt's inauguration in 1933, 5,500 banks (nearly 23 percent of all banks in the United States) had failed.[91] Second, and probably more important, bank robbery became a federal crime, and the FBI under J. Edgar Hoover began an effective war against bank robbers. Fewer banks and more cops greatly reduced the opportunity for successful bank robbery. In addition, as bank robbers got caught and went to prison, the population of bank robbers became severely depleted. After a few decades, though, as the numbers show, bank robbery eventually made a comeback. But the robberies and the robbers were of a different sort. The opportunities had changed, and so had the people willing to take them.

The postwar period of the late 1940s and the 1950s was the era of suburbanization. As the population shifted from cities to suburbs, businesses followed, banks included. In the 1930s, a city might have a half dozen different banks, all of them downtown. In the 1950s, each of those banks would spawn branch offices in all the surrounding suburbs. The new banks themselves were different. In the 1930s, banks tried hard to foster the image that money there was safe. Banks dramatized their security measures—armed guards, alarms, tellers behind iron bars, and so on. It was an understandable strategy since during the depression, many people had lost their life savings by putting all their money in a bank.

In the 1950s, with government-insured deposits, banks no longer needed to maintain a tough-but-safe image. To attract customers, banks began to soften their image. The austere banker and bank faded into history, replaced with "friendly" banking. The new banks were designed to be especially friendly to the automobile-based life of the suburbs, so it was now quite easy to drive up, transact business, and drive away—easy for customers and easy for robbers. Interior decor also played a part. Down came the iron bars, in favor of friendly counters. Of course these changes, too, were friendly not just for customers but also for robbers. "The lower the counter, the better I like it," said one robber. "You just hop over and hop back."[92]

Banks were not defenseless. By keeping less money on hand and keeping larger amounts in new, time-lock safes, they could prevent large losses. So while the number of bank robberies increased, the average take in a robbery decreased. The big-score bank heist gradually became a thing of the past. More and more robberies were solo, low-profit jobs—a robber handing a teller a note and walking out with a few thousand dollars or less. Today, the take might be less than $1,000, and if the teller, protected now by bulletproof glass, refuses, the robber might walk out empty-handed.

Banks' defense measures have also ensured that robbers will eventually be caught. Banks have cameras that make identification easier. Some banks have put time-delayed dye bombs in money sacks so that the robber who walks out of the bank with a bag of money may find himself on the street a minute later covered with bright red dye. Note-passers can get away with a few crimes, but since their take per robbery is so small, they must continue to commit crimes. As a result, most bank robbers today eventually get caught and go to prison. And here is another change from the golden age of bank robbery: prison does not solve the problem. In the 1930s, when the FBI put several professional bank robbers out of business, bank robbery nearly disappeared. However, sending today's casual bank robbers to prison has done nothing to decrease the number of bank robberies. Because the crime requires so little skill and because the robber usually can get away with the first few crimes, there are always others willing to get into the game.

HIGHWAY ROBBERY   While changes in banking, technology, and law enforcement altered the profile and numbers of bank robbers, some other types of robbery have been most affected by changes in transportation. Over the centuries, "highway robbery" has taken various forms. In England in the 1700s, "footpads" lurked along the major roads between towns. It is important to keep in mind the small scale of those cities. Today, the journey from central London to Hampstead is merely a passage through a city, from one section to another. In the seventeenth and eighteenth centuries, the road led through unpopulated stretches, ideal for highway robbers like Dick Turpin. Government policies also affected robbery rates, although in unintended ways. England's eighteenth-century enclosure laws, which forced large numbers of people off the land, probably served to swell the ranks of highwaymen—despite the extensive use of the death penalty for robbery and other crimes. In time, the city populations expanded greatly; the government improved road surfaces; and the new railroads provided safer, swifter passage. As a result, opportunities for highway robbery decreased. In the United States, stagecoach robbery flourished in the West during the early 1800s but faded with the expansion of the railroads. The early railroads also fell victim to train robbers like Jesse James and the Younger gang. But train robbery also decreased as railroads fortified their baggage cars and heavily armed their security men.

By the nineteenth century, the robbery problem was no longer on the highways but in the urban streets. In contrast to other types of robbery, street robbery has changed little over the centuries—probably because the targets are still the same. Banks may have changed in numbers, location, security systems, and amounts of cash on hand, but people in the streets have undergone no similar transformation. As for the methods of street robbers, guns and knives have been available for centuries. The most frequent form of street robbery is still the unarmed mugging. A century ago, it was called garroting, since the criminal usually placed his arm around the throat of the victim, a technique that remains popular among muggers today.[93] The criminals, however, may be of a different sort. In eighteenth- and nineteenth-century New York or London, garroters were probably men in their 20s and 30s who were part of a large criminal subculture. Today's muggers are frequently teenagers with no extensive commitment to a criminal underworld.

Some changes in robbery depend less on technology than on social structure. Consider, for example, the bandit-hero, the Robin Hood-like robber who is admired, sheltered, and aided by the common people. This type of banditry seems to arise in particular social conditions: It is usually rural, arising where a relatively poor, peasantlike population works on land owned by distant and wealthy persons. Some writers believe that train-robbing and bank-robbing gangs flourished in the American West not just because trains and banks were relatively defenseless but also because the general population condoned the robbers and even helped them avoid capture. Bandits like Jesse

James took on the aura of folk heroes, and ordinary people may have been honored to offer them a temporary hideout if they were being chased by the law. Why did people not despise them as evil criminals? Probably because of the robbers' targets. Farmers and ranchers in the West often resented the railroads, which had bilked the settlers out of their land, set unfair rates, and obtained vast amounts of land from the government only to resell it at much higher prices.

Later, in the depression, banks acquired a similarly unpopular reputation for foreclosing on mortgages and taking away farms and homes. People with little left to lose might disapprove of robbery, but they also might admire the person who could turn the tables on the bank. Banks were seen as institutions that took people's property. Robbers were people who took the bank's property.

Many countries have similar legendary figures—"social bandits," as one historian has called them. It is important to understand that these Robin Hoods, whatever their individual virtues or vices, are produced by particular kinds of economic structures: "Social banditry is universally found, wherever societies are based on agriculture ... and consist largely of peasants and landless laborers ruled, oppressed, and exploited by someone else—lords, towns, governments, lawyers, or even banks."[94]

SUMMARY AND CONCLUSION

Robbery comes in various forms, from the opportunistic mugging that might net only a few dollars to the highly planned and profitable robbery of institutions like banks. Although the FBI classifies robbery as violent crime (i.e., a crime against the person), in fact it combines elements of both property and violent crime. It consists of taking property from a person by force or threat of force. The element of force, whether threatened or actual, suggests that robbers are psychologically different from other criminals, who have no qualms about taking other people's money but wish to avoid violent confrontations. However, in looking at robbers and robbery, it is useful to try to distinguish between expressive violence and instrumental violence. Though any violent crime contains elements of both, expressive violence seems to be more characteristic of younger, opportunistic robbers, while the violence of older, more professional robbers is more likely to be instrumental. Still, even for older, career robbers, robbery may be important not only as a source of cash but also as a source of identity, a particular identity based on domination, control, and violence—the identity of the identity of the "hardman."

The demographics of robbery conform to popular notions about violent crime. Robbery is most common in the cities, especially those of the industrial Northeast. Robbers are almost entirely men, usually from working-class and lower-class areas. African Americans have exceptionally high rates of committing robbery. Since the majority of robberies are committed by opportunistic criminals who stay in their own neighborhoods, the profile of the victims closely resembles that of the robbers—men rather than women, poorer rather than middle class, and black rather than white.

ABOUT CRIME & CRIMINOLOGY

STICKUP AND THE SOCIAL STRUCTURE

It's fairly easy to see how the availability of targets contributes to bank or convenience store robberies (see Table 5–3, and remember, the parent company of the 7-11 stores is called the Southland Corporation). But can these structural factors explain street robberies? Surely the high rate of robbery among African-Americans cannot be attributed to a greater number of vulnerable people and stores in the black community.

According to criminologist Jack Katz, what matters is not the presence of these targets but the absence of other criminal opportunities for the "violent hardman." All ethnic groups have some version of this type of person, who gets his money through crimes based on violence and intimidation. But among most ethnic groups, the role of the hardman has taken the form of the gangster. Gangsters prey on the businesses in their own communities, and their crimes typically include protection rackets; political corruption; labor racketeering; loan-sharking; and racketeering in the areas of trucking, shipping, and other delivery and warehousing services. These crimes differ from simple robbery: Because of the economics of the business, the entrepreneur actually does need the services the gangster is forcing on him.

Black entrepreneurship, in contrast, "has offered comparatively few employment opportu-nities to black hardmen." What black businesses there are have been concentrated in small owner-operated services like repair shops and beauty salons. They have low capital requirements and therefore no need for loan sharks. They do not depend heavily on a flow of material or on organized labor, so they are not vulnerable to labor racketeering or extortion from the "representatives" of dock workers, truckers, or suppliers.

Finally, while other cultures have emphasized tightly knit associations based on kinship or region (families, tongs, etc.), African-American culture has celebrated either flamboyant individualism or a loyalty to all blacks.

It is these economic and cultural differences that cause the differences in robbery between African-Americans and other ethnic groups (remember that the gangster's victims are much less likely to call the police, and the crimes, even if reported, would rarely be classified as robbery).

Black hardmen, who parasitically stick up victims in or close to their byways of action, are social worlds away from the white and Asian-American violent hardmen who have historically exploited businesses, unions, and vice institutions developed by their ethnic kinsmen. In part, blacks have been historically overrepresented in robbery statistics because robbery is the form that the structure of the black community has given to its version of the violent hardman.

Source: Jack Katz, *Seductions of Crime* (New York, Basic Books, 1988), pp. 256–263.

Historically, robbery has been shaped by the broad forces in the society at large. In commercial robbery, there has been a steady evolution, with banks, transportation companies, and other businesses taking various defensive measures and different types of robbers adapting to the new targets. Bank robbery, for example, has changed from a crime committed by teams of well-organized professional criminals to one committed almost entirely by casual, unskilled criminals.

Though bank robberies make up less than 2 percent of all robberies, they could serve as an image of the bulk of the robbery problem today. The courts have sent more and more robbers to prison, but this policy has had little impact on the rate of robbery. Apparently, for every robber removed from the population, another stands ready to enter the field. In earlier generations, juvenile criminals who committed property crimes would, as they grew older, leave the streets for unskilled or semiskilled jobs in industry. Today, more of these juveniles graduate instead into robbery, especially the less skilled and potentially more violent robberies like muggings and convenience-store holdups.

CRITICAL THINKING QUESTIONS

1. In most killings, how clear is the killer's intent? How much planning goes into the homicide?
2. What role do guns play in homicide? How valid is the argument that "guns don't kill people; people kill people"?
3. Why has the South always had the highest homicide rate in the United States? Do the explanations also apply to the difference between the United States and other countries?
4. Are robbers different from other criminals, and if so, how did they get that way?
5. To what extent is the violence involved in robbery spontaneous and emotional and to what extent is it calculated and purposeful?
6. How have changes in the economic and social organization of society influenced different types of robbery?

KEY TERMS

cultural approach

expressive violence

felony murders

instrumental violence

interactionist approach

muggings

opportunists

primary homicide

professionals

structural approach

CHAPTER SIX

VIOLENT CRIMES, PART II

WOMEN AND CHILDREN

CHAPTER OUTLINE

RAPE

The issue of rape brings out the most contradictory reactions. On the one hand, people generally regard it as an extremely serious crime, even when the victim suffers no other physical injury,[1] and the laws on rape reflect this judgment. The crime carries very severe penalties. In fact, of all executions in the United States between 1930 and 1965, 12 percent were for rape.[2] On the other hand, because rape is a sexual crime, it can evoke in grown men the kind of sniggering humor usually found among seventh-grade boys. The "jokes" are often based on the idea that rape is not really a serious matter. For example, in 1979, commenting on the marital exemption (which made it legal for husbands to rape their wives), a California state senator said, "If you can't rape your wife, who can you rape?"[3] He was speaking to a group of women lobbyists.

But rape *is* serious. Rape victims suffer considerable psychological harm. The effects of rape—which can include extreme fear, sleep disturbances, and various sexual symptoms—sometimes last months and even years, in what psychiatrists call post-traumatic stress disorder.[4] Of course, not all rape victims react in the same way. The degree of violence and cruelty during the rape, the relationship between rapist and victim, the victim's general psychological health, her previous victimization (or lack thereof), her general expectations about male-female relationships, and the support she receives from others—all these factors can affect the victim's reaction.[5] Unfortunately, we do not know with any certainty the proportion of victims who suffer severe, moderate, or mild symptoms, for rape remains a largely

Battered women sometimes stay with abusive men because they have nowhere else to go. Even shelters in smaller cities (this one is in upstate New York) may not always have places for all the women seeking refuge.

hidden crime. Until recently, even criminology textbooks tended to give this serious crime relatively brief coverage.[6] Textbooks neglected rape, not necessarily because the authors were insensitive males, but because the evidence on rape was so insubstantial and so questionable.

HOW MUCH RAPE?

Before criminologists begin to build explanations of a crime, they start with some basic questions: What is it? How much of it is there? Who commits the crime? Who are the victims? How, when, and where does the crime occur? With rape, more than with any of the other Index crimes, all of these questions are matters of serious dispute. The Uniform Crime Reports, long our primary source of statistical information on crime, defines rape as "carnal knowledge of a female against her will." The UCR limits rape to penile-vaginal intercourse. It includes attempts, but it does not include forced oral or anal intercourse. Nor does it count rapes in which the victim was the wife of the rapist.

In addition, the UCR counts only crimes known to the police, that is, crimes that the victim reported and that the police recorded. Obviously, the rapes in the UCR (104,000 in 1993), are an undercount of the true number. The NCVS, too, appears to have been reluctant to discover rape. Until the early 1990s, the standard NCVS interview did not mention rape or sexual assault by name. While questions about other crimes were fairly specific ("Were you knifed, shot at, or attacked with some other weapon by anyone at all?"), the only question that might hint at rape was this: "Did anyone TRY to attack you in some other way?" The person being interviewed would then have to realize that "some other way" meant rape and then volunteer the information. Now the NCVS has revised the question: "Incidents involving forced or unwanted sexual acts are often difficult to talk about…. Have you been forced or coerced to engage in unwanted sexual activity by (a) Someone you didn't know before, (b) A casual acquaintance, or (c) Someone you know well?"[7] But the same reasons that keep a woman from reporting a rape to the police—shame, embarrassment, fear of letting others know, and the desire to avoid further questions—may also keep her from reporting the crime to a survey interviewer.

DATE RAPE   The rapes most likely to be missed by the UCR and the NCVS are rapes committed by husbands, lovers, or men with whom the victim had some social relationship—what has come to be called **date rape**. Although this kind of rape is probably far more common than rape committed by strangers, the 1991 NCVS estimated that the two types were equally frequent. Surely this estimate reflects women's reluctance, even in crime-survey interviews, to mention rape by someone they know, someone who may even be in the house at the time of the interview. Victims may also fail to report rape, even in a survey, because they apply a very narrow definition of the crime. In one study, what the researchers defined as rape was seen as rape by only 55 percent of the victims—and that was when the offender was a stranger. When the offender was an acquaintance, the percentage fell to 28 percent; and when the offender was a dating partner, only 18 percent labeled the act as rape.[8]

If a woman thinks of rape as a stranger jumping from the bushes, brandishing a knife, and brutally forcing himself on her, she may not apply that term to an incident of forced sex with someone she knows, even though the man's actions may meet the legal criteria for rape. "I didn't think it was rape," said one typical victim of date rape at a college, "I just thought I'd been bad."

Marital rape—where a man forces his wife to have sex—raises another problem with definition. Not only do wives often think of it as a personal matter rather than a criminal one, but until recently the law, too, has turned a blind eye to marital rape. In many states a husband's rape of his wife is not a crime. Some states have abolished the **marital rape exemption** entirely; other states still retain some form of marital exemption (e.g., in many states, the exemption applies only to married couples living together, not to cases where one spouse has filed for divorce or has moved out).[9] The extent of marital rape is most hard to estimate since wives who have been raped by their husbands are most likely not to report the rape to a crime-survey interviewer or to the police. In a 1990 survey 9 percent of rape victims said the rapist was a husband or former husband.[10]

FINDING MORE RAPE   Although the UCR and NCVS have made it difficult for victims to become rape statistics, other researchers, who emphasize the confidentiality of the interview, have tried other methods. Instead of introducing the questions in the context of crime, the interviewers ask about "unwanted sexual experiences," stressing that these might even involve friends, boyfriends, or family members, or that the woman might not have reported the incident to the police or even mentioned it to her close friends or relatives. The actual questions about the crime may also be different, focusing on specific behavior rather than labels like *crime* or *rape*. Since victims may not always define their experiences as rape, researchers do not ask, "Did anyone rape you this year?" but rather, "In the past twelve months, has a man made you have sex by using force or threatening to harm you? When we use the word 'sex' we mean a man putting his penis in your vagina even if he didn't ejaculate (come)."

The results of surveys like these produce numbers so astonishingly larger than other estimates that we must wonder what is going on. For example, the number of "yes" responses to the preceding question in 1986 was 37 out of a sample of 2,291 women in the Cleveland area, or 1.6 percent. That may not sound like much, but multiplied by the female population in the U.S., it means that 1.5 million women were raped—a figure at least fifteen times higher than that in the NCVS. The women in the sample were also asked how many times in the past year this event had occurred. The total number of victimizations from these 37 women was 216—an average of nearly 6 rapes for each victim. Even correcting for telescoping (i.e., the inclusion of incidents that happened over a year ago), the researchers estimated the rate of rape at 28.5 per 1,000 women. That would mean 2.7 million rapes annually in the United States, more than twenty-seven times the number recorded by the police.[11] A national telephone survey of 3,200 women asked, among other things, "Has a man or boy ever made you have sex by using force or threatening to harm you or someone close to you? Just so there is no mistake, by sex we mean putting a penis in your vagina." The annual rate estimated from this survey was 720 per 100,000, lower than the earlier study but still five times the victimization rate estimated by the NCVS.[12] Another survey, using a national sample of 4,000 women, reached a remarkably similar result: 710 per 100,000.[13]

TABLE 6-1 •
ONE-YEAR INCIDENCE FREQUENCIES OF SEXUAL EXPERIENCES

	WOMEN (N = 3,187)		MEN (N = 2,972)	
	INCIDENTS		INCIDENTS	
1. HAVE YOU GIVEN IN TO SEX PLAY (FONDLING, KISSING, OR PETTING, BUT NOT INTERCOURSE) WHEN YOU DIDN'T WANT TO BECAUSE YOU WERE OVERWHELMED BY A MAN'S CONTINUAL ARGUMENTS AND PRESSURE?	725	1716	321	732
2. HAVE YOU HAD SEX PLAY (FONDLING, KISSING, OR PETTING, BUT NOT INTERCOURSE) WHEN YOU DIDN'T WANT TO BECAUSE A MAN USED HIS POSITION OF AUTHORITY (BOSS, TEACHER, CAMP COUNSELOR, SUPERVISOR) TO MAKE YOU?	50	97	23	55
3. HAVE YOU HAD SEX PLAY (FONDLING, KISSING, OR PETTING, BUT NOT INTERCOURSE) WHEN YOU DIDN'T WANT TO BECAUSE A MAN THREATENED OR USED SOME DEGREE OF PHYSICAL FORCE (TWISTING YOUR ARM, HOLDING YOU DOWN, ETC.) TO MAKE YOU?	111	211	30	67
4. HAVE YOU HAD A MAN ATTEMPT SEXUAL INTERCOURSE (GET ON TOP OF YOU, ATTEMPT TO INSERT HIS PENIS) WHEN YOU DIDN'T WANT TO BY THREATENING OR USING SOME DEGREE OF FORCE (TWISTING YOUR ARM, HOLDING YOU DOWN, ETC.) BUT INTERCOURSE <u>DID NOT</u> OCCUR?	180	297	33	52
5. HAVE YOU HAD A MAN ATTEMPT SEXUAL INTERCOURSE (GET ON TOP OF YOU, ATTEMPT TO INSERT HIS PENIS) WHEN YOU DIDN'T WANT	143	236	72	115

How many rapes were committed last year? The 100,000 known to the police? Surely, this UCR figure is too low. But which victimization survey should we believe: the earlier NCVS, which found about 130,000 rapes; later NCVS surveys, which showed slightly more than 200,000; the two other surveys that put the number near 700,000; or the Cleveland survey, whose results extrapolate to 2.7 million rapes nationally? It is impossible to reconcile estimates that diverge so widely. The high estimates are swelled by large numbers of acquaintance rapes—incidents women mention in surveys about unwanted sex but which in other circumstances they

TABLE 6-1 •

ONE-YEAR INCIDENCE FREQUENCIES OF SEXUAL EXPERIENCES (CONTINUED)

	WOMEN (N = 3,187)		MEN (N = 2,972)	
	INCIDENTS		INCIDENTS	
TO BY GIVING YOU ALCOHOL OR DRUGS, BUT INTERCOURSE <u>DID NOT</u> OCCUR?				
6. HAVE YOU GIVEN IN TO SEXUAL INTERCOURSE WHEN YOU DIDN'T WANT TO BECAUSE YOU WERE OVERWHELMED BY A MAN'S CONTINUAL ARGUMENTS AND PRESSURE?	353	816	156	291
7. HAVE YOU HAD SEXUAL INTERCOURSE WHEN YOU DIDN'T WANT TO BECAUSE A MAN USED HIS POSITION OF AUTHORITY (BOSS, TEACHER, CAMP COUNSELOR, SUPERVISOR) TO MAKE YOU?	13	21	11	20
8. HAVE YOU HAD SEXUAL INTERCOURSE WHEN YOU DIDN'T WANT TO BECAUSE A MAN GAVE YOU ALCOHOL OR DRUGS?	91	159	57	103
9. HAVE YOU HAD SEXUAL INTERCOURSE WHEN YOU DIDN'T WANT TO BECAUSE A MAN THREATENED OR USED SOME DEGREE OF PHYSICAL FORCE (TWISTING YOUR ARM, HOLDING YOU DOWN, ETC.) TO MAKE YOU?	63	98	20	36
10. HAVE YOU HAD SEX ACTS (ANAL OR ORAL INTERCOURSE OR PENETRATION BY OBJECTS OTHER THAN THE PENIS) WHEN YOU DIDN'T WANT TO BECAUSE A MAN THREATENED OR USED SOME DEGREE OF PHYSICAL FORCE (TWISTING YOUR ARM, HOLDING YOU DOWN, ETC.) TO MAKE YOU?	53	96	19	48

Source: Mary P. Koss, Christine A. Gidycz, and Nadine Wisniewski, "The Scope of Rape: Incidence and Prevalence of Sexual Aggression and Victimization in a National Sample of Higher Education Students," *Journal of Consulting and Clinical Psychology*, vol. 55, no. 2 (1987) 162–170.

would not report as rape. But even for rape by strangers, the smaller surveys give a number twice as high as that in the NCVS. In some ways, these surveys are not comparable. Surveys that have an overrepresentation of young, single, or better-educated women will produce higher estimates of the prevalence of rape.

Table 6–1 illustrates some of the problems in estimating the amount of rape. The 98 incidents reported by 63 women in Question #9 qualify as completed rapes and yield a rate roughly 30 times higher than that reported in the UCR (of course, a sample of college women—young, single, edu-

ON CAMPUS

BUT IS IT RAPE?

During a dormitory lecture on acquaintance rape at Lehigh University recently, a male student was asked by a dorm official whether he had ever committed rape.

"Hell, no," the young man responded. But when the student was asked whether a woman he had dated had consented to having sex, he responded, "No, but she didn't say no, so she must have wanted it, too."

"Are you sure?" he was asked.

"Well, not really, but you can never be completely sure," the young man responded, adding that both of them had been drunk and that the woman had struggled initially before they had sex. "But they all do.... It's the way it works," he told the dorm official.

After the conversation, the young man admitted he was "very confused." He then concluded he had raped "some" of the women he had dated.

Source: William Celis III, "Students Try to Draw Line Between Sex and an Assault," *New York Times*, January 2, 1991, p. B8.

cated—is not representative of the U.S. population). Perhaps more interesting are the numbers on the male side (the questions are in the form given to women; they were reworded for men). Twenty males admitted to committing such rapes; their 36 rapes extrapolate to a rate ten times that found in the UCR.

TRENDS IN RAPE   Although we cannot be sure of the exact number of rapes, the different sources of information might be useful in identifying trends. By analogy, if I have three bathroom scales, none of them very accurate and all giving a different weight, I may not know how much I really weigh. But if the numbers on all three this month are higher than those of last month, it's a safe bet I've been gaining weight. For detecting trends, the smaller surveys—the ones that have produced such high estimates of rape—are no help since they have been one-time projects not repeated in the same form from year to year. Only the UCR and the NCVS are useful here, and unfortunately they give different results. For the two decades that we have had two sources of national data on rape, the UCR shows a steady increase, the NCVS a slight decrease. The rate of rapes known to the police between 1973 and 1992 rose from about 24 per 100,000 to nearly 43 per 100,000, a 75 percent increase. The NCVS rate in the same period fell from about 100 per 100,000 to a low of 60 per 100,000 in 1990 before rising to about 70 per 100,000 in 1992 (see Figure 6–1).

How can we explain these differences? Many people would guess that the increase in the UCR rate might be caused by an increasing willingness of victims to report the crime. But according to the victimization survey, the

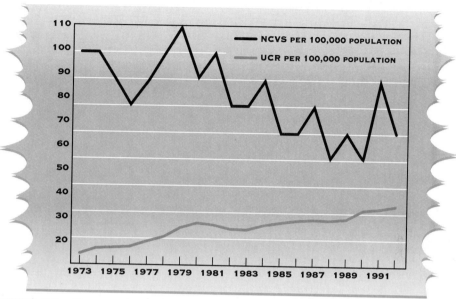

FIGURE 6–1   Rape 1973–1992 (Rates from UCR and NCVS)

Source: Maguire and Pastore, *Sourcebook—1993.*

reporting rate has remained fairly stable. Instead, the increase has probably resulted more from changes in the way police departments handle rape cases. Over the last twenty years, police departments have hired more civilians, especially female civilians, as dispatchers (the people who take phone calls and send out the information to patrol units). Some departments have also set up special sex crimes units that are more sensitive to the needs of rape victims. These changes have made it more likely that a reported rape will be officially recorded.[14] The bigger question, though, remains: Has rape really increased in the last twenty years? Unfortunately, with only two sources of data, neither very accurate and each giving a different answer, it is hard to draw any firm conclusions.

THE SOCIAL DISTRIBUTION OF RAPE

Because most sources of data leave out so many incidents, especially date rape, we should be fairly cautious about conclusions concerning the social correlates of rape, and we should look for other supporting evidence. International comparisons show that the United States has a rate between three and twenty times higher than that of other industrialized countries (see Table 6–2). It is possible that some of these countries, especially those where sex role differences are greater, may have more unreported rapes than the United States. But such factors cannot account for such large differences in

TABLE 6-2 •
RAPE IN SELECTED COUNTRIES, 1984

UNITED STATES	35.4
AUSTRALIA	13.8
SWEDEN	11.9
WEST GERMANY	9.7
DENMARK	7.7
BELGIUM	5.7
AUSTRIA	5.3
FRANCE	5.2
ENGLAND/WALES	2.7[a]
ITALY	1.8[a]
JAPAN	1.6

[a]1983 data.

Source: Interpol data in Carol B. Kalish, "International Crime Rates," Bureau of Justice Statistics, U.S. Department of Justice, 1988.

rape rates. Moreover, these differences parallel those of murder, whose statistics are much more reliable.

In fact, for many comparisons, the social map of rape resembles that of other violent crimes. Just as the U.S. rate is higher than that of other countries, within the United States, the West and South have higher rape rates than do the Midwest and Northeast. There are some interesting variations. For example, Oregon and Washington have fairly low rates of murder and aggravated assault, but their rates of reported rape are among the highest in the country. Victimization surveys show that poorer people are victimized more frequently than middle-class people, blacks more than whites. And because in most rapes the criminal and victim inhabit the same social space and often know each other, these differences hold true for rapists as well. In addition, women who are young and single are at a greater risk of rape than are those who are older and married (see Figures 6–2 through 6–5).

EXPLAINING RAPE

Rape is both a violent and a sexual crime, committed almost exclusively by men and almost always against women. Rape is most likely to occur among men whose feelings of sexuality and aggression are closely intertwined. There is some question about why these two feelings should be linked at all. Some sociobiologists argue that rape is a result of evolution. Rape, in their view, is a reproductive strategy for those males who could not otherwise attract a mate. They point out that rape occurs not only among humans but also

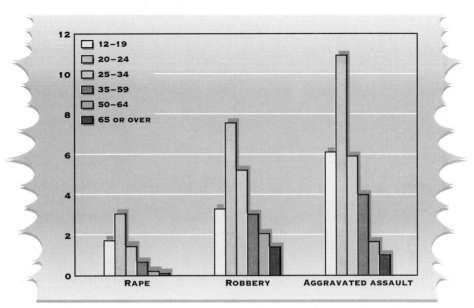

FIGURE 6–2   Average annual victimization rates per 1,000 females by Age, 1987–1991

Source: Derived from Ronet Bachman, *Violence Against Women* (Washington, DC: U.S. Department of Justice, 1994), table 3.

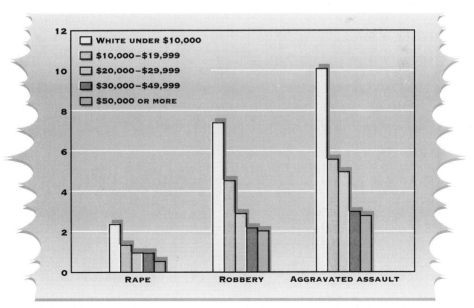

FIGURE 6–3   Average annual victimization per 1,000 females by Family Income, 1987–1991

Source: Derived from Ronet Bachman, *Violence Against Women* (Washington, DC: U.S. Department of Justice, 1994), table 3.

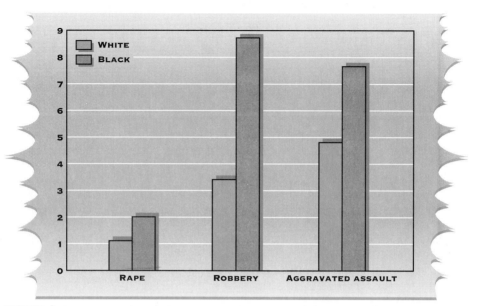

FIGURE 6–4   Average annual victimization rates per 1,000 females by Race, 1987–1991

Source: Derived from Ronet Bachman, *Violence Against Women* (Washington, DC: U.S. Department of Justice, 1994), table 3.

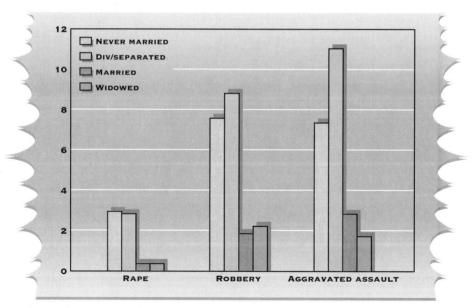

FIGURE 6–5   Average annual victimization per 1,000 females by Marital Status, 1987–1991

Source: Derived from Ronet Bachman, *Violence Against Women* (Washington, DC: U.S. Department of Justice, 1994), table 3.

among apes and in other species ranging from the bullfrog to the bluebird. Thus rape, the linking of sex and aggression, is a way of ensuring genetic survival, and over millions of years, evolution has programmed rape into human nature.[15] Needless to say, many people have criticized this idea.[16]

Even if the biological argument were correct, it still would be of little use in explaining the wide variation in rape among different human societies. For example, among the Minangkabau in West Sumatra, rape is virtually unknown,[17] while among the Yanomamo of Brazil, it occurs frequently. Yet there is no reason to think that there are important biological or genetic differences between the two societies. The question is not why rape exists at all but rather why rape is more frequent among some societies, groups, or individuals.

For many years, theories of rape were dominated by psychological ideas. Most researchers were psychologists, who saw rape as a sexual perversion. In keeping with psychological explanations of other sexual perversions, theories of rape looked for its causes in personality factors or traumatic childhood experiences. Unfortunately, psychological studies rarely gave consistent results; researchers have had to conclude that rapists come in a variety of psychological types—aggressive or insecure, abused or not, alcoholic or sober.[18]

In the 1970s, largely because of the resurgence of feminism, social scientists began rethinking theories of rape. One of the most important books in this period was Susan Brownmiller's legal and historical account of rape, *Against Our Will*. Brownmiller argued that rape was a social and political issue and not just a sexual one. Rape established and maintained the power differential between the sexes. Even though most men did not commit rape and even though most women were not raped, rape was basic to men's legal, social, and political domination over women. Through rape and the threat of rape, men created a system that forced women into permanent subjugation, dependent on men for protection from men.[19] Rape was not a sexual oddity of a relatively few psychological deviates. It was part of a society-wide protection racket.

During this same period, theories about individual rapists were following a parallel change in direction. Psychiatrists and psychologists came to view rapists' motives as not entirely sexual, perhaps not sexual at all. Although this psychiatric view still saw rapists as suffering from some psychological dysfunction, it also held that rape was a "pseudo-sexual" act. The rapist's real motivation was not sex but power and aggression.

Psychiatrists discounted the sexual motive because many of the rapists they interviewed did not need to rape in order to get sex. They had active sex lives, either with their wives or other consenting women.[20] However, this is hardly convincing evidence. After all, married men who regularly have sex with their wives may also have affairs or visit prostitutes. Although these liaisons may fulfill a variety of needs, it would be misleading to call their motives pseudo-sexual. Other evidence of nonsexual motives came from the rapists' own statements about their crimes. Typical of "revenge" rape is the case of the man who went to collect some money from another man and found his wife home alone. They started to argue about the money. Then, "I grabbed her and started beating the hell out of her. Then I committed the act. I knew what I was doing. I was mad. I could have stopped but I didn't. I did it to get even with her and her husband."[21]

For some rapists, rape was a way to assert strength and dominance and to deny feelings of inadequacy. For others, rape was a means of expressing anger.[22] "Rape was a feeling of total dominance. Before the rapes, I would always get a feeling of power and anger. I would degrade women so I could feel there was a person of less worth than me."[23]

Some rapists did see their acts as purely sexual; they used force or threat only as a means to obtain sexual intercourse. For the other rapists, the sex was a part of a more general goal of threat or actual violence.

THE NORMALITY OF RAPE

If we view rape as a crime committed by depraved individuals, our explanations will focus on psychological factors—the twisted mind of the rapist. Undoubtedly, some rapists fit this picture. They are warped by unusual, unique histories; they provide excellent examples for psychological explanations showing how childhood experiences shape later behavior. However, in many ways psychological approaches are not especially useful. Standard measures of personality (the Rorschach ink-blot test, the Minnesota Multiphasic Personality Inventory, etc.) find no consistent differences between rapists and nonrapists.[24] Even if there were a psychological profile of the rapist, it would have little predictive value. It might fit many rapists, but it would fit far more nonrapists as well. Moreover, psychological explanations tend to distract attention from the normality of rape. By "normality," I mean three related things: First, as the recent discovery of date rape has made obvious, many rapes are committed by men who are normal (i.e., not noticeably different psychologically from those around them). Second, rape is normal in the same way that traffic accidents are normal: The crime occurs with regular frequency, and rates of rape vary predictably according to demographic factors. Third, while most rapes appear to violate general social norms (everyday ideas about proper behavior), in fact the norms regarding forced sex are not so clear as we might hope or think they are.

RAPE AND INEQUALITY

The demographic facts of rape have led social scientists to offer the same kinds of explanations they apply to murder rates. But the usual structural explanations that see the crime as a product of inequality do not seem to fit as well with rape as they do with murder or robbery. The structuralist argument holds that economic and social inequality lead to increased aggression and violence among those on the short end of the inequality. But unlike murder, rape is not so clearly about anger and frustration, and unlike robbery, it is certainly not about money. Accordingly, the evidence—even using crimes known to the police as the measure of rape—does not always show a correlation between rape and poverty or economic inequality.[25]

Rape is also a sexual crime, and some sociologists argue that rather than abandoning structural explanations for rape we should expand them to include not just economic and racial inequality but sexual inequality as well. We should look at the distribution of power between the sexes. For example, in some simple, preindustrial tribes or societies women have a place roughly equal to that of men. They have an important part in religious rituals, and they take part in decisions both in the family and in the society. This equality between men and women characterizes the societies where rape is virtually unknown.

By contrast, societies where rape is most frequent are those characterized by male violence, greater social distance between the sexes, and sexual inequality. In these societies, men dominate most aspects of life, with women living a subservient and even segregated existence. Often, men sleep separately from women and children in special men's houses. Sometime in late childhood or early adolescence, boys are separated from their mothers and sent to an all-male group where they undergo a long initiation, a process that usually involves psychological terror, physical violence, tests of strength and agility, and the learning of tribal secrets known only to the men in the society. They may continue to live separately from women for the rest of their lives, even after marriage, continuing the pattern of sexual segregation.[26]

The most extreme illustrations for these ideas come not from strange "primitive" tribes visited by anthropologists but from accounts of soldiers—including European or American soldiers—in war. Combat soldiers often come to take for granted sexual practices that would bring reactions of horror in the civilian world—individual rape, gang rape, sexual torture, and rape-murder.[27] One American soldier told how seven men from his company had gang-raped a Vietnamese girl: "I know the guys and I know basically they're not really bad people, you know?... It was just part of the everyday routine."[28] In this case, the victim was not even from an enemy village.

War—especially war between nations—exaggerates all the conditions found in high-rape societies: violence, segregation, and inequality. For combat soldiers, violence is not just a part of life but its very center. Also, soldiers live in an all-male environment segregated from women. This social distance allows them to dehumanize women, to treat them as objects. The social distance is even greater when the soldier comes from a different culture, when rapist and victim cannot even understand each other's language. Finally, the power difference is absolute—conquering male soldier and conquered female civilian. The systematic rape of Bosnian women by Serbian soldiers in the early 1990s during the war in the former Yugoslavia revealed another link between rape and war: the use of rape as a deliberate policy.

In civilian life in complex societies, the relationship between rape and sexual inequality is less clear. Some societies may have great sexual inequality but little rape. In these societies, women, though powerless and dependent, are nevertheless protected by a strict code of male morality. This protection, however, may extend only to women of the upper class. (Of course, getting reliable data is a problem since rapes of women from the powerless classes are much less likely to be part of the record.) The South of the plantation era featured both sides of this chivalrous ideal. The rape of white women—especially those of the land-owning class—was probably quite rare. The rape of black women (slaves) was much more frequent, though such rape usually was not even considered a crime.[29] In the United States today, states vary in the degree of sexual equality, as indicated by measures of income, political position, and law (e.g., an equal rights amendment). Yet the correlation between sexual inequality in a state and its rate of rape is fairly small.[30]

ON CAMPUS

INEQUALITY, SEXUALITY, FRATERNITY

In anthropological films, preliterate societies characterized by much rape may seem bizarre at first, but the strangeness is superficial—a matter of dress styles and language. Socially and psychologically, they resemble some of the most cherished institutions of college life: athletic teams and fraternities. Fraternities mirror these "primitive" societies in their sex segregation, their emphasis on violence and strength (athletic ability), their power relations with women, and their affinity for rape.

Prompted by a gang rape at Florida State University, two researchers there began to look more closely at rape, especially gang rape, on college campuses. They interviewed students (fraternity and nonfraternity), college administrators, state prosecutors, and defense attorneys.

Their findings sound much like those from anthropology: Fraternity "practices that contribute to the sexual coercion of women include a preoccupation with loyalty, group protection and secrecy, use of alcohol as a weapon, involvement in violence and physical force, and an emphasis on competition and superiority."

The sexually segregated "men's huts" of simpler societies and the fraternity houses on U.S. campuses rest on the same idea: that there is something inhibiting, contaminating, or even threatening about sharing daily life with women. The pledging period and hazing, like the initiation period in other societies, serves to create

RAPE CULTURE AND RAPE MYTHS

The other leading sociological view of rape resembles the subculture of violence as an explanation of robbery and murder. Rape, in this view, occurs where cultural ideas condone it, where men (and even women) think that forced sex is legitimate. Some groups of young men consider gang rape to be just one more adventurous form of delinquent activity. They think of gang rapes not as loathsome, perverted crimes but as socially approved behavior. They may even avoid using the word *rape* to refer to their actions.[31] Similarly, in date rape, neither rapist nor victim may think of this forced sex as rape. And, as mentioned previously, in some states forced sex between husband and wife is not legally rape.

As these examples suggest, permissive ideas about forced sex are not confined to a single race or social class. These ideas—the **rape myths**—exist to varying degrees throughout American society so that even the lone rapist can find in the general culture a set of ideas that legitimize rape. These myths, besides defining rape to exclude date rape and other forms of the crime, usually shift the focus of attention from the man to the woman. The "cry rape" myth maintains that many charges of rape are false, that is, that women falsely accuse men of rape, either because they do not want to admit to having consented to sex or because they are seeking revenge.

strong bonds among the males (brotherhood), bonds based on shared secrets (handshakes, symbols, names) and stereotyped masculine traits.

The male violence against people and property is hardly a campus secret. University officials said that fraternities "are the third riskiest property to insure behind toxic waste dumps and amusement parks."

As for power, although women may be equal in the official rules of the college, fraternity culture places them in decidedly secondary roles. Privately and individually, a fraternity member may have a serious relationship with a woman, but the dominant public fraternity idea of women is that they are to be used socially or sexually. As one sophomore said of his frat's "little sis-

ters," "Their sole purpose is social—attend parties, attract new members, and 'take care' of the guys."

To this mixture of hypermasculinity and sexual exploitation, fraternities add one important element not consistently found in the high-rape societies: alcohol. Fraternity men typically drink to relax after class and on weekends to "get drunk," "get crazy," and "get laid."

As one fraternity member said, "We provide [women] with 'hunch punch' and things get wild. We get them drunk and most of the guys end up with one," hunch punch being "a girls' drink made up of overproof alcohol and powdered Kool-Aid, no water or anything, just ice. It's very strong. Two cups will do a number on a female."

Source: Derived from Patricia Yancey Martin and Robert A. Hummer, "Fraternities and Rape on Campus," *Gender and Society*, vol. 3, no. 4 (1989).

Other myths seek to shift the blame for the crime from the rapist to the victim. One such myth is the idea that any healthy woman could successfully resist a man if she really wanted to (the obvious corollary is that if a woman was raped, she must have wanted it). Another rape myth says that most women who are raped are promiscuous or "bad" women. Another holds that some women want to be raped and even enjoy it. Belief in these myths is not limited to men.[32] One survey asked college students, "If a woman were raped and nobody knew about it, would she enjoy the experience?" Thirty-two percent of the men answered yes, but so did 27 percent of the women. (When women were asked if they themselves would enjoy being raped, 98 percent said no.)[33]

Another variation of the blame-the-victim theme is the idea that women provoke rape by the way they dress or act. Consider the following letter from a convicted robber-rapist, who nevertheless thinks of his crimes as the fault of the woman:

I was more the victim in this case, this person came to the door, dressed with a towel wrapped around them. I told the person to go and get some clothes on, she went into her bedroom ... but she put the clothes on so I could see her. I was in the other room watching her more or less so she couldn't do nothing funny, and when she started putting on clothes, there she was right in front of my eyes.[34]

It is not only rapists or the uneducated who believe this idea. In 1977, a Wisconsin judge said that a 15-year-old boy who had raped a girl in the stairwell of the high school was "react[ing] normally" to the general sexual permissiveness of the society and the provocative clothing women wore.[35]

In 1984, four men were convicted of a gang rape in a bar in New Bedford, Massachusetts. (This incident was the basis for the fictional movie *The Accused.*) The victim had stopped at a bar to buy some cigarettes and have a drink. There was some testimony that she may have flirted with some of the men. When she tried to leave the bar, the men picked her up, put her on the pool table, and raped her. The jury found the men guilty, but a crowd of 10,000 to 15,000 people marched to protest the convictions. A newspaper reported one of their supporters as saying, "The girl is to blame. She led them on."[36] The man quoted was the local priest.

RAPE AND PORNOGRAPHY

Some feminists contend that **rape culture** extends to the most conventional ideas and practices, even traditional child rearing. By socializing boys and girls to adopt the "correct" sex-role behavior (aggressive for boys, passive for girls), even solidly law-abiding Americans contribute to rape culture. Another widespread element of rape culture is the male tendency to view women as sexual objects. Of course, men do sometimes relate to women as real people, but the sexual-object view is widespread, and more important, this attitude seems to bring very little disapproval. In fact, there is a multimillion-dollar pornography industry thriving on this tendency for men to dehumanize women into mere sexual objects.

If rape actions derive from rape ideas, it seems logical that anything that promotes rape culture will increase the amount of rape. As one antipornography slogan puts it, "Pornography is the theory, and rape the practice."[37] But does exposure to the theory turn people into practitioners? Does pornography lead to rape? Of course, rape is not the only issue in the pornography controversy. The debate ranges over a variety of legal and social issues—from the First Amendment (freedom of speech and freedom of the press) all the way to the general decline of morality. These are interesting and important topics, but for the purposes of this book, I am going to stick to one narrow topic—the connection between pornography and rape—and to one limited but important perspective: What is the evidence?

In 1970, a presidential commission that spent two years and $2 million studying the issue of pornography did base their conclusion on the available evidence: "Empirical research ... has found no reliable evidence to date that exposure to explicit sexual materials plays a significant role in the causation of delinquent or criminal sexual behavior among youth or adults."[38] Unfortunately, people—even those who eventually decide what kinds of movies and books will be available to us—do not necessarily decide on the basis of evidence. Especially on controversial issues, they may offer variations of the old slogan "My mind's made up; don't confuse me with facts." For example, the facts uncovered by research did not convince President Nixon, who rejected the conclusions of the commission. Nor did Charles Keating, the commission member appointed by President Nixon, wish to be bothered with facts: "Credit the American public with enough common sense to know that one who wallows in filth is going to get dirty. This is intuitive knowledge. Those who spend millions of dollars to tell us otherwise must be malicious or misguided, or both."[39] (This is the same Charles Keating who gained a certain amount of unwanted fame in 1990 as the director of savings and loans whose failure cost the government billions of dollars. Before the banks' collapse, Keating had contributed generously to five U.S. senators, who then urged government actions favorable to these banks. In 1993, Keating was convicted of various bank frauds, and sent to prison.)

Sixteen years later, another government commission investigated pornography. The Attorney General's Commission on Pornography (also known as the Meese Commission, after Attorney General Edwin Meese), which spent much less time and money in their research than the first commission, concluded that exposure to pornography did increase sex crimes. However, this conclusion went so far beyond the available evidence that some of the leading researchers publicly criticized the commission's use of their data.

The basic idea behind much of the research is that exposure to pornography changes men's attitudes and also their behavior. The evidence usually comes from experiments carried out in college psychology laboratories. Experimenters ask students to watch pornographic movies and then fill out questionnaires: How strongly do they agree or disagree with various statements about rape, violence, women, men, and so on? How long a prison sentence would they recommend for a convicted rapist?

Do the movies "desensitize" the viewers? On the one hand, the standard porno film—the kind found in the adult section of video stores, with much explicit sex but no violence—has a very small effect, if any. Some experiments have found small differences after subjects watch the films; other studies find no differences. "Slasher" films, on the other hand (the nonpornographic, R-rated blood-gushers you can see at the drive-in), do consistently make viewers less sensitive toward rape victims.[40]

As for behavior in these experiments, *some* pornography *sometimes* increased aggression toward women. The trouble is that this "aggression toward women" is a far cry from rape. Men who volunteered for the experiment thought that they were in an experiment to help another person, a woman, learn by administering a shock or loud noise when she gave an incorrect answer. This other person (actually a confederate of the experimenter) had previously insulted the subject. Result: The men who had been insulted and who had been exposed to *violent* pornography were more likely to select higher levels of shock or noise.

Is this result evidence that exposure to violent pornography increases rape? Did the "victim" resist or even ask the subject to lower the shock? Could the subject see how his action affected the victim? To equate this behavior with rape requires a large leap of the imagination, and the social scientists who conducted the experiments were careful not to jump to conclusions. The Meese Commission, however, felt no such inhibitions: "Finding a link between aggressive behavior toward women and unlawful sexual violence requires assumptions not found exclusively in the experimental evidence. We see no reason, however, not to make these assumptions."[41]

The evidence coming from outside the experimental laboratory also leads us to question the idea that pornography causes rape. In the late 1960s, Denmark legalized pornography, and consumption of pornography quickly increased. Sales of hard-core magazines rose from 20,000 in 1966 to 1,600,000 in 1968 before leveling off.[42] What effects would the Danish "pornography wave" have? Some people predicted that sex crimes would increase, but others thought that easily available pornography might cause sex crimes to decrease. They reasoned that men who might previously have played out their sexual fantasies in criminal acts could now gain safer satisfaction through pornography and masturbation. As you might expect, researchers and policymakers paid close attention to reports of sex crimes.

Although the statistics on the various sex crimes may have some inaccuracies, the results are fairly clear. The amount of rape in Denmark did not increase; it remained level, and other sex crimes such as peeping and sex crimes against small children decreased.[43] Although there is some disagreement among social scientists, the data from other countries also fail to show a connection between liberalized pornography policies and rates of rape.[44] Japan, for example, has a flourishing pornography trade. Japanese law prevents pictures from showing pubic hair or genitals, a policy that makes Japanese pornography less sexually explicit than that of America or Europe. However, Japanese pornography includes far more bondage and rape, and the victim in these sadistic scenes is frequently a high school girl. Moreover, the Japanese appear not to condemn these messages. Men read these books and magazines openly on the subways and commuter trains.[45] If violent pornography causes rape, or if the propagation, acceptance, and consumption of rape myths cause rape, Japan should have an extraordinarily high rate of rape. Yet Japan's rate has remained extremely low—less than one-quarter of the rate for Germany or Great Britain and one-fourteenth of the rate for the United States.[46] It is possible that some of the differences might be a result of differences in the willingness of victims to report rape. Perhaps in Japan, because of the position of women in society and because of the cultural importance of shame, rape victims are less likely to call the police. There is no way we can be certain. Still, the fourteen-to-one difference is too large to ignore.

In any case, new tests of the pornography-rape connection should be coming soon: Beginning in the early 1980s, the VCR greatly expanded the consumption of pornography throughout the industrialized world. Statistics on rape are, of course, inadequate, but for what they're worth, they show no dramatic increase in the rate of rape.

SUMMING UP AND CONCLUSION

Rape is both a violent and a sexual crime, committed almost exclusively by men and almost always against women. Our knowledge of rape is uncertain because so many victims do not report the crime to the police or to victimization survey interviewers. Especially underreported are rapes in which the rapist is an acquaintance or relative of the victim. The available data show that the social distribution of rape somewhat resembles that of other violent crimes.

ABOUT CRIME & CRIMINOLOGY

IRRECONCILABLE DIFFERENCES: ANECDOTAL AND SYSTEMATIC EVIDENCE ON RAPE AND PORNOGRAPHY

Shortly before his execution, Ted Bundy, who had committed a series of sexually sadistic murders, attributed his crimes in part to the influence of pornography. The Meese commission, too, heard testimony from law-enforcement officials, rape victims, and sometimes sex offenders themselves, all contributing examples to show how pornography led to rape. Police would tell of finding piles of pornographic magazines in the houses of rapists. "Victims of pornography" would tell of husbands or boyfriends who would watch pornographic videos and then force the women to replicate the scenarios.

It is difficult to reconcile such compelling anecdotal evidence with the more systematic evidence, which shows little explicit connection between pornography and rape. Why do all these bits of anecdotal evidence not add up to something that can be found by systematic research?

One possible answer is that the systematic research is not sensitive enough to discover these relatively small effects. First, the data are bad. If most of the porno-inspired rapes occur between nonstrangers, they will not turn up in the usual sources of data. Second, even if some of the porno-inspired rapes by strangers do come to light, their numbers will be too small to make a statistically significant difference, especially in nationwide or statewide studies.

Another possibility is that the sex criminals would commit their crimes anyway, taking their inspiration from whatever was available—if not X-rated videos then the images in *Playboy* or *Penthouse* or, failing those, the Victoria's Secret catalogue.

Finally, it may just be possible that pornography prevents as much sex crime as it provokes. This is one explanation for the absence of any increase in rape in Denmark following its porno explosion in the 1960s. Of course, getting clear evidence, even anecdotal evidence, for this proposition is extremely difficult. Presidential commissions are unlikely to hear from pro-pornography counterparts to the "victims of pornography," witnesses testifying that had X-rated videos not been available they would have been raping women rather than sitting safely at home by the VCR masturbating.

Public attitudes toward rape are strangely ambivalent. On the one hand, people generally consider rape an extremely serious crime. On the other hand, there is a widespread acceptance of rape myths—ideas about rape that place the blame on the victim rather than the rapist. The relation between rape culture ideas and rape itself is not clear. For example, though pornography embodies many of the assumptions of rape culture, there is little evidence that it increases the amount of rape. Rape myths do, however, have an influence on the treatment of rape in the criminal justice system—in the behavior of police officers, prosecutors, defense lawyers, and sometimes judges and jurors.

In the last two decades, laws and criminal justice policies regarding rape have begun to change. Some states have rewritten their laws to differentiate between several degrees of rape. Before, when anyone convicted of any type of rape faced severe punishment, the victims, police, and prosecutors were unlikely to pursue the less aggravated cases like date rape since the defendant, if convicted, was subject to the same sentence as the most brutal rapist. Now that there are different penalties for varying degrees of seriousness, the people involved may be more willing to pursue the case. Other changes in some states now protect the victim from being questioned about her sexual history, eliminate the requirement of corroborating evidence of force or coercion, and eliminate or restrict the marital exemption.

Other social changes may affect rates of rape in the near future: trends in economic and social equality between the sexes, changes in the availability of pornography, and changes in public awareness about marital rape and date rape. Criminologists interested in rape will be trying to determine what effects these changes will have on the actual incidence of rape, the amount of reported rape, and the outcome of rape cases in the criminal justice system.

DOMESTIC VIOLENCE

If you had picked up a criminology textbook fifteen or twenty years ago, you probably would not have seen a category for domestic violence. Textbooks might have noted the rather high percentage of murders between spouses, but generally criminologists devoted little attention to crime in the family. Their neglect of family violence was not surprising. It merely reflected the relatively minor place that domestic crime—wife beating, child abuse, and incest—occupied in the criminal justice system.

In the 1960s, family violence began to come out of the closet. It is not clear exactly what caused the "rediscovery" of child abuse in the 1960s, wife beating in the 1970s, and sexual child abuse in the 1980s. We still do not know whether it was the amount of domestic violence that increased during these decades or merely the rate of reporting. Nevertheless, these were years of tremendous changes at several levels—changes in public awareness of domestic violence as a social problem, changes in social science knowledge, and changes in the policies of the criminal justice system.

WIFE BEATING

Even when people are aware of domestic violence, they often think of it as special—different somehow from other crimes. Domestic violence also receives special treatment from those who make and enforce the laws. Legislators, police, and courts have often been reluctant to intrude—to extend the long arm of criminal law into the family. Of course, laws have always limited what family members may do to each other. Law and custom usually have also given extensive power within the family to the man. Patriarchy—the notion that the man is the ruler of his family—has long been a part of our Judeo-

Christian heritage. In biblical times, a man had rights over his wife and children much as he had rights over his other property, rights that included physical violence and even decisions of life and death.[47] Later centuries paid similar tribute to patriarchy. For example, just as the biblical law spelled out the conditions under which a man could kill members of his family, the "rule of thumb" of English common law defined the limits of proper wife beating: For that purpose a man could use a stick no thicker than his thumb. Modern society is less patriarchal, yet most people (officials included) see wife beating as different from other assaults. As for child beating, the great majority of Americans still approve of spanking and other forms of violence, although, as with the rule of thumb, Americans distinguish between legitimate and illegitimate instruments for these purposes.

CHANGES IN ATTITUDES

In the early 1970s, wife beating began to draw more public attention in the United States. (I am using the terms *wife* and *spouse* beyond their narrow legal meaning. The terms as used here should be understood to include *boyfriend-girlfriend* relationships as well.) Not only did the media carry more stories about battered women, but also concerned groups created women's shelters for the victims of abuse and at the same time urged changes in criminal justice policy. This was not the first such campaign in U.S. history. As early as the 1830s, the temperance movement had made wife abuse a prominent theme in the campaign against alcohol. Fifty years later, temperance organizations like the Women's Christian Temperance Union (WCTU) joined forces with feminists in the attack against domestic violence.[48] By 1870, according to one historian, wife beating was generally considered disreputable, and in most states it was illegal.[49] However, the issue gradually disappeared from public sight, only to be rediscovered a century later in the 1970s.

The new social consciousness was rooted in social change. As in the 1870s, wife beating was a major issue for a growing women's movement a hundred years later. In addition, women in the 1960s and 1970s were moving out of their traditional roles. They were delaying marriage and childbearing—that is, spending more years not being wives and mothers. They were getting more education, and they were taking paid jobs outside the home. At the same time, divorce rates were also increasing. So whether by desire or by default, women were becoming more independent, and this new independence contributed to the new emphasis on wife beating as a serious crime.

In 1994, wife battering again became the focus of much public attention. This time, the cause of the heightened awareness was not any social change or any campaign by feminist organizations but a single event: the murder of Nicole Brown Simpson. The prime suspect was her former husband, O. J. Simpson, and the police and media soon revealed that the football and media star had beaten or threatened his wife several times before. Of course, the media devoted most of their attention to the murder, but in between coverage of the police pursuit, the bloody trail of evidence, and the courtroom proceedings, they also surveyed the general problem of spouse abuse. Here was one instance in which a highly celebrated case could in fact tell us much about a crime that touches millions of people.

CHANGES IN KNOWLEDGE

Although the laws had long made wife beating a crime, enforcement of the law was another matter. In practice, the criminal justice system treated just about any spouse abuse short of death as a domestic rather than a criminal matter. Criminologists, too, largely ignored wife abuse as a topic for research, perhaps because they shared the same assumption that it was a domestic matter or perhaps because research on wife beating is especially difficult. For any crime, it's hard enough to get the most basic data—how much of it there is and who commits it—but this problem is even more difficult when the crime is wife abuse. The usual sources of information—police reports and victimization surveys—have some obvious shortcomings. Official police statistics are suspect since abused women frequently do not call the police. They may feel too ashamed, or they may fear retaliation from their husbands. Some victims may define the beating as a private matter rather than as a crime to be reported to the police. Then, even when victims do call the police, the officers may fail to write up the incident as a crime, preferring to handle it informally. Consequently, police data on wife abuse have been essentially worthless.

Victimization surveys, for similar reasons, also miss a great deal of domestic violence. These surveys ask about criminal acts. Therefore, they contain only those incidents that the victim herself both defined as a crime and was willing to report to an interviewer. A woman who felt that marital violence was "normal" or at least not criminal would not be counted in any of the statistics on wife abuse. The NCVS estimate of 500,000 wife-beating incidents per year is probably too low.[50]

More recently, social scientists have tried to estimate the amount of family violence through the equivalent of self-report studies. In 1975, a team of social scientists interviewed a national sample of 2,143 families. Interviewers asked people how often they used various ways of dealing with family conflict. There were twenty items in this **Conflict Tactics Scale (CTS)**, beginning with "We discuss the issue calmly." Number 16 referred to "slapping or spanking," number 20 to the actual use of a knife or gun. Nearly 4 percent of the couples reported serious violence, a figure that translates to nearly 2 million instances in the United States *each year*,[51] although a similar survey with a much larger sample taken ten years later showed a slight decrease in spouse abuse.[52] Other researchers have estimated that 20 to 25 percent of U.S. women have been abused at least once in their lives. That adds up to 12 to 15 million women.[53]

Table 6–3, based on the Conflict Tactics Scale, shows a slight decrease in violence between 1975 and 1985. However, we should be cautious about these results. For example, they also show that women are as likely as men to use each type of violence—and in some cases more likely. Do these results

TABLE 6-3 •

MARITAL VIOLENCE: COMPARISON OF SPECIFIC ACTS, 1975–1985

TYPE OF VIOLENCE	HUSBAND TO WIFE		WIFE TO HUSBAND	
	1975	1985	1975	1985
A. MINOR VIOLENT ACTS				
1. THREW SOMETHING	28	28	52	43
2. PUSHED/GRABBED/SHOVED	107	93	83	85
3. SLAPPED	51	29	46	41
B. SEVERE VIOLENT ACTS				
4. KICKED/BIT/HIT WITH FIST	24	15	31	24
5. HIT, TRIED TO HIT WITH SOMETHING	22	17	30	30
6. BEAT UP	11	8	6	4
7. THREATENED WITH GUN OR KNIFE	4	4	6	6
8. USED GUN OR KNIFE	3	2	2	2
NUMBER OF CASES	2,143	3,520	2,143	3,520

Source: Murray A. Strauss and Richard Gelles, "Societal Change and Changes in Family Violence from 1975 to 1985 as Revealed by Two National Surveys," *Journal of Marriage and the Family*, vol. 48 (1986), 471.

mean that husband abuse is as much a problem as wife abuse? The problem is that the questions do not distinguish levels of seriousness, and they leave much open to the interpretation of the person being interviewed. Imagine a couple in bed discussing some problem; the man says something teasing, and the woman playfully kicks his leg or swings the pillow at him. On the Conflict Tactics Scale, these acts ("kicked," and "tried to hit with an object") would qualify as "severe violence." In contrast, a slap counts as "minor" violence, but the man who occasionally "slaps his wife around"—even if she does not suffer serious injury—may be doing more than minor violence; he may be enforcing a domestic reign of terror.[54]

In most ways, the demographic breakdown on wife abusers resembles that for other violent crimes. They are male and young, the highest rates occurring among those aged 20 to 35. The data on social class and race are not so clear, though they seem to follow the pattern of other violent crimes: Higher rates occur among poorer people and among blacks. The 1975 survey found that serious marital violence was five times more likely in poor families than in families with above-average incomes.[55] However, other researchers have found wife battering to be nearly as frequent in the middle class as in the lower class.[56] At this point, we just do not have enough good data to be certain which estimates are closer to the truth. But we can say, at a minimum, that above-average income does not bring immunity from abuse.

EXPLANATIONS

Although each violent family is violent after its own fashion, two themes stand out in wife abuse. One is jealousy.[57] The abusive man often seems motivated by the most patriarchal kinds of ideas. He sees his wife as his property, and when she appears to be involved with another man, his jealousy can turn to violence—even deadly violence.[58] The woman's infidelity may be real or it may be merely imagined; in either case, the man is using violence to enforce his view that the woman is his property. The notorious double standard is often at work here. The man who uses violence to punish his wife's real or imagined adultery may feel no compunctions about his own infidelities.

Jealousy is only one special version of the more general theme in wife abuse: male dominance. Often the actual detail that sets an incident in motion—dinner not ready on time, some dust on the floor—is so trivial that we must suspect the violence to be about something other than good house-keeping. Instead, as the ensuing argument usually makes clear, the real issue is power. The man's goal is the establishment of his own dominance and the humiliation and degradation of the woman.[59] The man's anxiety over his position of dominance can be heightened by any of several other factors associated with wife battering—alcohol, drugs, lack of money, social isolation, and stress from setbacks like unemployment or illness.

WHY DO THEY STAY?

For most crime victims, the crime is a one-time, isolated event. For victims of wife battering, however, the crime can occur again and again. Media stories of wife abuse often depict women who are assaulted repeatedly by their husbands. A Texas study found that of men who beat their wives, nearly half did so three times a year or more.[60] The NCVS estimates that about one-third of the victims of domestic violence are assaulted again within six months.[61] Extending the follow-up period to a year or so would make this percentage even higher. These findings, like the media stories, raise a question: Why don't the women just leave? In fact, many do. Nearly half of all victims of wife battering are in their 20s, especially their early 20s. The higher the age group, the lower the rate of victimization. This means that older women (i.e., those over 30) either have done something to end the violence or have left.[62]

Still, many women do stay—hundreds of thousands each year. Why? Although some critics complain that merely asking this question tends to blame the victim rather than the batterer, it is still a question that needs to be answered. To begin with, many women stay because they want the relationship to continue, though without the violence. They believe that a peaceful future is possible. The abuse is not constant and is often followed with a period of apology and contrition. The man is once again the person to whom the woman was originally attracted. The woman may blame the abuse on her husband's drinking or his job. She may even blame herself or think that it is her job to save her husband from his own flaws, including his violence.[63]

IN THE NEWS

Psychological explanations of battered women often assume that the victim has some unconscious need for abuse. In 1993, a Boston woman bailed her abusive boyfriend out of jail, despite his threats, his past violence toward her, and her own restraining order. But as the news article makes clear, her actions were probably motivated less by unconscious, self-destructive urges than by quite conscious and legitimate fears.

BATTERING CASE FITS PATTERN: SOME SAY WOMAN APPARENTLY CAUGHT IN A BIND

by Lynda Gorov

Time and again, Anne Marie Yukevich let the man who beat her back into her life.

She took him back after he spent six months in jail for assaulting her. After more violence and threats she ignored her own restraining order and took him back again.

The last time he was arrested, on Aug. 4, she reportedly bailed him out herself.

"Maybe she cared for him, like people sometimes do no matter what someone does to them," said her father, Frank Cristello. "But I'd guess it's more that she was afraid of his threats."

Around midnight Monday, Michael Bowler of Watertown allegedly made good on his threats and suffocated Yukevich. The mother of two young children was three months pregnant with their third child.

The tendency, as advocates for battered women concede, is for outsiders to blame the victim.

But they also say that Yukevich, who would have turned 40 on Friday, was caught in a familiar bind: Her abuser had been released before, and he would be again.

By putting up the $200 bail, as Bowler's lawyer says she did, perhaps Yukevich hoped to try to avoid further harm.

"She knows as well as we do that they're not going to hold him forever," said Stacey Kabat, who heads Battered Women Fighting Back, a group that works for the release of women jailed for killing their abusers. "Put yourself in her shoes."

"Here's a guy who's beat her up badly before. I'm sure she thought she had to do what he wanted or he'd be really mad."

Source: Boston Globe, August 25, 1993, p. 22.

Another reason for staying is a very real and rational fear. The woman's attempt to leave is a gesture that threatens to undermine completely the man's domination and possession of her. Separation, actual or threatened, is the most dangerous point in the cycle, the time of greatest risk of extreme violence and even homicide. Some men threaten that if the woman does anything—goes to the police, seeks help, or leaves—they will commit even more violence on her, her children, or anything else she holds dear.[64] Since the man has already demonstrated that he is capable of violence, the woman must take his threat seriously.

Even without a threat, social and economic pressures make leaving difficult. Some women feel ashamed to admit that they did not have a proper, respectable marriage and that they married a wife beater. A woman may lack the social support to leave. In extreme cases, the husband may have forced his wife to limit her contacts with other people. More commonly, the woman's friends and relatives may encourage her to stay, to try to hold her marriage together rather than leave.[65] In addition, many women lack the money to leave. Where will she live, and how will she house and feed her children? Women's shelters are a fairly recent innovation, and some women may still not know about them. Even if a woman knows that shelters exist, she may not be able to get into one. Women's shelters in the United States have room for perhaps as few as 50,000 women, though some estimates put the figure at 150,000. Yet each year, over half a million women are severely and repeatedly battered.[66]

WHY DO THEY LEAVE?

Once established, the pattern of wife abuse can continue for a long time. Yet many women who have previously stayed with abusive partners do leave. In some cases, the woman just hits bottom and leaves out of utter despair, but usually the decision follows some other change in the woman's life: Her husband increases the level of brutality or becomes less repentant and loving in the periods following the abuse; she is no longer tied to her husband through children or economic dependence; or the violence becomes more visible, and family or friends say something to challenge the rationalizations which had allowed the woman to stay.

CHILD ABUSE

In 1963, 150,000 cases of child abuse or neglect were reported to public authorities. If ever a statistic deserved the cliché "tip of the iceberg," this was it. Even though the number of reported cases today is over 2 million, this probably still represents only a small portion of the total. The great bulk of domestic violence lies beneath the surface. Every so often, a case of family child abuse gains public attention through the media, though usually only when the child dies. Unfortunately, as with other media coverage of crime, these stories do not even attempt to answer some of the most important questions about child abuse—the kinds of questions we ask about any crime before we start to construct explanations: How much of it is there? Is it increasing or decreasing? Are there any systematic similarities among offenders or among victims?

With child abuse, these questions are very difficult to answer. Ordinary people and even experts may disagree strongly over such basic matters as definitions. Just what is child abuse? The extreme cases—the ones that get media publicity, the ones in which children are scalded, tortured, or killed—clearly and by any definition qualify as abuse. But what about spankings, paddlings, whippings, and other physical punishments? What is legitimate discipline, and what is abuse? Each society has its own definition of acceptability. Many of the standard childrearing techniques of our seventeenth-century Puritan forebears or even Americans of a century ago would today be condemned as severe child abuse.[67] Yet although most Americans no longer approve of severe whippings and beatings, there is no objective standard or even any clear consensus on where to draw the line between discipline, punishment, and abuse. Sweden, by contrast, has adopted a simple solution to the definition problem: The law forbids both teachers and parents from striking children. Of course, such a law could never be passed in America, where most people approve of at least some form of child beating. Ninety percent of U.S. parents report spanking their children, in many cases even children of high school age.[68] Most states in the United States permit teachers to hit students, and all states allow parents to hit their children. The only question is at what point the beating becomes abuse.

For purposes of criminology, the most likely strategy would be to define child abuse as an incident of aggravated assault where a child is the victim. Aggravated assault is defined as an assault that is likely to cause serious physical harm. This excludes psychological abuse, a category that would involve far too much disagreement over definition and which in any case would not fall into the area of criminal behavior. This definition also excludes negligence, even though child neglect has always caused more harm than child abuse. Even today, children suffer more from malnourishment, unhealthy living conditions, lack of supervision, and other forms of neglect than from direct physical abuse. Even "good" middle-class parents, who do not have poverty or lack of education as an excuse, may carelessly leave poisonous materials where children can get them, and although this is not a good thing, it hardly qualifies as violent criminal behavior. Nor does buying a child a skateboard or Rollerblades—even though more children are injured each year in skateboard accidents than by direct violent acts.[69]

HOW MUCH CHILD ABUSE?

If the usual criminological sources of statistics on crime are questionable for estimating spouse abuse, they are useless for child abuse. Police statistics depend on a victim reporting the crime—something that is fairly rare in all sorts of family violence but especially so when the victim is a child. Only when the abuse results in death can we trust police statistics to be accurate. The NCVS, our other national source of crime statistics, asks only about the victimization of household members aged 12 and over. Even for older children who are included, the survey will miss many cases of abuse because the person interviewed may wish to keep the abuse secret even from an interviewer.

Much of the data on child abuse come from other sources—social service agencies, hospitals, and doctors. In fact, the rediscovery of child abuse in the 1960s came about largely through the efforts of pediatric radiologists, doctors who specialize in X rays of children. Instead of accepting parents' statements about accidents or falls, pediatric radiologists began to suspect that certain

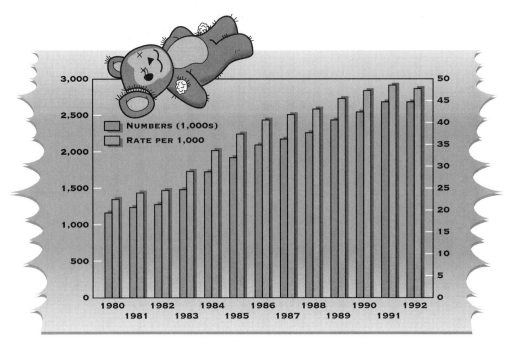

FIGURE 6-6   Child Abuse and Neglect Reporting (Number and Rate per 1,000 children under 14)

Source: American Humane Association; National Committee to Prevent Child Abuse.

fractures and blood clots were the results of beatings or other deliberate assaults by the parents. Social workers, pediatricians, and emergency room doctors and nurses quickly became more sensitized to the possibilities of child abuse, and the number of reported incidents rose rapidly. Still, hospitals and social agencies were not accurate sources for estimating the true extent of child abuse. They could provide valuable information on the families in which severe abuse occurred or the circumstances that led to the abuse. But the cases they saw were only a small percentage of the real number. Who could guess how many cases, some perhaps not quite so severe, remained hidden?

The social service agencies that keep data often lump abuse cases and neglect cases together. Thus, trends like those in Figure 6–6 may be more apparent than real. The data include child neglect, not just abuse; more important, much of the increase reflects an increase in reporting rather than in the actual amount of abuse. For example, in contrast to the dramatic upward trend in the graph (in twelve years, the number and rate of reported cases more than doubled), the number of deaths caused by abuse and neglect has steadily declined. In the late 1960s, between 3,000 and 5,000 children died from abuse and neglect; by 1987 the number had fallen to about 1,100.[70]

The national self-report survey of 1,146 families estimated that in the United States each year 4 percent of children are victims of abuse. Abuse, in this study, was defined as kicking, biting, punching, attacking with an object,

TABLE 6-4 •
PARENT-TO-CHILD VIOLENCE: RATES 1975 AND 1985

TYPE OF VIOLENCE	RATE PER 1,000 CHILDREN AGED 3 THROUGH 17	
	1975	1985
A. MINOR VIOLENT ACTS		
1. THREW SOMETHING	54	27
2. PUSHED/GRABBED/SHOVED	318	307
3. SLAPPED/SPANKED	582	549
B. SEVERE VIOLENT ACTS		
4. KICKED/BIT/HIT WITH FIST	32	13
5. HIT, TRIED TO HIT WITH SOMETHING	134	97
6. BEAT UP	13	6
7. THREATENED WITH GUN OR KNIFE	1	2
8. USED GUN OR KNIFE	1	2
NUMBER OF CASES	1,146	1,428

Source: Murray A. Strauss and Richard Gelles, "Societal Change and Changes in Family Violence from 1975 to 1985 as Revealed by Two National Surveys." *Journal of Marriage and the Family,* vol. 48 (1986), 469.

or threatening with or using a knife or gun (see Table 6–4). That means more than 2 million children are abused each year.[71] In a single year, the study estimated, 50,000 parents use knives or guns against children. Put another way, these figures mean that nearly half a million American children will be the victims of a knife or gun attack during their childhoods. (The sample for child abuse was smaller than the sample for spouse abuse since some of the families had no children. In addition, researchers limited the sample for parent-to-child violence to only those families with two parents present. Both the small sample size and the exclusion of single-parent families diminish the usefulness of this survey for estimating national rates of child abuse.)

WHO COMMITS CHILD ABUSE?

As with other types of violence, child abuse is more likely to occur among poor people, though the official statistics may exaggerate this difference. Doctors are more willing to define a case as child abuse when the parents are poor or black rather than middle class and white.[72] From our knowledge of other violent crimes, we might expect males and blacks to have higher rates of child abuse. The available data, however, paint a different picture. Abusers are more frequently women, probably because women spend far more time with children than do men. Also, black-white differences are smaller for child abuse than for other violent crimes. According to most research, blacks are

ABOUT CRIME & CRIMINOLOGY

THE CYCLE OF VIOLENCE

Since the discovery of child abuse in the early 1960s, one of the most popular and durable theories has been the "cycle of violence"—the idea that violence is transmitted across generations. Sometimes, people in the popular media will in passing mention the "fact" that 99 percent of abused children grow up to be abusive parents. Surely this is too high an estimate. But what is the actual rate of transmission, and how can we find out? Here, again, we are faced with the problem of getting evidence to test an obvious, commonsense idea.

Ideally, we would follow a large group of children from birth to adulthood, finding out the degree of abuse each one suffered as a child and later inflicted as an adult. Because such a study would take thirty years to complete and require accurate information about morally sensitive and largely private behavior, we have to make do with less perfect research. Perhaps because of these imperfections, the studies come up with rates of transmission that range from 70 percent to 18 percent.

The differences stem in part from the style of research. Methods that find high rates of transmission usually use a backward-looking strategy, taking abusive parents and looking back to their childhoods. For example, one study found that of a group of 282 babies, 10 had been abused by age 1. Of these 10 babies, 9 had parents with a history of maltreatment as a child. Nine out of 10—looks like a transmission rate of 90 percent. But when researchers reversed their strategy and looked first for parents abused as children, the result was much different. In their original interviews, 49 of the parents reported having been abused or neglected as children. These 49 included, of course, the 9 who went on to maltreat their own babies. In terms of rates of transmission, now instead of 9 out of 10, we have 9 out of 49—18 percent, or less than 1 in 5. That is, 82 percent of the parents who had been abused did *not* abuse their own children.

This estimate is probably too optimistic. Currently, estimates by experts in the field range between 30 percent and 40 percent—far from the 90 percent or more sometimes casually thrown around on talk shows, but important nevertheless. It means that abused children are more than ten times as likely as others to become abusive parents.

Source: Derived from R. S. Hunter and N. Kilstrom, "Breaking the Cycle in Abusive Families," *American Journal of Psychiatry*, vol. 136, (1979), 1320–1322. Byron Egeland, "A History of Abuse Is a Major Risk Factor for Abusing the Next Generation," in Richard J. Gelles and Donileen R. Loseke, *Current Controversies on Family Violence* (Newbury Park, CA: Sage, 1993), pp. 197–208.

no more likely than whites of similar income to commit child abuse, even though other forms of violence are more frequent in the African-American community. Some observers credit the African-American family structure for this lack of high rates of child abuse. The isolated nuclear family, typical among whites, places a great strain on all relationships within it—strains that can erupt in violence. Black family structure, however, is more extended or open. The basic family unit may include grandparents, aunts, and uncles. In this more extended family, the child has more caretakers and the mother has more support. Therefore, the intensity of strain is diffused among several people, not concentrated into a single parent-child relationship.[73]

WHY CHILD ABUSE?

The explanations for child abuse are often the same as those for spouse abuse. Psychological theories focus on the parent's anger and impulsiveness. Stress theories hold that when adults experience stress or oppressive conditions in the outside world, they may respond by becoming violent in the home, especially when they are isolated from family and friends, who might otherwise help diffuse the anger and tension. The target may be the child, the spouse, or both.[74] The "cycle of violence" theory (abused children grow up to be abusive adults) also applies to any sort of family violence, perhaps even more to child abuse than to wife abuse.

These theories assume that child abuse is an irrational, emotional response to current or past conditions: The parent takes out his or her own anger and frustration on the child. Yet child abuse is not a completely irrational act. Like many other violent crimes, it begins as an attempt to control someone else's behavior. However, unlike other violent crimes, the control of children is something we expect and even demand. Most people approve of parents who use some level of force in exercising this control. With no agreement on the level of force that constitutes abuse, it is little wonder that some parents, in trying to control a child's behavior, sometimes go beyond the line drawn by official institutions.

Child abuse, then, is not just a matter of emotions. It also involves a *cognitive* element—a matter of what parents know and how they think about children. "Parents who abuse their children seem ... less able to take into account their children's perspectives, to see their children as separate from themselves and having needs independent of the parent's needs."[75] The parent may not realize the limited extent to which children—especially young children—can control their own behavior. The child just may not be old enough to follow the parent's order, but the parent interprets the child's behavior as willful disobedience.[76] In addition, once parents do cross the line, there is often little to prevent their continued crossing of it. As one expert says, "People abuse family members because they can. There are rewards to be gained for being abusive: the immediate reward of getting someone to stop doing something; of inflicting pain on someone as revenge; of controlling behavior; of having power."[77] Parents may abuse children, first, because they do not know any better and, second, because they do know that they can get away with it.

SEXUAL CHILD ABUSE

Sexual abuse of children differs from physical abuse in several ways. Though statistics on both are only slightly more than "best guesses," the estimates of sexual abuse are far lower than those for physical abuse. For example, for the

ABOUT CRIME & CRIMINOLOGY

BELIEVE THE CHILDREN

Some people charge that prosecutors misuse their powers to plant false memories in children's minds. In prosecutions like the Michaels and McMartin cases, children frequently deny that the teacher did anything unusual. But, critics say, prosecutors and specialists coax and cajole, sometimes promising rewards if the child changes his or her story. Sometimes, the stories get out of hand ("Then she flew up in the tree"), but with a little help, the children get their testimony into something prosecutors can use. Perhaps the most frequent use of false accusations occurs not in criminal but in civil cases—bitterly contested custody battles, in which one parent accuses the other of abusing the child. The accusing parent may even hire "experts" who are skilled at eliciting stories of sexual abuse from children, even perhaps when no such abuse has in fact occurred. Can children's memories be so easily manipulated?

[One] study involved 75 children 5 and 6 years old and a man who cleaned the room while they watched. At one point he picked up a doll and cleaned it. In a later interview, the interviewer told some of the children that she suspected that the man had actually been playing with the doll, not cleaning.

A quarter of the children said the man was playing, not cleaning, at the first gentle suggestion by the interviewer. But the interviewer became more accusatory and persistent and by the end of the most pointed questioning, all but two of the children were completely swayed to the interviewer's version.

Source: Daniel Goleman, reporting on research by Alison Stewart-Clarke, "Doubts Rise on Children as Witnesses," *New York Times*, November 6, 1990, p. C6. Also Ellen Hopkins, "Fathers on Trial," *New York*, January 11, 1988, pp. 42–49.

year 1983, the U.S. Department of Health and Human Services estimated 72,000 cases of sexual child abuse.[78] A 1986 study said that professionals (doctors and others) saw 140,000 sexual child abuse cases, an extrapolation from the number of adults who say they were sexually abused as children would put the number at 300,000 to 400,000 victims annually.[79] Despite the difficulties of knowing the actual amounts, one historian argues convincingly that while the amount of physical child abuse probably has changed over the course of the last century, the incidence of sexual child abuse and incest probably has remained fairly constant.[80]

There are other important differences. In most cases of sexual abuse, the child suffers no other physical injury. Indeed, most cases involve only fondling rather than intercourse.[81] Also, while physical abusers are more often women than men, sexual abuse is nearly always committed by males. With physical abuse, the abuser nearly always is the child's parent. Sexual abuse, although committed mostly by fathers or stepfathers, is also committed by other relatives, people known to the parents and child (neighbors or baby-sitters), and even strangers. Finally, it seems that social class is not such an important factor in sexual abuse. Sexual abusers, on the average, have higher incomes than do physical abusers.[82]

SUMMARY AND CONCLUSION

This chapter and the previous one have been about individual violent crimes—murder, robbery, rape, and domestic violence. I have omitted collective forms of violence—gang fights, racial and ethnic violence, labor violence, and lynching. Riots, too, are sometimes designated as violence, a label that goes far beyond the FBI's definition of violent crime. Since the 1960s, the term *violence* has become stretched to the point of losing its specific meaning; instead it has come to mean anything the speaker does not like. It is now commonplace, in discussions and arguments about violence, for one person to interrupt with a phrase like, "No, the *real* violence is the malnutrition that still exists...." Other candidates I have heard declared as the *real* violence include racism, sexism, inadequate health care, pollution, pornography, communism, and capitalism. These things may be bad, depending on your point of view, but they are not in themselves violence. Rioters—whether poor townsfolk demanding lower food prices, angry ghetto dwellers, or exuberant college students—do most of their damage to property, not to persons. Collective violence seems much less mysterious than individual violence. It emerges from conflict between groups, each with its political agenda. The political conflict may arise over concrete economic issues like wages, or it may concern vague issues of status and respect. In either case, collective violence is pretty obviously "the furthering of politics by other means" (from Klausewitz's definition of that ultimate form of collective violence—war).

Individual violence is often no different. Murder and aggravated assault usually begin as disputes over seemingly trivial items, disputes that escalate into conflicts over "rights." Even rapists may feel that their crimes are in some way justified, and they may derive these justifications from ideas in the wider culture. The criminal, from his own point of view, is only trying to get the other person to act properly—to do something that she or he ought to be doing or to stop doing something that ought not to be done. Other forms of control—mediation or legal intervention—do not seem to be available, and violence appears as the immediate solution. It is the furthering of interpersonal politics by other means. The main difference between individual and collective violence seems to be the number of people who agree with the violent person's perspective. Relatively few people will accord full legitimacy to the goals or methods of the individual assailant or murderer. Certainly the state will not.

There is another important topic I have not explored here in any depth—the biological, evolutionary link with violence. The sociobiological view of human violence begins with the one outstanding demographic fact about violent crime: It is committed overwhelmingly by men. Sociobiologists see this aggressiveness in men as a legacy of evolution—a mechanism to determine whose genes are transmitted for survival in subsequent generations. From this perspective, murders and assaults that develop out of arguments resemble aggressive encounters between males of many other species. Add the crimes of passion and the fights over turf, and the difference between humans and "lower" species seems to disappear. The violent man's justification in terms of his "rights" begins to look like a thin veneer for the real reasons, reasons that exist in species from birds to baboons—dominance and sexual access to females.[83]

Of course, the sociobiological perspective does not directly address questions of different rates of violence. All human societies have roughly the same biogenetic heritage, but some of them have much higher rates of violence. Nor do biological theories suggest any policies that might reduce violence. Some critics of the subculture-of-violence theory complain that it does not point to any policy alternatives, for how can government policies change a widespread culture? But if changing culture is extremely difficult, changing evolution is impossible.

With other explanations of violence, it is easier to use our knowledge to point toward directions in policy. In fact, the trouble is not in coming up with ideas but in devising realistic policies. For example, if we know that violent crime occurs more frequently where people are poor, unemployed, and uneducated, it seems reasonable to expect that policies aimed at improving those conditions will reduce violence. At the very least, such changes will not increase violence. However, to date nobody has come up with politically and economically acceptable solutions to these problems. Similarly, we know that murder rates rise during disputes over the control of illegal markets—alcohol in the 1920s, drugs today. Yet it was not until the cocaine/crack crisis of the late 1980s that policymakers even began to think about reducing murder by legalizing drugs, for obviously decriminalization entails many problems, both practical and political. Instead, lawmakers chose to increase penalties for drug-related violent crimes, just as a decade before they had increased penalties for other violent crimes. To some limited extent the criminal justice system can reduce violence through the arrest and imprisonment of violent criminals. Yet get-tough proposals, too, run into political and economic problems: Do we want to be such a heavily policed and punitive society? And do we want to spend the billions of dollars required to build more prisons and to hire more police officers, lawyers, judges, and guards?

CRITICAL THINKING QUESTIONS

1. Why is it so hard to know how many rapes are committed, and why do estimates vary so widely?
2. In what ways is rape "normal"?
3. Does pornography cause rape?
4. Why do so many rape victims find the legal system inadequate?
5. Why are police reports and victimization surveys much less useful for measuring domestic violence than for measuring other crimes?
6. When a battered woman does not leave her abusive partner, is she motivated by unconscious masochism?
7. How and why do police officers and prosecutors treat family violence differently from the way they treat other crimes?

8. In what ways do rape and family violence fit with widely held beliefs about sex, about husbands and wives, and about child rearing? Are these differences of degree or differences of kind?

KEY TERMS

Conflict Tactics Scale (CTS)

consent defense

date rape

interracial rape

intraracial rape

marital rape exemption

rape culture

rape myths

CHAPTER SEVEN

PROPERTY CRIME

CHAPTER OUTLINE

BURGLARY

When criminologists want to focus on "real" street crime, they often pick robbery and burglary as the crimes to investigate. Robbery obviously qualifies as real crime. It is a violent crime (even when the violence is only threatened), usually committed by a stranger. Burglary—unlawful entry into a building, apartment, or other structure—is a property crime and it involves no confrontation between victim and criminal. Burglars take great precautions to avoid running into their victims. Yet victims of burglary, like the victims of violent crime, often say they feel personally violated—as though the house were an extension of the body. Burglary, like robbery, can increase people's feelings of vulnerability, for despite the person-property distinction, these two crimes have important similarities: Someone unknown, probably a stranger, unexpectedly violates the victim's personal territory to take valuable property.

The original laws defining burglary—as opposed to theft—were meant to protect the sanctity of the home. Since the 1700s, people have taken this sanctity for granted. We have all heard that "a man's home is his castle" (a phrase coined, by the way, in an argument for protecting homes not against burglars but against the government). Yet the concept of the home probably evolved gradually as society changed. In medieval times, people were less proprietary and private about their houses. The houses themselves were not separate living spaces apart from the outside world. The houses of the

Who is a thief? Under some circumstances, even usually honest people who do not think of themselves as criminals may decide to pay less.

wealthy might contain several families, both kin and servants; peasant quarters might house pigs and cows and other animals we now think of as belonging outside the house. For merchants and craftspeople, houses were workplaces as well as dwellings. The distinction between inside and out-side—especially during the daytime—was not so great, and people seemed to have conceived of this distinction more in terms of the town than of the individual house.[1] In fact the word *burglary* derives from the word for town (*burg*); in medieval England, *burgh-breche* was a breaking of the city walls. So while taking another person's property had long been against the law, it was not until the 1500s that burglary in English law began to focus on housebreaking.[2] Under such burglary laws, even if the offender did not take anything (or even if the state could not prove that there was theft), the unlawful entry itself was a crime. As society became more individualized and privatized, the home began to take on the qualities that we now take for granted. It became a specialized living space, a protected haven closely iden-tified with the self.

RESIDENTIAL BURGLARIES

Not all burglaries are alike. For example, they can be classified according to the type of target—residential or commercial (i.e., homes or businesses). Residential burglaries are far more frequent, if only because homes far out-number businesses. The FBI's Uniform Crime Reports for 1992 show about 1 million commercial burglaries and 2 million residential burglaries reported to the police. Of course, many burglaries are not reported. The National Crime Victimization Survey for that same year estimated 4.8 million residential bur-glaries, more than twice the UCR figure. This number means that 5 percent of the nearly 100 million households in the United States were victimized by burglary in a single year. Of course, victimization surveys turn up many bur-glaries that are less serious. In fact, nearly 1 million of the burglaries in the NCVS (20 percent) were unsuccessful attempts.[3]

The victimization survey also discovered something interesting about the social distribution of burglary. Since colonial times, the individual solution to the crime problem has been to move away from it—at least for those who can afford to. The solution works well for violent crime, as victimization statistics demonstrate: The wealthier a person is, the less likely he or she will be vic-timized by violent crime. But burglary rates are highest among the poorest groups and decrease among middle-income groups (Figure 7–1), but then the graph levels off and turns back upward; the risk of burglary for upper-income homes is greater than for middle-income homes.

Even this simple graph tells us some important things about burglary and burglars. In burglary (as in robbery and perhaps in noncriminal work as well), there is often a trade-off between the ease of the job and the size of the payoff. Burglaries run from the most opportunistic to the highly professional. Opportunists focus on convenience; professionals focus on payoff. The left side of Figure 7–1 reflects opportunists who pick targets close to home; the right side reflects the professionals, who go where the money is.

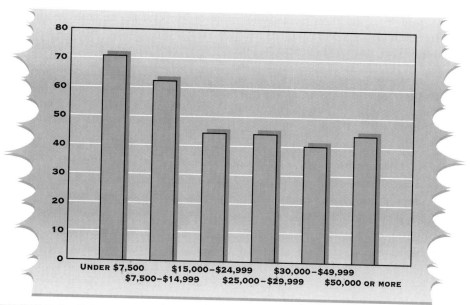

FIGURE 7–1   Burglary by Income, 1992 (Victimizations per 1000 Households)

Source: Bureau of Justice Statistics, *Criminal Victimization in the United States, 1992* (Washington, DC: 1994).

EASY COME—THE OPPORTUNISTS

The media—fictional TV programs and the news as well—convey an image of burglary as a high-payoff crime committed by fairly skilled criminals. In reality, as Figure 7–1 shows, most burglaries are not very glamorous or spectacular events. Remember, over 20 percent of burglaries are unsuccessful attempts. The burglars do not even manage to break in. Of successful burglaries, many do not involve forced entry; rather, the burglar enters through an unlocked door or window.[4] Most burglars, therefore, are not the determined and skilled professionals we might imagine. They are "door-shakers" making midmorning rounds of hotels or apartment buildings,[5] or they are neighborhood opportunists who can be deterred by securely locked doors and windows. If they find someone at home, they usually run away. Nor are their crimes very profitable. Most burglary victims estimate their net losses as less than $500 (and even that figure is higher than the sum that the stolen property will ultimately bring to the burglar). Most victims of these small-scale burglaries do not even bother to call the police.[6]

Thus the typical burglary is the kind of crime you are unlikely to see on television: Two or three boys, aged 15 to 18, wandering in their own low-income neighborhood, find a house or apartment with nobody home; they go in through an open door or window and take a television or tape recorder or something else they can sell quickly, probably to people they know.[7] Older burglars, too, may prefer to operate in this opportunistic way. They are constantly sizing up their immediate surroundings for possible targets, and when an opportunity looks ripe, they strike. One study of adult burglars in England found that half of them worked largely on impulse. "Spur of the moment," as one of them put it. "I saw the open window and took a chance."[8]

Many "older" burglars (i.e., those no longer in their teens) are drug users or addicts; and although they may derive much of their income from burglaries, they still prefer quick, minimally planned crimes. They don't know for certain what they will find, but their expectations are very modest.

> I get up every morning and go to "work." Before I comb my hair or brush my teeth, I go out and steal something to get $20 for a "fix." After I've fixed for the first time, I clean up and go to work again.

> Every house has got something worth stealing. I figure to get $50 every time I go in a place.[9]

Although the no-force walk-in is the most frequent type of burglary, more determined burglars use other methods. At a somewhat more sophisticated level are the burglars who are "kicking it in"—giving the door a sharp kick "just next to the latch. Burglars assert that most doors of both houses and business establishments are so poorly made that a kick-in will usually spring the door open."[10] The sliding glass doors on newer suburban houses can be silently popped out of their tracks with a crowbar or screwdriver.[11] Less sophisticated burglars will use a crowbar or simply batter at a door until it breaks. Like the burglars who merely walk in, kick-in burglars have little expertise and do not plan their crimes very extensively.

On the one hand, as haphazard and unglamorous as these simple burglaries may seem, from the burglar's point of view they do have certain advantages. The burglars are familiar with the neighborhood, so they know the easier targets and the better routes of escape. Also, since possession of burglar's tools is itself a crime, burglars who do not use crowbars, loids (a strip of celluloid that can be used to open a simple door catch), lock picks, or other tools are eliminating one more risk.

On the other hand, opportunistic burglary has some obvious disadvantages. The payoff of any one score is usually small, so opportunistic burglars will have to commit a fairly large number of crimes. This combination of high frequency and lack of skill or sophistication is a sure formula for getting caught. Juveniles or first offenders may receive probation, but because their skills for legitimate jobs are usually no greater than their burglary skills, they often continue to commit burglaries as well as other types of theft or drug crimes. Eventually, they wind up in prison.[12]

THE GOOD BURGLAR

These low-end, opportunistic crimes—walk-ins and kick-ins—account for the majority of burglaries. Slightly higher up the scale are the more professional burglars, less numerous but more committed to their work. I should note here that burglars themselves, like robbers, rarely use the word *professional* in this sense, just as they do not use the word *opportunist*. Instead, they speak of the **"good" burglar**[13] or the "better" burglar or—since these criminals commit other crimes besides burglary—the "better thief."

> Say we're talking to some females or to some people we know that is straight…. They knows we're burglars but don't know what kind…. So we say "professional"—means we got skills, know our s—, 'cause they understand the word…. Whereas if we'd say "good burglar," that they wouldn't understand…. More than anything you hear "good people"— means the guy is trustworthy but can mean he's into crime for a living…. Burglars main-ly say a guy is good or decent or is half-assed.[14]

A former burglar and fence makes the following distinction between "bet-ter" thieves and others he worked with: "Your better thief is choosey about what he takes. He ain't gonna carry a f—-ing sofa or TV out of a house. The run-of-the-mill burglar and the shoplifter, your common thief, will pretty much take what he runs across."[15] The same man, like the burglar quoted just before, also distinguishes between good burglars and those somewhat less professional, whom he calls "decent" burglars. For the common thieves, he uses a variety of words: *penny ante*; *bottom-barrel*; *ordinary* thief; or more sim-ply, *asshole*.

Good burglars, as the fence says, are more selective about what they steal. They prefer valuables like jewelry and silverware to bulky goods like televisions. Good burglars also tend to be older, and even if they use simple methods of entry, they may range farther from their own neighborhoods in search of larger payoffs. Professional burglars plan their crimes more careful-ly and use more sophisticated methods of entry. They are also more likely to be part of a well-developed criminal subculture—a group of people who share a set of ideas (norms, values, and beliefs) that differ from those commonly held in the wider society. Another dimension for differentiating the more opportunistic from the more professional is commitment. Opportunists might see crime as something to do for kicks and a few dollars, but they are not fully committed to a life of crime. Criminals in the good burglar subculture, in con-trast, see crime as a way of life. This professional subculture is also marked by a greater specialization, or division of labor. Good burglars may even spe-cialize in the type of loot they prefer: Some specialize in jewels, others in furs, still others in antiques. Division of labor extends to the job itself. Low-skill burglaries usually have a minimal division of labor—one person to act as look-out, one or two to go into the house. More sophisticated burglars may team up to combine different skills and roles in addition to just keeping watch: monitoring police calls, disarming burglar alarms, or opening safes.

A LITTLE HELP FROM THEIR FRIENDS

The criminal subculture extends beyond its central core of professional crim-inals, and the division of labor goes beyond the burglary itself. Professional burglars, whether they work in teams or alone, are usually connected with a loosely organized support system of other people. Fingermen, for example, provide information about lucrative targets. They do not have to be criminals themselves (nor do they have to be men). All that is required is the right information and a willingness to share it with a burglar. Night watchmen, window cleaners, gardeners, maids, deliverymen, prostitutes, and bartenders, as well as other thieves or ex-thieves, may for a percentage of the profits pass along tips about possible scores.[16] Even the more respected members of the community may act as fingermen.

> We always got a lot of tips on places to clip—like from a bartender, an insurance man, a salesman, maybe a guy that drives a delivery truck. But more from lawyers than anybody. See, your lawyers handle a lot of wills. And many times they know the house and the people exceptionally well. It's too bad, really, that people trust a lawyer that way. Your older people especially talk to their lawyers, open up an awful lot to them. Which they shouldn't, but they do.[17]

After a successful score, burglars need to get rid of the jewels, furs, art, or other valuables. Some burglars try to sell the items themselves, offering them to people at the bars where they drink. But what if a burglar has stolen several suits in a commercial burglary, expensive jewelry, or furs—items that are less easy to sell? The burglar needs to get rid of the stolen merchandise quickly since it constitutes incriminating evidence if the police make an arrest. For this reason, the good burglar probably will know at least one **fence**—a person who trades regularly in stolen goods. They offer burglars a safe and reliable outlet. They may pay only from 10 percent to 50 percent of the item's value, but the money is probably better and surer than what the burglar could get by selling the merchandise himself.

Finally, the burglar's network includes those he can turn to in case of misfortune. These are people at the criminal justice end of the system—bail bondsmen, criminal lawyers, and perhaps even corrupt police, prosecutors, or judges.[18] As one burglar says,

> To make it, really make it, now, as a burglar—not this penny-ante shit.... You need someone on the inside to give you information, say, a lawyer, or have a contact with somebody that works in a security agency or a place that sells burglar alarms.... Need a good partner unless you can hack working alone, which freaking few can do; a lawyer to get you off and help line you up with the right people; the right kind of fence unless you're going strictly after cash which is getting harder and harder to do; and a good woman to stand by you but not get in your way.[19]

CAREER PATHS IN BURGLARY

There are two principal paths into these networks. In a city neighborhood with a criminal tradition, a boy can serve something like an apprenticeship with an older, more experienced burglar. "[I] grew up with a lot of thieves, learnt off them,"[20] is a typical statement. Of course, other criminals do not accept the newcomer automatically. The apprentice may have to demonstrate his toughness and reliability and his willingness to break the law.[21] Through this apprenticeship, he can acquire the basic techniques of burglary and a generally more professional outlook on crime. More important, he can also meet the other people who provide the services and information **professional criminals** may need. Other young criminals lack these neighborhood connections. For them, the link to more experienced criminals occurs in another logical, inevitable place: prison. In prison, the young criminal can make connections, learn criminal techniques, and acquire the criminal worldview.

> In the adult penitentiaries you would be meeting guys who were a whole lot better.... With the better criminal, you don't hear that much talking, that much bragging. But, in a way, I learned how to crack a safe ... from hearing different ones talking about it. Main thing I got from the safecrackers was that crime was a business. I learnt that crime is a business.[22]

One study of thirty burglars in a Texas city (population 250,000) classified twenty-one of them as **journeymen**. They did only residential burglaries and often took items like VCRs, televisions, and whatever jewelry they could find.

> Journeymen are experienced, reliable burglars.... Rather than waiting for criminal opportunities to present themselves ... the journeyman searches out or creates opportunities. Selecting a community or neighborhood in which he or she feels comfortable, the burglar cruises around looking for a target site that looks vulnerable. The burglar may plan the act by casing the site for a period of a few hours to several days.... Assistance in the form of additional persons may be necessary and the burglar may require time to put a team together. He or she may also determine that the situation and circumstances make a there-and-then hit advantageous and commit the crime immediately after target selection.[23]

COMMERCIAL BURGLARIES

Burglars steal not just from houses but also from businesses. Commercial burglaries in 1993, according to police reports, numbered about 950,000, with an average loss of nearly $1,200. Like residential burglaries, commercial break-ins range from the highly profitable, highly planned, and technically sophisticated down to the spontaneous and simple. Teenagers may break into local factories and take what goods are around.[24] Older criminals, too, using simple methods, may also pick commercial targets: "Smash a window and if I hear an alarm run."[25]

Even opportunistic burglars have good reason to prefer commercial targets over residences. Some burglars find it less troubling personally to steal from businesses than from individuals—especially when the burglar realizes that the victims are ordinary people like him: "In one house, I found photos of people.... It didn't seem right [to steal]."[26]

For **opportunistic burglars**, the size of the score is always an uncertainty, but many think that commercial targets are more profitable than residences and less risky. They are more likely to find something of value and less likely to run into people. If the worst does happen, burglars who steal from businesses and factories can expect to receive more lenient sentences than those who break into houses.[27]

Naturally, businesses that have a lot to steal will take greater preventive measures, so burglars in search of these larger scores may have to develop more sophisticated methods. Some burglars may be deterred by alarms; other burglars will learn techniques that overcome them.[28] Once inside, some burglars may content themselves with the cash they can take from easy targets— the cash register, jukebox, and game machines. But burglars aiming for big commercial scores will have to learn how to open safes.

Even safecracking is not as glamorous as you might think. Few safecrackers these days can delicately feel their way through the combination to a lock. Besides, many safes yield to much simpler methods. Some safes can be peeled—a technique similar to peeling open a sardine can. The safecracker uses wedges and then a heavy bar to pry open a hole between the door and door jamb, peeling the metal back until he can put his hand through the hole. Another method, punching, attacks the lock directly. The burglar knocks off the dial with a hammer and then uses a long steel punch to knock in the spindle until the tumblers fall. If all goes well, he can then turn the handle and open the door.[29] "Actually, anybody with any kind of knowledge can crack an old type safe, the old square boxes. They're easy to punch or can peel.... And many of the new square boxes you buy even today are tin cans. They're fire protection, not protection from the good safeman."[30]

Some burglars who beat safes use explosives. This technique requires a good deal of knowledge and skill: how to make nitroglycerine from available chemicals, transport it to the job, load it into the safe, and detonate it. Blowing a safe is a complicated process. Use too little nitroglycerine and you will "bulge" the safe, leaving it unopenable. Use too much and you may literally burn the money or blow out a window, either decreasing the profit or increasing the risk.[31] The burglar who wants to learn how to blow safes, therefore, must become part of the criminal subculture. Some of the necessary information useful for safecracking is available from open, legitimate sources:

> *How did you learn to make the stuff [nitroglycerine]?*
>
> Oh, I'd hear about it—the thing that I actually studied was the *Encyclopaedia Britannica*—they've got a very good run-down on it.[32]

But generally, there is no substitute for experience—one's own or someone else's.

> *Did you know right away what had gone wrong on the first safe?*
>
> Well, we went back to a couple of safeblowers we knew and we talked this over with them, and they explained to us exactly what we had done wrong.
>
> *So next time you used less grease [slang for nitroglycerine]?*
>
> So we used less grease and less grease as we went along until we found that we could blow a safe and just have the door open instead of havin' it flyin' right off its hinges and across the hall![33]

Here again we see a criminal subculture—a group of people who share a set of values and a way of life different from that of the dominant society. In fact, within the broader criminal subculture, those few people who specialize in safeblowing seem to have their own subculture. They know one another and recognize one another's work. They share information about methods, though

IN THE NEWS

POLICE SAY ALBANIAN GANGS MAKE BURGLARY AN ART IN U.S.

by Matthew Purdy

The burglars sometimes visit a store beforehand, police investigators say, posing as foreign tourists interested in videotaping a modern supermarket for the folks back home. But they return when the store is closed, pound through the roof with sledgehammers, disable alarm systems and then break open the safe with hammers, crowbars, torches and specialized saws....

The crews are suspected of committing as many as 300 burglaries of supermarkets, jewelry stores, banks and other retail outlets in more than a dozen states....

Most often ... the burglars specialize in cash-rich supermarkets, usually shunned by thieves because they are rarely closed, and the estimates of their take are as high as $10 million. They have turned routine breaking-and-entering crimes into an art, investigators say, organizing burglaries with precision usually reserved for thefts of precious paintings.

They also frustrate authorities. Lookouts armed with police scanners and walkie-talkies outside the stores warn burglars inside when the police are coming....

The police said the crimes follow an unmistakable pattern. The burglars use ropes to lower themselves through the roofs. They rarely brandish guns, but they bring an array of tools to the scene, including, in some cases, tanks of oxygen and acetylene to fuel their torches. They usually leave their tools behind.

"If they find a location that they believe has $100,000 in it and it's in a $15,000 safe, they'll spend the money to go buy the same kind of safe and practice on it," said Thomas Leahy, the chief of the rackets bureau....

Law-enforcement officials said the burglars often cut the telephone lines to a store or bank, setting off the alarm, and then hide outside while the police arrive, waiting until they leave to actually break in. This allows the burglars to gauge the length of the response time and it also increase the chances the police will treat another alarm from the store as a false alarm.

Tom Walsh, a New Jersey safe salesman, said the work of the burglars had been eased because most food store chains have similar safes in every store. He said once the burglars learn how to crack the safe, it becomes routine.

Source: New York Times, December 17, 1994, pp. 1, 27.

---

they also believe that each safecracker develops his own particular style. Style is important. A safecracker can gain status in this subculture, not necessarily by the amount of money he takes but by the artfulness of his technique.

There is an ironic twist in this subculture. Usually subcultures form as a source of protection for their members. But the burglars' subculture may also work to the disadvantage of its members and even lead to arrest. Since members of the subculture must cooperate in various aspects of their work, they will know one another's crimes. The police, then, can pressure one criminal to divulge important information. When the police arrest a burglar, they may offer him a lighter sentence in return for information about other burglars, fences, or even (though rarely) corrupt officials. The police may also make deals with the fence. They will allow the fence to operate safely; in return the fence will occasionally inform on burglars or provide general information from the criminal grapevine.[34] In this way, the police may also come to have a fairly good knowledge about the criminal world. Individual criminal styles become known not just to other burglars but to police specialists as well. "Let's say four or five safes have been blown, the police can look at the jobs and it's just as if they've left their fingerprints—they know immediately who did it just by how it's done."[35] More important, the safecracker's need to gain recognition in the eyes of his peers can easily lead to his undoing:

> Conversation ... would be the biggest factor.... Seems like nobody is able to keep this to himself so you get in a big crowd, a whole bunch of you, and you're yakkin', and pretty soon it gets to be common knowledge and all the safecrackers all over town know who did just about every score, you see? And, well, this is alright if you was only talkin' amongst yourselves, but you get girlfriends and wives and other guys that aren't safecrackers and pretty soon—I think it's just a matter of time before it gets back to the police.[36]

PREVENTING BURGLARY

For individuals, preventing burglary is largely a matter of "target hardening"— making the house or apartment harder to break into. While better locks, guard dogs, or alarms may help, the best deterrent is having people at home. Of course, such measures may have less effect on the overall burglary rate since the burglar will merely keep looking for an easier target.

One of the first things burglars do, having selected a possible target, is to make sure nobody is home. In choosing the right time and place, they use general knowledge of people's routine activities.

> This neighborhood is full of families with kids in elementary school. I don't do this part of town in the summer. Too many kids around. But [in winter], the best time to do crime out here is between 8:00 and 9:00 [A.M.]. All the mothers are taking the kids to school. I wait until I see the car leave. By the time she gets back, I've come and gone.[37]

Burglars also look for visible signs announcing a safe target. In one town, the high school pep squads decorated the front yards of the homes of football team members—announcing to burglars that the family would be out on game night. "Man! wait until football season. I clean up then. When they are at the game, I'm at their house."[38]

Burglars also use specific methods to assure themselves that a house is empty. Knocking on the door is the simplest method; if someone answers, they pretend to have gotten the wrong address or ask to use the phone to call for help for a broken-down car. Nearly as simple is the ringing phone: They get the name from the mailbox, look up the phone number, call, leave the phone off the hook, and then go back to the house. The still-ringing phone is an all-clear signal to the burglar.

Reducing burglary rates would seem to be a job for the criminal justice system. Yet it is difficult to devise effective strategies against burglary. Prevention by police patrols seems an obvious answer, but a moment's reflection will show that this is probably not a very effective policy. Police patrols, whether on foot or in cars, are unlikely to deter a burglar. If a burglar can hit a house while the residents are in the back mowing the lawn,[39] he or she can certainly wait for a patrol car to drive out of sight. Besides, most of these patrols—especially cars—go down the street, while most burglars prefer to make their entrances from places that cannot be seen from the street itself. The following quotation from a black burglar illustrates how burglars—even black burglars in white neighborhoods—feel they have little to fear from the police:

> As long as we stay off the main drag, we're safe. It's the service entrances, the fire escapes. We know about back doors. Most people never question a black man walking through a service entrance. They kind of go together. That was Whitey's idea, you know, sending us in the back door.[40]

In any case, the burglar can always wait until the police go by. Then, once the burglars get inside, police patrol becomes irrelevant. Burglars, therefore, rarely even bother to get much information beforehand about police patrols.[41] Even citizen patrols and neighborhood crime-watch programs rarely take much of a bite out of burglary.[42]

Some policies aim at catching more burglars, especially the career criminals who commit so many crimes, and sending them to prison. This strategy, too, will have a very limited effect. Catching burglars is difficult. Police figures give the official clearance rate as 14 percent, and some independent studies estimate the real clearance rate as closer to 4 percent.[43] This low rate should hardly surprise us: Burglary victims do not see the burglar, and there are rarely other witnesses. In addition, by the time the victims arrive home and call the police, the burglars are long gone. For the same reason, if the police do pick up a suspect, it may be difficult to get enough evidence for a conviction; and even if a burglar is convicted, there is still the matter of sentencing. Not that judges have a soft spot in their hearts for burglars; but with prisons already overcrowded and with some states requiring mandatory sentences for drug crimes, judges prefer to save the available, valuable prison space for people convicted of violent crimes. Judges, therefore, may be lenient with burglars. Those caught for commercial burglaries or those with shorter records may receive light sentences or probation. Career burglars or those who have burglarized homes may serve some time, but far less than the law allows. In 1990, the average sentence for convicted burglars was more than six years, but the estimated average of actual time served was just under two years.[44]

Some people think that even if the courts did lock up more burglars, it would do little to decrease burglary. Much burglary is committed by teenagers, who do it as part of growing up. Getting a few professional burglars off the street will have little effect on the succeeding waves of adolescents coming of age in poor neighborhoods. To these opportunists, people at home or securely locked doors are probably a much surer deterrent than the arm of the law.

LARCENY

Larceny is the most basic property crime: taking something that belongs to someone else. The crime is also known as theft or, more simply, stealing. It is the crime you are most likely to be familiar with, either as victim or perhaps as perpetrator. If your bicycle has been stolen or if your pocket has been picked or if someone took a lawn chair from your backyard, you have been the victim of a larceny. If you have ever shoplifted or if you have ever walked off with a book or umbrella you found in a classroom, you have committed a larceny (see Figure 7–2).

Of the seven Index crimes that the FBI uses for comparison (arson is omitted), over half are larcenies. For example, in 1992, the police recorded a total of about 14 million Index crimes; of these, 7.7 million (about 55 percent) were larcenies. Another 20 million larcenies never became official statistics because the victims did not bother to call the police.[45] An unreported crime is usually less serious, and the victims feel it is not worth the bother to report it, especially since they think the police will be unable to catch the thief or recover the stolen property.

EXPLAINING LARCENY—SUPPLY AND DEMAND

How can we explain these 27 million or more thefts? Most explanations assume that crime rates are simply a function of the number of "bad guys" in the population. But larceny is largely an economic crime, and from the eco-

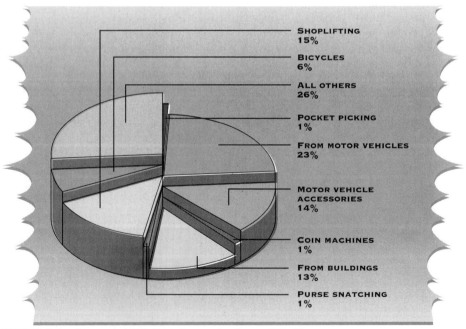

FIGURE 7–2   Larceny, 1993 (Distribution by Type of Theft)

Source: Derived from UCR, 1993.

nomic point of view, these explanations give only half the picture—the supply side, that is, the supply of criminals and their "services"—and neglect the demand side. Of course, it sounds odd to speak of a "demand" for theft; perhaps "opportunity" is more accurate. But just as legitimate jobs providing legitimate opportunities represent a demand for legitimate labor, so too opportunities for crime represent a demand for criminal labor; and just as the demand for legitimate labor is reflected in the pay, so too the demand for crime is reflected in the profitability of that crime. The full economic picture of crime, then, would have to include changes in opportunity or profitability (i.e., the demand), independent of the supply of bad people.

Consider the two forms of larceny that have grown the fastest in recent years (say, since 1985): thefts of auto parts and accessories and thefts of other items from automobiles. To explain this increase, most people (including most law enforcement officials) point to the supply side: The spread of drugs (largely cocaine and crack) increased the number of criminals; more drug users needing more money to pay for more drugs meant more larceny. For these and other opportunistic criminals, automobiles on city streets provided an easy target. The following excerpt from a news item exemplifies this supply-side explanation of car break-ins in New York City: "They have risen steadily since [1983]—in large part, the police say, because drug addicts can sell a car radio on the street, no questions asked, for the $10 or $20 it takes to buy a few vials of crack."[46]

Sometimes, however, auto break-ins have increased when drug use was *not* on the rise. For example, in 1980, nearly all of the increase in the Los Angeles crime rate was attributable to this type of larceny.[47] Drugs were an unlikely cause of this change, for the increase occurred well before the crack crisis; nor had theft from automobiles suddenly become easier. It has always been a fairly simple matter for a thief to smash the window of the car and take whatever is inside. Instead, the explanation probably lay on the demand side, particularly in the value of what thieves might steal. The fashion trend in luxury cars was moving away from Cadillacs toward BMWs and Mercedes, and the German imports came equipped with expensive, high-quality sound systems. For the potential thief, an AM radio that picked up mostly static hardly provided a tempting target. But a $600 Blaupunkt was quite a different proposition, as the Los Angeles crime statistics showed. Nationwide figures reflected a similar trend (see Figure 7–3). The value of the average theft of auto accessories, which had decreased in 1979, shot up suddenly by 75 percent in two years.

The trend in the quality of highway sound continued, and so did the trend in theft. Soon, Chevrolets and Hondas were sporting stereos equal to those of the BMWs of a few years earlier. The high-quality radios, tape decks, and CD players also opened up a new source of profit for opportunistic thieves. Equally important, a market in used car stereos arose, allowing thieves to convert the electronic gear into quick cash. Without this market, the new wave in larceny might have leveled off. Instead, the market and the crime both grew.

A similar pattern occurred in another form of larceny—chain snatching, which in some cities increased greatly in the 1970s. As with breaking car windows, the increase had little to do with new criminal populations or new techniques: Tearing a chain from someone's neck does not require sophisticated criminal skills. The most likely cause of this trend in crime was international economics. In the late 1970s, the price of gold on international markets rose from about $350 an ounce to nearly $800. This price translated to similar

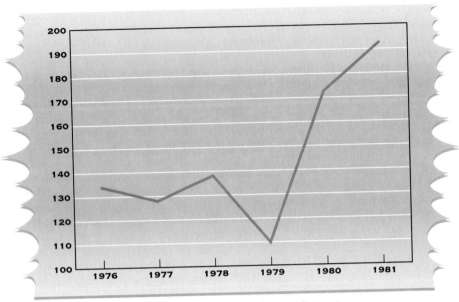

FIGURE 7–3   Average Value of Auto Accessories Theft (in Dollars)

increases at the retail level, where many jewelers were willing to pay cash for gold—and no questions asked about its origins. Unfortunately, crimes do not go out of fashion as quickly as they come in. The price of gold eventually fell, but chain snatching remained part of the urban scene.

Both these cases—car stereo theft and chain snatching—involve a similar interplay of criminal and legitimate elements: Changes in the legitimate world increase the profitability of an easily committed crime. Criminals then take advantage of the new opportunities. Finally, a regular market for stolen merchandise is created by people who straddle these two worlds.

SNITCHES AND BOOSTERS

With these and other types of larceny, we must distinguish among various types of crime and types of criminals. Not all thieves are alike. They differ in their levels of professionalism and in their motivation. At the low end is the casual, opportunistic thief—the person who steals relatively infrequently, taking things for personal use rather than resale. At the other end is the professional thief for whom theft is a regular source of income. In the jargon of shoplifting, these two ends of the spectrum are represented by the **snitch** and the **booster**.[48] Snitches are opportunists. They do not think of themselves as thieves and may have no intention of stealing when they enter the store. Yet the temptation of free merchandise, combined with a variety of "neutralizing"[49] justifications, may help them overcome their inhibitions. Some snitches steal out of need: They are poor people who simply cannot afford all the necessities of life. Not surprisingly, supermarkets and other food stores in low-income

IN THE NEWS

ACTING ARMY SECRETARY ACCUSED OF SHOPLIFTING AND IS PUT ON LEAVE

Washington, Aug. 27—The Acting Secretary of the Army [the Army's number two civilian posi-

tion], John W. Shannon, was placed on administrative leave today after being accused of shoplifting, the Army said.

Mr. Shannon was accused of shoplifting a skirt and blouse valued at about $30 from the Army post exchange at Fort Myer, Va....

A decorated Vietnam War veteran, Mr. Shannon was commissioned as a second lieutenant in the infantry in 1955 and served 23 years before retiring at the rank of colonel.

Source: *New York Times*, August 28, 1993.

---

neighborhoods have far more shoplifting losses than do those in better-off areas. More often, however, opportunistic shoplifting is a matter of convenience rather than necessity. The shoplifter could pay for the item but finds it more convenient not to. These snitches can come from all socioeconomic levels, even the highest. Every so often, the media will report on a case of shoplifting by a government official or celebrity or perhaps a member of some wealthy family.

Similar to these opportunistic shoplifters are juveniles, though often their motives may go beyond simply wanting something for nothing. These youths may shoplift for excitement or to impress friends with their daring and skill.[50] A colleague of mine told me that the teenagers who hung out at his local shopping mall had a "200 club": To be a member, a youth had to have shoplifted an item worth at least $200. (This was in the 1970s. Adjusting for inflation, it would today be something like the 400 club.) These were middle-class or even upper-middle-class teenagers, and, they were not necessarily unusual. Surveys of high school seniors find that nearly 30 percent have shoplifted in the last year, and nearly 10 percent have done it three times or more in that period.[51] Most of the time, these shoplifters do not try to convert their swag into cash, or if they do, they sell the items to friends or acquaintances, probably for a tiny percentage of the value.

Youths commit a substantial number of other thefts as well. In fact, 15-, 16-, and 17-year-olds, although making up perhaps 7 percent of the U.S. population, account for about 18 percent of all larceny arrests.[52] Accordingly, as the proportion of teenagers in the population decreases, we should find some predictable trends—especially in the area of opportunistic larceny for personal use. Bicycle theft, for example, should be especially sensitive to changes in the age structure of the population. Fewer young teenagers means both fewer kids who want to steal bicycles and fewer kids with bicycles to steal. As the baby boom children aged out of their teens between 1975 and 1986, the overall number of reported larcenies in the United States increased by 67 percent, but the number of bicycle thefts *decreased* from about 70,000 to about 48,000.[53] The smaller proportion of teenagers was only part of the decrease. The teenagers of the 1980s were not only fewer in number, but also less criminal than the baby boomers who preceded them. From 1975 to 1986, the percentage of high school seniors who said they had shoplifted dropped from 35.1 percent to 27.9 percent; the proportion who had done so three times or more fell from 14.3 percent to 8.9 percent.[54]

Besides these young and opportunistic thieves, more serious, professional criminals—boosters—also contribute to the larceny statistics. With theft, as with other crimes, several factors distinguish the more professional criminals from the opportunistic. Professionals use theft as a regular source of income. Therefore, their crimes often involve more planning and more sophisticated techniques. Professional shoplifters, for example, may have specially designed clothes or packages with compartments for hiding stolen items. Professionals also focus on the resale value of the item, not on how easily it can be taken or whether they personally want it.

Professionals also have a different self-concept. They think of themselves as criminals; opportunists do not. For this reason, the opportunistic shoplifter, when caught, may experience a social and psychological crisis. Perhaps by neutralization, or by mentally compartmentalizing the shoplifting, he or she might have been able to keep it from conflicting with a basically noncriminal self-concept. Other people, not knowing about the thefts, would confirm this good-citizen identity. Thus, the casual shoplifter could maintain a self-concept as a good, law-abiding person. Once caught, however, the snitch is forced to face a fact that utterly contradicts this self-concept, and the experience can be temporarily devastating.

> "This is a nightmare," said one woman pilferer who had been formally charged with stealing an expensive handbag. "It can't be happening to me! Why, oh why, can't I wake up and find that it isn't so," she cried later as she waited at a store exit, accompanied by a city and a store policeman, for the city police van to arrive. "Whatever will I do? Please make it go away," she pleaded with the officer. "I'll be disgraced forever. I can never look anyone in the face again."[55]

For professionals, by contrast, being caught is not likely to produce such a social and psychological crisis. They see arrest more as a technical problem to be solved than as a completely disorienting experience.

GOOD FENCES

Professional and casual thieves differ in their behavior not just when they are caught but when they are successful, too. A serious thief must have some way of converting stolen items into cash. Casual thieves sell their loot to friends or to local tradespeople. For the professional thief, however, these outlets are too irregular and uncertain a way of doing business. Most likely, he will take his swag to a fence, someone who buys and sells stolen goods. In official language, fences are called "receivers" because the crime they commit is officially known as "receiving stolen goods." Fences, much like retailers of legitimate goods, provide a crucial link between suppliers (in this case, thieves) and consumers. In fact, because fences create a market for stolen

One amateur fence we interviewed was a public-school teacher who began her part-time fencing when she was approached by a student who offered her a "really good deal" on certain items. She stated that the first time she bought something, she did so to help out the student, who had financial problems. Afterward, however, the student began to offer her bargains regularly and she became a frequent customer. Eventually she began to offer her colleagues the opportunity to "get in on a good deal" and even posted a note in the teachers' lounge stating:

> Need a TV, VCR, Microwave, Etc.????
>
> See me before you buy. 1/2 off retail.

She did not usually profit financially in this exchange, instead garnering the goodwill and appreciation of those to whom she afforded merchandise at well below wholesale prices. Although she admitted to the interviewer she "probably knew, deep down inside that the items were stolen," she had not admitted it to herself. In explaining her motivation for purchasing goods in such an unconventional manner, she ironically described these goods as "a real steal."

Source: Paul Cromwell, James N. Olson, and D'Aunn Wester Avary, *Breaking and Entering: An Ethnographic Analysis of Burglary* (Newbury Park, CA: Sage, 1991), p. 77.

---

goods, law-enforcement people have long thought that if fences could somehow be put out of business, property crimes would decrease dramatically.[56] With no reliable outlet for their goods, thieves and burglars would soon find their work unprofitable and move into other lines of work. As Henry Fielding put it nearly two centuries ago, "Nothing can be more just than the old observation, 'that if there were no receivers there would be no thieves.'"[57] (Note that even when Fielding wrote this in 1751, he acknowledged that it was already an "old observation.")

Since many people think fences are so pivotal in property crime, why doesn't the criminal justice system put them out of business? One part of the problem is that with fencing, as with theft, a large part of the market consists of small-time nonprofessionals. Some of these people may barter goods (like drugs) or services rather than pay cash. "A criminal defense attorney agreed to represent a burglar in a criminal prosecution, telling the client that he wanted a gold Rolex as his fee. [The burglar] later proudly displayed the watch to the interviewer, saying, 'This is a special order.'"[58] As a study of fencing in San Diego concluded, "Receivers of stolen property include a myriad of occasional receivers: the bartender at the neighborhood tavern, the gas station operator, the car salesman, the secondhand dealer, and the Sunday shopper at the swapmart."[59] Just as the arrest of occasional shoplifters will not take much of a bite out of the larceny rate, the arrest of these casual receivers, even if the arrest leads to conviction and imprisonment, will hardly affect the market for stolen goods.

Law enforcement is much more likely to focus on the professional fences, who provide an outlet for professional thieves and who handle stolen merchandise on a much larger scale. Yet despite the efforts of police and prosecutors, most fences manage to stay in business, operating at the intersection of legitimate and illegitimate worlds. That is, fencing is often only a part of an otherwise legitimate business. Consider the theft of car stereos—a form of larceny that has grown dramatically in the last ten or fifteen years. As noted, the increase occurred in part because of the increase in value of these stereos. The thieves, for the most part, are young males who need to get a little cash quickly to spend on the pleasures of the moment—drugs, food, liquor, movies, and so on. Stealing the stereo is simple enough, but then who can they sell it to? The most likely buyer is a store that sells car stereos and other car accessories. It certainly makes economic sense for the store owner to fence the merchandise. He or she pays the thieves a fraction of the dealer's usual cost, allowing for either greater profit or very attractive prices for customers. Without such stores to provide a regular market for stolen stereos, it is doubtful that the growth of this type of larceny would have continued for so long.

At the other end of the spectrum, financially speaking, are the fences for expensive items like jewelry and furs. Here, too, the fencing operation is often only part of a legitimate business. A jewelry store, for example, can sell items stolen from private homes or from other stores. Especially safe from prosecution is the jeweler who not only deals in finished pieces of jewelry but also buys and sells the actual gemstones. Once the jeweler removes the stones from their settings, they become very difficult to identify. Then, in trading with other dealers, he or she can easily include the stolen gems among those bought from legitimate sources.

A crucial element in a fence's success seems to be the legitimate front. Even fences who deal in a wider variety of merchandise will have a legitimate front that can cover this variety. For example, one of the widest-read and entertaining scholarly works on fences is Carl Klockars's case study of a man who ran a store that sold everything—clothes, luggage, electric appliances, toys, perfume, and so on.[60] The fence, to whom Klockars gave the pseudonym Vincent Swaggi, provided an outlet for all sorts of property crime—burglary, shoplifting, and employee theft. Burglars came to Vincent's store early in the morning, as did deliverymen who stole packages from their own trucks. Shoplifters came later in the day.

> Around half-past one, the boosters [shoplifters] start comin' in. Most of 'em work just a couple of hours a day. All of 'em work lunch time. That's when everything's so busy, customers shopping their lunch hours.... Things get so rushed the security guards don't know what they're doin'.... If I had a department store I'd keep a skeleton crew all day except for lunch hour. Then I'd flood the store with security.[61]

It is common knowledge around town that Vincent sells stolen merchandise, and he does nothing to change that image. It's good for business. "See, most people figure all of the stuff in my store is hot, which you know it ain't.... People figurin' they're gonna get something for nothing. You think I'm gonna tell 'em it ain't hot? Not on your life.... If they figure it's hot, you can't keep 'em away from it."[62]

STAYING FREE

If everyone, including police and prosecutors, knows that Vincent is a fence, how does he stay out of prison? There is an uneasy but symbiotic relationship among the three sides in this game—thief, fence, and law enforcement. Vincent, for example, counts among his regular customers several police officers, detectives, insurance adjusters, and even a judge or two. Besides offering bargain prices to law-enforcement people, the fence may also "take care of" them with outright bribes and payoffs. As a fence (not Vincent) puts it, "You can't be a dealer...without the police knowing and being taken care of. You can't operate without their cooperation. One way or another, they have to give you some slack, really a license to steal."[63]

Other fence and law-enforcement relationships may be more complicated. Fencing is a victimless crime, so neither buyer nor seller is going to complain to the police. But this also means that both buyer and seller know about each other's criminal activity. The police, therefore, can put pressure on a fence to inform on thieves. It's a convenient exchange: The fence gets a continued license to operate; the police get information that will make their arrest records look good.

> Makes the detective look good and the chief, too, 'cause in the public's mind they're solving all those crimes. It's all bullsh—. What they do is get the fence to snitch on a few burglars or a couple of dopers. And the ones the fence is turning in are usually ... the penny-ante thieves.... They will end up admitting crimes they didn't even do.[64]

Police officers can also pressure thieves to inform on fences, although arresting and convicting them may be another matter. The lack of a complainant makes the state's job more difficult. In addition for the state to convict a fence, it must prove that the goods were stolen and that they were in his possession. Fences can make such proof hard to establish. They can avoid possession by using a "drop" (some storage place that they do not own) until they are ready to sell the merchandise. As for the requirement that the fence knew (or could reasonably be expected to know) that the goods were stolen,[65] here, too, fences have some effective maneuvers. Vincent explains:

> Look, you got a store, I got a store. Some shine [thief] takes a load of merchandise from you and sells it to me. Even if detectives find out it's me that's got it, how you gonna know it's yours? Say it's suits, Botany suits. How are you gonna know they're yours? I got Botanys, you got Botanys, every store in town's got Botanys....
>
> Now of course, if you got suits nobody else is supposed to have, say Sears or Macy's, then you just cut the labels off and you own 'em. And there ain't a thing nobody can do once you got those labels off.

Vincent also uses his legitimate dealings to provide "proof" that can cover his illegitimate ones.

> Suppose some detectives come in and say somethin' I got ain't legit.... Chances are I got a bill for it. [How?] Look, how many things you think I buy legitimate, with bills, each year? Hundreds! I gotta keep all those bills, you know, for Uncle Sam. So two months ago I bought 75 suits at auction. You know what that bill says, "One Lot of Suits Sold to Vincent Swaggi, Paid in Full." It don't matter what those detectives have on their warrant then. Those suits are mine.
>
> I do that with bills a lot. Like a while ago I had a guy bringin' me electric razors and hot combs. Every day or so he'd bring me a dozen of each. So what did I do? I bought two dozen legitimate from the supplier he was workin' for. Now, if there's a backup, I'm covered.[66]

To prove that the fence bought the goods and knew they were stolen, the police may have to rely on the testimony of an informer, usually the person who stole the goods. The trouble is that burglars and thieves do not make good witnesses. They may be very valuable to the government for information, but for convicting fences they leave much to be desired. How much faith will a jury place in the word of a thief, who probably has a long record of arrests, convictions, and prison terms? To quote Vincent again, "See, that's my rule in court.... Swaggi's rule is always go after the informant. He's probably a rat bastard and the cops ain't gonna take no chances puttin' him on the stand."[67]

THE STING

In recent years, the police have introduced some variations in the strategy of setting a thief to catch a fence and vice versa. They have themselves set up **sting** operations, in which undercover cops pose as fences to attract criminals eager to sell stolen goods. They rent a warehouse, put out the word that they are in business, and wait for the thieves to come. The police secretly videotape each deal, and when they have accumulated enough evidence on enough criminals, they start making arrests.

These **buy-and-bust operations** have provided some interesting information. For example, they confirm popular ideas about the kinds of items thieves look for: The most frequently fenced items are cars, electronic goods, credit cards, jewelry, and silverware. But the police have also found that thieves, given a potential market, will steal just about anything. Stings have been offered everything from a 250-pound lion to nerve gas stolen from a government arsenal. Sting operations have proven highly effective in catching thieves and burglars—even (or perhaps especially) career criminals. A single operation will usually net between 100 and 300 criminals, most with prior arrests. Because the witnesses are police officers and because the evidence is on videotape, these sting arrests are far more likely than others to result in conviction. One Detroit sting, for example, recovered $3.3 million of stolen property and arrested 176 people. In court, only 8 percent of the cases were dismissed, compared with nearly 50 percent under ordinary conditions (see Chapter Fourteen). The other 92 percent, with no reduction in charges, all pleaded guilty.

For the police and courts, who are interested in catching crooks, the operation was highly successful. But for ordinary citizens interested in the safety of their property, the results were less clear: Although 162 of Detroit's serious burglars and thieves wound up behind bars, rates of property crimes did not go down. Sting operations in several other cities have produced similar results: many arrests and convictions, much stolen property recovered, and no reduction in crime.

Other stings have taken Fielding's advice to heart and have aimed at fences rather than thieves. Antifencing stings involve a slight change in the script: police posing as thieves with loot for sale. These **sell-and-bust operations** turn out much like the buy-and-bust stings. The police officers arrest the fences and the courts convict them, but rates of property crimes remain unchanged.[68]

The inability of the police to reduce theft, even using these undercover methods, brings us back to the idea that rates of property crimes are more than just a matter of the number of bad people in the population. They also indicate the profitability of property crimes. Police strategies are designed to affect chiefly the supply side by removing thieves from the population. These tactics have failed to lower crime rates probably because they can reach only a very small proportion of those who steal. At the opportunistic end of the scale, the millions of teenagers who swipe things are unlikely to be much affected by stings or any other type of police effort. Target-hardening measures such as car alarms or store detectives or better bicycle locks may deter some opportunistic theft, or they may just displace the theft to easier targets. In any case, most of these young, opportunistic thieves will age out of property crime just as the preteens coming behind them will age into it, though the criminality of each generation may be different. We don't really know why teenagers of the late 1980s were less criminal than those of a decade earlier. At the other end of the scale, the police may be able to arrest and convict career criminals, but if the market for stolen goods continues to provide a demand for the services of criminals, other enterprising thieves apparently move in to take up the slack. In fact, some observers think that sting operations, in creating a market for just about anything thieves bring in, may actually amplify theft rather than reduce it.[69]

Motor Vehicle Theft

The American love affair with the automobile began around the turn of the century and has continued unflaggingly ever since. Today, there are over 180 million private motor vehicles registered in the United States, an average of more than two vehicles for every three people in the country (including babies).[70] In 1985, 12 percent of all consumer spending was for buying and maintaining these vehicles—a total of $320 billion (about twelve times as much as consumer spending on all other forms of transportation).[71]

The invention of the auto also meant the creation of a new crime—auto theft. As the horse gradually gave way to the auto, the horse thief came to be replaced by the auto thief. And in the early years, stealing an automobile was not much more difficult than stealing a horse. There was no need to worry about locked doors because there were no car doors, at least not until after the turn of the century. Nor did thieves have to worry about having a key to start the motor; they just had to turn the crank in front and go. Nor was there any system of registration or serial numbers that would allow victims to identify their cars. It was not until the 1920s that states began to use the certificate of title to keep track of a car's ownership.[72]

COUNTING VEHICLE THEFTS

In 1993, the number of reported motor vehicle thefts in the United States was 1,561,047. Of all the Index crimes, except perhaps murder, this count is the most accurate, especially if we consider only the completed thefts. The UCR definition of motor vehicle theft includes attempts as well as completed thefts. Attempts account for about 15 percent of all reported auto thefts. People whose cars are stolen call the police—and for obvious reasons. In any type of crime, the greater the loss, the more likely people are to report it, and a car is a costly item. In addition, car-theft victims want to have an official police report to file an insurance claim or to be on record in case the police find the car. So while the reporting rate for most other crimes is about 50 percent, the reporting rate for completed auto theft is nearly 90 percent (attempts are reported only about 45 percent of the time).[73]

The real problem in computing motor vehicle theft rates is not the accuracy of the numerator of the fraction but the choice of a denominator. The UCR computes the rate per 100,000 population. The NCVS bases its rate on the number of households. However, basing the rate on either population or households may be misleading, especially for comparing times and places that may differ widely in the number of cars available to steal. Insurance companies compute the rate a third way. When they estimate risks, they use a rate based on the number of registered vehicles. These different ways of computing rates can lead to different results, as shown in Table 7-1. In the time period used in the table, police reports show a large increase in motor vehicle theft, the national victimization survey shows a fairly large decrease, and the

TABLE 7-1 •
CHANGES IN MOTOR VEHICLE THEFT RATES, 1973–1985

SOURCE OF INFORMATION	1973	1985	PERCENT CHANGE
UNIFORM CRIME REPORTS (PER 100,000 POPULATION)	442.6	462.0	+4.4
NATIONAL CRIME VICTIMIZATION SURVEY (PER 1,000 HOUSEHOLDS)	19.2	14.2	-26.0
NATIONAL AUTO THEFT BUREAU (PER 100,000 VEHICLES)	771.7	622.6	-12.5

Source: Timothy J. Flanagan and Katherine M. Jamieson, eds., *Sourcebook of Criminal Justice Statistics—1987* (U.S. Department of Justice, Bureau of Justice Statistics, Washington, DC: USGPO, 1988).

National Auto Theft Bureau (NATB, an arm of the insurance industry) shows a moderate decrease.

Understanding these differences is important in thinking clearly about the causes and prevention of auto theft. Obviously, the rates depend on the number of people willing to steal cars, but they are just as clearly a matter of opportunity. The more opportunity (i.e., the more households to steal from, the more cars to steal), the more theft.

JOYRIDING

The oldest and most common type of car theft is joyriding. Typically, two to four people—usually teenage boys—will steal a car; drive it around for a while; and then abandon it, sometimes not far from where they took it. The motives and explanation for the crime are transparent. It's a classic instance of anomie theory (see Chapter Eleven): Unequally distributed opportunities do not allow some people to achieve socially induced goals; some of these people then take illegitimate means to attain them.

In this case, the goal is driving, which undoubtedly is socially induced. Detroit and Madison Avenue spend billions of dollars each year to convey the message that a car is the most desirable thing in the world. The automobile is a symbol of independence, excitement, sex, and power. This not too subtle message may be especially alluring to the teenage boy eager to latch on to symbols of adult status. The effects can be read in the statistics on theft rates for different cars. Late-model Firebirds, Camaros, and other sporty cars have theft rates several times the national average. A Chevy wagon, especially if it's a few years old, is much less likely to be an object of envy for potential joyriders. Younger teenagers often lack legitimate means to this culturally valued goal: Economics denies many teenagers the ability to own a car, parents may deny them the use of a car, and laws deny them the right to drive a car. With legitimate paths closed, several hundred thousand American teenagers each year resort to illegitimate means to motor machismo: They steal a car. Little wonder that auto theft—especially joyriding—increased when the children of the baby boom reached their early teens.

There is a second type of opportunistic car theft: short-term transportation. The thieves steal a car not for the thrill of driving but to get from one place to another. Most thefts of this type are probably committed by teenagers who feel that there is no other convenient way of making the trip. In other, more serious cases, the thief may drive to another city or state and steal yet another car to continue his journey; he often leaves a trail of incidents in which he purchases gasoline and leaves the station without paying.[74]

FROM JOYRIDING TO PROFESSIONAL THEFT

Although we cannot be certain of the exact proportion of motor vehicle theft attributable to the opportunists, the best indicator we have is the percentage of stolen cars that are recovered. When professionals steal a car, it's gone for good.

When opportunists steal a car, it is more likely to be recovered. In fact, the NCVS estimates that in about one car theft in twelve, the offenders themselves return the car to the owner.[75] In the 1960s, over four-fifths of all stolen cars were recovered. By the early 1980s, that figure had dropped to about 53 percent,[76] and clearance rates fell from 25 percent to 15 percent. (Not all recovered cars are stolen by joyriders. In a few cases, professional criminals will steal a car for use in a robbery or burglary, then abandon it.) These statistics almost certainly reflect a change in the type of auto theft—from joyriding to professional crime.

Several factors caused this transition. First, demographic change undoubtedly played a part. Auto theft, perhaps more than other crimes, may have been sensitive to changes in the age structure of the population. The end of the baby boom, the year when birthrates started to decline, was 1957. Seventeen years later, the last of the baby boomers were finally passing out of their joyriding years. Second, opportunistic criminals by definition are those who commit a crime because it is easy. Up until the 1960s, stealing a car was very easy. A substantial number of people left their cars unlocked, often with the keys in the ignition. Locked cars were not much more of a problem. With equipment no more sophisticated than a coat hanger, any teenager could get into the car of his choice. Once inside the car, the thief could start the motor by crossing the ignition wires, which were within easy reach under the dashboard. This knowledge was part of teen culture. I grew up in a very low-crime suburb, and most of my upper-middle-class friends would discuss how to hot-wire a car, though I suspect that few of them used this knowledge to actually steal one.

As auto-theft rates increased, car manufacturers, car owners, and insurance companies all took steps to deter the casual car thief. Insurers pressured car owners to lock their cars, and manufacturers made locks more difficult to open without a key. They also began to install various kinds of steering-wheel locks, so that even if a thief managed to start the engine the car would still be undrivable. The previously loose ignition wires were now encased in the steering column. All these target-hardening devices served to deter the purely opportunistic, spur-of-the-moment thief. For the rest, it simply meant a few more sophisticated tools—a "slim jim" instead of a coat hanger, a special tool to remove the ignition switch from the steering column, and a screwdriver to start the ignition.

But the most important factor in the transition to professional auto theft was the creation of a market. It was a question of demand and supply. Before the 1960s, the demand for stolen cars was low. The person who stole a car could not do much with it besides drive it around for a while. He could not sell it as he might other stolen goods, for cars were easily traced. They had serial numbers, and they had to be registered with the state, with the appropriate license plates. A car couldn't be kept out of sight, like a television in the living room, nor could it be sold to a pawn shop, like stolen jewelry or furs.

THE MARKETPLACE: DEMAND AND SUPPLY

The late 1960s saw the expansion of two markets for auto theft: "new" cars for resale and auto parts. The demand for stolen cars increased, and suppliers (i.e., thieves) increased their output accordingly. The resale market also demanded a slightly different type of thief. Selling a stolen car to a consumer requires techniques and personal connections beyond those of the joyrider. It requires, first, that the car not be damaged during the theft, so professional thieves for this market need special skills and equipment. Second, the resale market also requires someone who can provide registration papers and someone who can find customers. Existing criminal organizations meet both these needs. Their other criminal dealings—loan-sharking, gambling, higher-level fencing—bring them into a network of people who don't mind buying merchandise of questionable origin. Of course, even many otherwise legitimate people might be unable to resist the offer of a nearly new Cadillac at half price. Criminal organizations can also obtain the necessary documents either by bribing people within the motor vehicle bureaucracy, by hiring skilled forgers, or by a method known as the salvage switch. "Salvage" cars are those that have been "totaled"; that is, the cost of repair would be higher than the car's book value. In the salvage switch, the criminals buy (cheaply) a salvage car of the same make and model as the stolen one. They do not want the car itself; they want the title and the vehicle identification number, which they then switch to the stolen car.

The business of theft and resale was so organized and the thieves so professional that they adopted the just-in-time system of supply long before it became fashionable in other industries. Rather than stealing cars randomly or on speculation, thieves would wait for an order from a dealer. Usually, they can find and steal a nearly new model to order (e.g., a dark green four-door Cadillac) more quickly than one can be supplied legitimately by Detroit—often in a matter of days. Some thieves keep a log of available cars. A thief might note that a late-model Buick Riviera is parked regularly in a particular lot. He records this information so that when he gets an order for such a car, he can consult his log and know where and when to find it.[77]

Although the market for stolen cars already existed to some extent before 1970, it was relatively small and confined mostly to the Northeast. When I first started looking at the UCR in the mid-1970s, I noticed that some cities with low rates for all other Index crimes had among the highest rates of motor vehicle theft—cities like Boston; Brockton, Massachusetts; Worcester, Massachusetts; and Providence, Rhode Island. Could New England teenagers be so fond of joyriding? I confess, it took me a while to figure out what was going on. Since then, organized auto theft has expanded, even to include overseas outlets, where cars stolen in the United States are unlikely to be discovered. Consequently, major port cities have been experiencing increasing thefts of these high-priced cars, which are often shipped to foreign countries. The advent of containerization has made it easier for criminals to export stolen cars. A 40-foot container, which can hold two cars, can be loaded and sealed anywhere in the country and then sent by truck or rail to a port. From there, the container, still sealed, can be loaded onto a ship and sent anywhere in the world (though Europe and the Middle East seem to be the most popular destinations). Although there is no way of knowing precisely how large this industry is, U.S. customs officials estimate that about 200,000 stolen vehicles (15 percent of all vehicles stolen in the United States) are exported each year.[78]

CHOP SHOPS

While the market for cut-rate luxury cars was expanding, another market for stolen cars was developing even more rapidly: the market for auto parts. It expanded on the supply side because thieves came to realize that parts were worth something, but other changes contributed to the demand side of the equation—changes in the noncriminal world. Americans were keeping their cars longer, fixing the old cars rather than buying new ones. Cars were becoming more complicated; parts that a mechanic might once have repaired now had to be replaced. In addition, legitimate parts became harder to get. For economic reasons, legitimate dealers cut back on their inventories, preferring to order parts from Detroit as the need arose. So repair shops calling a dealer for some part might find they had to wait two weeks. (To speed up the search, repair shops and salvage yards now have a network, called "the long line," for matching up those who need some part with those who have that part. Of

Without chop shops to provide a steady market, the for-profit sector of motor vehicle theft would probably shrink. Joy riding would, of course, be unaffected.

course, illegitimate suppliers can also subscribe to the "long line" and offer the needed part faster than the legitimate competition.)[79] As a result, the price of parts increased—so much so that the resale value of a used or even new car broken down for parts was often more than that of the car itself. The parts market has also made older cars more desirable as targets of theft. While joyriders go after newer cars, professionals keep their eyes on older models. In 1991, the most frequently stolen cars were those made in 1987 and 1986.[80]

The market in parts provided an enormous advantage to those with criminal inclinations. Stealing a car had always been fairly easy, but state requirements about documents made selling it difficult. However, it was fairly easy to sell stolen car parts. License and registration papers might be necessary for a 1980 Chevy but not for a 1980 Chevy transmission or door panel. The potential market in stolen parts was nearly all there—the potential supply of stolen cars and the potential demand for stolen parts. All that was missing was someone to match the supply and the demand, that is, someone who would reduce the stolen car into parts. So in time, at this central point in the market there emerged a new type of business—the **chop shop**.

A chop shop is essentially a fence operation; it buys and sells stolen goods. The only difference is that after it buys a stolen car, the chop shop quickly breaks it down into component parts. Jewel thieves or fences take similar precautions, removing valuable gems from their settings and thus making identification nearly impossible. Like other kinds of fences, the chop shop owner often trades in legitimate merchandise as well, thus providing a cover for the illegal side of his business, and typical of fencing, several others may be in the know. The employees who do the actual chopping and the buyers of the shop's reasonably priced parts probably know or at least suspect what's going on, and they are all part of the network that sustains the crime. However, the people who benefit the most—the chop shop owners—take the least risk. A few owners steal cars themselves, but most pay others—usually teenagers—to do this more exposed and riskier part of the work. The actual thief might get a few hundred dollars for a car whose parts will bring the chop shop anywhere from $500 to $2,500, depending on their condition.[81]

OTHER VEHICLES

Although cars make up the bulk of stolen vehicles, there has been a growing market in off-road vehicles—tractors, bulldozers, and farm machinery. The thief may find it somewhat more difficult to drive off in one of these big pieces of equipment, and there may be fewer potential buyers. But for the thief who can solve these problems, off-road vehicles make attractive targets. First, most off-road machinery does not require registration or title documents, and manufacturers do not have a uniform system of identification numbers. Once stolen, a tractor or log-skidder may be hard to identify, and the victim may have a difficult time proving ownership. Second, these pieces of industrial equipment are obviously much more expensive than cars. You may not know what a log-skidder is (I don't), but whatever it is, it costs upward of $100,000. A good bulldozer may be worth as much as half a dozen new Cadillacs. The value of all on-road vehicles stolen in 1987 was about $6.4 billion. That year, the value of all off-road vehicles (not including farm equipment) was $1 billion.[82]

INSURANCE FRAUD

Of the nearly 1.3 million reported motor vehicle thefts each year, perhaps as many as 190,000 have not really been stolen. Instead, the owner is filing a false report for an insurance claim. The insurance industry claims that fraudulent property and casualty claims cost more than $20 billion each year, two and one-half times the value of all stolen cars. Who are these fraud artists? Some of them are people who deliberately set out to maximize their profits through fraud. They buy a popular car, making a low down payment, export the car for sale overseas, and then report it stolen. In most "owner give-ups," however, the owners committing insurance fraud are not professional criminals. Instead, they are car owners who for one reason or another want the insurance money more than they want their cars. In New York City in 1988, for example, an investigation of insurance fraud resulted in the arrests of thirty people, among them executives, a respiratory therapist, a carpenter, a student, a secretary, and a homemaker. People like these turn to fraud for a variety of reasons. Some need cash, others have run into payment problems, and some just want to avoid the trouble of selling an unwanted car. In some cases, the owner is stuck with a lemon; tired of trying to get the car repaired, he or she arranges to give up the car, report it stolen, and file an insurance claim for a car in good condition. Some owners will add claims for a set of golf clubs or a fur coat that supposedly had been in the trunk of the stolen car.

These one-time defrauders may rationalize their act with the argument that unlike real auto theft, their scheme doesn't really hurt anyone. Of course, on the insurance company's bottom line, a claim paid is a claim paid, whether the theft was real or fraudulent. Then the insurer, through higher rates, passes its costs on to consumers. Still, most of these people probably do not think of themselves as criminals, and since they do not belong to groups that serve to reinforce their neutralizations, they may be easily deterred. For example, to reduce fraud, the Houston police instituted two small changes: They refused to take auto-theft reports by phone, so the victim had to file the claim face-to-face with a police officer; also the officer reminded victims that if the report proved false, they could be charged with theft. Theft reports dropped by 10 percent.[83] (Actually, proving false claims beyond a reasonable doubt is very difficult, a fact unknown to most of the one-time, nonprofessional criminals.)

Insurance fraud still leaves room for professional criminals, who act as middlemen. For a fee, they take the car and assure the owner that it will not be seen again. The middleman then hires a disposer to get rid of the car. Lakes and rivers are popular disposal sites since even if the car is eventually found, the water may have corroded it beyond recognition. Says one Florida official, "We have a 55-foot deep canal around here that gets filled up with cars at least once a year. The cars are stacked so high that a diver can stand on the top one, and he will be out of the water from the waist up."[84]

Summary and conclusion

Burglary, larceny, and motor vehicle theft account for nearly 90 percent of the serious crimes on the FBI's Index of crimes reported to the police and about 85 percent of all crimes reported in victimization surveys. The crimes vary from the trivial to the very serious. Because the motivation in property crime is largely economic, I have tried to look at the rates for these crimes both in terms of the criminals (the supply of criminal labor) and the opportunities for profit (the demand).

Increases in property crime reflect, at least in part, an increase in the opportunity for profitable stealing. Opportunity has three important components: the amount of stealable property, the ease of stealing it, and the existence of a market for converting the stolen property to cash. The first two elements depend almost entirely on the actions of law-abiding people. If more of them stock their houses with more VCRs and jewelry, and if more of them leave those houses empty during the day, they are creating more opportunities for burglary. The third element—the market for stolen goods—often depends on people who straddle the criminal and noncriminal world. They are the fences whose legitimate business provides a cover for traffic in stolen goods. Ultimately, the market must also be provided by consumers who are eager to take advantage of low prices, regardless of their suspicions (or knowledge) about the origins of the merchandise. Remember, some of Vincent Swaggi's best customers were police officers.

Of course, most of us more-or-less law-abiding citizens rarely think of ourselves as part of the crime problem. Crime is what "they" do. But occasionally we can get a closer view of crime as a free-enterprise market, and the invisible hand of supply-and-demand becomes a bit easier to see. For example, a student came up to me after class one day when I had discussed the idea of the demand for crime. He said that he had once bought a stolen Fuzzbuster (a radar detector). Only a few months later, his own car was broken into; the thief took the radar detector *and* the car stereo. It made the student realize the contribution he himself had made to car break-ins. "After that," he said, "I swore I'd never buy anything stolen again"; he added proudly that he bought his next radar detector from a legitimate source. I praised his honest policy, not bothering to mention that a radar detector, whatever its source, has only one purpose: to help people break the law.

On the other side of the equation are those who commit the crimes. They range from the opportunistic to the professional. Although the professionals—highly skilled, selective, and profit-oriented—make for more interesting stories, the bulk of property crimes are committed by criminals toward the opportunistic end of the scale. They spend little time in planning and make little money from their crimes. Many are younger people who commit property crimes but who quit in their late teens. Of those who remain in crime, a few become more professional in their attitudes and methods. Most, however, do not. They continue in their minimally planned, low-profit crimes and eventually wind up in prison.

Controlling property crime has proven a difficult task. Some strategies—such as target hardening or moving far from poor neighborhoods—may be effective for the individual. Good locks and other security devices may be enough to deter the casual criminal. But these strategies are unlikely to change the overall rate of crime in the society. Unfortunately, the policies available to the criminal justice system also seem to have only a modest effect, if any, on rates of property crime. Sting operations that aim at career thieves or at fences have been successful in arresting and even convicting these targets, but they have had no demonstrable effect on the rate of crime.

CRITICAL THINKING QUESTIONS

1. What makes a crime more opportunistic or more professional, and how well do these categories apply to the criminals who commit the crimes?
2. What role do noncriminals play in property crime?
3. What role do fences play in property crime; if fences occupy the central point in the economics of property crime, why have law enforcement officials been unable to do much about them?
4. Property crime is a largely economic enterprise. How do the laws of supply and demand apply? What is the demand for crime, and who creates it?

KEY TERMS

booster

buy and bust operations

chop shop

fence

good burglar

journeyman

opportunistic burglars

professional criminals

sell and bust operations

snitch

sting

CHAPTER EIGHT

ORGANIZED CRIME

CHAPTER OUTLINE

What is organized crime? For most topics in this book, I have skipped the formal definitions. They would have been unnecessary and, for the most part, irrelevant. It's pretty clear what stealing and burglary and murder are. Of course, for any crime there will be cases at the fringe. Is "assisted suicide" murder? how is "unauthorized use" different from "auto theft"? But these legal curiosities and distinctions are more relevant for lawyers than for criminologists. For most crimes our everyday concept is sufficient, and we need not worry about differentiating first-degree robbery from second-degree robbery or second-degree murder from voluntary manslaughter. We are interested in the broader categories—homicide or robbery—and most of the acts that fit the legal definition will also correspond to our everyday notion of these crimes.

Not so with organized crime. Legal definitions of organized crime are often so vague that they could include almost anything. They usually stress that organized crime is a pattern of crime (usually defined as two or more criminal acts) committed by more than one person. But these criteria are far too loose. They do not allow us to distinguish the Mafia from a group of kids who commit a few break-ins. This definition puts the Medellin cartel into the same category as a stock brokerage that violates some minor securities regulations. Of course, government lawyers may find that this broad definition greatly enhances their prosecutorial powers, but for criminological analysis we need a definition that can make better distinctions.

One obvious difference between a Mafia family and a burglary gang is permanence. The true criminal organization is institutionalized, not just organ-

Is the Mafia an anti-Italian myth? Clearly, John Gotti was more than just a plumbing-supplies sales representative. But many other ethnic groups have spawned their own independent criminal organizations. None, though, has approached the Mafia in its quasi-governmental capacity for settling disputes between organizations or individuals.

ized. It exists above and beyond the participation of any single member or group of members. It has different positions that will be filled if someone leaves—just like a baseball team. The Yankees are still the Yankees even though the names in the starting lineup are completely different from the roster of only a few years ago. So, too, in criminal organizations, individual members may leave, but the organization goes on. For example, what is called the Gambino family was until 1993 headed by a man named Gotti, and the Genovese family may no longer have any Genoveses in it (at least not in the top positions). However, permanence cannot be the only criterion since legitimate businesses, too, are institutionalized. We want a good definition of organized crime to distinguish between the Genovese family and General Motors.

Current laws do not make such a distinction. The most important statute in this area is a federal law known as **RICO** (Racketeer Influenced and Corrupt Organizations), passed in 1970. Under RICO, an organization that has engaged in a pattern of criminal acts (two or more crimes in a ten-year period) is subject to harsh penalties. The law was designed to make it easier for the government to prosecute organized crime, but it has also been used in various civil and criminal cases against companies like Shearson/American Express, Lloyd's of London, E. F. Hutton, and General Motors. RICO has been the basis of cases against antiabortion protesters, and it has been used by at least one woman in a divorce case.[1] Apparently, prosecutors or judges have used RICO as a very broad net to bring in a wide variety of offenders. Indeed, in some cases, notably some of the savings-and-loan (S&L) failures, the crimes of supposedly respectable people and organizations greatly resembled those of traditional organized crime groups.[2] For most purposes, however, we would prefer a definition that can distinguish between white-collar crime and organized crime.

Separating the gangsters from the stockbrokers is harder than it seems at first, as the history of RICO shows. For example, the financial firm of Drexel, Burnham, Lambert pleaded guilty to violations of the RICO law, but we do not really think of the firm as a corrupt organization, nor do we think of their executives and other employees as racketeers. One possible difference is that for the crime family, crime is its primary means of income. Merrill, Lynch brokers, in contrast, may have violated SEC (Security and Exchange Committee) regulations, but the company still makes most of its money legally. However, what of legal businesses that are dominated by organized crime? For example, in the New York City area, most private garbage collectors belong to a cartel—an association of businesses. The cartel divides up the territory and allocates sections to each member. Members do not compete against one another, so each member can charge higher prices in its sector. As a result, the cartel makes substantial excess profits, of which it pays a small percentage to the local Mafia.[3] Is the cartel part of organized crime? Most New Yorkers (including those in law enforcement) would say yes. Few people, on the other hand, consider Texaco or Shell Oil to be part of organized crime. Yet for many years the oil industry in the United States was dominated by a similar cartel arrangement, with the similar effect of high corporate profits at the expense of the consumer.[4]

Besides the size and permanence of the organization and its reliance on crime for income, the most significant and troubling aspect of organized crime is its use of violence. The large oil companies may have conspired to divide up

IN THE NEWS

In the 1980s, law-enforcement officials saw that it would take more than prosecution to break up the garbage cartel; it would take competition. They invited the top waste companies in the country to enter the New York hauling market. Waste Management, Inc., the largest, declined. But Browning-Ferris, second with annual revenues over $3 billion, decided to dip a toe into the possibly shark-infested waters.

BROWNING FERRIS BUCKS MOB, WARILY HAULS NEW YORK CITY TRASH

New York—If Browning-Ferris Industries Inc. thought breaking into the trash-hauling business here would be easy, that notion vanished in February.

Dumped on the suburban doorstep of...a company executive was a dog's severed head. In its mouth was a note: "Welcome to New York."

The entry of Browning-Ferris—despite such threats—did bring some competition to the market, and some customers even doubted that it was the Mafia who actually controlled the old cartel.

"I hope Browning-Ferris is here to stay," says Michael Downey of Mendik Realty Co., which has been aggressive in winning price cuts of 30% to 40% on trash bills. New York haulers, "would like you to believe they're connected [to organized crime] when they're in negotiations," Mr. Downey says. "But basically, they're just shrewd businessmen. They set up this whole cartel."

The New York cartel may have been violating antitrust laws,

but Browning-Ferris, the city's white knight, had similar tarnish on its armor, and some of its executive dialogue seems to have been scripted by Don Corleone.

The small-fry haulers accuse Browning-Ferris of having a "sordid reputation as ruthless, unscrupulous competitors," and they frequently cite its history of price-fixing and environmental violations. Browning-Ferris paid $30.5 million in a 1991 settlement of an antitrust lawsuit. And, trying to run a small Vermont hauler out of business, a Browning-Ferris executive told an underling, "Squish him like a bug," according to 1987 testimony in federal court in Burlington; the company was ordered to pay $6 in antitrust damages.

Source: Jeff Bailey, "Too Good to Refuse," *Wall Street Journal*, November 8, 1993, pp. A1, A6.

---

the market and fix prices; they may even have used their financial power to drive competitors out of business; but they did not use violence to create and enforce their cartel. The garbage cartel is another matter. On Long Island, for example, a single garbage hauler tried to compete against the cartel, offering lower bids and better service. At first, the cartel director encouraged him to join and share in the benefits of the cartel, but the independent hauler refused. Eventually, some of his trucks were sabotaged. When government prosecutors began investigating the cartel, he cooperated by providing information. Then, a year or so later, with the close scrutiny of the investigation past, he was murdered.[5] Of course, actual violence is the exception, not the rule. But the threat is always there, even when the gangsters make no explicit statements or even suggestions. The person who borrows money from a loan shark in a criminal organization knows that violence, although unlikely, is still a possible risk of not repaying.

To summarize: Organized crime involves large, long-standing organizations with diversified roles for its members; a criminal organization derives much of its income from crime; and it relies on violence, real or potential, to accomplish its goals. Some criminologists add a fourth element: corruption. Certainly, organized crime usually goes hand in hand with the corruption of government and police, but some criminal organizations do not participate. For example, biker gangs may derive much income from drug deals without paying off politicians or police officers. In any case, any definition will have flaws, and I am offering this one not as a perfect system for classifying all possible cases but as a help in understanding similarities and differences among criminal groups.

Mafia or myth?

The media often use *organized crime* and *Mafia* interchangeably, along with a variety of other terms: *the underworld, gangland, the syndicate, the mob, racketeers,* and *La Cosa Nostra.* Whether the story is tragedy (*The Godfather*), comedy (*Married to the Mob*), or history (John Gotti on the evening news), the media convey the impression that organized crime *is* the Mafia. However, in the definition I am using, organized crime includes not only the Mafia but other criminal organizations as well. Indeed, there are many such groups. What remains a matter of debate is the relative importance of the Mafia compared with these other organizations. The media, even when they recognize the existence of other criminal groups, still portray the Mafia as the largest, most powerful, most highly organized, and wealthiest criminal organization. In this picture, other criminal organizations are either dependent on the Mafia or exist only with its consent. They do not compete with the Mafia.

Opposed to this view are the critics who claim that the Mafia is a myth, an invention of law enforcement and the media, which also happen to be our principal sources of information about the Mafia. The critics question both the accuracy and the motives of these sources, for far from being neutral and disinterested, they derive much benefit from the **Mafia myth**. By building up the enemy as a single, giant criminal conspiracy, the police, FBI, prosecutors, and other law-enforcement agencies make their job look more important.

The media, for their part, are almost completely dependent on the police and prosecutors for their information. If a federal prosecutor tells reporters that someone is a captain in a crime family, reporters usually have no independent way of verifying this claim. In addition, the media, too, prefer big news. A story about a "godfather" far outweighs a story about ordinary criminals. And a story about a "boss of all bosses" is bigger news than a story about a gang leader.[6]

If information from law-enforcement and media sources is tainted, the other source of information—testimony from former members of the Mafia—is even less credible. These people are usually fairly low in the ranks and often do not have accurate information about activities elsewhere in the organization. They also may not be the most truthful of souls and may, for a variety of

IN THE NEWS

Under current law, a person who is granted immunity and still refuses to testify before a grand jury may be jailed for contempt of court. Such grand jury investigations, with the grants of immunity, are the principal way the government gets information and builds cases involving organized crime. Note also that the mother's statement at the end of the following excerpt exemplifies one of the stereotypes about the link between Italians and organized crime: that Italian-Americans uphold Italian cultural traditions even when these violate the laws and interfere with law enforcement. ("Basta" is Italian for "enough.")

KANSAS CITY GROUP FIGHTS JAILING OF 20

Kansas City, Mo.—It started with a banner with the words BASTA! BASTA! waving from a small airplane over Arrowhead Stadium during a Kansas City Chiefs football game.... Within a month the two-word message began appearing on T-shirts and billboards and at the steps of the Federal courthouse in demonstrations.

It is the slogan of the newly formed Kansas City Council Against Discrimination. The 850-member group banded together to oppose the jailing of 20 men, almost all Italian-Americans, who refused to testify about organized crime before a grand jury even though they were granted immunity from prosecution....

Kansas City has been well known for its organized crime since the 1930s.... In recent years there have been investigations of prostitution, extortion, and drug trafficking. An earlier investigation led to the conviction of 26 men on gambling charges.

But the most recent investigation has unified the city's small, close-knit Italian-American community as never before. The community recently began a public relations campaign calling the contempt cases a form of prosecutorial discrimination against Italian-Americans....

"I feel like they're abusing their authority," said Anna Marie Sciortino, whose son, Tom, is in jail. "They think he knows something about their investigation. I am proud of my son that he has stuck up for the teachings that you don't rat on anybody."

Source: New York Times, October 29, 1991, p. A22.

reasons, embellish or even invent stories. They may want to inflate their own importance or the importance of their former colleagues, they may be trying to tell the story the way they think the authorities want to hear it, or they may themselves be paying more attention to the myth than to the reality.

The critics of the Mafia myth see in it an even less savory motive—prejudice: The message contained in Mafia reporting is blatantly anti-Italian. Of course, some of these critics have motives that are less than pure. Joe Colombo, himself head of a New York crime family, formed the Italian-American Civil Rights League and, in his role as its chairman, complained openly to the press about the anti-Italian bias. Referring to a New York legislature report on crime, he said,

> This book lists only Italians. Is it possible in New York that only Italians have committed crimes?... If you know any Italian that's in jail, his records get stamped "O.C." for organized crime. O.C. means only for Italian people. They do the last day of their sentencin'. I got one to two-and-a-half for checking the wrong box on a form.[7] [In applying for a real estate license, he concealed his arrest record and was subsequently convicted of perjury.]

According to the Mafia myth, then, everyone has suspect motives. Law enforcement and the media use the myth to enhance their organizations. The public uses the myth as a source of fascination and moral comfort. Of course, even people with impure motives may be telling the truth, so the critics also challenge the factual basis of the Mafia myth. They charge that its purveyors have ignored many facts while exaggerating the importance of others. Certainly, some criminals are Italian, but most Italians, even those who commit crimes, are not part of any organization. Certainly, some criminal organizations are largely Italian, but they are not the only such organizations, and they are not all-powerful. Often the evidence turns up instances in which the supposedly all-powerful Mafia cannot get things done. For example, wiretaps on two high-ranking Mafiosi in New Jersey found Sam ("The Plumber") de Cavalcante constantly grumbling about his inability to control his own agents and Angelo "Gyp" De Carlo spending much time worrying about very small sums of money.

Evil empire or the gang that couldn't shoot straight? These contrasting views of the Mafia and organized crime raise some questions that I will try to answer in this section. How do criminal organizations make their money? Does the Mafia control these illegal operations? Does it control criminal infiltration of legitimate organizations? What is the relationship between the Mafia and other criminal organizations?

A BIT OF HISTORY

In 1890, David Hennessy, the police chief of New Orleans, was murdered. Before he died, he was heard to say, "The dagos shot me." New Orleans, whose population was 240,000, had 10,000 to 15,000 Italian-born inhabitants, most of them from Sicily, and Hennessy's murder was the occasion for much anti-Italian sentiment. The newspapers began to carry stories referring to a secret Italian organization so powerful that according to one news story, it constituted a government unto itself. The organization was called the Mafia. Eventually, a number of Italians were tried for the crime, but the jury acquitted all of them. Historians disagree over the reason for the verdict. Some say that the gangsters threatened the jury; others maintain that the evidence was too flimsy. In any case, when news of the verdict came out, a lynch mob invaded the prison where the men were still being kept and killed them.

The story came to national attention, bringing with it a debate over the existence of the Mafia. The *New York Tribune* said that the Mafia existed not just in New Orleans but also in most large cities nationwide. Denying the existence of any Mafia, either in Sicily or in the United States, were the Italian-language newspapers and community leaders.[8] This may have been the first such debate, but it was certainly not the last. For the next hundred years, this same question would crop up periodically, with journalists, law-enforcement figures, prominent Italian-Americans, and academics arguing about the nature, extent, and even existence of the Mafia. At one extreme are those who argue that the Mafia is a tightly controlled and organized national organization with orders emanating from a central commission.[9] At the other extreme are those who argue that the Mafia is largely the creation of the media and law enforcement, who weave a small amount of evidence into an improbable web of connections. In this skeptical view, Americans have a weakness for stories about secret, powerful, broad-based conspiracies. These theories, often tinged with prejudice or xenophobia, provide convenient explanations for the country's failings or difficulties.[10]

CRIMINAL GANGS

Even in 1890, criminal gangs were hardly new to U.S. cities. Earlier in the century, street gangs had become a regular feature in poorer neighborhoods of the cities. These gangs committed mostly small-time thefts and fought one another over turf. Although the prevalence of gangs has varied from city to city and from one historical period to another, gangs like these have continued to the present day.[11] The primary motive in the formation of gangs is social rather than criminal. Especially for young men, gangs provide an alternative to the recognized social institutions. It is from the gang, rather than from work or family, that these young men derive a sense of self. Usually, the gangs are very loosely organized, and their crime—like their noncriminal activity—is oriented less toward economic profit than toward demonstrating personal qualities like toughness. Sometimes the gangs become more serious about crime, more profit-oriented, and more vicious. In the 1800s, for example, New York had waterfront gangs like the Charlton Street Gang and the Short Tails, who specialized in theft and robbery of cargoes on ships coming into the city and who used violence, including murder, to accomplish their goals.[12]

These variants still exist today. The Westies, for example, an ethnic gang based in an old West Side neighborhood of New York City called Hell's Kitchen, often seemed to resemble the gangs depicted in *West Side Story*. But until a series of criminal convictions in the late 1980s slowed them down, they were committing a variety of profit-oriented crimes ranging from hijacking to contract murder.[13]

Gangs interested in high profits usually are better organized. They use violence in attempts to monopolize illegal enterprises like gambling or (more recently) drugs and to gain control of legitimate businesses. In fact, at the time of the New Orleans shooting in 1890, two rival gangs had been fighting over control of the Italian sections of the docks, where fruit was unloaded. Today, though the weapons, drugs, and businesses have changed, this pattern of ethnic gangs still persists. Similar gangs have arisen in the Southeast Asian communities of California, the Russian immigrant neighborhoods in New York, and perhaps in other communities of recent immigrants as well.[14] The major structural difference involves the link between gangs and politicians. In the nineteenth century, the political machines that dominated city politics were often allied with neighborhood street gangs, and the gangs were active on election day—voting several times and sometimes intimidating other voters. As machine politics has faded, so have the political connections of gangs.

THE MAFIA IN ITALY AND AMERICA

The Mafia shares many of the characteristics of other ethnic criminal gangs and organizations. However, in its historical development, its internal organization, its scope, and its position in the illegal world, the Mafia is different.

The rise of the Mafia in America is a product of historical forces. The waves of immigration from Italy, beginning in the late nineteenth century, obviously played an important role. Then as now, immigrant communities gave rise to their own criminal gangs, which often specialize in extorting their own compatriots. The gangsters may start by providing helpful services—settling disputes within the community or helping immigrants in dealings with nonimmigrants such as landlords, employers, or government agencies. (The movie *The Godfather II* has a scene where the young Don Corleone helps a poor woman in a dispute over her rent.) The gang owes much of its power— for both good and evil—to the unwillingness or inability of people in the community to go to the authorities. Perhaps the immigrants do not speak English, or perhaps they feel (often rightly) that the American bureaucrats or the police will not understand them or will not give them adequate protection. The gangster steps in to fill this government role. But just as governments levy taxes, the gangs extort regular payments from the merchants of the community.

Although Italian organized crime groups in the United States are descended from organizations in Italy, and while there may be some trans-Atlantic cooperation on specific deals, they are largely separate and operate on different norms. Assassinations of law enforcement officials—like the car-bomb killing of a judge in Palermo, Sicily—have never been part of the tactics of organized crime in the United States.

This mistrust of official institutions ran particularly high among Italian immigrants, who were mostly from the south of Italy, especially Sicily. Many Mediterranean cultures emphasize that a man does not turn to the government for help; instead, he takes action personally to defend his honor. In Sicily especially, with its history of repeated foreign domination, people were alienated from official governments. One historian quotes Palermo's police chief, Antonio Cutrera:

> Long domination by succeeding invaders had produced people who were suspicious, diffident, intolerant, and above all, enemies of government—any government—and of all law enforcement. Thus, disrespect for laws, hatred of authority, and contempt for all those who had dealings with authorities characterized Sicilians.[15]

Not only was government distant and untrustworthy in Sicily, but so was the economy. Most agricultural production took place on plantation-like estates called *latifundia*, whose owners were largely absentees and whose workers were little better off than slaves. Under such conditions, peasants might well turn to anyone, even criminals, who offered them any semblance of protection against exploitation by government and landowners. Not surprisingly, then, the Mafia arose not in the cities but in the agricultural sections in western Sicily. Eastern Sicily apparently did not experience the same rise of the Mafia. In the early 1900s, the eastern cities of Messina and Syracuse had rates of murder and robbery that were only one-third those of Palermo in the west. Mafiosi emerged from the peasantry but distinguished themselves from the rest by their ability and willingness to use violence. They portrayed themselves as protectors of the peasants, but soon protection became a protection racket, and their Robin Hood–like altruism came to be mixed with heavy portions of self-interest. They used their reputation for violence more for their own purposes, even as agents for landowners and eventually as landowners themselves. Their power spread, and different Mafia groups came to dominate different territories or different industries in the cities. Mafia figures also became influential in local politics, using their money and power to corrupt incumbent officials and to elect new officials they could control.[16] Naples and Calabria, the other two regions of heavy emigration to the United States, had similar customs and similar criminal organizations. The Camorra of Naples was more centrally controlled and tightly organized than the Sicilian Mafia. Like the Mafia, though, it operated on both the legitimate and illegal levels. It extorted money from small businesses both legal and illegal (waiters and porters as well as prostitutes and thieves). The Camorra also had influence among politicians and businesspeople.[17]

It is a matter of some debate whether the Mafia leaders who came to power in the United States had also been gangsters in Italy. Most of them probably had not.[18] However, the sociologically important point is that when the Sicilians emigrated to the United States, they brought with them a set of assumptions and expectations about government and nongovernment institutions. This culture allowed for a home-grown Mafia to spring up in the United States. It may have been different in both personnel and structure from Italian criminal organizations, but it was a Mafia nevertheless.

In the early 1900s, criminals in Italian-American communities began extorting money from Italian shopkeepers, workers, and professionals by sending threatening notes: "This is the second time that I have warned you. Sunday at ten o'clock in the morning, at the corner of Second Street and Third Avenue, bring three hundred dollars without fail. Otherwise we will set fire to you and blow you up with a bomb."[19] The notes were signed *Mano Nera*, or Black Hand. Black Hand extortion continued for more than a decade and spread to many cities and even to small towns. However, although their methods and signatures may have been the same, this was not necessarily evidence for the existence of a large, criminal conspiracy. In fact, most Black Hand crimes were the work of individuals or small gangs. The federal government stepped in around 1915 and began to enforce laws against using the mails to defraud, and the Black Hand gangs faded.[20]

PROHIBITION AND THE ROARING TWENTIES

Historical accident played an important role in the next evolutionary stage of the Mafia. Just when Black Hand groups were looking for new sources of money, Prohibition came along, opening up large-scale criminal opportunities. Before 1920, the typical arrangement between gangsters and politicians left politicians at the top. The local ward leader may have owed many of his votes to the cooperation of the gangs, but they in turn counted on him for protection from the police. (The politicians and police were predominantly Irish, the gangsters Jewish and Italian.)[21]

Prohibition reversed this relationship. The reversal was an unintended consequence of the vigorous reforms brought in with the triumph over liquor. For many who backed Prohibition, the issue was not clean living but clean government. The machine politics that dominated most cities had been revealed to be corrupt, and the source of that corruption was often the saloon. In the minds of reformers, cities were a tangle of intertwined pathological elements: the corrupt political machine, the ward boss, the saloons, and the crooks. By getting rid of the saloons, reformers would kick the support out from under the rest of the corrupt elements. There may have been an element of ethnic or religious politics as well; the reformers were largely Protestant, while the urban populations had become increasingly Catholic—first Irish, then Italian.

The irony, of course, is that Prohibition had the opposite effect. By creating a source of tremendous wealth for criminal organizations, it enhanced the power of criminals. It even gave them a certain respectability in the eyes of the public; illegal alcohol linked the bootleggers with the nongangster drinkers. Suppliers and consumers alike participated in evading the liquor laws. In a similar irony, the replacement of corrupt political machines with relatively honest city government sometimes transformed the criminal underworld from an orderly, controlled operation into an anarchic and bloody battlefield.

Chicago provides a good illustration of these processes. Chicago is important in itself, of course, if only because it was the base of operations of the most famous gangster in U.S. history, Al Capone. In the decades before Prohibition, different gangs dominated different parts of the city. With the protection of the politicians in their respective wards, the gangs ran various illegal enterprises, the most important of which, after 1920, was the importation, manufacture, and distribution of alcohol. Johnny Torrio, a master strategist among gangsters, created a system of cooperation among gang leaders in various parts of the city—on the North Side, Dion O'Banion; on the South Side, smaller groups like Ragen's Colts (they began as a baseball team), the Terrible Gennas (six brothers), and the O'Donells. Torrio's own territory included some of the South Side and the West Side, extending as far as suburbs like Cicero. In controlling this small enterprise Torrio had help from a young man he had recruited from New York—Al Capone.

The arrangements proceeded fairly peacefully under the corrupt administration of Mayor Big Bill Thompson. But in 1923 a reform candidate, William Dever, unseated Thompson. The new mayor and his chief of police refused to continue the old *modus vivendi* with the mobsters. In one raid, Torrio himself was arrested. Whatever other effects the gangbusting may have had, it demonstrated to other gangsters that Torrio was vulnerable. It was then that Chicago began to see the gang warfare that has become legendary. O'Banion was murdered in 1924 in his flower shop. Both Capone and Torrio were victims of attempted murder, probably by people from the organization of O'Banion's successor, Hymie Weiss. Weiss himself was killed in 1926, and eventually Bugs Moran took control of the O'Banion group. There was more violence over control of bootleg liquor, and there was violence during elections. In three years, gangsters killed over 200 of their competitors; police killed another 160. The gangland wars culminated in the famous St. Valentine's Day massacre of 1929, when men from Capone's organization murdered seven members of Bugs Moran's group. Soon, Capone solidified his control over the entire Chicago area, and the number of mob-related killings dropped. In 1931, Capone was jailed for income tax violations, but the organization he had built continued to control Chicago's underworld. Thus, one of the most violent and largest criminal organizations was shaped by one of the country's most idealistic programs—Prohibition.

After the St. Valentine's Day massacre and with the repeal of Prohibition in 1933, organized crime ceased to command the kind of public attention it had gotten in the 1920s. Interest dwindled partly because of a lack of characters as colorful or as willing to talk to the press as Capone had been; partly because (thanks to repeal) far fewer people were involved in mob-controlled services; and partly because law enforcement, especially the FBI under J. Edgar Hoover, channeled its efforts in other directions.

THE MAFIA IN THE AGE OF TELEVISION

Organized crime returned to the spotlight reluctantly in 1950, when Senator Estes Kefauver presided over hearings of a special senate committee. The hearings took the committee to a number of cities and lasted several months. Most of the 600 witnesses who testified were law-enforcement officials, but the roster also included bookmakers, pimps, enforcers, and others connected to organized crime. The star of the show was Frank Costello. The committee and the media built up Costello as the crime boss of the entire country, which was a considerable exaggeration. The Kefauver hearings gained special prominence because they were televised. Television was just becoming a prominent medium, and the possibility of seeing real live gangsters proved an unbeatable attraction (even though all that viewers could see of Costello, who objected to the cameras, were his hands).

Television gave the **Kefauver committee** a wide audience for its ideas about the nature of organized crime. The committee promulgated the view that organized crime was more centralized than had been thought previously, with the Mafia as the hub of the organization. Back in the days of the New Orleans lynching, there had been several "mafias," small associations of criminals who engaged in extortion and racketeering. But now, the word had taken on a new meaning.

> There is a sinister criminal organization known as the Mafia operating throughout the country with ties in other nations.... The Mafia is the direct descendant of a criminal organization of the same name originating in the island of Sicily. In this country, the Mafia has also been known as the Black Hand and the Unione Siciliano [sic].... The Mafia is a loose-knit organization specializing in the sale and distribution of narcotics, the conduct of various enterprises, prostitution, and other rackets based on extortion and violence. The Mafia is the binder which ties together the two major criminal syndicates [one in Chicago, the other in New York] as well as numerous other criminal groups throughout the country.[22]

As we have seen, the actual history of the Mafia is not quite the direct line that the committee portrays. The committee makes it sound as if the progression from Sicilian Mafia to Black Hand to American Mafia was merely a change in name and place—something like the Washington Senators baseball team becoming the Texas Rangers. In fact, few American gangsters, even in the early years, had been connected with Sicilian crime groups, and the Black Hand existed as many small, independent extortion operations rather than as franchises of a single, large organization. The Unione Siciliana was originally an above-board fraternal organization. In New York in the 1920s, gangsters who had come to power in the Unione forced members to operate stills, producing "bathtub gin" in their homes. The police appropriated the name to refer to the combination of the various Italian crime groups in New York.[23]

The Kefauver hearings ended in 1951, giving way in the media to Senator Joseph McCarthy's hearings. In the public eye, the menace of the Mafia conspiracy was replaced by the menace of the Communist conspiracy. The next brief flurry of publicity about a nationwide Mafia came in 1957. In Apalachin, New York, a small upstate town, approximately sixty men had gathered at the home of Joseph Barbara, a soft-drink bottler. None of the men was carrying a gun or was wanted by the police. They owned legitimate businesses. Their number included "a Man of the Year from Buffalo, a manufacturer of bleach, a grocery clerk ... the Eastern distributor for a national brand of whiskey, a bandleader, a Boston cheese purveyor, a trucking tycoon, and even a Manhattan hearse salesman."[24] However, when a curious state trooper pulled up in the driveway, the men bolted for the woods. They were soon rounded up but refused to answer police questions, for which refusal they were indicted and convicted. The convictions were overturned on appeal, the court ruling that the police had no probable cause to make the arrest in the first place.

But what did the **Apalachin conference** mean? To the most conspiracy-minded, it was evidence of a nationwide criminal organization. Although most of the Barbara guests were from New York, New Jersey, and Pennsylvania, a few had come from as far away as Florida, Texas, Colorado, and Cuba.[25] These men, many known to authorities as being involved in organized crime, may have been making decisions about underworld business. Or the "convention" may have been a mostly social gathering. At any rate, if this was a meeting of a structured organization rather than a reunion of people who happened to be in the same line of (illegal) work, it remained unclear what that structure was and what kinds of business decisions were to have been made.

Six years later, another Senate committee, this one headed by Senator John McClellan, tried to clarify the picture, though many people dispute its accuracy. The star witness of these hearings was Joe Valachi, a government informer who had been serving a sentence in a federal prison. Valachi was only a low-level member of one New York crime family; his testimony was inconsistent and at times vague; some of it—for example, his tale of a nationwide coup in which forty high-ranking Mafiosi were killed in a three-day period—turned out to be simply wrong; but the committee and the media generally accepted his story as the truth. He told of a secret ceremony, of oaths he had taken while holding burning scraps of paper, of the "kiss of death." It was Valachi who introduced the country to the term *La Cosa Nostra* (literally, "our thing"), and it was Valachi who put terms like *capo* and *consigliere* in the public glossary and added new meanings to words like *family*, *lieutenant*, and *soldier*. Only *The Godfather* (the novel and movies) has had more of an impact on public conceptions of the Mafia. *The Godfather* had an impact on the Mafiosi as well. One undercover detective reported, "They had a lot of things taught to them through the movie. They try to live up to it. The movie was telling them how."[26]

How is Organized Crime Organized?

The basic unit of the Mafia is the gang, known as a family, or *borgata*. According to law-enforcement officials, there are twenty-four families active in the United States, five of them in the New York area. Other cities have only one. Disputes between families are handled by a "commission" made up of high-ranking members of a few of the families. Most descriptions of the structure of a Mafia family agree that there are certain hierarchical relationships designated by the various titles. At the top are the boss (also known as the don); underboss; and *consigliere*, or adviser. At the next level are those with the title of *capo* (short for *caporegima*), also known as captains or lieu-tenants (some models put lieutenants in a separate rank below capos). Below them are the *soldati*, or soldiers (sometimes called buttons). Each family con-trols the number of these "made" members. According to the FBI, the total number of members is about 2,000 nationwide, a number that has remained basically unchanged since the 1930s.[27] In addition, many nonmembers work with or for the family.

What is a matter of some dispute is the nature of the relationships among these various roles. What does a boss or a capo or a soldier *do*? According to some models of the crime family, these positions function much like those in a legitimate business organization. The president (boss) makes decisions regarding the general strategy and direction of the company; the underboss acts as a sort of general operations manager. The capos are like division managers, and the soldiers, in cooperation with nonfamily employees, produce the actual product or service. This is the **bureaucratic model**, and it is the one favored by law-enforcement personnel. Here, for example, is the opening paragraph of a presidential commission task force report:

> [Organized crime] involves thousands of criminals working with structures as complex as those of any large corporations, subject to laws more rigidly enforced than those of legitimate governments. The actions are not impulsive but rather the result of intricate conspiracies carried on over many years and aimed at gaining control over whole fields of activity to amass huge profits.[28]

The image is of a corporation with several ongoing businesses, staffed with bureaucrats.

Unorganized Crime

The problem with the bureaucratic model is that it makes crime groups seem more organized than they really are. In reality, most organized crime businesses have a much looser, decentralized structure than the chain-of-command model suggests. How could it be otherwise? True business bureaucracies depend on routinized procedures, a large flow of information, and elaborate record keeping. Illegal businesses, because of their vulnerability to law enforcement, must minimize all these elements. The less predictable and routine they are, the less everyone knows; the fewer the records that might become evidence, the safer the operation is. But if illegal businesses like bookmaking and loan-sharking cannot be run like legitimate corporations, perhaps the popular image of organized crime is also exaggerated or just plain wrong. This image, often mirrored in the mass media, portrays the Mafia as a tightly run organization that dominates many forms of crime. However, the economic realities of crime make this kind of organization and domination unlikely. The difference between image and reality will become clearer if we look more closely at some of these crimes.

BOOKMAKING

Part of the conventional wisdom about the Mafia is that it controls vice. That is, most bookmakers, loan sharks, prostitutes, and other providers of illegal goods and services either belong to the Mafia or work for members of the Mafia. Nonmembers in these businesses must pay money to the Mafia and must accept orders from the Mafia. In return, the Mafia will use its resources to provide protection from law enforcement. Arrests will be rare, convictions even rarer, and serious sentences rarer still. This picture of Mafia control dominates popular ideas of illegal gambling—both numbers and bookmaking. Consequently, gambling is supposed to be the major source of Mafia income. A typical version of this idea can be found in the testimony of Vincent Teresa before a U.S. Senate subcommittee in 1971. Teresa was a criminal who worked with the Mafia in New England, though he never became an actual member.

> There is no bookmaker that can do business by himself; he couldn't survive. The mob would turn him over to the police, give him a few beatings, or even kill him if he's real stubborn. He has to go with them, because they run everything.
>
> Gambling is the single most important activity for organized crime. They control it all over the country and all over the world.[29]

Teresa was including legal casino gambling in Las Vegas and Europe, but the turf he knew firsthand was illegal bookmaking in New England.

Some scholars echo Teresa's views. According to criminologist Donald Cressey, "In most large American cities, the opportunity to gamble is provided by Cosa Nostra. Members of this organization do not themselves own and operate all the illegal betting and lottery enterprises, but those they do not own they control, or provide with essential services."[30] But does the Mafia control illegal gambling? Both economic logic and the available evidence cast doubt on this widely held assumption. From the economic point of view, any industry—legal or illegal—will be difficult to control if it is decentralized (i.e., made up of many independent entrepreneurs). If one element in the business is centralized, the organization that can control that element can also control the business. For example, for several decades, bookmakers derived most of their income from gambling on horse racing. They were subject to control from a single crime group because there was one element in the system that was centralized: information. The law prevented racetracks from broadcasting the races, and racetracks could not have public telephones. Bookies, therefore, had to get their information from a telegraph service, an illegal monopoly run by Moe Annenberg. A bookmaker who wanted to go into business had to have the wire service. Whoever controlled the wire controlled access to bookmaking.

Corruption, an essential part of most illegal businesses, was also centralized. Bettors on horse races found it more convenient to have a place to go—a "horse room" or "wire room," where they could bet, hang out, and hear the call of the race. (The 1973 movie *The Sting* depicts a fairly elegant version of a 1920s horse room.) Horse rooms were easy targets for raids, so bookmakers needed to pay off the police. The corruption often extended all the way through a city police department right to the top, and often to top politicians as well. Only a large organization (the Mafia) could buy such protection.

In the 1960s, both information and police corruption became more decentralized. More and more of the bookmakers' business came from gambling on football, baseball, and basketball—sports where information flowed freely over radio and television. Many bookmakers dealt exclusively by phone, so they no longer needed elaborate and semipublic places like the horse rooms that required protection from the police. At the same time, many city police departments were undergoing anticorruption reforms, which often had the effect of reducing or at least decentralizing corruption. A small-time bookie had only to pay off the local cops, if he had to pay anyone at all. In addition, as predatory crime burgeoned in the 1960s, the police and courts paid less attention to illegal gambling, so bookmakers had even fewer worries about payoffs. In this new atmosphere, the two sources of control—the wire and high-priced corruption, which had allowed organized crime to dominate in illegal betting—were things of the past. These changes should have made it more difficult for the Mafia or anyone else to maintain a monopoly on bookmaking. While horse rooms may have passed into history, some cities still have a latter-day counterpart: the after-hours gambling club, where patrons may drink and play casino gambling games (craps, roulette, and blackjack). These clubs, except for those with an exclusively Chinese clientele, are probably a Mafia monopoly.

There is another economic reason to question the idea that gambling is a Mafia monopoly. A monopoly must be a continuous, permanent enterprise, large and centralized. Such a structure may work in the legitimate world, but illegal businesses are different. If the police do make a raid, they can seize the operation's assets and arrest the employees. In the underworld, therefore, a large, centralized operation is potentially a liability.

The economic conditions of bookmaking would seem to make it an unlikely candidate as a Mafia monopoly. But what is the evidence? On the one hand, there is Vincent Teresa's statement. But some researchers have sought more diverse types of evidence: the books and betting slips seized from police raids, conversations from wiretaps, and interviews with both arrested and nonarrested bookmakers. This evidence shows that in most cities, the bookmaking industry consists of many small enterprises with a high rate of turnover. Some of the bookmakers are connected to the Mafia; others belong to other criminal organizations; but many are just independent entrepreneurs operating completely apart from any organized crime.

New York City offers an interesting example since, unlike most cities, it has five Mafia families. According to the conventional wisdom, these five families have divided the city among themselves so that each has exclusive control over the various illegal operations in its territory. Presumably, this control should extend to bookmakers. Yet the evidence suggests otherwise. If the Mafia controlled bookmaking, it would do what any other monopoly tries to do when it gains control of an industry: It would reduce competition and raise consumer prices. But prices have not gone up.

In bookmaking, the bettor is the consumer, and the price of making a bet takes the form of odds. The bookmaker makes his profit because the bettor must give odds of eleven to ten. That is, the bettor puts up eleven dollars to

ABOUT CRIME & CRIMINOLOGY

The organization of prostitution closely resembles that of bookmaking. At one time, it may have been centralized and dominated by a few criminal groups. Earlier in this century, prostitution was centered in brothels. Racketeers may even have moved prostitutes from one city to another—what was called the white slave trade. Independent brothels, like wire rooms, could be extorted. But in the latter half of the century, brothels gave way to call girls and streetwalkers, which, like telephone-based bookmakers, provided too decentralized a target for extortion. Organized crime groups lost interest in prostitution, even brothels (and their 1960s version, massage parlors). In Philadelphia, for example, in the 1970s, "an FBI informant opened three brothels in the central vice district. At no time did he have to 'get permission' from any other organization. In fact, the only people who called upon him for tribute were the police."

Source: Gary N. Potter and Philip Jenkins, *The City and the Syndicate: Organizing Crime in Philadelphia* (Lexington, MA: Ginn Press, 1985), p. 8.

the bookmaker's ten dollars. Or as some bettors think of it, there is a 10 percent surcharge on losing bets. If bookmaking were a monopoly, it could raise the surcharge to 15 percent or even 20 percent. In fact, some bookmakers have tried conspiring to change the standard odds to give themselves more profit. The result was a rapid loss in business as customers switched to bookmakers who offered competitive prices.[31]

There is one low-risk way for the Mafia to control bookmaking—extortion. The principal quality of bookmaking that makes it susceptible to Mafia domination is its illegality. People who make their money illegally make good targets for extortion since they are less likely to go the police for protection. However, social science studies have found little evidence for extortion. For example, an economist who studied illegal enterprises in New York concludes that although there is some Mafia extortion of bookmakers, "it is neither systematic nor unavoidable. Such extortion yields only modest sums to the Mafia members."[32]

It may be that in some cities, the Mafia does make an effort to control bookmaking by extorting money from bookmakers. In Boston, the territory Vincent Teresa knew best, the Mafia did manage to control most illegal gambling. As a result, Boston bettors had to give 6 to 5 odds.[33] In most cities, however, the bookmaking market is classic free enterprise. Some Mafia members run bookmaking operations, but they do not dominate the business, and the occasional attempts to raise prices have failed against the free market competition of bookmakers who continued to offer the usual odds.[34]

THE NUMBERS

A second type of gambling often thought to bring untold riches to the Mafia is the numbers. Today, many states run their own lotteries, but until the 1970s the only available lotteries were the illegal numbers rackets. In the game's most common form, the bettor selects a three-digit number and places the bet with a collector. The collector gathers the bets, turns them over to a pickup man, who in turn gives them to a middle-level manager called a controller. The controller is the link to the central "bank." That afternoon, the day's number is determined by some random process, and winners are paid off at odds usually between 500 to 1 and 600 to 1. Popular, heavily bet numbers get even lower odds, sometimes as low as 350 to 1. Different banks offer different odds, and a bank may change its odds.

Obviously, the numbers game requires a larger organization than does bookmaking. It is also more difficult to hide. Bookmakers operate by phone, but numbers runners collect bets in person. The size and visibility of the numbers game should make it a much more likely candidate for domination by a single criminal organization. In the 1930s, a single gangster, Dutch Schulz, did gain control of the numbers in New York City. A wave of anti-corruption reform had hit New York politics, and the police had raided several numbers banks in Harlem. Schulz seized on the banks' temporary weakness and, largely through threat, took over these formerly independent numbers banks. According to one historian, the numbers yielded Schultz $20 million a year.[35]

As with other forms of gambling, the numbers game has since become decentralized. In a large city like New York, fifty or more numbers banks may be operating at any one time. Even a single neighborhood may have three or four numbers banks that compete with one another. Some of the banks are Mafia run, but many are not; rather, they are neighborhood industries. Banks in black neighborhoods are run by blacks, those in Hispanic neighborhoods by Hispanics. No single group dominates or controls the industry.

How much does the bank make? If it pays out at 600 to 1, of every $1,000 coming in, it should pay out, on the average, $600 to winning bettors, $250 to collectors, and $100 to controllers. That leaves $50, or 5 percent of the total amount bet, as the bank's gross. The average numbers bank in New York in the 1970s was taking in about $7,000 a day, or about $2.2 million per year. The 5 percent gross works out to $110,000 annually, out of which the bank must pay for its operating costs (rent, clerks' salaries, police payoffs, etc.).[36]

How does this reality square with the image of the numbers racket as a huge profit center dominated by a relatively small central group of Mafia mobsters? The system as it really works features a diversity of banks, often competing in the same geographic area, and the competition can be serious. For example, one Cuban numbers organization in New York was, according to the FBI, using profits from drug smuggling to increase payoff odds to attract bettors.[37] Although numbers banks are more permanent than bookmaking offices, some of them go out of business (too many hits by customers or a raid by the police), and new ones may enter the field. The system also pays a high percentage of the income to the lowest-level personnel, the collectors, who also have a great deal of discretion. All of this suggests that the numbers business is a relatively free market, not one dominated by any one organization, such as the Mafia.

IN THE NEWS

Times change. So do the relations among numbers bankers, the Mafia, and the police—as the story of Raymond Marquez illustrates. In the 1960s and 1970s, when Marquez was still making payments to the Mafia boss who had given him his start, the police were also getting regular payments for protection. In the 1990s, Marquez was paying nothing to the Mafia (except $300 a week for information, not protection—almost nothing for a business grossing over half a million a week) and nothing to the police. Also changing with the times is the technology of illegal business and law enforcement.

FAX USE SPELLS NUMBERS ARREST TO HARLEM RING

For 30 years, Raymond Marquez was a thorn to law-enforcement agencies and a legend to countless gamblers in Harlem and East Harlem.

From a clientele whose wagers ranged from a dime to more than $1,000 a day on numbers games, the authorities say, Mr. Marquez, whose nickname is Spanish Raymond, built a gambling empire that raked in about $30 million a year....

[The illegal lottery] has remained popular despite the growth of legal gambling because taxes are not paid on the winnings, because numbers runners make placing a bet more convenient and because some of the games appeal to recent immigrants who played similar games in their homelands....

Reports on the daily operations were faxed ... to Mr. Marquez and his wife while they were in Fort Lauderdale, [a prosecutor] said. "We intercepted 30 to 40 faxes a day.... It spelled out in minute details everything about the organization."

Mr. Marquez, whose parents are from Puerto Rico, was born in New York City. His father was a numbers operator in the 1940s for Vito Genovese, a major Mafia boss, officials said. Detectives said Mr. Marquez ran numbers games for Anthony Salerno, a Mafia leader in East Harlem in the 1950s before branching out on his own.

Prosecutors ... said that in the 1960s and 1970s Mr. Marquez paid about 5 percent of his profits to Mr. Salerno but that he no longer makes payments to Mafia bosses. However, said the prosecutors, Mr. Marquez's organization paid $300 a week to the Genovese crime family for daily information on the parimutuel results used for the numbers games.

Source: *New York Times*, April 21, 1994, pp. A1, B4.

LOAN SHARKS

The classic movie *On the Waterfront* depicts a corrupt union that runs the docks, a union dominated by organized crime. Longshoremen who wish to continue to get work must borrow money at high interest rates from the union-connected loan shark, a thoroughly detestable character. In the movie *Rocky* the hero's physical and moral self-improvement seem all the more noble because the place where he begins is so contemptible: He is a bone-breaker for a loan shark (though, of course, our Rocky cannot bring himself to use actual violence against debtors).

Popular conceptions of the loan shark resemble these media images. The term itself summons up images of horror. We usually think of sharks as vicious creatures who prey on the innocent, and once the shark sets out to get his prey, the victim rarely escapes. Bloodshed is the rule. This picture of the loan shark has several notable elements. The loan shark

- charges usuriously high interest rates
- preys on innocent victims
- uses violence to collect debts
- uses loans as a means to take over legitimate businesses
- is closely tied to the Mafia.

How accurate is this picture? The first element—usury—is certainly true. While bank loans are figured on an annual interest rate (say 15 percent per year) and credit card companies charge a monthly rate on unpaid balances (1½ to 2 percent per month), loan sharks figure interest on a per-week basis. A typical rate is 3 percent a week, or more than 150 percent a year, though the interest rate depends on the size and repayment terms. The larger the loan, the less the interest. Very small loans go at the standard rate of six for five. Borrow $100 today; pay back $120 next week. The $20 weekly interest works out to an annual interest rate of over 1,000 percent. Very large loans might go for as little as 1 percent a week. In any case, whether the annual interest is 1,000 percent or "only" 50 to 100 percent, it is far higher than the interest that banks and finance companies may legally charge.

If the interest rates are so high, why would anyone borrow from a loan shark? The answer sometimes suggested in the media is that the loan shark somehow forces the client to take the loan. In reality, such victimization is extremely rare. The nearest version of this is the loan shark who hangs around card games or other gambling settings, ready to lend money to the gambler who has lost his capital and wants to continue playing. I suppose the moral thing for the loan shark to do would be to advise the gambler to quit before he loses any more. But dispensing wisdom is not the loan shark's role, and besides, few gamblers in that situation would heed the advice.

This example of the gambler illustrates some of the reasons borrowers go to a loan shark rather than to legitimate lenders. A borrower may need the money quickly or wish the loan to remain secret. Some borrowers need the money for purposes no bank would approve. Drug dealers may need money to finance a large deal; a numbers bank that undergoes a few heavily played hits may need money to stay in business; so might a bookmaker whose customers have had a run of good luck.

Even legitimate businesses or individuals may find that banks will not lend to them. Perhaps they already have an outstanding loan at the bank, they cannot put up enough collateral, or the loan looks too risky for a bank to approve. Or they may need the money quickly and for only a few weeks. Furriers, for example, have little income during the summer. If they need a few thousand dollars to buy pelts in the fall, their cash reserves will be too low. Other small businesses may have similar cash-flow problems.

Customers of loan sharks, then, come because they need the money, not because anyone is forcing them. In this sense, they come just as voluntarily as the customers of banks and finance companies. As for the extortionary interest, a loan shark charges high rates because he is taking a greater risk. Some of his clients are criminals, perhaps even unsuccessful criminals whose schemes have already gone sour (a losing bookmaker or gambler or a fence who is stuck with merchandise he cannot sell). His customers may be arrested and have their assets seized (or stolen) by the police, greatly reducing their ability to pay. If the criminal is convicted and imprisoned, the chances of repayment become extremely remote. Even the loan shark's noncriminal borrowers are high-risk customers, people whom Citibank and Household Finance wouldn't touch.

The most unsettling aspect of loan-sharking, however, is not the usurious interest (which may be understandable) but the potential violence. The media often portray threat and violence as the most frequent outcome when borrowers are late in paying. The reality is more complicated. Yes, violence and threat are part of the understood terms of a loan; actual violence, however, is rare. To understand both parts of this equation, consider the transaction from the loan shark's point of view. His clients are not reputable people, and the terms of the loan are neither legal nor officially recorded. If the borrower does not repay, what can the loan shark do? Against the risk of nonpayment, loan sharks often demand some sort of collateral, but often the resale value of the collateral is much less than the amount of the loan.[38] If the client does not pay, the loan shark cannot file a lawsuit in court; he simply has no legal means to get his money back. Under these conditions, what else but violence does the loan shark have to make sure he doesn't lose his money?

Nevertheless, violence is by far the exception rather than the rule. In my own research on compulsive gamblers, I met scores of men who had taken loans from "Shylocks"; a man might have loans from two or more loan sharks, an arrangement that usually left him deeper in debt and unable to keep up payments. "I owed more in vig (interest) than I was making each week," said one man who was only slightly worse off than many others. Many of these men had received continual reminders from the loan sharks; a few had been threatened, but none of them had actually been beaten up.[39] Peter Reuter, an economist who studied gambling and loan-sharking in New York, found a similar pattern.

> Violence is, in most cases, a very late stage of the collection process. Harassment is the most common first stage. The borrower is called with increasing frequency. Threats become more explicit and are made increasingly at night and at the borrower's home. It appears that the typical process of harassment may extend for a reasonable length of time, not less than a month in most operations.[40]

Some loan sharks are more prone to violence than others, and they are the ones the public is most likely to learn about. After all, only when a borrower is severely beaten are the police likely to find out about the loan-sharking. The anecdotal evidence in the media also suggests that debtors who cannot pay may even be murdered. This seems unlikely since it is so unwise economically. Dead men make no payments. If murder occurs at all, it would occur only when the borrower is trying to defraud the loan shark, that is, taking a large loan with no intention of repaying it.

Because loan-sharking is illegal and because it depends ultimately on violence, many people, including many in law enforcement, believe that it is controlled by the Mafia. There may be logical reasons for this belief. It is the kind of enterprise the Mafia would find attractive: It requires neither hard work, skill, nor intelligence. The only requirements are cash and access to violence. In addition, if successful loan-sharking depends ultimately on violence or threat of violence, the group whose threats are most credible will be most successful. And that group is the Mafia.

Despite these considerations, loan-sharking, like bookmaking and numbers, is probably a decentralized market rather than one that is centrally controlled. To be sure, many loan sharks are Mafia members or have Mafia connections, which can put them at an advantage. "To be able truthfully to tell a loanshark customer that 'this is Fat Tony's money' is a considerable asset."[41] ("Fat Tony" Salerno was head of the Genovese crime family in New York.) But what is to prevent other lenders from entering the market? For example, suppose that I am a businessperson with cash on hand, and another businessperson I know needs money quickly. What is to prevent me from lending him my money at 3 percent a week? (I might even tell him that the loan is backed by the mob.) Through referrals in the network of people in our business, I might get other borrowers. In fact, Reuter's research found non-Mafia loan sharks who started in just this way. If threat or violence became necessary, they could always hire enforcers on a free-lance basis.

So although the Mafia is active in loan-sharking, the market may also have many independent lenders. Unfortunately, since loan-sharking is one of the crimes least likely to become known to the police, the available evidence is quite limited. A study of organized crime in Philadelphia found the loan-sharking market to be made up of many independent lenders with no monopoly by the Mafia or anyone else.[42] Loan-sharking in other cities probably resembles this disorganized structure.

Finally, there is the idea, also popularly disseminated, that Mafia loan sharks use loans as a way of taking over legitimate businesses. In fact, such takeovers are rare, and it is not hard to imagine the reasons why. Why would a loan shark want to take over someone else's business? Running a business is hard work. When a Mafia loan shark takes over a business, it is for one of three reasons: (1) to sell off its assets and get cash, (2) to use it in a bankruptcy scam (see p. 275), or (3) to use it as a legitimate front for other illegal activity.

DRUGS

Drugs is one area in which even the mythology of the Mafia is divided. In a famous scene in *The Godfather*, the don (Marlon Brando) takes a principled position against drugs. As long as he remains in control, the family will not traffic in drugs; other Mafiosi want to take advantage of its easy profits. This ambivalence existed in reality as well. Some Mafia leaders ordered their members to stay out of the drug business, though their reasons may have been more practical than principled. In any case, the restriction seems to have been more often broken than observed.[43] For decades, the police and media have portrayed organized crime and the Mafia as deeply involved in the drug trade. Celebrated cases like the "French Connection" in the 1970s or the "Pizza Connection" in the late 80s offered a model of the drug distribution business as a sort of pyramid. The lowest and most visible levels— the small-scale distributors and street dealers—were for the most part blacks and Hispanics. The few at the top, the importers, who made the big money, were in the Mafia. However, in the late 1980s, when cocaine replaced heroin as the country's most feared drug, law-enforcement officials began to downplay the role of the Mafia and concentrate instead on other large conspiracies based in Colombia—first the Medellin cartel, then the Cali cartel.

The reality of drug importation and distribution differs somewhat from the image of a business controlled at the top by a small, immensely powerful group. As with other illegal businesses, Mafiosi may be involved in importing these drugs; certainly, however, they are not the only ones, nor do they control the market. The large shipments of drugs into the United States come from Latin American organizations, which seem to be doing quite well without the assistance of older American crime groups. In addition, much of the cocaine and marijuana from South America is imported by many independent entrepreneurs and small partnerships. The main reason organized crime does not dominate the market is that smuggling drugs does not require very much organization. Some importers smuggle in large quantities—thousands of kilos of cocaine aboard cargo ships. These operations obviously require a larger organization to coordinate the purchasing, loading, shipping, unloading, and storage of these large shipments. But large shippers are a fairly recent addition to the drug scene. For smaller-scale smuggling—less than a ton per shipment—just about anyone can become a cocaine importer.

The operation has three stages: buying the drugs in South America, bringing the drugs into the United States, and selling the drugs. The only stage that requires organization is the middle step—smuggling. The first step—connecting with a source—is a matter of networking through the distribution chain. Some would-be dealers actively look for ways to link up with sources. Low-level dealers or even nondealing drug users seek out a large dealer who is willing to take them as temporary partners. For others who become dealers, the opportunity arises almost by chance. Bartenders, waiters, even people in more upscale occupations like real estate brokers or lawyers may find their social or business paths intersecting with high-level dealers willing to cut them in.[44] Another type of networking occurs in prison. Other prisoners can offer information (who to meet or what bars to hang out in) valuable for making contacts with large dealers and even suppliers in Latin America.[45] As for the third stage—selling the drugs—if dealers have been using drugs or selling in small quantities, they will have little trouble finding buyers for their inventory.

It is the second part of the process—smuggling drugs into the country— that may require some degree of organization. The dealer must find someone willing to transport the drugs to the United States. Since cocaine is so expensive, even a $100,000 purchase (at 1990 prices) weighs only 5 kilos (11 pounds), takes up little space, can easily be carried on small airplanes or pleasure boats, and has a street value several times the initial cost.[46] A pilot approached by a drug dealer may well be tempted by the offer of $10,000 for a round-trip flight south of the border. However, the pressure can be unnerving, especially when things do not go precisely according to plan. As one dealer explained, "They burn out so fast I have to replace them every six months to a year."[47] Marijuana is much bulkier than cocaine and may require specially rigged boats or planes; or the importers may send the drugs on a commercial ship that lies offshore and downloads its cargo in smaller quantities to pleasure craft, which then run the drugs into the mainland. This method also is used for larger shipments of cocaine.

For a single criminal organization like the Mafia to control drug trafficking, it would have to control at least one part of the business—either sources, smuggling routes, or distribution networks. For cocaine and marijuana, all three elements are decentralized. However, if a drug comes from more limited sources and requires longer supply lines, it may be more susceptible to control by a single group. Until the 1970s, the market in heroin fit this description. The geography of heroin kept smaller entrepreneurs out of the market. The poppies were grown in the Middle East (Iran, Afghanistan, and Turkey), converted to heroin in Mediterranean ports like Marseille, and shipped to the United States in large commercial ships. Because the distance was much too far for importation by small aircraft or pleasure boats and because the Mafia controlled corruption on New York City docks, the Mafia could control the heroin market. Then in the 1970s, global politics (i.e., the war in Vietnam) opened up Southeast Asia as a source of heroin. Increased U.S. presence in the region allowed growers and dealers to establish links to American distributors.[48] The long distance between Indochina and the United States still meant that drug traffic could be dominated by large crime groups, but these new groups were Asian (Chinese and Vietnamese) or even African (Nigerian) rather than American or European.

OTHER CRIMES, OTHER RACKETS

I have gone into detail in the foregoing sections to cast doubt on one widespread image or model of the Mafia. In this model, the Mafia is a giant corporation that dominates the various businesses of vice—gambling, loan-sharking, prostitution, and drugs. As we have seen, there is much in the way of both logic and evidence to question these two assumptions. In fact, it appears that although Mafia members may be involved in these rackets, they usually do not control them. The supply side of the market in illegal goods and services consists of many independent entrepreneurs. In some cases, the criminal enterprises may be quite large, with dozens of employees and gross incomes of millions of dollars. Yet no one enterprise or organization controls the market.

CRIME, BUSINESS, AND LABOR

In addition to the sale of illegal goods and services, organized crime groups are sometimes involved in predatory crimes like theft and robbery. Most street crime, of course, is highly decentralized. Thieves, burglars, and robbers operate in small, temporary groups, and their income from crime is too low and too irregular to interest criminal organizations. Therefore, when these organizations are involved in street crime, they are more likely to direct or control the actual predators than to be out on the streets committing the actual crimes. The term *ring* frequently crops up in these kinds of operations: a car-theft ring, a burglary ring, a hijacking ring. Rings bring in money on a regular basis. Car thieves, for example, sometimes are professional criminals closely tied to the organization, but they are just as likely to be teenagers who get a few hundred dollars per car. The criminal organizations take care of the final disposition of the car—exporting it, selling it in this country (complete with forged documents), or breaking it down into parts for repair shops—for a profit of thousands of dollars per car.

Occasionally, the Mafia or other organized crime groups will be involved in a single theft or burglary, one that will have a very large payoff. For example, the best-seller *Wiseguy* shows the involvement of Mafia (and non-Mafia) criminals in the robbery of the Lufthansa terminal at JFK airport in New York City, a single crime that netted several million dollars. Truck hijacking or theft of shipping containers, which can be worth hundreds of thousands of dollars, also may be part of organized crime activities. The Mafia may get involved in large-scale theft when the proceeds cannot be immediately converted to cash—items like stock certificates, bonds, and other securities stolen from financial firms.

To some people, the most damaging Mafia activities are not these predatory crimes nor even the provision of illegal goods and services. The most threatening and insidious projects are those that involve legitimate businesses and labor organizations. Loan-sharking and drug importing are serious and illegal; large-scale robbery and theft obviously are serious crimes. But while these crimes may attack society, they do not undermine it. In other organized crime activities, however, the interweaving of legal and illegal becomes much more complicated. Indeed, the most problematic part of organized crime is its involvement in the legitimate world. It is here that the Mafia distinguishes itself from other criminal groups; no other criminal organization has entered into legitimate business on a similar scale. Various Mafia groups own several individual companies. In some cases, like garbage collection and concrete production in New York City, the Mafia has controlled an entire industry through a cartel. Through rigged bidding and suppression of competition, the companies (and organized crime) make millions of dollars in excess profits. Similarly with labor, the Mafia runs several union locals and in some cases controls the entire national union.

Frequently we hear officials warning us that organized crime has "infiltrated" or "taken over" legitimate businesses. Why is this bad? What is the harm if, say, a soap company is run by someone "with ties to organized crime"? Doesn't it still have to sell soap?

Law-enforcement officials usually give two answers to this question. The first is that the profits of the company may finance illegal operations like drug smuggling (though usually the officials warn of the reverse—that the Mafia will use its profits from drugs and gambling to take over legitimate businesses). The second answer is that the Mafia uses the legitimate enterprise as a front, which can serve as a legitimate cover for money that was really made illegally—a fairly simple form of money laundering. It can also provide the appearance of employment for people who otherwise have no way of explaining the source of their income.

There are other reasons to fear criminals in legitimate business. Most important, they are more likely to engage in illegal business practices like the **bankruptcy scam**. In this scenario, criminals will establish a corporation and buy out a legitimate company, paying only part of the purchase price in cash. The rest is to be paid off in mortgagelike installments. They then order merchandise from the company's regular suppliers, who are probably unaware of the change in ownership. The crooks then sell off all the company assets (including the new supplies) and transfer the cash from these sales to another corporation, also controlled by the criminal organization. The company then goes bankrupt, leaving its suppliers unpaid. The company and its good name have been destroyed, the suppliers have taken severe losses they can never recover, and the money winds up largely in the pockets of organized crime. In one variation of this scam, before the company declares bankruptcy a mysterious fire destroys its books and records and perhaps its buildings, which are of course insured.

Another criminal practice involves substituting inferior goods or services. Hauling companies in an organized crime cartel are more likely to violate environmental laws. In some cases, trucks hauling toxic wastes have simply discharged their toxic contents into ordinary city sewers or at the side of a road.[49] In the meat business, companies connected to the Mafia have used rotting or diseased meat in ground beef, frankfurters, and sausage. They have even used horse meat in place of beef.[50] Diseased meat is potentially harmful to consumers, as are the chemicals suppliers may use to mask its smell. That's why the government inspects meat. However, to avoid the inconvenience of having meat rejected, criminal companies bribe inspectors. Here is another common area for organized crime: corruption. Since organized crime operations—especially the fully illegal ones—require law enforcers to look the other way, bribery of the police and other public officials is an important part of organized crime. At higher levels, they may bribe officials who decide which companies get government contracts.

Ignoring regulations, bribing officials, and using cheap ingredients are ways to beat the competition. When the Mafia becomes involved in a legitimate business, it also seeks to eliminate competition altogether. Businesses run by organized crime may use violence (actual or threatened) as a method for accomplishing this goal. For example, in the 1970s, an organized crime outfit took over a not very successful detergent company. The soap was not very good, and the company tried to market it as a low-priced, supermarket house brand. By threatening stores with labor problems if they didn't go along, the Mafia managed to get the inferior soap into most of the New York markets. Only A&P refused to go along since the soap did not pass A&P's quality control tests. Soon, A&P stores and warehouses became the targets of a series of fires and explosions. Store managers were beaten, and two managers were murdered. The Justice Department stepped in, and although no one was convicted, the continual pressure of grand jury subpoenas and indictments convinced the mobsters to quit. However, the soap remained in other stores. Only when the FDA (Food and Drug Administration), some years later, ruled that the soap was corrosive to the skin did it disappear from the shelves.[51]

Of course, usually the Mafia does not have to go so far in carrying out its violence. Remember, the other supermarket chains gave in and stocked the inferior soap. In a similar way, the Mafia can use violence to gain control of a union. Once it has control, further actual violence is seldom necessary as the threat is usually sufficient to elicit compliance.

Control of a union by organized crime creates dangers that parallel those of Mafia firms in the legitimate marketplace. The Mafia can use the union to launder money, or it can provide the cover of employment for people who make their money illegally. Most crucial, the union will be run to enrich the criminals rather than to improve the lot of the rank-and-file membership. Union leaders can use their positions to extort bribes from businesses that must deal with the unions. Builders may find that unless they pay off certain people, they will have labor problems. Every nonwork day on a building costs them money, so they will save money by paying the bribe. The bribe, of course, stays in the pockets of the criminals; it does not go to any purpose that might benefit the rank and file.

Some bribes are detrimental to union members themselves. In these cases, the bribe does not ensure that the work goes on. Instead, the corrupt union leaders write a sweetheart contract—one that allows the employer to violate the usual contract terms by paying lower wages, hiring nonunion workers, or ignoring various rules. The union leaders who take the bribes benefit, and the employer benefits. But the workers themselves wind up working under less pleasant, more dangerous conditions and for less money.

Finally, when criminals run a union, they may steal the union's money. It's usually not so simple and obvious as embezzlement, but the effect is the same. The most notorious and large-scale examples come from the Teamsters Union. Through members' dues and employers' payments, the union has amassed large funds—well over $10 billion—to pay for each teamster's pension when he or she retires. In the meantime, the pension fund money must be invested. Much of the Teamster pension fund "investments" turn out to be risky loans, often to Mafia associates. If the borrower goes bankrupt, the union loses out, but someone has profited. At the same time, while Mafia figures easily tap into the pension funds, some retired union members have had great trouble getting the union to pay their pensions.[52]

"A GOVERNMENT FOR WISEGUYS"[53]

In many of these ventures—criminal or "legitimate"—the Mafia itself is not running the actual business. Instead, it sanctions the illegal work of others and in return gets a share of the profits. The picture of the Mafia we get here is not a business bureaucracy but a loose network of **patron-client relationships**, an authority structure.[54] Those below pay tribute to those above. This structure, rather than that of a corporation, is something like a (nondemo-cratic) government. The government licenses operations, and in return each level must pay a percentage or fee (like a tax or licensing fee) to the level above. The garbage company owner pays money to the cartel organizer, who in turn pays money to a Mafia member, who in turn passes some of that money to his capo (or captain, a patron higher up in the authority structure). The capo may not really care what kind of business his soldati are running, as long as they pay him his share. It may be a business cartel or a labor union, a hijacking ring or a stock fraud, but some of the profits go upward through the organization. In return, those who pay the tax or tribute receive the equivalent of a franchise. They operate their business with the backing of the Mafia, which provides any necessary protection.

Thinking of the Mafia as a licensing structure of power rather than as a bureaucratic organization points to what may be the Mafia's unique and most important function—not business but arbitration. The Mafia, unlike any other criminal organization, functions as a court for settling disputes in the under-world. In illegal circles, competition among different organizations can lead to conflict; and when there is no established way of resolving conflict, the result can easily be violence—as the experience of the 1920s and 1930s showed. What seems to have emerged from the gangland wars of that era is not so much the elimination of non-Italian, non-Mafia criminal organizations. Non-Italian gangsters (mostly Jewish and Irish) continued to run illegal business-es. But the Mafia came to occupy a central place in settling conflict. It became a sort of government.

A government—an official government—almost by definition has a monop-oly on the legitimate use of force. Consequently, the government acts as the ulti-mate settler of disputes, and the authority of the courts in settling disputes rests finally on the government's monopoly of force. Similarly, what distin-guishes the Mafia from other criminal organizations is its reputation for being able to command great force. It does not necessarily have a monopoly on heavy persuasion, but it does have the reputation of being the most effective. The Mafia earned this reputation in the 1920s during Prohibition, when Italian gangs won out over their rivals largely because of their greater willingness or ability to use violence. That reputation continues to this day. Thus, while the Mafia may not have a total monopoly on violence in the criminal world, it has carved out a large enough chunk of the market that it has come to function as a kind of government. After all, somebody has to fulfill this role since parties in these disputes cannot turn to the usual sources to resolve their differences. For example, if a legitimate liquor supplier has trouble collecting payment from a bar owner, the supplier can sue in court for the unpaid balance or he can recov-er the liquor and sue for the expense of shipping. But what if the supplier is a thief and the liquor is stolen? What recourse does the supplier have?

Because the Mafia arbitrates disputes, a Mafia member can provide a second service for the criminal who pays it tribute: If a dispute arises, he has representation. To have the backing of a Mafia member in such a dispute is an invaluable advantage. Only Mafia members may participate in settling dis-putes. Nonmembers must be represented by a member. The higher the rank of the person backing you, the better off you are. Remember, the Mafia is not a bureaucracy run according to rules. The "rules"—to the extent that they

IN THE NEWS

The power to settle disputes like a government is the hallmark of the highest level of organized crime, whether the criminal organization has its origins in Italy or in Russia.

TOP ECHELON OF MOBSTERS IS A THREAT

by Selwyn Rabb

In Russia, they are called Vory v Zakone, "thieves-in-law," the top criminal echelon. For American law-enforcement agencies, they are a new threat....

Russian organized-crime experts estimate that there are about 800 Vory v Zakone in the world, [Jim Moody, chief of the FBI's organized-crime section] said.

"They are the closest thing the Russians have to being a made guy in the Cosa Nostra," he said....

The Vory v Zakone are not necessarily members of the same gang but ... belong to an honored category of criminals who are empowered to resolve disputes among gangsters. Mr.

Moody said that the existence of the Vory v Zakone was believed to predate the communist revolution in 1917 and that all members were recruited while in prison and branded with a tattoo of an eagle with talons, usually on their hands.

"They had a sort of a coronation ceremony in prison or in the old gulags here they took an oath never to work and never to cooperate with the police or the military," he said.

Source: New York Times, August 23, 1994, p. B2.

---

exist at all—are ideals like respect, honor, loyalty, and secrecy; qualities that have more to do with personal relationships than with a highly specified set of procedures. The basic principles of the organization are personalistic rather than bureaucratic; it is a government of men, not of laws.

At the simplest level, a disputant with no Mafia backing has no chance in a dispute with a Mafia member. An independent loan shark or bookmaker, for example, who is owed money by a member of the Mafia (or someone fronting for one) has no way of collecting if the Mafioso decides not to pay.[55] The illegal entrepreneur has two ways of avoiding this problem—either screen customers carefully or make a connection with a member of the Mafia who will represent him if the dispute must be arbitrated.

When disputes arise between Mafia members or between people who are represented by members, things can become more complicated, as the following example shows.

> Michael Hellerman was a successful, young (Jewish) stock manipulator. He maintained a long-term relationship with Johnny (Dio) Dioguardi, a major Mafioso in the Lucchese family, whose main source of income seems to have been labor racketeering.

> Hellerman had been involved in an unsuccessful swindle that had lost money for two minor Mafiosi, Fusco and Burke, members of the Colombo family. He now began a new one and offered to let them share in the proceeds so as to compensate them for the former failure. The swindle required that Hellerman control all the sales of a certain stock. The other party, Stein, who had initiated the deal, now tried to cheat Hellerman through some undisclosed sales. Hellerman found out about this and confronted one of Stein's associates at a meeting in Miami.

Stein arranged for Fusco and Burke to be informed that he was being backed by a Mafioso of the Bonnano family, Evola. Stein, in the course of negotiations about arranging an adjudication, insulted Fusco. Fusco obtained permission from his own boss, Aloi, and Stein's mentor, to give Stein a beating for failure to show respect.

A meeting was arranged involving all the principals and their mentors. The other participants had not believed that Hellerman would be able to obtain Dioguardi's explicit help and had arranged that Hellerman would end up as the loser, being required to compensate everyone else. When Dio actually turned up at the meeting, Hellerman moved from being the least protected to the most protected, since Dio was the most senior of the Mafiosi present.

Dio ordered Stein to work out an acceptable arrangement with Hellerman; this yielded a total of $78,000 to be divided by the numerous parties. The division was extremely complicated. Hellerman ended up as the prime individual beneficiary, with $15,000. However, Dio, who had risked no money and invested minimal time, also received $7,500. Aloi and his associates, who had invested a great deal more time, received only about $1,500 each.[56]

This incident illustrates several points. First, not all scams work; Hellerman's original swindle had lost money. Second, notice the lack of honor among thieves. Stein tried to cheat Hellerman. One partner cheating another is a constant problem in illegal enterprises, as is the cheating of employers by employees. Third, the use of violence (especially against other Mafia members or associates) has to be cleared with a superior. This seems to be a general rule in the Mafia. Fourth, what mattered ultimately was not so much the facts of the case but the status of the representatives involved. Fifth, the high-ranking Mafioso winds up with nearly 10 percent of the money, all because of his position, not his effort. (Johnny Dio was involved in rackets ranging from corrupt unions to kosher meat and was widely believed to have been the one who, in a famous incident in the 1950s, blinded journalist Victor Riesel by throwing acid in his face. Hellerman eventually became a government witness and testified against Dio, who received a long prison sentence.)

Finally, the incident shows that the dispute-settling mechanism works not just within a Mafia family but also between different families, and that members of one family respect the rank designations of other families. Johnny Dio, because of his position in the Lucchese family, outranks the lower-level members of the Colombo family. In this sense, and probably only in this sense, is the Mafia a coordinated network of families. This coordination occurs primarily in settling disputes, usually between families but occasionally within them.

Summary and Conclusion

Although most crime is socially organized in some degree, the term *organized crime* refers to large-scale criminal organizations—especially those that rely on violence, threatened or actual, to make money through crime. Organized crime often goes hand in hand with the corruption of public officials. Nevertheless, precise, useful definitions of organized crime have proven elusive in both criminology and law enforcement. The principal law defining organized crime (the Racketeer Influenced and Corrupt Organizations Act, or RICO) is so broad that it has been used in criminal and civil actions that have nothing to do with what most people think of as organized crime.

In America, criminal organizations have often arisen in immigrant communities. Groups that start by providing real services for their fellow immigrants may end up extorting them. Protection can turn into a protection racket. Criminal organizations still make money by meeting the demand for illegal goods and services. However, the supply side of the market in illegal drugs, gambling, loans, and sex consists of a large number of small-scale entrepreneurs. Even the largest suppliers do not control the market in vice.

The Mafia is probably the largest and longest-lived criminal organization. Like members of other criminal organizations, Mafia members often make their money from vice. In addition, the various Mafia groups, probably more than other criminal organizations, make a great deal of their money from their influence in more legitimate organizations—unions and businesses. By manipulating the legitimate functions of these organizations (strikes and contract negotiations, bids for private and government contracts, investment of pension fund money, filings for bankruptcy, etc.), the Mafia-backed groups derive income far in excess of what an unrigged market and honest business practices would bring.

The degree of organization within the Mafia is a matter of much debate and uncertainty, as is its connection (past and present) with criminal organizations in Italy. Law-enforcement officials often portray the Mafia as a highly organized national and international conspiracy. Other observers see each Mafia "family" as a loose arrangement in which members independently seek out criminal opportunities and pay a portion of the profits to those above them in the organization. The organization in return provides backing, should any disputes arise. In fact, it probably would be more accurate to think of the Mafia not as an arrangement for committing certain types of crime but rather as an arrangement for regulating relations among people who do commit those crimes.

CRITICAL THINKING QUESTIONS

1. How are organized crime groups different from "legitimate" organizations whose criminal behavior is usually called white-collar crime?
2. What are our most important sources of information about the Mafia and organized crime and why might they be biased?
3. How did Prohibition reverse the power relationship between politicians and gangsters?
4. What special factors make it difficult to run a criminal organization in the same bureaucratic way in which legitimate large-scale organizations are run?
5. Some observers claim that the Mafia controls vice—prostitution, gambling, drugs, and loan-sharking. What aspects of the economic structure of each of these enterprises makes it more or less susceptible to domination by a single organized crime group?

KEY TERMS

Apalachin conference
bankruptcy scam
bureaucratic model

Kefauver
committee

Mafia myth

patron-client
relationships

RICO

CHAPTER NINE

WHITE-COLLAR CRIME

CHAPTER OUTLINE

Every so often, a bit of sociological language crosses over into general use. Despite criticism that sociology uses needless jargon—new and clumsy words that make the obvious seem obscure—sociological terms like *lifestyle* and *role model* are now part of the language. But of all the terms originating in sociology, none has passed into greater currency than *white-collar crime*. The phrase was coined by Edwin Sutherland and first used in his presidential address to the American Sociological Society in 1939. Clearly, white-collar crime was a concept waiting to be born and christened, and Sutherland, the father of white-collar crime, seems to have chosen precisely the right name. The term moved quickly and broadly into general use. The French now have *crime en col blanc*; the Italians, *criminalità in colletti bianchi*; and the Germans, *weisse-kragen-kriminalitat*.[1] Sutherland was chiding his colleagues for focusing their criminological theorizing and research almost exclusively on the crimes of the poor. This focus, he said, led them not only to ignore a great deal of crime but also to construct bad theories. These theories—reflecting ideas that are still popular—attributed crime to individual or social defects like poverty, low intelligence, psychological problems, or broken families. But how useful were these theories, asked Sutherland, if they could not apply to white-collar crimes?[2]

The criminal prosecution of white-collar crime poses special problems. In 1993, FBI agents posed as traders at the Mercantile exchange in Chicago in an attempt to uncover wrongdoing. Merc traders were immediately suspicious of these inexperienced yet high-rolling newcomers, and the operation resulted in only a handful of minor convictions.

Sutherland mentioned several crimes and topics that remain on the research agenda for white-collar crime today: bribery in government and business, unnecessary treatment in medicine, embezzlement, tax fraud, insider trading, and political corruption. These crimes, as Sutherland pointed out, are far more costly than the street crimes of the poor, and the comparison tends to contradict our usual assumption that "respectable" people in responsible positions are somehow more moral than those who live at the margins of society. But it takes only a moment of consideration to realize that as people become wealthier and more powerful, the more serious the crimes they can commit. The robber barons—the nineteenth-century giants of the railroads, banks, and other enterprises—provide the most glaring and costly examples of upperworld criminal greed, though in the opinion of many observers that dubious distinction must now go to those involved in the savings-and-loan (S&L) debacle of the late twentieth century. Only people with access to large amounts of money—especially if they have the support and approval of the government—could do so much financial damage. As the old saying puts it, "The best way to rob a bank is to own one." The respectability that comes with wealth and government backing also serves as a buffer against efforts to control white-collar crime, as Sutherland, writing over fifty years ago, pointed out. Not only do the wealthy and powerful influence the writing of the very laws that are intended to control their sins, but also their status protects them from harsh penalties when they do violate these laws.[3]

In the years following Sutherland's landmark article, white-collar crime remained relatively ignored among criminologists and sociologists. Instead, most theory and research continued to focus on juvenile delinquency and street crime. Perhaps this inattention to white-collar crime reflected the temper of the times, for in the two decades following World War II the large institutions of business and government in the United States enjoyed a position of popular confidence and respect. The only noticeable dark spot occurred in 1961, when several vice presidents of General Electric, Westinghouse, and other manufacturers of electrical equipment were convicted and imprisoned for price-fixing. Even this case probably did little to shift the public trust in big business. Only government prosecutors seemed to be complaining that the rules were being broken. The public could not find any victims to feel sorry for, and the executives on trial had not been taking any money for themselves.

However, beginning in the late 1960s the political climate began to change. Public reactions to the Vietnam War and then Watergate signaled the increasing suspicion and even resentment of the government. Business, too, suffered a loss of public confidence[4] as consumer activists and environmentalists began to document unsafe car design, indiscriminate use of chemicals, marketing of unsafe products, and other business shortcomings. The stories involved some of the largest corporations—General Motors, Ford, Firestone, Union Carbide, Eli Lilly, and A. H. Robbins. Their misdeeds—badly designed automobiles and tires, dangerous and improperly tested drugs and medical devices, and toxic pollutants released into the workplace and environment—did more than add a few dollars to corporate profits. They also cost human lives.

DEFINING WHITE-COLLAR CRIME

According to Sutherland's original definition, white-collar crime is "a crime committed by a person of respectability and high social status in the course of his occupation."[5] This definition distinguishes upperworld crime from street crime, but it still includes a diverse multitude of sins. For example, in Sutherland's definition, the bank teller who embezzles and the bank president who launders drug money are both white-collar criminals, although obviously their crimes differ in some important ways. Criminologists have tried to refine the definition to distinguish between these different types of crime. In doing so, they have looked at several aspects of the crime. Who is the victim—the public (as in consumer fraud) or the organization itself (as in embezzlement)? Who benefits directly from the crime—the individual or the organization? Does the criminal act independently or as a member of the organization? Is the crime the central part of the company's business (like fraudulent land sales), or is it only one part of an otherwise legitimate business (as in tax evasion and bribery)?

CATEGORIES OF WHITE-COLLAR CRIME

Some crimes that Sutherland might have classified as white-collar crime seem to resemble street crime. When workers steal from their employers, the crime is not much different from shoplifting, the principal difference being that the thief is an employee rather than a customer. These offenses are probably best categorized as **occupational crime**, meaning a crime that people commit at work. Usually, the victim is the employer.

When government employees and officials use their jobs to victimize people, their occupational crimes usually fall into the category of **corruption**. Police corruption, for example, usually takes the form of officers accepting or demanding money in exchange for not enforcing the law. In a similar way, government inspectors may take bribes in return for overlooking health and safety violations; inspectors may even extort payments from companies with no violations. In other cases, officials may take the public services of their agencies and sell them privately. Employees in the Department of Motor Vehicles have been caught selling driver's licenses and registrations; employees of the Immigration and Naturalization Service have sold phony green cards and other documents.

In occupational crime, the criminal is an individual misusing his or her position in an otherwise legitimate organization. In **organizational crime**, however, it is the organization itself that is committing the crimes. In some cases, the organization has no legitimate purpose; it is a front—a means of making money through fraud and deceit. Most **swindles** follow this pattern, for example bankruptcy scams and elaborate confidence games. The criminals misrepresent either themselves or their businesses to get people to hand over their money. In a Ponzi scheme, the swindler poses as an investment broker and promises a temptingly high return. Investors who put in $50,000 may find themselves receiving a divi-

ON CAMPUS

Nonprofit institutions like colleges and charities are less likely to be involved in corporate crime than are institutions oriented toward making money. However, they may still be sites for high-level employee theft. This case illustrates some general features of white-collar crime. The criminal is older—in this case much older—than the typical street criminal, and his profits are much larger. The crimes (let us assume that the charges are true) took place over a long period of time without being discovered. The discovery of the crime and the original actions against the criminal were carried out by others within the organization, not law-enforcement officials. Finally, the crimes are also the subject of lawsuits in civil court.

EX-HEAD OF BAPTIST COLLEGE PLEADS NOT GUILTY TO FRAUD

Jackson, Miss., Sept. 22—The former President of Mississippi College, a Baptist institution founded in 1826, pleaded not guilty in Federal District Court today to charges that he stole $1.7 million in college donations. The authorities said he used the money to buy stocks and pay for prostitutes and lavish gifts.

The 20-count indictment ... included charges of money laundering and viola-

tions of the Mann act, which bars the transportation of a woman across state lines for "immoral purposes."

The charges follow a yearlong investigation by the [FBI], which entered the case after college officials filed a lawsuit against Mr. Nobles, accusing him of embezzling more than $3 million....

The Federal indictment accuses him of diverting donations for 17 years. Mr. Nobles took over as president in 1968, publicizing the 3,000-student college ... as a place where virtue was valued.

"If you wish a college that will place no restrictions on your behavior, this is not your college," he told students in 1971. "If you wish freedom to drink on campus, you are in the wrong place."

Last summer, the authorities said, college officials started the action that led to the indictment when they entered his office and found $27,000 in cash. The Clarion-Ledger reported that officials also found Polaroid pictures of scantily clad women and a bottle of strychnine in his briefcase. Alongside his books on the Bible, the authorities said they found publications on how to hide money in bank accounts in foreign countries.

Source: New York Times, September 23, 1994, p. A16.

dend of $2,000 after only two months—an annual rate of 24 percent. Word spreads, more investors get in on the good deal, and for a while the dividends keep coming. The only problem is that there is no real investment. The swindler is paying the early investors' dividends out of the money received from new investors. When the swindlers have brought in enough capital, they disappear with the money. Ponzi swindlers are often so persuasive that their victims can scarcely believe that such kind and generous persons could have been stealing all their savings. Equally persuasive, although they operate almost entirely by phone, are salespeople in boiler room rackets. Working from carefully prepared scripts, they convince people to put their money into investments—penny stocks, real estate, art, or coins—that turn out to be nearly worthless. A psychologist who examined one such script said that it "taps into every human weakness ... every way to flatter, bully, cajole, intimidate," adding, "It would take a very secure person to say no to the pressure and manipulation."[6]

Individuals are not the only victims of fraudulent schemes. Bankruptcy frauds victimize other businesses, as do other forms of cheating or chiseling, in which a company inflates its bills or deliberately fails to deliver goods and services that customers have paid for. The victims may be individuals but more often they are other businesses or the government, as in Medicaid fraud, in which doctors file false bills or perform many unnecessary procedures.

In all of these swindles and scams, the criminals set out with the express purpose of getting money through fraud. Not so with **corporate crime**; here corporations that are by and large legitimate break some laws as part of their operations. Price-fixing, bribery, commercial espionage, misrepresentation of goods, and the violation of safety regulations all fall into this category. Although some of the criminals are fairly small-scale, this type of white-collar crime sometimes involves large, well-known corporations.[7] During the 1980s, at least twenty-five of the largest military contractors were found guilty of fraud in their dealings with the Pentagon. Several companies, including Teledyne, Boeing, and the Hughes Aircraft division of General Motors, illegally obtained Pentagon documents that allowed them to inflate their bids. Northrop falsified test results on some of the components of missiles and aircraft. Rockwell, GTE, and Litton, among others, were guilty of overcharging the government millions of dollars.[8]

HOW MUCH WHITE-COLLAR CRIME IS THERE?

The problems associated with counting street crimes are nothing compared with the difficulty of measuring white-collar crime. Just defining the crimes is difficult, and getting an accurate count is impossible. Suppose that a drug company suppressed the data from two different tests of its drug, that doctors then prescribed the drug to 250,000 patients, and that 500 of these patients suffered harmful side effects. How many crimes should we count? If a corporation violates fourteen safety regulations in three of its factories over the course of eighteen months, but no workers suffer harm as a result, how many crimes should we count?

Measuring the amount of damage can be just as difficult as counting the crimes. Early estimates of the cost of the S&L crisis ranged between $23 billion and $53 billion. Four years later the lowest estimate was $50 billion, and some experts were putting the cost at $1.4 trillion. Of course, since the victim in this debacle was the government, it could spread the cost over the entire population and over a period of many years rather than sticking each taxpayer with a single $2,000 surcharge. Because the cost of the crimes could be socialized and deferred, public outrage was surprisingly subdued.[9] Americans seemed more interested in electing legislators who would pass mandatory twenty-five-year sentences for a first-time drug offender than in punishing an S&L fraud artist who cost the public millions of dollars.

A few criminologists have used the FBI's Uniform Crime Reports as sources of data on white-collar crime.[10] The UCR has information on fraud, forgery, and embezzlement—often thought of as white-collar crimes. The UCR tally, however, does not come from crimes known to the police (i.e., crimes where the victim called the police) but from arrests. It is unlikely that these numbers reflect much of the reality of white-collar crime. Like the tallies for gambling, prostitution, and other forms of vice, the official count of white-collar crime—that is, arrests reported in the UCR—depends mainly on what the police do, not on what the criminals do. More important, these crimes are usually not sophisticated, corporate-level crimes but individual, small-scale offenses: Much fraud turns out to be nothing more than using a stolen credit card or even writing bad checks.[11] So when the UCR shows a high rate of fraud in the South—a rate 450 percent higher than that of Western states—it is telling us not that Southerners are five times more fraudulent than Westerners, but that they are more willing to use the criminal justice system against people who bounce checks. Still, UCR arrest data show that even these "white-collar" criminals differ from street criminals. The world of street crime is dominated by young men; but arrests for forgery, fraud, and embezzlement include substantial numbers of women as well as people above the legal drinking age (see Figure 9–1).

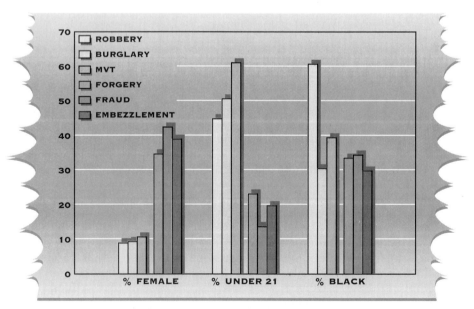

FIGURE 9–1   Arrests, 1992 (Street Crime and White-collar Crime)

One other source of information on corporate crime is the official records of the various inspection agencies that monitor certain industries for health and safety violations. These records, however, are subject to the selective bias of the inspectors. Probably most corporate misdeeds never come to light. Even so, despite all the crimes that escape detection or prosecution, the numbers are astonishing. The most complete records are those of the U.S. Mine Safety and Health Administration, which is required by law to inspect mines four times each year. The agency records about 140,000 violations annually.[12] Little wonder that miners have one of the highest rates of work-related deaths, much higher, for example, than that of the police.

As for nonsafety violations, Sutherland, in his pioneering work in the 1940s, examined the 70 largest corporations in the United States over a fifty-year period. Nearly all the companies (98 percent) had two or more violations, and the total number of violations came to 980—an average of 14 per company—mostly in such areas as restraint of trade, unfair labor practices, and false advertising.[13] Thirty-five years later, a study of the nation's 477 largest manufacturing corporations found that nearly half had committed at least one "serious or moderate" violation. This category excluded minor violations such as those concerning record keeping. One hundred and twenty of these firms had multiple violations,[14] and these are only the violations that resulted in some government action. Presumably, they represent only a fraction of the true number of violations. Some industries were more law breaking than others. Oil refining, for example, had a disproportionate share of the violations, financial as well as environmental. Motor vehicle and pharmaceutical manufacturers also had far more than their share of the total violations.[15]

EXPLAINING WHITE-COLLAR CRIME

Several years ago, the political journalist Jack Newfield wrote that when it comes to crime, nobody's a liberal anymore. That is, nobody still believes that robbers and burglars are basically good kids who turned to crime merely because of their social circumstances. But with white-collar crime, or at least corporate crime, it seems that nobody's a conservative. The conservative view of crime tends to attribute crime to defects within the individual, deemphasizing the effects of the social environment. In the much-quoted phrase of conservative criminologist James Q. Wilson, "Wicked people exist." However, nearly all analyses of large-scale white-collar crime barely consider individual motives or morals at all. In fact, the critics most willing to blame corporate crime on the wickedness of individuals are those usually thought of as liberals. Ralph Nader, for example, objects to the use of the word "crisis" in connection with the S&L debacle, referring instead to "crimes" and "the looting of the savers' monies."[16] With street crime, criminologists have exhaustively researched every aspect of criminals' lives, from their parents' employment histories to their brain waves. Yet until very recently, theory and research

IN THE NEWS

Some people think that corruption and other types of white-collar crime are more widespread in the United States than in other industrialized countries like Germany or Great Britain and that the differences are attributable to certain aspects of American culture.

AMID A HERITAGE OF GRAFT, A TAXI BRIBERY SCANDAL SEEMS SHOCKING TO FEW

by Dennis Hevisi

In 1653, the Dutch settlers of Manhattan hired a retired pirate to build a wall at the north end of what was then New Amsterdam to ward off Indians who, perhaps, had soured on the original $24 deal.

Within two years the wall—which later gave Wall Street its name—was crumbling.... The Pirate ... was accused of using low-grade lumber and pocketing half of the colonial equivalent of $1,300 that had been appropriated for the project. (The Indians, by the way, never attacked.)

So last week's accusations that more than half of New York City's taxi inspectors took bribes to overlook safety and pollution violations in yellow cabs, and that three top officials in the Board of Education's school security office were involved in illegal real-estate deals, pension abuses and nepotism came as no great shock.... "If you take most European cities, there is a

burgher mentality, a belief that municipal service is a very high calling," Dr. [Richard C.] Wade [professor of the history of cities] said. "It's for a life time. You train for it. It's nonpartisan. And it creates a culture of service rather than one of opportunity."

In the United States, public service has always been more politicized, Dr. Wade said,...

Joseph D. McNamara, a former police chief ... who is now a research fellow ... pointed out a paradox: that often efforts to halt corruption by citizens often create opportunities for corruption. "The more society passes regulations, the more power is given to inspectors to shake someone down."

Source: *New York Times*, July 26, 1992, sec. IV, p. 28.

about individual white-collar criminals was noticeably absent. Few criminologists bothered to investigate the characteristics of individual white-collar criminals, assuming that these criminals are psychologically and biologically no different from white-collar workers who do *not* violate the law; and in fact, the few psychological studies of white-collar criminals find them to be quite normal.[17] So rather than thinking in terms of wicked people or lack of opportunity, criminologists searching for explanations of white-collar crime, especially corporate crime, have turned their attention to institutional forces, both external and internal. External forces include the pressures and opportunities of the market; internal forces refer mostly to the culture of a particular company or organization.

Some external pressures permeate the entire society. Emphasis on competition and the profit motive predominate in U.S. businesses. In addition, as Robert Merton suggested in his classic 1938 essay, American culture places a higher value on goal attainment than on strict adherence to proper procedures, a value that may get the job done but one that also produces more crime.[18] Of course, these aspects of American culture affect all businesses. Studies that try to show the effect of external forces, therefore, usually focus on factors that vary from one business to another. For example, by using these ideas we might test the hypothesis that corporate crime will be less frequent in nonprofit organizations or government agencies, where the profit motive is unimportant, than in for-profit corporations.

EXTERNAL FORCES—THE MARKET

Even among profit-oriented businesses, external factors may influence corporate crime. For example, we would expect that violations would be more frequent when business is bad, and in fact, some research does find that firms in depressed industries and firms with declining profits are more likely to violate antitrust laws.[19] Because fixing prices is easier in some industries than in others, another factor that might be related to price fixing and other antitrust violations is **market concentration**—the degree to which the market is concentrated in the hands of a few producers. Criminologists assume that despite all the patriotic statements from business executives and politicians about the virtues of free enterprise, those who run the business would rather not leave such an important matter as profit to the uncertainties of a free market. As Adam Smith, the father of free enterprise economics, wrote nearly 300 years ago, "People of the same trade seldom meet together ... but the conversation ends in a conspiracy against the public or in some contrivance to raise prices."

In an industry consisting of many sellers, antitrust violations seem unlikely since the conspiracy, if it is to be effective, must involve so many participants. When an industry is highly concentrated, with a few large firms dominating the market, collusion to reduce competition becomes more possible. The 1960s price-fixing of electrical equipment, for example, required the collusion of only a few manufacturers. However, despite this intuitive and anecdotal evidence, actual research into antitrust violations has not been able to provide systematic evidence for the relationship between market concentration and price-fixing.[20]

Market concentration can create pressures for other crimes apart from antitrust violations. When a few manufacturers dominate the market, they can squeeze distributors, who in turn resort to shady practices to make a profit. For example, two studies from the 1970s illustrate the way in which automobile dealers, who were in a truly competitive market, were squeezed by Detroit. The manufacturers, through the use of sales quotas, bonuses, and threats of cutting off the low-sales dealerships, pressured dealers to sell cars at low prices. The dealer could scarcely take his business elsewhere; a Chevrolet dealer could not quickly switch to Ford, and if he did, he would probably find himself under similar pressures. So to avoid losses, dealers engaged in service and repair frauds: phony labor charges, unnecessary repairs, used parts billed as new, and so on. Sometimes the victim was the manufacturer (if the car was under warranty), but manufacturers, by paying

IN THE NEWS

The structure of the auto industry—even though no longer dominated by the Big Three—puts pressure on local dealers. In this case, government regulations also played an important part in creating these pressures. Note also that the criminal investigation began, as in many white-collar crime cases, only after a disgruntled competitor initiated a civil suit and that much of the evidence came from people within the organization who have themselves taken part in the crimes.

PAYMENTS BY CAR DEALERS

Concord, N.H. March 14—Federal prosecutors are uncovering a long-running fraud in which American executives of the Honda Motor Company pocketed more than $10 million in bribes and kickbacks paid by car dealers. In return, the dealers received permission to open lucrative dealerships and obtained scarce Honda automobiles that they could sell at a large profit.

Prosecutors said that the largest amount of cash and gifts went to Honda's top sales executive in the United States.... Eight other executives also agreed to plead guilty

today to Federal crimes connected to the illegal payments. [The] United States attorney ... said the eight executives agreed to cooperate in a widening investigation in return for recommendations of leniency in sentencing.

Corrupt practices by Honda officials were almost certainly facilitated by the sensational demand for Honda's cars throughout the 1980s. Starting in 1981, the importation of Hondas and other Japanese cars was limited by a voluntary restraint agreement between Japan and the United States. That agreement, meant to ease competitive pressure on the Big Three auto makers, created a risk-free environment for Honda dealers, who could sell at a profit nearly every car they could get on their lots.

Many dealers kept long waiting lists for each Honda they received, and they often sold the cars for more than the sticker price—sometimes for thousands of dollars more. Having more cars to sell automatically meant more profit.

Since all dealers wanted more cars, Honda supposedly distributed its cars equitably, on the basis of how quickly dealers sold

what they had. But some dealers were apparently willing to bribe the Honda executives in charge of distribution for extra vehicles and additional franchises....

The guilty pleas ... lend credence to rumors about Honda activities that have circulated for years among dealers and auto industry executives but only recently have been exposed as a result of civil litigation....

Richard M. Nault, a car dealer from ... Manchester, sued Honda in 1989 after his Acura dealership first foundered and then was canceled by Honda.... Mr. Nault contended that one reason his Acura store had done poorly was that he could not get enough cars.

While Mr. Nault's franchise was failing, a rival Acura dealer in Nashua was getting plenty of cars and doing well. Mr. Nault had heard that the owner of the Nashua showroom ... was friendly with an Acura sales executive ... and that was why [he] received more cars.

Source: Doron P. Levin, "Prosecutors Link Honda Fraud Cases to U.S. Executives," and "How 2 Dealers' Squabble Broke a Scandal at Honda," *New York Times*, March 15, 1994, pp. A1, D19.

---

only set rates for each repair or by offering rewards to dealers who underspent their warranty budget, could protect themselves. Usually the victim was the car owner.[21] Pressures on dealers have probably not changed much in subsequent decades. Car dealers still sell unsuspecting car buyers extended service contracts at inflated prices.

INTERNAL FORCES—CORPORATE CULTURE

The other major explanation of white-collar crime is cultural. The earliest version is Sutherland's own theory of differential association, which he saw as an explanation for both street crime and white-collar crime. Sutherland stressed the learning aspect of crime—that both criminal techniques and criminal ideas were learned from other people. Other theorists extended this principle of differential association, explaining different crime rates by looking at the values and norms of different cultures or subcultures. Applied to white-collar crime, particularly corporate crime, these theories suggest that an organization, like different groups or subcultures in society, develops a particular **corporate culture**. Some of these cultures may be more tolerant of crime. In fact, the employees may find themselves under great pressure to participate in various forms of unethical or even criminal behavior.

The case for cultural explanations seems much more applicable to corporate crime than to street crime. Corporations, in contrast, are a more closed environment. They have clearer boundaries, and within those boundaries the organization exerts far more control. One business expert has compared the executive levels of the corporation to a monastery or the army—the sameness of people one meets socially, the emphasis on loyalty, and the great demands on the executive's time.[22] The area of the employee's life that the corporation touches may be more limited, but the leeway for individual choice in that area is much narrower. Those who resist corporate pressures for unethical or illegal behavior may not be promoted or may be given less attractive assignments. Whistle-blowers may find themselves demoted or even fired. There is another difference between corporate culture and subcultures in the wider society. Because corporate culture exists in a more structured environment, those at the top can exert more direct control over it. As several researchers have found, the highest levels of management, particularly the CEO (chief executive officer), set the tone of corporate culture, including its tolerance for breaking the law.[23] Therefore, compared with the less structured subculture of a neighborhood or social class, corporate culture is easier to change—*if* the managers want to change it.

Although the general culture of the organization may be the most important aspect in corporate crime, it provides a difficult target for law-enforcement agencies. After all, you can't prosecute a cultural atmosphere; you can prosecute only specific acts by specific people. Usually, top executives are able to use the structure of the organization to keep themselves insulated from any legal responsibility. Typically, they pressure middle-level managers for results with no word about whether the results must be achieved ethically and legally. In such a climate, employees understand that results are more important than methods, and this message easily travels down through the levels of management. At the same time, the corporate structure often prevents bad news from traveling up. If test results show a product to be ineffective or unsafe, if bribes have been paid to clients or government officials, or if managers have colluded with other corporations to fix prices, this sort of information may never reach the top levels of a company's management—at least not in any way that is traceable.

IN THE NEWS

Often, white-collar cases come to the attention of the authorities when someone inside the offending company blows the whistle, usually after he or she has made unsuccessful attempts within the company to stop the illegal behavior. As this example shows, despite recent federal laws to protect whistle-blowers, insiders who try to do the right thing may still be risking their jobs. Note also that the effective action was taken by a regulatory agency, not the criminal justice system.

REBUKE AND REVENGE AT MET LIFE

by Michael Quint

Butler, Pa.—Rick Sabo came from a family in which all three sons went to work selling life insurance for the Metropolitan Life Insurance Company....

But within a few years, the seamy sales practices of some fellow agents who were favorites among the Met Life hierarchy in western Pennsylvania started to trouble Mr. Sabo. Unlike many of his colleagues, he began complaining to his superiors, thinking that management would be grateful. His reward: he was fired.

Mr. Sabo got his revenge. He gave state regulators evidence that led to an investigation and a blistering report that forced Met Life to offer restitution this past spring to more than 60,000 customers who could show they were improperly persuaded to replace their old policy with a new one or were improperly sold life insurance in the guise of a retirement or savings plan.

The Pennsylvania report and the $1.5 million fine levied on Met Life are part of a growing crackdown by state regulators—there is no Federal regulation of insurance companies—on sales practices by the country's 600,000 sales agents and the 3,000 life insurance companies they represent. Met Life has recently taken the brunt of the criticism and earlier this year was fined a record $20 million in a multistate settlement of improper sales activities conducted from its Tampa, Fla., office.

Source: New York Times, June 22, 1994, pp. D1–2.

Two American executives I interviewed explained that they had held the position of "vice-president responsible for going to jail" and I was told of this position existing in a third company. Lines of accountability had been drawn in the organization such that if there were a problem and someone's head had to go on the chopping block, it would be that of the "vice-president responsible for going to jail."[24]

CONTROLLING WHITE-COLLAR CRIME

In the last decade or so, the prosecution of white-collar crime has become more visible. Nearly every week, it seems, the financial section of the newspaper carries word of some new investigation, grand jury indictment, or trial. Of course, the misdeeds of the rich and famous have always provided the media with good headlines, and perhaps these stories reflect the ambitions of prosecutors who want to pursue newsworthy cases.[25] Even so, the sales of newspapers and the TV ratings, along with more systematic surveys, tell us that the public takes a generally punitive position on white-collar crime.[26] We may even hear complaints that the prisons for white-collar criminals are not dismal enough, that swindlers and inside traders and others convicted in federal courts spend their sentences in the country-club atmosphere of "Club Fed." Yet despite the desires of both the public and law-enforcement officials, those who commit white-collar crimes—especially corporate crimes— rarely wind up behind bars.

PROSECUTION AND ITS ALTERNATIVES

Corporate crime is different from street crime; not only are the crimes and the people who commit them different, but so is the official response. Street crime is largely the province of the criminal justice system—police, courts, prisons, and probation—agencies whose chief weapon is the criminal law. Corporate crimes and misdeeds are much more likely to come under the control of non-criminal agencies—civil courts and government regulatory agencies like the Federal Trade Commission or the Securities and Exchange Commission. In addition, the penalties for corporate crime rarely involve incarceration. Corporations and their executives may have to pay fines, recall products, or change the way they do business. But seldom do they go to prison.

Bringing corporate criminals to justice is no simple matter, often because the crime itself is not detected. Even in cases where corporate decisions cause physical harm or even death—the individuals who suffer will usually not realize that they are victims of corporate wrongdoing. Only later, when someone else (usually a lawyer, sometimes a government agency) begins to see a pattern, will questions of corporate criminal liability emerge. In bribery and illegal political contributions, in money laundering, insider trading, and price-fixing, the criminals are the only ones who know about the crime. The victims—other investors, the public, the taxpayers—have no way of knowing that their reduced government services or higher taxes, their lower profits or higher prices, are the result of a criminal conspiracy. Some criminal cases begin when a business competitor complains to law-enforcement officials that a rival company is skirting safety regulations or using bribery. But when the charges are conspiracy—an antitrust collusion to drive out true competition—Department of Justice officials are usually suspicious of the complainant's motives and are unlikely to take action.[27] Complaints from disgruntled or conscience-stricken insiders are more likely to bring action, probably because the insiders can also provide concrete evidence.

CRIMINAL LAWS AND CORPORATE CRIMES

Suppose that a government agency does find of evidence of corporate crime, for example, that a drug company is marketing an unsafe drug. What should the government do? Our first response would probably be criminal prosecution of the chief executives of the corporation. Surely, such a prosecution would have a deterrent effect. Many people (criminologists included) think that while prison may not do much to deter street criminals, even the possibility of a prison term may scare white-collar criminals into ending their crimes.[28] Yet despite the desire of both the public and prosecutors to see white-collar criminals punished, a very small proportion of corporate criminals ever see the inside of a prison.

The first problem is the law. An action can be a crime only if there is a law against it. Laws are made by legislators, and legislators are open to influence. Large, wealthy corporations or entire industries can wield a great deal of influence. For example, when Congress, in response to public pressure, drafted the Motor Vehicle Safety Act in the mid-1960s, it originally included criminal penalties for manufacturers who willfully marketed unsafe cars. The automobile industry used its influence to have this provision removed.[29] More recently, in 1990 the U.S. Justice Department, after a long study, proposed much larger fines for corporations convicted of white-collar crime. A business lobby met with White House officials, and the next day the Justice Department withdrew its support for the stiffer penalties.[30] Tax law is another area in which corporations, business lobbies, and some powerful individuals have been able to get changes so that they can avoid taxes without breaking the law. Local governments, especially, often give tax breaks to big businesses, usually with the justification that these generous tax policies will attract or keep the industries that provide jobs. Not just for taxes but for most types of laws, the ability of corporations to influence legislation and prosecution is probably even greater at the state and local levels. As one Alabama state senator explained:

> I don't know whether you want to call it corrupt money or not, because we have a very gray line in this state. What is corrupt? It's legal in Alabama, for instance, if there is a bill on the floor to address an envelope [to me], and I'm walking out of the Senate floor, and one of these people can walk up to me and hand me a check for $10,000 and say to me: "Senator, now this is for your next campaign. This is not for anything to do with trying to sway your vote on the bill." And I can simply say, "Well, look, I'm going to tell you, I'm going to take your money and I appreciate it, but this has nothing to do with the way I vote because I was going to vote for the bill before you gave this check." That's legal in Alabama. It's rotten.[31]

New laws specific to corporate crime are often necessary because ordinary criminal laws are difficult to apply to corporations. Criminal laws derive mostly from individual crimes. They are designed to allow for the prosecution of a single criminal (or small group of criminals) whose crimes have a direct victim. These laws are not well designed for prosecuting people who, as employees in corporations, play a limited part in a complicated process that eventually causes some sort of harm. Murder statutes, for example, fit cases where one person directly kills another. But consider a death that results from a series of decisions taken by a variety of people who work for a corporation that creates a workplace environment in which accidents are more likely to occur? The usual legal concepts of murder may be inadequate for these cases. In addition, many of the due process regulations that protect individual defendants also protect corporations, and corporate lawyers make excellent use of them.

CONTROLLING CORPORATE CRIMES

Because of the difficulties in bringing criminal prosecutions against corporate criminals, the control of corporate wrongdoing falls largely to **regulatory agencies**. At various times in U.S. history, Congress has established an agency to regulate a particular industry. Sometimes the legislators were responding to pressures from interest groups, sometimes to a more general need. For example, over a century ago, Congress set up the Interstate Commerce Commission (ICC) mainly in response to farmers and merchants, who had no other effective way to fight the high shipping fees that the railroads charged. The Securities and Exchange Commission (SEC) was created in the depths of the depression to prevent another stock market crash. The federal bureaucracy includes many other such regulatory agencies, some smaller and less noteworthy than others. In the area of corporate wrongdoing, the Federal Trade Commission (FTC), the Food and Drug Administration (FDA), the Occupational Safety and Health Administration (OSHA), and the Environmental Protection Agency (EPA) are among those with potentially important roles.

"I always thought white-collar crime was done by computer."

IN THE NEWS

The "captive agency" problem can become exacerbated when, as happened during the 1980s, presidents appoint top-level administrators who favor deregulation. "Under Reagan and Bush we never had the support from Washington that we needed to be a strong regulatory agency. It's gotten worse in the last year." So says the chief of the Knoxville, Tennessee office of the federal government's strip-mining regulatory agency.

U.S. MINE INSPECTORS CHARGE INTERFERENCE BY AGENCY DIRECTOR

by Keith Schneider

Dunlap, Tenn.—Federal mining inspectors here and in five other states say the head of the agency that oversees the $20 billion coal industry has repeatedly interceded on behalf of coal companies to thwart enforcement of the law regulating strip mining.

The inspectors, who head regional offices of the Office of Surface Mining, Reclamation and Enforcement, said in interviews that the director, Harry M. Snyder had ordered them to end investigations of violations, reduce fines, eliminate penalties, divert prosecutions and prevent inspections....

Here at [Skyline Coal] Tennessee's largest strip mine, a huge shovel heaves aside tons of rock and earth to lay bare a seam of black coal. But mixed with the discarded material are deposits of sulfur and iron, manganese and aluminum that with moisture form a red acid brew that finds its way into streams and destroys fish and plant life for miles downstream. The Federal strip mining law was meant to eradicate it, but countless mountain streams in the mining regions of West Virginia, Kentucky and Tennessee have been polluted in this way....

Last July, after the streams around the Skyline mine turned red, Federal inspectors from the Office of Surface Mining's Knoxville office ordered the mine closed until the company came up with a plan to stop the pollution. The stop-work order, one of the strongest penalties available to Federal officials, followed more than two years of effort by the Knoxville office to compel Skyline to deal with the problem....

Under the strip-mining law, when a stop-work order is issued the company must either eliminate the problem or seek temporary relief from a Federal judge before resuming operation....

But three days after the stop-work order was issued, say mine inspectors here, Skyline was back in business without having taken either step. Federal officials in Knoxville were directed by their superiors in Washington to lift the order, an action that meant Skyline and its 60 employees could continue mining more than 1,400 tons of coal, valued at more than $38,000 a day.

Source: New York Times, November 22, 1992, pp. 1, 30.

These agencies can create rules and regulations that industries must follow. Often, the congressional act that creates the agency gives it a general direction and establishes the scope of its actions but leaves the specific methods up to the agency itself. Of course, if a regulatory agency adopts an unpopular policy, Congress can pass a law to change it. Agencies may require companies to provide various types of information—about their financial dealings, the contents of the goods they produce, the specific safety precautions in their workplaces, and so on. Agencies can also undertake more thorough investigations when they suspect a violation. When regulators do uncover violations, they have a number of options. The most extreme is to turn the matter over to the Justice Department for criminal prosecution. The problem with prosecution, as we have seen, is that it requires extraordinary amounts of time and may not be successful.

Agencies also may seek civil fines against corporations, but the maximum penalties allowed are so small that they have no real deterrent effect, nor do they seem to square with most ideas of justice. For example, in the early 1970s, Firestone began selling a steel-belted radial tire called the 500. The problem with the tire was tread separation. After only a few thousand miles of use—sometimes less—the tread would become distorted, the tire would bulge, and in some cases it would blow out. Firestone's own testing had revealed the defect, but the company marketed the tire anyway and for years thwarted the efforts of the National Highway Traffic Safety Administration (NHTSA) to stop its production and sale. Under the 1966 law that created the NHTSA, there simply were no criminal penalties that could apply. The NHTSA had really only two ways to get Firestone to remove its dangerous 500s from the roads: It could create bad publicity by releasing its own information about the tires, and it could go to court to force Firestone to recall the tire. The maximum fine the agency could have imposed was $50,000, a trifling sum for a corporation that had made millions of dollars from its tires. The NHTSA eventually did get Firestone to recall the tires in 1980, and Firestone did pay the $50,000 fine. By that time, millions of consumers had paid good money for defective tires—tires that caused thousands of accidents, including at least thirty-four fatalities.[32]

Sometimes, regulatory agencies become captive to the industries they are supposed to regulate. The members of the agency come to see their role as not only controlling the abuses of the industry at all costs but also as promoting it and providing a climate in which it can flourish. In addition, in both the creation and enforcement of regulations, agencies depend on information. Usually, the industry to be regulated has a near monopoly on that information, so the agency becomes dependent on the industry it is supposed to regulate. In a similar way, the people who are appointed to an agency should ideally be those with a great deal of knowledge about the industry. Unfortunately, most people who meet this criterion will have gained their knowledge as *members* of the industry. Moving into a government regulatory agency, they bring with them the worldview of the industry they are supposed to supervise. In addition, those whose interests would be served by stricter regulation—for example, the potential victims of exploding tires or polluted rivers—are seldom in a position to offer a well-organized and convincing response to the views presented by the industry, nor do they usually have the same access to regulators, legislators, or presidents that executives of large corporations enjoy.

DETERRENCE OR COMPLIANCE?   Besides seeking criminal or civil penalties, regulatory agencies may also take administrative actions at an administrative hearing before a judge. Administrative courses of action often begin with an official warning. Agencies can seek an injunction requiring the corporation to halt its illegal practice immediately, pending further court decisions, or they may try to force the company to issue a recall of its unsafe product. A fairly common administrative device is the **consent decree**, whereby the officers of a corporation do not admit any guilt but do agree not to commit further violations. Such an alternative is much less threatening to the corporation and its executives. For the general public, it may also be less satisfying morally. How would we react to news that the directors of a company that had cheated others out of hundreds of thousands of dollars were punished by nothing more than having to sign a statement that they wouldn't do it again? On the other hand, these noncriminal sanctions may be much quicker and more effective in reducing white-collar crime. The path of criminal prosecution is long and expensive, and the outcome is never certain. Especially if the case involves physical and not just financial harm, the regulators may be more interested in ensuring public safety than in punishing the guilty. The recall of a faulty product may seem too light a punishment for a corporation that has put the public at risk, but the recall may save more lives than would a prolonged criminal case. Regulators, therefore, may face a choice: to seek justice or to save lives.[33] Often they choose the path of compliance rather than that of punishment. Of course, as the Firestone and the Dalkon Shield cases show, if executives want to "stonewall," both courts and regulatory agencies may find company practices very difficult to change.

Summary and conclusion

The category of white-collar crime is a fairly recent one in criminology, dating only to Sutherland's coinage of that term in 1940. It includes a variety of crimes—from small-scale individual crimes like embezzlement to deliberate business fraud to corporate crimes like antitrust conspiracy. It is impossible to know the true extent of white-collar crime, though certainly it costs several times more than street crime. We probably will never know just how much of the $300 billion lost in the S&L collapse was criminal fraud and how much was merely poor judgment.

Explanations of white-collar crime should distinguish between the different levels of crime. Those crimes committed largely by individuals acting alone (embezzlement and certain types of fraud) resemble other types of theft and probably do not require special theories. Corporate crimes are different—both in the way they are committed and in the types of people who commit them. Theories of corporate crime take two general approaches. Some emphasize the external conditions that make it more attractive for even relatively affluent people to commit crimes in their work. The general profit orientation and competitiveness of business in America, the threat of declining profits or even losses, the ease of fixing prices when a few firms dominate a market, the impersonality and diffusion of responsibility in large firms—all can affect corporate decisions to violate the law. The other type of explanation focuses on the internal dynamics of the corporation and the ways in which employees learn both the methods of violating regulations and the justifications for doing so.

The problems involved in controlling white-collar crime are even more frustrating than those connected with street crime. The criminal justice system may have no effective means for lowering rates of burglary, robbery, or murder, but at least it can usually punish the individual street criminals it does pursue. With white-collar crime, especially corporate crime, the situation may be reversed. That is, law-enforcement agencies often have a difficult time dispensing justice, even in those cases where they have "caught" the criminal corporation. However, the increasingly powerful role of regulatory agencies probably has, over the long run, reduced illegal corporate behavior. Regulators, therefore, are more likely to seek compliance on the part of corporate offenders rather than justice in the form of some penalty proportionate to the offense. Those concerned about corporate wrongdoing probably have less to fear from a weakening of the Justice Department than a weakening of the regulatory agencies.

THE LAST WORD—THE DALKON SHIELD

The Dalkon Shield case illustrates two points in white-collar crime. First, it reminds us that corporate misdeeds sometimes go beyond illegal profits; they can cause human suffering and loss of life. Second, the case shows all the difficulties in bringing justice to bear on corporate wrongdoing.

Beginning in the late 1960s the A. H. Robins company marketed an intrauterine contraceptive device (IUD) called the Dalkon Shield. Within the first two years of production, Robins learned of several drawbacks to their IUD. More than one-fourth of the women who used it suffered bleeding and severe cramps. About 5 percent became pregnant while wearing the Shield, and of those who did, more than half suffered miscarriages. Others delivered stillborn babies with serious birth defects. But the most dangerous side effect of the Shield was pelvic inflammatory disease, an infection that can cause chronic pain, sterility, hemorrhaging and other severe medical problems, or even worse. Eighteen Shield users in the United States died. So did many hundreds more outside the United States, where Robins vigorously marketed the Shield, especially in Third World countries. Yet Robins continued to market the device, ignoring or covering up warnings of its harm, until the FDA in 1974 urged it to take the product off the market. Robins continued to maintain that its IUD was safe "when properly used," and the company made no effort to alert women who might still be wearing the Dalkon Shield. Six years later, it finally urged doctors to remove existing Shields from their patients, and in 1984 it issued a full recall.

Following are excerpts from a statement read in February 1984 by Judge Miles W. Lord, chief U.S. district judge for Minnesota, to three officers of A.H. Robins. Judge Lord had heard much of the evidence in the court cases involving the Dalkon Shield, and his statement details some of the techniques corporations can use to avoid or minimize criminal and civil penalties: the diffusion of knowledge and responsibility, the legal delay, and the special out-of-court settlements to prevent victims from sharing their knowledge. The Robins officers were E. Claiborne Robins, Jr., president and CEO; Carl D.

Lunsford, senior vice president for research and development; and William A. Forrest, Jr., vice president and general counsel.

You, Dr. Lunsford, as director of the company's most sensitive and important subdivision, have violated every ethical precept to which every doctor under your supervision must pledge as he gives the oath of Hippocrates and assumes the mantle of one who would help and cure and nurture unto the physical needs of the populace.

You, Mr. Forrest, are a lawyer—one who, upon finding his client in trouble, should counsel and guide him along a course which will comport with the legal, moral, and ethical principles which must bind us all. You have not brought honor to your profession, Mr. Forrest.

Gentlemen, the results of these activities and attitudes on your part have been catastrophic. Today as you sit here attempting once more to extricate yourselves from the legal consequences of your acts, none of you has faced up to the fact that more than nine thousand women have made claims that they gave up part of their womanhood so that your company might prosper. It is alleged that others gave their lives so you might so prosper. And there stand behind them legions more who have been injured but who have not sought relief in the courts of this land....

If one poor young man were, by some act of his—without authority or consent—to inflict such damage upon one woman, he would be jailed for a good portion of the rest of his life. And yet your company, without warning to women, invaded their bodies by the millions and caused them injuries by the thousands. And when the time came for these women to make their claims against your company, you attacked their characters. You inquired into their sexual practices and into the identity of their sex partners. You exposed these women—and ruined families and reputations and careers—in order to intimidate those who would raise their voices against you. You introduced issues that had no relationship whatsoever to the fact that you planted in the bodies of these women instruments of death, of mutilation, of disease....

Under your direction, your company has ... continued to allow women, tens of thousands of them, to wear this device—a deadly depth charge in their wombs, ready to explode at any time. Your attorney, Mr. Alexander Slaughter, denies that tens of thousands of these devices are still in the bodies of women. But I submit to you that Mr. Slaughter has no more basis for his denial than the plaintiffs have for stating it as truth, because we simply do not know how many women are still wearing these devices, and your company is not willing to find out. The only conceivable reasons you have not recalled this product are that it would hurt your balance sheet and alert women who already have been harmed that you may be liable for their injuries. You have taken the bottom line as your guiding beacon, and the low road as your route....

The policy of delay and obfuscation practiced by your lawyers in courts throughout this country has made it possible for you and your insurance company, Aetna Casualty and Surety Company, to delay the payment of these claims for such a long period that the interest you earn in the interim covers the cost of these cases. You, in essence, pay nothing out of your pocket to settle these cases. What other corporate officials could possibly learn a lesson from this? The only lesson could be that it pays to delay compensating victims and to intimidate, harass, and shame the injured parties.

Mr. Robins, Mr. Forrest, Dr. Lunsford: You gentlemen have consistently denied any knowledge of the deeds of the company you control. Mr. Robins, I have read your deposition. Many times you state that your management style was such as to delegate work and responsibility to other employees in matters involving the most important aspects of this nation's health. Judge Frank Theis, who presided over the discovery of these cases during the multidistrict litigation proceedings, noted this phenomenon in a recent opinion. He wrote, "The project manager for Dalkon Shield explains that a particular question should have gone to the medical department, the medical department representative explains that the question was really the bailiwick of the quality-control department, and the quality-control department representative explains that the project manager was the one with the authority to make a decision on that question." Under these circumstances, Judge Theis noted, "it is not at all unusual for the hard questions posed in Dalkon Shield cases to be unanswerable by anyone from Robins."

Your company seeks to segment and fragment the litigation of these cases nationwide. The courts of this country are now burdened with more than three thousand Dalkon Shield cases. The sheer number of claims and the dilatory tactics used by your company's attorneys clog court calendars and consume vast amounts of judicial and jury time. Your company settles those cases in which it finds itself in an uncomfortable position, a handy device for avoiding any proceeding which would give continuity or cohesiveness to the nationwide problem. The decision as to which cases to try rests almost solely at the whim and discretion of the A. H. Robins Company. In order that no plaintiff or group of plaintiffs might assert a sustained assault upon your system of evasion and avoidance, you time after time demand that able lawyers who have knowledge of the facts must, as a price of settling their cases, agree to never again take a Dalkon Shield case nor to help any less experienced lawyers with their cases against your company.

Minnesota lawyers have filed cases in this jurisdiction for women from throughout the United States. The cases of these women have waited on the calendar of the court for as many as three years.... Yet your company's attorneys persist in asking that these cases be transferred to other jurisdictions and to other judges unfamiliar with the cases, there to wait at the bottom of the calendars for additional months and years before they have their day in court. Another of your callous legal tactics is to force women of little means to withstand the onslaught of your well-financed, nationwide team of attorneys, and to default if they cannot keep pace. You target your worst tactics for the meek and the poor....

Please, in the name of humanity, lift your eyes above the bottom line. You, the men in charge, must surely have hearts and souls and consciences. If the thought of facing up to your transgression is unbearable to you, you might ... confess to your Maker, beg forgiveness, and mend your ways.

Please, gentlemen, give consideration to tracing down the victims and sparing them the agony that will surely be theirs.

Judge Lord's statement did not have its intended effect. Instead, Robins filed to have the judge's remarks removed from the record, claiming, "The company believes it has acted responsibly in the handling of the Dalkon Shield." Robins hired President Reagan's former attorney general, Griffin Bell, to represent it. Some months later, a panel of the federal circuit court ordered Judge Lord's statement stricken from the record.[34]

CRITICAL THINKING QUESTIONS

1. Some criminologists have based their conclusions about white-collar criminals on the UCR's information about arrests for embezzlement, fraud, and forgery. Do these data give an accurate picture of white-collar criminals?

2. How do explanations of white-collar crime differ from explanations of street crime, even in their basic assumptions about the important factors to look at?
3. In controlling white-collar crime, how effective are the criminal laws and criminal courts compared with civil and administrative processes?

KEY TERMS

consent decree	corruption	organizational crime
corporate crime	market concentration	regulatory agencies
corporate culture	occupational crime	swindles

CHAPTER TEN

BIOLOGICAL AND PSYCHOLOGICAL THEORIES

CHAPTER OUTLINE

THEORIES OF CRIME—AN INTRODUCTION

Everybody has a theory about crime. Even before you had read one word in this book or in any other book about crime, you had some ideas about the kinds of questions it was important to ask, questions like, Why is there so much crime? Who commits crimes, and why? What influence does the peer group have? What is the connection between crime and the economic situation, family, psychology, age, race, or education of the criminal? Why do some countries have much less crime or much more crime than others? What can

Biological and psychological explanations of crime seem best suited to the highly unusual criminals like Jeffrey Dahmer or Richard Speck (shown in the photo). They are less useful in explaining more common crimes or changes in crime rates.

be done to reduce crime? What is an effective way of dealing with criminals?

These questions may seem like rather obvious ones to ask, even if the answers are not obvious. However, although crime has existed for thousands of years, it was not until the eighteenth century that people began to think systematically about it. Philosophers as far back as the ancient Greeks had written about the law. But they did not pay special attention to criminal law and they ignored questions about crime itself—its causes and cures.

People in centuries past left little written record of their theories of crime. However, even though we may not know exactly what they thought about crime, we do know what they did about it, so perhaps by looking at their actions we can reconstruct the ideas that inspired them. For example, in medieval times, a criminal dispute might be settled through trial by combat, in which the accused and accuser fought to the death. Presumably, since God would not allow a liar to prevail, whoever was right would win. In some cases, courts decided guilt on the basis of trial by ordeal, in which the accused could prove his or her innocence by surviving some test. In one such test, the ordeal of cold water, a priest would sanctify a body of water, and the accused would be bound and lowered into it. Sanctified water would not receive a guilty person; that is, a guilty person would be buoyed up by the water. Therefore, a person who floated was obviously guilty; a person who sank was innocent.[1]

Since the criminal justice process depended on supernatural signs of guilt or innocence, we can reasonably assume that people—at least those who ran the courts—thought that crime was caused by supernatural forces. The criminal had fallen from grace with God or had been influenced by the devil. Authorities must surely have used this theory to explain crimes associated with witchcraft, but they probably applied it to other crimes as well. The idea that criminality was essentially a spiritual matter also justified torture—and not merely as an effective way to get a confession; torture also saved the soul, which was so much more important than the body. For the good of the accused, his or her body had to be purged, however painfully, to save the soul.[2]

Like the treatment of the accused, the punishment of the guilty in other times and places can also seem irrational and brutal to us. I will spare you detailed descriptions of these tortures and methods of execution. When I read about them, I have three different reactions. First, I am horrified and appalled at the cruelty of which people were capable. (Of course, I should not be surprised since I know that torture still persists today, inflicted by "educated" people in "modern" societies.) Second, I imagine that perhaps there was some rational justification for the practices; perhaps people believed that public torture and execution might deter others from crime. Third, I am convinced that the cruelty must have been based on ideas that go beyond the merely rational since the transformation and destruction of the body often continued long after the victim had died. Sometimes the actions seem so alien that it becomes difficult to imagine the ideas that lay behind them. For example, in medieval Europe, the same sorts of punishments were also inflicted on animals for their misdeeds. A pig that killed a child might be subjected to a trial, and if found guilty sentenced to hanging, dismembering, or burning alive.[3]

The purpose of the punishment must have been something other than the prevention of crime. Certainly, retribution was part of it. The judges reserved the most horrible deaths for those crimes they thought most offensive. Perhaps another component was just a sort of sadistic curiosity, like that of the kid who pulls wings off a fly, to show what could be done to the body. Or perhaps by beheading offenders or cutting out their internal organs or burning them, the society was protecting itself against the return of the evil spirits of the dead. Certainly much about punishment was ritualistic and based on invisible forces like spirits, demons, the soul, and the hereafter. Behind all of it seems to be a view that the person had committed a crime because of supernatural forces, especially possession by the devil, for during medieval times and even later, many of the crimes for which people were tortured and executed were religious crimes like blasphemy, heresy, and witchcraft.

BECCARIA AND CLASSICAL THEORY

The eighteenth century brought in the Enlightenment, the Age of Reason. In the 1700s, philosophy in general began to emphasize rationality and logic rather than mystery. The most influential thinkers on crime and justice shared this approach, creating what came to be called **classical theory**. Probably the most famous writer of the classical school was Cesare Beccaria, an Italian who in 1764 published an essay called "On Crimes and Punishments." Many of Beccaria's ideas may seem unexceptional or obvious to us today, but we must remember that although the Middle Ages had waned and the Renaissance had come and gone, some of the same brutalities had persisted. Beccaria was writing at a time in which a judge might find a person guilty on the flimsiest of evidence and impose a sentence of "breaking on the wheel"; a time when torture was used to extract confessions; a time when in England raucous crowds turned out to watch the public hanging of criminals, several at a time, whose crimes might have been nothing more serious than stealing a fish.[4] The time was ripe for just such an essay as Beccaria's, which included the following proposals:

- The only purpose of punishment should be the prevention of crime.
- In preventing crime, the severity of the punishment is not so important as the swiftness and certainty of punishment.
- Punishments should be proportional to the seriousness of the crime.
- Punishments should be just severe enough to offset the utility to be obtained by committing the crime.
- The penalty should depend on the nature of the crime, not on the nature or position of the offender. A penalty should be applied equally to anyone found guilty of that crime.[5]

The basis of Beccaria's ideas was a philosophy known as **utilitarianism**. For the individual, according to this belief, life was a highly rational and calculated pursuit of pleasure and avoidance of pain. Society, however, had to stress the general good rather than individual pleasure. For society to maintain itself, it had to find a way to "counterbalance the passions of the individual which oppose the general good."[6] The counterbalance was to be found in punishing people for their crimes. Note here that in the utilitarian view, society punished a criminal not for purposes of retribution—not because the criminal had done something wrong—but because the punishment was useful in preventing crime. As the English utilitarian Jeremy Bentham argued, punishment was not a matter of what someone deserved but rather a matter of what was necessary. Unnecessary punishment was irrational and should be eliminated.

Beccaria's essay outlined an idea whose time apparently had come. European criminal procedures, though in need of change, already had become somewhat more rational. In fact, Beccaria probably had exaggerated the irrationality and atrocity of the courts of his day.[7] Nevertheless, his ideas found an immediate welcome in the courts of Europe, from Russia to England, and in the American colonies as well. In 1770, John Adams, as the attorney for British soldiers accused in the Boston Massacre, opened his defense with a quote from Beccaria.

Later theorists and policymakers rejected or modified some of Beccaria's ideas, for example, his opposition to the death penalty and his approval of corporal punishment for people convicted of violent crimes. New laws also rejected Beccaria's utter inflexibility about basing penalties entirely on the crime and not at all on the criminal. Had Beccaria been writing the laws, he would not have allowed flexibility in a penalty because the offender was insane or very young. Nevertheless, many of his ideas remain relevant, and some of the most influential criminological research in recent years represents a return to classical theories.

Beccaria was much more concerned with justice and prevention than with the causes of crime. It was not until a century after the publication of his essay that criminological theory began to explore ideas about why a person breaks the law. These newer theories of motivation see criminals not primarily as rational individuals making choices but as creatures who differ in the most basic ways from law-abiding people.

BIOLOGICAL AND PSYCHOLOGICAL THEORIES OF CRIME

In the mid-nineteenth century, a new "science" of personality came to enjoy considerable popularity. It was called phrenology, and it was based on the idea that different behaviors were controlled by specific areas in the brain. For example, if the "destructiveness" area were overdeveloped, the person would be aggressive. The more developed an area was, the larger it would be. These larger areas of the brain would push out on the skull in particular places, causing slightly different skull shapes, depending on the aggressiveness, amorousness, and other qualities of the individual. By feeling for the location of the bumps on a person's skull, the trained phrenologist could discover which areas were most developed. It was a hands-on method of personality assessment.

Although phrenology may seem ridiculous to us now, in its time it was just as scientific as anything else in medicine or psychiatry, and it was just as legitimate. Prisons, for example, did phrenological analyses of inmates. However, phrenology was also a popular science. Some phrenologists worked in road shows, as do tarot readers today. Others adopted a more distinguished manner, traveling from town to town giving lectures and demonstrations. After explaining the scientific basis of his work, the phrenologist would call a person from the audience up to the stage, carefully run his hands over the person's skull, and then give an account of the person's character. Before leaving town, the phrenologist might also do private readings—personality assessment coupled with advice. Then the next week, the town would get a hypnotist or a Shakespearean troupe or a lecture and slide show on the mysterious East.[8] My point here is not to poke fun at phrenology or those who believed in it. I want merely to show the appeal of an idea that keeps cropping up in different forms: the idea that differences in character reveal themselves in the body.

This mind-body idea has appeared in several forms, both in scientific research and in more popular notions. The basic idea remains this: If people behave differently, their minds must work differently, and therefore their physical makeup must also be different. If the behavior is extremely different—like violent, predatory crime—the person may be so different in both mind and body as to be less than fully human. It may be more than just a figure of speech, therefore, when people refer to criminals as animals. There is a certain logic to the label. If someone does something that we cannot imagine ourselves doing, the person must be a different order of being, not quite a human like us. Even a phrase like *cold-blooded killer* implies that the criminal's physiological responses are different from our own warm-blooded reactions, which in turn are not to be confused with those of "hot-blooded," impulsive types. Of course, few people really believe that blood temperature determines a person's temperament. Nobody still believes in the ancient notion that temperament is determined by a mix of four "humors," each corresponding to a body fluid—phlegm, black bile, yellow bile, and blood. Most people today do not know such a theory ever existed. But words can stay in use long after a theory is forgotten. Words like *phlegmatic, melancholic, bilious*, and *sanguine* remain part of the English language—if not in most daily speech, then at least on the SATs. What some people may believe, however, is that criminals differ from the rest of us in some very basic, essential, and physiological way.

LOMBROSO DISCOVERS THE BORN CRIMINAL

It was just such an idea that inspired the man sometimes called the father of criminology, Cesare Lombroso. Lombroso was born in Italy in 1835 and studied medicine and psychiatry there (remember that at this time these were very ineffective and inexact sciences). In 1870, Lombroso had one of those "aha!" insights, when different notions and observations suddenly come together to create an idea. By that year, Darwin's theory of human evolution (published eleven years earlier) had become of interest not only in biology but in the social sciences as well, and no doubt Lombroso was familiar with it. At the same time, Lombroso was working with his medical knowledge of anatomy in an attempt to differentiate physically between criminals and the insane. One day, he was doing a postmortem examination of the skull of a notorious criminal and noticed that not only was it different from a normal skull but also the differences resembled those of "primitive men and of inferior animals." In a flash, it all became clear: "At the sight of that skull, I seemed to see all at once ... the nature of the criminal, who reproduces in civilized times characteristics not only of primitive savages, but of still lower types as far back as the carnivora."[9] Here was the basis for a new theory. The criminal was an **atavism**; that is, although he lived in the present time, he was biologically and physiologically a throwback to an earlier stage of evolution.

Lombroso's next step was to begin studying the heads of criminals in search of other such atavisms, or what he called born criminals. After much research he concluded that they made up one-third of the criminal population and could be distinguished by their facial features: thick skull bones; protruding chin; low, sloping forehead; large ears; abundant and curly hair; thin beard. In his later research, Lombroso even claimed that specific types of criminals had different kinds of faces and bodies. For example, "Thieves have mobile hands and face; small ... frequently oblique eyes." Rapists "are of delicate structure and sometimes hunchbacked." Among murderers, "the nose, always large, is frequently aquiline or, rather, hooked; the jaws are strong ..." and so on (see Figure 10–1).

Lombroso also included in his description characteristics such as laziness, which we would think of as social or psychological. The list continues with a mixture of physical, psychological, and social traits. Lombroso saw them all as part of the same basic underlying pattern of atavism:

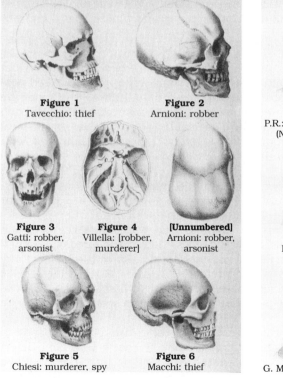

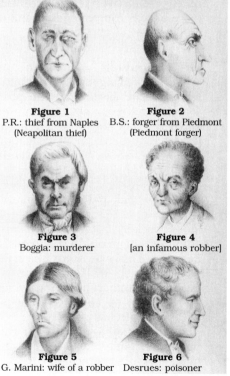

FIGURE 10–1   Skulls and Heads of Criminals

Source: From Cesare Lombroso, *L'Uomo delinquente*, 1876. Reproduced with permission from the New York Public Library.

great agility; relative insensibility to pain; dullness of the sense of touch; ... ability to recover quickly from wounds ... precocity as to sensual pleasures ... absence of remorse; impulsiveness ... excitability ... improvidence, which sometimes appears as courage and again as recklessness changing to cowardice ... great vanity; a passion for gambling and drinking; violent but fleeting passions; superstition; extraordinary sensitiveness with regard to one's own personality ... the custom of tattooing; the cruelty of their games; the excessive use of gestures.[10]

Lombroso reasoned as follows: (1) Criminals have these characteristics (e.g., impulsiveness and tattoos); so do savage peoples; (2) savage peoples are at a lower point in the evolutionary ladder; (3) therefore, criminals must also be evolutionary throwbacks. Criminals, at least these atavistic ones, were essentially savages who through some accident of nature happened to have been born in nineteenth-century Europe.

At this point you may be asking, If Lombroso, with his ideas about criminal ears and jaws, is the father of criminology, what can we expect of subsequent generations of criminologists? But Lombroso's importance lay not so much in the specifics of his theory of atavism. In fact, his ideas were criticized as soon as they appeared, and by the time of his death in 1909 few people believed them. We now know the basic error in Lombroso's theory: Humans in nineteenth-century Italy—criminals and noncriminals—were biologically no more or less evolved than humans in other times and places that Lombroso may have read about.

POSITIVISM   Lombroso's primary idea was not very fertile, but what remained was a general approach to studying crime—an approach called **positivism**. The essence of the positivist school of thought was the *empirical* search for the causes of criminal behavior. In both respects, this approach departed from that of Beccaria and the classical thinkers. Beccaria's classical theory may seem more reasonable to us today, especially compared with Lombroso's ideas, but Beccaria did no research to generate or to support his views. His work may have been logical, but it was not scientific in the modern sense. Beccaria also took a rather simple-minded view of the causes of behavior: People calculate the pleasure and pain to be gotten from any particular act and then decide accordingly. In the view of the positivists, human behavior—especially criminal behavior—had causes that were more complex and subtle. If they could ever identify these causes, they could predict criminal behavior. This may seem like an innocent enough idea since the basis of any science lies in identifying causes and predicting results. But if that science deals with human behavior, it casts doubt on our idea that we have free will, that is, that we can freely choose what we will do and what we will try to become in life.

The debate over free will and determinism was a long-standing issue in philosophy and religion, and some thinkers took the view that God determined, or predestined, an individual's fate. In a similar way, the positivist approach raised questions of determinism, in this case scientific rather than religious. Even though the positivists looked to worldly forces rather than to God, their ideas challenged everyday assumptions about free will. After all, if my behavior is the predictable, inevitable result of biological or social or economic causes, and if I have no power to alter those causes, how much control do I have over my behavior? Do I really have free will? The positivists, then, far beyond Lombroso's wrongheaded ideas about evolution, were raising very basic philosophical questions in social science.

More important, the positivists based their search for causes on empirical evidence. Lombroso himself studied and measured the facial features of hundreds of criminals and noncriminals. The results, he claimed, confirmed his belief that about one-third of all criminals have atavistic features. But in response to criticism, he also gathered data on all sorts of factors that might be associated with crime: climate, economics, type of government, religion, alcoholism, education[11]—the same sorts of factors a criminologist might investigate today.

Lombroso's approach far outlasted his ideas of atavism in one other important area: his emphasis on the individual criminal. Lombroso was interested in how criminals differed from noncriminals. He also argued that since crime resulted from individual defects, special treatment might help the criminal overcome his or her handicaps. Even atavistic tendencies might be channeled into noncriminal activities. It followed logically that prisons should be places of rehabilitation and treatment, not just punishment. This view, at least in principle, remained a dominant ideology of prisons through the 1960s, though in recent years it has been on the decline. The focus on individual deficiencies (rather than on social ills) influenced not only prison policy but also later criminological theory and research. Positivism began a line of biological and psychological studies on crime that continues to this day.

THE LOMBROSO LEGACY   The search for criminal features did not end with Lombroso. Early in this century the English researcher Charles Goring spent eight years measuring chins, foreheads and ears, as well as education, alcoholism, and standard of living. Goring had set out to prove that Lombroso's atavism theory was wrong and that his research methods were sloppy. Starting in 1901, Goring took his micrometer and other measuring instruments to English prisons and elsewhere, eventually compiling data on 3,000 prisoners and a comparison group of noncriminals. The research had grown out of Lombroso's challenge to his critics to set up an impartial committee to test his ideas. The atavism challenge never occurred since Lombroso's conditions for the committee were impossible to meet. By the time Goring published his own findings, Lombroso had been dead for four years. Goring spent another two years analyzing his data with modern statistical techniques, and in 1913 he published his conclusions: "There is no such thing as a physical criminal type." Goring added, "The physical and mental constitution of both criminal and law-abiding persons of the same age, stature, class, and intelligence, are identical."[12]

Definitive as this statement sounds, Goring was rejecting only the idea of atavism. He did not abandon the biological approach to crime. On the contrary, his data showed that while English convicts were "normal," they were nevertheless marked by "defective physique" (i.e., they were smaller) and "defective mental capacity."[13] Goring also saw no relationship between crime and the environmental factors he had measured, and he went on to develop his own theory that crime was largely a genetically inherited tendency.

MIND AND BODY IN AMERICA

In the United States, the search for a crime-body link was led by E. A. Hooton, a Harvard anthropologist. In the 1930s, Hooton conducted a large study of 17,000 people in ten states. He did not mention atavism, but in many other respects his work echoes themes from Lombroso. American criminals came from "the physically inferior element of the population"; their inferiority was "principally hereditary" and led them to "gravitate into unfavorable environmental conditions," where the weakest turned to crime. Criminals were "inferior" to noncriminals on most measures of body and mind. The two groups differed on facial features—lips, ears, jaws, and so on. Criminals were less likely to have purely dark eyes or blue eyes; instead, they usually had mixed-color eyes, a sign that criminals, instead of being "pure racial types," were more of the mixed type. They also more frequently had thin eyebrows; long, thin necks; sloping foreheads; and tattoos. (Lombroso, too, had noted criminals' tattoos. You might think that a tattoo is not so much a physical factor as a somewhat uncomfortable social custom or fashion—something like shaving or having pierced ears or wearing high heels. Lombroso and Hooton thought otherwise, and they are not the last in this line of thinking.) The broader noses of criminals were evidence of "infantilism and primitivism." Like Lombroso, Hooton claimed he could distinguish between different types of criminals: Forgers, for example, were tall and heavy; robbers, tall and thin.[14]

POLICY AND IDEOLOGY

When Hooton published his work in 1939, most criminologists disagreed with his ideas and criticized his research. But it is important to understand why his work caused such controversy. By 1939, Americans had already come to know something about racial theories and where such ideas had led under Nazism and fascism. The Nazis had used biology and physical anthropology to support their claims to racial superiority, and American scientists feared that the same ideas might be used against blacks, Jews, and others in America. Today, when prejudice is based largely on sociological data (e.g., that blacks in fact have higher rates of crime), we may have lost sight of the extent to which prejudice in the 1930s in this country relied on ideas about the biology of race. Hooton claimed that it was wrong to confuse his ideas with Hitler's and that the Fascist misuse of biology was no reason to stop all research into the biological sources of human behavior. He felt that his innocent baby was being thrown out with Hitler's dirty bathwater.

But how different were they? Hooton wanted "to investigate seriously the racial anatomical characters which are the outward signs of inheritance"; in the case of crime, this meant the study of racially inherited inferiority. The same idea and virtually the same vocabulary about "racial purity" lay at the heart of Nazi studies on racial inferiority. Moreover, Hitler's solution to the presence of low-grade, inferior humans was to exterminate them or to lock them away in concentration camps. How different was Hooton's solution? Let's let him speak for himself.

Criminals are organically inferior. Crime is the resultant of the impact of the environment upon low-grade human organisms. It follows that the elimination of crime can be effected only by the extirpation of the physically, mentally, and morally unfit; or by their complete segregation in a socially aseptic environment.[15]

BODY TYPES

The idea that physical features reflect personality took a somewhat different approach in the 1940s with the technique of the **somatotype**. William Sheldon, a doctor and something of a fan of Hooton, developed a scheme for classifying people according to their body build. The theory of somatotyping holds that there are three basic body types—endomorphic, mesomorphic, and ectomorphic—each linked to a type of temperament.

- Endomorphic: soft and round body; extroverted, easy-going temperament
- Mesomorphic: muscular, athletic body; active, aggressive temperament
- Ectomorphic: slender, small-boned body; introverted, sensitive temperament

Every person contains a combination of the three characteristics. What is important is their proportion (or somatotype profile), which varies from one person to another. In his research on crime, Sheldon compared the somatotype profiles of 200 delinquents with those of 200 college men, and he found that delinquents, on the average, were much more mesomorphic and much less ectomorphic than the collegiate control group.

There may be some validity to Sheldon's results. The group of delinquents probably did have more of the mesomorphic "jock" types and fewer of the skinny, nervous types. However, some aspects of Sheldon's research muddy its implications for the study of crime. First, Sheldon used an odd definition of delinquency. Rather than measure the amount of crime or the seriousness of crime, he defined delinquency as "behavior disappointing beyond reasonable expectation."[16] Second, Sheldon recognized that this body type is far from unique to criminals. He found the same physical and psychological traits among salesmen and politicians. (This similarity among salesmen, politicians, and criminals may no longer seem like an odd coincidence.) Third, Sheldon shared the belief of others going back to Lombroso that the criminal was an "inferior human organism" and that this inferiority lay in the person's basic physical being.[17] Obviously, a person does not acquire these physical characteristics by learning them; he or she is born with them. By implication, the "behavioral inferiority" that accompanies them must also be part of the person's basic biological make-up. In other words, more than seventy years after Lombroso's theory of atavism first appeared in print, some social scientists were still talking about born criminals.

ON CAMPUS

HOOTON AND SHELDON AT COLLEGE: THE STUDENT BODY

One fall afternoon in the mid-60's, shortly after I arrived ... at Yale, I was summoned to ... Payne Whitney Gym. I reported to a windowless room on an upper floor, where men dressed in crisp white garments instructed me to remove all of my clothes. And then—and this is the part I still have trouble believing—they attached metal pins to my spine. There was no actual piercing of skin, only of dignity, as four-inch metal pins were affixed with adhesive to my vertebrae at regular intervals from my neck down. I was positioned against a wall; a floodlight illuminated my pin-spiked profile and a camera captured it....

I soon learned that [the posture photo] was a long-established custom at most Ivy League and Seven Sisters schools. George Bush, George Pataki, Brandon Tartikoff and Bob Woodward were required to do it at Yale. At Vassar, Meryl Streep; at Mount Holyoke, Wendy Wasserstein; at Wellesley, Hillary Rodham and Diane Sawyer....

Another Wellesley alumna Judith Martin, author of the Miss Manners column ... confessed ... "I do remember making a reunion speech in which I offered to sell them back to people for large donations. And there were a lot of people who turned pale before they realized it was a joke."

Source: Ron Rosenbaum, "The Great Ivy League Nude Posture Photo Scandal," *New York Times Magazine*, January 15, 1995, pp. 26–31, 40, 46, 55, 56.

NUDE PHOTOS ARE SEALED

New Haven—The Smithsonian Institution has cut off all public access to a collection of nude photographs taken of generations of college students, some of whom went on to become leaders in American culture and government.

The pictures at first were taken to study posture. Later they were made by a researcher examining what he believed to

CRIME AND BIOLOGY—SEEING THE INVISIBLE

The question under discussion here is whether there is a biological basis for human behavior, especially criminal behavior. So far (we're up to about 1950), researchers have looked for evidence in physical features that are visible to the naked eye: ear shape, eye color, body type, and so on. Although the researchers themselves claimed that their evidence supported their ideas, they met with a variety of criticisms: The theory was absurd; the methodology was shoddy; the ideas seemed too congenial to fascist, racist politics. The idea that some babies were born with criminal tendencies and were morally inferior contradicted many of our most noble sentiments ("All men are created equal"). It also contradicted much evidence that showed the importance of environmental factors in crime.

be a relationship between body shape and intelligence....

The frontal and profile "posture" photos were taken beginning in the early 1900's as part of physical education classes, because poise and balance were considered an integral part of health.

Later, other photographs were taken by W. H. Sheldon, a researcher who believed that there was a relationship between body shape and intelligence and other traits.

Mr. Sheldon has since died, and his work has long been dismissed by most scientists as quackery. But it was apparently respected from the 1940's through the 1960's, because highly regarded colleges like Yale, Wellesley, Harvard, Princeton, Vassar and Swarthmore allowed him access to their students. Much of Mr. Sheldon's work was destroyed by various colleges years ago. But an article last Sunday in *The New York Times Magazine* disclosed that the *Smithsonian* still had some of the photos.

Source: *New York Times*, January 21, 1995, p. 11.

Is there anyone ... who will step forward to defend Sheldon's posture photos?

Of course there is: Camille Paglia [a literature professor].

"I'm *very* interested in somatotypes," she said. "I *constantly* use the term in my work. The word 'ectomorph' is used repeatedly in 'Sexual Personae' [Paglia's recent book]. That's one of the things I'm trying to do: to rescue them from their tainting by Nazi ideology. It's always been a part of classicism. It's sort of like we've lost the old curiosity about physical characteristics, physical differences....

"See, I'm *interested* in looking at women's breasts! I'm *interested* in looking at men's penises! I maintain that at the present date, *Penthouse*, *Playboy*, *Hustler*, serve the same cultural functions as the posture photos."

Source: Rosenbaum, "Great Ivy League Posture Photo Scandal."

CHROMOSOMES, TESTOSTERONE, SEROTONIN The search for the born criminal was not abandoned entirely, and researchers in the latter half of the twentieth century found new physiological areas to explore. Technological and scientific advances made it possible to look for previously invisible biological factors that might be associated with crime. Instead of measuring the slope of a person's forehead, researchers could now measure hormones in the blood, Galvanic skin response, brain waves, or chromosome structures.

In the 1960s there was a flurry of interest surrounding the possible link between crime and genetic abnormalities, specifically, what was called the **XYY syndrome**. A person's sex is determined by one of the twenty-three pairs of chromosomes inherited from parents. Everybody inherits an X chromosome (so called because under a microscope it looks like an X) from the mother. Some people inherit a second X chromosome, also from the mother. These people (XX) are called women. Others inherit a Y chromosome from the father. These people (XY) are men. That takes care of almost everyone. However, about one person in every thousand inherits a third chromosome. Those with an extra X chromosome (XXY) are basically male but have some female characteristics—they may even develop breasts—and are often mentally retarded. Now if males with an added X chromosome are more feminine, what about males with an extra Y chromosome (XYY)? Will they be "supermales," exaggerating all those masculine tendencies that can lead to aggressive, violent crime?

Such speculation grew when research on inmates in a British maximum-security prison turned up a much greater frequency of XYY males (one or two in a hundred instead of one or two in a thousand), some of whose crimes "would supply material for a series of horror films."[18] It began to look as though indeed there was a genetic component to crime. However, as more research data on more XYY men accumulated, the supermale idea looked less and less plausible. The XYY males were different: They were generally taller and had lower IQ scores; they were even somewhat more likely to commit crimes than were normal (XY) males of similar IQ, social class, and other demographic traits. However, their crimes generally were not of the violent, supermale type. In addition, the XYY abnormality occurs so rarely that these findings are probably more relevant to the field of genetics than to criminology. The XYY males account for very little of the total crime in our society. The second Y chromosome is nowhere near as important for crime as the first one.

> Some years ago, there was a bitter controversy over whether men with an extra male-determining Y chromosome—the XYY syndrome—were hypermasculine. One not-so-subtle humorist wrote in to Science that it was silly to get so excited over the extremely rare XYY syndrome, when 49 percent of the species was already afflicted with the XY syndrome—an uncontroversial disorder known to cause hyperactivity and learning disabilities in childhood, premature mortality in adulthood and an egregious tendency to irrational violence throughout life. "Testosterone poisoning," a colleague of mine calls it.[19]

The idea of linking crime to the supermale was based on the well-known fact that men commit far more crime than women. It is also a well-known fact that men are biologically different from women. These two facts (biological differences and crime differences) led to the chromosome studies. The same line of thinking has also led to research on one of the key hormones that makes men different from women: **testosterone**. Since men have more testosterone than women, would criminals have higher levels of testosterone than noncriminals? The research findings are not extensive, and they often rely on very small samples. A 1970 study of twenty-one prisoners found that those who had committed violent crimes as juveniles had higher levels of testosterone.[20] More recent studies on larger samples have found that high testosterone levels were associated not just with crime but also with traits like dominance and competitiveness. So although testosterone is clearly a biological factor and contributes to a certain kind of motivation, the specific form that this motive takes depends on social factors. Men who have high levels of testosterone and are poorly integrated into society may well wind up committing crimes. But for other men, high-testosterone traits will emerge as socially acceptable aggression in athletics or business.[21]

Most recently, biological research related to crime has focused on the role of brain chemicals called **neurotransmitters**. One of these, **serotonin**, seems to moderate people's responses to emotional stimuli. People with low levels of serotonin are more likely to respond impulsively and violently.[22] Of these two characteristics—impulsivity and violence—most serotonin research has focused on the latter, but if there is a connection between serotonin and crime, it may well be the link to impulsivity. Even with property crimes, most criminals are opportunistic. The crimes are at best minimally planned, and the criminals are acting more on impulse than on any long-term consideration of their actions.[23]

ALL IN THE FAMILY   For much of the last forty years, most biological research was all but ignored in mainstream criminology. By the 1950s, the dominant view in the behavioral sciences—sociology, psychology, and anthropology—was decidedly opposed to biological explanations of behavior. The prevailing ideology held that all behavior was learned rather than innate and that environmental factors exerted by far the most influence on human behavior. Still, there were a few researchers who continued to look for biological factors in crime. Some of them, as we have seen, pursued the biology of crime by using traditional clinical (i.e., laboratory) methods, analyzing blood samples. But other biologically oriented researchers chose the epidemiological approach, that is, studying the distribution of crime as though it were a disease and using the methods of social science. Instead of looking for specific biological elements (e.g., testosterone) that might be related to criminality, these researchers tried merely to show that behavior and personality do have biological and hereditary bases, even though we may not know the specific genetic factors involved.

Most of this research tries to link biological similarity with behavioral similarity. If there is a genetic factor in crime, the greater the biological similarity between two people, the greater will be their similarity in crime. For example, people in the same family are biologically more similar to one another than they are to nonfamily members. So we might look at the criminal records of brothers. If one brother has a criminal record, will the other brother have one also? Of course, you can immediately see the problem here. Even if the brothers are similar in crime, the causes for that similarity could just as easily be environmental as hereditary. They inherited similar genetic material, but they probably also grew up in the same environment. How can we know which was causing the similarity in crime?

TWINS—FRATERNAL AND IDENTICAL   There are two general research strategies for untangling the strands of environment and heredity. The first method compares pairs of fraternal twins with pairs of identical twins. Fraternal, or dizygotic (DZ), twins are the result of two separate eggs being fertilized at the same time. Genetically they are no more similar than two separate eggs fertilized at different times; that is, fraternal twins are no more similar genetically than ordinary brothers and sisters. They share about half their genes. However, in some cases, a single fertilized egg divides into two embryos, which develop into identical, or monozygotic (MZ), twins. They share all the same genetic material, which is why identical twins are always the same sex; fraternal twins may be of opposite sexes.

Researchers have looked at the degree of similarity, or **concordance**, between twins of each type. Generally, they find greater similarities of crime between identical twins than between fraternal twins. For example, a Danish study of 3,500 sets of twins found that the concordance for MZ twins was more than twice that for DZ twins. If one MZ twin had a criminal record, the other had a record 52 percent of the time. For DZ twins, the figure was only 22 percent.[24] It is unlikely that MZ twins grow up in a more similar environment than DZ twins, so the stronger similarity must come from the greater genetic similarity. Of course, other factors must play a part since even among MZ identical twins, only about half the pairs were concordant.

PARENTS AND CHILDREN   The second strategy has been to look at the criminal similarity of parents and children. If there is a genetic component to crime, it will be transmitted from parent to child along with other genetic material. Here again, we face the problem of untangling heredity from environment. If we find that children resemble their parents in criminality, the cause might be some genetically transmitted traits, but the cause might also be a variety of social factors. Children might pick up their parents' ways through imitation, or parents who are more criminal may also be ineffective parents. How, then, can we know to what extent the similarity is biological and to what extent it is social?

One way of separating heredity and environment is to have two separate sets of parents, one for heredity and one for environment, and then see which one the child most resembles. Of course, we cannot deliberately perform such an experiment, but as you may already have realized, something very close to this experimental design already exists: adoption. All we need to do is find out the criminality of the adoptive parents, the biological parents, and the child. Table 10–1 shows the results from one such study of adopted sons and parents in Denmark.

First, look at the columns in the table. Raising the child in a criminal home has only a very small impact—differences of 1.2 or 4.5 percent points, depending on the criminality of the biological parents. However, reading across the rows, you can see that the effect of the biological parents is much greater. (In this study, "criminal" meant having one or more criminal convic-

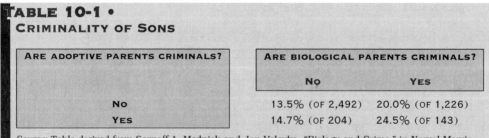

TABLE 10-1 •
CRIMINALITY OF SONS

ARE ADOPTIVE PARENTS CRIMINALS?	ARE BIOLOGICAL PARENTS CRIMINALS?	
	No	Yes
No	13.5% (OF 2,492)	20.0% (OF 1,226)
Yes	14.7% (OF 204)	24.5% (OF 143)

Source: Table derived from Sarnoff A. Mednick and Jan Volavka, "Biology and Crime," in Norval Morris and Michael Tonry, eds., *Crime and Justice: An Annual Review of Research* (Chicago: University of Chicago Press, 1980), pp. 85–158.

tions. Criminal adoptive parents usually had only one conviction; criminal biological parents often had two or more.)

BIOLOGICAL EXPLANATIONS OF CRIME: METHODS, USEFULNESS, AND IDEOLOGY

These twin studies and adoption studies, like the other biological research mentioned in this chapter, have come in for much criticism. Critics point out that in the adoption studies the differences between groups are small; that the initial studies, which used only fathers rather than both parents, found no significant differences; and the researchers had to keep adjusting their sample until they found the desired link between biological parents and children.[25]

Even if we allow that the biological studies are accurate, we must still ask questions about their interpretation and usefulness. Nobody, not even the most biologically oriented criminologists, claim that genetic or biological factors absolutely cause crime. After all, many people with high testosterone or low serotonin or other factors possibly linked to crime do not become criminals. Instead, some criminologists say that these factors "predispose" a person toward crime. Whether that tendency takes the form of crime or whether it gets channeled into noncriminal pursuits depends on social forces.

It may be easier to picture this interaction between biochemical and social factors by looking not at hormones or other chemicals produced inside the body but at more familiar chemicals produced externally that people take into their bodies—chemicals like cocaine, amphetamines, PCP (phencylidine, or angel dust), and alcohol. Obviously, these substances produce chemical changes that affect the way a person feels and reacts (if they didn't, they wouldn't be so expensive), and equally clearly, they play a role in crime and violence. We might say that they "predispose" people toward crime, although they do not affect everyone in the same way. More important, even when a drug does raise a person's aggressive or antisocial feelings, the person may be restrained from acting out those feelings by his or her own morality or by the influence of others in the situation.

So the debate over biology and environment (or nature and nurture) is really a matter of emphasis. And most researchers agree that biological factors play a less important part in criminality. Even Lombroso estimated that two-thirds of criminals were *not* biologically different from noncriminals. More currently, Sarnoff Mednick, one of the leading American biologists doing research on crime, said, "Social factors are much more important in the etiology [causes] of crime and everybody knows this, especially the biologists."[26]

In addition, biological theories have a limited relevance; they can help explain individual differences, but they are almost useless in explaining the social facts about crime, such as large changes in crime *rates*. Remember, the biological and genetic makeup of the population does not change. The gene pool in the United States in 1970 was substantially the same as it was in 1960, although during that decade crime rates more than doubled. Something must have changed, but it wasn't biology.

Finally, biological theories are a political issue. The political objections to biological theories begin with the claim that biological ideas divert attention from the social sources of crime. First, if crime is a matter of biogenetic inheritance, we need not worry about poverty, inequality, race relations, or other matters of social reform. Second, critics fear that some people will take biological theories to mean that certain individuals and groups are inferior. The assumption of biology, whether in the latest studies or in the writing of Lombroso, is that people are different in their essential biological makeup and that these differences may be inherited. The person who is a criminal may be biologically and morally inferior. What if we applied this idea not just to individual criminals but to crime rates? For example, if crime rates are higher among the poor, might that not mean that poor people are biologically inferior?

The question becomes even more controversial concerning racial differences in crime. African-Americans today, Italian-Americans a century ago, the Irish in Great Britain—all of these groups have higher rates of crime than the majority of the society. Moreover, these racial or ethnic groups, unlike different social classes, are possibly biologically different from the majority. They have different physical features, which are transmitted genetically from parent to child. The question is whether behavioral or moral traits are also part of the biogenetic inheritance. Right now, no responsible biologist would claim that one racial group can be morally superior on the basis of its biological inheritance, but some biologists do claim that there may be a biogenetic component in criminality. The critics fear the abuses to which such an idea can lead. Some of the worst atrocities in history have resulted from ideas of racial inferiority.

Few people, even the most vigorous critics, really believe that biological theories of crime could lead to a revival of anything resembling the killing of millions of "racially inferior" people under nazism or slavery. But some people do fear even the less extreme policies that could emerge from these ideas. These policies might involve the use of biological information to determine what kind of treatment an offender will receive. An offender who has been biogenetically identified as a high risk would receive a sentence different from that given a low-risk offender convicted of the same offense. This policy, however, would be punishing someone for his biogenetic makeup rather than for his crime.

FROM BIOLOGY TO PSYCHOLOGY

Studies of twins and adopted children may show that there is some biological basis for crime, but they make no attempt to identify the precise physiological component that leads to crime. As a way of explaining crime, these more sophisticated studies are less satisfying than Sheldon's ideas about body types. At least Sheldon could link a specific physique to a higher rate of delinquency. Yet even Sheldon does not say exactly what it is about the mesomorphic, athletic types that makes them more prone to delinquency. We have to go all the way back to Lombroso to find a theory, even a silly one, that explains why a particular type of body is linked to crime. Lombroso thought

IN THE NEWS

Biological ideas about crime remain politically controversial. In the following incident, the controversy was not even about the results of the research but about the possibility of researchers coming together to present their research and discuss ideas.

CONTROVERSY FLARES OVER CRIME, HEREDITY: NIH SUSPENDS FUNDING FOR CONFERENCE

by Lynn Duke

The National Institutes of Health, embroiled in a controversy over racial implications of genetic research, has suspended funding for a conference on heredity and criminal behavior until organizers can reshape the program to make clear that NIH does not advocate a genetic explanation for crime.

The conference, originally scheduled for Oct. 9 at the University of Maryland, has come under fire from NIH officials, a mental health activist and some concerned citizens. Because blacks are disproportionately represented in crime statistics, some of those who oppose the conference fear that such research could revive discredited theories that blacks are biologically inferior.

Other critics see biological approaches to crime as an attempt to blame people who are victims of social conditions such as poverty and racism.

NIH Director Bernadine P. Healy last month ordered the $78,000 earmarked for the conference put on hold until confusion about the conference's intent is adequately addressed.

Source: Washington Post, August 19, 1992, p. A4.

---

that criminals were less evolved in both body and mind; being more like savages or even animals, criminals naturally preyed on others without regard to modern law or morality.

CONSCIENCE AND CONDITIONING

In the 1960s, the connection in crime between mind and body became the focus for psychologists interested in **conditioning**. The term refers to the process by which a learned reaction becomes automatic and internalized. Much of the research and theory in this area falls within a tradition in American psychology known as behaviorism, a perspective that stressed behavior rather than thought, and ever since Pavlov conditioned a dog to salivate at the sound of a bell, psychologists have been conditioning the behavior of laboratory animals, caring little for what might be going through the creature's mind. From the behaviorist point of view, the mind—whether of beast or human—was merely a set of conditioned reflexes.

The behaviorist perspective on crime rests on two key assumptions: first, that people commit crime because of a weak conscience; and second, that people acquire a conscience in the same way that rats can be conditioned to turn right in a maze or dogs can be conditioned not to mess up the carpet. In the words of psychologist Hans Eysenck, "conscience is a conditioned reflex."[27]

PHYSIOLOGY AND PSYCHOLOGY   What does any of this have to do with physiology, aside from the obvious fact that reinforcements—especially in the conditioning of laboratory animals—are often physical (e.g., food, electric shocks)? If you have ever tried to train an animal, you know that there are two sides to the process—the trainer and the trainee. From the trainer's side, if the rewards and punishments are not strong enough or do not come consistently or promptly, the conditioning will be less effective. For example, child-rearing manuals these days strongly condemn parental inconsistency. Imagine a parent who ignores the child's misbehavior much of the time or gives only threats that are never carried out; but every so often, long after the misbehavior, the parent blows up and punishes the child severely. Bad parenting, say the manuals; with such inconsistent discipline, a child is unlikely to learn to behave correctly.

The quality of training may vary from one trainer (or parent) to another. But the trainees also differ. The exact same techniques that work with one breed of dog, for example, may not work so well with another. Children, too, differ from one another. Some may be harder to "condition" than others, and some may respond differently to different types of reward or punishment. Some of these differences are a matter of temperament or personality. But what if there were also physical differences that made some people less "conditionable"? For example, what if some people were less sensitive to pain? Since punishments would be less painful, they would have less effect. In fact, some psychologists claim that there are people who generally feel less physical sensation. These people can tolerate a greater level of stimulation; they may prefer or even need such heightened stimulation. They gravitate toward contact sports and loud music. And of course, they are more likely to commit crimes. Their "greater immunity to pain ... explains, in part, their inability to sympathize with the pain of others. This might underlie their greater involvement in accidents, their noisiness, and even [their] preference ... for tattooing themselves."[28] Does this description—taken from a 1984 criminology textbook written by a prominent criminologist—sound familiar? Go back and check Lombroso's inventory of criminal traits (p. 312).

RESPONSIVENESS AND SWEATY PALMS   A variation on this idea comes from studies of **skin conductance**; that is, how easily a person's skin will conduct electricity. Skin conductance is an indicator of the arousal of the "autonomic nervous system," the mechanism that controls reflex-like responses such as heart rate and breathing. When a person is nervous or afraid, the surface of the hands becomes more moist, and skin conductance increases. For this reason, it is one of the measures used in polygraph ("lie-detector") tests. Basically, this part of the polygraph is just a very sensitive device for detecting sweaty palms.

Researchers have found that criminals and noncriminals differ from each other in what is called **skin conductance recovery**. This is the length of time it takes for the skin conductance to return to its normal level following arousal. Typically, a person in such an experiment receives an "aversive stimulus"—is given a hypodermic injection or an electric shock, is told that such a stimulus will be given, or is shown someone apparently reacting to a painful shock or injection. Under these conditions, people become nervous, their hands become more moist, and skin conductance increases. The question is how much it increases and how long it takes for it to return to normal. Generally, in these studies, criminals show less arousal and a longer recovery time.[29]

According to the theory, a person with low arousal and slow recovery time is less easily conditioned. Take the example of the child who starts to do something wrong, such as hitting another child. The parent intervenes, scolding, threatening to withhold love or to punish the child; in any case, the parent presents an "aversive stimulus" that arouses the child's fear. The child stops hitting, the parent approves, and the child no longer feels fearful. In other words, the child feels fear when misbehaving and relief upon ceasing the misbehavior. The child who will be most affected is the child who feels a great arousal of fear and then a quick and equally great reduction in fear. But what about the child who feels less fear-arousal and whose fear-reduction comes more slowly? That child will not feel such a big difference between punishment and relief, or between good and bad behavior. The "conditioned reflex" of conscience will not be as strong. That child will be more likely to misbehave and eventually to break the law. And in the sweaty-palms theory—as in the theories of Lombroso, Hooton, Sheldon, and others—this weakness of conscience is rooted in the physical differences in the criminal's body.

THE FREUDIAN PERSPECTIVE

Outside of the research labs, psychology came under the influence of a much different theory: psychoanalysis. Psychoanalytic theory and therapy were largely the creation of Sigmund Freud, whose ideas developed out of his treatment of middle-class patients suffering from neurotic symptoms like phobias, obsessive behavior, and hysteria (that is, physical symptoms—paralysis, anesthesia, and coughing—for which there was no physiological cause). Freud himself wrote little about crime or criminals, but his ideas do offer a very general explanation. Freud, like the behaviorists, believed that what prevented people from committing crimes was conscience (and this may be the only thing these two schools of thought share). Freudian theory, however, offers a much different model of the psyche (i.e., mind or soul). It sees the mind not as a set of conditioned reflexes, but as a three-part structure. Without conscience, people would be ruled by the id—the part of the psyche that serves as a sort of reservoir of sexual and aggressive energy. The ego, the second component of the psyche, is the part we are most likely to think of as the self. The ego deals with everyday reality, negotiating in the real world to gratify the instinctual desires of the id. The id operates on the pleasure principle; it cares only about pleasure or its absence in the immediate present. The ego must operate on the reality principle, delaying gratification.

If the psyche consisted only of ego and id, people would do anything they could to satisfy their impulses. However, most people do not commit crimes—even ones they can get away with. Either the thought does not even enter their (conscious) minds, or if it does, it is accompanied by fear or guilt— the pangs of conscience. This unconscious mechanism that automatically keeps people from doing the forbidden is called the **superego**. In Freud's theory, the superego is not part of a person's original mental makeup; rather it develops in early childhood as the child internalizes the demands of parents. The strength of the superego will depend on the relationship between child and parents. Criminals who ignore the rules of society, who show no remorse, who care nothing for the suffering of their victims or anyone else in pursuing their own pleasures—these are the types who fit the description of weak superego. Their crime, like symptoms of neurotics, is a symbolic way of dealing with unconscious wishes and conflicts, and their motivations are complicated and often unconscious.

Discovering the particular unconscious ideas that are symbolically expressed in a crime may be very interesting. For example, a psychoanalytically trained psychiatrist may discover that stealing was a symbolic compensation for the love the criminal felt his mother had withheld from him in childhood. The difficulty with this kind of interpretation is not in its accuracy (though Freudian ideas have long come under attack, and prisoners treated with Freudian types of psychotherapy do not seem to do any better than other prisoners at keeping out of trouble). The real problem is that the interpretation cannot be generalized beyond the individual case. Psychoanalysis can tell us much about the individual criminal but very little about crime.

Both the Freudian model and the behaviorist model attempt to show how criminals fail to acquire conscience. Both theories also focus on development. They start with the assumption that we are *all* born criminals (compared with Lombroso's estimate of a paltry one-third of the criminal population) but that in our early years, most of us develop the psychological mechanisms that make us noncriminals. These theories are a noble effort—the attempt to define the process of becoming a moral person—but one for which conclusive evidence is hard to come by. Both theories would require careful, systematic observation of the daily interaction of children and parents. They would also require turning vague ideas like "internalization" or "reinforcement" into specific items of behavior that any observer could recognize.

Perhaps because developmental theories are so hard to prove, other psychological theories have placed less emphasis on how a child develops into a criminal and more emphasis on searching for common psychological or personality traits among criminals. Is there some identifiable collection of traits that distinguishes criminals from noncriminals? In essence, is there a criminal mind?

PSYCHOPATHY AND SOCIOPATHY—THE BORN CRIMINAL REBORN

In the early twentieth century, psychiatrists and social workers began to use the term *psychopath* to describe certain criminals. Derived from the Greek words for "mind" and "disease," the term implies mental illness and has been used to describe people who commit senseless crimes, who act on no apparent purpose, and who seem to have no sense of guilt. But the term has been used to designate a wide variety of criminals. On the one hand, psychopaths are said to be impulsive, unable to control themselves. On the other hand, they have been described as cold people who manipulate others for their own ends. In either case, they are impervious to influence by others and feel little remorse for their crimes. In actual use, **psychopathy** has been somewhat difficult to pin down, an understandable difficulty given that the label could be applied to both the impulsively violent criminal and the slick, calculating con artist. It often seemed that the diagnoses of psychopathy had more to do with the person doing the diagnosing than with the person being diagnosed. For example, in 1925, a clinic for troubled youths had been diagnosing as psychopathic about 1 percent of the cases brought to it. Suddenly, in one year, the clinic had six times that proportion of psychopaths. The children brought to the clinic were probably no different from those of previous years. What had changed was the fashion in psychiatric diagnosis.[30]

Because of the abuses of the term *psychopathy*, some psychiatrists and social workers substituted the term **sociopathy**, though the meaning was not much different. In either case, the concept explains antisocial behavior by seeing it as a symptom of an underlying disease—a more or less permanent condition that makes someone unable to follow social rules.

DISCOVERING PATHOLOGY   How can we know such a disease exists? We can't do lab tests as we would for a physical disease. The principal evidence must be the person's behavior. But how can we know that the behavior comes from the disease and is not simply a response to the pressures of the situation? One way is to see how the person behaves in a variety of situations and over a long period of time. In other words, we are asking two kinds of questions: Are criminals "bad" in most social areas? And do bad kids grow up to be bad adults? If so, these consistencies would be evidence that the behavior was caused by something within the person, something like a permanent disease.

Probably the most extensive research on these questions is Lee Robins's thirty-year follow-up of children—more than one-fourth over 18—who had been brought to a child guidance clinic. Some had been referred by the juvenile court, others by parents or teachers. Robins had not been around in the 1920s for the original diagnoses. However, she had salvaged the files and was able to get information on 524 of these problem children, who had now grown up. In many cases, researchers were able to interview the people themselves or relatives who could fill them in on the course of their later lives. For comparison, the researchers also interviewed a control group whose members had not had serious behavior problems as children but who otherwise matched the clinic children in age, race, IQ, and social class.

Did criminal children become adult criminals? Did children who were diagnosed as psychopaths in the 1920s turn out to be the worst adult criminals in later years? Unfortunately, Robins's book does not directly answer these questions. However, her report does give us some evidence relevant to the concept of misbehavior as a disease. Robins was more interested in sociopathy, a general pattern of antisocial or deviant behavior, than in predatory crime or even crime in general. In fact, to be diagnosed a sociopath, the person had to be antisocial in several areas. So when Robins writes about sociopaths, it is not always clear whether she is referring to an armed robber or just someone with a poor work record, a series of unstable marriages, a drinking problem, bad health, and few friends. Nevertheless, some facts emerge from her study. First, compared with a control group of adults, the clinic children when grown up committed more crimes and spent more time in prison. Second, there was some consistency from childhood to adulthood. Among the children with six or more antisocial symptoms (lying, stealing, running away, bed-wetting, truancy, etc.), 33 percent were diagnosed thirty years later as sociopathic, compared with 22 percent of all clinic children and only 3 percent of the control group. In other words, children with a lot of problems often became adults with a lot of problems.

When I see figures like these, I sometimes wonder about the other troubled children, the 67 percent who did *not* wind up as sociopaths. Let me give some rough figures based on this study and some other studies that focus just on crime. Suppose we take two groups, each with 100 children: One group has the most troubled and troublesome children; the other group shows no serious misbehavior. Among the "good kids," perhaps 20 will wind up in trouble with the law, and few of these will be serious or frequent offenders. In the other group, as many as half will be arrested, and of these, 20 will be serious offenders who spend more than a year in prison.[31] Of course, these numbers mean that half the bad kids grow up having no further arrests and that 20 percent of the good kids wind up being arrested as adults. So knowing whether a child misbehaves can help predict later criminality. Even for children as young as 3, 4, or 5, there are tests that predict future delinquency with some accuracy. That is, the preschoolers predicted to be antisocial will, on the average, commit more crimes than those predicted to be less troublesome. But group averages can be deceiving, for among the children predicted to be antisocial will be many who turn out relatively well.[32]

CRIME AS A DISEASE   Is there really such a disease as psychopathy or sociopathy? If so, does it contribute to crime? First, if sociopathy is a disease, it should turn up in several different types of situations. Unfortunately, Robins's study is of no use here since she used trouble in several areas as her criterion for defining the disease. If we select as sociopaths those people who are deviant in several areas of life, we cannot also use that sample of people to prove that the disease *causes* deviance in several areas of life. It may be true that people in prisons are often general failures—with a history of bad marriages, unsteady and low-paying jobs, and drinking or drug problems—but there are two ways to interpret this fact. On the one hand, we can say that all these problems are symptoms of a single underlying disease, much in the same way that fever, chills, aches, tiredness, and sneezing are all symptoms of the influenza virus. On the other hand, it may be that a setback in one area makes it harder for a person to succeed in other areas. Losing a job puts greater pressure on a marriage; a broken marriage makes it hard to have a stable home life; moving around a lot makes it difficult to maintain friendships.

Second, if sociopathy is a disease, unless it is cured people will carry it from childhood through adulthood. But do they? Here, on the one hand, we have Robins's research: One-third of the children who showed up at a child guidance clinic with several symptoms were diagnosed thirty years later as sociopathic. As adults, they had high rates of arrest (as well as other non-criminal problems—alcoholism, unemployment, etc.). On the other hand, two-thirds of the problem children (those with six or more symptoms) did not become sociopaths; and even the sociopaths, although they may have led unenviable lives, were not all predatory criminals. If sociopathy is a disease, then it is one from which most of its sufferers spontaneously recover.

It also might be worth noting that although the words *psychopathy* and *sociopathy* denote disease, these conditions are different from physical disease. They carry a heavy moral connotation. Unlike physical illness, a "moral disease" is an intrinsic part of the afflicted person. In fact, the person *is* the disease. Normally, we speak of someone as *having* a cold or *having* the measles. Putting it this way means that the disease is not a part of the person; it's just something he or she has. But even the most committed believers in the concept of psychological disease do not say that someone *has* sociopathy. Instead, they say that the person *is* a sociopath.

THE "CRIMINAL MIND"

Is there a special criminal personality? Behind this question are two crucial assumptions: first, that the "criminal mind" is different from the normal, non-criminal mind; and second, that these differences are rooted in largely unconscious ways of thinking and reacting that can be discovered only through subtle psychological tests. The brief answer to the question is yes. Many studies using personality tests do find differences between groups of criminals and groups of noncriminals. Looking only at the results, we might think these tests had the ability to probe deeply into the mind and discover important psychological differences, to discover who is a criminal and who is not, and even to predict who will commit crimes. However, when we look more closely at the tests themselves, these diagnoses sometimes appear to be the result of much less profound processes.

THE MMPI

The most popular test in all of psychology is a personality test called the **Minnesota Multiphasic Personality Inventory** (**MMPI**). It was developed in the 1940s at the University of Minnesota, and here's how it works.

If you take the MMPI, your results will give your score on ten traits, among them schizophrenia, introversion, masculinity-femininity, hypochondria, and paranoia. The test itself consists of 556 true-or-false questions, such as the following:

- I refuse to play some games because I am not good at them.
- I worry over money and business.
- It takes a lot of argument to convince most people of the truth.

Did you say "true" on the first question or "false" on the second? If so, your answers would increase your score on the schizophrenia scale.

You might wonder what not worrying about money has to do with schizophrenia. In fact, in the way that the MMPI was developed, there does not have to be any obvious, logical connection. The reason the money question counts toward a diagnosis of schizophrenia is that the test makers, in trying out questions on people, discovered that schizophrenics often answered this question "false" while normal people tended to answer "true." Of course, one question is certainly not enough for a firm diagnosis. Instead, the MMPI diagnosis rests on a pattern of answers over the course of the 80 questions that make up the schizophrenia scale. The closer your pattern of answers resembles that of the schizophrenics, the more likely it is that you, too, are schizophrenic. A "false" on the third question listed above counts toward the masculinity-femininity scale—not because there is anything inherently masculine or feminine about argument but because women and homosexual men answered it "false."[33]

Can the MMPI diagnose crime? Can it trace a profile of the criminal personality? Typically, researchers have given the test to a group of noncriminals and to a group of prison inmates or juvenile delinquents and then compared scores. They have been especially interested in the psychopathic-deviate (Pd) scale, and here the MMPI confirms their suspicions. Offenders often (though by no means always) score higher on the Pd scale. The implied conclusion is that lawbreakers have a different personality, one marked by psychopathic-deviate tendencies. The twisting and turning paths of their minds, formed long ago and now difficult to change, lead them to commit crimes.

But is that what the MMPI really tells us? The Pd scale itself has 50 questions. Because of the way the test is scored, a difference on only 4 questions will put you into the psychopathic deviate category. (Of course, you would not know which items among the 556 counted on which scales; and in addition, some of the questions are there just to check on whether you are taking the test seriously and answering consistently. These questions count on the validity scales.) One of the 50 questions is "I have never been in trouble with the law." Another is "I like school." Yet another is "Sometimes when I was young I stole things." Looking at the actual questions takes some of the mystery out of personality assessment. After all, it's one thing to say that delinquents suffer from a mental condition measurable on something called the psychopathic-deviate scale. It's quite another to say that they don't like school, commit petty theft, and get in trouble with the law.

Are these questions getting at personality, or do they merely reflect a set of attitudes and life experiences? To define the problem as personality implies that the criminal has a deeply ingrained set of psychological traits acquired early in life. However, to see the MMPI as measuring attitudes implies something less mysterious. Attitudes are ways of looking at the world, ways that a person learns from others and from experience. Anybody in the same position as the delinquent, anybody experiencing the same world, would tend to share the delinquent's typical point of view. In fact, MMPI research confirms this idea. We know that delinquents and normals score differently on the Pd scale of the MMPI. But what would happen if we compared delinquents with noncriminal youths from poor neighborhoods? In such comparisons, the differences are greatly reduced, and in some cases not significant.[34]

One final comment about criminal personality as shown by the MMPI: It is not just on the Pd scale that criminals score higher than normals. They score higher on every scale, making for somewhat confusing results. Most studies have painted criminals as impulsive, unrestrained, and aggressive. They pursue a faster lifestyle, complete with liquor, drugs, and women.[35] But why then should criminals outscore normals on the masculinity-femininity scale, where high scores "often correlate with homosexuality"[36] and indicate more feminine interests and attitudes? Why should these extroverted, free-wheeling criminals score high on "tendency towards obsessive ruminations, guilty feelings, anxiety, indecision, and worrying" (the psychasthenia scale)? Or on the depression scale? Criminals even scored slightly higher on the social introversion scale, though the difference was significant only for the most deviant group of prisoners. Still, unless all the other personality assessments are wrong, the scores should have gone the other way—toward extroversion, not introversion.

THE CRIMINAL PERSONALITY

The MMPI is objective and empirical. A computer can score the test and make the diagnoses. In fact, had a computer existed in 1940, it could, without any fancy programming, have come up with the original scale itself. In this way, the MMPI technique differs from the more clinical approaches based on observation and interviewing. The MMPI is a standardized tool used primarily for putting the person into some diagnostic category. A clinician, in contrast, listens at length to the patient and interprets the thought processes and motivations that lie behind what the patient says and does.

For nearly three decades, the objective MMPI-style approach dominated the psychological study of crime. However, in 1978 two clinicians, Samuel Yochelson and Stanton Samenow, published a two-volume study called *The Criminal Personality*.[37] It was based on long and repeated interviews with 240 male criminals, some of whom had been committed to a mental hospital as not guilty by reason of insanity.

Yochelson and Samenow concluded that none of these men was insane. They did not hallucinate or hear voices, and they were clearly in touch with the real world. Eventually, the clinicians also discarded several other conventional ideas. They had apparently started out with the notion that these criminals were victims of deprived environments or bad child rearing, men who, with the insights gained in psychotherapy, could rehabilitate themselves to noncriminal life. After much effort at changing the criminals, the two clinicians gave up these notions. Most important, they abandoned the idea that the criminal was a victim of environment. Instead, they came to the conclusion that the causes of crime lay entirely inside the criminal's mind and were not much affected by the environment. In their book, Yochelson and Samenow do not speculate on what causes a person to arrive at a criminal mentality, but they do say that the process occurs very early in life. They even use the phrase "the criminal child" to refer to the criminal in his early years. He is not an innocent child led astray by bad companions. If he has bad companions, it's because he has sought out others like himself. If schools or parents reject him, it is only because he has first and repeatedly rejected them.

They go on to list fifty-two of the criminals' typical "thinking errors," though these also sound like personality characteristics that other researchers have noted.

- Fearfulness—fear of rejection, of injury, of death
- Superoptimism—the complete absence of fear that takes over when he commits crime, even a very risky one
- Zero state—a sense of worthlessness, hopelessness; however, unlike depression among noncriminals, this zero state is linked not to resignation but to anger
- Anger—constant; sometimes expressed, often just under the surface
- Pride—usually put in terms of manhood, independence, superiority to everyone else
- Present-orientation—no thought to long-term consequences

If some of these seem contradictory (fearfulness vs. superoptimism; zero state vs. pride), it is merely a sign of the fleeting quality of the criminal's emotions ("I can change from tears to ice in a minute"). The criminal constantly sizes up situations to see whether they can be exploited for crime, and he takes the same exploitative, manipulative view of other people. His thinking is dominated by self-centeredness and selfishness; although he demands that others treat him with respect and consideration, he shows no regard for the rights or feelings of others. He is incapable of anything resembling a close, trusting relationship with other people. Nevertheless, he also maintains a belief in himself as a good person, though he can commit brutal crimes without a twinge of conscience or remorse.

The problem with this description is not its accuracy. There must be something going on when we find such a striking similarity between the qualities described here and those found by observers over the course of a century, going back to Lombroso. The problem is representativeness. The criminals described by Yochelson and Samenow are only a small proportion of the criminal population, though they probably committed a substantial proportion of the crime (exactly how much we have no accurate way of knowing). In any case, they are not typical of all criminals. Very few criminals are judged not guilty by reason of insanity. These criminals, called psychopaths or sociopaths or chronic offenders, are the most serious 10 to 15 percent of the criminal population. Mednick estimates these psychopaths as 10 percent of the criminal population. Wolfgang's chronics were about 18 percent of all criminal youths. Of Robins's 524 criminals, 243 (45 percent) were referred for stealing; of these, 31 percent were diagnosed sociopathic—about 15 percent of the total.

CRITICISMS AND CONCLUSION

Biological and psychological theories of crime focus on two basic questions: In what ways are criminals different from noncriminals, and what accounts for these differences? The theories emphasize individual traits, and the research usually focuses on those characteristics that criminals have in common but that are much rarer among noncriminals. Rather than seeing crime as a possibly normal response to situational pressures, the individual-based perspective seeks essential, underlying differences or abnormalities within the person that predisposes him or her toward criminal behavior. Some theories have found the abnormality in the criminal's facial features or physique, others in the criminal's blood chemistry or brain paths.

A generation ago, criminology textbooks tended to dismiss biological and psychological explanations of crime. It was easy to chuckle at Lombroso; and most of the later studies, as I have tried to show in this chapter, had methodological flaws that left them open to question. By the 1950s, criminology had become dominated by a more sociological view that emphasized environmental factors and disparaged individual-based explanations for crime. The anti-individual approach was a response to the available evidence, but it was also a response to larger historical events. The horrors of Nazism lingered in the consciousness of social scientists, who remained sensitive to the political implications of theories about biological differences.

Still, the evidence from biological and psychological sources gradually accumulated. What is striking about all these studies and what lends support to their assumption about essential differences, is that no matter how unscientific and wrongheaded the theories behind them may now seem, the descriptions of criminals are remarkably similar. Of course, nobody takes seriously Lombroso's theory of atavism, but many of his observations of social and psychological lives of criminals sound much like those of more scientific observers more than a century later.

Stated in various ways, the portrait of the criminal that emerges is that of a person—almost always a man—with little self-control. He is quick to anger and impulsively acts on that anger. He also acts impulsively on his desires for money or sex; he has little ability to delay gratification. He is not intelligent. He is restless and likes high-risk, dangerous activities. These traits show up in childhood. Even as an adult, he is unable to commit himself to long-term efforts, and as a result he has no stable relationships. He is also self-centered to the point that he seems to lack a conscience and is unable or unwilling to think about the consequences of his own actions for other people and even for himself beyond the immediate situation.

Today, individual-based theories have returned to mainstream criminology. The consistency of antisocial behavior from childhood to adulthood; the similarities among family members, even those raised in different environments; the link between delinquency and performance on physiological and neurological tests—these and other sources of evidence point to a place for psychological or biological factors in the explanation of crime. The environment cannot explain everything. Some criminals have fairly enduring biological and psychological characteristics that are different from those of the rest of the population.

ABOUT CRIME & CRIMINOLOGY

LEARNING PSYCHOPATHY

Sometimes what looks like psychopathic or sociopathic behavior is clearly a product of learning or socialization, part of a criminal's on-the-job training. The following excerpts are taken from an interview with a "road hustler"—a skilled card cheat. These hustlers usually work in teams so that the one actually manipulating the cards is not the one who wins the money.

When I first got involved in hustling, my attitudes were less calloused. I might be at a stag of some sort, and say some fellow is losing a little money. Through the course of the evening, talking back and forth, you find out that maybe he just got married, or that he has some kids and here he's writing checks, and I would slow down. If you pull something like this with a crew, the other guys will want to

know what the hell you are doing. They're waiting for you to take him and you're saying, "Well, gee, the guy doesn't have much money." You would get the worst tongue lashing! The position they take is that "You can't have feelings on the road." And it's true. If you start saying to yourself, "Well, maybe I better not beat this guy or that guy," you would soon be out of business or at least you would really cut down on your profits.

When a crew is on the road, they have no feelings for the other players.... When I first started out, I had some feelings for the people I was beating, but later on I didn't, because then you think, "This is my money."

I remember one time when I had just started working with this one top crew. We were playing poker and there was this cripple there. He was deformed and on crutches, but the guy

The criticisms of biological and psychological theories focus mostly on what individual factors *cannot* explain. Most researchers in these areas acknowledge that environmental factors are more influential on criminal behavior. Individual factors may predispose a person toward selfish, antisocial behavior, but the social environment will determine whether that behavior takes the form of crime. Nor is it clear just what part of the criminal population is affected by the various biological or psychological factors that may influence crime. Lombroso put the ratio of born criminals at 33 percent. Later studies have estimated that psychopaths make up about 10 percent of the criminal population. We must wonder about the other 90 percent.

A second problem with the psychological approach is that many people, not just the most extreme 5 percent or 10 percent of the population, are capable of behavior that an observer would label cold-blooded or even psychopathic. This possibility—that normal people can commit pathological deeds—is now well established. One of the most frightening experiments in social science created a mock prison, with college students assigned to the roles of guard and prisoner. Although none of the students could have been diagnosed as anything near to psychopathic, within only a few days some of the guards were deliberately humiliating prisoners far loved to play poker. Anyway we started to beat him, and I felt sorry for the guy. I said, "Leave the guy alone, he's crippled." They looked at me and said, "Are you kidding? His money is just as good as anyone else's."

Priests, we beat priests, oh yeah.... When I was just starting out, I would say, "I'm a Catholic, I can't beat this priest." Like I had been an altar boy. So later, when I was with this crew and the first time a priest came and got into the game, I wasn't manipulating towards him. These guys sensed it and let me know they weren't happy with me. It ended up that we really took advantage of him, it was like a circus. There's been monks, priests, brothers, we've beaten.... Women, it's the same thing. Sometimes you don't want to beat a woman, but you might as well, you can't afford to have feelings about the people you are going to beat....

Now, say I was with a crew and noticed that a new man was tightening up with a cripple or a priest or whatever, and he didn't want to take advantage of him, I would give him shit! Just like I got shit. You have to, because you can't afford to feel sorry for people. Like you'll hear these sob stories over the table. The guy may go to the toilet and sure enough the guys will be saying, "Gee, he can't afford to lose all that money. He's got this to pay, or that to pay."... But if you slow down, it will definitely get in your way.

It's like when they started me on boosting [shoplifting], if you don't boost, they are going to take you for a sucker. "If something is laying there, pick it up, it's money to you! What's the matter with you! Don't you understand that's money in your pocket.... It's not that I've been an angel, but hustling pool or cards or craps seemed different than stealing from a store."

Source: Robert C. Prus and C. R. D. Sharper, *Road Hustlers* (Lexington, MA: D. C. Heath, 1977).

beyond what the experimenters expected. Not all the guards did so, but even the ones who did not brutalize the prisoners did nothing to restrain the brutality of their colleagues.[38] Of course, even though the guards and prisoners seemed to be taking their roles seriously—too seriously—this prison was just an experiment. In real life, too, war atrocities and police brutality provide evidence that normal people can act in ways that seem sadistic or psychopathic, but we needn't go so far afield for examples. College fraternity initiations have often featured psychological or physical torture (under the euphemism "hazing"), with the torturers showing no guilt, compassion, or remorse. They regard the sufferings of the pledges— both at the time and in retrospect—with amusement. Are the fraternity brothers sadists or psychopaths?

If normal college students and others can behave pathologically, we must question another basis of these theories. Psychology assumes that the personality traits precede and cause the criminal's behavior. But the process may also work in the other direction. That is, criminal ways of thinking are part of the job. Just as people who join the football team often acquire a taste for violence (a "good hit"), at least on the field, criminals, too, may acquire their typical ways of thinking on the job. Or if they bring some of these psychological traits with them, their life as a criminal tends to reinforce these traits. The same reversal may be present in biological and neurological factors as well. Higher testosterone levels may make a man more dominant, but behaving in a dominant way can, at least in the short run, raise a man's testosterone levels.[39] Similarly, a criminal lifestyle may cause a neuropsychological deficit.[40]

A third criticism, one I have already mentioned, is political; it looks at the policies that psychological theories might create. Such policies would ignore social factors like economic inequality. They might also use psychological tests to decide the fate of individuals—punishing them on the basis of their responses to psychological tests rather than on the basis of the crime committed. Would society or the courts tolerate such policies? I hope not. However, when public fear and concern rise, people may accept any proposal that claims to offer a convenient solution. For example, in 1970, in the wake of the urban riots of the late 1960s, a national commission issued a report pointing to social conditions (unequal opportunity, education, housing, etc.) as the cause of the riots and calling for social change. Not everyone agreed with this sociological analysis. For example, the president's own personal physician preferred a more individual-based explanation and offered

> another direct, immediate and ... effective way of tackling the problem at its very origin by focusing on the criminal mind of the child. The government should have mass testing of 6- to 8-year-old children to help detect the children who have violent and homicidal tendencies. Corrective treatment could begin at that time.[41]

From the perspective of the person sent to a special program or institution, it's often hard to tell the difference between "corrective treatment," on the one hand, and punishment, on the other. In fact, in many states, prisons are still officially known as correctional institutions. This proposal never became policy. But given the influential position of its author, it did provide substance for fears about the misuse of psychological theories of crime.

The fourth criticism of psychological explanations of crime is the most critical: Psychological theories of crime, like biological theories, cannot account for the most important demographic facts. If crime is the result of certain personality traits, why should those traits be more common to urban people than to those in the suburbs? Or to 15- to 20-year-olds rather than to 30-year-olds? Why should those traits be so much more prevalent in the United States than in Canada? And even in the United States, did the large increase in crime in the decade 1963 to 1973 mean that a greater proportion of psychopaths had been born into the population?

Psychological concepts may help us to understand the differences between serious criminals and those who commit few or no crimes. But none of the psychological theories seems well equipped to explain the important facts about the social distribution of crime. For this reason, we now turn to sociological explanations of crime.

CRITICAL THINKING QUESTIONS

1. What were the classical theories lacking in their explanations for crime?
2. Which of Lombroso's ideas and observations still seem relevant today?
3. Why are biological theories of crime so controversial? What are their possible political implications?
4. What are the similarities and differences between behaviorist psychology and Freudian psychology in their explanations of crime?
5. Is there a criminal personality? How can it be diagnosed or measured?
6. What facts about crime are psychological theories best suited to explain, and what facts are they least useful in explaining?

KEY TERMS

atavism	neurotransmitters	somatotype
classical theory	positivism	superego
concordance	psychopathy	testosterone
Minnesota Multiphasic Personality Inventory (MMPI)	serotonin	utilitarianism
	sociopathy	XYY syndrome

CHAPTER ELEVEN

SOCIOLOGICAL THEORY TO 1960

OPPORTUNITIES AND ASSOCIATES

THE SOCIOLOGICAL PERSPECTIVE

What makes a theory sociological? Of course, no simple answer could possibly satisfy all sociologists. But to oversimplify, we might say that if biological and psychological approaches try to show how criminals are different from you and me, sociological theories try to show how they are similar to us. Psychological theories see crime as the result of abnormal people doing abnormal things. Sociological theories tend to see crime as the product of normal people going through normal social processes in normal (though perhaps not ideal) social environments.

Psychological and biological theories look for the differences between individuals. According to these theories, the important causes of crime are to be found within the *person*. Deficiencies or defects inside the person make him or her different from other people and cause him or her to break society's rules. Sociological theories, in contrast, tend to emphasize causes found in the *environment*. Certain environments will produce more crime, regardless of the characteristics of the people living there. Individual differences hardly enter into these theories.

Many sociological theories of crime that emerged in the 1940s and 1950s sought to explain lower-class juvenile delinquency. Later research has found that delinquency—especially property and status offenses—may be equally common in other sectors of society.

The sociological approach raises an important question: If sociologists believe that crime is largely a result of environmental causes, does this mean that sociologists also believe that criminals are not responsible for their crimes since the causes lie not in the person but in the social environment? The answer is no, although many people have just such an image of sociology. I once spent a frustrating two weeks on jury duty—frustrating because the district attorneys prosecuting the cases always rejected me as a prospective juror after the voir dire. (In principle, you are not told which lawyer—prosecution or defense—rejected you, but it was not hard for me to guess.) One afternoon, in the hall, I ran into a district attorney who had kept me off a jury that morning. "Why did you toss me off your case?" I asked innocently.

"Are you kidding?" he said. "A sociologist? You people don't think anyone's responsible for what they do."

At the time, I didn't know what to say, and the conversation ended there. But what I should have said is that he was confusing two separate questions. It's one thing to understand the social forces that may have caused a person to commit a crime. It is quite another matter to absolve that person of all blame. For a lawyer or a juror (even a juror who is also a sociologist), the question of guilt is paramount. But for the sociologist who is thinking about crime as a social problem, the issue of individual guilt or innocence is much less important. Sociological theory often dodges the problem of assigning moral or legal blame, just as it also avoids the issue of individual differences. In this way, sociological theorizing is different from everyday thinking about crime. Often, when we read about some horrible crime, our first thought is a moral one (this is a bad person), and our second response may be to look for individual differences and defects (what's wrong with him that made him so bad?). Sociological theory often sidesteps both these issues.

How can sociology, if it wishes to explain crime, ignore both the question of individual differences and the issue of moral guilt and blame? The answer is that sociologists look not just at individuals but also at groups.

RATES AND CASES

If we are acting as jurors or psychologists, we must focus our attention on a single case, a single criminal. But if we are sociologists, we want to look for larger patterns. We look not at this or that crime but at crime in general. One way of gaining this broader view is to step back from the individual crime or criminal and look instead at crime **rates**. When we do, we often notice something interesting: Although the rate is made up entirely of individual **cases**, it seems to have an existence of its own, apart from any individual case. In other words, although individuals may change their behavior unpredictably from day to day or year to year, a society's overall rates of behavior show a remarkable consistency; and when these rates do change, they do so gradually. For example, most people who commit murder do so only once. There is a great variation in the murderer's behavior: This year he killed; he had never done so before and will probably never do so again. Yet, despite this great variation in each murderer's behavior, the overall murder *rate* every year is quite close to that of the previous year. So we can predict that next year in the United States the homicide rate will be between 9 and 10 per 100,000, that is, that about 24,000 people will be murdered. We also know that different societies or different sections of the country will have predictably different rates. And these rates are predictable on the basis of social, not psychological, factors.

Of course, knowing rates allows us to predict only other rates, not individual cases. We can roughly predict the number of homicides, highway deaths, births, or whatever, but we cannot specify which individuals will become part of these statistics. Here's a useful analogy: Suppose that a casino spins a roulette wheel 38,000 times. I know that since there are 38 numbers in the wheel (counting the 0 and 00), my lucky number will come up approximately 1,000 times. Unfortunately, I do not know exactly on which spins it will come up. (If I did, I would probably not be writing this book.) But I do know that the total will be very close to 1,000.

This is one of the basic and most important insights of the sociological perspective: We can predict the collective number, or rate, of these events in a given population even though each individual event may be unpredictable and unintended. For example, we can predict that the number of people who will die in traffic accidents next year will be roughly 40,000. This estimate is not exact, but we can be sure that the number will be closer to 40,000 than to 50,000 or 30,000. The first use of this insight—at least in the area of criminology—came over 150 years ago. In 1835, a French writer, Alfonse Quetelet, published a book called *A Treatise on Man and the Development of His Faculties*. As the book's title implies, Quetelet wanted to explain how physical changes that occurred as people grew older affected their moral or psychological life. However, while trying to find out the age at which human passions are strongest, Quetelet reviewed the statistics on murder and on crime in general, statistics that the French government had just begun to compile in 1825. When Quetelet examined the first few years of these annual figures, he discovered that the numbers stayed remarkably stable from one year to the next. Differences among the various regions of France, differences between the sexes, differences among age groups—all showed consistent patterns. For example, year after year, women committed about 14 percent of all violent crimes and 21 percent of property crimes.[1]

Today, we take these consistencies for granted. But to Quetelet and other "moral statisticians," as they were called, these were discoveries that raised important questions. The statistics added a new element to the philosophical debate over free will. Today, most of us assume that, as individuals, we have free will. But if our behavior—even our seemingly impulsive, unpredictable behavior—falls into a consistent, predictable pattern, is our sense of free will merely an illusion? Are we perhaps merely parts in some larger design?

For purposes of criminology, the philosophical questions are less important than the sociological ones. Quetelet and Guerry (a Belgian who lived during the same period and explored much of the same statistical territory)—along with others of this cartographic school of thought—mapped out the geographical and social distribution of crime rates (see Table 11–1). The data they gathered set what should have been the agenda for criminology. Unfortunately, their work was largely ignored. The dominant ideas in thinking about crime focused on the individual criminal, and it was nearly a century before sociologists began to pick up the trail blazed by the cartographic school.

TABLE 11-1 •
CRIME IN FRANCE, 1825 TO 1830

CRIMES AGAINST THE PERSON								
REGION	1825	1826	1827	1828	1829	1830	POPULATION	PERCENT OF POPULATION
NORTH	25	24	23	26	24	25	8,757,700	27.6
SOUTH	28	26	22	23	25	23	4,826,500	15.2
EAST	17	21	19	20	19	19	5,841,000	18.4
WEST	18	16	21	17	17	16	7,008,800	22.1
CENTER	12	13	15	14	18	14	5,238,900	16.5

CRIMES AGAINST PROPERTY								
REGION	1825	1826	1827	1828	1829	1830	POPULATION	PERCENT OF POPULATION
NORTH	41	42	42	43	44	44	8,757,700	27.6
SOUTH	12	11	11	12	12	11	4,826,500	15.2
EAST	18	16	17	16	14	15	5,841,000	18.4
WEST	17	19	19	17	17	18	7,008,800	22.1
CENTER	12	12	11	12	13	13	5,238,900	16.5

Source: A. M. Guerry, "Essai sur la statistique Morale de la France," in Terence Morris, *The Criminal Area* (London: Routledge & Kegan Paul, 1957), p. 46.

EVIL EFFECTS, EVIL CAUSES?

Besides emphasizing rates rather than cases, sociological theories take an interesting perspective on the moral issue. Individualistic theories usually assume that criminal behavior arises from some deficiency, from something wrong—bad genes, bad psychology, bad family, bad environment. Sometimes called the **evil-causes-evil assumption**, this way of thinking seems to come naturally. If something is wrong, we assume that it must have both evil causes and evil consequences. Some of the theories we will be looking at directly challenge the evil-causes-evil assumption, even in the study of crime. Some theories find causes of crime in some of the most valued aspects of our society. One theory says that something good (an emphasis on success and results) causes something bad (crime). Other theories hold that something bad (crime) can cause something good (social cohesion). They argue that crime has positive consequences for society—that a society *needs* a certain amount of crime, and if the criminals fail to meet their production quotas, the society will create more crime. For example, people may raise their moral standards; although they once accepted a behavior, they may later think of it as a problem to be corrected. In the end, they will have created whole new categories of crime and criminals.[2]

MERTON AND ANOMIE

In 1938, Robert Merton, an American sociologist, published an essay enti-tled "Social Structure and Anomie."[3] It proved to be one of the most influ-ential articles in sociology. Every sociologist has read it; it has appeared in the footnotes and references of other sociological articles more often than any other title.[4] Nearly every criminology textbook outlines it (the book you are now holding is no exception). Yet Merton had never claimed to be a criminol-ogist, and he presented no new information about crime. Nevertheless, this article remains important because it explains something about crime by using purely sociological ideas.

Merton begins his essay by rejecting psychological and biological theo-ries since they cannot explain why different social groups consistently have different amounts of crime. As Merton puts it, "Our perspective is sociologi-cal. We look at variations in the *rates* of deviant behavior."

The basic fact Merton is trying to explain is the connection between social class and crime. He assumes that in America, poorer people commit more crime than wealthier people. (Although many people now question this assumption, at the time it was widely accepted and supported by the available research.) He set out to explain not individual differences (criminals vs. non-criminals) but rather the different crime rates of different social groups.

MEANS AND ENDS

Why, then, are poorer people more likely to commit crime? The obvious answer is, because they need the money. But the problem in that answer is the word *need*. After all, there are many populations in the world who by any objective standard are much needier than the lower classes of the United States; yet they commit far less crime—and not just because there is less available for them to steal.

The crucial factor is not how much money you have, but rather how you *feel* about what you have. Do you feel satisfied or frustrated? This feeling about the satisfaction of needs comes down to the match between ends and means, that is, between your goals and the means you have to achieve them. If the available means allow you to move toward your goals, you will be satis-fied; if those means are not sufficient for your goals, you will feel frustrated. All this is obvious. It is also fairly obvious that society does not distribute the same package of means to everybody. Children born to poor parents will not have the same opportunities as children born to middle-class or wealthy par-ents. Poor children's chances even of surviving the first few years of life are not as good; they will not get as good an education; they may not meet the "right" people or learn how to deal with them in the "right" way. They are more likely to wind up in dead-end, low-paying jobs. If you think these environ-mental factors make no difference, imagine that you could choose the family you will be born into in your next life. Would you choose to be the child of poor, uneducated, and unwed teenagers?

Few people would argue with the idea that society—something over which the individual has little influence—greatly determines the means a person has available to reach his or her goals. But Merton reminds us of something less obvious: that goals, too, are socially distributed. Usually, when we think about our goals—what we want, what we think is good—we see them as ideas that we have arrived at by ourselves. If we admit to being influenced by someone else, it is usually the kind of influence we can control, such as specific advice we can accept or reject. However, society influences our ideas in a more general and subtle way. To take a trivial example, consider our ideas of beauty. If you look at movie stars of seventy years ago—or clothing of seven years ago—you may wonder how people could have thought them the pinnacle of attractiveness. Yet years from now, the same will be said of the bodies, faces, and clothes that are today's ideals. Obviously, in our ideas about what looks good, we have been influenced by other people, that is, by society. In the same way, society also shapes our more abstract ideas of what is good or worth pursuing—our values and goals.

CONDITIONS FOR THE CLASS-CRIME CONNECTION

Crime rates are higher in the lower class, then, not merely because lower-class people have less money. For a society to have a strong connection between crime and lack of money, three other conditions must exist:

1. Poorer people must share the same goals as better-off people.
2. These goals—the things people want—must be easily transferable.
3. The society must emphasize attaining goals rather than using approved means.

America meets these three conditions so well that we may have difficulty imagining a society where they do not hold true. However, not all societies resemble ours in these respects. Consider, for example, the first condition. The important point to remember here is that *both* means and goals are socially distributed. In other words, society creates these goals and means and instills them in people. In some societies, different social groups may have different goals—different standards of success. Poor people there will not compare themselves enviously with better-off people. But in America, according to Merton, people on all rungs of the social ladder place a high value on financial success—or, in a word, money. Every child is taught—at home, in school, and later at work—that anyone can and should work hard and become wealthy. Even the poor adopt this ideology of individual success. They will compare themselves not just with one another but also with those at a higher level, and they will feel that they are missing something. Although Merton does not identify this concept by name, he is using the idea of **relative deprivation**—the notion that how deprived you feel depends on the people you are comparing yourself with. Although the comparison will be more stressful for the poor, Americans at all economic levels, says Merton, tend to compare themselves with people who are somewhat more successful; and everybody measures success chiefly in terms of money.

Money provides a very good means of comparison. Not only is it easily calculated, but also it has the advantage of being easily transferred from person to person (the second condition), unlike membership in a particular family or possession of a title of nobility. Money is money, regardless of who is holding it, regardless even of how the person got it. Americans, in Merton's view, are rather tolerant of ill-gotten gain—especially if the amount is large enough and if it has been handed on to the next generation. A Mercedes-Benz costs $80,000 and looks classy no matter who is driving it. But it's not just that money can buy things; in America, "money has been consecrated as a value in itself." No matter how much we have, we always want just a little (or a lot) more.

RELATIVE DEPRIVATION AND SOCIAL STRUCTURE

Not every society has this correlation between poverty and crime. People with lesser means need not feel envious or deprived as long as they are in a society "where rigidified class structure is coupled with *differential class symbols of success*." Imagine a strict caste society, one where the caste you are born into largely determines your lot in life. Different castes will have different ideas and symbols of success, and the institutions of society—especially the family—will reinforce these differences. In each caste, the family will teach its particular goals to its children. Members of a lower, poorer caste would not necessarily feel deprived relative to someone in a higher caste. Instead, they would judge themselves by the unique standards of their particular caste. Even in some industrialized societies, the working class may have a strong class consciousness; its members may feel that the working-class way of life is every bit as legitimate as middle-class life. In such a society, working-class parents, instead of hoping for their children to move up into a better class, will hope for the position of all working-class people to become more comfortable—but with no basic changes in their way of life. In the United States, however, according to Merton, everyone shares the same basic goal.

When we think of money and the things it buys—houses, cars, vacations, furniture, and other standard prizes of TV game shows—we may find it hard to believe that there are societies where some people would not want these desirable consumer goods that other people enjoy, or where the members of a lower caste do not constantly look with envy on the goods of another caste. We can scarcely imagine such a system. The closest analogy I can think of in our own society is that of male-female differences. Gender is perhaps the nearest thing we have to caste. What one sex might strive for (bulging biceps or soft, luxuriant hair) members of the other sex might not find at all enviable for themselves.

More to the point, not all societies base the status of the individual on such impersonal, transferable things as money and the things it buys. In simple societies, people's positions in the world—their work, their relationships with others, the respect others give them—may be determined almost entirely by their age, sex, and family. These sources of status are nontransferable. Factors like age and position in a family structure cannot be acquired through hard work: If you are not born as the eldest child of a chief, no amount of talent and hard work will get you there. Consequently, in these societies, striving for success will not be so important.

Not just in small-scale, simple societies, but in those based on aristocracy as well, a person's place may be largely determined by the family he or she is born into. Even in modern European societies, the faint traces of an aristocratic tradition, where position in society is based on family, may make for somewhat less emphasis on money as a measure of who a person is. Modern Europeans visiting America today still seem surprised by our preoccupation with success.

America has much less of an aristocratic tradition. Our democratic, egalitarian ideals extend from the political arena into economics and society. We judge all people by the same standards. But at the same time that our society leads us all to want similar goals, we do not all have the same opportunities to achieve them. People with less opportunity will feel a certain amount of strain between their culturally prescribed goals and the socially structured means available to achieve them. Something will have to give. In the extreme case, the result will be **anomie**, a condition of normlessness in which the rules of the game no longer make sense. Short of this kind of social chaos, there may be less drastic adaptations. When legitimate means and goals do not mesh, people may give up one or the other or both.

ADAPTATIONS TO ANOMIE

Merton outlines five logical "modes of adaptation" to the means-ends conflict. A person can either accept (+) or reject (0) a culturally prescribed goal; he or she can also accept or reject the legitimate means toward that goal; or the person can both reject the means and substitute a different one (0/+).

MODES OF ADAPTATION	CULTURAL GOALS	INSTITUTIONALIZED MEANS
CONFORMITY	+	+
INNOVATION	+	0
RITUALISM	0	+
RETREATISM	0	0
REBELLION	(0/+)	(0/+)

Conformity—law-abiding behavior—is probably the most common adaptation and does not much concern us here. But innovation—keeping the goal of financial success while adopting illegitimate means to achieve it—obviously includes many forms of economic crime. Merton expects that this adaptation will be found most frequently in the lower class, although he also mentions upper-class crime—from the robber barons of the nineteenth cen-

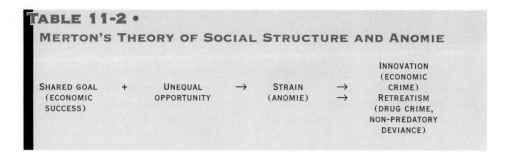

TABLE 11-2 •

MERTON'S THEORY OF SOCIAL STRUCTURE AND ANOMIE

SHARED GOAL (ECONOMIC SUCCESS)	+	UNEQUAL OPPORTUNITY	→	STRAIN (ANOMIE)	→ →	INNOVATION (ECONOMIC CRIME) RETREATISM (DRUG CRIME, NON-PREDATORY DEVIANCE)

tury to contemporary white-collar criminals. The pressure toward innovation is characteristic of American society at all levels. When the goal cannot be achieved by legitimate means, we still keep the goal. Since the goal (producing goods or making a profit) is worthwhile, Americans tend to overlook some corner cutting and questionable business practices: Break a few rules if you have to, but get the job done. Other societies, even those with greater inequality, may stress means over ends. People will do things in the proper or traditional way, even though this may not be the quickest way to the goal. At the extreme, this leads to what Merton calls ritualism. Ritualists, in Merton's scheme, are the people who abandon success goals while continuing to follow the rules of society, paring down their aspirations and not taking chances. The lower middle class is the most likely place to find ritualism since these people discipline their children to conform to society's rules even though their chances for real financial success remain small.

Rereatists have given up. They are "psychotics ... outcasts ... vagrants ... drunkards ... addicts." They do not pursue success, nor do they conform to the approved ways of doing things. Surely, the skid-row wino, who moves from the street to drunk court to jail and back to the street, is neither pursuing success nor following approved means (see Table 11–2). Rebels, too, have become alienated from the goals and means of society, but unlike retreatists, they are organized, and they take collective action to bring about change in the values and laws of the society.

CRITICISMS OF MERTON

I have outlined Merton's essay at length here, primarily because it has had so much influence on criminological thinking but also because it presents a truly sociological view of the issue of crime. Merton begins not with criminals but with society and culture, that is, the social class system and the widely shared ideas and ideals of a society. He directs his attention not to the individual criminal but to the different crime rates among social classes. People at certain places in the class structure will experience a strain between the goals society has taught them and the means society has made available to them. For this reason, Merton's theory and others like it are often referred to as **strain theories**. Merton also refuses to condemn criminals. Too often, we

ABOUT CRIME & CRIMINOLOGY

In 1938, Merton attributed crime in the United States to its value on financial success and the things money can buy—a value that the society inculcates even in those who cannot come close to achieving it. Over a half century later, Carl Husemuller Nightingale spent six years with children in a poor, African-American neighborhood of Philadelphia and wrote of the role that materialism, generously nurtured by advertising, plays in their lives.

The importance of materialistic values to inner-city youth seems to have increased steadily throughout the late twentieth century.

As soon as they are able, kids begin to demand the basic building blocks of the b-boy outfit. Already at five and six, many kids in the neighborhood can recite the whole canon of adult luxury—from Gucci, Evan Piccone [sic], and Pierre Cardin, to Mercedes and BMW (some people say these have replaced Cadillacs as "*Black Man*'s Wheels").

Though kids in [the] neighborhood can often achieve moments of glamour and pride through consumption, much bigger parts of their day-to-day existence are preoccupied with dreaming about those moments, desperately trying to find ways to get enough money for the things they want, feeling frustrated with parents who cannot regularly afford food and rent, let alone discretionary items like hundred-dollar sneakers, and feeling jealous of others who have found some way to dress "fly" for their own fleeting moment. It is difficult to exaggerate the intensity of feeling that can come from this mixture of a seductive sense of hope and expectation (so rare in the neighborhood as it is) and reconfirmed humiliation, frustration, and envy. Once, while he was visiting my house shortly after I first met him, eleven-year-old Georgie disappeared, and only after a ten-minute search was I able to find him, hiding deep inside the hall closet of my house with old coats pulled over his face. We had been fixing up his and his brother's homemade skateboards (scrap plywood and sawed-apart roller-skate wheels), and another kid had just ridden by on a hundred-dollar Hot Rod Wheeler. Georgie, as far as I know, had not learned to write at the time, but somehow he produced me a note in red crayon that said, "I a bich cause they state bod better." ["I'm a bitch because their skate board is better."]

Source: Carl Husemuller Nightingale, *On the Edge: A History of Poor Black Children and Their American Dreams* (New York: Basic Books, 1993), pp. 143, 153–154, 158.

think of criminals as some sort of alien race that has invaded our basically noncriminal society. In Merton's view, criminals are just as much a part of society and just as much a product of it as anyone else. By suspending the usual moral condemnation of criminals, Merton also avoids the evil-causes-evil assumption. In fact, according to his theory, both the worst street crimes and the greatest capitalist achievements flow from the same sources. By putting street thieves in the same category with the robber barons and calling it innovation, Merton is implying that both the burglar and the great industrialist are products of the same aspects of American culture: the value placed on economic success and the emphasis on goals rather than means.

Merton's views can be criticized at both the theoretical and the empirical levels. For example, his theory does not include any explanation of violent, noneconomic crime. It might be possible to place murder, rape, and assault under the heading of innovation, but this classification would stretch that category considerably. Merton himself never suggests this inclusion, nor do these crimes fit into any of his other adaptations. In addition, even crimes that do have an economic goal may be motivated as much by the immediate experience of the crime itself as by a desire for money and what it buys.[5] As for the empirical evidence on social class and crime, it is not exactly overwhelming. The poor probably commit more crimes than the middle class, but the difference is not as large as Merton's theory would lead us to expect. Furthermore, the difference is probably greatest for crimes of violence—precisely those crimes about which Merton's theory has the least to say.

In addition, Merton makes some assumptions about goals and means that are fairly difficult to prove. It might be possible, though certainly difficult, to see if the class-crime correlation was weaker or stronger in other societies. But how could we show that in the United States, compared with other countries, all social classes place a high value on financial success? Or that Americans are more likely than people of other cultures to let the ends justify the means? These perceptions may seem accurate; they may correspond well with what we think of ourselves, and visitors from other cultures may remark on these same ideas. But it is difficult to measure these variables in any systematic way, especially for purposes of comparison among different countries.

Some studies do provide evidence that for Americans of every social class, money is the principal measure of social standing,[6] and there are many studies that show to what extent our class system limits a person's opportunities.[7] But in order to compare the United States with other countries, we need the same measures for these other societies, and at least at present, these measures have not been devised.

A final criticism of Merton's theory concerns his picture of the relationship of the individual to society. Whenever I read this essay, I picture the individual as isolated, not in contact with other people. If he finds his opportunities too limited, his path blocked, then all by himself he "innovates" some illegal method of getting money. However, we know that most crimes are not very innovative in the usual sense of that word. In fact innovation, as we usually think of it, would apply much more to upper-class, white-collar crime than to ordinary street crime: the frustrated computer programmer who, working alone, electronically and undetectably credits his own account. Most burglars, robbers, and thieves today use techniques that have been around for hundreds of years.

This lack of real innovation and the tendency of street criminals to learn their crimes from other people bring up another gap in Merton's theory. Oddly enough, this weakness in Merton's theory is also its strength—its purely sociological approach. By drawing back from the individual, it allows us to discover patterns that we might have missed. However, it thus cannot explain very well how a person at whatever place in the social structure becomes a criminal. Because of its distance from actual behavior, this viewpoint also ignores the individual's capacity for thought and free will. As Howard Becker wrote several years later, "The people sociologists study often have trouble recognizing themselves in the sociological reports written about them" (his criticism was not directed specifically at Merton).[8] Sociology often runs the risk of treating people as "conceptual boobs," that is, as mere extensions of abstract social forces like social class or values rather than as people who can think and talk about what they do and why they do it.

ON CAMPUS

ANOMIE IN THE CLASSROOM

Several years ago, a student I was talking with began complaining about her Accounting I class, required of all accounting majors and a prerequisite for Accounting II, which was also required. The professor, it seems, was terrible. He taught his classes at so high a level that the students could not learn anything. Worse yet, he was very strict in his grading. As a result, according to my informant, at least half the students were failing.

Some of the students had talked to the department chair, who had told them there was little he could do. The teacher was an adjunct, hired to teach one or two courses for one semester, and although he would certainly not be rehired, he had a contract and couldn't be fired now. And even if firing were possible, there was no way the department could find someone to teach the remaining weeks of the course.

The students were in a bind. The department head did offer them a deal: If they took the final exam and passed, even with a D, he would allow them to move on to Accounting II.

"What are you doing?" I asked her.

"I guess I'll take the exam," she said without much hope. "Some of the kids won't. They just stopped coming to class." Then she added, "Some kids are talking about

CRIME AND CULTURE

During the same period that Merton was writing about the crime-causing strains in the American social structure, another sociologist, Edwin Sutherland, was creating what was to become the other dominant theory in American sociology—the theory of **differential association**.

Most social theories are elaborations of some commonsense notion. As such, they can be summarized in a sentence or two in a way that makes them sound so obvious they're hardly worth writing about. For example, we might reduce Merton's theory to this: Poorer people commit more crime because they want more money. Of course, Merton's essay is valuable because it shows the conditions in which this statement will and will not be true. In a similar way, Sutherland's theory of differential association boils down to the idea that a person becomes a criminal because he or she falls in with the wrong crowd. However, to understand the importance of Sutherland's ideas, it helps to know the kinds of views about crime he was reacting against. Perhaps a little history is in order here.

hiring accountants to come in and take the exam for them. The teacher doesn't know who we are anyway."

It occurred to me that this was a good example of Merton's model of anomie: goals, means, and adaptations. The goals in most classes are to learn something, get a decent grade, and move on. The means are being smart, going to class, studying, and taking exams. Most of the time, the means are proportionate to the goals. The smarter you are, the more attention you pay in class, and the more you study, the better your grade.

But in this case it had become clear, after many weeks, that these traditional means were not going to allow the students to attain their goals. This discrepancy

between means and ends is the classic recipe for anomie, and from my student's description it certainly sounded as though that term applied to her accounting class.

The student's adaptations, too, seemed as though they had been taken straight from Merton's essay. The few conformists would somehow manage to pass. But many students had become ritualists; they kept going to class and would take the exam, even though they were almost certain they would fail. The retreatists had dropped out—written off their tuition and blown off the course, perhaps to try again next semester. Then there were those who chose innovation—cheating in one form or another, keeping the legitimate goal of a decent grade but taking illegitimate means to get there.

SOCIAL PATHOLOGY, SOCIAL DISORGANIZATION

In the early twentieth century, much writing about crime took a perspective known as **social pathology**. The word *pathology* means disease, and as the name *social pathology* implies, this school of thought saw society as something like a living organism. Social pathologists were concerned with crime, drunkenness, divorce, and mental illness—what sociologists today call social problems. But by calling them social pathology, these writers likened the deviant behavior to a disease in an otherwise healthy society. Of course, they were primarily concerned with "curing" the disease, and their writings, therefore, provided the intellectual basis for practical social work during this era. But whatever its good intentions, social pathology as a theory suffered from a major flaw: It assumed that there is an objective state of health for society, just as there is for a single organism. On closer inspection, this standard of health turned out to be American, small-town, middle-class values.[9]

To sociologists of that time, the idea of social pathology did not *explain* the origin or persistence of the behaviors it intended to correct; it merely labeled them, using an analogy (society as body) based on a basically conservative view of society. Sociologists took a more tolerant view of things like drinking and divorce. They did not consider them forms of pathology. More important, they wanted a better explanation for crime and deviance. Therefore, in place of social pathology, sociologists of the 1920s developed the concept of **social disorganization**. In this view, society is not an organism; it is an organization. Just as formal organizations are based on rules, the basis of society also lies in its rules, written and unwritten, which are called **norms**. When people are closely tied to one another, as in small villages, they will be less likely to deviate from these rules; but when relationships become less personal and less permanent, an individual will feel less constrained.

Although social disorganization theory does not have an explicit central metaphor as does the organism metaphor of social pathology, it does have its own unstated image of society. It reminds me of those pictures of iron filings in the presence of a magnet. Social norms are like a central magnet, keeping people in line. But some members of society are further away, at the edges of the magnetic field, where the norms of society do not pull them as strongly. It is in these areas that deviance will flourish. Modern society, in contrast to a rural village, is particularly likely to develop pockets of disorganization, farther from the pull of social norms, where people (just like those iron filings) would get "out of line." The main causes of the breakdown, in this theory, were industrialization, urbanization, and immigration—processes that weaken personal ties and increase anonymity. Sociologist Robert Park included the automobile, movies, and newspapers in this list of "demoralizing" aspects of progress (he was writing in 1925, long before television): "Apparently, anything that makes life interesting is dangerous to the existing order."[10]

The idea of social disorganization was particularly influential with sociologists at the University of Chicago in the early part of this century. Some of their research took the form of close observation and description of life in less respectable social areas—places and groups that outsiders might well have seen as examples of pathology or disorganization: the taxi-dance hall, "hobohemia," juvenile gangs, inexpensive rooming houses, and other disreputable settings. However, their research showed that far from being disorganized, social life in these areas also had its rules. These rules might have differed from those of conventional society, but they nevertheless provided a basis for social life.

SOCIAL ECOLOGY AND NATURAL ZONES

Another style of research that emerged in Chicago was sometimes called **social ecology**. It was based on the idea that social life in cities, like plant and animal life in the wild, conformed to regular patterns that could be mapped by geographic area. Cities developed natural areas according to the functions that would be performed there. These zones tended to take the form of concentric circles radiating from the central business district (Zone I) to the better residential area farthest away (Zone V). In between lay the area of middle-class housing (Zone IV), one of working-class housing (Zone III), and one of transition (Zone II). As the central industrial area expands, owners of buildings in this transitional zone expect to sell their property. Therefore, they

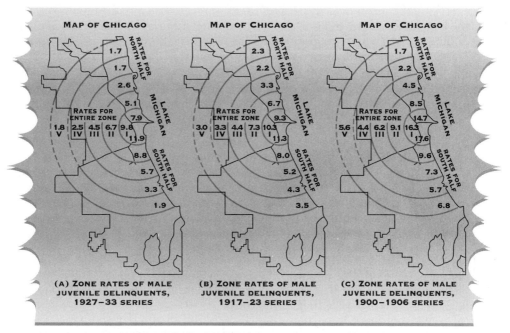

FIGURE 11–1 While the ethnic makeup of the zones in Chicago changed over the course of three decades, the distribution of delinquency among those zones remained remarkably stable.

Source: Clifford R. Shaw and Henry D. McKay, *Juvenile Delinquency and Urban Areas*, rev. ed. (Chicago: University of Chicago Press, 1969).

do not invest much in maintenance or improvement, and buildings deteriorate. Rents are low. The residents tend to be recent immigrants, who move on as soon as they can. There is rapid population turnover, and few people feel any strong attachment to the area or to the people in it.

Zone II is the picture of social disorganization, and it is here that social problems are most likely to occur (see Figure 11–1). The important point to remember is that the ecological view stresses the geographic and social area itself, more than the people who happen to live there, as a source of crime. This may not seem like a very unusual idea to us; we expect some neighborhoods to have predictably higher rates of crime and delinquency, mental and physical illness, poverty, marital breakup, and so on. But at the time, some popular explanations of crime tended to emphasize ethnic factors, sometimes in a way that sounded downright racist. To show the superiority of the ecological approach, two sociologists, Clifford Shaw and Robert McKay, collected statistics on delinquency over a period of several decades. During these years, the ethnic makeup of Zone II in Chicago changed from predominantly German and Irish to Polish and Italian. Yet Shaw and McKay found that regardless of ethnicity, Zone II always had the highest rates of delinquency.

Why did crime and delinquency persist in the zone of transition despite the changing population? Shaw and McKay emphasized two factors. First, social disorganization means that conventional, noncriminal people cannot exert much control over those who break the law. Second, criminals can pass their ideas and way of life to others in the neighborhood. This idea of a "way of life," however, implies that social life, even in this most unstable zone, is not *dis*organized but rather that it is organized on a different set of norms. What some people saw as social *dis*organization could be better seen as (in Sutherland's phrase) "*differential* social organization." Different geographic areas and different social groups have different sets of norms for conducting everyday life. In a word, they have different cultures.

This line of thinking laid the basis for cultural theories of crime. As opposed to Merton's view of America as a land with a single set of means and goals that individuals either accept or reject, cultural theories see America as a collection of different subcultures. In regard to crime, the essence of cultural theories is that while all subcultures have norms, the norms of some subcultures allow or even demand behavior that violates the law. For example, during Prohibition, a culture in which drinking was a basic part of social life would inevitably come into conflict with the law. It may not be purely coincidental that the theories based on the ideas of culture and organization were developed during the 1920s, the era of Prohibition. Not only did Prohibition mean that the pursuit of culturally approved activities would lead some people to violate the law or to help others to violate it; Prohibition also gave rise to the first extensive organization of crime.

Probably more important than Prohibition in the development of sociological views of crime was the phenomenon of immigration. The vast numbers of immigrants who came to America in the period roughly between 1890 and 1920 transformed the social landscape. Earlier generations of immigrants had come largely from northern Europe and, except perhaps for the Irish, had tended to settle in rural areas. The new immigrants came in unprecedented numbers; they came from southern and eastern Europe (Italy, Poland, Russia, and Slavic countries), and they settled in the large cities. It would have been difficult for anyone—especially University of Chicago sociologists studying cities—to ignore this cultural diversity.

SUTHERLAND AND DIFFERENTIAL ASSOCIATION THEORY

Of course, we cannot be sure to what extent these historical events influenced sociological theory. In any case, the ideas of differential social organization and cultural transmission came together in the work of Edwin Sutherland, sometimes referred to as the dean of American criminology. In the first edition of his *Principles of Criminology*, published in 1934, Sutherland stated, "The conflict of cultures is ... the fundamental principle in the explanation of crime."[11] In the full formulation of the theory, Sutherland eventually dropped the explicit mention of culture and conflict.

Though neither Merton nor Sutherland intended it, their theories complement each other. Sutherland's theory focuses on an aspect of crime that Merton avoids—the social and psychological process of becoming a criminal. While Merton begins with the large-scale elements of society such as social class,

Sutherland starts from the smallest element: a person who, in some specific situation, decides to break the law. The decision is based on a particular way of seeing that situation. To understand crime, therefore, we must understand why that person sees that situation as an occasion for crime. However, in saying that criminals see things differently than noncriminals, Sutherland does not mean that there is anything abnormal about them. Their thought processes have evolved in the same way as anyone else's. In other words, Sutherland, too, refuses to assume that the causes of crime must be evil or abnormal. Instead, crime, like any other form of behavior, is learned, and criminals are socialized into criminal life just as noncriminals are socialized into conventional ways of life.

This may seem rather obvious, but it goes against the idea, prominent since Lombroso, that criminals are essentially different from noncriminals. In fact, as late as the 1950s, a well-known criminologist, Sheldon Glueck, criticized Sutherland on just these grounds. According to Glueck, since criminal behavior was "antisocial," those who committed it had not been "socialized" to *any* culture. Consider Glueck's picture of the young criminal: "Unsocialized, untamed, and uninstructed, the child resorts to lying ... hatred, theft, aggression, attack ... in its early attempts of self-expression and ego formation."[12]

Sutherland took a sharply different view. He continued to reject the idea that criminals were somehow abnormal or deficient. Crime, according to Sutherland, is not some nearly instinctive, unsocialized act. It is learned behavior. Law-abiding behavior, street crime, white-collar crime—they are all learned. (Sutherland, incidentally, coined the phrase, "white-collar crime" and was one of the first sociologists to study the topic.) It is here that Sutherland begins the nine-point statement of his theory.

1. Criminal behavior is learned. Crime and deviance are learned in the same way as conventional behavior.

2. Criminal behavior is learned in interaction with other persons in a process of communication.

3. The principal part of the learning of criminal behavior occurs within intimate personal groups. Sutherland emphasized the primary group as the chief source of social learning. Impersonal agencies of communication (e.g., films, newspapers, and other media) play a relatively unimportant part in the specific process of deviant learning.

4. When criminal behavior is learned, the learning includes techniques of committing the crime (which are sometimes very complicated and sometimes very simple) and the specific direction of motives, drives, rationalizations, and attitudes. Deviant attitudes and motives prepare the way for the movement into a deviant career.

5. The specific direction of motives and drives is learned from definitions of legal codes as favorable and unfavorable. Values in modern society may be contradictory, conflicting, or ambiguous. Legal codes reflect value splits, and, for some groups, encourage positive attitudes toward breaking the law.

6. A person becomes deviant because of an excess of definitions favorable to violation of law over definitions unfavorable to violation of law. This

is the principle of *differential association*. It refers to the "counteracting forces" between criminal and anticriminal association. Sutherland believed that the crucial conditions for entrance into deviance were contact with criminal persons and codes, and exclusion from conventional patterns.

7. Differential associations may vary in frequency, duration, priority, and intensity.

8. The process of learning criminal behavior by association with criminal and anticriminal patterns involves all of the mechanisms that are involved in other learning.

9. Although criminal behavior is an expression of general needs and values, it is not explained by those general needs and values, since noncriminal behavior is an expression of the same needs and values. This position runs counter to the poverty-causes-crime notion, which views criminality as an expression of economic want.[13]

LEARNING AND MEANING   By saying that behavior, even criminal behavior, is learned, Sutherland is saying quite a lot. From the sociological point of view, behavior is like language. It is not just an action; it also has a meaning. When we learn a word, we learn not only how to make the sound but also what the sound means. Similarly, when we learn some behavior, we learn more than just how to do it. We learn what that behavior means; that is, we learn the ideas that people in our society have about it, including why it is done. When we learn the behavior, we also learn a set of ideas, attitudes, and even feelings that allow us to repeat the act. Other people play an important part in this process, even if they are not consciously teaching. They explain, make suggestions, help us conquer doubts, and give encouragement. This function applies to both conventional and law-breaking behavior. Why, for example, do you go to school now that it is no longer compulsory? As a child, you may even have complained about having to go; perhaps later in your career as a student you wondered why you were staying in school. At these times, the culture—in the form of parents, friends, and teachers—explains the motives and attitudes that justify going to school. You have probably learned these ideas so well that if somebody were to ask you now why you are in school, you probably could give a convincing, and predictable, answer about the value of education.

In a similar way, people who commit crimes learn the "motives, drives, rationalizations, and attitudes" (Sutherland's fourth point) that allow them to perform that behavior. Many studies of criminals—muggers, drug users and drug dealers, armed robbers, and professional murderers—find that during their first crimes the perpetrators felt afraid. However, they overcame their reluctance in the same way that students overcame their doubts about school. The crime and the decision to commit it usually occur in a group, with the more experienced members showing the novices how things are done and helping them over rough spots. Even so, the novices may still feel uneasy after the crime, and it takes the reassurances of others (and the absence of negative consequences) to convince them that the behavior was worthwhile. It is only after several crimes that they begin to become "hardened criminals," who have put aside conventional ideas about crime.[14]

This is not to suggest that school and crime are morally equivalent; only that the same normal social process—the same evolution of ideas, attitudes, and feelings—occurs in each. Of course, crime, by definition, is against the law; schooling is required by law. Perhaps a better example would be the custom of going on dates since no written law requires it. In fact, children of 8 or 9 may make fun of the child who shows an attraction to the opposite sex. A few years later, however, they must learn to reverse this attitude, and this learning resembles the way young criminals overcome their initial reluctance about crime. Social pressures cause people to do something (mugging or dating) that left alone they might prefer not to do. You may already be familiar with how it works. First dates (and first muggings) are frequently group events so that the others can keep the novice from making too many mistakes. Afterward, others may discuss the date with the novice, trying to convince him or her that what felt like a frightening and unnerving experience was really a lot of fun, or at least that it will be fun "once you get the hang of it."

In other words, people come to have different views of the same situation. One person may see it as a source of discomfort and even humiliation; another may see it as an opportunity for social and perhaps physical enjoyment. But in either case, they have *learned* their view with the help of others. This learning of different definitions of a situation is the key to Sutherland's theory of crime. Suppose you are in a store, waiting to buy something, but the clerk is out of sight in the back of the store. Although you realize that it might now be possible to shoplift an item or two, your principal reaction would probably be to define this situation as an inconvenience—having to wait to pay. But some people might define it primarily as a chance to steal. This is what Sutherland means in point 6 by "an excess of definitions favorable to violation of law over definitions unfavorable to violation of law."

EVALUATING DIFFERENTIAL ASSOCIATION THEORY   Over the years, differential association theory has come in for its share of criticism. One obvious point is that by placing so much emphasis on the social environment, this theory has trouble explaining differences between individuals. This shortcoming would not matter so much to a purely sociological theory, like Merton's, which sought only to explain different *rates* of crime. But differential association theory is basically a social-psychological theory; that is, while the causes it emphasizes are social or environmental, the behavior it seeks to explain is individual. Suppose that two brothers grow up in the same environment—same parents, same friends, and so on—but one becomes a criminal and the other does not. How can the theory of differential association explain these different outcomes?

One way of resolving the problem is to refer to the statement in point 7 that associations may vary in frequency, duration, priority, and intensity. We might then say that the criminal associations of one brother had a greater priority and intensity. If we probe into the criminal's past, we might find that he did feel more strongly tied to his criminal friends than did his brother. Their associations merely looked the same to an outsider; internally, one brother was giving his criminal associations much more intensity. One criminologist has developed this idea into a theory of **differential identification**; that is, who you *associate* with is not as important as who you *identify* yourself with.

A boy growing up in a largely law-abiding area may still identify himself with John Gotti.[15] If we look closely enough, say these theorists, we can find the pattern of associations that led to crime.

Putting the matter in these terms—that associations or reinforcements or identifications lead to crime—makes these ideas sound like theories of cause. Sutherland explicitly phrases it that way: "A person becomes delinquent *because....*" Yet speculation about the intensity of association or identification or the balance of definitions is frequently an after-the-fact explanation masquerading as a prediction. In fact, points 6 and 7 provide an escape clause, a heads-I-win-tails-you-lose gimmick that allows the theory to "predict" or at least to explain any outcome. If someone commits a crime, we can always say that he had an excess of criminal definitions; if he does not commit the crime, we can say that he had an excess of noncriminal definitions. Then we can search the person's history for the associations or reinforcements that led to those definitions—and of course, we will be able to find them.

In this way, the theory can explain any outcome. But far from being a strength, this flexibility points to the central weakness of the theory. It is not "falsifiable," that is, there is no way to prove it wrong. In principle, a theory should be testable. A theory says, given these conditions, I predict this specific outcome. If the outcome is as I predicted, the test supports the theory. If my prediction is wrong, the test serves to falsify the theory. But if a theory can—after the fact—"predict" *any* outcome, it can never be disproved.

A real test of Sutherland's theory would have to have a way of measuring beforehand the quantity of criminal and noncriminal definitions each person had and then seeing whether people with more criminal definitions committed more crimes. As yet, nobody has come up with any such measurement.[16]

SOCIAL LEARNING THEORY

Of the various theories derived from Sutherland's basic approach, the one most currently of interest today is **social learning theory**. It starts from Sutherland's first point—that criminal behavior is learned. But in addition to Sutherland's concepts of associations and definitions, social learning theory uses well-established psychological principles of conditioning to explain how the learning occurs. According to this approach, people learn criminal behaviors and ideas through the same mechanisms by which laboratory animals learn to press a bar or turn right in a maze—through reinforcement. At first, people may imitate the criminal behavior of some model. Then, if that criminal behavior meets with the approval, affection, or respect of other people, these social rewards will reinforce the behavior.[17] Like Sutherland, the current proponents of social learning theory reject the idea that criminals are essentially different from noncriminals. Instead, what distinguishes lawbreakers is the amount of time they spend with other criminals (known in much of the research as *deviant peers* or, since so much of the research focuses on juveniles, as *the delinquent peer group*). Ronald Akers, the primary exponent of social learning theory today, summarizes this research:

Other than one's own prior deviant behavior, the best single predictor of the onset, continuance, or desistance of crime and delinquency is differential association with conforming or law-violating peers.... More frequent, longer-term, and closer association with peers who do not support deviant behavior is strongly correlated with conformity, while greater association with peers who commit and approve of delinquency is predictive of one's own delinquent behavior.[18]

Of course, most people might wonder what all the fuss is about since it is common sense that if you hang around with a bad crowd, you're going to be more likely to get in trouble. But Akers, like Sutherland fifty years earlier, is arguing against the idea that the youths who commit crimes do so because they are inherently bad. The similarity between a kid and his peer group may arise because the bad kid will choose to hang around with other bad kids; it is similar for good kids. As the commonsense cliché puts it, birds of a feather flock together. But Akers, reviewing the research on delinquency and peer groups, maintains that the association with delinquent peers comes first and that these peers provide the newcomer with both models and reinforcement for delinquency.[19]

The ideas of differential association and social learning theory also underlie some of the most popular programs for reforming individual delinquents, criminals, and other deviants. Some of these programs have been derived specifically from criminological theory—gang intervention, peer counseling, group counseling, and so on. Other programs—like Alcoholics Anonymous and the many twelve-step programs modeled on it—have arisen from completely noncriminological, nontheoretical origins, yet they employ the basic concepts of differential association and social learning theories. What all these programs do is offer the individual new ways of thinking about his or her behavior (in Sutherland's terms, new "definitions") and support ("reinforcement") for these new ideas and new behavior. However, these programs are not overwhelmingly successful. Generally, as long as people remain in the program, they stay closer to their goal; they drink less, cut down on drug use, commit less crime, or whatever. However, long-term success is more rare. Of course, a supporter of differential association could well take these results as support for the theory: When people go back to their old associations, they also go back to their old definitions and behaviors. This line of argument may save the theory, but it does little to turn the theory into an effective policy.

Even if learning theories have not led to any sure-fire method of rehabilitation or crime prevention, and even if they add little to our ability to predict trends in crime rates, Sutherland nevertheless laid the groundwork for *understanding* crime and criminals. His theory urges researchers to understand the world in the way the criminal sees it. Following Sutherland, researchers have gotten inside the world of a wide variety of criminals and have come to see them not as the inert objects of abstract social forces, nor as monsters gratifying their animal impulses, but as people who act on the basis of a certain world view. It may be true that this kind of understanding has not added much to our power to predict or change criminal behavior, but supporters of Sutherland would argue that crime policies that are not based on such understanding are doomed to failure.

To sum up: In the 1930s sociological thinking about crime had moved far away from the social pathology outlook of earlier decades. By looking at rates of crime rather than at individual criminals, sociologists had been able to apply ideas about social structure, social change, social organization, norms, and values to the study of crime. In addition, empirical evidence was confirming the notion that crime was more prevalent in the lower social classes. By the 1940s, two lines of thinking had developed to explain the class-crime link. Structural or strain theories (e.g., Merton's) emphasized the conflict between culturally prescribed goals and socially distributed means. Cultural theories focused on the ways in which people learn ideas that lead them to commit crimes. In the next decade, sociological thinkers tried to combine the insights of these two points of view.

CLASS AND CULTURE

Although Sutherland and Merton had major differences in their approach to crime, they both wrote mainly about rational, economic crime. Merton's emphasis on means and ends is best suited to economically motivated crimes, and Sutherland's criminals—whether thieves or executives—usually have economic gain as their principal motive. "Senseless" crime does not figure heavily in either theory, perhaps because when these theories appeared (the late 1930s and 1940s), violent crime and crime in general were at a relatively low ebb in America.

The next major contribution to criminological theory—at least in America—came in the mid- to late 1950s and had a slightly different focus. First, these theories stressed juvenile crime; second, they gave the idea of culture a central place in their explanations.

Historical changes may have influenced this shift in emphasis. The 1950s brought a rise in public concern with juvenile gangs. American cities have always had gangs—young men who hang out together and sometimes break the law. But during the 1940s, World War II took many of these young men off the streets, and the trend away from gangs continued even in the immediate postwar years. During the 1950s, however, juvenile delinquency once again began to attract public attention. There was nothing basically new about this concern. Parents in America have, since colonial days, felt threatened by their children's independence and seeming rejection of parental ways. But the 1950s may have exaggerated the usual anxieties, if only because of the sheer numbers of children. Even in the early 1950s, when the children at the leading edge of the baby boom were barely counting their ages in two digits, they nevertheless were making an impact on society. Products aimed at them began to occupy more of the culture; there was a lot of money to be made selling Davy Crockett hats and hula hoops. Before long, things took a more ominous tone. Movies like *Rebel Without a Cause* or *The Wild One* drew large audiences by depicting rebellious, destructive, sullen young men. The news media gave more attention to juvenile delinquency, and one of the most popular Broadway shows of the decade—*West Side Story*—was set in the context of juvenile gang warfare.

ALBERT K. COHEN AND THE DELINQUENT SUBCULTURE

Sociologists were not deaf to these cultural messages and responded with their analyses of this "new" old problem. In 1955, Albert K. Cohen published a book called *Delinquent Boys*. As the title implies, Cohen was looking not at career criminals or white-collar criminals or people who stole to get much-needed money but at "boys" whose crimes consisted chiefly of vandalism, fighting, or other low-profit activities. "Nonutilitarian, malicious, and negativistic" are the adjectives Cohen used to describe this behavior. Such seemingly senseless crime seriously challenges Merton's theory. Bashing storefronts, school windows, or other boys hardly fits with any of Merton's adaptations: These crimes are not a means toward some conventional goal like money (innovation), and although the boys are not following accepted norms, their behavior does not look like retreatism or rebellion as Merton describes them.

More to the point are the ideas of differential association and cultural transmission introduced by Chicago sociologists like Sutherland. In fact, Cohen offers his theory as a fuller version of a well-known, everyday explanation for juvenile delinquency: "My Johnny is really a good boy but got to running around with the wrong bunch." The idea of a "wrong bunch" is at the heart of Cohen's theory. It is part of a more general phenomenon Cohen calls the **delinquent subculture**.

A subculture is a group of people within a society who share a set of ideas and ways of doing things that differ from those of the dominant society. A subculture provides its members not just with a sense of belonging but also with solutions to certain problems. The delinquent subculture, as Cohen describes it, differs in at least two crucial ways from nondelinquent ways of life. For one thing, it is "negativistic." Delinquents enjoy activities that break rules or inconvenience other people. "There is an element of active spite and malice, contempt and ridicule, challenge and defiance." In addition, the subculture is based on "short-run hedonism" (i.e., pleasure seeking). "There is little interest in long-run goals" or anything that requires consistent practice or study.[20]

How can a subculture based on nonutilitarian, malicious crime solve the problems of life? To answer this, Cohen reminds us of two facts in addition to the low-profit, negativistic quality of much juvenile crime. First, juveniles usually commit their crimes in groups, rather than alone. That is, delinquency is not merely a matter of individual maladjustment or psychological problems. Second, juvenile crime and the delinquent subculture are found primarily in "the lower socioeconomic strata of our society." But although he recognizes that social class is obviously a factor in delinquency, the lack of money, in Cohen's view, is not the basic problem. If it were, lower-class boys would commit crimes that were more profitable. Instead, the delinquent subculture forms to provide a solution to the problems of *status*— "respect in the eyes of one's fellows."

Schools function as peer pressure cookers. Not all teenagers can find success in conventional areas—academics, sports, looks, or personality. The delinquent subculture can provide an alternate set of definitions of success and alternate routes to an enhanced self-concept.

MIDDLE-CLASS AND LOWER-CLASS CULTURE　People gain the respect and recognition of others by living up to some set of standards. In America, the dominant standards of the society are middle-class values and norms. As these norms apply to teenagers, they emphasize ambition and success, academic achievement, responsibility for oneself, delay of gratification, control of physical aggression, and respect for property. Although people at all levels of society feel these norms to some extent, the realities of life for those in the lower class often require them to live by a different set of norms. Ambition and planning must give way to the pressing needs of the moment. People must depend more on others. They will be less eager to leave the group to go off on their own, even if such a move might mean a step up the socioeconomic ladder. This group orientation also means that the middle-class ethic of responsibility gives way to an ethic of reciprocity, or sharing. These cultural differences pervade social life, and school is no exception. School, regardless of the social class of its students, is a thoroughly middle-class institution, and the message it sends (intentionally or not) to the working-class or lower-class boy is that he is inferior. It is a message he cannot ignore.

ADAPTATIONS　Faced with the daily problem of confronting an institution that defines him as inferior, the working-class boy can adapt in one of three ways. He can strive for middle-class goals (like college); or he can accept his lower status but not commit crimes, hanging out with his friends and

TABLE 11-3 •

COHEN'S THEORY OF THE DELINQUENT SUBCULTURE

SHARED GOAL (ECONOMIC SUCCESS)	+	UNEQUAL OPPORTUNITY	→	SUBCULTURE BASED ON REJECTION OF MIDDLE-CLASS NORMS	→	NEGATIVISTIC CRIME

eventually taking whatever kind of job comes along. Both of these solutions accept the superiority of middle-class norms. The delinquent solution, however, challenges the assumption that middle-class ways are better. By the negativism of their delinquency, these boys are saying that it is the middle-class norms and institutions that are inferior (see Table 11–3). "The delinquent subculture takes its norms from the larger (middle-class) culture, but it turns them upside down." If middle-class norms define something as good, the delinquent subculture defines it as bad, and the subculture reinforces the idea through words and actions. Since it is middle-class values that threaten their self-esteem, these delinquents reward and esteem each other for behavior that attacks the symbols of the middle class: vandalism (schools are a favorite target); terrorizing "good" kids; stealing things not for their value but "for the hell of it," because it is "wrong."

WALTER MILLER AND LOWER-CLASS CULTURE

Cohen's theory was only one of several influential theories that used the notion of subculture. However, not everyone agreed that the delinquent subculture was a reaction against middle-class standards or an inversion of them. In an article published in 1958—three years after Cohen's *Delinquent Boys*—Walter Miller challenged Cohen's idea that lower-class delinquents cared deeply about middle-class values and therefore had to act out their frustrations in negativistic crime. Yes, there was a delinquent subculture, Miller said, but it stood independent of middle-class culture. Instead, it drew its ideas and institutions from lower-class ways of life.

The title of Miller's essay, "Lower-class Culture as a Generating Milieu of Gang Delinquency," sounds a bit awkward, but it concisely sums up his argument: first, that there is a distinct lower-class culture in America; second, that this culture is an environment (milieu) that causes gang delinquency to flourish.

FOCAL CONCERNS   Over the course of years of research, Miller and his coworkers spent many hours hanging around juvenile gangs in poor areas of cities, listening, observing, and talking with them. From this research, Miller concludes that poor people do not think about the world in the same way that middle-class people do. It is not a question of different values, certainly not in the way that Cohen saw delinquents as reversing middle-class values, nor even

ABOUT CRIME & CRIMINOLOGY

STREET CULTURE AND DECENT KIDS

According to anthropologist Elijah Anderson, black inner-city neighborhoods contain two competing cultures. One culture is based on "a strong, loving 'decent' (as inner-city residents put it) family committed to middle-class values." The other culture, echoing Albert Cohen's idea of a negativistic delinquent subculture, is "an oppositional culture, that of 'the streets,' whose norms are often consciously opposed to those of mainstream society." Even consumer objects like clothing and jewelry take on a special meaning that is different from the meaning assigned to them in mainstream culture.

These two orientations—decent and street—socially organize the community.... Even youngsters whose home lives reflect mainstream values—and the majority of homes in the community do—must be able to handle themselves in a street-oriented environment.

At the heart of the code is the issue of respect—loosely defined as being treated "right," or granted the deference one deserves.

By the time they are teenagers, most youths have either internalized the code of the streets or at least learned the need to comport themselves in accordance with its rules.... Its basic requirement is the display of a certain predisposition to violence.... To maintain his honor [a person] must show he is not someone to be "messed with" or "dissed."

Objects play an important and complicated role in establishing self-image. Jackets, sneakers, gold jewelry, reflect not just a person's taste ... but also a willingness to posses things that may require defending. A boy wearing a

in the sense of not valuing things like money or education or happiness. The differences lie not so much in what people think is good but in what people think *about*—the mental categories people used to perceive their world and themselves. To these categories Miller gives the name **focal concerns**.[21]

For example, one focal concern of middle-class Americans is success or achievement. Some middle-class people seem almost to worship the idea of success. But Miller's point is not that success or achievement is a value. Rather, it is a focal concern. It dominates middle-class thinking. Middle-class people tend to see other people and situations in terms of their potential for achievement. They use this framework for judging not just their careers but even their personal lives. They talk about "working" on a marriage that is "going nowhere" in order to have a "successful" relationship. Lists of best-selling books always have a few titles on self-improvement and career advancement. Parents worry about their children's performance in similar terms: Is the child keeping up? Is the child behind or ahead?

For lower-class Americans, according to Miller, achievement is not such a focal concern. Lower-class people might *value* success; they would certainly agree that it is better than failure, but it is not an idea that commands as much of their attention. "Trouble," however, is. "'Getting into trouble' and 'staying out of trouble' represent major issues for male and female, adults and children." Trouble, for fashionable, expensive jacket, for example, is vulnerable to attack by another who covets the jacket.... However, if the boy forgoes the desirable jacket and wears one that isn't "hip," he runs the risk of being teased and possibly even assaulted as an unworthy person. To be allowed to hang with certain prestigious crowds a boy must wear a different set of expensive clothes—sneakers and athletic suit—every day.

In this context, seemingly ordinary objects can become trophies imbued with symbolic value that far exceed their monetary worth. Possession of the trophy can symbolize the ability to violate somebody—to "get in his face," to take something of value from him, to "dis" him, and thus to enhance one's own worth by stealing someone else's.

So when a person ventures outside, he must adopt the code—a kind of shield, really—to prevent others from "messing with" him.... It is sensed that something extremely valuable is at stake in every interaction.... For people who are unfamiliar with the code, the concern with respect in the most ordinary interactions can be frightening and incomprehensible. But for those who are invested in the code, the clear object of their demeanor is to discourage strangers from even thinking about testing their manhood. And the sense of power that attends the ability to deter others can be alluring even to those who know the code without being heavily invested in it—the decent inner-city youths. Thus a boy who has been leading a basically decent life can in trying circumstances, suddenly resort to deadly force.

Source: Elijah Anderson, "The Code of the Streets," *Atlantic Monthly*, vol. 273, no. 5 (May 1994), 81–94.

women, means "sexual involvement with disadvantageous consequences"; for men it often means fighting or criminal behavior. A mother, for instance, might want to know of her daughter's fiancé, not how successful his career will be, but how much "trouble" he's likely to bring. Parents will ask of their schoolchildren not "Are you getting good grades?" but "Are you staying out of trouble?"

The other focal concerns of the lower class, as Miller outlines them, are the following:

- Toughness: "The almost obsessive lower-class concern with 'masculinity.'"

- Smartness: Not scholarly achievement or knowledge but rather "street smarts," the ability to outfox, outwit, or "con" others.

- Excitement: Lower-class culture has its own rhythm of life. Middle-class life runs on a regular rhythm, work alternating with home life or relaxation in a fairly even way. By contrast, the rhythm of lower-class life consists of long periods of boredom punctuated by brief periods of excitement. Lower-class people, especially males, spend a lot of time just "hanging out," waiting for the opportunity for some more risky adventure.

■ Fate: Lower-class people have much less of the sense that they are ultimately in control of their lives. Middle-class people tend to believe that what happens to people in life depends on their own abilities and efforts. Lower-class people see life more in terms of fate—either you're lucky or you're not.

■ Autonomy: In lower-class life, there is a strong resentment of external controls ("No one's gonna push me around"). Autonomy also involves independence or a denial of dependence ("I can take care of myself").

COVERT COMMITMENT   Even if we accept this picture of lower-class culture, we must still ask how it promotes delinquency. Trouble may be a concern, but why should it lead to crime? Why not just stay out of trouble? As for gang delinquency, why not just demonstrate autonomy by staying out of gangs?

In response, Miller says that it is precisely to avoid this theoretical problem that he uses the idea of focal concern rather than the usual sociological concept of value. A value can have only one positive side. To talk of focal concerns, however, allows us to see the more complex reality: Either side of each dimension can be positive, depending on circumstances. Most of the time, it is rather obvious which side is positive. On the trouble dimension, getting into trouble is bad, staying out of trouble is good. Therefore, people usually maintain an "overt" (or open) commitment to law-abiding behavior. They say that they want to stay out of trouble. But, says Miller, they may also share a "covert commitment" to the other end of the dimension, that is, a hidden or even unconscious attraction to the negative side (law-breaking behavior).

The dimension of autonomy provides a good example. Lower-class males will voice strong commitment to independence and freedom from constraint. But what are we to make of the delinquent in reform school who, with only a week left to his sentence, tries to escape? He gets caught, of course, and receives an additional sentence of several months. In Miller's view, he is expressing an *overt* commitment to autonomy ("They can't keep me locked up here") but a *covert* commitment to dependence since his behavior has the predictable effect of keeping him even longer in a state of confinement and dependence.

The same is true of trouble. "'Getting into trouble,'" says Miller, "achieves several sets of valued ends."[22] It demonstrates a boy's toughness, smartness, and autonomy, as well as his capacity for excitement. And getting caught need not be evidence of his lack of these qualities since it was just "bad luck" (fate).

LOWER-CLASS INSTITUTIONS   A culture is more than just a set of ideas or ways of looking at the world. It also consists of institutions that organize people's behavior. Institutions differ from one society to another. For example, all societies must educate their youths, but the institutions for education vary widely from one time and place to another. Had you lived in America two centuries ago, you would probably have been apprenticed at an early age to some trade rather than going to school for a minimum of ten or twelve years as you do today. Even in our own day, different countries vary in the way they organize such institutions as education, religion, health care, and family.

Within American society as well, the constellation of institutions can differ from one social class to another. For the middle class, the most important institutions are family, work, and—for the child—school. In the lower class, there is another institution that plays a crucial part in people's lives: the one-sex peer group. In Miller's view, it is the principal institution of lower-class life. "Lower-class society may be pictured as comprising a set of age-graded one-sex peer groups which constitute the major psychic focus and reference group for those over 12 or 13." Lower-class people usually spend their free time (and often their work time) with groups of the same sex. For women and girls, this means female friends or relatives; for men, it means "hanging out with the guys"; for boys, it is the juvenile gang.

These groups are the heart of lower-class social life, more so than work or school or even family. Young men and women may get married (or as Miller puts it, "form temporary marital alliances"), but after trying out the more middle-class two-sex family arrangement, they "gravitate back to the more 'comfortable' one-sex grouping."

The gang has two important functions. First, it gives a sense of belonging; second, it awards status. For both of these, the boy must show that he possesses those qualities that are valued within his culture. The more a boy can show that he has the right stuff, the higher his status in the group. For the lower-class male, the right stuff consists of toughness, smartness, capacity for excitement and trouble, and so on. Younger males—teenagers—share the additional concern of "adultness." For these boys, drinking, sex, driving, and ready cash take on a special importance, not just because they are pleasurable in themselves, but also because they are the symbols of adult status (see Table 11–4).

It is easy to see how the focal concerns and the institutions of lower-class life foster delinquency. The crimes that gang members commit (gang fights, mugging, purse snatching, shoplifting, and auto theft) are ways of achieving status by living up to the standards of the peer group. And both this peer group and its standards are versions of institutions and focal concerns that exist throughout lower-class culture.

In understanding juvenile crime in this way, Miller is also arguing against two other views of delinquency. First, he is saying that delinquency is not a reaction against middle-class culture. Lower-class youths do not violate the law for the sake of being bad. Rather, some of the things that they must do in following their own culture just happen to be illegal. As Miller puts it,

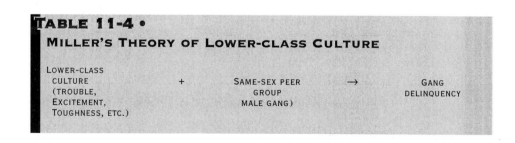

TABLE 11-4 •
MILLER'S THEORY OF LOWER-CLASS CULTURE

LOWER-CLASS CULTURE (TROUBLE, EXCITEMENT, TOUGHNESS, ETC.)	+	SAME-SEX PEER GROUP MALE GANG)	→	GANG DELINQUENCY

"The 'demanded' response to certain situations recurrently engendered within lower-class culture involves the commission of illegal acts." Second, delinquency is not the product of some kind of individual deficiency. These delinquents "are not psychopaths, nor physically or mentally 'defective'; in fact, since the corner group supports and enforces a rigorous set of standards which demand a high degree of fitness and personal competence, it tends to recruit from the most 'able' members of the community."

SUBCULTURES AND OPPORTUNITIES

Amid all this emphasis on culture or subculture, the issue of opportunity seemed to have disappeared. In 1960, however, two years after Miller's essay, Richard Cloward and Lloyd Ohlin published a book, *Delinquency and Opportunity*, that helped bridge the gap between opportunity theories and cultural theories.

Cloward and Ohlin also start from the assumption that delinquency is primarily a lower-class phenomenon. Not only is delinquency more serious in the lower class but also it receives "support and approval" from various groups there. Since a subculture is a group that values (supports and approves of) particular forms of behavior, and since these groups (such as gangs) support and approve of delinquency, we can talk about a delinquent subculture. Most delinquency, of course, takes place outside of delinquent subcultures. Most youths who break the law nevertheless believe that crime is wrong (just as most students who glance at someone else's paper during an exam probably think that cheating is wrong). They have not substituted a set of criminal norms and values for the conventional ones. The delinquent subculture, in contrast, is based on just such a rejection of conventional norms. Even though it includes only a small proportion of juveniles, it is important to understand the delinquent subculture because these youths account for a disproportionate share of the most serious crime.

Cloward and Ohlin reject Miller's notion that the delinquent subculture is just one more version of lower-class culture. They argue that no large part of American society, not even the lower class, has a set of values that supports or approves of crimes like burglary, robbery, murder, and drug addiction. Cloward and Ohlin also reject the idea that members of delinquent subcultures are psychopathic or in any other way deficient or unable to meet middle-class standards. "The available data support the contention that the basic endowments of delinquents, such as intelligence, physical strength, and agility, are the equal of or greater than those of their nondelinquent peers."[23]

Cloward and Ohlin instead start with the same ideas Merton proposed: first, that modern, industrial society—especially that of the United States—"emphasizes common or universal success goals"; second, that "structural barriers" come between lower-class youths and the pursuit of these goals. The most important means to success is education, but economic pressures force lower-class youths out of the educational system. They drop out not because they are less intelligent but because they are poorer. "In a family that can scarcely afford food, shelter, and clothing, pressure is exerted on the young to leave school early in order to secure employment and thereby help the family." The result of this clash between goals and means is "intense frustration," which can lead to crime.

OPPORTUNITY—LEGITIMATE AND ILLEGITIMATE

So far, this analysis echoes Merton's. But while Merton gives the impression that the lower-class person *individually* chooses innovation or retreatism, Cloward and Ohlin recognize that deviant behavior, too, has its own social organization. That is, not only are there structures of legitimate opportunity (schools, colleges, and jobs), but there are also structures for *illegitimate* opportunity. And not all lower-class people will have the same access to those illegitimate opportunities.

Cloward and Ohlin identify three distinct types of delinquent subcultures that evolve as adaptations to the lack of legitimate opportunity:

- The criminal subculture, based on economic crime as a source of income

- The conflict subculture, based on fighting as a way of gaining status

- The retreatist subculture, based on drugs as a means of detachment from conventional society.

The fate of a lower-class boy with few chances for legitimate success will depend on the kind of subculture available in his neighborhood (see Table 11–4).

THE CRIMINAL SUBCULTURE   In some lower-class neighborhoods, there is a flourishing criminal subculture. Crime here is *organized* as a way of making money. Some forms of crime (e.g., gambling) are run almost like businesses. Even predatory crimes like burglary have an organization that coordinates different roles. A burglar who works alone, outside of a criminal subculture, runs great risks and is not always sure of a large haul. Much safer and more profitable is a system in which there are fingermen, who tip off the thief to big scores; fences, who provide a safe place to convert stolen goods to cash; and should anything unfortunate occur, bail bondsmen, lawyers, and perhaps corruptible police officers, district attorneys, or judges.

In a neighborhood with a well-developed criminal subculture, boys may see crime as a means to financial success, and they may look up to successful criminals as role models. Boys may even serve the equivalent of an apprenticeship, with older criminals teaching them about the world of crime. In such an environment, say Cloward and Ohlin, even what looks like "malicious, negativistic, nonutilitarian" behavior may really be an attempt to catch the eye of adults in the criminal subculture.

THE CONFLICT SUBCULTURE   The criminal subculture thrives mostly in neighborhoods that, although poor, have a certain amount of stability. In less stable neighborhoods, crime, like the rest of life, tends to be less organized. The population is more transient, and people have fewer ties to one another or to the community as a whole. A person may turn to crime, but the kind of unorganized economic crime that he can commit will be less profitable and less protected. He will make less money, and he will spend more time in prison. In such neighborhoods, the young, according to Cloward, "are deprived of *both* conventional and criminal opportunity."

Cut off from both legitimate and illegitimate resources for economic gain, young men must fall back on the resources they do have—resources that are not part of any organization. They can win status primarily on the basis of personal qualities. Thus, interpersonal contests—from basketball to the dozens (a rapping game involving verbal ability, quick wit, and a repertoire of clever insults)—make up an important part of life in these groups. In interactions like these, income and connections count for nothing.

Obviously, there is another type of contest in which a youth can show his character and thereby gain status: fighting. Through violence, young men can demonstrate not just physical skill but also courage or "heart"—a "willingness to risk injury or death in the search for 'rep.'" In some neighborhoods, violence becomes the primary basis of the status system for young men. This is what Cloward and Ohlin call the "conflict subculture."

THE RETREATIST SUBCULTURE   In both of these delinquent subcultures (criminal and conflict), late adolescence is a crucial period. The criminal subculture does not have room for every boy who wants to join. Those who lack the necessary skills, character, or connections will find themselves excluded. In the conflict subculture also, some boys may not have what it takes, or they may not like fighting and its sometimes unpleasant consequences. Older boys—even those who excel at fighting—face an additional problem: Violence may bring status among 15-year-olds, who think that they can prove their manhood in one-on-one or gang fights, but this attitude and behavior will be inappropriate for the older youth. After all, by virtue of being 18 or 19, he *is* a man; he should not need to resort to "kid stuff" like fighting in order to prove it.

What can become of the older teenagers who are rejected by the criminal world? Or those who have outgrown gang fighting? These young men have reached the point where they are "double failures," unable to find success in either the legitimate or the illegitimate world. Something has to change (see Table 11–5).

Many youths as they approach their 20s replace "youthful preoccupations" with "more individual concerns about work, future, a 'steady' girl, and the like." (Given their chances for success, we might classify them as ritualists, though Cloward and Ohlin do not mention this.) But some of these young men will join the retreatist subculture, a culture based on the use of drugs and on being "cool." Cloward and Ohlin, writing in 1960, identified addictive drugs as only one of the many sources of "kicks" (i.e., "ecstatic experiences") sought by retreatists. Other kicks included marijuana and alcohol, but also jazz music and "unusual sexual experiences" (Cloward and Ohlin do not go into detail). As for money, retreatists ("cats" as Cloward and Ohlin call them, using the lingo of that era) will do anything that does not resemble work. They hustle; they beg, borrow, steal, pimp, deal drugs, and

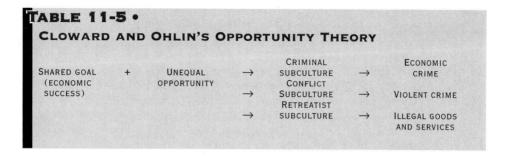

TABLE 11-5 •

CLOWARD AND OHLIN'S OPPORTUNITY THEORY

SHARED GOAL (ECONOMIC SUCCESS)	+	UNEQUAL OPPORTUNITY	→	CRIMINAL SUBCULTURE	→	ECONOMIC CRIME
			→	CONFLICT SUBCULTURE	→	VIOLENT CRIME
			→	RETREATIST SUBCULTURE	→	ILLEGAL GOODS AND SERVICES

run petty con games. It's a way to get by, and it's a way to gain status. In the world of the retreatist subculture, kicks and hustling provide the bases for winning the admiration of others.

OPPORTUNITY AND POLICY

Although Cloward and Ohlin's theory sounds plausible, empirical evidence was not overwhelming. Nevertheless, *Delinquency and Opportunity* did have the advantage of offering recommendations for policy. The message was clear just from the book's title. If boys move into delinquent subcultures because of barriers to legitimate opportunity, we should remove these barriers and provide that opportunity. If violent gangs arise because neighborhoods are disorganized, we must organize these lower-class communities.

In fact, Cloward and Ohlin had designed a program, based on their ideas, for New York's Lower East Side. Named Mobilization for Youth (MFY), it called for improved education, expanded job opportunities, community organization, and special social work services for adolescents as well as for other individuals and families. Their proposal came at the right time. The new president, John F. Kennedy, gave it his support, and eventually the federal government, New York City, and the Ford Foundation provided a three-year grant of $12.5 million (nearly $100 million in current dollars and a lot of money at the time). At the ceremony launching the program in 1962, President Kennedy sounded very much like Cloward and Ohlin when he announced that "juvenile delinquency is ... really a question of young people and their opportunity."

By the time MFY went into effect, it had become part of the nationwide War on Poverty. The most important idea in the various programs in this "war" was the Community Action Program, in which poor people themselves would help run the programs (as in the MFY plan for community organizing). Had it worked according to design, these programs would have shifted a significant amount of power from old, entrenched politicians to the poor. Of course, the politicians were not going to give away their power easily. Consequently, MFY became snarled in political battles, and eventually it "sank in a sea of conflict."[24] To accommodate the various political interests, MFY had to make several changes that took it further and further from the model designed by Cloward and Ohlin.

If MFY could not redistribute power, neither could it reduce crime; in fact. crime rates in MFY areas increased. Critics see this failure as more evidence against opportunity theory. The problem, they say, is not in opportunity structures but in the delinquents. Those who defend opportunity theory say that MFY, coming in the mid-1960s, was going against a tremendous rising tide of crime, especially juvenile crime. Given this nationwide trend, the MFY experience in New York was not so bad. In addition, because of all the changes that were forced on it, MFY in practice was never a true test of opportunity theory. It was more like a case study in urban politics. With its more radical features compromised, MFY was also an example of the failure of halfway efforts. Unless there can be real change in the structures of power and opportunity, these critics say, piecemeal reforms will do little to reduce lower-class crime.

WHERE DO WE GO FROM HERE?

The influential criminology theories of the 1950s turned from the topic of crime in general to the more specific problem of juvenile delinquency, especially lower-class delinquency. There were probably good historical reasons for this shift in attention. For one thing, crime rates, which had fallen during the 1940s, remained fairly low (by U.S. standards) for nearly two decades following World War II. In addition, the usual candidates for causes of crime seemed to be things of the past. The great waves of immigration had ended in 1925. Urbanization had slowed as the population shifted to the suburbs. The economy was thriving, and unemployment had decreased far below the prewar levels of the 1930s.

The apparent persistence of juvenile crime amid all this well-being called for an explanation. It was a sign of things still wrong in the society. For generally liberal sociologists, delinquency showed that not everybody was happy, that there was still a lower class, and that the general affluence had bypassed many people. The poor continued in a way of life that was all but hidden from public view, one that had its own problems and satisfactions, its own norms and values, and consequently its own high levels of crime and delinquency.

But theories of strain and theories of culture gradually faded into the background. Not only did they fail to provide effective programs for reducing crime and delinquency, but also new evidence was mounting to suggest that social class differences in crime were not so large. Perhaps more important, the general social and political climate of the United States was changing. The 1960s was a decade of great turmoil and conflict. People who had previously been powerless and silent—women, blacks, youths—began to challenge the accepted authorities and the accepted truths. In criminology, too, people with new viewpoints were questioning some of the certainties of sociological knowledge. Could we trust the official statistics on which theories were based? Could we even define crime, and could we study it while ignoring the officials who made and enforced the laws? Was crime really such a lower-class phenomenon as the official data claimed? Sociologists began to question basic concepts like *norm, value,* and *culture.* How did these ideas apply in real life? These questions, as we shall see in the next chapter, led to a radical critique of both society and conventional criminology. At the same time, however, a more traditional, individual-based, and even conservative criminology was also in the making.

CRITICAL THINKING QUESTIONS

1. Why is the consistency in rates of behavior so important to the sociological perspective?
2. How do everyday assumptions about the causes of evil limit the questions and ideas most people have in thinking about crime?
3. How are the individual's goals and the means to those goals socially distributed?
4. Why is it important to point out that crime is learned behavior?
5. What part does economic inequality play in cultural theories of crime?
6. What are the major differences between structural theories and cultural theories of crime?
7. Different theories of crime draw different pictures of social class in America. What are these pictures, and how are they important in the different explanations of crime?

KEY TERMS

anomie

cases

delinquent subculture

differential association

differential identification

evil-causes-evil assumption

focal concerns

norms

rates

relative deprivation

social disorganization

social ecology

social learning theory

social pathology

strain theories

CHAPTER TWELVE

SOCIOLOGICAL THEORY SINCE 1960

CONFLICT AND CONTROL

CHAPTER OUTLINE

CRIME AND CULTURE RECONSIDERED

The previous chapter presented several theories of crime based on the concept of culture. These theories might disagree on exactly how the delinquent subculture is different or why it forms or its relationship to the conventional, law-abiding culture. Nonetheless, all these cultural theories share the idea that crime arises and persists because group norms and values permit or encourage it. In other words, people who commit crimes believe in a different set of ideas, and these ideas precede and cause their criminal behavior.

The evidence for this conclusion comes mostly from participant observation research, in which a researcher hangs around high-crime areas or groups and listens for people expressing ideas that tend to justify crime. Evidence gathered in this way suffers from some major flaws. First, it depends on the perceptions of the researcher. Perhaps another observer might have heard people expressing different ideas. Second, it does not measure the two variables—culture and crime—separately. Third, even if people do voice criminal values and norms, does that necessarily mean that they have rejected conventional ideas?

More convincing research would first specify which values and norms should lead to crime; then it would discover people's values or norms; finally, it would see whether individuals, groups, or geographic areas with pro-crime ideas actually did produce more crime. Unfortunately, very few studies follow this pattern. In addition, it is difficult to measure such abstract notions as values or norms in a meaningful way. The studies that do try to measure values have gotten mixed results. They find that poor people, even gang members, share middle-class values and aspirations.

It shouldn't surprise us that the poor and criminals subscribe to conventional norms. After all, if cultural theories were absolutely accurate, that is, if a

Rather than condemning those who break social rules, labeling theory asks: How do some behaviors come to be labeled as deviant or criminal? Harmfulness is only one element. Some deviant behavior may be quite harmless, while the behavior of conventional people (ie., those involved in corporate crime) may cause far greater harm.

significant portion of the population valued crime and tried to live up to that value, there would be far more crime than actually occurs. But in fact, most people at every social level, and even most juvenile gang members, spend most of their time in nondelinquent activity.

Not only do delinquents spend much of their time well within the boundaries of the law, but in their thinking, too, they often support conventional ideas and symbols. They look up to noncriminal culture heroes—astronauts, sports heroes, and rock stars (even straight ones); they resent being called criminals; they hope for noncriminal futures; and they admire such highly conventional qualities as honesty and loyalty. Yet they can also behave and think in ways that seem to be solidly rooted in the criminal world.

DRIFT AND NEUTRALIZATIONS

It was just this kind of apparent contradiction that led sociologist David Matza to the concept of drift. Matza argues that the terms *criminal* and *conventional* or *delinquent* and *nondelinquent* can be misleading when they are applied to people. We must recognize that these terms are abstract concepts that refer to sets of norms rather than to individuals. In the real world, most delinquents live at the border of the conventional and the criminal worlds. Delinquents exist in a state of **drift**, not firmly committed to either set of norms.[1]

Since even delinquents support conventional norms, the question becomes this: How can people violate norms that they themselves believe in? Matza's answer (contained in his book and in an earlier essay written with Gresham Sykes)[2] is that delinquents use **neutralizations** that allow exceptions to the norms. For example, if you believe that cheating on exams is not such a good thing, you might justify copying someone else's paper by saying that the professor is such a creep that she deserves to be cheated on. Thus, you have "neutralized" the norm against cheating, and you now feel free to copy a few answers.

Sykes and Matza identify this neutralization as "denial of victim"—the idea that certain people or institutions (e.g., the unfair professor) do not deserve the usual protection of the norms of society. This idea neutralizes norms against theft and even violence. By denial of victim, delinquents in their own minds turn stores that supposedly charge rip-off prices into fair game for theft, turn homosexuals into targets for assault, and turn the phone company and its booths into objects of vandalism.

Sykes and Matza insist that these neutralizations are not mere rationalizations that occur after the fact. These ideas *precede* the crime and make the crime possible. By using neutralizations, the delinquent does not reject the conventional norm; he merely makes an exception in this particular case. Other neutralizations include the following:

- Denial of responsibility: "The others made me do it" or "I had to—it was self-defense."

- Denial of injury: "Nobody was hurt" or "It was a private quarrel" or "The graffiti makes the building look better" or "The store is insured."

■ Condemning the condemners: "The police are corrupt, so why shouldn't I steal, too?"

■ Appeal to higher loyalties: "I had to help my buddy in the fight."

Seeing delinquents in this way makes them seem more like you and me since we, too, neutralize norms we believe in ("The 55-mph limit on this road is a good thing, but I have a one o'clock appointment"). Even the law recognizes these exceptions. For instance, both the law and juvenile delinquents recognize the principle of self-defense as a legitimate neutralization. But the legal definition of self-defense is much narrower than the version recognized by delinquents. The boy who pleads self-defense by saying, "I had no choice: He called me a faggot so I had to beat the s—- out of him," may get nods of agreement from his peers, but he is unlikely to win his case in court.

TWO KINDS OF NORMS

People who hold conventional norms yet commit deviant acts present a paradox. The concepts of drift and neutralization are only one explanation for this contradiction. Another way of explaining it is to distinguish between kinds of norms—namely, norms of *pre*scription and norms of *pro*scription. Prescriptive norms define what a person *should* do; proscriptive norms define what a person should *not* do. Most people in this society follow the same prescriptive norms. But in the lower class, proscriptive norms are much looser, and people tolerate a wider variety of behavior.[3]

The same idea is contained in the concept of the lower-class "value stretch," a phrase coined by Hyman Rodman.[4] Rodman was writing not about crime but about other aspects of lower-class life, like work and family; nevertheless, the concept is useful. It recognizes that while values are ideals and guidelines for action (they tell you in which general direction you want to go), they are also justifications for behavior. We appeal to values to justify what we have done. Therefore, we want as little discrepancy as possible between our values and our behavior. For the poor, this means that although they hold the same values as the middle class, they must reinterpret, or "stretch," these values to fit the way they must live their lives. For example, in *Tally's Corner*, a classic study of poor, black, streetcorner men, Elliot Liebow mentions a man who at Christmastime went shoplifting for his children's presents.[5] Among middle-class parents, shoplifting would clearly have fallen outside the norms: It would have been proscribed. In the lower class, however, traditional family values were stretched to justify this obviously illegal behavior.

NORMS AND ENFORCEMENT

Just what are values and norms? How many different sets of values and norms are there in our society? How do people relate to them? These questions underlie most sociological theories about crime. Different views on norms and values are central to the debate between structural theories and cultural theories. This debate sometimes comes down to a single question: Do people who commit crimes share a different set of values and norms from the rest of society? To oversimplify, cultural theories say, "Yes, lower-class people have different values"; structural theories say, "No, we all share in a single culture, and the real problem is unequal opportunity in the social structure." Other theories try to bridge the gap by arguing, "Yes, there are different subcultures, but they have come into existence as adaptations to the inequality that is built into the social structure."

The other way of answering the question, as we have just seen, is to recognize that values (ideas about what is good) and **norms** (rules for behavior) are only general guidelines. Even a single, unified culture will have competing and contradictory norms. Therefore, which rule is applied and how it is interpreted depends on the specific situation and the people involved in it. For example, there are laws against speeding, yet not everyone who breaks the law is stopped or fined. If a cop stops you for speeding, you probably will not question the general principle of speed limits, but you probably will wonder why you have been selected. That is, you will realize that values, norms, and even laws are abstract; they are different from rules in use.

This difference leads to a whole new set of questions: not "Who breaks the rules and why?" but "Which rules are enforced, by whom, against whom, how, and with what effect?" In the hypothetical case just mentioned, you are unlikely to search for the sociological or psychological causes of driving 75 mph. You are much more likely to ask, "Why is this cop picking on me instead of going after real criminals?"

LABELING THEORY

The questions about rule enforcement are the basis for what is sometimes called labeling theory. (The term *labeling theory* may be incorrect. A theory, strictly speaking, is a set of logically connected propositions. It identifies important factors and predicts outcomes. A theory says, in effect, where such-and-such conditions exist, certain other results will occur. In this sense, labeling theory is not really a theory. It is not a tightly connected set of propositions, and it does not predict. Instead, it suggests outcomes that may possibly occur. It sensitizes us to possibilities that other theories ignore. It is not so much a theory as it is a way of looking at crime and deviance. For these reasons, some sociologists prefer to call it the *labeling perspective*.) Labeling theory begins by recognizing that no act is inherently criminal; it is a crime only if there is a law against it. Crime, therefore, is not just a matter of rule breaking but also of rule making and rule enforcement. In other words, crime is a joint product of the interaction of those who create and enforce the rules and those who break them. If we want the full picture, we have to look carefully not just at criminals but also at the criminal justice system and other forms of social control. Traditional criminology theories look at only one side of the interaction—the criminal. Labeling theory, in contrast, has usually focused on law enforcers and law creators—the people that Howard Becker, whose *Outsiders* is one of the basic texts of the labeling approach, calls **moral entrepreneurs**. They are in the business of making and enforcing morals—rules about what people should and should not do.[6]

By referring to the police, legislators, and reformers as moral entrepreneurs, Becker is taking an attitude of irony and skepticism toward the sorts of people and institutions that usually receive automatic and uncritical respect, not just from the public but from other criminological theorists as well. Law creators and law enforcers usually present themselves as working for the general good, as motivated by abstract principles of right and wrong, without regard to the particular interests of any one group. But the term *entrepreneur* implies that this enterprise brings them some profit. The profit need not be financial; it may be more abstract, perhaps the confirmation of one moral position over another. In any case, labeling theory questions both the motives and effects of these moral entrepreneurs. It does not take them at face value but looks for the discrepancies between what they do and what they say they do. For example, instead of accepting crime statistics as a true and objective measure of criminal behavior, labeling theorists long ago pointed out that these numbers also depend on the behavior of the police. This skepticism led to the many studies (some described in Chapter Three) showing how crime statistics reflect not just crime but also the public relations interests of the police department, its routine procedures for handling complaints and arrests, and the general expectations and prejudices of police officers.

This skepticism and irony are basic to much of labeling theory.[7] Even with law enforcement, labeling theory takes a somewhat ironical approach. It asks, "What does law enforcement really do?" The official position of law enforcers is, of course, that they prevent crime. Indeed, sometimes they do. But often enforcing the law has unintended consequences—both for individuals and for crime in general. The criminal justice process is supposed to keep people from committing crimes. However, labeling theory argues that this process, by defining the person as a criminal, may push him or her toward crime rather than away from it. Other people will respond to the label rather than to other facts about the person, and this response will make it more difficult for the labeled person to move easily into noncriminal society.[8]

Some people reduce this idea to the oversimplified notion that labeling a person a criminal or homosexual or whatever will inevitably make the person become that label. This process is called the self-fulfilling prophecy since the prophecy (person X is a criminal) makes itself come true (person X then becomes a criminal *because of the prophecy*). It *can* happen, but labeling theory does not claim that it *must* happen. Labeling theory merely suggests that researchers explore this as one of a number of possible outcomes. These theorists want to see exactly how the labeling process can work and what other factors can affect the outcome. People with enough money, power, status, or organizational support may be better able to resist the negative effects of labeling. For example, Richard Nixon's involvement in the Watergate scandal ended his presidency. However, not long after his resignation, he was being treated much more like a statesman than as an unindicted coconspirator in a series of crimes.

Labeling theory also differs from most other theories in that it sees crime control as a possible source of crime. Labeling research examines the unintended effects law enforcement can have not just on individuals but on the broader organization of crime as well. A study might investigate how Prohibition helped organized crime to expand and consolidate its powers or how making a drug like heroin or cocaine illegal has contributed to street crime: Since the drug's illegality drives up its price, users may turn to crime to get money for drugs. If they were cheap or free, nobody would need to steal to support a habit. (Of course, a free-drug policy might create other problems.)

Some research in the labeling tradition looks closely at the criminal justice system itself—at police officers, lawyers, or prison workers—as thoroughly as other research has looked at criminals. Rather than accept the statements of officials (that they just enforce the law), researchers investigate what people in the criminal justice system actually do. The police, for example, often do not arrest lawbreakers; officers have a great deal of discretion in responding to crimes. A labeling theorist would want to know just what determines whether a cop will make an arrest. A violation of the law is only one of many factors influencing that decision. In fact, sometimes an officer may make an arrest even though the person has *not* broken the law (chiefly as a means of defusing a potentially explosive situation).[9]

Besides examining the enforcement of the law, labeling theory also has directed its attention to the creation of laws. If law enforcement is a process of human interaction, so is lawmaking. Laws do not write themselves: They are created by people with a particular interest in having such laws passed. In *Outsiders*, Becker devotes two chapters to the history of the federal law, finally passed in 1937, that outlawed marijuana. The law was not the result of some spontaneous and broad-based democratic sentiment against the drug. Instead, it could be traced to the efforts of only a few people in law-enforcement agencies. They drafted legislation for Congress; but more important, they also managed, through an influx of stories in the popular press, to create an exaggerated image of marijuana and its dangers. (The 1936 movie *Reefer Madness* has provided cable TV and VCR viewers an opportunity to see a film version of the kinds of magazine articles that began appearing at about the same time.) The point is not whether marijuana is more or less harmful than it was portrayed. More important is the general insight that moral entrepreneurs try to use the law—especially the criminal law—as a tool to promote their moral view of the world. An obvious example today is the continuing battle in the courts and the legislatures over the issue of abortion. Still more obvious are the issues that are purely symbolic—issues like the death penalty, a ban on assault weapons, prayer in the public schools, and flag burning. People argue about these issues as though the very survival of the nation were at stake, when in fact the legal decisions one way or another will have no real impact on behavior. What is at issue in these debates (regardless of the claims of the debaters) is not public safety. Instead, the moral entrepreneurs are slugging it out to see whose version of morality and reality will be written into law.[10]

Conflict and consensus

Conventional theories, in one way or another, all start from questions like, "Why do people commit crimes, and how can we get them to stop?" You may have had similar questions in mind when you signed up for a course in criminology. But if you put together some of the observations from the last several pages, you may arrive at a much different viewpoint. Take the idea, from neutralization theory and elsewhere, that the rules of society are not uniform and obvious but are instead diverse and even contradictory. People select and interpret these rules in each situation, and which rule is enforced depends on the people involved. Add labeling theory's idea that the creation of laws and their enforcement is the product of human interaction and that different groups may have different interests. Add the observation that the more power a person has, the better he or she will be able to resist being labeled; and the more power a group has, the better it will be able to have its morality written into law and enforced. The conclusion from these propositions is that the enforcement of rules is not a matter of **consensus** or agreement, but rather that rule making and rule enforcement are matters of **conflict**.

Once you no longer assume that criminal laws and their enforcement are matters of consensus, you ask a much different set of questions. Instead of asking why some people break the law, you ask questions like, "Who has the power to create and enforce laws?" and "In whose interests are particular laws created and enforced?" and, more crucially, "In whose interests are particular laws *not* created or *not* enforced?"

These kinds of questions are at the heart of a style of criminological theory that grew to prominence in the 1970s. Some of the theorists with this point of view called their approach the conflict perspective or conflict theory. Others referred to their ideas as critical theory, Marxist criminology, radical criminology, or the new criminology. There are distinctions among some of these titles, and the criminologists involved address a variety of issues. They even differ with one another on some points. Nevertheless, I will try to sketch here their common ground.

In criminology, they turned their attention away from questions about crime and toward questions about justice. Instead of accepting the assumptions of the criminal justice system, they asked whether that system was in fact doing justice in the broadest sense of that word. They also preferred to examine the actions of the wealthy and powerful rather than those of the poor and powerless. These theorists had been influenced, even radicalized, by the political events of the 1960s. After all, if you see police officers enforce the law by clubbing antiwar demonstrators or civil rights marchers, you might come to question the basis of law enforcement and the law itself rather than accept them automatically as legitimate—especially if you are among those being clubbed.

THE MARXIST LEGACY

One unifying theme in radical criminology is its critical view of the basic foundations of society. I mean *critical* here in both the neutral and the negative senses of that word. Radical criminologists call their theory critical because it proposes a critique, an evaluation, of the entire society. They seek the origins of crime in the basic economic, historical, and political arrangements of society. Traditional criminology, the "old" criminology, takes these arrangements for granted. In the opinion of the new criminologists, this is a crucial omission: "The analysis of particular forms of crime, or particular types of criminal, outside their context in history and society, has been shown ... to be a meaningless activity."[11]

Dismissing most criminology as a meaningless activity is a fairly heavy charge, so let me offer a hypothetical example. Imagine that we are going to study crime in South Africa. If we use the models of conventional criminology, we ask questions like, "Who commits crimes and why?" and "How can we get them to stop?" Our research might show us that young black males have high crime rates; that they commit most of their crimes in their own towns against the persons or property of other blacks; that crime increased in the mid-1980s; that some townships have more crime than others. Our explanations for these findings might center on the culture of certain townships, on the ethnic backgrounds of the criminals, on rates of unemployment, on the failure of the criminal justice system to catch and punish offenders, or on the family backgrounds of offenders.

What is missing here? You don't have to be a radical Marxist to see a glaring defect in all these explanations and in our basic research: They say nothing about the history of apartheid. Apartheid was, until the early 1990s, the basis of South Africa's legal, political, and economic systems. Under apartheid, the white minority (about 15 percent of the total population) completely controlled the country. Blacks could not vote, move freely about the country, or receive an adequate education; they got the lowest-paying jobs, and generally lived in conditions of enforced inferiority. Although the laws of apartheid disappeared in 1993, the overwhelming social and economic inequalities remain. Do we really think that we can explain the *tsotsis* (muggers) of a black township like Soweto by looking at their differential associations or their probability of escaping punishment? These theories may have some relevance, they may even be supported by research data, but they are too shortsighted. They ignore or take for granted South Africa's historical economic and political arrangements.

Radical criminology would not make this omission. It generally tries to keep these basic historical and structural factors near the center of attention, a focus that is part of the Marxist orientation of most radical criminologists. Marx himself wrote little about crime, but he did hold that the basic economic structure of a society (its "social relations of production") provided the basis for all social (and antisocial) behavior. It is this fundamental idea, derived from Marx, that underlies much radical criminology. Radical (or critical) criminology makes the economic basis of society a central factor in the analysis of crime.

In principle, critical criminologists should take this approach whether they are analyzing crime and justice in South Africa or America or China; whether the system is capitalist, socialist, communist, or anything else. Their first task should be to relate the problem to the social relations of production. In practice, since most of these new criminologists are British or American, the societies on which they cast their critical eye are their own, the Western capitalist societies. And they have often found fault with what they see. Therefore, the writings of radical criminologists have also been *critical* in the negative meaning of that word. In explaining crime, they have pointed to some of the less attractive features of Western capitalism, focusing far more on its faults than on its virtues. Moreover, they argue that these faults are essential, fundamental parts of the capitalist system, not just a few flaws in a basically good society. Radical theorists hold little hope that reforms will bring about real change. Only a transformation of the economic basis of the society will bring a large reduction in crime.

A TOUCH OF CLASS

Another Marxian point central to radical criminology is the concept of social class. Other theories use the notion of social class only in seeking to explain why the lower class does (or does not) have a higher rate of crime. Radical criminology starts from a different conception of class. For Marxists, class is not a matter of income or education, nor do terms like *upper middle class* have much meaning for them. These all imply differences of lifestyle or patterns of consumption (i.e., how people spend their money). Marxists look instead at production and see two major classes: those who own or control the means of production and those who do not. Those who own the land, resources, machinery—what Marx called capital—are in a position to exploit those who have only their own labor. The interests of the two classes do not coincide. In fact, they are in conflict, and each class will use the tools at its disposal to further its own interests.

The law is an important tool in this conflict. One class will have a tremendous advantage if it can have laws passed against actions that harm its interests. The law adds to the power of the class by enlisting the machinery of the state; the class that can control the law now has the police and courts to do its work. Not only does the law then serve one class, but it drapes that class interest in the cloak of universal legitimacy. The law, since it applies to all people, has an air of neutrality and equality. Of course, in some cases, that neutrality barely hides the class bias of the law. As Anatole France said, "The law, in its majestic equality, forbids both the rich and the poor to sleep under bridges."

Radical criminologists are less interested in who *breaks* the laws and why than in who *makes* the laws and why. Much of the best research to emerge from radical criminology shows how particular criminal laws or patterns of law enforcement have fit into the conflict between social classes. A classic example is the antivagrancy law that appeared in the mid-1300s in England. The laws forbade begging and required that men or women without visible means of support should work for anyone who needed workers ("shall be bounded to serve him which shall him require"). The question is "Why this law at this time?" It helps if you remember that in 1348 the plague wiped out about 40 percent of the population of England. At the same time, the feudal system, which tied peasants to the manor estates of the lords, was beginning to break down. If laborers were free to refuse low wages and to wander about in search of the best situations, landowners would have to pay higher wages. However, the new vagrancy laws, by forcing peasants to take whatever work was offered, provided landowners with a continued supply of affordable labor.[12] Obviously a law that prohibited idleness served the interest of the owners. Even in the twentieth century, when there are too many laborers rather than too few, vagrancy laws have served to control poor people who are not committing predatory crimes. Merchants might ask the police to clear vagrants from shopping areas, where their appearance might keep customers away.

Other historical research on the development of English law has shown how laws were changed to accommodate the interests of owners against the interests of commoners. For example, by long-standing custom, common people had been able to take wood, game, and turf from the forests. But in the eighteenth century, much of this land was designated as the king's or was turned over to private owners, and Parliament passed antipoaching laws to protect their rights. For the landowners, these lands became a source of greater income. But for ordinary people, the laws meant that what had once been a way of life was now a crime punishable in some cases by death.[13] In the United States, laws permitting slavery or restricting unions or prohibiting boycotts promoted the interests of those who control the means of production.

The relationship between criminal law and economics is sometimes less direct. Drug laws, for example, would seem at first to have little to do with relations between labor and capital. We might assume that a drug becomes outlawed when it is shown to be harmful. However, one Marxist has argued that the passage of drug laws depends more on the economic position of the group that uses a particular drug than on the dangers of the drug itself. For example, antiopium laws in America first appeared in the West in the late 1870s, not because opium was any more harmful than it had been ten years earlier but because the position of Chinese laborers had changed. Chinese workers had been brought to America to provide cheap labor, virtually slave labor, for building the railroads. As long as this labor was needed, smoking opium was legal. However, when the railroads were largely completed and the country sank into economic depression, Chinese workers were no longer needed. In addition, some Chinese were opening businesses that competed with those of white merchants. The result was a flourishing of anti-Chinese prejudice and the criminalization of opium smoking. Of course, people urging antiopium legislation said nothing about the economic position of the minority group (the Chinese). Instead, their fears resembled those of the anticocaine panic of the 1980s: that a drug that had previously been confined to a minority group was now ruining the lives of "respectable" men and women. It is especially noteworthy that these laws did not ban opium itself. Liquid opium, widely drunk by whites in various patent medicines, remained legal. Only smoking, the form of opium ingestion preferred by the Chinese, was outlawed. A century later, the legal treatment of cocaine took a similar path. People convicted of offenses involving cocaine in powder form—the form more popular among the white middle class—on average received lighter penalties than those convicted of offenses involving crack, the form of cocaine more popular among poor African-Americans. Antidrug legislation in the Southwest in the 1930s followed a similar pattern, except that the laborers were Mexicans and the drug was marijuana.[14]

WHAT ABOUT STREET CRIME?

Many nonradical criminologists have come to accept some of this historical research and its conclusions. Radical criminology must be credited for showing how powerful groups use the law to secure their own interests. But for most citizens, the crime problem is not vagrancy in the fourteenth century or poaching in the eighteenth century; it is mugging in the twentieth century. What do radical criminologists say about the ordinary street crimes—the burglaries and robberies and rapes—that the majority of people see as "the crime problem"? Surely the laws against these crimes are meant to protect all people, not just the wealthy. Searching for the origins of laws is all very interesting, but how about explaining the origins of crime as well?

Radical criminologists respond to these questions in several ways. One of the most obvious answers is that street crime is a product of poverty, unemployment, and inequality. From the Marxist viewpoint, these economic problems are inherent in a capitalist economy. Radicals argue that the U.S. government could in fact ensure that all people had adequate income and employment. In that case, crime would drop dramatically. Why, then, does the government not take such action? Because, say the radicals, it would require a restructuring of the economy. The change would greatly benefit the poor and would reduce crime, but it would also diminish the position of the corporations and individuals that are now wealthy and powerful—the people radicals refer to as the ruling class. In other words, those who have the power to eliminate unemployment and poverty have no reason to do so and many reasons not to do so.

As for the laws against street crime, radicals make a variety of observations. First, remember the epigram about sleeping under bridges. The law forbids both the rich and the poor to commit burglary, but it often fails to criminalize many of the harmful acts committed by the wealthy in their pursuit of greater wealth. It was not criminal for Ford to build the flammable Pinto, even though the engineers and executives knew that the location of its gas tank would make rear-end collisions unusually dangerous. (The state of Indiana did bring criminal charges against Ford for reckless homicide after three teenage girls burned to death in a Pinto crash. The jury found Ford not guilty.) It is not criminal for politicians to vote tax breaks for a business that contributes heavily to their campaign funds. It is not criminal for a defense contractor to charge the government $200 for a $5 hammer, or for a drug manufacturer to charge $40 for a bottle of pills that costs a dime to produce. The laws that do restrict business practices are usually regulations, not criminal laws. So even if these various profiteers are caught, they may be embarrassed, they may be sued, and they may be fined, but they do not go to prison.[15]

Second, this selective attention, focusing on the evils of the poor rather than those of the rich, continues well beyond the creation of laws. For those who do break the existing laws, each step of the criminal justice process—arrest, indictment, trial, conviction, incarceration—allows the wealthy to slip out. Those left to receive the full force of the system are the poor and powerless.

This bias in the criminal justice system drops an added benefit in the lap of the ruling class. From the creation of laws to the imprisonment of criminals, the system conveys an image that the crime problem consists of the crimes of the poor. Thus, in two ways, street crime is good for business. It is an inevitable result of the levels of poverty and unemployment that are necessary to our capitalist system, and it diverts public attention away from the much more harmful acts of the wealthy and allows them to continue with business as usual.[16]

There is a third reason that the ruling class need not take drastic action to reduce crime: This crime rarely touches them. Street crime consists mostly of poor people victimizing other poor people. It does not affect corporations directly, and the people who run those corporations have been able to buy their way to safety. Their suburban homes or city apartments are well protected by police or private guards.

CRITICISMS OF RADICAL THEORY

Radical criminology has come in for a good deal of criticism. To talk about a ruling class in America offends many people, including some sociologists. After all, the United States is a democracy—a government of, by, and for the people—and our free enterprise economy, in principle, reinforces the democratic distribution of power. The argument between radical and mainstream criminologists, therefore, goes beyond questions of crime; it is about different pictures that people have of how society works. The most extreme radicals offer a model where a small ruling class runs nearly every part of the society to reinforce its position—a sort of collective J. R. Ewing.

Let's put it a bit more reasonably. First, power and wealth are not evenly distributed in society; some people and institutions have much more than others. Second, those who have power will use it to enhance their position. At a minimum, they will not do things that go against their economic or political interests; they will use the institutions they control to keep their positions of dominance. Third, this ruling class controls not only the economic institutions but also, ultimately, the institutions of justice. Therefore, the law and the criminal justice system, like other institutions in a society controlled by the powerful, will tend to reproduce these basic inequalities of wealth and power.

This model does not assume that the executives of corporations like General Motors and Citicorp necessarily get together with high-level politicians and scheme to get richer. Instead, it requires only that they share a similar way of looking at the world and a similar set of interests. That is, the ruling class is not a closed conspiracy; it is a set of powerful people whose interests are served by similar policies.

But is there really a ruling class? Granted that some people have far more power than others, do all these powerful people have the same goals? Is the state merely a tool of the ruling capitalist class, or does it represent other interests as well? Even some Marxist criminologists dismiss the idea that a unified and all-powerful ruling class is making all the decisions. Instead their model of society, though it still runs on power, sees that power as somewhat dispersed. They speak of "the partial autonomy of the state." The criminal justice system is not just one more instrument the ruling class can use for domination and exploitation. Instead, "law and law enforcement are ... products of shifting alliances. The superior financial resources of capitalists naturally give them an advantage over other classes in conflicts over legislation and enforcement, but this advantage is not always decisive."[17]

Another criticism of radical criminologists is that they have not produced much empirical data to support their ideas. Marxist criminology may offer a perspective for viewing the historical development of laws, but does it lead to propositions that can be tested with empirical evidence? If so, does the available evidence confirm the Marxists' statements?

There may be something to this criticism. Marx's ideas are not always easy to turn into measurable variables. However, the same can be said of non-

Marxian concepts as well, as we have seen with differential association theory.[18] Some sociologists have tried to show that the United States does in fact have a ruling class, but this research does not focus on crime.[19] Some criminologists have tried to show that the criminal justice system is used to oppress the poor; but despite many empirical studies, there is little conclusive evidence that, other things being equal, the courts treat the poor more harshly. It does appear, however, that the police (though probably not the courts) deal more harshly with African-Americans, especially in areas where there is a large black population.[20]

Radical criminologists have sometimes used the empirical data from conventional criminology to support their ideas. For example, early research using self-report studies showed that middle-class youths were committing as much crime as lower-class youths, while at the same time arrest data showed that more lower-class youths were arrested. Radicals interpreted the difference to mean that the police were biased against the lower class. One of the best examples of radical criminology is an essay by Marxist criminologist David Greenberg, entitled "Delinquency and the Age Structure of Society." Greenberg uses data and ideas from mainstream sources, but he reaches a more Marxist conclusion: Delinquency is a result of the particular position of youth in the capitalist labor market.[21]

Finally, some critics have taken radical criminologists to task for their ideas on capitalism and crime. As with their ideas on the ruling class, radicals do not all agree on the specific connection between capitalism and crime. Again, the most romantic, extreme versions are the easiest to criticize. A handful of radical criminologists argue that crime is solely a product of capitalism. Some even go so far as to say that under socialism, crime as we know it will disappear. "As we engage in socialist struggle, we build a society that ceases to generate the crime found in capitalist society."[22] Statements like this fly in the face of reality. Before the fall of communism in eastern Europe around 1990, those countries had little or no private, capitalist ownership; however, they had crime. The USSR had one of the highest rates of imprisonment in the world (perhaps even higher than that bastion of capitalism, the United States). The Marxists, however, may have a point. Since the demise of communism and the increase in both private enterprise and personal freedom, crime rates have risen sharply. At the same time, some vigorously capitalist countries have very low rates of crime (e.g., Japan and Switzerland). More flexible, less romantic Marxists recognize that socialist countries may have inequality, conflict between different classes of people, and alienation. In other words, they use Marxist concepts to understand crime in socialist countries, too.

CONTROL THEORY

Most of the sociological theories outlined here so far assume that individual differences play an insignificant part in crime rates. These theories locate important causes of crime in environmental factors such as the social structure or subcultural values, rather than in individuals or families. If these theories point to any kind of policy, it is one of reforming society rather than punishing individuals through the criminal justice system. Some of these theories—labeling theory, for example—even question the assumptions on which the criminal justice system is based. In political terms, these theories are usually classified as liberal since they question or criticize society and hesitate to see individual criminals as the cause of the crime problem.

In recent years, some criminology theories have taken a more conservative turn. One of the most influential is control theory, which rejects some important assumptions and strategies of the other sociological theories discussed here. First, when these other theories begin by asking, "Why do some people violate the rules of society?" they are making one important assumption: that the natural way of the world is for people to follow the rules; it is only the addition of certain unfortunate factors (e.g., inequality) that causes people to break laws. Control theory begins from a different assumption: namely, that people are by nature self-interested and antisocial, and unless this human nature is strongly controlled, we will have "the war of all against all." This phrase is from Thomas Hobbes, an eighteenth-century philosopher whose book *Leviathan* was an attempt to answer the question of why we do not have such chaos. "Why do [people] obey the laws of society?" is often referred to as the Hobbesian question. So we must turn the crime question around and ask not why criminals commit crimes but why other people do *not* commit crimes.

In this way, control theory resembles psychological theories of crime. Most psychological theories, too, start with the Hobbesian question. They assume that children come into the world with neither knowledge of society's rules nor an inclination to follow those rules. If society cannot instill the necessary controls by the time these children begin to acquire the physical strength of adults, society is facing an invading army. The leading psychological theories—Freudian, conditioning, and so on—try to explain how the child is socialized into automatically and largely unconsciously controlling these natural, antisocial, selfish impulses.

Second, control theory sees the legal and moral aspects of crime as clear and unambiguous. According to most other sociological theories (except perhaps Merton's), different groups have different concepts of the law and morality. Sutherland's statement that culture conflict is the basic cause of crime; other cultural theorists' ideas that delinquent subcultures value certain law-breaking activities as a route to status within that group; labeling theory's idea that rules, both in the abstract and in actual use, depend on which group has the power to enforce its morality—all these see definitions of crime or morality as something shifting and flexible, different from one group to the next, or a matter of conflict rather than consensus.

Nonsense, says control theory. Such ideas are either irrelevant or wrong. The simple truth is that for most crimes there is a clear morality of right and wrong, and some people choose to violate that morality. They know full well that what they are doing is wrong. In some special cases, there may be genuine disagreement over the legitimacy of a law (particularly with victimless crimes), but everyone, including the criminal, agrees that predatory crimes like robbery, assault, theft, and burglary are wrong.

Third, control theory rejects the usual environmental causes cherished by traditional sociological theories. Social class and race, as well as economic status and culture, have at best a secondary place in control theory. This challenge to the sociological tradition is based on empirical grounds as much as on theory, for control theory arose when criminological research—especially research based on self-report studies—began to show that lower class and middle class, white and black, were much more similar in their law-breaking than had previously been thought.

TRAVIS HIRSCHI'S CONTROL THEORY

Control theory comes in a variety of styles, and I cannot outline all of them here. Still, the one I will describe—that of Travis Hirschi—contains most of the basic ideas. Like many of the other theories, most control theories are trying to explain the behavior of younger criminals, that is, delinquents. This is probably a legitimate strategy, first, because most adult criminals started as delinquents, and second, because juveniles commit such a disproportionate amount of crime.

Hirschi's book, *Causes of Delinquency*,[23] presents both a statement of the theory and empirical support based on a sample of some 2,000 high school boys in the San Francisco–Oakland area. The boys filled out questionnaires covering a variety of attitudes and behavior, including, of course, crime.

Since race and social class did not seem to be important factors in delinquency, was there anything else that might distinguish delinquents from non-delinquents? In answering this question, Hirschi went back to the original Hobbesian question: Why do people obey social rules? Hirschi's answer is that there is a **social bond** that ties us to society: "Control theory assumes that delinquent acts result when an individual's bond to society is weak or is broken."

Hirschi specifies four elements in the abstract concept of the social bond and measures each. Then he correlates the boys' scores on each element with their delinquency. The four elements of the social bond correspond with four levels of analysis: feeling (called *affect*—accent on the first syllable), cognition (based on rational calculation), behavior, and belief or values (see Table 12–1).

TABLE 12-1 •
ELEMENTS OF THE SOCIAL BOND

LEVEL	ELEMENT	DESCRIPTION
AFFECTIVE	ATTACHMENT	EMOTIONAL CLOSENESS TO FAMILY, PEERS, SCHOOL
COGNITIVE	COMMITMENT	RATIONAL CALCULATION OF THE COSTS OF LAWBREAKING FOR FUTURE GOALS
BEHAVIORAL	INVOLVEMENT	TIME SPENT IN CONVENTIONAL ACTIVITIES (E.G., HOMEWORK)
EVALUATIVE	BELIEF	IDEAS THAT LEGITIMIZE DELINQUENCY

ATTACHMENT   The most important element of the social bond is the affective (emotional) component—what Hirschi calls attachment. Of course, a person is attached not to society in general but to specific institutions and people. Hirschi, therefore, measured attachment to three distinct groups: parents, school, and peers. His questionnaire had several items like these:

- Do you like school?
- Do you share your thoughts and feelings with your mother (father)?
- Would you want to be the kind of person your father is?
- Do you care what teachers think of you?

The theory says that the closer a boy is attached to family, school, and peers—or, in fact, to anything—the less likely he will be to break society's norms. There should be nothing startling about the idea that attachment to parents is a buffer against delinquency. Even lower-class parents, even parents who are themselves lawbreakers, prefer their children to stay out of trouble. But in giving attachment the central spot in his theory, Hirschi was going against the prevailing sociological theories, which downplayed the family as a source of delinquency.

Attachment to peers, though, is a different story, at least where delinquents are concerned. For boys with law-abiding friends, there is no argument. All theories would expect closer friendships to reduce delinquency. But what about those boys whose friends are delinquent—should strong attachment bring more delinquency or less? Common sense and most of the cultural theories (especially differential association theory) would predict that stronger attachment to delinquent friends should make a boy more likely to break the law. But Hirschi predicts that attachment to peers (like attachment to anything else) will dampen delinquency, even if those peers are hoodlums.

The evidence has not been kind to Hirschi's idea. Most studies confirm the commonsense notion. Hanging around with delinquent friends increases a youth's delinquency.[24] Even Hirschi had to sift his data thoroughly to find some small bit of support for his hypothesis. Nevertheless, his ideas about attachment among delinquents may help to correct one popular image of the juvenile gang. The media, both in fiction and in the news, like to portray these gangs as tight, supportive, highly organized, permanent groups, with special colors and a fairly regular schedule of confrontations with other gangs—something like a football team. This image may play well on the screen, but it rarely resembles reality. Instead, most research finds that gangs are fairly loose associations. It's true that delinquents commit most of their crimes in groups of two, three, or four. Most gangs consist of several of these sets of friends who hang around together, usually because they live in the same neighborhood. The military type of organization depicted in movies is rare.[25] More important, relationships among gang boys are based not on warmth and respect but on defensiveness, constant threat, insult, and aggression.[26]

As for attachment to school, the results in this area are exactly what anyone would expect: There is a strong negative correlation between delinquency and attachment to school (more attachment, less delinquency). Or stated simply, kids who like school commit fewer crimes. The question is, which is causing which? The sociological theorists of the 1950s and 1960s (e.g., Cohen, Miller, and Cloward and Ohlin) insist that delinquents are just as smart as nondelinquents. However, they say, school is culturally stacked against lower-class boys; as a result, they do poorly, and some of them withdraw into delinquent groups. In other words, the initial cause is the school's rejection of the lower-class boy. If schools were more tolerant of lower-class youths, if somehow schools were run so that these students would feel more at home there, if teachers could reach their lower-class students rather than humiliate them, there would be less pressure toward delinquency. In essence, delinquency is the school's fault.

Hirschi, in contrast, locates the causes of delinquency in the delinquent, not in the school. First, he argues that since delinquency is not related to social class, the school's supposed anti–lower-class bias cannot be blamed for delinquency. Second, Hirschi claims something that all of the other theories reject: that delinquents are less intelligent (and cites a substantial amount of research showing that on the average delinquents have lower IQ scores than those of nondelinquents). This academic incompetence means that they will do poorly in school and therefore resent and reject the school and its authority. The rejection of authority will loosen the social bond and leave them free to commit crimes.

COMMITMENT   In Hirschi's theory, commitment is the part of the social bond that involves a person's rational calculation of the costs and benefits of violating laws. Commitment links choices in the present to goals in the future. For a boy who has high future goals, the costs of crime (if he is caught) are much greater. He has more to lose. He has a greater **stake in conformity**.

Hirschi is interested in two aspects of a boy's "commitment to conventional lines of action": What aspirations does he have for college and career? And how willing is he to give up adult privileges in the present to attain his future goals? Hirschi's data show that boys with higher aspirations commit less crime. This result should not surprise us, except—as Hirschi reminds us—if we really believe theorists like Merton, Cohen, or Cloward and Ohlin. All of these theorists, you may recall, say that boys who become delinquent start out with the same aspirations, the same desire for success, as do nondelinquents but lack legitimate means to their goals. If these cultural theorists are right, delinquents should have high aspirations. But they don't.

Hirschi sees commitment not just in large future goals but in everyday choices, such as saying no to cigarettes, alcohol, and cars. The earlier a boy begins to smoke or drink, the more likely he is to become delinquent; the more important a boy thinks a car is, the more delinquent he will be. Of course, Hirschi is not saying that cigarettes cause delinquency but rather that smoking signals a lack of commitment to conventional goals. Boys who become delinquents think that adult pleasures in the present are more important than future goals.

INVOLVEMENT   Involvement is the behavioral component of the social bond. The theory says that the more time a boy spends in conventional activities, the less likely he is to break the law. Hirschi's research supports this

Smoking, drinking, driving, and having sex are not predatory crimes even for young teenagers. But, say control theorists, youths who refuse to defer these adult pleasures signal their more general antisocial view, a lowered "stake in conformity," and for that reason they are more likely to be the ones who commit other crimes as well.

idea up to a point. Boys who spent less time doing homework and more time riding around in cars were more likely to have committed crimes. However, Hirschi's own data often did not support his general ideas about involvement. Watching television, reading comic books, playing games—behaviors that show a lack of involvement in conventional activities—were very poor predictors of delinquency, and having a part-time job was positively correlated with delinquency. That is, the boys with part-time jobs were somewhat more delinquent than those without jobs. This result, along with more recent research, deflates one bit of conventional wisdom—the idea that having a job somehow automatically makes kids more virtuous. Apparently, this popular notion is highly overrated.[27] Conventional activities per se do not reduce delinquency. Involvement works only when the activity also shows commitment to future goals.

BELIEF   Belief, the fourth part of the social bond, refers to abstract ideas people hold about conventional authority, on the one hand, and crime, on the other. Conventional beliefs dampen the urge toward crime. Delinquency is "made possible by the absence of (effective) beliefs that forbid delinquency." Some of these delinquent beliefs resemble the neutralizations that Sykes and Matza defined. Boys were asked to agree or disagree with statements like, "Most things that people call delinquency don't really hurt anyone" (denial of injury) or "Policemen try to give all kids an even break" (disagreeing here would be condemning the condemners) or "I can't stay out of trouble no matter how hard I try" (denial of responsibility). As you would expect, those who took the neutralizing positions were more likely to have broken the law.

The problem with belief is that even if certain beliefs go hand in hand with delinquency, how can we know which is cause and which is effect? Hirschi says that lack of conventional belief "makes crime possible." But it is also possible that the boy who, for whatever reasons, commits crimes will come to adopt ideas that justify breaking the law. In this case, the belief is a consequence of crime, not a cause.

EXPLAINING IT ALL: SELF-CONTROL THEORY

Twenty years after he wrote *Causes of Delinquency*, Hirschi joined with Michael Gottfredson to produce a more streamlined version of control theory. This theory dismissed biological, psychological, and especially sociological explanations of crime, even to the point of abandoning Hirschi's earlier idea of the social bond. Instead, it reduced all of crime and delinquency to a single factor: **self-control**. (Properly speaking, self-control theory probably belongs in the chapter on psychological theories since it attributes crime to a single trait of the individual. But Hirschi and Gottfredson come from sociological backgrounds and are well versed in sociological theories. Their book, *A General Theory of Crime*,[28] is based mostly on sociologically derived data and seems addressed primarily to sociologists.) People commit crimes not because something is added (socioeconomic strain, cultural ideas, or a biochemical factor) but because something—self-control—is lacking. People who have learned self-control can control their impulses because they can see the long-term consequences of their behavior. People with low self-control are concerned only with gratification in the here and now.

Self-control accounts for many of the findings of criminological research. First, since self-control is a relatively enduring trait of the individual, the theory fits well with the research on sociopathy (i.e., antisocial personalities), research showing that deviant children often become deviant adults. Moreover, self-control theory accounts for the variety that deviance can take—not just crime but problems with drinking and drugs, job instability, failed marriages, family violence, accidents, and early death. All of these stem from the same inability to suppress immediate impulses in the interests of long-term goals.

Self-control theory also explains why criminals do not specialize in a single type of crime, even though from a purely economic point of view such specialization would make sense. By increasing his skills, a criminal could do fewer, well-planned, high-profit jobs, thereby increasing his income and reducing his odds of being caught. Instead, most criminals commit a variety of crimes and commit them in a way that requires little skill or planning. So even though a person is caught for a burglary, to label him a burglar would be misleading since he has probably committed a variety of other crimes as well. Criminologists who spin out special theories for the robber, the rapist, the drug dealer, and even the white-collar criminal are missing the fundamental point. All these crimes are manifestations of the same characteristic—lack of self-control. The difference lies entirely in the opportunities for quick gratification that a particular situation offers. Extending this same logic, Gottfredson and Hirschi dismiss the usual distinctions between serious crimes and petty crimes, violent crimes and property crimes, or victimless crimes and predatory crimes.[29] A criminal is a criminal, regardless of how the lack of self-control may manifest itself at any one time. "Our portrait of the burglar applies equally well to the white-collar offender, the organized-crime offender, the dope dealer, and the assaulter; they are, after all, the *same* people."[30]

SOURCES OF SELF-CONTROL

In the song, "Gee, Officer Krupke" from *West Side Story*, teenage gang members mock fashionable theories about the causes and cures of the delinquent—he's psychologically disturbed and needs a psychoanalyst, he's economically deprived and needs a job, and so on, discarding each theory and replacing it with another until in the last verse they conclude, "Deep down inside him, he's no good."

Gottfredson and Hirschi echo this rejection of popular theories of crime. According to these researchers, sociological ideas about class and culture fall apart in the face of the evidence: There is little, if any, correlation between class and crime; there is no cultural group that approves of crime; and criminals do not conform even to the norms of their own groups. Nor do cultural theories explain why only some members of a culture become criminals. Economic or rational-choice theories cannot apply since criminals do not calculate their costs and benefits beyond the immediate situation, and in any case, crime is not an economically rational career choice. Gottfredson and Hirschi also have no use for psychological theories of learning (i.e., that crime is learned through conditioning, imitation, and reinforcement); crime requires no such learning, and the reinforcement is inherent in the crime itself.

> [Our] view appears to fly in the face of the widely reported "peer pressure" phenomenon, where adolescents are heavily influenced by the wishes and expectations of their friends, often in a direction contrary to their own inclinations (or to the desires of their parents). However, the evidence also flies in the face of this interpretation; for example, adolescents who commit delinquent acts show less rather than more inclination to live up to the expectation of their peers. In matters of fashion in dress, speech, and music, they appear to be generally unfashionable or to take peer fashions to such extremes that they become objects of derision rather than admiration. (If the current fashion calls for short hair, they will tend to shave their heads; if long hair is in style, they will wear very long

hair; and so on.) In these matters, then, delinquents do not appear ordinarily concerned about the expectations and approval of others. Concern for the opinion of peers ("peer pressure"), it turns out, promotes conformity. Adolescents who care what other adolescents think of them in terms of their choice of dress, speech, and music are less rather than more likely to be delinquent.[31]

Nor can crime be a biologically inherited trait any more than accidents (not so different from crime, according to Gottfredson and Hirschi) can be a biologically inherited trait.[32]

The trouble with criminals is not to be found in their social or economic environment or in their history of learning or in their biological makeup. They commit crimes because deep down inside them, they lack self-control.

But where does this lack originate? "The major cause of low self-control ... appears to be ineffective child-rearing."[33] Parents must recognize and correct deviant behavior. If the parents do not care much about the child or if they do not have the time and energy to watch for deviant behavior or if they do not recognize the problem behavior, the child will be less likely to develop self-control. Parents who let their children watch too much television, avoid their homework, or skip school are failing to instill self-control.

> When children steal outside the home, some parents discount reports that they have done so on the grounds that the charges are unproved and cannot therefore be used to justify punishment. By the same token, when children are suspended for misbehavior at school, some parents side with the child and blame the episode on prejudicial mistreatment by teachers. Obviously, parents who cannot see the misbehavior of their children are in no position to correct it, even if they are inclined to do so.
>
> That many parents are not now attentive to such behaviors should come as no surprise. The idea that criminal behavior is the product of deprivation or positive learning dominates modern theory. As a consequence, most influential social scientific theories of crime and delinquency ignore or deny the connection between crime and talking back, yelling, pushing and shoving, insisting on getting one's way, trouble in school, and poor school performance. Little wonder, then, that some parents do not see the significance of such acts.[34]

▌THE LAST WORD

These last three chapters have offered an overview of theories of crime—biological, psychological, sociological, and a few others that don't quite fit into any one category. Future theories may try to combine some of the different approaches.[35] One recent approach, called the routine activities approach, is a variation on opportunity theory, although it addresses a slightly different set of questions from those examined by Merton or Cloward and Ohlin. Instead of asking who commits crimes and why, this approach seeks to explain the amount and distribution of crime by focusing on the ways in which the routine activities of ordinary people offer opportunities for criminals.[36] Mapping the location of crime takes us back to the ecological approach, although its explanations are different from those of the sociologists of the old Chicago school. Other ecological approaches try to incorporate ideas of control theory and differential association.[37] Other theories may emerge from the study of white-collar crime or organized crime or drunken driving—the kinds of crime largely passed over by earlier theories. In any case, the theory will try to do what any good theory does—to bring together and explain different sets of facts.

If you come across other theories or if you've read these chapters, you might be tempted to ask two questions: "So what?" and "Which of these theories is right?" The first question, though it sounds much less sophisticated, is probably a better one. Certainly it is the more difficult question. To ask of each theory whether it is right or wrong misses the point. Theories in social science are not like theories in the hard sciences, where one theory gains ascendance and replaces another, and old theories are like quaint objects gathering dust in an attic, interesting only for historical curiosity, much like the vintage automobile. The Model T Ford had a great impact in its field; it might even be elegant in its own way, but you wouldn't want to have to rely on one for your daily commute on the interstate. Similarly, no chemists today would pursue phlogiston theory, nor are there any physicists who base their research on Rutherford's model of the atom. These ideas are left to historians of science.

In social science, though, old theories never die, and if they fade away they have a strange way of returning. For example, Beccaria's utilitarian ideas on crime (1764), although helpful in the reform of courts and laws in the eighteenth century, had little influence on theories of crime in the nineteenth and early twentieth centuries. But roughly two hundred years later, what were the "new" trends in criminology? Economic cost-benefit analyses of crime, sociological theories of rational choice, and research on the deterrent effects of punishment. Utilitarianism was back in fashion.

In the natural sciences, new research may prove a theory wrong. Then, a new theory that can explain the new facts replaces the old theory entirely. With theories of human behavior, however, research seldom "proves" a theory wrong. When the results contradict a theory, supporters of the theory can (and frequently do) argue that the research was methodologically flawed. Research on human behavior (especially criminal behavior) can almost never approach the precision of experiments in the chemist's laboratory. In addition, the abstract concepts of a social theory are often difficult to define and measure in actual research. If a particular piece of research appears to contradict my theory, I can always argue that the researchers used a misleading definition of crime or social class or attachment or identification. An idea in social science comes and goes not so much because of its validity as demonstrated by research but because of its interest or usefulness.

Instead of a single theory dominating an entire field, as in the natural sciences, many social science theories may exist side by side at the same time. It looks as if these theories are competing with one another. Their proponents criticize one another, sometimes in the most caustic terms. They dismiss one another's research as methodologically shoddy, politically biased, or simply irrelevant. But this conflict may be more apparent than real. The different theorists are like the blind men discussing the elephant. They are not really talking about the same part of the subject. To take a slightly closer analogy, imagine theories about the problem of highway accidents. Some theorists might come up with principles of automobile construction. Other theorists would concern themselves with the perceptions, reactions, and mental states of drivers. Still others would point to the relationship between the powerful auto industry and the government's regulatory agencies. And each group would have research findings to support its ideas.

Is my analogy off the mark? Look at two of the more influential theoretical positions in criminology today, the two I have discussed at length in this chapter: conflict theory and control theory—one radical, the other conservative. Control theory concentrates on differences between criminals and noncriminals; it asks why some people commit crime and others do not. Conflict theory largely ignores questions about why people commit crime. It does, however, question the political and economic structure and its effect on crime. Control theory, in comparison, accepts the status quo and all but ignores the effects of social institutions (including even the criminal justice system). In their disputes, Marxists and control theorists may not be able to speak to each other in any meaningful way since they are addressing different questions. But an apparent dispute does not always mean that one side is right and the other wrong. Each theory may be useful in understanding the questions it has selected. The real dispute is whether those questions are the right questions.

How do we decide whether a set of questions is worthwhile? Frequently, the answer depends not on the facts but on our values and general worldview. In other words, instead of saying that a theory is wrong, those who disagree can merely say, "So what?" Even professional criminologists may take this approach. For some criminologists, the ultimate test of a theory is whether it leads to policies for reducing crime, especially street crime. If it doesn't, then so what?[38] But applicability is not the only test of a theory, nor even necessarily the best test. By this criterion, physicists should have dismissed Einstein's ideas when he proposed them in 1905, for at that time there were few useful applications for a theory of relativity. For other criminologists, a theory is worthwhile mostly insofar as it clarifies the economic and political structure of society. For still others, a theory must further our understanding of how people think; it must help us understand the subtle forces that influence the thoughts of criminals, police, judges, and others in the criminal justice area.

In other words, if a theory—a set of questions and answers—fits with our worldview, if it is useful for clearing up some of the puzzles of that worldview, then we find it interesting and important. Otherwise, we find it boring and irrelevant; we say, "So what?"

In discussing theory especially, this is the question I most fear, the question for which my answer will be the least satisfactory, for if you do not already think that the facts or issues addressed by a theory are relevant or interesting, I probably have little hope of convincing you otherwise.

CRITICAL THINKING QUESTIONS

1. Do people who commit crimes believe in the rightness of the laws they break? If so, how can they break them?
2. How do the actions of lawmakers and law enforcers contribute to crime?
3. In what ways are street crimes like robbery or drug dealing political?

4. How might street crimes be beneficial to the ruling class?

5. Do different social groups have different definitions of right and wrong? Why is the answer to this question important to theories of crime?

6. Is there a single factor underlying all criminal behavior? What facts about crime and criminals fit with a single-factor explanation, and what facts do not fit so well?

KEY TERMS

conflict	moral entrepreneurs	self-control
consensus	neutralizations	social bond
drift	norms	stake in conformity

CHAPTER THIRTEEN

THE POLICE

CHAPTER OUTLINE

The 1994 crime bill, proposed by President Clinton and passed by the U.S. Congress, provided money for 100,000 new police officers in cities across the country. The total cost to federal, state, and local governments over the five years of this program is estimated at $30 billion. Even before this legislation, the price tag for the roughly 700,000 police officers already on police forces around the United States was about $30 billion a year. Although most of this money comes from state and local governments rather than from Washington, it is ultimately the taxpayers who foot the bill.

The police are the most expensive sector of the criminal justice system; we spend more for police than for courts or corrections. Since $30 billion is a lot of money, maybe I ought to start this chapter by asking why: Why do we have police? Why not get rid of them and save the money? Think about it for a moment, and try to come up with an answer before you read the next few paragraphs.

When I ask students this question, they sometimes look at me as if I were impossibly stupid. "What do you mean, 'Why do we have police?'" they say. "You have to have police."

"But why?" I repeat.

"To enforce the law. To prevent crime. To catch criminals." These are the typical responses, and probably your answer was similar. However, to a great extent, the police do not enforce the law, do not prevent crime, and do not catch criminals. Since this is a fairly provocative and unusual statement, I should explain it fully.

Although most definitions of the police center on their role as crime-fighters, much of their work on the street involves maintaining public order.

IN THE NEWS

The possibility of increasing police visibility by hiring more officers is governed by a 10-for-1 rule: to get one officer on the street at all times throughout the year, at least 10 have to be hired.... They work different shifts, go on vacation, take sick leave, and are sent for periodic training.

Generally police departments estimate that it takes 5.5 officers to provide one officer around the clock throughout the year.

Add to this the fact that many uniformed patrol officers work away from the street ... and it quickly becomes obvious that 10-for-1 is a conservative estimate of how many bodies are needed to create a single visible police officer.

If Mr. Clinton's additions were doled out across the country, as politicians would probably insist, each town or city would get at most one or two more. Even this almost invisible increment is prohibitively expensive. A patrol offi-

cer costs about $50,000 per year, salary and benefits together. Following the 10-for-1 rule the cost of one more street officer is really $500,000.

The policy of deterring crime through increasing the visible presence of the police is bankrupt—a political nostrum that sounds good but is ineffective and costly.

Source: David H. Bayley, "The Cop Fallacy," *New York Times*, August 16, 1993, p. A17.

ENFORCING, AND NOT ENFORCING, THE LAW

Of course the police do enforce the law—sometimes. But think of all the times you have seen police officers. What were they doing? When I ask students this question, I get such answers as

- Riding around in their cars
- Directing traffic
- Giving me a ticket
- Sitting in Dunkin' Donuts drinking coffee
- Helping out after a traffic accident

Except for the speeding ticket (which was probably from a state trooper, not a city officer), none of these activities requires the enforcement of laws. Of course, these observations of the police are both unsystematic and unintended. Would we find something different if we looked at the jobs we specifically call on the police to do? In other words, have you ever called the police, and if so, why? When I ask students this question, most of the answers have little to do with enforcing the law, preventing crime, or catching criminals:

- I locked myself out of my car.
- There was a dead animal in the street somebody ran over.
- My little brother got lost.
- Someone broke into our house.

WHAT THE POLICE DO

These examples are not unusual. People call on the police for a wide variety of services. In poor neighborhoods especially, police officers may be called on for all sorts of social services—the kinds of things for which middle-class people call doctors or psychologists or social workers or lawyers. These requests for services, services that have little do with crime, make up the majority of calls to the police. When crime does occur, people may call the police, sometimes. But as you may remember from the chapter on crime statistics, in over half of all crimes the victim does *not* call the police.

These different questions—"Why do we have police?" and "Why have you called the police, and what have you seen the police doing?"—evoke strikingly different images. We refer to the police as law-enforcement officers; we think of them as our defense against crime; and yet most of the things we call on them to do, and most of the things we see them doing, have very little to do with crime and law enforcement.

One possible way to explain the contradiction is to say that, of course, we—the good, law-abiding citizens—rarely see the police in their crime-fighting, law-enforcing roles because we stay on the right side of the law. We don't have a complete view of police work. For that, we would have to follow the police through an entire working day to see what they actually spend their time doing.

In fact, there have been just such studies. Here is the breakdown from one study of police officers in a city with a population of about 400,000.[1]

ACTIVITY	PERCENT OF TIME CONSUMED
CRIMES AGAINST PERSONS	2.96%
CRIMES AGAINST PROPERTY	14.82
TRAFFIC	9.20
ON-VIEW	9.10
SOCIAL SERVICE	13.70
ADMINISTRATION	50.19

"On-view" refers to investigations initiated by the officer (rather than in response to a call)—checking the locks on buildings, stopping automobiles or people on foot if they seem suspicious—so these hours might reasonably be included as crime-related activity. "Social service" calls were mostly for family crises, drunkenness, or mental illness. "Administration" included activities related to crime—taking reports and serving warrants—but it also included other paperwork, time in the precinct house, meals, and coffee breaks.

Actual crime fighting, the sort of action that comes close to our image of "real" police work, took up only about 18 percent of the police officers' time. Similar studies have estimated that they spend 10 to 25 percent of their time in crime-related activities. More recent studies put the figure closer to 50 percent, partly because the police are in fact spending more time on crime, but partly because these studies have taken activities once classified as "administration" and redefined them as "crime related."[2] Whatever the exact figure, an actual 8-hour shift is a far cry from the exciting, action-packed image of police we get from "NYPD Blue" or *Lethal Weapon*. As one city officer put it, "Most of the time, this job is as boring as can be. You just sit behind the wheel and go where they tell you.... Your mind kinda wanders and some nights it's a bitch to stay awake."[3]

POLICE DISCRETION

To say that the police enforce the law is misleading in still another way. The definition of the police as law-enforcement officers implies that they size up situations by asking what law is being broken and how can they enforce it. The officer in this definition becomes more or less a tool of the law. The legislature passes laws, and the police go out and enforce them. But this definition overlooks the importance of police.

Time after time during their eight-hour shift, police officers come upon violations of laws and ordinances: public drunks, loitering teenagers, fights among acquaintances or family members, delivery trucks blocking the street, construction equipment blocking the sidewalk, and many others. Most of the time, the officers do not enforce the law as it is written in the statute books. They do not arrest the drunk; they do not bring assault and battery charges against the guy who punched out his friend; they do not write a summons for every sidewalk violation. All this nonenforcement should make us revise our ideas about the relationship between the police and the law. Instead of seeing the officer's primary function as enforcing the law, we might better think of it the way most police officers do—as "handling situations." The officers are not interested in applying all the available laws and ordinances. Instead, the law—the power to make an arrest—is just one tool they have for achieving their primary goal of restoring *order*. Instead of the officer being an instrument of the law, it's the other way around: The law is an instrument used by the officer.

POLICE—A DEFINITION

Recognizing this relationship between the law and the officer leads to a slightly different way of defining the term *police*. One criminology professor, Carl Klockars, begins his course on police by asking students to write down a brief definition of "police." Answers range from the serious ("an agency of government which enforces the law and keeps the peace") to the cynical ("The police are a bunch of hotshots who get their kicks by hassling blacks, students, and most other people who are trying to have a good time.").[4] When I borrow this exercise for my own class, someone usually says that the police are the people you always see hanging out in doughnut shops. My favorite is, "The police are the people you call when you call the police." Like the 5-year-old's definition of a bathroom as "a place where you go the bathroom," this definition is not so dumb as it sounds, as I will try to show.

The other definitions, the more typical ones, all define the police in terms of *goals*—what the police *should* do. Even definitions about hassling students or eating doughnuts have a "should" behind them. They imply that the cops should be doing something else, so even these sarcastic definitions still focus on goals. But no goal definition could possibly encompass all the things the police do or should do. What makes the police unique, what differentiates them from civilians, lies not in their goals but in the *means* they have at their disposal to accomplish those goals. Unlike anybody else, the police are allowed to use force.

Klockars gives a more elaborate definition based on this basic insight about means: "Police are institutions or individuals given the general right to use coercive force by the state within the state's domestic territory."[5]

When we define the police in terms of means—the legitimate use of force—we can see what all the different goals of police work have in common. Controlling crowds at parades or ball games; responding to reports of accidents or dog bites; driving drunks home; removing dead bodies from houses; intervening in arguments between landlord and tenant, customer and merchant, and husband and wife; removing children from abusive or negligent parents; getting a reluctant but seriously ill person to go to the hospital—the list is endless. What they all share is that somebody—a civilian, a social worker, a doctor—has called the police because the situation may require coercive force. That's why I liked the idea that "the police are who you call when you call the police." Beneath this circular definition is an intuitive recognition about who possesses the legitimate use of force. Another sociologist, Egon Bittner, has summarized this idea:

> Many puzzling aspects of police work fall into place when one ceases to consider it as principally concerned with law enforcement and crime control.... It makes much more sense to say that the police are nothing other than a mechanism for the distribution of situationally justified force in society.[6]

Bittner goes on to say that people call the police when a situation might require the legitimate use of force—situations in which "something ought not to be happening about which something ought to be done NOW."[7]

Obviously, one of these "somethings" that ought not to be happening is crime. But crime occupies only a part—and in many departments only a small part—of police time. Nevertheless, most people, including the police, see crime fighting as the core activity of the police role in society. Accordingly, the next sections of this chapter will examine the two major parts of the crime-fighter image: preventing crime and catching criminals.

PREVENTING CRIME—DETERRENCE

The idea that the police prevent crime is basically the idea of deterrence (there is a more thorough discussion of this topic in Chapter Sixteen). The question is not simply whether the police prevent crime. Undoubtedly they do. The questions are these: How much crime? What kinds of crime? Under what conditions? At what cost? Here is a somewhat oversimplified summary of the evidence:

■ Ordinary police-car patrol deters little, if any, crime.[8]

■ An officer on foot patrol deters more crime than no patrol at all. Further increases in the number of foot patrols add very little deterrent effect.[9]

■ Greatly increasing the number of police and arrests—i.e., police "crackdowns"—reduces the targeted crime, especially crime visible to police in the streets, e.g., illegal parking, street-level drug dealing, drunken driving.[10]

■ For crimes that usually occur out of view of the street (murder, rape, assault), police patrol makes little difference.[11]

■ Police deter crime in enclosed environments, like subway cars or subway stations.

■ The cost of police, relative to the financial cost of the crimes they deter, is very high.

So to the question "Do the police prevent crime?" the answer must be "Yes, but...." The "buts" include only certain crimes under certain circumstances and at great cost. For example, in 1965, New York City increased police patrols in subway trains and stations. Crime went down, but the cost of the patrol was such that each deterred felony cost the city $35,000—and that was in 1965 dollars, the equivalent of roughly $100,000 per deterred felony today.[12] As a Maryland police chief summarized the relationship between the police and crime, "We are not letting the public in on our era's dirty little secret: that there is little the police can do."[13] (Street cops, of course, may think otherwise. In their view, they could do some-

TABLE 13-1 •

"HOW MUCH CONFIDENCE DO YOU HAVE IN THE ABILITY OF THE POLICE TO PROTECT YOU FROM VIOLENT CRIME?"

	GREAT DEAL/QUITE A LOT	NOT VERY MUCH	NOT AT ALL
NATIONAL	45%	45%	9%
RACE			
WHITE	47	43	9
NONWHITE	33	53	13
REGION			
EAST	51	40	9
MIDWEST	53	39	8
SOUTH	42	48	9
WEST	35	53	11

Source: Data from The Gallup Organization, Inc., in Maguire and Pastore, *Sourcebook—1993*, p. 165.

thing about crime if only the courts or the police management "downtown" would let them.)

The ineffectiveness of the police may not be such a secret after all. As Table 13–1 shows, the majority of Americans have little or no confidence in the ability of police to protect them. The table also shows understandable differences between blacks and whites and a curiously high rate of skepticism in the South and West.

Perhaps in recognition of the relative ineffectiveness of police patrols as a deterrent, some police departments have developed special teams often called anticrime units. My first reaction on hearing of these was to ask, "Aren't *all* police anticrime?" In fact, the name acknowledges the "dirty little secret" that most police on general patrol have little effect on crime. The idea behind these units is not deterrence but incapacitation—getting the worst criminals off the streets. By going after habitual offenders, career criminals, or dangerous offenders, the police would be getting the most crime reduction for each arrest. Here, at last, is something that matches our TV image of cops. ("We know Smith's a one-man crime wave, so we just stake out his usual places, wait for him to make his move, then we nail him.") The idea sounds good, but the results have not always been encouraging.

Making arrests is not the problem. The special units do arrest criminals, nearly all of them for felonies. But arrests do not keep criminals off the streets; convictions and sentences do. However, only about a third of the arrests made by anticrime units result in convictions. This seems paradoxical. The anticrime unit is collaring the worst criminals, the ones that prosecutors and judges as well as police want to put away. Still, two out of every three of these criminals "walk." Why?

One reason is that although it's easy to arrest a criminal for *something*, it's much harder to catch him for a serious crime. Suppose that the police have identified Criminal Smith as a repeat offender and make him a target for arrest. Officers in the special unit may be so intent on arresting Smith that they are willing to bring him in for a less serious offense or for a crime with flimsy evidence. The district attorney looks at the case and either lets it drop or must bargain it down to a less serious charge.

Because of the small percentage of "quality" arrests, these special programs may have problems of cost efficiency and the department winds up spending a lot of money for a few good arrests. For example, in Washington, D.C., sixty-two officers worked on a repeat offender project (ROP); by the end of the year, they had produced sixty-six convictions, or only about one per officer per year.[14] Even so, not all of these convictions were for felonies. In 1981, only 19 percent of the arrests produced felony convictions. Even with innovative improvements in the next two years, the ROP still got felony convictions in only one of every four arrests. Thirty-eight percent of the repeat offenders received misdemeanor time, and 37 percent were released outright.[15] The ROP officers may have nabbed serious offenders, but they could not get them for serious crimes. In Kansas City, the police instituted a program that aimed specifically for quality arrests; the goal was to convict career criminals for serious crimes. But the special unit netted only six such convictions, and the police power spent on the project amounted to 240,000 hours. That is, each conviction cost an average of 40,000 officer hours—the equivalent of one officer working twenty years.[16]

ABOUT CRIME & CRIMINOLOGY

Using the police to prevent violence by strangers has a long, if not always noble, history.

In the 1930s ... New York police operated "Strong Arm Squads" against violent criminals ... just as other jurisdictions operated "Goon Squads." The target "goons" ... were probably contract workers who committed stranger violence against people who had broken business deals or failed to pay extortion money. The preventive action consisted of beating the goon up, taking his gun away, and telling him to leave town or at least watch his step.

Detroit maintained a similar tradition well into the 1960s with the "Cruiser" unit.... Its demise was followed shortly by the creation of the STRESS unit (Stop the Robberies—Enjoy Safe Streets). Its record of killing black suspects (and nonsuspects), if not of reducing crime, made the unit a central issue in the next mayoral campaign.... The results included the election of Detroit's first black mayor and abolition of the unit.

Source: Lawrence W. Sherman, "Attacking Crime: Policing and Crime Control," in Michael Tonry and Norval Morris, eds., *Modern Policing* (Chicago: University of Chicago Press, 1992), pp. 184–185.

Outside of such special units, the ordinary officers patrolling their beats rarely come upon a crime in progress. A 1967 study found that the average Los Angeles officer detected a robbery once every fourteen years, though perhaps this means that the officer's presence does deter (or at least delay) the criminal.[17] But even if the police are something of a deterrent, this crime prevention is not readily visible to the naked eye. By definition, a prevented crime is one that would have taken place but didn't, and it's very hard to see something that didn't happen. The cynical student I quoted saw cops sitting in the doughnut shop and concluded that they were loafing. He could not see quite so easily that just by sitting there, they may also have been keeping the doughnut shop from being robbed or from being disrupted by rowdy customers. This insight, however, was probably not lost on the owner, who was only too glad to provide the police with coffee and doughnuts at no charge.[18]

However, even the police may find it frustrating that most of their crime prevention is invisible. Aside from the doughnuts, it goes unrewarded and unrecognized even in departmental reports. "You can't put down the number of times you prevented a burglary by parking the radio car in the right place and questioning a guy in the street. It's not on the radio. It's never known."[19]

This officer is suggesting that it's not so much the quantity of police patrol that deters crime; it's the quality—what the officer actually does. Several studies back him up. In some cities, the police are more aggressive; they give out more traffic tickets, arrest more people for minor violations like disorderly conduct, and make more field interrogations—that is, questioning suspicious-looking people. It turns out that these tactics have an impact not just on public-order offenses and traffic violations but on predatory crimes like robbery as well. In a controlled study in San Diego in the early 1970s, in the sector that stopped its field interrogations for nine months, suppressible crimes (those that might be deterred by field stops—robbery, burglary, auto theft, malicious mischief, etc.) increased from 75 to 104 per month, nearly a 40 percent increase. When field interrogations were reinstated, the number of these crimes receded to previous levels.[20]

Unless you look at the statistics, which few people do, an increase or decrease of twenty-five crimes a month may still be hard to perceive. In any case, crime prevention remains the less dramatic component in the crime-fighting image of the police. It's certainly not good material for TV shows. Catching criminals, on the other hand, comes much closer to our idea of what real police work is all about. We want cops and robbers, where the cops nab the bad guy. But do they?

CATCHING CRIMINALS

When I said at the beginning of this chapter that the police do not catch criminals, I was, of course, exaggerating. The police do catch criminals. In 1993, police officers in the United States made 14 million arrests (see Table 13–2). The category with the highest total arrests was "driving under the influence" (1.5 million). Another 3 million arrests were for simple assault, disorderly conduct, liquor law violations, and drunkenness, offenses for which arrest is often used as a means of handling a situation or keeping order. Arrests for vagrancy and loitering also used to contribute to this category, but court decisions from the 1970s have greatly restricted the use of vagrancy and loitering laws. The police did make 2.8 million arrests for Index crimes, but these produced a **clearance rate** of only 21 percent. That is, of all Index offenses, known to the police, one in five resulted in an arrest.[21] Whether .210 is a good batting average is a matter of opinion. But what lies behind these 2.8 million Index crime arrests? How do the police manage to catch criminals at all? Let's start by looking at how criminals were caught before cities had police forces.

CRIMINALS WITHOUT POLICE   The first city police force that we might recognize as such did not come into existence until 1829 in London. By then, the population of London had grown to over 1 million, and street crime and riots occurred with alarming regularity. In the United States, Boston organized a small police force in 1837, patterned after that of London. Several other cities followed in the late 1840s. At that time, there were at least a dozen cities with populations over 25,000, and they, too, could be fairly rough places. Before cities had a regular police force, who caught the criminals? Who made arrests?

For the most part in nineteenth-century America, the responsibility for solving crimes fell on the victims. There were constables, but they were really more like servants of the court than servants of the people. A person who had been wronged could go to court and swear out a warrant. The victim would take the warrant to the constable and tell him who had committed the offense and where that offender might be found. The constable would then make the arrest. Not only the solution of the crime but even the administrative costs of processing the case fell to the victim.

TABLE 13-2 •
TOTAL ESTIMATED ARRESTS,[a] UNITED STATES, 1993

TOTAL[b]	**14,036,300**	EMBEZZLEMENT	12,900
MURDER AND	23,400	STOLEN PROPERTY; BUYING, RECEIVING,	158,100
NONNEGLIGENT		POSSESSING	
MANSLAUGHTER		VANDALISM	313,000
FORCIBLE RAPE	38,420	WEAPONS; CARRYING, POSSESSING, ETC.	262,300
ROBBERY	173,620	PROSTITUTION AND COMMERCIALIZED VICE	97,800
AGGRAVATED ASSAULT	518,670	SEX OFFENSES (EXCEPT FORCIBLE RAPE	
BURGLARY	402,700	AND PROSTITUTION)	104,100
LARCENY-THEFT	1,476,300	DRUG ABUSE VIOLATIONS	1,126,300
MOTOR VEHICLE THEFT	195,900	GAMBLING	17,300
ARSON	19,400	OFFENSES AGAINST FAMILY AND CHILDREN	109,100
		DRIVING UNDER THE INFLUENCE	1,524,800
		LIQUOR LAWS	518,500
VIOLENT CRIME[c]	754,110	DRUNKENNESS	726,600
PROPERTY CRIME[d]	2,094,300	DISORDERLY CONDUCT	727,000
CRIME INDEX TOTAL[e]	2,848,400	VAGRANCY	28,200
		ALL OTHER OFFENSES	3,518,700
		SUSPICION (NOT INCLUDED IN TOTALS)	14,100
OTHER ASSAULTS	1,144,900	CURFEW AND LOITERING LAW VIOLATIONS	100,200
FORGERY AND	106,900	RUNAWAYS	180,500
COUNTERFEITING			
FRAUD	410,700		

[a]Arrest totals based on all reporting agencies and estimates for unreported areas.
[b]Because of rounding, figures may not add to totals.
[c]Violent crimes are offenses of murder, forcible rape, robbery, and aggravated assault.
[d]Property crimes are offenses of burglary, larceny-theft, motor vehicle theft, and arson.
[e]Includes arson.

Source: Federal Bureau of Investigation, *Crime in the United States: The Uniform Crime Reports, 1993* (Washington, DC: 1994).

England had a similar system but coupled it with a cash reward—the equivalent of over a thousand dollars today—for people who caught felons. The reward system gave rise to the specialized occupation of **thief-taker**. Ideally, thief-takers would catch thieves and collect a reward from the government; or they would deal directly with the victim, catching the thief and, for a fee, returning the stolen property.

ARRESTS: WHO SOLVES THE CRIME?   The modern system of catching criminals is, at least in principle, much different. The responsibility now belongs not to the victim or private thief-takers but to the agents of the state, namely, the police. The police are specialists in this enterprise and are therefore presumably much better at it. Television shows provide endless examples of well-planned murders, organized crime, or high-level drug deals—crimes that often require specialized police work. Street crimes like robbery, larceny, or burglary do sometimes crop up in movies or TV shows, but here too the media portray crime solving as clever criminals being outwitted by even more clever and hard-working cops. Through sophisticated techniques of forensic science—fingerprints, ballistics, and so on—the detectives manage to figure out the identity of the killer or burglar, or they arrange to be in the right place at the right time to catch a robber in the act. Through it all, the citizens stand aside and watch with respect and gratitude as the police nail the bad guy. Reinforcing this idea of the cop as a crime-fighting specialist, the media usually have the plainclothes detectives doing all the real police work while the uniformed patrol officers play secondary roles.

To assess the reality of this picture, researchers have looked not just at the most spectacular cases but also at a more representative sample of the crimes reported to the police. The conclusion from these studies is that most arrests result from very routine and unexciting methods.

In real life, in contrast to the TV image, it is the citizen or the patrol cop, not the detective, who usually solves the crime. A RAND study of detectives found that in 30 percent of solved crimes, the officer arriving at the scene of the crime makes the arrest, either because citizens have stopped the criminal or because the criminal is still roaming the area. More to the point, in *half* of all crimes cleared by arrest, "the perpetrator is known when the crime report is first taken, and the main jobs for the investigator are to locate the perpetrator, take him or her into custody, and assemble the facts needed to present charges in court."[22] In other words, the most common way in which crimes are solved very much resembles the methods of the prepolice era: The victim or a witness tells the officer who did it; the officer goes and makes the arrest. Things haven't changed much in 200 years.

A surprisingly large proportion of crimes involve family members and acquaintances. Only 14 percent of murders are clearly between strangers (in another 40 percent, the victim-offender relationship is unknown).[23] A New York study found that about one-third of the arrests for burglary or robbery involved crimes between people who knew each other. (When the victim does not know the offender, the police are less likely to make an arrest, so statistics based on arrests tend to inflate the true number of crimes between people who know each other.) Consider the following robbery:

> A woman reports that her sister and her sister's boyfriend assaulted her, threatened to kill her baby, and took her purse and $40. Later, she explains that it was a misunderstanding. Previously the boyfriend had bought the woman a baby carriage; she had thought it was a gift, but he did not. The crime was his attempt to get what he thought was rightfully his.[24]

Burglaries, too, may be ways to settle personal scores. An angry man breaks into his ex-wife's house, steals her clothes, and drives them to his new home several hundred miles away.[25] Even burglaries intended for profit may have this element of personal revenge that makes them easier to solve. John Allen, the street criminal, says of his early burglaries, "We always tried to get the dude that the neighbors didn't like too much or the guy that was hard on people who lived in the neighborhood.... I like to think that all the places we ... broke into was kind of like the bad guys."[26]

OTHER CRIMES, OTHER METHODS   In most burglaries and robberies, victims or witnesses cannot immediately identify the criminal. Many of these crimes are "cold"—that is, the police arrive too late to arrest a suspect, and the victim cannot name the criminal—and most of them are not solved. In New York City, police manage to clear only 2 percent of these cold cases,[27] though other cities may have slightly more success. However, even when the police do solve these crimes, their investigations rarely resemble the glamorous or high-tech detective work that makes for exciting television. The methods are almost always routine.

In crimes where the victim has seen the criminal, if any procedure can lead to an arrest it is the routine method of having the victim look through mug shots. For other crimes, the routine methods include tracing gun ownership or pawn shop slips, checking a person's identification against a list of persons wanted on outstanding warrants, and checking auto registrations against a hot-car file. Many other reported auto thefts are solved when the officer asks the victim three questions: Did you lend the car to anyone? Might a relative or friend have borrowed it? Could it have been repossessed for nonpayment?[28] These rather unspectacular techniques resolve more cases and produce far more arrests than does intensive detective work. Sophisticated techniques like fingerprinting account for only about 2 percent of all crimes solved.[29] In fact, a police detective whose house has been burglarized probably would not want the fingerprint squad to come in. They rarely get a usable print, and they leave a big mess.[30] Even if the police do get a fingerprint, it becomes useful only *after* they have a suspect. They can then match the suspect's prints against the one found at the crime scene. But if they don't have a suspect, checking the fingerprint against all existing prints on file is a hopeless task. Only if the crime is particularly important will the police go to such extraordinary lengths.

Today, fingerprinting brings results in only a small percentage of cases. In the future, however, now that computers can be programmed to read and match fingerprints, searching for this kind of physical evidence may become much more worthwhile. Computers also may speed up the tedious search through mug shots.[31] Similar technological advances have turned hot-car checks, ID checks, and weapons tracing into routine procedures.[32] Even these advances will probably do little to make real crime solving more like television, with its glamorized and fashionably dressed detectives. Detectives have their place in the small minority of hard-to-solve crimes that receive extraordinary attention. But for most crimes, if they are solved at all, the patrol officer who arrives first at the scene to interview the victims and witnesses will be the one who gets the valuable information. The detective's job is usually not so much to solve the crime but to gather evidence that will convict the suspect. Patrick Murphy, who has been chief of police departments in Detroit, New York City, and Washington, D.C., puts it more bluntly. A *Newsweek* article quotes him as saying, "The truth about detectives is that ... they are not likely to be effective police officers." The article continues to paraphrase the chief: "They [detectives] spend much of their time in bars, supposedly seeking information, or buttering up politicians and the press, which gives them strong allies when they need to resist reform."[33]

Keeping the Peace

Let us return to the original question, "Why do we have police?" To enforce laws? To prevent crime? To catch criminals? Police officers' enforcement of laws is very selective, their effectiveness in preventing crime is at best hard to demonstrate, and their ability to catch predatory criminals depends mostly on the help of civilians. The police do perform all these functions, but not to the extent that we might think, though it's not exactly clear what we think of the police. Most people express support and approval of them, but four out of ten Americans rate the police as "only fair" or "poor" at preventing crime and catching criminals.[34] Of course, somebody has to do these things, even if imperfectly; but somebody also had to do them in the centuries before 1830. So why do we have police?

One way of answering the question is to look at the origins of the police. If we understand why this institution came into being, perhaps we also can understand something about why it continues to exist. Of course, we must also trace the evolution of the police to see what has changed and what has remained the same.

THE NEW POLICE—LONDON

The uniformed, patrolling police force is a relatively recent invention. It was not until 1829 that London instituted the first version of what we now take for granted—a uniformed, patrolling police force. The idea quickly caught on in America, and by the 1870s, most U.S. cities had police forces.[35] Obviously, the police force was an idea whose time had come. But why? Cities had existed for centuries, and as early as 1750, there had been proposals in England for an urban police force. But it was nearly another hundred years before the idea was put into practice. Why had people resisted their formation? What other institutions allowed cities to get by for so long without them? And what was happening in the nineteenth century to make police forces acceptable or even desirable?

To a great extent, the prepolice era depended on private means for doing the work that today is done by the police. Catching criminals was the responsibility either of the individual or of the community collectively. In London there were private detective agencies and thief-takers. In the countryside, the system resembled the posse of the American West. When the parish constable needed help in putting down a disturbance or chasing a criminal, he would "raise the hue and cry," and all men in the parish were required by law to come to his assistance.[36]

The job of catching criminals, then, did not belong to a single, specialized occupation; neither did the responsibility for crime prevention, which was also largely a matter for the individual or the community. The most common form of crime prevention—the precursor of the cop patrolling a beat—was the **watch system**. The person on watch walked about the town on the lookout for fires and other dangers, including disturbances and suspicious persons. In some towns, the watch had the power to arrest people and hold them until a hearing the next morning. He might also ring bells, call the hour ("eleven o'clock and all's well"), or light the lamps. It was not an attractive job, and in some towns men were forced to serve by a sort of draft: Any male over 18 was liable to serve for a period of time or pay someone to substitute for him. In most towns, the wage was low and, consequently, so was the quality of the watch. Elderly, sleepy, corrupt, or just incompetent, the night watch—since Shakespeare's time and before—has probably provided more comic relief than real security. In London, watchmen were routinely taunted and occasionally murdered by rich young men, who thought it great sport. As a result, the watchmen tended to spend much of their time out of sight—an understandable strategy but hardly an effective deterrent to crime.[37] In Boston, the watch was so ineffective that merchants either paid for extra watchmen or hired their own private patrols.[38]

In any case, the system did little to reduce crime. By some accounts, London in the 1780s was a far more dangerous place than any present-day American city, although the actual amount of crime is a matter of dispute among historians and criminologists.[39] At the very least, many influential people at the time saw crime as a widespread problem. From time to time, crime waves would seize public attention and create an atmosphere of crisis. One such crisis arose in the 1730s, when gin became widely available. Previously, the only liquors available (mostly brandy) were upper-class drinks, too expensive for the masses, who got by with less potent beverages like ale. But the availability of cheap gin democratized drinking, and the new drunkenness among the poor caused some alarm. In the view of the wealthy, gin had brought new levels of violence, crime, laziness, family disruption, and general moral and physical decay to great numbers of people. In response, the government passed anti-gin laws, which had little effect on the flow of gin but did add a new source of corruption for the constabulary.[40] (You may have noticed that the gin crisis of London in the 1730s sounds a lot like the drug crisis of the United States in the 1980s: A drug of the wealthy (cocaine) becomes democratized in potent form (crack); the elites (lawmakers et al., greatly aided by the media) declare a crisis and call for more severe penalties and more law enforcement. It is an open question whether the similarity lies more in the nature of the drugs and their effects or in the relations between social classes.)

In addition to the continual presence of crime, riots, too, posed a regular danger. Since the poor and even the middle class were largely powerless (they still did not have the right to vote), they made their position known through riots: riots over specific issues like wages or the price of bread; politically motivated riots, like the extremely violent, anti-Catholic Gordon riots of 1780; and riots based on vague, general feelings—"the belief in a rough sort of social justice, which prompts the poor to settle accounts with the rich by smashing their windows, or burning their property," as occurred in the 1760s and 1780s.[41]

Yet despite all this crime and rioting, and despite several royal commissions on police and legal reform, London still did not replace the watch system with uniformed police until 1829. And the reason behind their reluctance is important: Upper and lower classes alike saw the police as a threat to political liberty.

Those who resisted the establishment of a police force believed that there was an inherent conflict between the power of the state and the freedom of the people. If the state were granted more power—in the form of a police force that could, for purposes of controlling crime, intrude into people's lives—freedom would be diminished. Their fears are well grounded. In principle, a police force may be a neutral enforcer of the law, but it can also use its extraordinary power to keep tyrannical governments in power. The police have always been such a danger, and they still are. Look at any dictatorship today and you will see a regime that depends on its police, uniformed or secret, to suppress opposition. In Haiti under the Duvaliers, the most hated symbol of tyranny was the *tonton macoutes*, the secret police. In the relatively nonviolent revolutions in eastern Europe in 1989–1990, the people were most vengeful toward the secret police—the *stasi* in East Germany, the *securitate* in Romania. Similarly, in England and America in 1800, people feared the authoritarian use of the police; and to confirm their fears they had only to look at France, where the police acted as spies, informers, and *agents provocateurs*, brutally stifling political dissent. Americans wary of police could also look at their own recent history as colonies policed in part by the British army.[42]

Overcoming such resistance required a combination of historical factors. The creation of the London police force, like any historical change, arose from a combination of large social forces and the efforts of individuals. The social changes, which had been building for a long time, involved the rise of both the lower and middle classes. Large numbers of peasants, forced off the land by government policies, had come to the city, where they formed an urban lower class uprooted from the traditional village forms of social control. The upper classes felt threatened by the crime and rioting they associated with the "dangerous classes." In addition, a changing economy had expanded the middle class—merchants and professionals, whose business demanded a more regulated, coordinated, and orderly society, rather than one marked by unpredictable outbreaks of riot, disorder, and violence.

As for the individuals involved, the person credited with creating the police was the young Home Secretary, Robert Peel. To win passage of the law creating the new police force, Peel had to overcome popular fears about possible police repression. He had excellent credentials for the task. Earlier in his career, he had worked for the reform of the old criminal laws. Prior to Peel's efforts, a person could be hanged for crimes as minor as theft of much-needed food, and the fate of a person convicted of a crime often depended on the whim of the judge.[43] Like these reforms, his plan for the new police also served to allay fears of arbitrary and cruel government power. The law creating the police imposed three important limitations on this new force.

- The police were to be unarmed. They carried truncheons but no firearms.

  This provision meant that the officers would have to rely on their authority, not their power. Authority, unlike power, depends on its acceptance by the other person. Unarmed, the police cannot act unless the people accept their role as legitimate.

- The police were to be uniformed.

  This requirement obviously kept the police from being used as political spies or informers.

■ The police were to be confined to preventive patrol.

They were there principally to keep order. Only to a much lesser extent were they criminal catchers or crime solvers. They were more like the watch, except that they would patrol both day and night, and, it was hoped, they would be more effective.[44]

Thanks to Peel's good political sense in limiting police power, a police force was established. More important, from the very first the London police officers did their job in a professional manner—fair, impartial, impersonal, detached, and relatively incorrupt. After a short while, they won fairly wide approval. The people of London even invented two affectionate terms for them—nicknames derived from the name of their founder: *Peelers* or (the one that stuck) *bobbies*.

THE POLICE IN AMERICA

The image of the London bobby—unarmed, impartial, restrained, going by the book—stands in contrast to the image of his American counterpart. Perhaps you know the picture I have in mind: the (usually) Irish cop who knows everybody in the neighborhood and runs his beat pretty much the way he wants to. He got his job through political patronage, carries a gun, deals out street justice with his nightstick, and takes payoffs from various crooks operating in the area. This image has much basis in reality, especially for nineteenth-century America.[45] As professional as the bobbies appeared, American police officers seemed the opposite. New York City police even wore street clothes rather than uniforms. Not until ten years after the force was founded, and with the patrolmen still protesting, did the commissioners succeed in imposing the blue symbol of discipline. The police also became known for their tendencies toward brutality and corruption, misdeeds that largely went unpunished.[46]

For all their differences, the London and New York police shared one important similarity—the reason for their existence. They were needed to impose a more orderly existence on riotous sections of the population. As the economy and urban society became more complex, the need for order increased. At this time, America, too, had its "dangerous classes," and respectable folk welcomed a police force to deal with them. In part, the dangerous classes consisted of tramps and paupers (what today we call the homeless). For them, the police might provide lodging for a night or two and then force them to move out of town.[47] But from the perspective of the middle class—white, Protestant, nondrinking, and clinging to an image of America as small town or rural—the dangerous classes also included the immigrant, urban poor. Their threat lay not just in their higher rates of predatory crime. The years in which more and more cities felt the need to establish police forces—roughly from 1840 to 1870—were probably the most riotous decades in U.S. history, and the chronic threat of civil disorder raised fears that the dangerous classes might undermine the entire political system.

The urban industrial revolution of the nineteenth century simply demanded more orderly, rational, cooperative behavior than the previous economic system, in which farmers, craftsmen, and small merchants operated in relative independence. In a preindustrial society, high levels of drunkenness, and erratic or violent behavior hurt only those most immediately involved. In an industrializing society, in contrast, they were intolerable, as the work of each, in mill or office, was dependent on the predictable behavior of others. The state was called in then, and cops in part created to help tame a formerly unruly population—with special emphasis on drunkenness, the kind of victimless crime that private citizens did not prosecute on their own.[48]

The urban immigrants were largely the Irish, who voted Democratic, and the slogan labeling the Democrats as the party of "Rum, Romanism, and Rebellion" neatly summarizes these fears. The issue for "nativist" Americans was not just a different view of drinking (rum) or a different religion (Romanism); it was rebellion, the stability of the whole society. (By analogy, imagine Jesse Jackson winning the Democratic presidential nomination and the Democrats being labeled the party of "Race and Rap, Crack and Chaos." The phrase is less succinct than its nineteenth-century counterpart, but it does convey the ethnically based fear and resentment directed at the urban poor.)

The police were a response to this threat. They were there to keep the civic peace. They wound up doing many other things—finding lost children, catching criminals, putting down labor strikes, and so on—but the original reason for existence was to preserve social order.

THE POLICE AND THE POLITICS OF ORDER

Preserving order or keeping the peace sounds like a politically neutral activity, hardly a matter for debate. But in reality, policing is neutral only when there is substantial agreement about social matters among all members of society. What happens, though, when some people think that current social arrangements are not right and that there is systematic injustice? What happens when these people agitate for social change?

Usually, when such conflict arises, the police find themselves protecting the status quo. They are ultimately representatives of the state, the government, and when people challenge its legitimacy the police naturally find themselves opposing the challenge. That is their job. They do that job not in the name of some political ideology—police officers do not see themselves as oppressing minorities or stifling social change—but in their traditional role as crime fighters, peacekeepers, and law enforcers. The police see themselves as neutral, enforcing the law and keeping order, but in effect they are conservative—conservative in the literal sense of conserving things as they are. The politically conservative function of the police seems fairly clear in totalitarian societies, where they represent the interests of the government against those who seek change. To outsiders it may seem clear that they are repressing politically uncomfortable ideas and the people who express them. But there as elsewhere, the police probably believe sincerely that they are protecting society: controlling crime, maintaining order, and enforcing the law. Certainly, those in authority justify police work in the name of these legitimate and seemingly neutral goals.

In democracies also, conflict usually puts the police on the side of the establishment. In the United States in the mid-nineteenth century, preserving

IN THE NEWS

The existence of the police—the branch of the government allowed to use force—always poses the possibility of the expansion of government power at the expense of the people's freedoms. In some cases, a more effective police force means a more tyrannical government. This threat of tyranny looms especially large in countries with little or no democratic tradition. After the United States invaded Haiti in 1994 to restore a democratically elected president, some people looked to the police to protect democracy. In the opinion of Charles Maechling, Jr., a former State Department official, such a view is dangerously optimistic.

The pentagon is still committed to "professionalizing" the Haitian police.... Yet we have been down this road before in other countries, with unhappy results....

In 1963 ... the Public Safety program ... got caught up in the Kennedy Administration's obsession with countries confronting left-wing political movements.

Endowed with an internal-security mission, and "professionalization" being the watchword, it offered equipment and training in radio communications, riot control and automatic firearms to police officers of South Vietnam, Thailand, Colombia, El Salvador and Iran....

The Public Safety Program represented an unthinking projection of a conventional police force into environments where policemen have often been the harsh enforcers of a repressive class structure....

To the recipients, "professionalization" meant squad cars, two-way radios, record-keeping systems and modern command-and-control—all the apparatus for setting up a police state....

When over the next two decades the military in several Latin American countries overthrew civilian governments and established murderous dictatorships, it should have been no surprise that

modernized police forces became the front line of state terrorism.

In Argentina, Chile, El Salvador and Guatemala, to name only a few countries, the police engaged in the systematic torture, murder and "disappearance" of dissidents who were only tenuously, if at all, associated with guerrilla movements. The notorious death squads were mostly off-duty officers in unmarked vehicles....

The former New York City Police commissioner, Raymond Kelly, who is leading a team of monitors in Haiti, remarked that the crime rate there is not particularly high and in fact is much better than in many U.S. cities. It follows that we should limit the role of the Haitian police to community law enforcement. The last thing Haiti needs is a police force with high-tech equipment ready and waiting for the next despotic regime.

Source: Charles Maechling, Jr., "Can't Haiti's Cops Just Fight Crime?" *New York Times,* November 29, 1994, p. A25.

---

order meant enforcing the position of the established Protestant majority against the threat posed by the immigrant, urban Irish. Later, it meant protecting the interests of the owners of factories and mines against union organizers and striking workers. In the 1950s and 1960s, police in the South enforced segregationist Jim Crow laws against civil rights workers. During the Vietnam War, they confronted antiwar demonstrators—all in the name of maintaining order and enforcing the law.

Much has changed over the years. The police cultivated their image as crime fighters rather than peacekeepers, and they managed to separate themselves from the obvious politics of urban political machines. (In the nineteenth century, the officer's principle loyalty was not to the law, the city, or the people but to the political party that gave him his job.) However, regardless of party politics, the police force, as an arm of the state, is a conservative political force. The bulk of police work still consists of preserving order, and when there is social conflict, that means preserving the status quo.

POLICE MISCONDUCT—GUARDING THE GUARDS

BRUTALITY AND THE USE OF FORCE

When a society grants the police the right to use force, it also creates the possibility for the misuse or excessive use of force. In the United States, brutality was a part of policing from the very beginning. Dispensing street justice has always been simpler than making an arrest, especially before the police had call boxes and might have to walk a prisoner a mile to the station house. In Chicago of the 1880s, "It was not customary for a policeman to arrest anyone for a small matter. The hickory had to be used pretty freely."[49]

From time to time, reformers would investigate and find systematic brutality. In 1903, a former police commissioner spoke of a "procession of citizens with broken heads and bruised bodies…. Many of them had done nothing to deserve an arrest…. The police are practically above the law."[50] Yet for long periods of time, police brutality received little attention in the press and even among sociologists. A doctoral thesis published in the 1950s was virtually the only scholarly research on the topic, and it was all but ignored for fifteen years. The general public may have been dimly aware of police brutality, but there was little demand to stop it. The people on the receiving end of the violence were generally poor and powerless: street criminals, drunks, homosexuals, juveniles, the mentally disturbed, and the homeless—people who could not or would not make an issue of it.

Public opinion has usually been complacent about the police use of force, especially when crime rates are high. In the 1993 poll shown in Table 13–3, over three-quarters of the people approved of a police officer "striking" a man, which is not quite the same thing as brutality, and asking about "any situations you can imagine" leaves much to the imagination of the respondent. Nevertheless, the poll shows that those in position of greater social power—the wealthier, the white, and the male—are more tolerant of the use of force by the police.

In the 1960s, police violence came to public attention inescapably and in a way that often tarnished the image of the police. In the early 1960s, millions of Americans saw TV news film of Southern police using violence against civil rights workers—blacks and whites who wanted nothing more than to register to vote or eat a hamburger at Woolworth's. Against them, preserving the status quo and Jim Crow, were the police, using tear gas, fire hoses, cattle prods, attack dogs, and clubs. Later in the decade, the media brought pictures of

TABLE 13-3 •

"ARE THERE ANY SITUATIONS YOU CAN IMAGINE IN WHICH YOU WOULD APPROVE OF A POLICEMAN STRIKING AN ADULT MALE CITIZEN?"

	YES	NO
NATIONAL	77%	22%
SEX		
MALE	81	16
FEMALE	68	27
RACE		
WHITE	77	19
BLACK	51	40
INCOME		
$50,000 AND OVER	83	16
$30,000–$49,999	74	23
$20,000–$29,999	77	20
UNDER $20,000	65	29

Source: Data from NORC in Maguire and Pastore, *Sourcebook—1993*, pp. 168–169.

urban riots. In some cases, riots began when police, making an arrest in a black ghetto, used more force than the people thought appropriate and some observers and participants maintained that previous patterns of police brutality were an underlying condition that contributed to the riot.[51] Then in 1968, outside the Democratic presidential convention in Chicago, crowds of antiwar demonstrators (mostly peaceful, mostly white and middle class) were attacked by the Chicago police in what some commentators called a "police riot." It was all on television ("The whole world is watching," chanted the demonstrators), and police brutality became a topic of much greater concern.

Important as these scenes were, they provided little information about violence in everyday police work. When do the police use force, in what situations, against whom, and with what justification? Getting that kind of information requires more systematic observation, not just the spectacular events that make TV news. So in the 1960s, criminologists began to turn their attention not just to criminals but also to the police. In one 1968 study, a team of thirty-six researchers rode with police in high-crime neighborhoods of four large cities for a period of seven weeks. In that time, they saw thirty-seven instances, involving forty-four citizens, where the officers used improper force. About 3 percent of all suspects encountered by police were unnecessarily brutalized. Half the victims suffered bruises but no major injuries. Three citizens had to be hospitalized.[52]

Why do the police abuse people? The reasons haven't changed much since officers first started patrolling. Some cops still see street justice as more

ABOUT CRIME & CRIMINOLOGY

The following excerpt from an interview with a police officer illustrates the different perspectives on police violence—the citizen's view, the legal view, and the cop's view. It also touches on other topics, such as lying, police solidarity, and the officer's sense of isolation, all as part of the police culture each cop learns.

Policemen are taught very early that truth rarely, if ever, can be helpful....

They don't know how much force they can use, so they lie to protect themselves....

The cop gets called into a review board and they ask him, "Did you hit this guy?"

"No, I didn't hit him. I never hit him. Nope....

"There's 19 witnesses here who say you were doing a number on this guy in the street."

"Who you going to believe, those people there or me?...

His PBA lawyer and his PBA delegate are sitting there with him.... He spoke to these two guys and he said, "Look, I banged the guy. I

didn't want to, but the guy was robbing an old lady and he gave me some s—- and I hit him."

"You can't tell them that," the lawyer and the delegate say. "No way. You can't punch him. You can't hit him with your nightstick."

"Then what have I got a nightstick for?"

"You got a nightstick so you can probe with the nightstick. You can't hit somebody over the head with it. Hit them over the head and ... you're trying to kill them. So just say he's lying."

But that cop has every right to use that nightstick. He has every right to hit someone in a situation where he feels threatened or the guy is threatening him. The cop has the right to say, "Hey, I'm forty-nine and I go 145 pounds. I got somebody here six-four and two-thirty or forty. He's going to take me apart. So, yeah, I beat him up. My partner grabbed him and I hit him. It was great." That's okay, that's not bad. You're allowed to do that. But they'll never admit it. Instead, they make up all sorts of stories.

Source: Mark Baker, *Cops: Their Lives in Their Own Words* (New York: Simon & Schuster, 1985), p. 280.

effective and less troublesome than arrest—especially if the officer believes that the punishments imposed by the courts are not certain or severe enough. But brutality is much less likely to stem from these abstract notions of justice and deterrence than from a highly personalized sense of justice. Violence is particularly likely after a chase, fight, shootout, or anything else that might give the cop a "combat high" or "adrenalin rush," as in the Rodney King beating.[53] Cops may inflict severe brutality against people arrested for crimes that offend their own morality: certain sex crimes, crimes against women and children, or assaults against the police.[54] Cops may also use force to get information from suspects. After all, solving crimes is the essence of the real police work that officers rarely get to do. Given the chance to get credit for an arrest, they might be willing to break the rules.

Sometimes violence arises when the person arrested initially challenges the officer or resists arrest. Then, even after he is handcuffed and subdued he may be

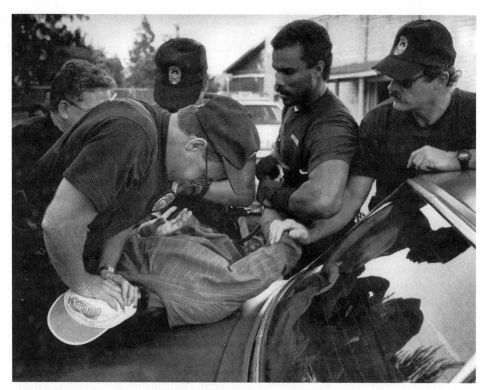

The police, unlike anyone else, have a general right to use force. But how much force? Sometimes, police behavior that civilians and the law define as excessive may be defined by the norms of police culture as legitimate and even noble.

beaten. In one such case, a boy was beaten after the police had taken him to the station house. As one of the cops told the researcher, "On the street you can't beat them. But when you get to the station, you can instill some respect in them."[55]

The officer's comment about respect provides a clue to some of the reasons for police brutality. First, by discussing the action, the officer shows that he thinks it was legitimate. Second, he is also telling us that although civilians on the street would condemn his actions, the other officers in the station house would see the beating as justifiable. It's not that the police approve of *all* violence done to prisoners. Like anyone else, they have a moral code that distinguishes between legitimate and illegitimate violence, between normal and excessive force. "But the police draw the lines in extremely different ways and at different points than do either the court system or the public."[56] This means that most police brutality is not the result of the psychological quirks of a few isolated rotten apples; it is a group phenomenon. The officer commits the brutality in the presence of other officers and sometimes with their assistance. In addition, the morality shared throughout the department not only justifies but also sometimes demands excessive and illegal force. "For the street cop, it is often a graver error to use too little force and develop a 'shaky' reputation than it is to use too much force."[57]

Finally, the officer's emphasis on respect represents one of the most common police justifications for violence. By far the greatest number of brutality cases arise not from actual threats or attacks on the police or even from resisting arrest but rather from "disrespect"—the challenge to the cop's authority.[58] For a person stopped by the police, showing respect may mean the difference between a warning and an arrest or even a few blows with a nightstick. This preoccupation with respect does not mean that our cities are being patrolled by a bunch of Rodney Dangerfields in blue. There is good reason for it. Respect is an acknowledgment of the cop's **authority**, and authority is the most important tool the police have for doing their job.

Remember, people call the police when "something ought not to be happening, about which something ought to be done NOW." Frequently in these situations, the officer must persuade people to do something they would rather not do—and to do it quickly. Whether it's getting spouses to stop assaulting each other or kids to turn down their radio or putting an arrested person into a patrol car or keeping a crowd at bay—whatever the situation, the cop needs to be in control, to maintain his or her "edge,"[59] in order to do the job. Sometimes officers may believe that they must use actual force: "In general, it's the cop who hits first. You say, 'Nah, cops react, they don't act first.' Not if they've been on the street for a while and they know how to handle the situation."[60]

The cop's ultimate weapon in staying on top of the situation is the gun. But the more important and more useful tool is authority—the agreement by the citizen that the officer is to be obeyed. Without authority on the street, suddenly the cop is vulnerable, for despite all the hours of boredom and tasks that are not real police work, there is always the risk of danger. Police lore is full of stories of cops losing control of the situation and ending up at least embarrassed and sometimes seriously injured. But the issue of authority goes beyond personal safety, for in the officer's mind, the authority is also that of the state. Respect confirms the cop's authority and the legitimacy of the state. Disrespect not only carries a threat of injury to the officer but also resonates with undertones of potential chaos for the state. In the eyes of the officer, therefore, the citizen who challenges authority might just as well have made a grab for the officer's gun. Little wonder, then, that the police generally approve of using violence to instill respect, even though the officer is no longer in danger and even though neither the law nor the public generally recognize this as a legitimate use of force.[61]

POLICE CORRUPTION

Eskimos supposedly have fourteen different words for snow. The police vocabulary for corruption is equally rich, and for much the same reason: It is part of the environment. Words meaning corruption include *graft, the pad, taking, bribery, chiseling, mooching, paying with your badge, extortion, shakedown, scoring*, and probably others I do not know. What they all share is that in one way or another, the officer receives something in return for not enforcing the law.

It is impossible to get an accurate measure of police corruption. Observational studies by sociologists or complaints from victims may provide at least a rough estimate of police brutality. But corruption usually has no obvious victim, certainly not one who will complain. Only when there is a full-scale investigation—such as the **Knapp Commission** in New York City in 1970—does the public get an idea of the amount and variety of police corruption. Even so, the measurable part—the dollar value of illegal payments—may be the least important aspect.

> In economic terms, the total impact of police graft is insignificant. The real cost is the degradation of the job, the destruction of morale, the erosion of supervision, and the breakdown of clear standards of what constitutes "good work" which allows some policemen to become criminals in every sense of the word.[62]

As with crime, the least serious forms of police corruption are the most common—variations on the theme of the old cop on the beat who takes an apple from the sidewalk grocery as he walks by. A legitimate business is granting a small favor. In return, the merchant expects the cop to help if the need arises and not to enforce petty laws and ordinances against the merchant. "I used to eat hamburgers and drink coffee in the sector for nothing.... Was it corruption? Yes.... There was a fire hydrant in front of the place ... and we didn't hang tags on [illegally parked cars]."[63]

Officers also learn which stores and movie theaters in their sector will allow them to "pay with the badge." At Christmas time merchants may give them gifts, often cash. Large-scale legitimate businesses may have similar arrangements with the upper levels of the police department or even of city government. A precinct captain who orders officers to ticket the illegally parked trucks at a large distribution center may get a call from "downtown" to "lay off."[64]

Illegal businesses or those that operate on the fringes of the law invite more serious corruption. After-hours bars, gambling, prostitution, drug dealing—all these victimless crimes that fall into the category called vice have long been sources of corruption. In New York, it's called the "pad"; in Philadelphia, the "steady note"; other cities may have still other names, but the idea is always the same: People who sell illegal goods and services pay the police on a regular basis not to enforce the law. The Knapp Commission found the pad to be particularly pervasive among plainclothes divisions. Detectives on the pad would each get from $300 to $1,500 (roughly $1,000 to $5,000 in today's dollars) every month from gambling establishments. Uniformed cops on a pad generally got much smaller amounts—perhaps $20. In addition to a regular pad, detectives sometimes received one-time payoffs called "scores." For example, a narcotics dealer stopped by detectives might offer them a large amount of cash in exchange for retaining his freedom and his inventory. The largest such score uncovered by the Knapp Commission was $80,000; shakedowns for several thousand dollars were also common. Even when the detectives made an arrest, they often would hold back some of the confiscated cash and drugs for themselves.[65]

Nonvice work also brings opportunities for acquiring goods cheaply. Officers arriving at the scene of a burglary might finish the job the burglar had begun. One cop told of a supermarket where

> there had been a legitimate break-in, and one particular detective had been so busy loading the back seat of his car full of hams and picking up sides of beef that he was stumbling and falling down back and forth from the cooler to the alley, and he didn't even know who was around him he was so busy carrying things out.[66]

Of the cops involved in corruption, most settle for the opportunities that come their way in the course of their work. In New York at the time of the Knapp Commission, they were referred to as **grass-eaters**, and most of what they did was condoned by the others in the department. However, the commission also found a smaller number of **meat-eaters**, officers who aggressively sought out sources of illegal income or created their own opportunities. It was a short step from cleaning up after a burglary to planning and carrying out the whole operation, from making drug deals as undercover cops to doing the same thing for personal profit.[67]

EXPLAINING POLICE MISCONDUCT— PERSONALITY AND OPPORTUNITY

The distinction between grass-eaters and meat-eaters implies that individual integrity is important in determining how corrupt, if at all, a cop will be. Certainly, individual character makes a difference, especially with the most corrupt and the most incorruptible. Sociological ideas are not much help in understanding a cop like Frank Serpico, who resisted taking payoffs himself and then risked his life to help expose the widespread corruption among his fellow detectives. Nor can sociological ideas fully explain the cop who is unusually corrupt or sadistic.

However, explanations that look only at individual personality have some important shortcomings. First, these explanations offer little in the way of a solution. Aside from the screening that departments already use, no test yet developed can distinguish those who will make good cops from those who will go beyond the norm in brutality or corruption. Second, even successful screening will do nothing to reduce the payoffs and the use of force that the law and the public see as wrong but which the police accept as normal, acceptable, and even unavoidable. Police misconduct is more than just a few bad apples in an otherwise blemish-free barrel.

Although it's true that some cops are more honest than others, it is also true, and perhaps more important, that some kinds of police work present far more opportunities for corruption than do others. As one Knapp Commission witness said, commenting on the honesty of officers in the Central Park precinct, "What are you going to do—shake down the squirrels?" At the other extreme, in neighborhoods with a flourishing drug trade, officers regularly come across mountains of cash or drugs easily converted to cash—a temptation that often proves irresistible. (Some people think that the FBI managed to remain free of corruption because J. Edgar Hoover deliberately kept it out of those areas that were likely to tempt agents. During most of Hoover's tenure, the FBI concentrated on bank robbery and political subversion, not gambling, drugs, or organized crime.)

For the more common corruption involving street-level criminals and much smaller payoffs, we must look to another aspect of detective work, namely, the relationship between cop and criminal. When an officer arrests a mugger or burglar, neither one has a stake in continuing the relationship, nor will the criminal have much to offer. In narcotics work, however, even the poorest street junkie may be able to offer something the cop legitimately needs: information that will eventually lead to an arrest of top-level dealers. Since the detectives can never know just when the right bit of information may come along or who will have it, they must maintain their relationships with criminal informants. The informant can provide information or introductions to higher-level dealers; the cops can provide immunity from arrest. However, once the relationship is established, cop and criminal are no longer just adversaries; they are also partners. They may then find other things to exchange. Cops can provide drugs to the addict; the addicts, who may also be stealing to support their habit, can offer free stolen merchandise.[68]

WORKING PERSONALITY AND POLICE CULTURE

Previously, I downplayed the importance of the personality the cop brings to the job. Much more important in understanding police behavior (and misbehavior) is the personality the job brings to the cop. That is, police officers, because of their work, develop a particular way of looking at the world, a particular set of attitudes and beliefs, a particular way of thinking and responding. These components closely resemble the psychology textbook definition of personality. But this personality, this way of looking at the world, is too widely shared among police officers to be mainly a matter of individual psychology. Jerome Skolnick called it the officer's **working personality**.[69] It is a product of the experiences the officers have on the job and the understanding of those experiences that they learn from the other cops.

I have already mentioned the central place that authority has in this working personality, and we have seen how it can lead to the use of excessive force. Other types of misconduct can involve other aspects of the working personality. For example, when antivice work requires the police to enforce laws that they themselves violate, the result may be a type of cynicism. Moreover, this cynicism and disillusionment may be deepened by other aspects of police work. Police may become cynical about the criminal justice system when they see criminals they have arrested getting off lightly. They may become disillusioned by their own very limited ability to improve the world they patrol. Being a cop, perhaps more than any other role in society, brings one face to face with the darker side of human nature. Deceit, crime, insanity, misery, suffering, and cruelty are all part of the daily round. "The job runs against every good impulse you ever had.... That's probably the greatest single tragedy that every cop faces. You find out that nothing is on the level. You find out that people die for nothing."[70]

The feeling that nothing is on the level combines with another important element—the sense of danger—to produce another facet of the working personality: suspiciousness. Police are keenly sensitive to things that don't look quite right. They also have a sense of isolation from the general public, the feeling that "nobody loves a cop." Danger, suspicion, and isolation produce one other characteristic—solidarity with other cops.[71]

IN THE NEWS

Two decades after the Knapp Commission report, police corruption in New York City once again began making headlines, and once again, the city formed a commission to hear testimony on the subject. The Mollen Commission of 1993–1994 found that although police corruption had not disappeared, its organization had changed. In addition, it was no longer distinct from police brutality. Corrupt officers were protected by police culture, by the police union (officials of the Police Benevolent Association tried to hinder corruption investigations and tipped off cops who were being investigated), and even by the department's own anticorruption mechanisms, including Internal Affairs.

The problem of police corruption extends far beyond the corrupt cop. It ... has flourished in parts of our city not only because of opportunity and greed, but because of a police culture that exalts loyalty over integrity; because of the silence of honest officers who fear the consequence of "ratting" on another cop no matter how grave the crime; because of willfully blind supervisors who fear the consequences of a corruption scandal more than corruption itself; because of the demise of the principle of accountability that makes all commanders responsible for fighting corruption in their commands; because of a hostility and alienation between the police and community in certain precincts which breeds an "us versus them" mentality, and

because for years the New York City Police Department abandoned its responsibility to insure the integrity of its members....

Twenty years ago, the most common form of corruption was relatively minor. Officers of all ranks took bribes to allow gamblers, prostitutes and others to avoid the law and escape arrest. These "grass-eaters" ... constituted the majority of cops in the department at that time; serious corruption committed by ... "meat-eaters" was relatively rare. Today the situation is reversed.... "Meat-eaters" are the rule rather than the exception among corrupt cops today.

There is nothing today that corresponds to the long-running, institutionally perpetuated "pad" of 20

Since cops generally share this view of the world, there is a considerable overlap between the working personality of the individual cop, on the one hand, and police culture, on the other. To a great extent, the traits of the working personality and the norms and values of police culture are indistinguishable from each other. For example, police solidarity is not just an individual feeling; it emerges as a set of norms, an unwritten code, that governs behavior. A primary rule of this code expresses the norm of solidarity: "Watch out for your partner first, then for the rest of the guys working that tour."[72] Police solidarity grows out of the sense of danger and the need for mutual protection. On the street, protection can mean the difference between safety and injury, or even between life and death. But cops are also vulnerable administratively since all of them have in some way or other violated the rules.

> How the f—- can I tell anyone who ain't a cop that I lie a little in court or that sometimes I won't do s—- on the street 'cause I'm tired.... The only people who can understand are people who've had to pull the same s—- ... and there ain't nobody in this department from the Chief on down who hasn't pulled some tricks in their time on the street.[73]

years ago. And the simplest, most common form of narcotics corruption today—lone officers "stealing" drugs and money from dealers—does not involve much group planning or organization.

Virtually all of the corruption we uncovered, however, involved groups of officers—called "crews" that protect and assist each other's criminal activities. This was accomplished in a variety of ways, including: identifying drug sites; planning raids; forcibly entering and looting drug trafficking locations, and sharing proceeds according to regular and agreed-upon principles....

[A] former police officer ... told the commission how he and various members of his crew of approximately 12 police officers routinely burgled drug locations and beat local residents as well as suspected criminals....

This "crew" corruption displays a new and disturbing form of organization. Whereas pads were standardized and hierarchical—almost bureaucratic—crews are more akin to street gangs: small, loyal, flexible, fast-moving and often hard hitting. They establish areas to plan and discuss their operations. They often structure their legitimate police work to generate the leads they need to locate promising targets. They use police radio network, and code names, to mount and coordinate operations. They often use department equipment to force entry. They manipulate fellow officers, their supervisors and the courts to their advantage. And they fuel each other's corruption through their eagerness to prove their loyalty and toughness to one another.

Oversight of Internal Affairs was virtually nonexistent, intelligence-gathering efforts were negligible, corruption investigations were often deliberately limited and prematurely closed, and the appearance of integrity was more important than the reality. In short, genuine commitment in fighting corruption had virtually disappeared and Internal Affairs had abandoned its mission to remove serious corruption from the department.

Source: The Mollen Commission Report, *New York Times*, July 7, 1994, p. B2.

Solidarity and the sense of isolation also make it almost impossible to get one cop to testify about another's misconduct. Even when an officer's brutality goes far beyond what other officers find acceptable, they still will do nothing to expose the wrongdoer to outside forces. They may avoid that officer, but they won't report him or her. This solution may be adequate for the problem of the officers in the precinct, but it is hardly ideal for the citizenry.

> I told the bosses... "He's crazy.... Let the next guy who comes in work with him."
>
> That's what they did. The new guy would work with him for two months and then the next new guy would work with him for two months. I saw him years later. I was going into a precinct and he was coming out with a prisoner. His prisoner looked like he'd been through a meat grinder.[74]

In some departments, the officer who refuses to take payoffs, like the one who is reluctant to use force, may become suspect in the eyes of others. Supervisors or superiors may shunt the unusually honest cop to some unattractive post. So to our corruption explanations—individual, structural (temptation), and cultural—add one more: the lack of deterrence. The department often has no effective way to combat police misconduct.

There is nothing new here. This combination of factors goes back to the earliest days of the police, and at its worst it can resemble what a journalist wrote in 1869:

> [The police] are compelled to associate with vulgarians and scoundrels of all grades; are exposed to every species of temptation; act unfavorably on each other, and have no restraining influence beyond their own intelligence, which is not very great, and their fear of exposure, which is not probable.[75]

Varieties of policing

So far, I have been treating the police and police departments as though they were all the same. Obviously, they are not. I only wished to point out some of the problems inherent in the institution. Society puts into police care a set of tasks and limitations, what is sometimes called the "police mandate."[76] At the heart of this mandate is the maintenance of order, the essence of everyday police patrolling. It also includes fighting crime and providing certain social services. Different departments serve different kinds of communities, and the balance among the various aspects of the mandate will differ according to the demands of the community.

Several years ago, James Q. Wilson outlined three types of police departments. One style of patrol exists mostly in homogeneous communities. The *service* style, usually found in middle-class suburbs, emphasizes community relations. The department's concern is to patrol against burglaries. It also tries to handle the transgressions of its citizens (offenses involving too much drink, juvenile delinquency, etc.) in a discreet way that does not embarrass or damage them.[77] The *watchman* style of policing represents a kind of holdover from previous eras, dating back to the nineteenth century. The department is closely tied to a political machine, and getting a promotion depends on political connections. The pay is low (officers often moonlight), the training minimal, and the turnover high. The patrolling style stresses order rather than law. Officers follow their own informal ways of getting things done rather than following formal procedures, especially in dealing with juveniles and with minor offenses. The department does not bother illegal businesses like gambling, except perhaps to take payoffs. The cop prefers to avoid trouble and "keep his nose clean." The department's preference, similarly, is not to rock the boat since the department has strong ties to the locally dominant political party.[78]

However, around the turn of the century, progressive reformers offered a new model: the professional police department—a disciplined, militarylike organization with centralized authority, separated from politics, and focused on the impartial enforcement of laws. The movement had some success, and gradually police departments began to adopt some of these reforms. Then in the 1930s, the notion of police reform began to take a narrower focus: the control of crime through the application of scientific knowledge.[79] Several developments gave a boost to this idea. "Criminalistics" (fingerprinting and other crime-detection techniques), telephones, radio cars, the police academy, crime statistics—all these contributed to the image of the cop as a crime-fighting technician.[80] Sergeant Joe Friday of the old "Dragnet" TV series was the perfect example of this image. He dealt only with serious crime, and he did so in a highly efficient, technical way ("Just the facts, Ma'am"). Of course, despite this image, even professional departments must deploy most of their officers in routine patrol.

The result is what Wilson calls the *legalistic* style. Legalistic departments operate by the book. Authority, both within the department and between the officer and the public, is formal, not personal. Officers dealing with minor offenses are more likely to make an arrest than use some informal procedure. The police in legalistic departments are neatly dressed, formal, and polite. The department keeps extensive records, and officers must fill out daily logs and a variety of reports.[81]

BUREAUCRACY AND THE DILEMMA OF PROFESSIONALISM

In practice, every department will be a combination of these styles. What will vary will be the proportions in the mixture. Given the mandate of police in a large and diverse city, no style of department or patrol will be perfect. Each solution will create its own particular problems. The pitfalls of the watchman style are fairly easy to see, especially in light of the historical record. But the professional model, with its legalistic style, also has its shortcomings. The most serious is that it does not fit well with what the police are most often called on to do. Remember, most police calls do not involve crime. They involve disorder, where frequently no crime has been committed—the sort of trouble where a watchman would intervene. But if the police take a purely legalistic approach, they end up shortchanging the traditional watchman tasks, and it is these peacekeeping tasks, not crime fighting, that make people feel safer.[82]

> There are no streetlamps to light anymore, but there are a large number of constabulary functions—maintaining order in public places (parks, buses, subway platforms), resolving marital disputes, disciplining noncriminal but harmful juvenile behavior, preventing public drug and alcohol use—which no other public organizations have taken up since they were abandoned by the police. These jobs simply are not done.[83]

This quotation overstates the case. The police mandate still includes maintaining public order. The trouble is that the professional, legalistic style of policing is ill suited to these tasks. Police professionalism works on a bureaucratic model, and bureaucracy means, among other things, playing it by the book. This phrase, "playing it by the book," implies a set of rules and procedures that the worker learns and then uses in dealing with the various cases that come up. The worker sees how the specifics of each case fit with the rules and then acts accordingly.

The principle involved here is called **universalism**, and it is the basis of the rule of law and of fairness. It places the law above any particular individual. It applies the same set of rules equally to all people, regardless of race, social class, sex, or other individual differences.

What is wrong, then, with universalism, with playing it by the book? The first problem is that no book could possibly cover all the situations that the officer must handle. All the training in the police academy does little to prepare the new officer for the variety of situations that arise. In fact, many officers feel that the academy is useless for learning about street patrol. What the academy can and does teach well is the bureaucratic part of the job—how to do the paperwork.

What everyday policing requires in practice is the opposite of universalism: **particularism**. This term means treating each situation as a special case and dealing with it according to its particular needs rather than according to some abstract set of rules. Particularism places people or situations above rules. It means recognizing all the special characteristics of a situation or person, not just those that fit some set of rules. It allows for flexibility. Under the principle of particularism, if the rules don't fit the needs of the person or situation, too bad for the rules. Under the principle of universalism, if the needs of the person don't fit the rules, too bad for the person.

If policing really were a legalistic activity—the universalistic enforcement of the law—any officer who has learned the rules of policing could be sent to any sector and do a good job. This was the idea behind the early reforms. Reformers saw that police corruption arose when the close ties between officers and the people in their areas led to the selective enforcement (or nonenforcement) of the law. Professionalism would defeat corruption by centralizing authority, so that the cop's major ties would be to the department. Officers might be moved from one beat to another to prevent corruption. After all, it's harder to offer a bribe to a perfect stranger than to someone you know—especially if the stranger is wearing a uniform. Professional policing, then, meant "stranger policing."

But good police work depends on a thorough and highly particularistic knowledge of an area and the people in it. Certainly this is true for the peace-keeping side of police work. Domestic disputes, drunkenness, juvenile delinquency, and other situations of disorder are probably better handled by an officer who knows the people involved. He or she may even be able to work out a decent solution that has nothing to do with the legal aspects of the situation. Crime fighting, too, requires the same particularistic knowledge. Knowing the streets and alleys that can give the quickest route to the scene of a crime, knowing which gang controls which turf, knowing people who can provide information about different sorts of crime—all make the officer more effective in preventing and solving crimes.[84] Given also that the police generally depend on citizens for the information that solves crimes, the better they know the people, the more effective they will be as crime fighters.

There is another way in which the professional model does not fit the reality of police work. Professionalism assumes a militarylike chain of command, where the most experienced and highest-ranking officers who give the commands have the most influence over what the force does. The army may work like this, but a city police force, despite its weapons and uniforms and military ranks, does not. Unlike officers in the army, police captains and lieutenants do not lead their troops into battle. The troops are out there alone—an arrangement that has crucial consequences concerning who really has the decision-making power. Because of the wide variety of situations patrol officers must respond to, they have a great deal of discretion in deciding what to do. The police department, therefore, in actual practice turns the army model upside down: The greatest amount of discretion flows to the people at the lowest rank.

COMMUNITY POLICING: EVERYTHING OLD IS NEW AGAIN

As we approach the end of the century, professional policing is in decline, in theory if not in practice. The persistence of high crime rates for nearly three decades has changed ideas about the police—among police administrators, criminologists, and the public at large. It has gradually become clear that having uniformed strangers riding around in glass-and-steel cages does little to reduce crime or to make citizens feel safer. The more modern impersonal, bureaucratic style of patrol has also downplayed or even ignored some important needs that the nineteenth-century, preprofessional style of policing— despite its glaring flaws—did address. While reformers of a century ago sought to replace undisciplined, politicized policing with professional policing, reformers today talk about abandoning the professional model in favor of **community policing**.

In the professional policing model, the police officer is a sort of uniformed Lone Ranger—a stranger who comes into the community to deal with some crime while the ordinary folk watch appreciatively. Community policing, by contrast, conceives of the officer more as an agent for the community. Where the professional officer was a crime-fighting specialist, the community police officer is a problem-solving generalist.

In practice, community policing encompasses several elements. First, there is an emphasis on community relations, that is, making citizens feel closer to their police department. Of course, most departments have long had community relations officers, but most cops dismissed such work as "Mickey Mouse bullshit."[85] However, departments that follow the community policing model recognize that accessible storefront precinct houses, newsletters distributed door to door by officers who chat briefly with the people, and other community relations gimmicks can make the residents feel less fearful of crime and more positive toward the police. Proponents of community policing also maintain that citizen involvement enhances both aspects of crime fighting: preventing crime and catching criminals. These functions are most evident in programs like civilian patrols and crime-watch groups. Criminals, after all, usually prefer to do their work with as few observers as possible. So law-abiding people, just by coming out into the neighborhood rather than sitting behind locked doors even when they are not organized into formal groups, prevent crime. And if they feel that police officers are also part of the community rather than strangers, they will more readily call the police when they

ABOUT CRIME & CRIMINOLOGY

Citizen-oriented Police Enforcement (COPE) is based on the ideas of community policing: the police as proactive problem-solving agents for the community rather than as outsiders called in to react to individual incidents of crime.

No one ever seemed to use the Belmont Community park. Casual passersby would rarely see a child in its playground, or a jogger on one of the parks' tree-shaded walks. Had they looked closely, they might have seen the reason: rowdy youths frequented one corner of the park. They used drugs and drank, and resisted all attempts by patrol officers to remove them. Neighborhood residents kept their children—and themselves—far away, fearing intimidation and exposure to alcohol and drugs. Residents had complained to various local government agencies for years with no response. Finally one of the residents read about COPE in his community newspaper and called the unit.

COPE Officers Sam Hannigan and James Chaconas were assigned to handle the Belmont problem. Their survey of neighborhood residents revealed that the problem did not focus on the park, after all; instead, it centered on a shed, dubbed the "treehouse," that older youths had constructed in the vacant wooded lot next door. The treehouse was often used as a crash pad and drinking place by a few, local teenagers.

Hannigan and Chaconas felt that the public nature of the drinking and drug abuse was mostly responsible for the residents' fears. So, at the suggestion of several neighborhood residents, they decided to make the drinking and drug abuse less visible by removing the treehouse.

Their first efforts went nowhere. The County Roads Department agreed that the treehouse posed a hazard and was in violation of city codes. They refused to take the problem seriously, however, since no one lived there. The Health

see something amiss, and they will be more likely to provide information about the perpetrators.

A second element, related to the first, is the return to foot patrol—the cop on the beat. As with other community relations efforts, foot patrol is no guarantee of reduced crime, but it does make citizens feel safer, partly because people will have more contact with the police but also because cops walking the beat are more effective than patrol cars at maintaining order. Many departments make order-maintenance a high priority for their foot-patrol officers.

A third element of community policing is a problem-solving approach to crime. Under older models, the policing was largely *reactive*: Something happened, someone called the cops, and they reacted. But by making police work a series of responses to individual incidents, the department was ignoring the background conditions that allowed crime to flourish. By "background conditions," community policing advocates are not referring to the usual liberal litany of unemployment, inequality, poverty, and other root causes. Instead, they mean the specific aspects of some particular place that make it easier for a particular crime to occur. Under community policing, departments pay close attention to patterns of crime. If, for example, there is an increase in car thefts in a particular location, they try to figure out what it is about that place that and Fire Departments felt the same way. Even if they had been willing to condemn the shack, the formal process would have taken months.

Instead, the officers decided to work with the owner. They searched through tax records to find the owner of the vacant lot.... The owner readily admitted that the treehouse was a nuisance and a hazard, and that he had no use for it whatever. Still, he feared retaliation from the kids who had constructed it, and was unable to pay the costs of demolishing the building.

Hannigan and Chaconas [and a COPE lieutenant] agreed that the two officers should demolish the treehouse themselves. Two employees of the County Roads Commission agreed to help out. Next Saturday morning, the four, armed with saws and sledgehammers, quickly reduced the treehouse to rubble. Then they carted the pieces to a waiting county truck and took them to the dump.

The kids still drink and use drugs, and most of them have stayed in the neighborhood. They now meet in private places, however, where they are not visible to their neighbors. Most important, residents are no longer subject to their unpredictable, loud, and threatening behavior. The ... residents are less fearful. One tangible result of the fear reduction is that, for the first time in years, the park is filled with children.

The Belmont case shows that an apparently intractable problem—here, fear created by teenage drinking and drug abuse—can be ameliorated with a little analysis, and through some simple actions. The treehouse case took two weeks from start to finish. The key was to accept the neighborhood's definition of the problem (threatening public behavior) rather than the usual police definition (illegal drinking and drug abuse).

Source: John E. Eck and William Spelman, "Who Ya Gonna Call? The Police as Problem Busters," *Crime & Delinquency*, vol. 33 (1987), 31–52.

has made it an attractive target for criminals. Then they design some *proactive* plan to change those conditions rather than just reacting to calls about stolen cars.

THE PROBLEM OF PROBLEM-SOLVING POLICING

Not everybody welcomes the community relations approach. Much resistance comes from the police themselves, especially the street cops. Aside from the possible inconvenience of walking a beat rather than patrolling by car—especially in cold or wet weather—the police cling to the idea that the essence of police work is fighting crime. And they have a point. Press releases from "downtown" may extol community relations, but it is still crime work—catching criminals—that brings rewards. The officer who makes arrests for important crimes gains the admiration of the public and other police and wins the more tangible rewards of promotion. Therefore, officers often dislike changes that deemphasize their own role as crime fighters. They also may dislike volunteer patrols sponsored by the department. As police themselves say, "Cops don't like civilians, and especially they don't like them inside the station house where they can get to know a cop's business."[86] Nor do they care much for an independent group, like the Guardian Angels, that encroaches on the police department's crime-fighting turf.

Another problem of community policing lies in the nature of the community itself. The term implies a great deal of homogeneity or at least consensus; it summons up nostalgic images of the old neighborhood, where folks were pretty much alike and agreed about what they did or did not want. But urban neighborhoods often present a mix of ethnic groups, age groups, and even social classes—all with conflicting ideas about the community norms that should be enforced.[87] It is quite likely that under these circumstances the police will identify with the power structure of the neighborhood.

Some critics fear that the autonomy that community policing gives to the patrol officer will lead to the same kinds of misconduct that characterized policing in its early days. Community policing stresses peacekeeping; it often involves "aggressive order maintenance"—the name one social scientist has given to activities the police officers referred to more simply with the phrase "We kick ass."[88] This mandate, coupled with wide discretion, seems like an invitation to brutality. And the asses kicked will likely be those of the poor and the young.

SUMMARY AND CONCLUSION

In contrast to the excitement, clever crime solving, and glamorized violence of the police shown in the movies and on TV shows, the bulk of the police officer's work time has little to do with crime. In most cities, the police patrol in cars, waiting for the radio to dispatch them, usually in response to citizens' calls. People call on the police for a variety of services, especially when situations may require the use of legitimate force. Police work, therefore, is now and historically has always been more a matter of keeping the peace than of enforcing the law. Restoring peace and order is the goal, and enforcing the law is only one of several available tools to accomplish that task. As for crime, the police have some deterrent effect. Adding officers can reduce only certain types of crime and only under certain conditions—usually at great financial cost. The police do catch criminals, clearing by arrests about 20 percent of all Index crimes. The methods of catching criminals, however, are usually routine and depend much more on civilian cooperation than on sophisticated crime-solving techniques.

Since the police are empowered to use force and the law in carrying out their work, the potential abuse of this great power is a constant problem. The most notable abuses are brutality and corruption. Brutality is most likely to occur when civilians challenge the officer's authority, for authority is the officer's primary tool. Without it, even the ordinary aspects of police work—directing traffic, controlling crowds at parades, and settling family disputes—become difficult and dangerous. Ordinary corruption arises from the great amount of discretion built into the police role and the mandate to enforce laws against victimless crimes. Severe corruption combines these two elements with the temptation of large amounts of money. Both brutality and corruption can continue unchecked because police solidarity—the blue wall of silence—makes prosecution difficult.

There is no ideal solution to all the dilemmas of police work. The long trend toward professionalism may reduce corruption and brutality, but it also makes for "stranger policing." The more recent trend toward community policing goes in the opposite direction. Putting the cop back on the beat and in touch with the people of the community may make the public feel better, but it also may be resisted by the officers themselves, who prefer the "real" police work of crime fighting over the Mickey Mouse of community relations—especially if it means more civilian knowledge or control over what they do.

Finally, we should not forget that ultimately the police are an agency of the state and as such they are a political institution. In times of political consensus, this political role is almost invisible. However, when the consensus breaks down, when large numbers of people question the legitimacy of the government and the law, the police are on the front line defending the political status quo. Even in times of general consensus, dissenters who see the state as illegitimate or unjust will see the police as the enforcers of injustice.

CRITICAL THINKING QUESTIONS

1. We often think of the police role as enforcing the law, preventing crime, and catching criminals. How—and how well—do the police perform these functions? What limits their ability to carry out these tasks?
2. What are the differences between the way criminals were caught before police forces were established and the way they are now usually caught?
3. Why for so long did the English resist the establishment of a police force, and what convinced people to change their minds?
4. Are police brutality and corruption a matter of the few bad apples that might be found in any barrel? What aspects of police work make police misconduct more likely?
5. What is police professionalism; when and why did it arise? What are the flaws in the theory behind professional policing?

KEY TERMS

authority	Knapp Commission	universalism
clearance rate	meat-eaters	watch system
community policing	particularism	working personality
discretion	reward system	
grass-eaters	thief-taker	

CHAPTER FOURTEEN

COURTS AND RIGHTS

CHAPTER OUTLINE

A DAY IN COURT

Courts, more than any other topic in this book, present the biggest contrast between the ideal and the reality. I didn't appreciate how large the difference was until I spent a day in court observing the proceedings. I had been there before, on jury duty or to meet a friend who worked there. But I hadn't really noticed my surroundings. I had to take another look.

From the outside, the court building looks just like a courthouse in the movies: its broad stone steps rising to the entrance; the stone columns a 100 feet tall; the sculpted facade carved with noble quotations. Several movies have in fact used this exterior for courthouse scenes. It conveys the majesty of the law and justice.

Inside, it was a different story. What I saw reminded me of what you see at other city agencies. The floors were dirty, the walls scarred. In some rooms, the cushioned theater-style seats for jurors were ripped or broken. But what most reminded me of other city agencies were the people. What you see in the criminal court building is what you see at the public hospital or the welfare department: poor people waiting. They sit on long, wooden benches. Most of them are relatives of accused people scheduled for court that day. They do not know when their son or daughter, husband or wife, will be brought from the holding pen into the court. By the afternoon session, some of them will have been waiting six or seven hours. A court officer walks through the room waking up people who have fallen asleep.

A trial represents the adversarial system of justice in its ideal. Yet of all the arrests made by the police, only about three percent result in trials. Many are dismissed before final adjudication. Most of the rest are settled by guilty pleas.

At the front of the room, defendants are brought to the courtroom in groups of four or five, handcuffed, to wait on a bench to the right of the judge. The clerk calls a name. The prisoner is unshackled and led before the judge, district attorney on one side, defense attorney on the other. The clerk reads numbers that indicate the charge. The people who have been waiting cannot get close enough to the judge's bench to hear what is happening. The lawyers, judge, and clerk often speak in what sounds like a code anyway: "Charged with one-six-five-four-oh," "waive the reading," "vacate the warrant," "deponent is informed by complainant," and so on.

The defendants themselves often seem to have little grasp of what is going on. The attorneys make very brief statements about the case. Sometimes the judge sets bail; sometimes there is a plea of guilty and a sentence: five days or time served. Papers are shuffled. A police officer leads the defendant out the door, and the next defendant is brought forward. The whole process takes only a few minutes. Lower courts that deal with less serious crimes—misdemeanors—work in a still more impersonal way. There, a judge may dispose of dozens of cases, at the rate of a few seconds each, rarely spending more than a minute on a case.[1]

The whole scene is far removed from the image of courts that we see on television—no prosecutors cleverly cross-examining witnesses, no defense lawyers jumping up and shouting, "objection." Nevertheless, there is a logical and sometimes real connection between these two pictures of justice—the ideal, civics-book version of the criminal process and the everyday reality of a big-city court.

THE ADVERSARIAL SYSTEM

Our court system has long distinguished between two kinds of cases, civil and criminal, but both run on what is called the **adversarial model**. According to this model, the court is an arena for a conflict between two adversaries. *Civil* cases are disputes between two private parties. For example, if Jones beats up Smith and injures him, Smith may sue in civil court. The case will be *Smith v. Jones*, naming the two adversaries. Smith is the plaintiff (the one who brings the complaint), Jones the defendant. If Smith wins, the court will require Jones to give Smith some compensation, usually money, for the damages caused. Of course, beating up somebody also violates criminal laws against assault, so the case may also be brought to criminal court. But in *criminal* cases, the plaintiff is always the state (i.e., the government). The state, not the victim, brings charges against the defendant. The case will be called *State of New Jersey v. Jones*, and if Jones loses, the court will impose some punishment. Even if that punishment is a fine, the money goes to the state, not to the victim. These distinctions are not absolute. Some criminal cases involve compensation: The criminal must make restitution to the victim. And some civil cases involve punishment in the form of punitive damages, although this money—unlike the fine in criminal cases—goes to the victim, not to the state.

In criminal cases, the state charges a person with breaking a particular law, and in front of a jury (or impartial judge), the state produces whatever evidence it can legally find to establish guilt; the defense tries its best to discredit the state's evidence and testimony. The burden of proof is on the state. That is, the state must prove guilt beyond a reasonable doubt; the defense does not have to prove innocence but only that the state's case does not prove guilt beyond a reasonable doubt. A verdict for the defendant, therefore, is not "innocent"; it is "not guilty." The news media almost invariably miss this distinction. They report that "the defendant pleaded innocent," or that "the jury found the defendant innocent of all charges." Wrong. As a lawyer lecturing in my class said, "In the entire history of this country, not one person in a criminal trial has ever been found innocent."

Since most of us have not been exposed to other models of justice, we might assume that the adversarial model is the best, if not the only, model for determining guilt. But is this really the best way to find out if a person has broken the law? A trial, at least in theory, is a truth-finding process. Is the adversarial system the best way to discover the truth? How can it be, when neither side has truth as its primary goal? By definition, an adversarial proceeding means that the primary goal of each side is to win. In this respect our modern courts resemble the medieval trial by combat. Six hundred years ago, in legal disputes between nobles, the adversaries would fight to determine the verdict. Often the nobles themselves would not fight; instead "champions" would represent them in battle. When one person brought criminal charges against another, the accuser and accused themselves would fight it out, usually to the death. (If the loser was not already dead, he would be immediately hanged on the gallows.)[2] The logic behind trial by combat was, obviously, that God would never let the wrong side win. The truth would prevail. From today's more secularized perspective, it seems equally obvious that in fact the outcome depended on fighting ability, not on truth. But our adversarial system runs the same risk: We no longer have champions in armor, but we do have lawyers in three-piece suits; and many people feel that in at least some trials, the winner may be merely the side with the best lawyer, not necessarily the side with the truth.

Adding to this danger, the adversarial model puts the final decision in the hands of a jury of ordinary people. Jurors are not lawyers. They do not know the law, nor do they have any special knowledge that makes them the best judges of the evidence. In fact, to become jurors, they must be almost completely ignorant of any of the evidence. Furthermore, while our system places the responsibility of decision on the jurors, it bars them from asking questions of the witnesses, even though the jurors might consider the answers crucial to their decision. Only the lawyers (and occasionally the judge) question witnesses. Nor do jurors have to be very intelligent. In most jurisdictions, the only requirement for serving on a jury is a social security number. It is possible that a jury may decide a defendant's fate on the basis of irrationality, prejudice, faulty logic, or misunderstanding of the facts of the law. Since juries deliberate in secret and keep no records, we do not know how often jurors make these errors.

For these reasons, some societies have based their trial process on a more **inquisitorial model**. This system is designed not as a battle but as a cooperative effort, an inquiry to discover the truth. The role of discovering the truth is assigned to a person or committee of people who are trained both in the law and in criminal investigation. These experts do not take sides; they are not on the side of the defendant or the plaintiff but on the side of the

ON CAMPUS

In an adversarial system, people accused of crimes have the right to a public trial with a lawyer to represent them; they also have the right to present their own witnesses and to confront witnesses against them. Most college disciplinary hearings, by contrast, are more inquisitorial than adversarial. Usually, a special committee investigates the misconduct, hearing one by one from the alleged wrongdoer, witnesses, and victims if any—all behind closed doors. The goal of this system is to discover the truth while at the same time protecting students from further embarrassment. Victims, witnesses, and wrongdoers often prefer these committee inquiries to adversarial and public questioning and cross-examination. Lately, however, students punished under these systems have begun suing colleges for ignoring due process.

CAMPUS DILEMMA: THE RISK OF LAWSUITS DISHEARTENS COLLEGES FIGHTING DATE RAPE

MEASURES TO ASSIST VICTIMS LEAD TO BITTER WRANGLES OVER RIGHTS OF OTHERS: AMATEURS ON HEARING PANELS

by Edward Felsenthal

When the new sexual assault policy [at Valparaiso College in Indiana] was invoked last fall, the aftermath severely tested the university's resolve to deal with date rape.

Shortly after the semester began, a woman accused a man she had known since high school of raping her. In late August, she told campus authorities, she asked the man to dinner at the student union because he had been making advances toward her and she wanted to explain that she wasn't interested in a romantic relationship. Later that week, assuming she had made the message clear during the dinner, she accepted the man's invitation to a fraternity drinking party where, she said, the man led her into a small room, locked the door and raped her.

The man told a very different story. He said that the woman had been flirting with him and that she had participated voluntarily in a fraternity-party drinking game. Around 3 a.m., he said, the two of them had sexual intercourse. He maintained that the sex was consensual and that she accused him of rape after having "second thoughts and guilt" about betraying her boyfriend....

truth, whatever it may be. They have broad powers of inquiry to ask any questions of anyone—the police, the defendant, and the witnesses. The defense lawyer may present witnesses, but it is the expert, the inquisitor, who asks the questions and who recommends a verdict.[3]

Which sounds like a better system—a direct quest for the truth by skilled and trained persons or a decision made by twelve untrained people who, in getting the relevant information, must depend on the wrangling of two adversaries more interested in winning than in finding the truth? Because of its advantages, the court systems of many European countries, and even our own grand juries, follow a model that is more inquisitorial and less adversarial. Why, then, has the Anglo-American legal system followed the adversarial tradition?

The Valparaiso disciplinary panel convened to hear the case in a small classroom in Christ College, home of the university's academic-honors program.... The panel, composed of four administrators, listened to testimony from several students and eventually ruled that the man had violated Valparaiso's sexual-assault guidelines and would be suspended. Two weeks later ... the male student sued the school and the panel members, calling the hearing a sham and seeking $12 million in ... damages. The man charges that in the school's zeal to assuage campus concerns about date rape, it violated his rights by refusing to allow testimony from several students he wanted to speak on his behalf. The school also unreasonably refused to delay the hearing for a week so that the man could prepare his case, he contends.

A second woman who accused a fellow student of rape early in the school year says Valparaiso's concern with avoiding further lawsuits negated the purpose of having a date-rape policy in the first place. She says her hearing was postponed for six weeks, during which time she repeatedly encountered the man she accused and suffered flashbacks of the assault. She also says that when it came time for the hearing, the school was going to permit the man to bring his lawyer into the room during testimony. School policy forbids outsiders to sit in on a disciplinary hearing, but the man had hired an adjunct professor in Valparaiso's law school. When she learned that the lawyer was to be allowed in the hearing room because he was a faculty member, the woman says she dropped her charges.

"I felt by the time it was over that I was more victimized by the school than I was by that man," she says. "They catered to him simply because someone else was suing them."

Source: *Wall Street Journal*, April 12, 1994, pp. 1, 12.

Whatever its strengths for truth finding, the inquisitorial system has one large flaw: It places an immense amount of power in the hands of a single person, the investigator. In any social system, large or small, centralized power may allow for speed and efficiency in reaching decisions. But the system works well only as long as the person in power is both very capable and very fair. If that person is incompetent, the system does not accomplish its task; if that person is not fair, the result is tyranny, especially when he or she is an agent of the government. For this reason, trial by a jury of one's peers, for all its inefficiency and possible error, may be the most important institution we have to prevent tyranny—more important even than the vote.[4]

THE RULES OF THE GAME

The founders of the United States, recognizing that the centralization of power carries the potential for tyranny, created a constitution that structured the government on the separation of powers, thereby limiting the power of any one branch. In their desire to prevent tyranny, the founding fathers also continued the English adversarial system—with its diffusion of power among state, defendant, judge, and jury. But the framers of the Constitution recognized something else about the adversarial system of criminal justice. It turns the justice process into a contest, and in contests the rules of the game become very important. These rules are called procedural law, as distinguished from substantive law. **Substantive law** refers to laws that specify what people may not do; they define and set penalties for offenses like robbery, fraud, and conspiracy. **Procedural law** refers to those laws that specify the procedures the government must follow in prosecuting defendants. For example, procedural law forbids the government from torturing people to get evidence.

Some of the rules of U.S. procedural law are descended from English **common law**. Common law is not created by legislation; rather, it is a body of judicial precedents and principles that has accumulated over the centuries, ever since King Henry II, in the twelfth century, instituted a system of law common to all people in England. Many of the principles of English common law were incorporated into principles of law in the United States, including some restrictions on the government that are written into the U.S. Constitution.

When we look at courts, we must also distinguish between **factual guilt** and **legal guilt**. A person may be factually guilty; that is, he or she committed the crime. But for the person to be legally guilty, the prosecution must present evidence to prove that guilt beyond a reasonable doubt and must gather and present this evidence in accordance with the procedural law.

THE BILL OF RIGHTS AND DUE PROCESS

Because of their concern about tyranny or at least about the dangers of a too-powerful government, the first Congress elected under the new Constitution proposed a set of constitutional amendments specifically designed to limit the powers of the government. In 1791, the states ratified ten amendments, known as the Bill of Rights. The First Amendment, as most people know, concerns freedom of religion, speech, and the press. But it does not say merely that these freedoms are good things and that people should have them. The specific language of the amendment is important: "*Congress shall make no law ... abridging the freedom of speech, or of the press.*" In other words, it strictly limits the power of the legislative branch of the government. Four of the amendments deal with the procedures in criminal cases, and like the First Amendment, these too limit the power of the government. Because a criminal case is contested between the government and the individual, the framers of the Constitution stressed that the government must follow correct procedures in bringing criminal cases. The cornerstone of procedural law is the Fifth Amendment:

No person shall be held to answer for a capital, or otherwise infamous crime, unless on presentment or indictment of a Grand Jury ... nor shall any person be subject for the same offense twice to be put in jeopardy of life or limb; nor shall be compelled in any criminal case to be a witness against himself, nor be deprived of life, liberty, or property without due process of law....

This amendment contains many familiar ideas; you have probably heard phrases like "double jeopardy" or "taking the fifth" (refusing to testify against oneself). But it is the last phrase that is crucial: "due process of law." *Due process* means "procedure." The government must follow the correct procedures in proving a person guilty.

The due process clause serves the same function as the ideal of "innocent until proven guilty," a phrase that, by the way, does not appear anywhere in the Constitution, although it was part of English common law. But the Fifth Amendment goes beyond "innocent until proven guilty." It says that in order to deprive a person of life (i.e., to execute), liberty (i.e., to imprison), or property (i.e., to fine), the government must follow due process. If the government does not follow the correct procedures, it cannot punish. So if someone asks, "Where does it say that a criminal should go free just because of a technicality?" the answer is there in the Fifth Amendment. No matter how vicious the person, no matter how clear the guilt, if the government doesn't follow procedure, if it doesn't observe due process, it cannot fine, imprison, or execute that criminal.

CRIME CONTROL AND DUE PROCESS

The Constitution has built a basic contradiction into the role of the courts. On the one hand, the justice system is supposed to protect the community from criminals. On the other hand, the Constitution spells out specific protections for individuals accused of crimes. This contradiction is at the heart of many current debates about the role of the courts. In the view of Herbert L. Packer, a prominent legal authority, these debates often come down to a choice of two models of how courts are supposed to work: the crime-control model and the due-process model. In the **crime-control model**, the main purpose of the courts is to do something about crime, that is, to prevent crime by punishing criminals. In the **due process model**, the main purpose of the courts is to protect constitutional rights, making sure that the government respects the rights of all individuals, even those accused of crimes. If you are arrested and demand your right to an attorney, or if you ask the judge to throw out the confession you made because the police forced you to talk, you are invoking the due process model. On the other hand, if you demand that the courts pay more attention to the rights of victims or the right of the public to be safe from muggers, you are invoking the crime-control model.

Of course, the rights of victims or potential victims are not of the same order as the rights of the accused. The rights of the accused are constitutional rights, spelled out in the various amendments. Nowhere in the Constitution is there any mention of the rights of victims or of the public, rights that are the province of substantive criminal law and civil law. The Constitution says nothing about substantive criminal law, probably because the framers of the Constitution did not consider it to be basic to the structure of government. They left such law for later legislation by the states and the federal government. However, the Constitution does speak to issues of procedural law. It says specifically what must occur if the government fails to follow the rules. The framers of the Constitution apparently were much more worried about protecting citizens from the government than from one another.

Due process is the overarching concept in establishing the boundaries of criminal procedure. The phrase itself goes back many centuries to well before the founding of the United States, and it has encompassed a variety of definitions. At one time, torturing a suspect was a legitimate part of due process. In the United States three crucial questions have shaped the development of criminal procedure: What specific practices violate the principle of due process? How shall the government enforce the restrictions of due process? And how much latitude do the states, as opposed to the federal government, have in determining their own versions of due process? To illustrate the evolution of the answers to these questions, consider what is nowadays called the right to privacy—a right not explicitly stated anywhere in the Constitution.

SEARCH AND SEIZURE

THE WRITS OF ASSISTANCE AND THE FOURTH AMENDMENT

"Taxation without representation is tyranny"; the Boston Tea Party; the Stamp Act—clearly, one of the important issues leading to the American Revolution was taxation. The king needed more money and levied taxes on the colonies to get it. As a way of making sure that the colonists were not avoiding taxes, the English prime minister empowered customs agents with **writs of assistance**, which in effect gave officers the power to search anyone, anywhere, for anything. These writs and general warrants also allowed English officials, both in England and in the colonies, to ransack people's houses looking for antigovernment literature.

From the colonists' point of view, these legal practices gave the government far too much power to intrude into the lives of citizens. They were part of a style of government that we today call totalitarian or authoritarian and that the colonists more bluntly called tyranny. So when it came time for the former colonists to create a government for their own new nation, they were still sensitive to the possibility of tyranny. They feared concentrated power and therefore designed a government, under the Articles of Confederation, with a very weak center, so weak in fact that after barely a decade the most influential and thoughtful Americans met to revise its basic structure. The outcome of this 1787 convention was the U.S. Constitution, a document that balances the need for government power on the one hand with the fear of tyranny on the other. The system of separation of powers, of checks and balances, among three branches of government diffuses power within the federal government, and the Constitution further limits that power by granting sovereignty over many matters to the states. But to win ratification by the states and further accommodate those who still feared the power of the central government, the creators of the Constitution promised a Bill of Rights—ten amendments that sought to protect specific civil liberties. These include the famous freedoms of speech, press, religion, and assembly. Four of the ten amendments, though, concern criminal procedure. One of the most important and controversial is the Fourth Amendment:

> The right of the people to be secure in their persons, houses, papers, and effects, against unreasonable searches and seizures shall not be violated, and no warrants shall issue but upon probable cause, supported by oath or affirmation, and particularly describing the place to be searched and the persons or things to be seized.

The amendment in itself is not controversial. Nobody favors unreasonable searches. But what makes a search unreasonable? What constitutes probable cause? More important, what should the courts do when the police make an unreasonable search? Consider the following example:

> On the night of April 23, 1973, Herbert Joseph Giglotto, a hardworking boilermaker, and his wife, Louise, were sleeping soundly in their suburban house in Collinsville, Illinois. Suddenly, and without warning, armed men broke into their house and rushed up the stairs to the Giglottos' bedroom. Giglotto later recalled, "I [saw] men ... dressed like hippies with pistols, yelling and screeching." The night intruders threw Giglotto down on his bed and tied his hands behind his back. Holding a loaded gun at his head, one of the men pointed to his wife and asked, "Who is that bitch lying there?"... The men refused to allow the terrified couple to move from the bed or put on any clothes while they proceeded to search the residence. As books were swept from the shelves and clothes were ripped from hangers, one man said, "You're going to die unless you tell us where the stuff is." Then the intrusion ended as suddenly as it began when the leader of the raiders concluded, "We made a mistake."

The raiders were from a federal antidrug agency set up under President Nixon. That same night, another group from the same agency

> kicked in the door of the home of Donald and Virginia Askew.... Virginia Askew, who was then crippled from a back injury, fainted as the men rushed into the frame house. While she lay on the floor, agents kept her husband ... from going to her aid. Another agent kept their 16-year-old son ... from telephoning for help by pointing a rifle at him. After the house was searched, the agents admitted they had made another mistake and disappeared. (Virginia Askew the next day was rushed to a mental hospital for emergency psychiatric therapy.)[5]

The government agents had no warrant to search either of these houses, so the searches were clearly unreasonable under the Fourth Amendment. We find them especially offensive because the victims were innocent. But since everyone is presumed innocent until proven guilty, such searches would have been just as unreasonable if the houses had contained illegal drugs. It was exactly such government invasion of people's homes that the Fourth Amendment sought to prevent; and the authors of that amendment knew full well that to protect the innocent, the right to be secure against unreasonable government searches had to extend to *all* persons. The amendment does not say, "The right of good, innocent, law-abiding people who don't possess illegal materials to be secure in their persons, houses, and so on, shall not be violated; but bad people like drug dealers, it's OK for the government to search them whenever it wants to." It says, "The right of the people to be secure in their houses ... shall not be violated."

What if the police do conduct an unreasonable search like the ones in Collinsville and find illegal drugs? Suppose, for example, that the agents had found a gram of cocaine in Herbert Giglotto's drawer. The search was illegal, but the government now has evidence of a crime. What should happen? Here the language of the Fourth Amendment offers no explicit instructions. It says only that the government should not conduct unreasonable searches; it does not say what should happen if the government does violate a person's Fourth Amendment rights.

Common law had few provisions on the matter. Under English common law, the victim of a search could sue for trespass or for the return of stolen property. But the evidence, however the police obtained it, could be used in court. After all, evidence is evidence. The defendant could argue that the evidence was irrelevant or insufficient, but he or she could hardly claim that it didn't exist.[6]

Critics of the common law view argued that if the courts continued to allow such evidence, the Fourth Amendment was meaningless. It could not keep the police from making unreasonable searches since they had nothing to lose and might gain a conviction. In 1914, the Supreme Court agreed. In a unanimous decision in the case of *Weeks* v. *United States*, the Court established the **exclusionary rule**: Evidence seized in violation of the Fourth Amendment could not be used against the defendant.[7]

Although law-enforcement officials criticized the Court's decision, *Weeks* did not revolutionize police procedure. The reason was simple: *Weeks* was a federal case. The evidence against Weeks was seized by a U.S. marshal, and the case was tried in federal court. However, most criminal cases—typical street crimes like burglary and robbery—are violations of state laws. In 1914, the Supreme Court's decisions on criminal procedure applied only to federal courts. States were still largely free to establish their own versions of due process. In other words, the local police could still make illegal searches and use the evidence.

The federal-state distinction raises a central constitutional question. The language of the Bill of Rights clearly restricts the *federal* government, but to what extent do its protections apply to the *states*? Advocates of states rights argued that these constitutional restrictions apply only to federal cases. They based their argument on the Tenth Amendment: All powers not specifically granted to the federal government belong to the states. For example, the First Amendment says only that "Congress shall make no law respecting an establishment of religion ... abridging freedom of speech, or of the press." The amendment says nothing about the state legislatures. In fact, when the Bill of Rights was written, a state constitution might establish religion, providing state support for some sects. Many states had, on their own, disestablished religion, but nobody thought that the Bill of Rights required such disestablishment; the Bill of Rights restricted only Congress and the federal government. For over a hundred years, therefore, the Court refused to apply the restrictions of the First Amendment to the states.[8]

In criminal cases, too, the Court applied constitutional guarantees only in federal courts. In the years following *Weeks*, the Court stood by this state-federal distinction. Occasionally, a particularly offensive police action would be appealed to the Court. For example, in 1952 the Court reviewed the case of a man named Rochin who had been convicted of a drug offense in state court. How had the police obtained the evidence? They entered Rochin's house illegally, and having seen him swallow some capsules, arrested him and forcibly pumped his stomach. Rochin was *factually* guilty since the capsules had contained illegal drugs. The local court had convicted him, and the California Supreme Court had upheld the conviction. But the U.S. Supreme Court ruled that even though this was a state case, the search was so outrageous that the evidence must be excluded despite state-federal differences.[9] Still, the Court refused to make any general policy binding on all states.

The stage was set for one of the most important and controversial cases in criminal law: *Mapp* v. *Ohio*. In 1957, in Cleveland, Ohio, the police received a tip that a suspect in a recent bombing was hiding in the home of Dolree Mapp and that the house also held illegal gambling equipment. The police went to the house, but Mapp, on the advice of her lawyer, refused to admit them without a search warrant. The police kept the house under surveillance and returned to the door three hours later, this time forcing their way in. When Mapp demanded to see a search warrant, one of the officers waved a piece of paper, which she grabbed and stuffed in her bosom. The officers, with some struggle, retrieved the paper (at the trial, no warrant was ever produced). They then handcuffed Mapp to a railing and continued to search the entire house. They found no bombers and no gambling equipment. However, in the basement of the building, they found some pornography. Mapp was eventually convicted of possession of obscene materials, and the Ohio Supreme Court upheld the conviction. She appealed the case to the U.S. Supreme Court.

In a five-to-three decision, the Court reversed the conviction. The constitutional reasoning is crucial because it had implications far beyond the fate of Dolree Mapp. Obviously, the Fourth Amendment occupied a central place in the Court's reasoning since this warrantless search was illegal. The question was whether the evidence could be excluded. By 1960, nearly half the states in the country had adopted some kind of exclusionary rule, but Ohio was not one of them.[10] The search, although illegal, was not unusual or repulsive—nothing like the stomach-pumping case where the Supreme Court had stepped in before. So if the Court were to overrule, if it were to make sure that the Fourth Amendment protected Ohio residents, it would have to extend the exclusionary rule to state courts as well. Was there any constitutional basis for such a broadening of Court rulings?

The answer lay in the Fourteenth Amendment, which, along with the Thirteenth and Fifteenth, was passed in the aftermath of the Civil War—a war whose major aim and justification had been the preservation of the Union. If the Tenth Amendment was meant to guarantee the rights of each state, the Thirteenth, Fourteenth and Fifteenth amendments—often called the Civil War amendments—were meant to protect individuals, especially African-

Americans, from discrimination by the states and to force certain minimum, uniform standards on all the states in the Union. The Thirteenth Amendment banned slavery in all states. The Fifteenth Amendment guaranteed that in all states, all races would have the right to vote.

The Fourteenth Amendment is far longer and broader in scope than the other two. Its first section says in part, "No State shall make or enforce any law which abridges the privileges and immunities of the citizens of the United States." This phrase seems to say that no state can deny the basic rights of a citizen of the United States. The next phrase of the amendment seems to extend the due process clause of the Fifth Amendment to all states: "Nor shall any State deprive any person of life, liberty, or property, without due process of law; nor deny to any person within its jurisdiction equal protection of the laws."

So if the due process clause of the Fifth Amendment protects the rights of the accused against the federal government, the due process clause of the Fourteenth Amendment seems to protect those same rights against state governments.[11] I have used the phrase "seems to" here because for nearly a century the Supreme Court had interpreted the amendment very narrowly. In effect, the Court allowed each state to make up its own version of due process.[12] Only when particularly ugly procedures came to light did the Supreme Court step in.

However, by 1960 the membership and philosophy of the Court had changed, and under Chief Justice Earl Warren, it was making important changes in its interpretation of some parts of the Constitution. In *Brown* v. *Board of Education*, probably the most famous Supreme Court decision in this century, the Court had reversed the previous interpretation of the equal protection clause (the doctrine of separate but equal) to ban segregation in public schools. The school decision of 1954, while having no direct impact on criminal law, did have three features that should have given Mapp and her lawyers some encouragement. First, it sought to protect individuals from abuses by *state* governments; second, it imposed a national standard on all the states; and third, it based its decision on a new interpretation of the Fourteenth Amendment. Mapp's case hinged not on the equal protection clause of this amendment but on its due process clause. However, in 1961, a bare majority of the Court held for Mapp (the decision was five-to-three; the decision in the school segregation case had been unanimous). The Warren Court extended a federal standard to protect the individual's rights against the state. The Court ruled in effect that the exclusionary rule would apply not just in the federal courts but in all state criminal procedures as well.

THE EFFECTS OF MAPP V. OHIO

The reaction to *Mapp* was immediate and predictable. It was a classic example of conservative versus liberal, crime control versus due process. Police and other hard-liners spoke out vigorously against it, claiming that the Supreme Court had handcuffed the police. Criminals would be freer to commit crimes; they would be released on these technicalities and return to the streets to commit more crimes. Civil libertarians, in contrast, applauded the decision as a step toward preserving the right to privacy and as a way to ensure that the police, too, would abide by the law of the land, the Constitution.

It is difficult, if not impossible, to learn the truth about all these claims. We could easily find anecdotal evidence to support either side—stories of criminals being released because of search-and-seizure technicalities or stories of police officers continuing to make illegal searches. What we need here, however, is good, systematic evidence, which unfortunately, is not always easy to find.

On the issue of whether *Mapp* changed the nature of police work, the answer is probably this: not immediately, not universally, and not for most arrests for street crimes. While the warrantless police search in the O. J. Simpson murder case was challenged in court, most arrests for Index crimes like murder, robbery, and burglary rarely involve questionable searches. The police either are lucky enough to catch the criminal in the act or they rely on information from other people. Searches are not so important in these cases, and where warrants are required, the police can get them easily enough—as they could and did before *Mapp*.

However, we shouldn't ignore the strength of the reaction against *Mapp*. In part, the police were reacting to the symbolism of the Court's decision since it seemed to side with the criminal against the cop. But perhaps they also objected to *Mapp* because it forced them to change the way they conducted themselves. Remember, *Mapp* did not change the rules about whether a search was illegal; it said only that the fruits of illegal searches could not be used. So perhaps the police reaction to *Mapp* amounted to an admission that they had in fact been making a lot of illegal searches and were irked that they would no longer be able to use their illegally seized evidence.[13] All this is speculation, however, not proof. In any case, most observers believe that *Mapp* did have its intended effect, and that to some extent police departments have become more professional in the way they carry out searches. Patrick Murphy, who was police commissioner in New York City at the time of the *Mapp* decision is quite emphatic about its impact on police procedures: "I can think of no decision in recent times in the field of law enforcement which had such a dramatic and traumatic effect as [*Mapp*].... I was immediately caught up in the entire program of reevaluating our procedures.... Retraining sessions had to be held from the very top administrators down to each of the thousands of foot patrolmen."[14] In some cases, however, *Mapp* had less impact on the actual search than on the way the police described the search in their reports and in court.

There is a further problem with the exclusionary rule: it will deter police officers from making illegal searches only in those cases in which it is important to get a conviction in court. Sometimes the police may use their power of search and arrest to relieve a drug dealer of his cash and inventory or to show potential criminals (and the public) that the police are getting tough on crime. These searches may be illegal, but since they do not lead to criminal charges, the exclusionary rule is irrelevant. The same is true if the police make an illegal search of a truly innocent person. Suppose that they illegally search a house or person, find no evidence, and let their victim go, as in the Collinsville raids described earlier. With no arrest, no charges, and no trial, such misconduct cannot be deterred by the exclusionary rule.

ABOUT CRIME & CRIMINOLOGY

The one notable exception to the marked honesty of a good police witness, the only point in the legal process where law officers can be expected to lie routinely or, at the very least, exaggerate, is probable cause.

For narcotics or vice detectives in particular it's become a ridiculous game, this business of establishing the correct legal prerequisites for a search or arrest. Not surprisingly, it isn't enough to say that the suspect was a squirrel who'd been out on that corner about ten minutes too long. No, the law of the land requires that the arresting officer had the opportunity to observe the defendant operating in a suspicious manner on a corner known for drug trafficking

and that upon closer inspection, the officer noticed a glassine envelope sticking out of a sweatshirt pocket as well as a bulge in the front waistband indicative of a weapon.

Yeah. Right.

Probable cause on a street search is and always will be a cosmic joke, a systemic deceit. In some parts of Baltimore, PC means looking at a passing radio car for two seconds longer than an innocent man would. The courts can't acknowledge it, but in the real world you watch a guy until you're sure he's dirty, then you jack him up, find the dope or the gun and then create a legal justification for the arrest.

Source: David Simon, *Homicide: A Year on the Killing Streets* (Boston: Houghton Mifflin, 1991), p. 462.

> The [Mollen] commission [which investigated police corruption in New York in 1994] … said perjury and falsifying records had effectively become part of "police culture."…
>
> "No one looks down on it," said one former prosecutor…. "Taking money is considered dirty, but perjury for the sake of an arrest is accepted. It's become more casual. And the civil libertarians have no effective response to it. It's almost an intractable problem."[15]

Most discussions of the *Mapp* decision focus not on its impact on the police but on the question of justice, of factually guilty people getting off on technicalities. Fortunately, for this question—unlike questions about the number of illegal searches—we can base our answers on systematic evidence. How many criminals—and what kinds of criminals—go free because of *Mapp*?

One of the first studies of the exclusionary rule found that its impact on court cases was very small. Of all felony arrests filed, less than 1 percent were rejected for Fourth Amendment reasons. Drug arrests accounted for nearly three-quarters of the more than 4,000 rejected cases rejected cases (see Figure 14–1). Similarly, Table 14–1 shows the number of arrests for violent crimes in San Diego in 1987. It also shows the number of cases dropped (either screened out by the prosecutor or dismissed in court) and the reason for this decision. The last column shows the number of cases dropped because of due process problems.

Most violent crimes (nearly 80 percent) do not result in arrest but remain unsolved. Of the arrests the police do make, prosecutors reject or dismiss about 40 percent, but only a handful (18 out of the original 16,284 arrests) are rejected because of due process problems. Even assuming that all the cases in the last column were search-and-seizure problems, it is obvious that the exclu-

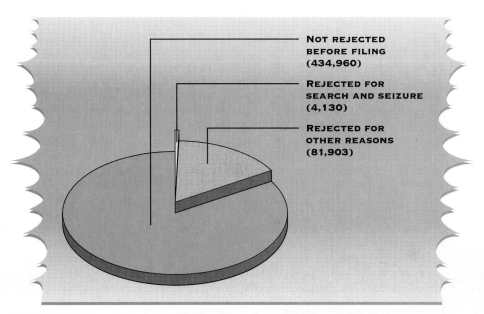

FIGURE 14–1 Outcome of 520,000 felony arrests in California, 1976–1979

TABLE 14–1 •
INDEX CRIME IN SAN DIEGO, 1987

	REPORTED CRIMES	ARRESTS	REJECT AND DISMISS	REASONS FOR REJECTIONS/DISMISSAL		
				EVIDENCE	WITNESS	DUE PROCESS
MURDER	176	132	20	12	1	0
RAPE	801	482	219	64	113	1
ROBBERY	5,421	1,137	365	124	104	7
AGGRAVATED ASSAULT	9,886	1,684	799	187	332	10
BURGLARY	35,214	4,123	1,006	344	93	53
LARCENY AND MVT	106,263	2,374	746	245	61	20
VIOLENT CRIME	16,284	3,435	1,403	387	550	18
TOTAL	157,761	9,932	3,155	976	704	91

Source: Barbara Boland, Catherine H. Conly, Paul Mahanna, Lynn Warner, and Ronald Sones, *The Prosecution of Felony Arrests, 1987* (Washington, DC: Abt Associates, 1990). *UCR*, 1987.

sionary rule does not hamper the state's ability to prosecute violent crimes. These cases, in which individuals arrested for crimes are released because of due process "technicalities," account for much less than 1 percent of all reported crimes or arrests and only about 1.25 percent of all cases dropped.

If the exclusionary rule affects any area of crime, it should be crimes of possession—of stolen property, drugs, weapons, or gambling materials—cases that often hinge on evidence found in searches. In San Diego, about 10 percent of all drug arrests were dropped because of due process problems; for stolen property and weapons offenses, the proportion was much smaller. In many other cities even the proportion of drug offenses affected by due process is small. In Seattle, for example, in the same year (1987), the police filed over 1,800 drug arrests. Prosecutors screened out or dismissed nearly 45 percent, but only two of these cases were dropped because of due process violations.[16]

If a case does get to court, the defendant may still try to have evidence excluded (or in legal terms, "suppressed"). Motions to suppress evidence occur in only a handful of cases—probably fewer than 10 percent—and 80 to 90 percent of the time, judges deny these motions and allow the contested evidence. Even when evidence is excluded, about half the time the defendant is convicted anyway on the basis of other evidence and testimony.[17]

BEYOND <u>MAPP</u>: OTHER ISSUES IN SEARCH AND SEIZURE

Although the *Mapp* decision settled the question of how to enforce the Fourth Amendment, it raised a host of other questions about how to interpret its language. Just what makes a search "unreasonable" and what constitutes "probable cause"? When may a police officer "stop and frisk" someone in the street? In the years following *Mapp*, the Supreme Court has had to settle borderline cases and establish the boundary between legal and illegal searches. In the 1970s and 1980s, conservative justices appointed by conservative presidents (Nixon, Reagan, and Bush) moved that boundary to allow searches that the Warren Court would probably have found unreasonable. Still, the Court held to the principle of the exclusionary rule: If a search is defined as unreasonable, the evidence may not be used. That position, however, has changed.

In 1984, the Court began to allow **good faith exceptions** to the exclusionary rule. That is, if a police officer acts in good faith, the evidence may be used *even if the search warrant is not valid.* In one case, the police officer had used the wrong form and had filled it out incorrectly.[18] In another case, the police seized evidence on the basis of a warrant, but it later turned out that the information used to get the warrant in the first place was not sufficient to establish probable cause. In yet another case, the police had a warrant but searched the wrong apartment by mistake, one on the same floor but not named in the warrant, and found illegal drugs. Had a lawyer challenged any of these warrants *before* the search, a judge would probably not have allowed it. Nevertheless, the Supreme Court ruled that the exclusionary rule did not apply because the police had acted in good faith; that is, they had thought that they were correctly executing valid warrants.[19] Early in this chapter, after describing the Collinsville

IN THE NEWS

Police searches are not always calm, polite events, which is why the Constitution requires a "technicality"—that the police must have a warrant signed by a neutral magistrate and that the warrant must be based on well-established probable cause. In this case, a 75-year-old retired minister died of a heart attack after police officers broke into his apartment, chased him into a bedroom, and hand-cuffed him.

DETECTIVES HAD PREVIOUSLY REJECTED RAID INFORMANT

by Sean Murphy

The informant who led police to the wrong apartment on a drug raid in which a retired minister died last month was rejected as unreliable just two months earlier when he offered detectives information about illicit gun dealing....

Even though the informant was brushed aside in January by

detectives assigned to the Area C-11 police station in Dorchester, detectives in the drug control unit relied on him for the ill fated ... raid....

In January, the informant told police an acquaintance was selling 9mm Glocks ... from an apartment....

The detectives determined the informant's information was poor and did not trust him....

The drug control detectives, however, had a long relationship with the informant, dating back to 1990 ... the informant has supplied police with information leading to the arrests of at least five suspects, records show.

Drug detectives were aware that the same informant lied to them in 1991 when he offered to act as a confidential informant while blaming a shooting at two police officers on another teenager....

In fact, the informant was responsible for the shooting....

[Lisa] Lehane [the detective who led the raid] cited the informant without naming him as describing four heavily armed drug dealers and a kilo of cocaine in the second-floor apartment....

In her application for a search warrant, Lehane specifically characterized the informant as "reliable" and named three instances in 1991 and 1993 when the informant's tips led to successful drug raids....

But, unlike virtually all other applications for search warrants she sought over the past two years, Lehane did not attempt to corroborate the informant's tip through surveillance or an informant's drug buy....

A team of SWAT officers and drug control detectives who broke into the second-floor apartment found Rev. Accelyne Williams, 75, a frail retiree who died of heart failure minutes after being handcuffed.

Source: Boston Globe, April 16, 1994, pp. 1, 22.

---

raids, where federal agents raided the wrong houses, I asked what would have happened if they had found drugs—traces of cocaine powder or a marijuana seed. If those raids had taken place today rather than before 1984, the logic of the good faith exception would make the evidence admissible.

The reasoning of the Court is especially interesting. Instead of holding the police to strict procedures, the Court adopted a balancing approach. It weighed the defendant's right to due process against the truth-finding functions of a trial. It weighed the benefits of deterring unreasonable searches against the cost of letting a guilty person go free.[20] In effect, the Court was asking a different set of questions. Instead of asking, "Was this search legal?"

IN THE NEWS

As in cases like Mapp, *sometimes the only weapon the court has in curbing illegal behavior is to hamper the prosecution of a person who may be factually guilty. The following incident shows how easily the police can get around the probable cause requirements for obtaining a search warrant.*

DEAD OFFICER, DROPPED CHARGES: A SCANDAL IN BOSTON

by Allan R. Gold

Boston—The Police Department here has been rocked by scandal since a judge last month dismissed murder charges against a man accused of killing a detective in an abortive drug raid 13 months ago.

When Judge Charles M. Grabau dismissed the indictment, he acknowledged it was "a drastic measure" but he had to act because of "egregious misconduct" by the prosecution and the police.

The judge based his decision on the state's failure to produce, after repeated requests and months of delay, an informer that the defense wanted to question. The raid in which the killing occurred was carried out with a search warrant the police obtained based on information they said came from the informer....

Mr. Luna [a detective] had applied for the search warrant using information the police said was supplied by an informer, "John."...

Since then, Mr. Luna has admitted he invented "John" and never made two undercover purchases of cocaine that he swore to in his application for the warrant....

Mr. Luna's admissions have revealed the possibility of abuse of search warrant process, particularly the ease with which a magistrate will grant a warrant. It is information ... that never would have emerged if Mr. Griffiths [a detective] had not been killed....

Source: New York Times, *March 20, 1989, p. A12.*

---

it asked, "What will be the effect of excluding the evidence? Will it greatly deter police misconduct? Will a guilty person go free?"

In the closing years of this century, we can probably expect further eroding of *Mapp*. A majority of the justices appear to be relatively tolerant of police misconduct in the interests of fighting crime. But giving the police a freer hand in searches will have little effect on this battle. First, the exclusionary rule affects relatively few cases. Second, the cases in which the exclusionary rule makes a difference are not predatory crimes in which innocent citizens are victimized. They are, like the *Mapp* case itself, crimes of illegal possession, most of them drug possession. If the Supreme Court were to abolish the exclusionary rule completely, it would have very little effect on street crimes like robbery or burglary, much less on the most serious violent crimes of murder and rape. As for drug trafficking, it is a dishearteningly robust industry, remarkably unaffected by arrests, convictions, or confiscations.[21] Moreover, the police are already making so many arrests for drug crimes that the courts and prisons don't know what to do with all these cases; so it seems unlikely that eliminating the exclusionary rule would take much of a bite out of drug crime. It is harder to know how easing it would affect violations of people's rights. At the least, it seems logical to conclude that as the police are given greater latitude in their searches, there will be no decrease in such violations.

MORE RIGHTS

The *Mapp* decision was only one of the historic and controversial rulings on criminal law made in the 1960s by the Warren Court. Two others that have become well known are *Gideon* and *Miranda*. As with *Mapp*, these later decisions also involved a conflict between the due process model and the crime-control model of the criminal justice system. But the *Gideon* case also brought to light a third view—what might be called the administrative model. As with *Mapp*, the case hinged on the conflict between federal standards and state standards, and therefore the decision also involved new interpretations of the Bill of Rights and the Fourteenth Amendment.

GIDEON AND THE RIGHT TO COUNSEL

In the early hours of June 3, 1961, in the small town of Bay Harbor, Florida, somebody smashed the window of the poolroom, entered, took some wine and beer, and broke into the coin boxes of the cigarette machine and jukebox. Following a lead from an eyewitness, the police arrested Clarence Earl Gideon, a drifter who sometimes ran poker games and who had a record of crimes and prison terms dating back to his youth in the 1920s. Gideon pleaded not guilty to the break-in. At his trial that August, he requested that the court appoint a lawyer for his defense since he had no money to hire one. The judge refused, telling Gideon, "Under the laws of the state of Florida, the only time a court can appoint a counsel to represent a Defendant is when that person is charged with a capital offense."

Gideon, with little choice in the matter, acted as his own lawyer. Considering that he had never had much formal education of any kind, let alone legal training, he did about as well as could be expected. He lost. The case against him came chiefly from the eyewitness testimony of the young man who claimed to have seen Gideon inside the poolroom at 5:30 A.M. He said that Gideon came out with a bottle of wine in his hand, phoned for a cab, and left in the cab. Acting as his own lawyer, Gideon called eight witnesses, but his questioning of them seemed rambling and inconclusive. The jury found Gideon guilty, and the judge imposed the maximum sentence—five years.

Gideon appealed to the Supreme Court. The Court receives many such letters—handwritten in pencil on prison stationery—and it rejects most of them. But the Court decided to hear Gideon's case and appointed as his attorneys one of the best Washington law firms.

Gideon's appeal rested on the Sixth Amendment, which says in part, "In all criminal prosecutions, the accused shall enjoy the right ... to have the assistance of counsel for his defense." But what did this mean? In Florida, it meant that if Gideon wanted to hire a lawyer for his defense, he had every right to do so. If he did not have the money, well, that was no concern of the state.

By the time the Supreme Court decided to hear Gideon's case, an earlier decision (1938) had already ruled that the Sixth Amendment required a court-appointed counsel when the defendant was too poor to afford one.[22]

Since the Gideon decision in 1963, indigent defendants have had the right to free legal representation. Most felony defendants avail themselves of the Sixth Amendment right to counsel. Only a few—like Colin Ferguson, on trial for shooting several people on a Long Island commuter train—defend themselves, and for good reason. Ferguson refused the advice of experienced criminal lawyers, constructed and carried out his own defense strategy, and was convicted on all charges.

However, the Court limited this interpretation to federal courts; state courts were not required to provide lawyers for poor defendants. As in the development of search-and-seizure standards, the Supreme Court had overturned some convictions in state courts when the denial of counsel had been "fundamentally unfair"—for example, when the defendants were mentally unfit to conduct their defense, either because of feeble-mindedness, illiteracy, or ignorance or because the case was too complex for a nonlawyer. The Court had also required free counsel in state trials for capital offenses (i.e., those carrying the death penalty). The poolroom break-in was not a capital crime, Gideon was mentally competent; the case was not legally complicated, and there were no special circumstances. So at the time of Gideon's trial in Florida, the judge's denial of his request for a lawyer was perfectly in accord with the law.

Gideon's attorneys, therefore, were asking the Supreme Court to change its previous interpretations of the Sixth Amendment. They argued that if the right to counsel meant a court-appointed lawyer in federal courts, it should mean the same thing in state courts. They based this argument on the due process clause of the Fourteenth Amendment ("nor shall any state deprive ... without due process of law").

The state of Florida argued that the Constitution provided for diversity among the states and that the Court should not change the policy that had guided it for nearly 200 years. Florida also made an argument on practical as well as constitutional grounds: If Gideon and thousands of other poor defendants like him were given the right to counsel, there would be a flood of not-guilty pleas requiring court time for jury trials even in minor cases. "The entire undertaking would result in an unnecessary expense to taxpayers."[23]

This practical argument is not a very strong one from a moral or a constitutional point of view. Imagine yourself in the position of a poor defendant being told, in effect, "No justice for you because we want to keep taxes down." However, the argument does reveal something else about the criminal justice system: that in reality, courts operate along the lines of neither the due process model nor the crime-control model. Instead, most of the time they run on what might be called the **administrative model**.[24] Regardless of ideological statements about justice and crime, the primary goal of the courts is not to implement due process nor to control crime. Instead, a court is like any other public bureaucracy, say, the department of motor vehicles or the welfare department. Its principal goal is to process a large number of cases rapidly, and it accomplishes this goal by establishing a routine procedure. The routine procedure for handling criminal cases requires that defendants plead guilty rather than go to trial.

This system has come in for a good deal of criticism. Liberals insist that it shortchanges the poor, who are pressured to plead guilty rather than have their day in court. Conservatives grumble that the criminals who plead guilty are rewarded with sentences that are far too short. However, for at least seventy years (i.e., since well before the current high levels of crime), most criminal cases have been settled by guilty pleas. To do otherwise, some argue, would clog the courts and bring the machinery of justice to a grinding halt so that it could neither protect the rights of the accused nor punish the guilty.

The Supreme Court ignored Florida's argument and sided with Gideon. In its historic 1963 decision of *Gideon* v. *Wainwright* (Wainwright was the Florida district attorney at the time Gideon submitted his appeal), the Court remanded Gideon's case to Florida to be retried, this time with a court-appointed attorney. But the Court's decision had implications far beyond the fate of Gideon. The ruling meant that in all state proceedings for felonies (i.e., crimes punishable by a year or more in the state prison), poor defendants would have the right to a court-appointed lawyer. (Nine years later, in *Argersinger* v. *Hamlin*, the Court extended this right to all cases that carry any jail sentence.)

The constitutional history of the right to counsel resembles that of the exclusionary rule: First the Court sets a standard for federal courts; then it extends that standard to state trials involving unusual circumstances; finally it imposes the standard in all state trials. In *Gideon*, as in *Mapp*, the Court did not say that *all* aspects of the Bill of Rights would now be incorporated into the Fourteenth Amendment and therefore held to be binding on the states. Instead, it held that the right to counsel was so "fundamental and essential to a fair trial" that it was to be "absorbed" into the Fourteenth Amendment.[25] "In our adversary system of criminal justice, any person haled into court, who is too poor to hire a lawyer, cannot be assured a fair trial unless counsel is provided for him." If the state has a lawyer, then the defendant must also have one; otherwise, since our system is adversarial, the trial would be unfair.

Clarence Earl Gideon was tried again for the Bay Harbor Poolroom break-in, and the difference between the first and second trials offers an excellent illustration of the reason for the Supreme Court's decision. The second trial, this time with an experienced defense lawyer, made it clear that Gideon was not *legally* guilty. That is, the prosecution could not prove its case beyond a reasonable doubt. For every other bit of evidence the prosecution offered, the defense had a reasonable explanation. After an hour's deliberation, the jury found Gideon not guilty. But the trial also showed that Gideon was more than legally not guilty of the break-in. He was probably *factually* innocent as well, that is, he didn't do it. The trial was an example of our adversarial system of justice operating at its ideal.

But did the *Gideon* decision create a return to the adversarial ideal in all cases, or even in most cases? The state of Florida had argued that it could not afford this ideal. Was its argument correct? Did run-of-the-mill street criminals, thinking that they would get a free Alan Dershowitz, suddenly start pleading not guilty? The answer is clearly no. By the time of the *Gideon* decision, most states already had some kind of arrangement to provide free counsel. In fact, only five states (Florida, Alabama, Mississippi, North Carolina, and South Carolina) did not provide attorneys for poor defendants.[26] But providing free lawyers for the poor makes very little difference in everyday court proceedings. The vast majority of defendants plead guilty. Both before and after *Gideon* and *Argersinger*, about nine out of ten cases that end up in court are settled by guilty pleas. The percentage may vary from city to city, but the average is about 85 percent, and the figure rarely falls below 75 percent.[27]

Defendants plead guilty largely for two reasons. First, pleading guilty usually is more convenient and less painful than going to trial. Second, most defendants plead guilty because they are guilty—both factually and legally. If they went to trial, even with a good lawyer, they would lose. These are open-and-shut cases, or as they are known informally among public defenders in Los Angeles (and perhaps elsewhere), **deadbang cases**.[28] Public defenders get mostly deadbang cases because the prosecutor has already screened out the others.

DISCRETION: THE BETTER PART OF PROSECUTION

Prosecutors have a great deal of discretion in deciding what happens to people who have been arrested, and there are several points along the way from arrest to trial where the prosecutor can drop a case. Soon after an arrest, the arrested person must appear before a magistrate for an initial hearing to be formally notified of the charge and to have bail set. Many jurisdictions have done away with the initial hearing to save time. Instead, the accused goes directly to the preliminary hearing, where a magistrate determines whether there is probable cause to charge the suspect.

The next step is the determination of formal charges. The prosecutor presents evidence to a grand jury, which either returns an indictment (a true bill), specifying the charges, or returns a no bill, freeing the accused. In some states, and especially for less serious crimes, instead of a grand jury indictment the prosecutor presents evidence in an information before the magistrate. The magistrate then decides whether the evidence is sufficient to bind over the defendant for trial.

At any point in this process the prosecutor may drop the case. If the prosecutor lacks the evidence or witnesses to win a conviction or if it appears that the arrested person is really innocent, the prosecutor may enter a **nolle prosequi**, a statement that the case will not be further prosecuted. For example, in New Orleans (a jurisdiction that screens cases very carefully at the initial stage), about half of all felony arrests are "nolled out."[29] If the case is a felony, the prosecutor may also decide to reduce the charge to a misdemeanor or to divert the case to juvenile court if the offender is a juvenile.

Once formal charges have been filed, the prosecutor (or a defense lawyer) may still file for dismissal of the case, usually for the same reasons that cases are rejected earlier in the process—lack of witnesses or evidence. Manhattan (New York) prosecutors reject only 3 percent of cases at the initial screening, but 32 percent of the cases are dismissed later. In New Orleans, where most weak cases don't get past the initial screening, only 5 percent of cases are dismissed.[30] In other words, at some point early in the process, prosecutors drop nearly half of all felony arrests and, as a result, ensure that they are left with only the strongest cases. As one prosecutor put it, "We have them cold-cocked. They plead guilty because they are guilty. That's something that people don't understand. Basically the people that are brought here are believed very definitely to be guilty or we wouldn't go on with the prosecution. We would *nolle* the case."[31] Given such a strong position, prosecutors do not really have to bargain. In fact, most of the time, the defendant pleads guilty to the top charge.[32] Contrary to the popular image, for most defendants the plea bargain isn't much of a bargain.

Figure 14–2 shows the importance of prosecutorial discretion. Prosecutors reject, dismiss, or divert nearly half of all felony arrests brought in by the police. Nearly all the cases that are carried forward are settled by guilty pleas. The figure illustrates the fate of an average 100 cases, the average being based on data from over a dozen jurisdictions with different operating procedures, crime rates, populations, and demographics. For any one jurisdiction, the actual percentage of cases at each stage may vary significantly from this average.

The defendant who insists on a trial incurs risks and costs. In a plea bargain, defendants are offered fairly specific sentences. If they accept, they know how much time they are facing. If they choose instead to go to trial and are found guilty, they will probably receive a much longer sentence. One study found that for the same crime, defendants who lost in jury trials received sentences twice as long as those who pleaded guilty.[33] Some people have argued that such a system is unfair to defendants since they are being penalized for exercising their Sixth Amendment right to a trial. Nevertheless, the Supreme Court has given its approval to the prosecutor's use of this bargaining chip.

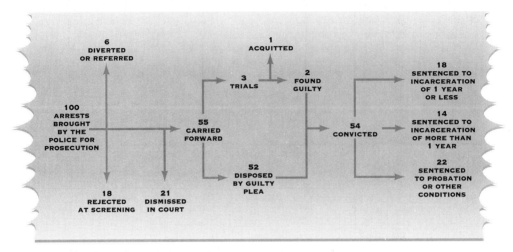

FIGURE 14–2 Typical outcome of 100 felony arrests brought by the police for prosecution

Source: Barbara Boland, Paul Mahanna, and Roland Sones, *The Prosecution of Felony Arrests, 1988* (Washington, DC: U.S. Department of Justice, 1992).

There are many criticisms of the current system. Conservatives argue that plea bargaining allows wicked people to get off too lightly. This lenience both denies justice to the public and encourages crime. In the good old days, they argue, people who were arrested went to trial; if they were found guilty, they received sentences appropriate to their crimes. Critics from another perspective argue that too often plea bargaining denies justice to the defendant. The administrative style of justice means that the defense lawyer is less interested in providing the best defense for the defendant than in handling a large volume of cases.

Consider the following transcript from a New York City courtroom:

Judge: But the offer is 90 days, only 90 days.

Defendant: I said I won't take more than 60.

J: My God, this is arrogance. A Class A felony drug sale, punishable by a sentence of 15 years to life, and they are offering you a plea to a misdemeanor and 90 days. That's very generous, sir.

D: You offer me 90 days because you ain't got no case. And if you ain't got no case, why can't I go home right now?

Legal Aid lawyer: They are not offering to send you home.

D: Hey, you my lawyer, ain't you?

LAL: Yes.

D: Then how come you never talk to me?

LAL: I am trying to determine your circumstances. What you say doesn't mean s—. What matters is what's on the court papers and the record.

[The defendant continues to protest.]

IN THE NEWS

WINNING VERSUS TRUTH

In our adversarial system, defense lawyers have only one goal—the best possible outcome for the defendant. But prosecutors, at least in principle, have a dual role: They must represent the state in an adversarial proceeding—that is, they must win the case for the state—but they must also seek justice and the truth. What happens when these two goals conflict, when some of the evidence weakens the state's case? Apparently, the "straight-shooter" is something of a rarity.

Robert T. Johnson, who ... join[ed] the race for District Attorney in the Bronx, is described by ... former colleagues as ... "a straight shooter...."

[His] impartiality became apparent to Mr. Alperin [president of the Bronx Criminal Bar Association] six years ago when, a defense lawyer in a manslaughter case, his opponent was a young prosecutor named Robert T. Johnson.

"He produced a witness who looked around the courtroom and said, 'I can't identify anybody.'..." Of course that's favorable testimony for the defendant. "During recess ... the witness was in the

D.A.'s office and he told the D.A. that the defendant was actually not the person who committed the crime. *Now a lot of D.A.'s would have sent the witness home.* Mr. Johnson brought him back and told the judge and myself that the witness had even more favorable testimony to give for the defense. The point is, he wasn't concerned with winning and losing, but with doing the right thing."

Source: Dennis Hevesi, "'Straight-shooter' Enters Bronx Race," *New York Times,* June 24, 1988, p. 33 (emphasis added).

Not all prosecutor's would be as scrupulous as that DA, especially in emotionally charged cases, as this item shows.

A state appeals court has unanimously upheld the overturning of a conviction of a man wrongfully imprisoned for seven years in the rape of a 5-year-old girl at a day-care center.

The ruling...says that prosecutors ... withheld documents that could have led to the defendant's acquittal....

Mr. Ramos [the defendant] had been working as a teacher's aide at the ... day-care center in the Bronx. He was convicted ... and sentenced to a maximum term of 8 1/3 to 25 years in prison....

The prosecution's case, led by Assistant District Attorney Diane Farrell, centered on the child's description of a sexual act and the testimony of the examining doctor, who concluded that the child could only have known about such behavior if she had been molested. In her closing remarks, Ms. Farrell asked the jury, "Where else could the child have learned such conduct?" The withheld documents, which the defense learned about only after the conviction, contained statements by other workers at the day-care center that the girl masturbated openly in class, watched explicit cable-television movies, described sexual conduct to her teachers and other children and placed dolls in positions mimicking sexual conduct. "Her teachers regarded her sexual knowledge as being well beyond that of a 5-year-old and she could and did descriptively communicate that knowledge in class," Judge Collins said in overturning the conviction....

[The appellate court, in upholding that overturning, said] "The people's failure to fulfill their obligation to insure that a fair trial was had and justice done is inexcusable."

Source: Dennis Hevesi, "Overturning Conviction Is Upheld," *New York Times,* July 17, 1994, p. 25.

J: The matter will have to be litigated. Is the district attorney asking for any bail?

District attorney: $500.

J: $500 bail.

D: I'll take the 90 days. I'm guilty.[34]

This small case, typical of hundreds that come through city courts every month, illustrates several points. First, the defendant's final statement tells us that this is probably a deadbang case. Second, the transcript shows the way in which the prosecutor—with the judge's cooperation—can use bail to force a reluctant defendant to cooperate—probably a common, though clearly unconstitutional, use of bail. Third, as the judge points out, there is a large difference between the penalty the defendant would risk in a trial and the penalty he receives for a guilty plea.

But how are we to interpret this discrepancy? On the one hand, it looks as though a serious criminal—one guilty of a fifteen-year-to-life felony—is getting off very lightly. On the other hand, a mere $500 bail—which he will get back—is sufficient to persuade this drug dealer, this "serious felon," to accept a sentence 50 percent longer than his original demand.

Finally, notice the relationship between the defendant and his lawyer. The lawyer virtually ignores the defendant; instead he is interested in the factors that will determine the outcome of the case: the prosecutor and the court papers. More important, the lawyer seems to have no interest in helping his client bargain for a shorter sentence. If the DA has, with no explicit bargaining, already reduced a 180-month sentence to 3 months (15 years to 90 days), why does the defense lawyer not join his client in trying to get the DA to knock off another 30 days? Why does this defense lawyer seem to abandon his adversarial role? Whatever happened to *Gideon* v. *Wainwright*?

As for the DA and the judge, why should they resist the defendant's counteroffer of 60 days? Will the extra 30 days really do more to rehabilitate the defendant, deter other drug dealers, or reduce drug sales? If the answer is no (as it almost certainly is), why should the DA and judge insist on 90 days? The answer becomes clear if in thinking about what happens in court we abandon the adversarial model in favor of the administrative model, if we think of prosecutor and defense lawyer not as adversaries but as part of a work group—co-workers trying to process cases quickly by fitting them into routine, normal categories.

"NORMAL CRIMES" AND THE COURTROOM WORK GROUP

In the 1960s, just as research on the police had provided evidence of a sharp contrast between their ideal role and what they actually do, research on courts also offered some sobering views of what really occurs there. Two of the most famous sociological articles from this period analyzed the role of the defense lawyer. In "Normal Crimes," David Sudnow argued that the pressure of having to handle a large volume of cases forced the district attorney and the public defender (PD) to create a kind of shorthand—a set of categories into which most cases would fit. "Over the course of their interaction and repeated 'bargaining' discussion, the PD and DA have developed a set of unstated recipes for reducing original charges to lesser offenses." The recipes include not only the crime itself but also the motives and the characteristics of the offender and victim; for example, "most ADWs [assault with a deadly weapon] start with fights over some girl."[35]

This system allows a quick disposal of those cases that fit into the typical categories. **Normal crimes** are "normal" in the sense that they are typical—they fit the stereotype the lawyers have of these crimes and the people who commit them. Using these stereotypes allows the lawyers to dispose of these cases almost automatically. "'Typical' burglaries are reduced to petty theft, 'typical' ADWs to simple assault, 'typical' child molestation to loitering around a schoolyard, etc." The burglary might not actually have involved petty theft, and the child molestation might have occurred far from any schoolyard; nevertheless, if the accused seems to be a "typical" burglar or "typical" child molester, that's how the charge is bargained.[36] The classifications of the law as written in the statute books take a secondary place to the set of categories that the DA and the PD have worked out.

Sometimes, the crime does not fit into the normal category. The deadly weapon was not a knife or a handgun but a machine gun. The burglary took place in a wealthy neighborhood or involved much property damage. The molestation went beyond fondling. These distinctions may not make the crime any different in terms of the written law. But for the prosecutor and defender, these special circumstances mean that the usual plea bargain cannot automatically go forward. The case requires its own special bargaining or, especially if the crime is more serious, perhaps even a trial.

When the court works in this way, the prosecutor and defense lawyer are working less like adversaries and more like colleagues. In principle, the public defender's role is no longer to fight tooth and nail for his or her client. Instead, "the major job of the public defender, who mediates between the district attorney and the defendant, [is] to convince his 'client' that the chances of acquittal are too slight to warrant this risk [of trial]." The PD does not really try to determine if the facts of the case fit the law the defendant is accused of violating; instead, the PD tries to determine if the crime fits into the profile of a normal crime. Instead of a courtroom in which the defense attorney and the prosecutor are adversaries and the judge a referee, the three are now working together. They constitute what some observers call the **courtroom work group**.

Let's return to the questions I posed about the drug trial cited earlier. To understand it, we would do better to stop thinking in terms of justice and adversarial bargaining and think instead of normal crimes and the courtroom work group. To plead this case out at anything other than ninety days would upset the established routine for this kind of case. It would be a violation of the unspoken understanding between prosecutor and defense about what this case was worth. The defense lawyer argues so forcefully against his own client ("What you say doesn't mean s——") because he knows that the prosecutor would never settle for a sixty-day sentence. However, if the prosecutor had asked for six months instead of three, the defense attorney might have taken a more adversarial stance. He probably would not have gone to trial (assuming that this was a deadbang case), but he could use various legal devices to cause delays and generally give the prosecutor a hard time—if not in this case, then in one of the many other cases in which he would be confronting the same prosecutor.

In the courtroom work group, the DA and PD share a common language and a common knowledge of the law, both in the ideal and in the way it works in their particular court. They also share an interest in disposing of a great number of cases. In other words, the defense attorney has much more in common with the DA than with the defendant—the client whose interest the public defender is representing.

A similar irony or contradiction is built into the role of prosecutor. Remember, the DA represents the state, the people. The view of the people about what sentence a crime deserves is, presumably, expressed in the penal code (i.e., in the laws written by the legislators the people elect). But prosecutors soon acquire a different courtroom perspective. "It's like nurses in emergency rooms. You get so used to armed robbery that you treat it as routine, not as morally upsetting.... The nature of the offense doesn't cause the reaction in me that it would in the average citizen."[37] Prosecutors may enter the job with the same perspective as the public, but they soon adapt to the system. Other prosecutors, supervisors, defense attorneys, and other courtroom regulars socialize the newcomer. Learning the ropes means taking a different view of human behavior, at least for purposes of disposing of cases. Here is a prosecutor talking about "a serious crime ... a crime that I thought was serious at one time, anyway":

> He ... is charged with aggravated assault. One guy got 25 stitches, the other 15. And the [defense] attorneys would want me to reduce it. I'd go talk to [the chief prosecutor]. He'd say, 'They both are drunk, and both got head wounds. Let them plead to breach of peace, and the judge will give them a money fine.' Things like that I didn't feel right about doing, since, to me, right out of law school, middle-class, you figure 25 stitches in the head, Jesus Christ.[38]

THE GOING RATE

This insider's view of the courtroom offers an interesting contrast to the criticisms that come largely from outside the court. Those criticisms frequently claim that the justice system does not do justice, especially in sentencing. Conservatives often complain that the courts are too lenient; liberals may see the courts as unjustly severe. Critics from both camps argue that the courts are inconsistent: The same crime can receive widely different sentences.

In reality, when a court disposes of cases in a routine, administrative fashion, it should achieve a high degree of consistency. Similar crimes or criminals will receive a similar sentence—the **going rate**. The sentences in a court may not conform strictly to the law, but they will conform to the sense of justice of the members of the courtroom work group. That sense of justice, however, is influenced much less by the law than by experience and by the number and kinds of crimes that they must deal with every day. Prosecutors and defense lawyers in high-crime jurisdictions get used to knife wounds and muggings. In low-crime areas, the going rate for these crimes might be much stiffer.[39]

In recent years, some states have tried to reduce the disparity in sentences by reducing the discretion of prosecutors and judges. Some jurisdictions have placed limits on the prosecutor's discretion in plea bargaining. More commonly, states have reduced judges' discretion by moving away from indeterminate sentences and toward mandatory, determinate, or presumptive sentencing. The loss of discretion over sentencing may be more apparent than real. By using their discretion at an earlier stage in the game (e.g., by deciding which charges, if any, to file against the defendant), prosecutors have often been able to maintain control over their courts. Judges, prosecutors, and even defense attorneys have cooperated to protect "their" courtrooms from the intrusion of the legislature and to continue coping with a large volume of cases while dispensing justice as they see it.

PRIVATE ATTORNEYS: PERRY MASON AS CON ARTIST

Private attorneys, too, have been criticized for their role as members of the courtroom work group. Two years after Sudnow's article appeared, Abraham Blumberg published a cynical view of private defense lawyers: "The Practice of Law as a Confidence Game."[40] In most con games, con artists deceive you into believing that they are on your side, when they are only out to get your money and in are fact teamed up with someone else. Defense lawyers, says Blumberg, are no different. Private attorneys, much like public defenders and Legal Aid lawyers, are much more in league with the court system than with the defendant. "The accused's lawyer has far greater professional economic, intellectual and other ties to the various elements of the court system than he does to his own client." Like any con artist, the lawyer must keep these ties hidden from the client and appear to be doing his or her all to help the client. Like the public defender, the private lawyer makes a more or less standard deal—the going rate—with the district attorney and then tries to sell that deal to the defendant. Of course, when he or she talks to the client, the lawyer makes it appear that the deal is extraordinarily attractive, attainable only through the lawyer's particular craftiness and connections. True, private defense attorneys may deliver in court ringing defenses of their clients or condemnations of the police or community, but these rhetorical exercises may be mostly a show put on to convince clients that they are getting what they paid for. And pay they must, for the private attorney, unlike the public defender or Legal Aid lawyer, must also make sure to collect whatever fee he or she is charging—"a sum which bears an uncanny relationship to that of the net proceeds of the particular offense involved."

Perhaps these studies paint too bleak a picture of criminal defense. Not all private defense attorneys are "copout" lawyers, incompetents who know only how to plead a client guilty. Not all public defenders go along with the prosecutor. Generally speaking, defense attorneys are more willing to go to trial than prosecutors. In some cities, relationships between public defenders and prosecutors really do remain adversarial, even hostile.[41] However, the system creates pressures so that even the most able and committed public defenders may not be able to give their clients the best defense. The caseload is high; most clients are guilty, factually and legally; and the lawyer has neither the time nor the money to make an independent investigation of every case.

Gideon was an important case. It was an example of how our system of justice works in its ideal version. It vindicated the adversarial system and the necessity for the presumption of innocence. It pointed out the importance of having a lawyer, and by guaranteeing lawyers even to the poor, it gave substance to our ideal of equality before the law. In practice, however, it did little to change the reality of how courts operate. Most cases continued to be handled in an administrative rather than an adversarial way. But the *Gideon* decision was important in one other way. It provided a basis for some much more controversial Supreme Court rulings in criminal law.

THE <u>MIRANDA</u> DECISION

Probably the most famous decision in criminal procedure made by the Warren Court was the case of *Miranda* v. *Arizona*. We have all seen TV cops reciting the Miranda warnings to people they arrest, that is, reading them their rights. *Miranda* concerns, among other things, a suspect's right to remain silent, a right explicitly provided in the Fifth Amendment against self-incrimination. This right is rooted in the adversarial system, in which the defendant's role is to defend himself or herself, not to help the state in its prosecution.

The history of the right not to self-incriminate in the United States resembles that of other aspects of due process. The framers of the Constitution were aware of the history of forced testimony. It was a useful tool for convicting criminals, but it increased the power of the government at the expense of liberty. The Star Chamber of sixteenth-century England, for example, was basically a way of enforcing the law without bothering with the inconveniences of the usual procedures—inconveniences such as defendants who refused to testify and juries that did not always convict.[42] The Star Chamber, with its forced testimony and secret, nonjury trials, may have been swift and effective, but the framers of the Constitution were less concerned with the efficiency of government than with the liberty of the people.

By the time of *Miranda*, the Supreme Court had overturned convictions based on forced confessions. In 1936, in *Brown* v. *Mississippi*, it reversed a murder conviction in which one suspect had confessed after being hung twice by the neck to a tree (being let down each time before he died), tied to the tree and whipped, and two days later being arrested and severely whipped again. Other defendants in the case were also whipped in the jail; the deputies used leather belts with buckles that cut the men's backs to pieces. (The deputy in charge testified that such whipping was "not too much for a Negro; not as much as I would have done if it were left to me.") These defendants were persuaded when told that the whipping would continue until they confessed.[43]

In later years, the Court rejected confessions extracted by psychological pressure, lying, and deceit. As with other provisions in the Bill of Rights, the Warren Court in the 1960s broadened the Fifth Amendment protection to include state courts, not just federal courts.[44] And, as with some of the other constitutional protections, the Supreme Court in the 1980s began to allow some exceptions.[45]

CONFESSIONS AND THE COURT

One objection to forced confessions is that they are unreliable. A person being tortured might say anything, regardless of whether it is true. Some people have argued that a confession should be allowed in court if it is "voluntary." The Supreme Court, however, in its landmark decisions in the 1960s, went beyond this narrow, practical reasoning. It enforced the Fifth Amendment not because the confession might be unreliable but because the police must not be allowed to deny people their constitutional rights, including the right against self-incrimination. This right, combined with the Sixth Amendment right to counsel, formed the basis of the *Miranda* decision, and its precursor *Escobedo* v. *Illinois*, decided in 1964.

A year before, the Court had already ruled in *Gideon* that everyone has the right to counsel. The question the Court faced in *Escobedo* was this: When does that right begin? The police arrested Danny Escobedo in connection with a murder and questioned him for fifteen hours, releasing him only after his lawyer, who had not been present, had gotten a writ of *habeas corpus*. Eleven days later, the police again brought in Escobedo for questioning after another suspect in the case had identified him as the murderer. Escobedo asked for his lawyer to be present, and the lawyer himself asked to be present, but the police refused these requests.

After more questioning, a Spanish-speaking officer told Escobedo that if he pinned the murder on one of the other defendants, he could go home. So in a confrontation at the police station, Escobedo said to the other defendant, "I didn't shoot Manuel. You did it." But by saying this, Escobedo was admitting his own part in the murder, and under Illinois law, this complicity made him as guilty as the actual killer. Obviously, if Escobedo's lawyer had been there, he would have told Escobedo to keep his mouth shut under any circumstances. However, by the time Escobedo was allowed to see his lawyer, he had already incriminated himself. He was convicted of murder and sentenced to twenty-two years.[46]

In a five-to-four decision, the Supreme Court reversed Escobedo's conviction, ruling that the police had violated due process. Specifically, the police had denied the Sixth Amendment right to counsel, a right that was "made obligatory on the states by the Fourteenth Amendment." This right to a lawyer, the Court said, begins when the inquiry into a crime "has begun to focus on a particular suspect" and that suspect has been taken into custody. Furthermore, if the police deny a suspect's request for a lawyer or fail to warn the suspect of the right to remain silent, they have violated the Sixth Amendment.

Two years later, the Court heard the case of Ernesto Miranda. Miranda was a suspect in the kidnapping and rape of an 18-year-old woman in Phoenix, Arizona. The victim had identified him in a lineup. The police questioned him without telling him of his right to an attorney. After two hours, they emerged with Miranda's written confession, which stated, among other things, that the confession was voluntary and made in full knowledge of his legal rights. The confession was used at his trial, and Miranda was convicted and sentenced to twenty to thirty years. The Supreme Court overturned the conviction, holding that the government must get evidence against a defendant "by its own independent labors, rather than by the cruel, simple expedient of compelling it from his mouth." In addition, the Court, in this now famous (or infamous) decision, outlined specific procedures that the police must follow when they take a suspect into custody:

> Prior to any questioning, the person must be warned that he has a right to remain silent, that any statement he does make may be used as evidence against him, and that he has a right to the presence of an attorney, either retained or appointed. The defendant may waive effectuation of these rights, provided the waiver is made voluntarily, knowingly and intelligently. If, however, he indicates that he wishes to consult with an attorney before speaking, there can be no questioning. Likewise, if the individual is alone and indicates in any manner that he does not wish to be interrogated, the police may not question him.[47]

Nobody, not even the toughest crime-control proponents, advocates scrapping the Fifth and Sixth amendments. However, the constitutional right to a lawyer and the constitutional right to remain silent can be real only if individuals know about them and can exercise them. What *Miranda* did was to ensure that people arrested by the police be informed of these rights and allowed to use them. Apparently, what bothers the critics of *Miranda* is that suspects may actually become aware of and assert their constitutional rights and that the police must respect those rights.

THE EFFECTS OF MIRANDA

Apart from the legal basis of *Miranda*, we must also ask what practical effects the decision had. Did it change the way police operate? Did it allow more suspects to go free? Like many of the other cases we have looked at in this chapter, *Miranda* overturned the conviction of a person who was factually guilty. Rochin did indeed possess the illegal drugs the police pumped out of his stomach; Dolree Mapp had been in possession of obscene materials; Danny Escobedo had been guilty of murder under Illinois law; Ernesto Miranda had committed the crimes he confessed to. (The Court, by the way, did not free Miranda. It merely ordered that Arizona retry him, this time without his confession as evidence. At his second trial, on the basis of other evidence, Miranda was again found guilty of the same rape and kidnap charges and sentenced to twenty to thirty years. He was paroled after a few years and arrested a couple of times—weapons, drugs, and parole violation. In 1976, at the age of 34, he was killed in an argument over a card game in a Phoenix skid-row bar.) The Court has reversed convictions in crimes even more horrible than the kidnap and rape Miranda committed.[48] In all these decisions, the Court has placed procedure ahead of results, an emphasis based on the due process clause of the Constitution (no person shall be punished without due process of law).

Undoubtedly, in some of these celebrated cases, the guilty have gone free. But the Supreme Court rarely gets cases in which the police have violated the rights of the truly innocent—not necessarily because they do not make such violations but because such abuses, like the outrageous search that produces no valid evidence, rarely result in arrest, much less in a court appearance. There is no conviction to overturn.

However, these due process considerations count for very few of the cases in which criminals go free. As the data in Table 14–1 show, in San Diego in 1987, nearly 10,000 arrests for Index crimes, 91 (or less than 1 percent) were dropped because of due process problems. In Manhattan the proportion was even smaller: four cases out of 21,000 arrests, or less than two one-hundredths of one percent.

A FINAL WORD: JUSTICE FOR ALL?

This chapter has focused on two large questions: What is the constitutional basis for criminal courts in the United States? And how do the courts actually deal with criminals? One way of reviewing is to look at the question of whether the system does justice, especially in light of the many criticisms leveled at it. Let's look at the complaints from liberals and conservatives and try to estimate the extent to which they are valid.

LIBERALS

The complaint: Adversarial justice exists only for the rich. Most defendants, too poor to afford an all-out adversarial defense, get free lawyers, who force them into plea bargains. These lawyers must help the system process cases, even if it means sacrificing the interests of a particular client. Even what looks adversarial may be merely a show meant to impress the client.

Another view: public defenders and other free lawyers do fight for their clients, although much of the adversarial work may be invisible. Some of it occurs in the early stages following arrest, when charges are dropped or greatly reduced. If defense lawyers were less vigorous, prosecutors might *nolle* out far fewer cases. Remember also that the going rate, which looks like assembly-line justice rather than a vigorous defense, is the outcome of adversarial bargaining on similar cases that came before. Finally, the defense lawyer is usually playing a losing hand. The DA has eliminated all but the deadbang cases. The defendant is guilty factually and legally, and it is doubtful whether even a Perry Mason or an Alan Dershowitz could get a better deal.

CONSERVATIVES

The complaint: The courts are too lenient. Bad people who have committed bad crimes go free because of legal technicalities. Other serious criminals wind up with overly lenient sentences—a few months or even probation, the proverbial slap on the wrist—because prosecutors plea-bargain rather than prosecute.

Another view: the raw data on this question at first glance seem to support this very popular notion. Picture the criminal justice system as a corridor or a sequence of branching corridors with the crime at one end, the prison door at the other, and many other doors along the way. For 100 serious crimes like burglary and robbery at the beginning of the corridor, more than 90 never get to that final, steel-barred door. Of course, it's important to understand why these cases leave the system, and it turns out that these reasons do not conform to the image of a criminal justice system soft on crime and hamstrung by the restrictions of due process.

Most of the crimes never really make it into the corridor as actual people. Only 20 percent of Index crimes result in an arrest; the other 80 percent exist only as uncleared crimes on police records. Still, of those arrested, nearly half exit the system fairly quickly. The prosecutor holds open the door marked "reject" or "dismiss" or "divert to juvenile court," and out they go. But these rejections occur largely in the interests of justice. Remember, the most frequent problems that cause rejection and dismissal of cases concern evidence and witnesses. The lack of evidence may mean that the crime was not very serious to begin with. Witness problems usually arise when the victim, and perhaps other witnesses, know the defendant. After tempers cool, they may wish to settle the matter privately rather than pursue it in court, or witnesses may feel that the crime is not important enough to bother with. In other words, the cases that disappear are likely to be those whose dismissal would not upset even the most conservative critics. And as we have seen, the constitutional restrictions of due process, those infamous "technicalities," account for only the tiniest percentage of dropped cases.

Who is still left in the corridor? People who commit the more serious offenses, those who commit crimes against strangers, or those who have a long criminal history. They are the people who must actually face charges and either plead guilty or go to trial.

As for plea bargaining, there is some truth to this criticism. Certainly, those who plead guilty get shorter sentences than those who go to trial. But the serious criminals, repeat offenders who commit serious crimes, do receive stiff sentences. New policies that "close the loopholes," eliminate plea bargaining, institute mandatory or determinate sentencing, or generally "get tough" seldom change the fate of these criminals. The courts are already dealing with them severely. The defendants most affected by these tough policies are the less serious offenders.[49] Prosecutors and judges use their discretion to differentiate between more serious and less serious defendants whose crimes nevertheless look the same on paper. Consider the following case, a man charged with grand larceny who nevertheless walks out of court free.

> Bridgeman: Charged with 155.30, grand larceny and 165.40, criminal possession of stolen property....
>
> Legal Aid lawyer: (turning to the prosecutor) Petit larceny and time served?
>
> DA: Fine. Let's go.

LAL: Okay, Mr. Abramson. If you admit you did it, they're willing to let you go home.

Defendant: I did it, but I ain't got no home.

LAL: Well, do you want to go to jail?

D: No....

DA: Mr. Adamson,* is that your lawyer standing next to you?

LAL: Say yes.

D: Yes.

DA: Did you discuss the case with him adequately?

D: Yes.

DA: Do you understand that a plea of guilty is the same as a conviction after trial, and that by pleading guilty you give up your right to trial, your right to call witnesses on your own behalf, and your right to cross-examine witnesses brought against you? Do you understand that you are giving up all those rights?

D: Yes.

DA: It is charged that on the night of April 23, on the corner of Broadway, you acted disorderly and took a purse from Viola Simpson. Are the facts true as stated?

D: Your honor, I didn't have nothing to eat for two days, and she was coming out of a restaurant, so I know she just ate. I snatched her purse.

Judge: And no one threatened you or made any promises to get you to enter this plea?

D: He told me I could go.

Judge: That's right. The plea is acceptable to the court. Sentence of the court: time served.[50]

First, notice how quickly the district attorney and the defense attorney apply the normal crimes recipe. Were it not for the defendant's confusion, this case would have been disposed of in a matter of seconds. But then imagine what might have happened under a system that did not allow the prosecutor the flexibility to reduce the charges and did not allow the judge such discretion over the sentence. Imagine further that this defendant had committed a similar purse snatching ten years earlier and had also been caught once with a small amount of cocaine. Under the increasingly popular three-strikes laws, he might be occupying a state prison cell for the next thirty years.

The basic function of the criminal courts is to determine guilt and then decide what punishment to assign the guilty. This chapter has focused on how the people in the court reach those decisions. The next chapters will try to answer a question that has been strangely absent in the discussion so far: What effect does punishment have on crime?

■ *The confusion over the defendant's name is perhaps not such a rarity, especially in a case such as this, in which, as the transcript makes clear, everyone (except perhaps the defendant) is concerned mostly with bringing the case to a rapid conclusion.

CRITICAL THINKING QUESTIONS

1. What are the advantages and disadvantages of an adversarial system? What structural similarities are there between our adversarial court system and our constitutional form of government?
2. The Fourth Amendment became part of the Constitution in 1791, yet it was not until 1961, 170 years later, that a state was required to exclude illegally seized evidence. Why did it take so long? What change did the Supreme Court make in its interpretation of the Constitution to justify this new requirement?
3. No other country has an exclusionary rule like that of the United States. Why do we have it? What are its flaws and what alternatives are there?
4. Nearly half of all arrests are dismissed before they reach some judicial decision. Why? Would we be better off if prosecutors prosecuted more cases?
5. What is the legal reasoning behind *Mapp*, *Gideon*, and *Miranda*? What impact have these decisions had on criminals and on the criminal justice system?
6. Forty percent of Americans favor an end to plea bargaining. What's wrong with plea bargaining, both from the perspective of the defendant and of the public? What good does it accomplish? Does it do justice?

KEY TERMS

administrative model	due process model	legal guilt
adversarial model	exclusionary rule	*nolle prosequi*
common law	factual guilt	normal crimes
courtroom work group	going rate	procedural law
crime-control model	good faith exceptions	substantive law
deadbang cases	inquisitorial model	writs of assistance

CHAPTER FIFTEEN

REHABILITATION

CHAPTER OUTLINE

PUNISHING CRIMINALS

People convicted of crimes receive some punishment. That is how we know it is a crime. If the misdeed were a tort (or civil wrong), the defendant would make some sort of restitution to the plaintiff. But when a defendant loses in a criminal case, the state imposes a punishment. The U.S. Constitution specifically mentions three types of punishment: deprivation of "life, liberty, or property"—in other words, execution, prison, and fines.

At the time the Constitution was written, courts could impose several other types of punishment, including whipping, branding, and mutilation. These are forms of **corporal punishment** (i.e., punishment to the body of the convicted person). Some Moslem countries and others still impose whipping and even (though rarely) mutilation, but all modern industrialized countries, East and West, have abolished corporal punishment. Most Western democracies have also abolished capital punishment (i.e., the death penalty). The United States, of course, is the main exception, though Japan has executed a handful of criminals over the last forty years. Capital punishment is much more likely to be found in countries like Iran, Iraq, or China—countries with authoritarian, totalitarian, or otherwise oppressive forms of government.

Rehabilitation programs have long been a part of prison life. In the seventeenth century, prisoners in Pennsylvania were given Bibles. Today, prisons offer computer training. The question is whether any of these programs has a significant impact on recidivism.

Today in the United States, the most common forms of punishment are fines (money paid to the state, not to the victim) and incarceration (i.e., being locked up) or some other form of supervision. The United States currently has about 1 million people in prisons and jails, but an additional 3 million convicted criminals are on **probation** and **parole**.[1] Probation and its close cousin, the **suspended sentence**, do not involve any incarceration at all. Parole is a form of early release for those in prison. Probation and parole are forms of **conditional release**. That is, instead of spending time in prison or jail, the offender must fulfill certain conditions. The courts may impose a wide variety of conditions, especially with probation: reporting to a probation officer, participating in a drug or alcohol rehabilitation program, working a specified number of hours in community service, avoiding certain places or people, holding a job, and sometimes making restitution to the victim. If the convict violates the conditions of probation or parole, the court may impose a prison sentence. The total cost of these punishments now runs to over $25 billion a year.

PRACTICAL MATTERS—REHABILITATION, DETERRENCE, INCAPACITATION

Why impose any of these punishments, which cost so much money? Why shouldn't we just let criminals go? Probably your first answer to this question was a practical one: We punish criminals to reduce crime. If we didn't punish them, crime rates would increase. This is an empirical proposition—one that can be tested against evidence. Accordingly, this section of the book will try to present the reasoning and evidence on how punishment affects crime.

The practical effects of punishment fall into three categories. One justification for punishment is **rehabilitation**—providing prisoners with the skills, education, self-control, or whatever so that they will not commit crimes. For more than a century, rehabilitation was the dominant ideology of prisons. In recent years, however, it has lost much support, and for good reason: There is precious little evidence to prove that prisons can in fact rehabilitate criminals or correct their behavior. Nevertheless, governments still place prisons under the heading of "corrections"; prisons are still officially known as correctional facilities, and they still offer a variety of rehabilitation programs. Later in this chapter, I try to trace the history of rehabilitation—the long road to its ascendancy and the shorter path of its decline.

A second justification for punishment is **deterrence**, the idea that the pain or threatened pain of punishment will prevent people from committing crimes. Probably the best-known arguments about deterrence center on the issue of capital punishment, with its supporters maintaining that if people knew they would be executed for murder, murder rates would not be so high. They also apply this same logic to other crimes and penalties, arguing that if punishments were more certain and more severe, crime rates would drop. In the last twenty-five years, public support for deterrence, and especially for the death penalty, has risen steadily. However, the evidence on deterrence, like the evidence on rehabilitation, is not so clear or encouraging.

Finally, even if prisons do not rehabilitate and even if they do not deter, they may still reduce crime by keeping criminals off the streets. This function, known as **incapacitation**, has been the topic of much recent research in criminology. The logic of incapacitation is irrefutable: As long as criminals are in prison, they cannot be on the streets committing crimes. Incapacitation as a policy, however, depends on two questions that are not so easily answered: How much crime can prisons prevent? And at what cost?

JUSTICE—THE MORAL DIMENSION

Punishment is not just a matter of practical effects. For example, several years ago, Jean Harris, a prep-school administrator, shot and killed her lover, who was a physician and the author of a best-selling diet book. A jury convicted Harris of murder. What sentence should the judge have given her? Assume that if released, Harris would never commit another crime; and assume also that her immediate release would not affect anyone else's behavior; it would not inspire anyone else to commit a murder. In other words, locking her up would have no effect on crime; letting her go would not increase the danger to anyone at all. Should the judge have let her walk out of court free?

If you said no, you could not be basing your answer on any of the practical reasons for punishment. I already stipulated that rehabilitation, deterrence, and incapacitation were not at issue. Instead, you were basing your decision on the morality of sentencing rather than on its practical effects. It just would not be "right" to let a convicted murderer go. Much of the debate over capital punishment concerns concepts of right and wrong. Opponents of the death penalty argue that it is not right for the state to be in the business of killing people, especially in the absence of evidence that execution is a deterrent that saves other people's lives. Supporters of the death penalty argue that even if capital punishment is not a deterrent, a person who commits an exceptionally brutal or cold-blooded murder deserves to die.

This fourth reason for punishment is usually called **retribution**. It resembles revenge, but ideally it is based less on personal feelings than on general principles. Criminals should receive the punishment that they justly deserve; they should get their **just deserts**. Although the concept of justice plays a large role in people's views of crime and punishment, it is also the area where social science and empirical evidence are the least relevant. When we talk about "justice" and what people "deserve," we are no longer in the world of factual information, of cause and effect. We are no longer in the world of science, where we ask, "What is?" We are in the world of philosophy and ethics, where we ask, "What ought to be?" There is another important difference between retribution (or justice) and the other goals of punishment. Rehabilitation, deterrence, and incapacitation refer to the impact on criminals. But retribution refers to the impact of the punishment on the rest of society: Does it make us feel that justice is being done?

The following discussion is not an attempt to answer questions of justice, for these are not a direct concern of this book. It is important that we examine our notions of justice, for too often we take them for granted and assume that everyone agrees, as though justice were a matter of fact rather than a matter of philosophy. However, although I certainly hope that you take time (and perhaps a philosophy course) to examine your own ideas about what is just, in this text I try to stay closer to matters of fact.

REHABILITATION: THE EVOLUTION OF AN IDEAL

Over 150 years ago, a young Frenchman wrote what is still probably the best book ever written about the United States—its people, its culture, its government, and its problems. But Alexis de Tocqueville had not set out to write *Democracy in America*. He had sailed to America in 1831 for much narrower purposes: to study its prisons. Nor was he the only one. In that same decade, England and Prussia also sent experts to look at U.S. prisons; even nonexpert tourists made prisons a part of their travels.[2] What was it about American prisons that drew such international attention?

America had not always had such exemplary forms of justice. Punishments in colonial times resembled those of England since America was still under English rule. The most frequent were fines and whipping, although there were other punishments, some that may now seem quaint, others brutal. The *ducking stool* was a chair in which the offender was repeatedly lowered into a pond or river. Other offenders were sentenced to sit in the *stocks*—a wooden board with holes for immobilizing the hands and feet. The *pillory* was similar to the stocks, except that the offender stood rather than sat. Here is a description from Boston 1771.

> A little further up State Street was to be seen the pillory with three or four fellows fastened by the head and hands, and standing for an hour in that helpless posture, exposed to gross and cruel jeers from the multitude, who pelted them constantly with rotten eggs and every other kind of repulsive garbage.[3]

Punishments could also be quite brutal by modern standards. A pilloried offender might have his ears or tongue nailed to the board or cut off entirely. Others might be branded on the forehead, cheek, shoulder, or hand—*T* for theft, *M* for manslaughter, *SL* for seditious libel; *B* might mean burglar or blasphemer, depending on the jurisdiction.[4] In other cases, the offender was not branded but had to wear a letter sewn onto his or her clothing to indicate the crime. Fiction has given us the best-known example: Hester Prynne's scarlet *A* for adultery (though *D*'s for drunkenness were far more common).

Finally, and frequently, there was the gallows. In the 1700s, both in England and in America, criminals were put to death for crimes like burglary, theft, and counterfeiting as well as for more serious crimes like murder. Many of those executed were third-time offenders. A first offense would bring a fine and whipping. A second-time offender would be sentenced to more whipping and perhaps a few hours sitting in the gallows with a rope about his or her neck, presumably as a warning against a third offense.[5] Capital punishment occurred far more often than it does today. And America was, if anything, more tolerant than Europe, where in the seventeenth century those accused of witchcraft were executed by the tens of thousands.[6] As late as 1805 in England, about 13 percent of all convictions (7.6 percent of all indictments) resulted in the death sentence.[7] However, of those sentenced to die, many were granted reprieves. Only about one in four actually went to the gallows. At a 13 percent rate, the United States today would be putting over 100,000 people on death row each year. In 1993, there were nearly 900,000 felony convictions in state and federal courts; if 13 percent were executed, that would be 117,000 deaths. Executions were public events. In England, crowds of people turned out, giving the event a riotous, almost festive atmosphere. In America, too, hangings were public, though the mood was usually more solemn.

England did have recourse to one other form of punishment—transportation. Some countries today occasionally deport a few criminals (especially noncitizens). But from the time of the first American settlement until 1776, England shipped tens of thousands of convicts to America. After American independence, Australia became the favored destination. As for prison, it was not widely used in colonial America. In England, prison terms became fairly common by 1800, though most sentences were for less than a year (see Table 15–1).

DIFFERENT SOCIETIES, DIFFERENT PUNISHMENTS

If you had walked into a town square in eighteenth-century America or England, you would have seen the focal points of community life—the courthouse and the church—but you also would have noticed the stocks, the whip-

TABLE 15-1 •

SENTENCES FOR PROPERTY CRIMES IN SURREY, ENGLAND, 1740–1748

PUNISHMENT	PERCENTAGE OF TOTAL SENTENCE
HANGING	9.8
TRANSPORTATION	49.3
WHIPPING	31.0
DISCHARGING	8.8
IMPRISONMENT	1.0

Source: J. M. Beattie, "Crime and the Courts in Surrey, 1736–1753," in J. S. Cockburn, ed., *Crime in England, 1550–1800* (Princeton, NJ: Princeton University Press, 1977), pp. 155–186.

ping post, and the pillory. Many colonies had laws requiring each town to build these devices. Probably you would not have seen a jail, and if you did, it would have looked much like any other house rather than like a secure lockup for hardened criminals. Today, by contrast, we have no pillory, no ducking stool, no tongue piercing, no branding. Even whipping is outlawed. Instead, we spend billions of dollars to build prisons.

Why did these other punishments disappear, and how did incarceration become the preferred way of punishing criminals? First, look at the differences between punishment 250 years ago and punishment now. The older punishments were physical, and they were public. Today, punishment is private. The stocks and pillory exposed offenders to the rest of the community. Prison deliberately removes them from public view. Even capital punishment, where it exists today, is a far more private event—execution behind prison walls with only a handful of witnesses rather than a public hanging preceded by an uplifting sermon.

One reason for the change may be that the stocks, the pillory, and other public punishments are best suited to small, stable communities—towns where everyone knows everyone else and where people depend on one another in a variety of daily interactions. Public punishments depend on shame—shaming the offender in the eyes of the community. Corporal punishments, too, took place in public, literally adding insult to injury. Flogging was done either at the whipping post or with the offender tied to a cart and pulled through the town. These punishments, in one important way, resemble the punishments schoolteachers inflict on pupils (though, of course, the Puritan punishment of criminals was more severe): The punishment is public, and it involves the entire community. The dunce cap may have disappeared from classrooms, but teachers still respond to misbehavior with open criticism, sarcasm, and even name-calling—all forms of humiliation in the eyes of the community (i.e., the other fourth-graders). Some teachers still make the gum-chewing child stand in front of the class with the chewing gum stuck on his or her nose. In many schools teachers are still allowed to use corporal punishment, sometimes carried out in front of the other children.

What is the point of such humiliation? Its effect on the offender is at best questionable. Nevertheless, public punishment serves an important function for the rest of the community. It marks the boundaries of proper behavior, and it enlists the entire community in supporting them.[8] However, this form of punishment can work only in a small community where everyone generally shares the same values and beliefs. If opinion is already divided, the punishment may make the divisions even sharper. If the criminal is something of a hero to many members of the community, it does little good for authorities to punish him or her publicly. Such an event, instead of uniting people in support of the laws, is more likely to cause an outpouring of support for the criminal and resentment against the authorities. In London (already a large city by 1700), when Daniel Defoe was pilloried for writing an antichurch satire, crowds pelted him not with rotten food but with flowers.[9]

Public shaming worked in colonial America because towns were usually stable, uniform communities. People knew one another's business and shared a fairly narrow range of ideas and opinions.[10] This uniformity was no accident. To prevent diversity, towns enacted laws to restrict the flow of outsiders into the community, and they closely monitored people's daily behavior. Those with unorthodox ideas might be banished from the town. The right to privacy and freedom of expression as we know them today were alien concepts in early America. However, by the nineteenth century, this small-town uniformity was falling victim to historical demographic changes. The population was growing rapidly, and Americans were becoming a "people on the move."[11]

Demographic change often brings social change. As societies become larger, the division of labor becomes more complex. What had been a job for the whole community becomes a task for specialized individuals or institutions. In the 1800s, as the population became more mobile and as communities grew larger and less unified, towns developed special agencies to perform the tasks once performed by the community at large. Where once citizens patrolled on the watch, now police officers walked a beat. Where once the shaming of offenders had been a task for the whole community, now punishment became the province of a specialized institution, the prison.[12] (Similarly, when pupils graduate from the grammar school, where they spend all day in the company of the same twenty-five children, to the more individualistic, mobile, and diverse society of the high school, shaming punishments give way to the school equivalent of prison—detention.)

PUNISHMENT AND PATRIOTISM

The change in America from public punishments and executions to incarceration has another source: the American Revolution—its underlying philosophy and sentiment. In the aftermath of the Revolution, both leaders and the general public were filled with feelings of optimism for their new nation. Philosophically, America was a product of the Enlightenment, the Age of Reason. Politically and emotionally the Revolution represented a rejection of things British, including the English system of punishment. The Bill of Rights, with its prohibition of "cruel and unusual punishments," is one result of the spirit of those times. The Americans felt that the extensive use of capital and corporal punishment was the mark of a government and a society based on privilege, tradition, and tyranny rather than equality, reason, and freedom.[13]

The Enlightenment ideas that inspired the Revolution and the new republic also provided the philosophical basis for criminal reform. In the area of crime, the most important Enlightenment document was Beccaria's essay "On Crimes and Punishments." Beccaria criticized extreme punishments, torture, and execution; they were irrational, out of all proportion to their utility as deterrents to crime. Instead he advocated that lawmakers see the law more as a matter of prevention than of punishment; he also recommended more use of incarceration and less use of corporal punishment. One of the colonies, Pennsylvania, had taken this direction much earlier, in 1682, because of the Quaker influence of its founder, William Penn. The Pennsylvania criminal code abolished capital punishment for all crimes but murder, and it replaced corporal punishments with incarceration or other more humane punishments. The experiment did not last long, however. Pennsylvania was still a colony dominated by England, and twenty-five years later, a political conflict between the colony and the crown resulted in the instatement of the English criminal code, with its long list of capital crimes.[14]

ABOUT CRIME & CRIMINOLOGY

WHY DON'T WE FLOG CRIMINALS?

In 1994, a young American in Singapore was found guilty of spray painting some cars. The sentence for his vandalism was six strokes with a rattan cane, a punishment that by most accounts is extremely painful and permanently scarring. Because the young man was an American, the case—and Singapore's use of flogging—drew international attention. Objections came not only from Amnesty International, which opposes all forms of torture, but also from President Clinton.

Yet many Americans said they approved of the punishment, and as of early 1995 legislatures in at least six states were considering laws that allowed whipping, paddling, or caning. The proponents of these punishments base their arguments almost entirely on the grounds of deterrence: If we had these punishments, our crime rate would be lower. Typical is columnist Georgie Ann Geyer: "Here at home, where we feel good about our form of punishment so long as it doesn't work, we are close to drowning in crime. Forty thousand murders a year (Singapore had 58 last year)."[*]

Forget the exaggeration of our murder statistics (Geyer is too high by at least 15,000). Forget that London and Tokyo, cities with a population roughly three times that of Singapore, have about the same number of murders despite the absence of torture as a criminal penalty.

In the United States, the government may not flog people for crimes. If the corporal punishment laws are passed, they will eventually be tested in the Supreme Court, and the Court will probably rule that they violate the Eighth Amendment prohibition of "cruel and unusual punishment" (though it will be interesting to see the reasoning of both the majority and the dissenters). As with the other practices, the framers of the Constitution objected to "cruel and unusual punishment" not because it was ineffective, not even primarily because it was morally wrong, because these grotesque corporal punishments were one more tool by which despotic governments kept themselves in power.

Singapore is a case in point. The government made vandalism punishable by flogging—a punishment previously reserved for serious violent offenses like rape and murder—in the wake of an outbreak of antigovernment graffiti. It was not a matter of public safety; it was a matter of tyranny—an autocratic government violently suppressing any expression of ideas it didn't like. Yet today, many people—even those who oppose flogging simply because it is cruel—fail to see something that was obvious to the framers of the Constitution: that there is a connection between tyranny and the ways of apprehending, trying, and punishing criminals.

■ [*]*Newark Star-Ledger*, April 12, 1994, p. 18.

Besides rejecting the older, English criminal codes, Enlightenment ideas of punishment also contradicted earlier ideas of crime and justice widely held in America. The Puritans who founded the New England colonies in the 1600s saw crime as the outcome of the devil's temptations and the natural sinfulness of humans. Theirs was a pessimistic view, for it saw little hope for reform. A century later, however, the dominant philosophy held not only that society could prevent crime but also that it could reform individual criminals. The principal instrument of this reform would be the prison.

Jails, prisons, and other houses of correction already existed in the eighteenth century, but they were not widely used in colonial America.[15] Some prisons looked like houses, and were about as easy to escape from. Others resembled those in England—horrid places where men and women, children and hardened adults, were all kept together under inhumane conditions.[16] However, in the 1790s, the prevailing spirit of optimism led many states to revise their criminal codes and to build new houses of detention based on new philosophical principles. It was these new institutions that drew observers like Tocqueville to America.

PRISONS—IDEOLOGY AND ARCHITECTURE

At the time of Tocqueville's visit, the United States was the site of two different models of prison, both of them new: the Pennsylvania model and the Auburn model. It may be difficult for us, looking back across nearly two centuries, to appreciate the differences, and perhaps these differences don't really matter. What is important to note about both systems is that they were attempts to design a prison specifically for the purpose of rehabilitation.

The Pennsylvania system, in its theory and its architecture, relied on one basic idea—separating the prisoner from evil influence. Pennsylvania had two main prisons, the Eastern Penitentiary near Philadelphia and the Western Penitentiary near Pittsburgh, both built in the 1820s. Each prison housed several hundred prisoners, but the prisons were designed so that the inmates never saw one another. For his entire term, a prisoner was isolated in an 8-by-12 foot cell. In that cell, a prisoner would eat, sleep, and work at some kind of craft. His only human contact would be with guards or clergy; the only book permitted was the Bible. For exercise, each cell had an equally small yard adjoining it.

This system may seem cruel to us, but it has a certain logic, especially for rehabilitation purposes. First, the solitude allowed the prisoner, uninfluenced by any other forces, to reflect on his sins. The isolation was also intended to prevent contamination by other prisoners. A prisoner could not learn criminal techniques and ideas from other prisoners, nor could he establish criminal contacts that might influence him after his release. (Incoming prisoners were even blindfolded on the way to their cells so that they would not be able to glimpse other prisoners.) The isolation also made it easier for the staff to control inmates and made the prisoner an eager worker when he was finally allowed some kind of handicrafts in his cell.[17]

Pennsylvania's separate, or solitary, system offered one way of reforming the criminal and preventing his contamination by other prisoners. However, it was not the only model for accomplishing these goals. In Auburn, New York, a prison built in 1823 offered a different solution. As in Pennsylvania, the New York prison tried to reform the criminals through religious instruction, work, and isolation from evil influences. Also as in Pennsylvania, the New York prison permitted no contact with the outside world and no books except the Bible. However, at Auburn, prisoners worked and ate together; they moved from cell to dining hall to workplace together. What prevented the spread of evil ideas from one prisoner to another was Auburn's silent system. Prisoners

The prison in Auburn, New York, built in 1823, was a model for rehabilitation, though many of its practices hardly conform to the rehabilitative ideal today. Prisoners were forbidden to speak to one another, wore prison stripes, and marched about in lockstep.

were absolutely forbidden to speak to one another. The New York prison also introduced the lockstep (a tight-formation shuffle in which prisoners marched from place to place) and prison stripes, the uniform that remained part of prison life into the next century.

Experts debated which system was better. Supporters of the Pennsylvania system pointed out that the New York model tempted prisoners to speak to one another by packing them together and then punished them cruelly for breaking the silence. In fact, Auburn guards did resort to a variety of punishments for those who spoke: flogging with rawhide or wire whips, sudden drenching with icy water, and other tortures.[18] Supporters of the New York system criticized Pennsylvania's isolation as inhumane; but more important, they pointed out the economic advantages of the New York prison. It was far cheaper to construct a block of small, inside cells (7 feet by x 3 ½ feet) than the outside cells of the Eastern Penitentiary. Eventually, with the rise in prison populations in the 1840s and 1850s, more and more states followed the Auburn model. Even Pennsylvania finally abandoned its solitary system.

THE INDETERMINATE SENTENCE

The reform movements of the 1790s had culminated in the widespread construction of prisons. By the 1820s, capital and corporal punishments had almost disappeared. Instead of these pessimistic versions of justice, state governments turned to the prison, with its potential for rehabilitating criminals. Before too long, however, the pressure of numbers compromised the ideas of both the Pennsylvania model and the Auburn model. In a pattern that by now has become all too familiar, the practical problems of running a prison soon undermined the lofty goal of rehabilitation. To prison authorities faced with overcrowding, underfunding, poor discipline, and the possibility of riot and escape, it didn't make much difference whether the prison had been designed to rehabilitate prisoners through silence or through separation. Their first goal was the smooth running of the prison. So rehabilitation gave way to discipline, and the new prisons came quickly to resemble the old—complete with degraded living conditions and brutal punishments.

The stage was set for the next round of reform, which came in the 1870s. Like the reformers of the previous century, prison experts of this decade saw prison as a place for rehabilitation rather than punishment. Toward this goal, they emphasized two new ideas: first, that prisons should provide decent living conditions and a variety of rehabilitation programs; second, that instead of **determinate** (fixed) **sentences**, courts should impose **indeterminate sentences**. Instead of a sentence of five years (no more, no less), a prisoner might be sentenced to three to 10 years. The actual date of release would depend on the prisoner's own individual progress.

This kind of sentence may seem unfair, but from the standpoint of rehabilitation, indeterminate sentencing was the most logical policy. If the purpose of punishment was rehabilitation, it made little sense to keep a person in prison after he or she was reformed. Similarly, releasing a prisoner too early (i.e., before complete rehabilitation) was harmful both to the prisoner and to society. Since different criminals would need different lengths of time to reform, determinate sentences were inappropriate. Instead, what was required was a system of indeterminate sentences coupled with parole.

The U.S. reformers of the 1870s were not the first to propose or even to try out these ideas. In 1840, the British government assigned a reformer, Captain Alexander Maconochie, to run its Norfolk Island penal colony off the coast of Australia. An earlier investigation by Maconochie had made the British aware of the degraded conditions in its Australian prisons, and Norfolk Island was the most extreme. Inmates sentenced to death would drop to their knees and praise Jesus for their deliverance. Catholic prisoners, whose religion strongly prohibited suicide, would sometimes draw straws, the winner being killed immediately; the runner-up would do the killing, thereby assuring his own conviction and execution.[19] Maconochie tried to humanize the prison and institute rehabilitation programs. Under the new system, prisoners would earn marks through their labor and good behavior; when a prisoner accumulated the required number of marks, he would be given a "ticket of leave" equivalent to parole. Unfortunately, Maconochie governed only a short time at Norfolk Island, and when he left the prison reverted to its old, brutal ways.

Maconochie's ideas received a warmer welcome in the United States, where reformers of the 1870s proposed similar changes. By that time, the failure of prisons was not exactly a secret. A New York Prison Commission report in 1852 concluded that long-term imprisonment "destroys the faculties of the soul"; long-term prisoners were "distinguished by a stupor of both the moral and intellectual facilities…. Reformation is then out of the question."[20] Here again was the idea that the principal goal of prison should be rehabilitation. Nearly twenty years later this idea was echoed at a convention in Cincinnati, which set the agenda in prison reform for nearly a century. Prisons were to achieve the goal of protecting society by means of rehabilitating prisoners. Zebulon Brockway, an influential prison administrator, said, "The supreme aim of prison discipline is the reformation of criminals, not the infliction of vindictive suffering."[21] Brockway also held that reformation could be brought about by education, religious instruction, and industrial training (which is probably better understood as hard work rather than job training).

In 1876, Brockway had a chance to put his ideas into practice. He was appointed superintendent of a new prison in Elmira, New York. His plans for the prison embodied the principles announced at the Cincinnati conference six years earlier: indeterminate sentences, education, job training, better living conditions, and a mark system in which inmates earned marks toward greater privileges and eventually release. Elmira became a shining example to prison reformers, even though the reality of prison life rarely matched the ideal. In 1894, an investigation at Elmira revealed that prisoners were regularly whipped, thrown into solitary confinement, or shackled to the cell door.[22] Apparently, even in a reformer's prison, ideals took second place to the pressures of maintaining order and security.

While actual conditions at Elmira may have degenerated, the rehabilitative ideal continued to gather support. By the early twentieth century, most states had some form of parole and indeterminate sentencing. The ideology of rehabilitation fit well with two typically American traits—optimism and the belief in progress through science. This is the era when psychology and sociology were becoming popular. These new social sciences held out the same hope for social problems that the hard sciences offered for technological problems. Reformers of this period (the late nineteenth century) could also look to medicine as an example. Recent discoveries in germ theory had led to the birth of scientific medicine and to real hopes for curing and preventing many diseases. Reformers, therefore, tended to see the problem of crime and criminals in terms of a medical model. That is, the criminal, rather than being evil or sinful, was sick. Prisons could be most useful if they tried to cure rather than punish. Psychology and sociology would provide the scientific basis for this cure, especially through individualized treatment. So instead of talking about punishment, prison reformers began to talk about treatment and about the needs of different kinds of prisoners. By the 1920s, the idea of psychiatry was a well-established part of prisons, and many prisons had at least part-time psychiatrists.

The greatest success of the reformers seems to have been not a practical but an ideological one: They convinced legislators, prison administrators, and the general public that prisons should be and could be places for rehabilitation. Reformers also succeeded in getting prisons to expand rehabilitation programs. In practice, however, the new programs were often not really new. Even in the eighteenth century, proposals for prison reform had included work, religion, and education. More important, the reformers' programs often turned out to be far different from the shining ideals set forth at the 1870 conference in Cincinnati. For example, prisons have always tried to provide work for prisoners. Usually, however, the prison work experience fell far short of any rehabilitative ideal.

Many southern states, especially after the Civil War, contracted inmate labor to private companies. The prisons got money, and the private companies got cheap, slavelike labor. Obviously, the purpose of this arrangement was economic rather than rehabilitative, and after investigations revealed the cruelty and high rates of death, states began to outlaw this form of prison work. In northern states, where reformers had more influence, prisons set up prison industries. But before long, these came to suffer from inadequate (or nonexistent) machinery, lack of supervision or training, and various other problems. Investigations in the 1920s found that work programs existed mostly on paper. For much of the day, prisoners had nothing to do. Education programs followed a similar pattern. The reform movement of the 1870s had inspired many prison systems to offer some sort of education, but by the 1920s most such programs had inadequate classrooms, too few books, too few teachers, and too few students.[23]

REHABILITATION—ONE MORE TIME

In the 1950s, the rehabilitative ideal came to dominate thinking about prisons, both among those who worked in the criminal justice system and among the public as well. In 1970, nearly three-quarters of the public thought that the main emphasis of prisons should be rehabilitation. Less than 20 percent wanted punishment or protecting society to be the main focus.[24]

By the time that poll was taken, prisoners had available a variety of rehabilitation programs. Depending on the prison and state, a prisoner might be able to choose from several psychotherapies, both individual and group. Newer therapies like transcendental meditation and behavior modification were added to the list along with drug and alcohol counseling and religious programs. Education programs offered basic education, GED (general equivalency diploma) studies, and even college courses. Job-training programs included instruction in trades like baking, TV repair, sheet-metal work, printing, and many others (see Table 15–2). In recent years, prisoners have been able to sign up for training in more modern areas like computers.

REHABILITATION PROGRAMS—"WHAT WORKS?"

The important question about all these programs is this: Do they work? Do they rehabilitate criminals? Perhaps the most noteworthy attempt to answer this question began in 1966. A New York State commission hired a team of researchers, headed by Robert Martinson, to find out what works. This seems like a logical thing for the state to do since it is spending money on several different types of rehabilitation programs. If it could find out which ones were most successful, it could expand those programs and let the unsuccessful ones wither away.

But how do we measure the success of a program? Education programs might give tests to find out how well students had learned. Psychotherapy programs could try to measure personality change or general adjustment

TABLE 15-2 •

ENROLLMENT IN ACADEMIC, WORK, AND COUNSELING PROGRAMS IN STATE CORRECTIONAL FACILITIES

TYPE OF PROGRAM	1984	1990
ACADEMIC PROGRAMS		
ADULT BASIC EDUCATION	8.3%	8.8%
SECONDARY	7.6	5.9
COLLEGE	5.5	4.9
WORK PROGRAMS		
PRISON INDUSTRIES	11.5	7.1
FARMING, ETC.	5.3	4.1
VOCATIONAL TRAINING	8.7	8.7
WORK RELEASE	0.8	0.8
COUNSELING PROGRAMS		
PSYCHOLOGICAL, DRUG, AND ALCOHOL	14.0	30.3
EMPLOYMENT	2.9	5.0
LIFE SKILLS	7.7	4.4

Source: Maguire and Pastore, *Sourcebook—1993*.

inside prison and out. Job-training programs could evaluate specific skills. But the most important question, one that cuts across all programs and gets at the basic idea of rehabilitation, is this: Did a program help prisoners keep out of trouble once they were released?

The usual way to answer this question is to measure **recidivism**. How many released prisoners were rearrested or reconvicted, and for what kinds of crimes? How many were returned for parole violations? Parole violations are not necessarily crimes; they are merely violations of the conditions of parole and may include nothing more serious than getting drunk, hanging around with old acquaintances, losing a job, or failing to meet with the parole officer. In New York, more than half the parolees whose paroles were revoked were returned to prison for these kinds of technical violations. In other states, the figure might be less than 25 percent.[25]

Martinson looked at every study he could find published in English from 1945 to 1967 that evaluated a rehabilitation program. It turned out that many of these "evaluations" had no scientific validity. Some did not adequately describe the treatment program; others did not bother to include data on recidivism or used unreliable measures of success. Still others made a crucial omission by failing to include a **control group**—a group of similar prisoners who did not go through the particular program. Suppose a treatment program claims a 75 percent success rate (i.e., that only 25 percent of released prisoners who had completed the program were subsequently convicted of a crime). If a control group also had a 75 percent success rate, we might as well scrap the program and use the money for something else; we would still have a 75 percent success rate. Only a study with a control group can really tell us whether a program is effective.

After Martinson had thrown out all the evaluation studies marred by shoddy research methods, he was left with 231 acceptable studies. Here is what he found: "With few and isolated exceptions, the rehabilitative efforts that have been reported so far have had no appreciable effect on recidivism."[26]

This finding was only the beginning. Or perhaps it was not even the beginning, for the New York State planning agency refused to publish Martinson's study. It even tried to prevent Martinson from publishing it on his own. Apparently the results threatened more than just current theories about prison; Martinson's conclusion also threatened the vested interests of those involved in the planning and operation of rehabilitation programs.

Eventually Martinson, with the help of a lawyer, was able to publish his results in a 1974 article entitled "What Works?" Although the title strongly implied that the answer was "nothing works," the truth is a little more complicated. What he found was "no clear pattern to indicate the efficacy of any particular method of treatment." In other words, if ten job-training programs reduced recidivism but ten others did not, Martinson could not say that job training "works" since there was no "clear pattern" of positive results, even though ten of the programs did work.

Although other researchers had previously reached similar conclusions, Martinson's article created quite a stir. It appeared in a widely read journal, and the history of the research itself showed the seamier side of prison politics. Moreover, the rehabilitative ideal was already beginning to fade, and Martinson's article added scientific support for those who wanted to abandon rehabilitation. Indeed, by 1978, four years after Martinson's article, when a Harris poll asked, "What should be the main emphasis in most prisons?" support for rehabilitation had declined to 48 percent, and punishment and protecting society had risen to 46 percent. In 1970 (four years before "What Works?") the figures had been rehabilitation, 73 percent; punishment and protect society, 20 percent. By 1982, the figures had changed further: rehabilitation, 44 percent; punishment and protect society, 51 percent (see Figure 15–1).

I do not mean to imply that Martinson's article caused this shift in public opinion, only that in both social science and public opinion the terms of the debate had changed. At mid-century, rehabilitation had been taken for granted, and the burden of proof lay upon those who doubted. Twenty-five years later, the burden of proof had shifted. Now, proponents of rehabilitation would have to prove that the idea was still valid.

Critics did attack Martinson's methods and conclusions—so much so that five years later, Martinson himself revised his views. He took into account the variability of different programs, both for better and for worse. "Some programs are indeed beneficial; of equal or greater significance, some programs are harmful."[27]

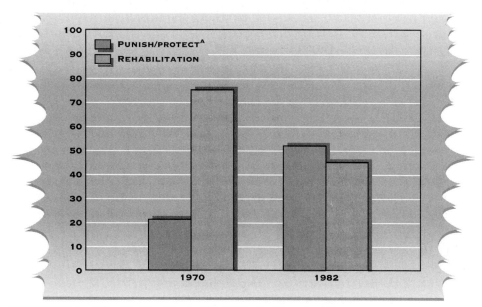

FIGURE 15–1   What Do You Think *Should* Be the Main Emphasis in Most Prisons?

ᴬPercentages do not add up to 100 because those saying "not sure" were not included.

Source: Louis Harris, in Edmund F. McGarrell and Timothy J. Flanagan, eds., *Sourcebook of Criminal Justice Statistics—1984*, U.S. Department of Justice: Bureau of Justice Statistics (Washington, DC: U.S. Government Printing Office, 1985).

WHY REHABILITATION FAILS

Perhaps "What works?" was not quite the right question to ask. In any case, it should not have been the only question. Instead, two related questions immediately arise. First, why did no one type of program show consistently positive results? Second, what are the characteristics that distinguish treatments that work from those that do not?

CURES AND CAUSES   One general answer to the first question is that the cure (rehabilitation) may have little to do with the disease (crime). Treatment assumes that crime arises because of a defect, a curable defect, in the criminal. However, if crime is caused largely by environmental factors, treatment will be ineffective. Suppose, for example, that lack of a job leads to crime. Rehabilitation programs, even if they work, can create only job skills, not jobs. If there are no decent jobs for released prisoners, the program will be ineffective, no matter how well the prisoners have learned.

In the same way, a psychotherapy program in prison may help a prisoner to understand his or her problems, but psychological problems may have had nothing to do with that person's involvement in crime. Group counseling may help prisoners learn to talk to others about problems and to interact as group members. But if the released prisoner returns to the same neighborhood and the same friends that led to crime in the first place, the effects of group counseling will quickly dwindle to nothing.

THE BEST-LAID REHABILITATION PLANS   There is another reason why rehabilitation programs fail. A program as it actually takes shape in prison may be very different from the one that was originally drawn up on paper. Sometimes the actual program differs from the planned version because of the people who run it. Generally, prisoners are not an easy group to work with, and rehabilitation programs will require a highly dedicated staff—teachers, counselors, psychologists, and administrators. If these people do not have the proper training or the motivation, if they are merely going through the motions, the program has little chance of success.

Even when the staff members are competent and dedicated, they may find that they cannot run the program as it was intended. The prison may lack sufficient space or facilities. It may not have money for the necessary equipment, supplies, or books (see Table 15–3). Job-training programs may have to make do with outdated, secondhand equipment. Some job-training programs will end up training inmates in outdated skills for jobs that no longer exist. Also, if some part of the rehabilitation program conflicts with the security needs of the prison, the program will be the loser. Suppose, for example, that an idealistic welding shop outside the prison proposes to train inmates and to give them jobs upon their release. The warden looks over the equipment—acetylene torches, masks, and a lot of plate steel—and realizes that while this program may provide job training, it is also furnishing material that prisoners can easily convert to weapons. I suspect that few wardens would allow such a program in their prisons.

Another possible reason for failure is that most rehabilitation programs occupy only a small part of a prisoner's time. If a program teaches specific job skills or basic education, it might work, at least in the sense of educating prisoners. But if a program aims to convert prisoners to a different set of attitudes and ideas about crime, it is competing with most of the rest of prison life. A prisoner may spend at most a few hours a day in some rehabilitation program but live the rest of his or her life in the inmate world. There, the inmate culture that dominates most prisons does not place a high value on staying away from crime.[28]

We should not be surprised at the failure of rehabilitation programs. The conditions in most U.S. prisons range from brutal and inhumane at worst to boring and monotonous at best. Prisons are overcrowded and understaffed; prisoner culture is dominated by resentment toward both the legitimate world in general and prison authorities in particular. In addition, few rehabilitation programs, if any, extend beyond prison. Prisoners who leave are on their own, frequently back in their old environments. Perhaps we should be surprised that recidivism rates are not even higher than they are.

Despite these conditions, some rehabilitation programs do work. What makes them work, I suspect, has little to do with the content or design of the program. The key factor is probably the quality of the people involved. People who are good at working with prisoners have some chance of success, even in

TABLE 15-3 •

PROPOSED CORRECTIONS BUDGETS IN SELECTED STATES, 1993–1994

STATE	TOTAL BUDGET	AMOUNT FOR TREATMENT	PERCENT OF TOTAL BUDGET
ALABAMA	$141,579	$1,500	1
ARIZONA	303,691	40,273	13
ARKANSAS	93,158	5,480	6
CALIFORNIA	3,178,339	68,016	2
FLORIDA	1,170,419	51,115	4
NEW JERSEY	622,342	28,128	4
NEW YORK	1,426,698	157,249	11
OREGON	192,881	19,958	10
PENNSYLVANIA	604,400	55,482	9
TEXAS	2,123,889	182,075	9
VIRGINIA	515,252	14,327	3

Source: Maguire and Pastore, *Sourcebook, 1993*, p. 14.

a program that on paper looks quite ordinary. On the other hand, people who are less dedicated will have no success even in better-funded and well-designed programs.

PAROLE

As belief in rehabilitation waned, so did the idea of indeterminate sentences. Indeterminate sentencing rests on two assumptions: first, that prison can rehabilitate criminals; second, that parole boards can tell when a prisoner is rehabilitated. The first assumption, as we have seen, was much too optimistic. Prisons and rehabilitation programs, as they are currently run, do little to reduce recidivism. The second assumption is equally shaky. To some extent, social science can identify factors that make a prisoner a greater risk: a history of alcohol and drug abuse, a crime career that begins at an early age, and a record that includes very serious offenses. These factors, however, are unchangeable parts of the prisoner's biography and have nothing to do with rehabilitation or anything else that goes on in prison. If these biographical factors are our best predictors of parole success, it makes little sense to talk of granting parole when the prisoner is ready—that is, when he or she will no longer return to a life of crime. Using these predictors, a parole board could just as easily make the decision at the time the prisoner is admitted.

UNDER ATTACK

The policy of indeterminate sentencing and parole has come under criticism from both the public and the prisoners, from conservatives and liberals. The conservative view of punishment generally focuses on deterrence, incapacitation, and retribution. By reducing the actual time served, parole undermines these purposes of punishment. Some liberals and prisoners themselves also object to parole. Prisoners, like conservatives, argue on the basis of just deserts—the principle that says that punishment should be based on what the person has done. But parole punishes a person on the basis of what the parole board predicts he or she will do in the future. Prisoners also object to parole because of its unfairness. The system, which grants so much discretion to a handful of people on a parole board, carries a great potential for inequity. Two prisoners with identical records sentenced for the same crime might wind up serving very different lengths of time. Prisoners also say that the uncertainty in parole is demoralizing; they never really know when they will be released. They may become even more cynical than they were to begin with, and conclude that the system depends not on principles of justice but on how well you can "con" a parole board.

Parole is one of the least popular aspects of the criminal justice system. When public opinion polls ask about criminal justice policies, eliminating parole gets more support than any other proposal, including the death penalty for murder.[29] Nevertheless, the number of prisoners on parole and other forms of supervised release continues to grow and currently stands at more than 350,000.[30] (Another 2.6 million are on probation.) The chief supporters of parole are the people who run the prisons. They see parole as a useful tool for controlling prisoners. If release depends on good conduct in prison, the prisoner will do what the prison administration wants him or her to do. Prison officials fear that without the reward of parole or the threat of withholding it, they would find prisoners less easy to control.

Given the conditions in prisons today, parole may even be a necessity. As prisons become more and more overcrowded, some prisoners must be released to make room for new ones. Parole acts as a safety valve for dangerously overcrowded prisons. In some cases, courts have ruled that prison conditions constituted cruel and unusual punishment, and they have ordered prisons to start releasing convicts as a matter of law. As inexact as parole board hearings may be, they at least provide some semblance of rationality in deciding which prisoners to release.

COST AND EFFECTIVENESS

From the state's point of view, parole has a distinct advantage over prison: It is much cheaper. In 1992, it cost, on the average, $18,000 a year to keep a person in prison. The average cost for a person on parole was less than $1,000 a year. Both figures vary according to the jurisdiction; in some states, the cost of parole is less than $400 per parolee.[31] Of course, we must ask what we get for our money. Could we just as easily abolish parole? Is parole effective? Do paroled criminals refrain from committing crimes? Obviously, parolees commit more crimes than prisoners who are still locked up, but how many more crimes do they commit?

As with rehabilitation, the principal measure of parole's success or failure is recidivism, and different ways of measuring recidivism give different answers. Some studies estimate that two-thirds of released prisoners eventually return. However, one study of parole found an overall success rate varying from a high of 90 percent for paroled murderers to a low of 65 percent for paroled car thieves. That's a recidivism rate of only 10 percent to 35 percent. Generally the more serious the crime, the greater the success rate; those paroled from manslaughter and rape convictions did far better than those paroled from burglary or check-passing convictions.[32]

Parole has two aspects—early release and subsequent supervision. Abolishing parole, therefore, can mean two very different policies: Prisoners serve their full term without hope of parole, or prisoners are released at an earlier date but are not required to report to parole officers.

Keeping everyone in prison is, of course, a very costly proposition. It would reduce crime—somewhat. For example, a 1985 study looked at about 150,000 people sent to prison. One-third were ex-convicts who had served out their terms. They had "max'd out" of prison and had then gone on to commit other crimes for which they were convicted. Another 28 percent (about 43,000 prisoners) were parolees, about 15 percent of whom were sent back to prison for technical parole violations. But 36,000 were sentenced for real crimes they committed while still on parole. These recidivists were not model citizens; most of them had four or more prior convictions. Nevertheless, compared with the other convicts, they were less likely to be entering prison for violent crimes. Instead, they were being returned to prison for property crimes like check passing and possession of stolen property.[33] Therefore, abolishing early release would have prevented the crimes and technical parole violations of these 43,000 people—at a cost of $645 million per year. This is a low estimate, based only on maintenance costs. In reality, without early release, prisons would quickly run out of space, and governments would have to build new prisons—at the cost of $75,000 per cell.

These numbers tell us only what parole does compared with what prison does. Obviously, prison prevents more crime, although at great financial cost. But how effective is parole compared with doing nothing? Does parole supervision make a difference? To find out, criminologists compared parolees with criminals who were released without any supervision (in most cases because they had served their full terms). The study found two important facts. First, recidivism rates for both groups were much higher than in other studies; second, parolees did somewhat better than those who left prison unsupervised (see Table 15–4).

According to the figures in Table 15–4, three years of parole supervision lowered recidivism from 85 percent to 77 percent. Assume that parole costs $1,500 per parolee, per year. If we release 100 convicts unconditionally, we spend nothing, and in three years 85 of them will have been reconvicted. If instead we grant the 100 convicts parole, in three years 77 of them will have been reconvicted, and we will have spent $450,000 ($1,500 × 100 convicts × three years). Are the 8 convictions we prevented worth

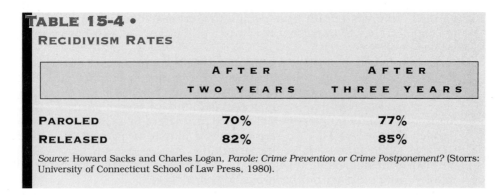

TABLE 15-4 •
RECIDIVISM RATES

	AFTER TWO YEARS	AFTER THREE YEARS
PAROLED	70%	77%
RELEASED	82%	85%

Source: Howard Sacks and Charles Logan, *Parole: Crime Prevention or Crime Postponement?* (Storrs: University of Connecticut School of Law Press, 1980).

$450,000? Calculations like this, combined with the other arguments against parole, have led some people to call for its abolition, except as a way of reducing sentences.[34]

One of the problems with parole (and probation) is that the released offenders receive so little actual supervision. Current caseloads allow very little time for any real supervision or help. The average amount of face-to-face interaction between parole officers and parolees can average as little as three minutes a week.[35] Perhaps if caseloads were smaller so that officers could

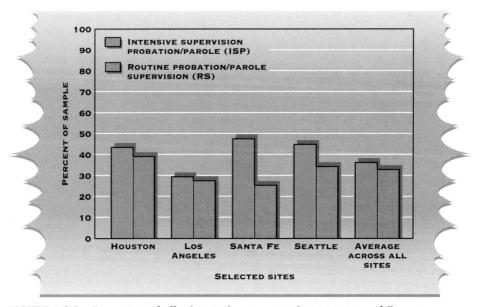

FIGURE 15-2   Percentage of offenders with any arrest during one-year follow-up.

Source: Joan Petersilia and Susan Turner, "Intensive Probation and Parole," in Michael Tonry, ed., *Crime and Justice: A Review of Research*, vol. 17 (Chicago: University of Chicago Press, 1993), pp. 281–335.

IN THE NEWS

Systematic evidence from social science is usually no match for the prevailing political sentiment. When everyone "knows" that drug rehabilitation doesn't work and when the politicians can win votes by promising to get tough on drugs, evidence about cost effectiveness will have little impact on policy. Instead, we will continue to get laws whose main goal seems to be to demonstrate our representatives' hatred of crime—like the 1994 crime bill, which added over fifty new federal death penalty offenses, including growing marijuana.

STUDY SAYS ANTI-DRUG DOLLARS ARE BEST SPENT ON TREATMENT

by Joseph Treaster

A dollar's worth of drug treatment is worth seven dollars spent on the most successful law-enforcement efforts to curb the use of cocaine, researchers say in a new study.

The study by Rand, a California research organization that has worked closely with the Federal Government, was partly financed by the White House, which immediately rejected its main points....

Rand estimates that Federal, state, and local governments this year will spend nearly $13 billion to combat the importation, distribution and consumption of cocaine, which, it says, runs about 330 tons a year.

The researchers ... said that for every $34 million allocated to treatment, cocaine consumption would be reduced by 1 percent, or a little more than three tons. To achieve the same effect with enforcement, the study said, the Government would have to spend $246 million on domestic law enforcement or $336 on anti-smuggling programs or $783 for anti-drug programs in countries where cocaine was produced.

The Rand researchers ... made their projections by reviewing data on treatment and by calculating the decline in cocaine consumption while addicts were in rehabilitation programs and, afterward, for a conservatively estimated 13 percent who stayed off the drug or sharply curtailed use.

Though the number of people using cocaine has steadily declined since the mid-1980s, the researchers say, total consumption is largely unchanged because the number of heavy users has increased.

Source: New York Times, June 19, 1994, p. 19.

maintain **intensive supervision** of parolees or probationers, these programs would be more effective. In the early 1980s, Georgia reported that its Intensive Supervision Program had achieved both crime reduction and cost reduction. Other states, inspired by this news, set up similar programs, reducing caseloads to between twenty and forty offenders per officer, at a reported cost of $5,000 to $8,000 per offender (in reality, the true cost was higher)—more than parole but still less than half the cost of prison. However, a large-scale study of several of these programs found that they were rarely more effective than regular supervision at reducing recidivism. After one year, the average rearrest rate for those under intensive supervision was 37 percent. For the control group under routine supervision, the rearrest rate was 33 percent (see Figure 15–2).[36]

Summary and conclusion

For about 150 years, the idea of rehabilitation dominated the ideology of imprisonment in the United States and in other industrialized countries. Before the 1800s, prisons had been used to house people awaiting trial; prisons also served as workhouses where those arrested for vagrancy or begging were forced to work. In England, jails (spelled then and now *gaols*) were also used as punishment for criminals, though only a fraction of those convicted went to prison. Other punishments included whipping, public humiliation, banishment, and death.

In the nineteenth century, reformers spread the idea that prisons could rehabilitate criminals. Rehabilitation, they said, required decent living conditions and effective programs. Toward this goal, prisons over the years have instituted everything from silent religious meditation to computer programming. Unfortunately, there is little evidence that any of these programs consistently reduce recidivism. This is not to say that criminals are never reformed. But whether a criminal "goes straight" depends more on the criminal than on any program he or she might have taken in prison. And if a program is effective, the reason is more likely to be found in the quality of the staff than in the program itself.

Reformers were only slightly more successful in changing living conditions than in rehabilitating prisoners. Discipline, economy, and security usually take precedence over humanity and idealism. There seems to be a never-ending cycle of exposé and reform. Periodically, reformers or reporters will expose the degraded conditions that exist in the jails and prisons. Prisons then will be cleaned up, only to disappear from public view. The old conditions will return, and the cycle will begin again. Doubtless the prisons in the United States today are vastly more humane than the bridewells of two centuries ago. Still, many of them remain places of boredom and violence.

The idea of rehabilitation also affected other aspects of the criminal justice system. Rehabilitation provided the ideological basis for the current system of indeterminate sentences and parole. The evidence on the effectiveness of parole is no more encouraging than the evidence on rehabilitation. Parole boards are not very good at predicting who will commit further crimes if released, nor is supervised parole much more effective than unconditional release.

The ideology of rehabilitation has been declining since about 1970. This change is probably linked to the rise in crime rates in the 1960s. As crime rates rose and remained high, people became more cynical about the ability of the prisons to reform criminals. Public attitudes, including support for capital punishment, became more punitive. Almost nobody called for restoration of the pillory and whipping post, although in the late 1980s, amid the panic over illegal drugs, some state legislators proposed the reinstatement of whipping as a punishment for drug crimes. However, more people began to demand that prisons punish criminals, isolate them from society, or execute them. If crime rates ever return to the low levels of the 1940s and 1950s, perhaps we will see a revival of interest in rehabilitation. For the moment, the public, the policymakers, and many criminologists seem more interested in two other functions of punishment: deterrence and incapacitation (which, coincidentally, are the topics of the last two chapters of this book).

CRITICAL THINKING QUESTIONS

1. Some people advocate a return to public punishment and corporal punishment, such as existed in colonial days. Why did these forms of punishment disappear? Under what conditions might they be effective today? Under what conditions might they not be effective?
2. Prisons in America seem to go through regular cycles of reform, reversion to brutal conditions, exposé, and reform. What makes it so difficult to maintain reforms and so easy to impose brutal treatment?
3. Why do prisons retain rehabilitation programs? How might supporters of rehabilitation counter the conclusions of Martinson's research?
4. Parole is a very unpopular policy. What are the arguments for and against it?

KEY TERMS

conditional release

control group

corporal punishment

determinate sentences

deterrence

incapacitation

indeterminate sentences

intensive supervision

just deserts

parole

probation

recidivism

rehabilitation

retribution

suspended sentence

CHAPTER SIXTEEN

DETERRENCE

CHAPTER OUTLINE

GETTING TOUGH

As the public's belief in rehabilitation declined, state legislatures and the federal government as well began to move toward fixed, or determinate sentences. Determinate sentencing takes various forms, some more determinate than others. The strictest version does away with minimum and maximum terms (e.g., four to ten years). Instead, anyone convicted of the crime receives the same fixed sentence (e.g., five years), with no parole or early release. Sometimes this policy is called **flat sentencing**. Along similar lines, some state legislatures have changed their criminal laws so that some offenses carry **mandatory sentences**. When a sentence is mandatory, the criminal

must spend a certain amount of time in prison; nobody convicted of the crime may receive probation or a suspended sentence. States have instituted mandatory sentences for drug offenses, gun crimes, violent crimes, and kidnapping.

Fixed and mandatory sentences remove discretion from judges and parole boards. These sentences have the apparent virtue of fairness and impartiality: People convicted of the same crime serve the same sentence. The weakness of this system is its inflexibility. It may lump together the hoodlum who robs a stranger at gunpoint with the teenager who takes another kid's pocket money by threatening him with a stick; technically, they are both armed robbers. Some jurisdictions, therefore, combine determinate sentencing with devices that bring discretion back into the system. In some states with fixed sentencing, a prisoner may become eligible for parole after serving some percentage of the sentence, usually one-third to one-half. Other states and the federal government have **presumptive sentencing**—guidelines that resemble determinate

Deterrence has long been a goal of punishment, and the theory is no doubt correct in principle: increased certainty, swiftness, and severity of punishment will reduce crime. Unfortunately, although severity is the element that the criminal justice system can most easily manipulate—in the form of longer sentences—it also contributes least to the deterrent effect.

TABLE 16-1 •
MINNESOTA'S SENTENCING GUIDELINES GRID

Conviction Offense	Severity Level	0	1	2	3	4	5	6 or More
							Criminal History Score	
Unauthorized use of motor vehicle / Possession of marijuana	I	12[a]	12[a]	12[a]	13	15	17	19 18–20
Theft related crimes ($250–$2,500) / Aggravated forgery ($25–$2,500)	II	12[a]	12[a]	13	15	17	19	21 20–22
Theft crimes ($25–$2,500)	III	12[a]	13	15	17	19 18–20	22 21–23	25 24–26
Nonresidential burglary / Theft crimes (over $2,500)	IV	12[a]	15	18	21	25 24–26	32 30–34	41 37–45
Residential burglary / Simple robbery	V	18	23	27	30 29–31	38 36–40	46 43–49	54 50–58
Criminal sexual conduct, 2d degree (a) and (b)	VI	21	26	30	34 33–35	44 42–46	54 50–58	65 60–70
Aggravated robbery	VII	24 23–25	32 30–34	41 38–44	49 45–53	65 60–70	81 75–87	97 90–104
Criminal sexual conduct, 1st degree / Assault, 1st degree	VIII	43 41–45	54 50–58	65 60–70	76 71–81	95 89–101	113 106–120	132 124–140
Murder, 3d degree / Murder, 2d degree (felony murder)	IX	105 102–108	119 116–122	127 124–130	149 143–155	176 168–184	205 195–215	230 218–242
Murder, 2d degree (with intent)	X	120 116–124	140 133–147	162 153–171	203 192–214	243 231–255	284 270–298	324 309–339

Numbers in the table refer to the length and range of the presumptive sentence. Cells above the dark line represent the area of the grid in which the presumptive sentence is a stayed prison term. Below the dark line a prison term is the presumptive sentence. The presumptive durations of confinement are in months.

[a]One year and one day.

Source: Minnesota Sentencing Guidelines Commission (1984): 2.

sentencing except that judges have some discretion to increase or decrease the presumptive sentence by a few months, depending on the circumstances of the crime and the criminal (see Table 16–1).

Determinate sentencing and mandatory sentencing probably owe their popularity to their promise of eliminating leniency. A person convicted of a crime will receive at least some prison time and will serve the sentence narrowly specified in the law, no matter what. These sentences appeal to the public's sentiments about justice, but people who blame high crime rates on the leniency of the courts, also look to them to reduce crime. The logic of this widely held, commonsense notion of crime and punishment goes something like this:

> People turn to crime because they can get away with it. They cannot control their impulses for easy money or for angry retaliation. The best and perhaps only way to force them to control these impulses is to punish them. If criminals are not punished, they will commit more crimes. Worse still, the lack of punishment will encourage other potential criminals to join the criminal ranks. Crime rates remain high because criminals are seldom caught; when caught, they are seldom punished; when punished, they get off too lightly. If the criminal justice system (the police, courts, and prisons) did its job of catching and punishing criminals, fewer people would risk committing crimes.

Like other commonsense ideas, this one is perfectly logical, and it corresponds well with the picture many people have of street crime today. The media regularly provide stories that confirm this picture: Citizens complain that the police can't or won't solve crimes ("They didn't even look for fingerprints"); demoralized police officers complain about the futility of arresting criminals when they are back on the street while the officers are still doing the paperwork; perpetrators of terrible crimes plea-bargain for light sentences; other criminals spend little or no time in prison despite a long record of prior arrests; crimes are committed by people who are out on bail or parole. Judged only on this kind of information, the truth of this theory appears obvious. But as with other seemingly obvious truths, we must test this one by more systematic evidence. So in the following pages, I will consider the ideas in this theory one by one and see what evidence exists to support or contradict them.

The underlying idea of the theory is **deterrence**, an idea you can probably find in the earliest writings on human behavior. The first formal statement of it for criminological purposes is Cesare Beccaria's essay "On Crimes and Punishments," first published in 1764. Beccaria emphasized that the purpose of punishment is not to demonstrate the evil of the criminal but to prevent crime. The penalty for a crime should be just severe enough to offset its possible gain. His utilitarian theory takes an essentially economic approach. Basically, it is the idea that crime pays. The theory assumes that criminals rationally calculate their costs and benefits. If the benefits outweigh the costs, people will commit crimes.

Beccaria also outlined the variables that are still considered the basis for research on deterrence: the **certainty of punishment**, the **severity of punishment**, and the **swiftness of punishment**. Research on deterrence asks this question: If criminals' chances of getting caught increase or if their punishment is more severe or if the punishment more quickly follows the crime, will crime decrease? To give a preview of the results (and an oversimplified answer to a complicated question), the answer is not much. The research provides only modest support for the theory. It seems that although the notion of deterrence is simple and straightforward, conclusive evidence for it in the criminal justice system is hard to find. Therefore, besides reviewing the results of the various studies, I will also outline some of the reasons deterrence is so difficult to prove.

Some of these reasons are methodological. There are many variables besides punishment that may affect crime, and it is very difficult to isolate a single variable and assess its impact apart from the others. It's a little like asking how much difference the manager of a baseball team makes in the team's success. There are many factors (hitting, pitching, fielding) over which the manager has little control but which affect the team's performance. However, after a bad season, it's the manager who gets fired. This may satisfy the owner or the fans, but how much better will the team do next year? And more important, even if the team improves, how can we be sure it was the new manager who made the difference?

In the same way, different thinkers about crime have their favorite targets to blame. Whatever the emotional satisfaction of pointing a finger at the police or courts or television or unemployment (the list is endless), it is the job of social scientists to measure these presumed causes and determine how much difference each one makes. Unfortunately, even the most advanced statistical techniques cannot give us solid answers, especially when several causes are operating at the same time and when we do not have the luxury of performing tightly controlled experiments.

In discussing this research, I will sometimes mention methodological problems or suggest other possible explanations for the findings. These points may seem merely technical, but they are often crucial to understanding not just the piece of research at hand but also the real world that the research is trying to describe. Usually, that world is not the scientific laboratory; it is the real world of crime and criminals, of cops and courts.

SPECIFIC DETERRENCE

In considering the effects of punishment, criminologists distinguish between **specific deterrence** and **general deterrence**. The idea of specific deterrence is that punishing a person for a crime will deter that person from committing a crime again. The idea of general deterrence is that punishment will affect the general population, not just the individuals who are caught and punished.

Specific deterrence seems especially simple and logical; it is essentially what psychologists call operant conditioning—punishing undesirable behavior and rewarding good behavior. If you have ever tried to housebreak a dog, your goal was a form of specific deterrence, and the principles you used were those of operant conditioning. And these principles work, at least with most dogs and laboratory animals. To know whether punishment is an effective specific deterrent to crime, we need to measure two variables—the punishment and subsequent crime—and look for a correlation between them. We look for an increase or decrease in the severity of the punishment, the certainty of the punishment, or the swiftness of the punishment, and then we see whether that change led to a change in crime. Usually, researchers and lawmakers have focused on the severity of punishment. When legislators want to show that they are getting tough on crime, they write laws changing sentences; they can do little about the certainty or swiftness with which these sentences are imposed.

Researchers usually measure severity in the same way that courts and criminals do: by sentence length. Measuring a criminal's further crime, called **recidivism**, presents a tougher problem. Ideally, we would measure the frequency and seriousness of all crimes committed by released prisoners, whether or not they get caught. Getting this information would require extensive self-report interviews with people who are sometimes very hard to find and who, for one reason or another, may not be too accurate in their self-reporting. So researchers usually settle for measuring recidivism by arrest or even by return to prison. These measures may not be perfect indicators of crime, but they are far more available.

PRISON AS A SPECIFIC DETERRENT

The data on recidivism do not give much cause for believing that prison is a good specific deterrent. Most criminals (about 60 percent) sent to prison have been there before.[1] Most released prisoners are rearrested, and about 40 percent of released prisoners wind up back in prison.[2] (The difference between these two statistics (60 percent and 40 percent) is not a contradiction. They represent different ways of measuring recidivism. By analogy, if I wanted to measure academic recidivism, I might measure the percentage of students getting a D or F on the final exam who also got a D or F on the midterm. To measure it another way, I might take the percentage of students who got a low grade on the midterm and then got a low grade on the final. The two percentages will not necessarily be the same.) These data are not quite a test of deterrence. We must take a closer look. According to our commonsense theory, the more severe the punishment, the more effective it will be. A light sentence— the proverbial slap on the wrist—will do little to deter a criminal from further crime. Other things being equal, prisoners who had served longer sentences should have less recidivism than those who served shorter terms. However, most research on this question has failed to find any connection between time served and recidivism.[3] Parolees are no more likely to commit further crimes than prisoners who serve out their full terms.[4] A Wisconsin study of three juvenile cohorts (a cohort is a group of people all born in the same year—in this case, groups born in 1942, 1948, and 1955) concluded, "What we found, in a variety of analyses and with considerable regularity, was an increase in frequency and severity of misbehavior in the periods following those in which sanctions were administered."[5] In other words, youths were *more* delinquent after being punished than they had been before. This reverse deterrence effect of punishment may hold for adults as well. One study of 4,000 released prisoners showed that among those locked up for the same crime (e.g., robbery), those who served longer sentences were, if anything, more criminal after release than those who served shorter terms.[6]

Why doesn't punishment deter? One problem with the research on specific deterrence is that it focuses on the severity of punishment. But while severity may be the easiest element to control and measure, it is also the least important. As most psychologists and dog owners know, the certainty and swiftness of punishment matter much more than the severity. If you can catch your puppy immediately every time he makes a mistake, you need do nothing more severe than rattling a newspaper in his face. But if you can punish only one mistake in twenty, and that only several hours after it occurs, even the most severe punishment will not teach your dog proper etiquette.

Another reason why prison might fail to deter, in fact why it might even increase recidivism, comes from differential association theory and labeling theory, or what might more simply be called the schools-for-crime argument. In prison, inmates learn the techniques, attitudes, and values of the criminal world. Then, once they are released, they may find that other people are less willing to accept them into the straight world. In this view, especially for juveniles who have not yet become "hardened criminals," prisons might do more harm than good, and we should be looking for ways to reduce incarceration rather than increase it.

Politically, the call for less punishment is obviously part of a generally liberal position on crime, a position that would concentrate on changing society rather than punishing individual criminals. Conservatives, by contrast, would focus on getting tough with lawbreakers. One study of deterrence (one conducted by political conservatives) did find evidence for the deterrent effect of punishment. Instead of just asking whether a person was ever rearrested, these researchers measured the number of rearrests. They reasoned that even if punishment did not reform a boy entirely, it might still reduce the amount of crime he would commit. Their sample was a group of 317 boys classified as serious delinquents. (How serious? Although the average age was 16, their combined arrest records included 14 homicides, nearly 200 armed robberies, and over 700 burglaries. And those were only arrests. The actual number of crimes probably was much higher.)[7]

Under the program studied, a boy could be sentenced to one of five alternatives—anything from group homes to wilderness experiences to intensive counseling. Boys who did poorly in these programs might be sent to ordinary juvenile prisons. Comparing the boys' arrest rates before sentencing with their arrest rates after release, researchers found a surprising result. Everything "worked." Boys averaged fewer arrests after release, no matter what type of institution they had been sent to. Some programs produced less recidivism than others. Prison was more effective than in-home supervision, but rural camps were more effective than prisons.

Apparently, the reduction in crime shows that arrest, sentencing, and punishment—any sort of punishment—act as a specific deterrent. However, some critics have questioned this conclusion. There may be other reasons the boys committed less crime after serving whatever type of sentence they received. Suppose that delinquents who commit crimes are something like streak hitters in baseball. Sometimes, for reasons we do not understand, they commit crimes fairly frequently; at other times they go into a slump and commit fewer crimes. Since delinquents are much more likely to get caught during a high-frequency period, the boys coming into the program were probably on a streak. They might have cooled off afterward, no matter what. It was time, more than imprisonment or wilderness, that caused the decrease in their crime. As one critic says, "Why should ... three months of counseling at a community center cause a long-time, repeat offender to cut his crime rate in half?"[8]

My own conclusion is that prison is not much of a specific deterrent. A high proportion of released prisoners, despite their best intentions (or at least their statements to parole boards), return to crime. Many people believe that prison is more of a deterrent to white-collar criminals. However, white-collar crimes are discovered so infrequently that measuring recidivism accurately or even usefully is almost impossible. The problem of infrequent arrest also makes it hard to assess the impact of punishment on drunk drivers.

GENERAL DETERRENCE

Societies create laws and punishments not just to punish, and perhaps reform, those who are caught. These laws are also intended to reduce crime through general deterrence. This term refers to the effect of punishment on the general population, not just on those who are actually punished. That is, the mere possibility of being caught and punished should make people refrain from crime.

To assess general deterrence, criminologists use the same basic variables as for specific deterrence, except that instead of measuring the effect of punishment on individuals they look at its effect on the general population. In other words, instead of measuring the crimes of each individual (i.e., recidivism), studies of general deterrence measure the crimes of the general population, that is, crime rates.

To take a simple example, suppose that to reduce illegal parking on campus, a university raises the fines for violations, instructs the campus police to issue tickets more frequently, and even tows away illegally parked cars. The administration has increased both the severity and the certainty of punishment. To see if the crime rate has changed, all we have to do is check the parking lots before and after the new policy and count the number of illegally parked cars. The chances are that more people—even those who have not been ticketed or towed—will obey the parking rules.

Assessing general deterrence of more serious crime can be far more complicated. Some of the problems involved can be seen in the research on one special topic—one that is not a typical example of general deterrence but is worth exploring since it is the subject of so much controversy: the death penalty.

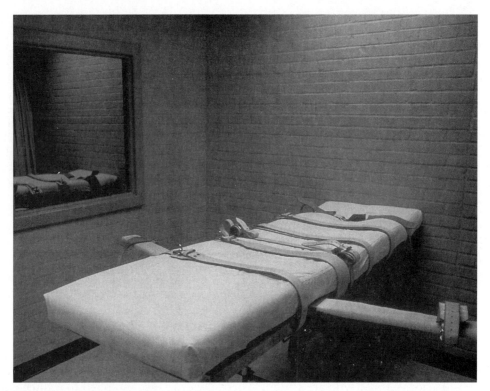

The death penalty has no measurable impact on crime and as currently administered is more costly than its alternatives. If excution sends a message, it is a message aimed at the feelings of the public at large, not at potential murderers. What then is the message of lethal injection, the medical, "humane" method that has come to be the predominant mode of execution in the United States?

CAPITAL PUNISHMENT AS A GENERAL DETERRENT

As fear of crime and concern over crime have risen in the past three decades, so has support for the death penalty (see Figure 16–1). The debate over capital punishment raises several questions. Is it effective? Is it fair and just? Is it moral? Is it legal? Most people taking sides on the issue base their decision on morality; legislatures and courts must consider additional questions of legality. On these moral and legal questions, scientific research counts for little. Social science cannot tell us whether capital punishment is morally right or wrong—whether a criminal deserves to die or whether the state has a moral right to kill. These are not **empirical** questions; that is, they do not rest on evidence. Nor can social science settle legal questions about the constitutionality of capital punishment.

In addition to questions of justice, this debate involves general deterrence. Proponents of the death penalty often claim that it will reduce crime in general or at least murder. They reason that potential killers would be less likely to kill if they knew they were risking execution. Opponents argue that

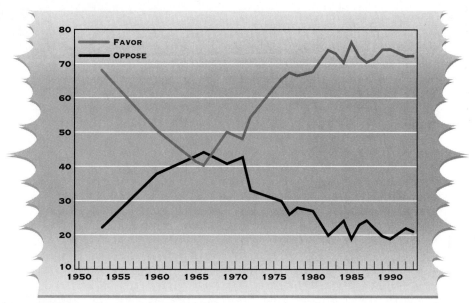

FIGURE 16–1   Attitudes Toward the Death Penalty for Persons Convicted of Murder, 1953–1993

Source: Kathleen McGuire and Ann L. Pastore, eds., *Sourcebook of Criminal Justice Statistics—1993* (Washington, DC: Bureau of Justice Statistics, 1994), based on data from National Opinion Research Center.

the death penalty is no more a deterrent than long prison terms. Both sides are making statements of cause and effect, so at least in principle these statements about deterrence can be tested by empirical evidence. Ideally, a research study would conclude that, other things being equal, the death penalty does (or does not) reduce the rates of those crimes to which it applies. Unfortunately, actual research is not so simple, for—especially in the case of the death penalty—other things are seldom equal.

How can we know whether the death penalty deters the crime to which it applies—murder? One of the first systematic studies on the subject compared murder rates of states with the death penalty and states without it. If the death penalty is a deterrent, states with the death penalty (other things being equal) should have lower rates of murder. In fact, it turned out to be the other way around.[9] The murder rates in states without a death penalty were lower than the national rate and lower than the average rate for their respective regions. Table 16–2 is based on data from 1993, when only twelve states had no death penalty. Still, of those twelve states, only two had murder rates higher than the national average of 9.5. Among states with a death penalty, fourteen of thirty-eight (39 percent) had murder rates above the national average. The positive correlation (more death penalty, more murder) was even stronger ten or fifteen years ago, when fewer states had the death penalty. If the correlation had been negative— that is, if states with this penalty had reported lower murder rates—we would have taken it as evidence that the death penalty reduces murder. Does the actual positive correlation mean, then, that the death penalty *increases* murder rates? Probably not. Some research has explored the idea of brutalization—that state-sponsored killing makes the population more brutal and thereby increases

TABLE 16-2 •
MURDER RATES IN STATES WITH AND WITHOUT THE DEATH PENALTY, 1993 (BY REGION)

STATES WITH THE DEATH PENALTY		STATES WITHOUT THE DEATH PENALTY	
CONNECTICUT	6.3	MAINE	1.6
NEW HAMPSHIRE	2.0	VERMONT	3.6
		MASSACHUSETTS	3.9
		RHODE ISLAND	3.9
NEW JERSEY	5.3	NEW YORK[a]	13.3
PENNSYLVANIA	6.8		
ILLINOIS	11.4	MICHIGAN	9.8
INDIANA	7.5	WISCONSIN	4.4
OHIO	6.0		
MISSOURI	11.3	NORTH DAKOTA	1.7
NEBRASKA	3.9	MINNESOTA	3.4
SOUTH DAKOTA	3.4	KANSAS	6.4
		IOWA	2.3
DELAWARE	5.0	WEST VIRGINIA	6.9
FLORIDA	8.9		
GEORGIA	11.4		
MARYLAND	12.7		
NORTH CAROLINA	11.3		
SOUTH CAROLINA	10.3		
VIRGINIA	8.3		
ALABAMA	11.6		
KENTUCKY	6.6		
MISSISSIPPI	13.5		
TENNESSEE	10.2		

the murder rate but the evidence, for the most part, does not support this idea. The positive correlation may also logically mean that murder causes the death penalty. Look again at the table. Many of the states contributing to the positive correlation (high murder rates accompanying the death penalty) are in the South. Most southern states have the death penalty, and most also have above-average murder rates. It may be that these states have the death penalty because they have had high murder rates—just as the increase in murder rates in northern states has led to a demand for the death penalty there.

Does the death penalty affect the murder rate? Or does the murder rate affect the death penalty? Perhaps both effects are occurring at the same time,

TABLE 16-2 •
MURDER RATES IN STATES WITH AND WITHOUT THE DEATH PENALTY, 1993 (BY REGION) (CONTINUED)

STATES WITH THE DEATH PENALTY	
ARKANSAS	10.2
LOUISIANA	20.3
OKLAHOMA	8.4
TEXAS	11.9
ARIZONA	8.6
COLORADO	5.8
IDAHO	2.9
MONTANA	3.0
NEVADA	10.4
NEW MEXICO	8.0
UTAH	3.1
WYOMING	3.4
ALASKA	9.0
CALIFORNIA	13.1
HAWAII	3.8
OREGON	4.6
WASHINGTON	5.2

[a]By the time you are reading this, New York, and its above-average murder rate, will be in the death penalty column.

Source: Maguire and Pastore, *Sourcebook—1993*. Federal Bureau of Investigation, *Crime in the United States: The Uniform Crime Reports, 1993* (Washington, DC: 1994).

creating a tangle known as **simultaneity**. Or perhaps there is a third explanation. When A and B are correlated, there are at least three possible explanations: A causes B (the death penalty causes higher murder rates); B causes A (higher murder rates cause the death penalty); a third factor, C, is causing both A and B (X causes both high murder rates and the death penalty). Theorists who favor the idea of the subculture of violence might argue that this third factor is culture. In Southern culture, according to this view, people see violence, even deadly violence, as a more acceptable means of resolving conflicts, both for individuals in settling personal matters and for the state in settling criminal matters. Therefore, the South will have both more murders and more executions. Proponents of this idea also extend it to the western states since these states were originally settled by emigrating Southerners, who took their cultural ways with them.

The national figures on murder and capital punishment may not be a fair test of deterrence theory, for to a great extent they are really comparing the

South and West with other regions. A good test would control for geographical region and for other factors that might be associated with murder rates: poverty, economic inequality, percentages of blacks and whites, or urban and rural populations. A better study would compare states similar in all respects except the death penalty—some with, some without. Or, since some states have abolished the death penalty, and other states have instituted it, a study might trace murder rates in a single state when that state changes its death penalty laws. Of course, a state's decision on the death penalty may depend on changes in its murder rate—again, the simultaneity problem. Conveniently for social scientists, however, in 1967 the federal courts ordered a moratorium in all states on all executions. The courts, facing several death penalty cases, ruled that until the Supreme Court resolved the constitutionality of the death penalty, nobody would be executed.

Raymond Bowers took advantage of this moratorium to assess the deterrent effects of capital punishment. Figure 16–2 shows his graph of the murder rates in neighboring (and presumably similar) states with and without the death penalty. If the death penalty is a deterrent, we should find that in states without it, 1967 should not mark any change in the murder rate. Rhode Island, for instance, had no death penalty before 1967 and no death penalty after. Neighboring Massachusetts and Connecticut had the death penalty until 1967, when it was suspended by the moratorium. If the death penalty had been deterring murders in Massachusetts and Connecticut, we should see an increase in murder after its removal in 1967.

As you can see from Figure 16–2, no such change occurred. Murder rates rose gradually before 1967 in all three states and continued to rise at

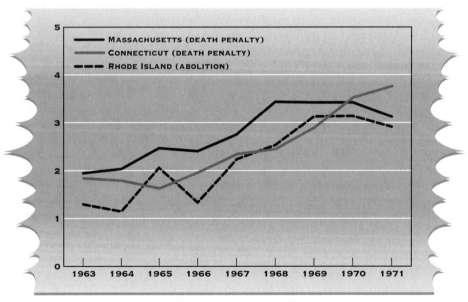

FIGURE 16–2   Murder Rates in Three States, 1963–1972

Source: Raymond Bowers, *Executions in America* (Lexington, MA: D.C. Heath, 1974).

about the same rate after 1967. There was no difference between the states with the death penalty and those without it that was attributable to the moratorium. Bowers compared other sets of states, and none of the comparisons showed evidence for a deterrent effect (see Figure 16–3).

SEVERITY OR CERTAINTY   Some critics (generally those who favor the death penalty) point out that this kind of research focuses only on severity; it completely ignores the question of certainty. Suppose a state has the death penalty but never actually applies it or applies it rarely. The penalty is severe, to be sure, but its certainty is low, undermining any possible deterrent effect. In fact, during the years covered in Bowers's research, many of the death penalty states executed the same number of people as those without a death penalty: zero. The other states executed only one or two each. Even for murderers in the South, execution was hardly a certainty.

In 1972, in the case of *Furman* v. *Georgia*, the Supreme Court ruled that the death penalty, as it was then administered in the various states, was unconstitutional. The Court based its decision partly on the lack of deterrence. It reasoned, in part, that the death penalty was so extreme that if it provided society no more protection than did long prison terms, it constituted "cruel and unusual punishment" and was therefore in violation of the Eighth Amendment of the Constitution.[10]

Soon after this decision, Isaac Ehrlich, an economist, published an article in which he claimed that the death penalty had a deterrent effect. Proponents of the death penalty quickly seized on this research as support for their position. Controlling for other variables, Ehrlich looked at executions

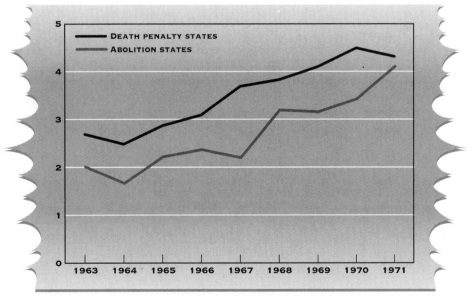

FIGURE 16–3   Murder Rates in Death Penalty and Non–Penalty States, 1963–1972

Source: Raymond Bowers, *Executions in America* (Lexington, MA: D.C. Heath, 1974).

and homicide rates in the United States between 1932 and 1969. He estimated that "an additional execution per year ... may have resulted in ... seven or eight fewer murders."[11] Subsequently, however, other economists and sociologists reanalyzed Ehrlich's data and methods and found cause to question his conclusions.[12] Most of this analysis is too technical to summarize here, but to cite one criticism, the (negative) correlation between executions and murder rates occurred only in the years 1962 to 1969.

Figure 16–4 shows both the murder rate and the number of executions for 1932 to 1992. Beginning in about 1940, the number of executions dropped steadily—from nearly 200 in 1938 to fewer than 60 in 1960 to only 2 in 1966. With the court-ordered moratorium, the number of executions from 1967 to 1976 was zero. What happened to murder rates during this period of decreasing executions?

Cover up the left part of the graph, leaving visible only the years after 1960. The evidence for deterrence looks impressive: Executions drop off to nothing, and the murder rate rises drastically. Now cover up the last thirty years of the graph and look only at 1932 to 1960. As executions decreased, so did the murder rate. What happened to the deterrent effect? If the death penalty is a deterrent, fewer executions should have meant increases in the murder rates in the 1930s, 1940s, and 1950s, not just in the 1960s. Similar studies using data from Canada (1926–1960) and Australia (1915–1975) have also failed to find any deterrent effect.[13] If the death penalty is a deterrent, it should deter Canadians and Australians as well as Americans.

Even in the 1960s, the decrease in executions was probably not the cause of the increase in murder. This was, after all, a decade in which all crimes were increasing dramatically. Since the death penalty does not apply

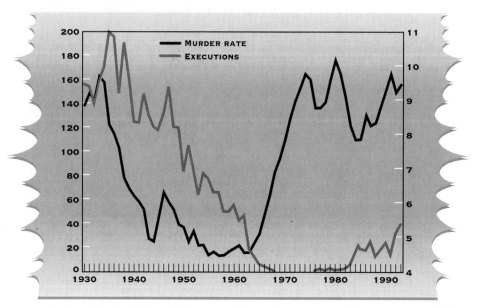

FIGURE 16–4   Murder Rate and Numbers of Executions in the United States, 1930–1993

ABOUT CRIME & CRIMINOLOGY

DEATH PENALTY RESOLUTION DEBATED AND ENDORSED

by Joan Petersilia

At the 1987 ASC [American Society of Criminology] meeting in Montreal, the following resolution was introduced and recommended at the business meeting:

> *Be it resolved that because social science research has demonstrated the death penalty to be racist in application and social science research has found no consistent evidence of*

crime deterrence through execution, the American Society of Criminology publicly condemns this form of punishment, and urges its members to use their professional skills in legislatures and courts to seek a speedy abolition of this form of punishment.

... Four papers were presented which summarized existing death penalty research.

Following the session, the ... resolution was reintroduced ... and passed by the members present (28-aye; 0-no; 3-abstain). The matter was then brought before the 1989 ASC Executive Board, who passed the resolution (8-aye; 3-no; 0-abstain).

Source: The Criminologist, January–February 1990, p. 2.

to robbery, larceny, or auto theft, the rise in these crimes must have been caused by some combination of factors other than the decline in executions. It is likely that these other factors, and not the decrease of executions, also caused the increase in homicide.

Can we conclude, then, that the death penalty has no deterrent effect? In 1990, the American Society of Criminology officially took that position. Yet some social scientists state their conclusions more cautiously, saying instead that if there is a deterrent effect, nobody has yet demonstrated it. In any case, research on the death penalty will continue, and the next few years may be quite important. Beginning in 1976, the Supreme Court began to uphold several death penalty statutes, and although the 600 prisoners on death row at the time of the *Furman* decision were released from death row, many others have been sentenced under new laws. As of the end of 1994, over 3,000 inmates were on death row, though most of them would not be executed quickly. It usually takes many years before a convicted murderer is executed. Many state and federal legislators and many judges—including the chief justice of the United States—have become impatient with the appeals process and have tried to streamline the course to the death chamber by limiting these legal appeals. So while it is doubtful that we will ever see the average of three executions per week as in 1935, the number will rise and, in some states, rise rapidly. If more executions do deter, murder rates should drop dramatically. The evidence as of this writing is hardly convincing. In the first seven years after the Supreme Court began allowing executions again (1976 to 1983), only 11 people were executed and the murder rate dropped from 8.8 to 8.3 per 100,000. In the next seven years, 132 people (12 times as many) were executed and the murder rate rose from 8.3 to 9.4.

GENERAL DETERRENCE AND OTHER CRIMES

Even if capital punishment were a sure deterrent, it would have little impact on the overall crime rate. Capital crimes constitute only a small fraction of all crime. Moreover, while the Supreme Court in recent years has upheld a number of death penalty statutes, it has also restricted the crimes punishable by death. In effect, the death penalty applies only to crimes that involve the taking of life in a particularly horrible or cold-blooded manner. Rape, which used to carry the death penalty, especially in the South, is no longer subject to capital punishment. Even the typical homicide—an argument leading to a fight in which someone gets killed—is not sufficiently aggravated to warrant the death penalty.

Advocates of deterrence call for stiffening penalties for other crimes too on the grounds that "getting tough" will reduce crime. The empirical questions are the same as for the death penalty: Will greater severity or certainty of punishment keep more people from committing a crime?

Research on the general deterrence of noncapital crimes runs into the same kinds of problems that complicate death penalty research. First, it is hard to measure punishments and crimes accurately. Second, it is very difficult to isolate the variables we want to examine—certainty or severity of punishment—from other factors that may affect crime rates: poverty, inequality, geography, age, and culture. Third, even when we find a correlation, it will not always be clear what is causing what.

THE POLICE AS A DETERRENT

The police represent the first step in deterring crime. Citizens look to the police to prevent crime: In 1994, President Clinton's proposal to add 100,000 new officers to state and local police forces was one of the most popular parts of his anticrime bill despite its high price tag. The police, too, may think of themselves as a thin blue line separating civilization from chaos or at least from crime. Police represent the certainty factor in deterrence: In theory, the more police there are, the more likely a criminal will be caught; the greater the certainty of being caught, the less crime. In reality, this logical idea—more police, less crime—may be highly overrated.

To begin with the ratio of police officers to population varies among U.S. cities. Some cities have fewer than 2 officers per 1,000 people; other cities have as many as 7 per 1,000. If nothing but deterrence were involved, the higher the ratio of officers to people, the lower the crime rate should be. In fact, there is no such correlation.[14] Of course, these intercity (or cross-sectional) comparisons run into the simultaneity problem: Higher crime may cause cities to hire more police. The question might better be answered by time-series data that trace crime rates when a single locality receives extra police.

KANSAS CITY STREETS, NEW YORK SUBWAYS Two well-known experiments on this question have demonstrated the limits of police deterrence. One took place in Kansas City, where, as in most U.S. cities, preventive patrols took the form of squad cars cruising the streets. Five of the fifteen beats studied continued this practice. Another five beats, similar to the first five in other respects, received what were called proactive patrol; that is, the number of squad cars patrolling the area was doubled or tripled. The remaining five beats, also matched for similarity to the others, received only reactive patrol: Police cars entered the area only in response to calls; there was no routine cruising. The experiment stayed in effect for a year.

At the end of the year, researchers could find no conclusive evidence of deterrence. Neither intensifying nor eliminating routine patrols significantly affected the crime rate one way or the other. Researchers measured crime both by official police statistics and by victimization surveys.[15] There were some differences in crime rates, but they were not large enough to be statistically significant. Some criminologists think that if the experiment had used more than fifteen sectors, the results would have passed the statistician's criterion. It also turned out that for the reactive (no patrol) areas, the police patrolling around the borders or responding to a call did so in a highly visible way. So, ironically, in the interest of preventing crime (or doing what they thought would prevent crime), the police may have helped prove that they do not prevent crime.

The other experiment involved a different type of police patrol. In 1965, in response to an increase in subway crimes, New York City put special patrols on the subways during the high-crime nighttime hours—the 8:00 P.M to 4:00 A.M. shift. Police statistics soon showed a substantial reduction in crime during these hours. Some of this decrease occurred on paper only; police administrators subtly encouraged patrolling officers writing up crime reports to downgrade the seriousness of the crime or even to change the time of occurrence so that serious crimes would fall outside the target hours.[16] Even so, crime really did decrease on this shift; for a short while crime even decreased during the hours when patrols had not been increased. However, the cost was enormous. It was estimated that each deterred felony cost an additional $35,000 (and that was in 1965 dollars; allowing for inflation, that sum would be equal to more than $100,000 today).[17]

These two studies illustrate several points about deterrence. They show, first, that in actual practice, experiments in the field don't always go exactly the way sociologists draw them up on paper. Workers in the criminal justice system may muddy the scientific purity of experimental design and data gathering. Second, the studies demonstrate the difficulty of generalizing about deterrence. Increased patrolling reduced crime in the New York subways but not in the streets of Kansas City. These contradictory results mean that we need to be more specific in the way we ask questions. Instead of asking the broad question "Do the police deter crime?" we must specify the type of patrolling, the setting, and the type of crime. Subway cars and stations offer criminals opportunities different from those offered by city streets. Cops on foot pose one kind of threat to potential criminals, patrol cars another.

EXPLAINING THE WEAKNESS OF POLICE DETERRENCE What started out as a simple question—do the police prevent crime?—has become quite complicated, and the obvious answer now seems to be in doubt. The deterrent effect of the thin blue line is, apparently, fairly weak. It is not hard to think of reasons the police might not be such an overwhelming deterrent. First, they can deter only those crimes that they might see. Indoor crimes—especially assaults, rapes, murders, and other nonutilitarian crimes between acquaintances—will not be affected by more cops in the street. Second, they cannot be everywhere at once. Even the most impulsive, opportunistic criminals can wait until there are no blue uniforms in sight. That is, rather than a reduction in crime, the police may cause a **displacement of crime** to another time or place. During the New York subway crackdown, for example, subway crime diminished, but apparently some of that crime was displaced to city buses, which experienced an increase. Criminals who are more professional may be especially likely to displace their work or to switch to lower-risk crimes. A special program to reduce robbery, for example, may merely drive criminals into other lines of work, like burglary.[18] The evidence from police crackdowns on specific areas or types of crime shows that a massive police effort does have a deterrent effect but that much crime is merely displaced (depending on the type of crime) and that the economic cost is considerable.[19]

Another possible explanation is that mere police presence does not necessarily increase the certainty of punishment. For punishment to be certain, the police must actually catch the criminals. Therefore, we ought to count not the number of police officers but the number or proportion of arrests.

ARREST RATES AND CRIME RATES   When the police arrest someone for a reported crime, the crime is said to be cleared by arrest. The clearance rate is the percentage of crimes known to the police that are cleared by arrest. Researchers have sometimes used this rate as a measure of certainty of punishment. If criminals think they can easily avoid arrest, they will be bolder about committing crimes. Deterrence theory would predict that when the police clear a greater percentage of crimes, the crime rate will decrease. In fact, research has generally found an inverse correlation between the two: The higher the clearance rate, the lower the crime rate. The obvious conclusion is that arrests by the police deter criminals.

SIMULTANEITY   However, this conclusion might not be the only explanation for the correlation. As in death penalty research, we must beware of problems of simultaneity. The data for most of this research come from the 1960s, when clearance rates were falling and crime rates were rising. One plausible explanation is that the lower risk of getting caught encouraged more people to commit more crimes: A causes B. But it is equally plausible that B causes A, that is, that rising crime rates led to lower clearance rates. Advocates of deterrence explain the huge increase in crime in the 1960s by pointing to the decrease in the proportion of crimes that resulted in arrest or imprisonment. They argue that crime increased because the chances of getting away became much more favorable. The other way of interpreting these numbers is that the increase in crime was caused by social forces and that the size of the increase overwhelmed the capacity of the criminal justice system. So although the *number* of persons arrested and imprisoned rose, the increase could not keep up proportionally with the increase in crime. Instead of a decrease in arrest and conviction rates causing an increase in crime, it was the other way around. An increase in crime was causing a decrease in the rates (but not the absolute numbers) of robbers arrested and convicted.

IN THE NEWS

Rudolph Giuliani was elected mayor of New York City after running on a strong anticrime platform. He promised to focus attention on visible crimes and disorder—everything from squeegee men (who clean the windshields of cars stopped for a light and then demand money from the drivers) to street-level drug traffic. He especially criticized the incumbent mayor for allowing drug arrests to decrease. A year after taking office, however, Giuliani had to cancel a strong antidrug program, a decision that reflects the problems of cost and displacement that often accompany efforts at deterrence.

DRUG SWEEP INTO QUEENS IS POSTPONED

by Clifford Krauss

Facing a persistent budget gap, Mayor Rudolph W. Giuliani has shelved at least temporarily a Police Department proposal to mount an ambitious sweep against mid-level drug dealers in Queens....

Mr. Giuliani's shelving of a plan that officials have said for weeks could make a major impact on drug dealing underscored the strains on the city's budget....

The policy review began last month when Police Commissioner William J. Bratton submitted to Mr. Giuliani a proposal that would put an additional 600 undercover and uniformed police officers in Queens. A series of simultaneous sweeps aimed at drug sellers who operate on street corners and out of apartments would have begun around Jan. 15 in high-crime neighborhoods....

The proposal also included reinforcing Brooklyn precincts bordering Queens to arrest dealers forced to move their operations in response to the initial raids. After arresting dealers in Queens and bordering neighborhoods, the plan called on the police to repeat similar operations—ranging from undercover buy-and-bust sting operations to saturation uniformed patrols—in a second and then a third borough.

Aides to Mr. Giuliani said he expressed concerns that the operation might do little more than push drug dealing out of one borough and into another, much as an effort to attack drug dealing in Washington Heights a few years ago drove up drug-related crime in neighboring Harlem.

He also cautioned that the sudden arrest of thousands of dealers could overwhelm the city's prisons and court system, which are already taxed by 45,000 more arrests in 1994 than the year before.

But Mr. Giuliani's primary concern ... is the cost.... The Police Department estimated that the program in Queens would cost about $10 million to begin, including spending for police overtime, fingerprinting suspects, processing arrests, and moving prisoners.

District Attorney Richard A. Brown of Queens said that he, too, would need additional money, to hire more prosecutors and new personnel for an additional arraignment courtroom and an additional grand jury.

Source: New York Times, December 26, 1994, p. 41.

One method of resolving this simultaneity problem is to allow for a certain time lag between a change in arrest rates and a change in crime rates. Will a change in this year's clearance rate affect next year's crime rate? Will a change in this year's crime rate affect next year's clearance rate? This kind of research requires statistical techniques too complicated to review here, but the answer from at least one study is that "arrest rates have no measurable effect on reported crime rates."[20]

THE POLICE AND CRIME—A SUMMARY   Despite the thousands of research studies, many important questions about the deterrent effect of the police have no conclusive answers. Still, there are a few points on which most criminologists agree. First, it is likely that without the police our cities would eventually have large increases in crime. Second, increasing police patrols beyond present levels can deter some crimes that patrol officers might happen on, such as auto theft or street robbery, but more squad cars cruising the streets and more routine foot patrols do little to decrease crimes in more private or indoor places. Some studies suggest that more police effort and more arrests may reduce crime, but methodological issues make this conclusion uncertain. In addition, the number of crimes deterred may be relatively small, while the cost of added police will be large. Police crackdowns usually have an overall deterrent effect, though some of the crime will be displaced to other areas; as costs force the withdrawal of the massive police presence, crime may gradually increase.

CONVICTION AND IMPRISONMENT AS DETERRENTS

Proponents of deterrence also argue that the police can deter crime only if the arrests they make lead to real punishment. The image of revolving-door justice, with criminals leaving the system almost as soon as they are caught, has an important place in some deterrence arguments. If the courts do not convict and imprison criminals, the lack of punishment will undermine the deterrent value of arrest (and also undermine the morale of the police). But if the courts get tough on criminals, so the argument goes, crime will decrease.

Getting tough usually means increasing the severity of punishment. Legislatures rewrite the criminal statutes, raising minimum sentences and allowing harsher sentences, including the death penalty. As for certainty of punishment, while lawmakers can do little to increase the ability of the police to catch criminals, they can make punishment more certain by requiring mandatory sentences and by calling for the abolition or restriction of plea bargaining.

Unfortunately, the way courts actually work makes it difficult to evaluate most of the evidence on the effect of these changes. In general, the few available research studies point to a deterrent effect: Higher rates of conviction and imprisonment accompany lower crime rates.[21] But as with other deterrence research, these studies have problems of simultaneity—of what is causing what.

DETERRING SPECIFIC CRIMES   Conservatives often argue that the criminal justice system undermines any possible deterrence because of its soft sentences. In fact, punishment in the United States is no less severe or less certain than in other industrialized democracies, which have lower crime rates. Prison terms in the United States—both official sentences and actual time served—are longer than those in other Western industrialized countries, and no other industrialized democracy allows capital punishment. Nor is punishment in those countries more certain than in the United States. The ratio of imprisonment to the number of reported crimes is about the same in

England or Germany as it is in the United States. Still, these countries generally have much lower rates of crime—especially violent crime—than those in the United States.[22]

The call to get tough often specifies a particular crime or criminal that has become the object of public attention. Since the 1960s, drugs, guns, and violent criminals have been the most popular targets of new laws and policies. The story of these efforts is an uneven one. Sometimes, prosecutors and judges find ways to get around the mandatory requirements. Yet, even when courts impose tougher sentences, the results are mixed. For example, in Massachusetts, a gun law—called Bartley-Fox, after its two authors—required a one-year minimum sentence in some gun offenses. A follow-up study of the law's first year showed that Massachusetts judges had followed the spirit of the law in sentencing offenders. The report also found that the law had caused "a small but demonstrable reduction of violent crime." Even so, the law was not necessarily a cure-all. Gun robberies decreased, but other robberies increased; assaults with and without guns followed a similar pattern. It looked as if criminals were responding to the new law by changing their weapons rather than by closing up shop. Then, in the third year that Bartley-Fox was in effect, gun robberies increased.[23] As more and more robbers were sent to prison for gun robberies, the effects of deterrence should have increased and gun robberies should have gone down even more sharply. But that is not what happened.

WHY DETERRENCE IS HARD TO FIND   Deterrence, which at first seems so obvious a factor in crime, has turned out to be very difficult to demonstrate conclusively. No wonder the public becomes so frustrated with social scientists. Instead of being able to confirm an obvious idea, researchers bring back little more than uncertainty and tentative conclusions.

The absence of solid evidence may be more than just a matter of research difficulties. Perhaps criminals cannot be deterred. Or to put it more accurately, perhaps our criminal justice system cannot increase the certainty, severity, or swiftness of punishment sufficiently to have a noticeable impact on crime rates. This is a controversial view. After all, if a change in the system could deter even one additional criminal out of ten potential criminals, or deter a criminal so that he or she commits nine crimes instead of ten, the crime rate would drop by 10 percent. That would mean a reduction of 1.4 million serious crimes (including 65,000 robberies and 2,400 murders) in the United States each year. But consider why criminal justice policies may not deter criminals.

DETERRENCE, KNOWLEDGE, AND PERCEPTION

Most research on deterrence tries to find correlations between certainty and severity of punishment, on the one hand, and crime rates, on the other. Usually, the correlations are very weak. One reason for the lack of deterrence might be that criminals are not aware of clearance rates, conviction rates, or sentence lengths. Suppose you, for example, were thinking of committing a burglary. Do you know what your chances of getting caught are; and if caught, your probability of being convicted and sentenced; and if sentenced, the minimum, maximum, and average terms for burglary? Do you know whether your local clearance rates for burglary have increased or decreased recently? Most likely, there are serious gaps in your knowledge on these crucial questions.

According to deterrence theory, however, what you know—or think you know—about these matters is extremely important. If increased certainty or severity is to deter criminals, the potential criminals must know about these factors. That is, criminals should be deterred if they *perceive* a high probability of being caught and punished, regardless of the reality of these risks. For example, many juvenile delinquents reduce their crimes or cease altogether as they get to be 17 or 18, and one reason may be that they know they face adult courts and prisons rather than the juvenile system. The same is true for adult criminals with prior convictions. As one serious (though not professional) thief said, "I know I'll grab big time if I go up again." (He also listed other, nondeterrence reasons for his early retirement from crime.)[24]

On the other hand, knowledge of harsh penalties may have little effect on those who commit crimes. A questionnaire given to California prisoners included the following item: "If prison time were a lot harder, most men who've done time would go straight when they got out." Only 13 percent agreed; 83 percent disagreed (and most of these checked "strongly disagree").[25] Nor do criminals think that certainty of punishment has much effect on their decisions. The same questionnaire had the following statement: "It's possible to get so good at crime you'll never get caught." Nearly 80 percent disagreed.[26] Criminals know they are going to get caught and go to prison. As a common saying in the criminal world advises, "If you can't do the time, don't do the crime."[27] Of course, criminals do not ignore the problem completely. They try to minimize the likelihood of getting caught by committing their crimes when nobody else (especially a police officer) will notice, but they rarely make a careful assessment of their actual chances.

If criminals think that getting caught is so certain, why do they commit the crimes? If asked later about the contradiction, a criminal might say, "If you thought about getting caught, you'd never do the crime." Opportunistic criminals may be too impulsive to think about consequences, but even older, more professional criminals say that they use this psychological tactic on themselves. Putting aside all negative thoughts is one way to neutralize the fatalistic view that prison is an eventual certainty. Not that it makes a difference: The California study found that criminals who thought that arrest was likely committed just as many crimes as did those who estimated a low probability of arrest. That is, perceptions of the certainty of punishment had no effect on actual levels of crime.

A second psychological process insulates criminals from their own knowledge that eventually everyone gets caught and goes to prison. Despite the odds, criminals often develop a belief in their own invulnerability. In part, this belief, this confidence, develops as the criminal commits more and more crimes successfully. A young mugger may approach his first crimes with much fear and may assess his chances as only fifty–fifty. But by the time he has committed several muggings with no trouble, he may come to feel nearly certain of his safety from the law.[28]

In any case, the long-range statistical probabilities indicated by clearance rates have a very weak influence on someone's moment-to-moment decision to commit a crime. For criminals, the most important deterrent factors are those in the visible present. In fact, the best interpretation of all these deterrence studies may be that the closer some element of deterrence is to the crime, the greater its power to deter. People in a house deter burglars and cops on the subway deter subway criminals more effectively than increased clearance rates, conviction rates, or imprisonment rates. If I am a criminal in search of an opportunity, police or even civilians in the area will affect me directly. I can see them; they can see me. But an increased imprisonment rate in my city will have touched only other criminals, not me (at least not yet). Some theorists think that "each arrest … has a relatively large effect on the perceptions of a small number of potential criminals,"[29] implying that if my criminal friend is arrested, I will be deterred. However, most criminals do in fact know others who have gone to prison; and despite the fate of their friends, they go on committing crimes. My hunch is that the possible deterrent elements of the criminal justice system do not seem as real, especially compared with other forces—the desire for money or excitement or the pressure from friends—in the immediate situation.

SCARED STRAIGHT?   In recent years, some law-enforcement agencies have tried deterrence policies aimed at first offenders and juveniles on the theory that they are not yet "hardened" criminals, that they may have committed their crimes out of a mistaken perception of the realities of crime and punishment, and that if arrested early enough, they will reduce or stop their crimes[30]—if only there were some way to punish them without at the same time allowing them to become socialized into the school-for-crime atmosphere of prison. One federal program for adult offenses instituted the practice of **split sentences**—a short term in jail followed by probation. Follow-up studies found that "a taste of the bars" had no extra deterrent effect. A similar program of **shock probation** in Kentucky had the same lack of effect: Offenders who received a brief, shocking term in jail followed by probation were no more successful than offenders sentenced to straight probation.[31]

A more widely known type of program has been used on juveniles, even those who have not been in trouble with the law. These programs try to change juveniles' perceptions of the certainty and severity of punishment by exposing them to real criminals in real prisons. In the late 1970s, a television documentary entitled "Scared Straight!" presented one such program—the Juvenile Awareness Project at Rahway State Prison in New Jersey, now probably the best known of these programs but certainly not the only one. Typically, youths are taken inside a prison, where a select group of convicts graphically explains the horrors of prison life. As the TV film shows, the convicts are indeed frightening as they depict, and to a certain extent enact, the humiliation and abuse many prisoners endure at the hands of guards and other prisoners. From the point of view of deterrence, the prisoners' message emphasizes the severity of punishment (prison is not a vacation; it is a physically and psychologically horrible experience). Their message also conveys the certainty of punishment (I was a smarter criminal than you'll ever be, and I got caught; therefore, if you don't straighten up, you will certainly wind up in here, too).

The original TV show and a sequel five years later gave mostly glowing reports on the thirteen juveniles it followed through the Rahway program. Unfortunately, the show did not have a control group (i.e., a group of similar youths who did not undergo the experiment). However, since not all adolescents in New Jersey had participated, there was a ready-made experiment waiting to be done: Match a group of scared straight kids with a control group—youths who had not undergone the program—and see who stays out of trouble. Compared with the control group, those who have been scared straight should be less likely to commit crimes.

SYSTEMATIC EVIDENCE VERSUS TELEVISION   Criminologist James Finckenauer followed two groups—one experimental (i.e., they went through the program) and one control—for six months after the subjects had visited the prison. He counted as successes youths who had no recorded offenses in that six-month period; failures were those who had one or more offenses. Table 16–3 compares only nondelinquents—youths who had no record of offenses prior to the study. Table 16–4 compares those who did have prior records of delinquency.

Clearly, the "scared straight" group did worse. Among the "good" kids (no previous offenses), 31.6 percent of the experimental group had offenses in the six-month follow-up period, compared with only 4.8 percent of the unscared control group. For youths with prior offenses, the failure rate was experimentals, 48.2 percent; controls, 21.4 percent. The "scared straight" kids had proportionally more than twice as many failures. Finckenauer's finding that experimentals did worse may have been caused by methodological problems. There had originally been fifty subjects in each group. During the experiment and follow-up period, four experimentals and fifteen controls disappeared from the data. They moved out of state or in some other way became impossible to trace. But at the very least, even if all the missing data had gone in the direction predicted by deterrence theory, the two groups would have had identical success rates.

These results surprised and in some cases angered the people who ran the Juvenile Awareness Project. Even some people without a vested interest in the project—perhaps those who had seen the TV show—had similar reac-

TABLE 16-3 •
OUTCOMES FOR NONDELINQUENT EXPERIMENTALS AND CONTROLS

	SUCCESSES	FAILURES	TOTAL
NONDELINQUENT EXPERIMENTAL	13 (68.4%)	6 (31.6%)	19
NONDELINQUENT CONTROL	20 (95.2%)	1 (4.8%)	21
TOTAL	33	7	40

Source: James Finckenauer, *SCARED STRAIGHT! and the Panacea Phenomenon* © 1982, pp. 137, 152. Adapted by permission of Prentice-Hall, Inc., Englewood Cliffs, NJ 07632.

TABLE 16-4 •
OUTCOMES FOR DELINQUENT EXPERIMENTALS AND CONTROLS

	SUCCESSES	FAILURES	TOTAL
DELINQUENT EXPERIMENTAL	14 (51.8%)	13 (48.2%)	27
DELINQUENT CONTROL	11 (78.6%)	3 (21.4%)	14
TOTAL	25	16	41

Source: James Finckenauer, *SCARED STRAIGHT! and the Panacea Phenomenon* © 1982, pp. 137, 152. Adapted by permission of Prentice-Hall, Inc., Englewood Cliffs, NJ 07632.

tions. The results are upsetting because they contradict two very appealing notions. First, these results strongly question the obvious, commonsense view of crime and punishment that began this chapter. Second, if the results had shown the project to have the 80 to 90 percent success rate it claimed, we would be looking at a very cheap solution to the crime problem. "Scared Straight!" suggested that for the mere cost of a bus trip to the nearest state prison, we could significantly reduce crime. Such a solution sounds too good to be true. It was.

The results of this systematic research on "Scared Straight!" may have been disappointing. However, the findings probably did not surprise people familiar with research on similar programs.[32] None of this research has found a deterrent effect. Nor should this surprise us if we recall the results of other studies of specific deterrence, which have consistently failed to show large deterrent effects. Juvenile awareness programs differ from these other studies only in that they do not allow the people being punished to become part of the inmate culture, with its criminal values. Apparently, however, even when youths are kept apart from inmate culture, the brief exposure to prison wears off quickly and has far less influence than do other factors in their day-to-day lives. Here is a typical example—a boy with a prior record of delinquency who went through the Rahway project but later committed a crime.

> Sixteen ... black, and in the county youth home. He was referred [to the project] by his probation officer for stealing and for a breaking and entering.... He said [referring to the prisoners at Rahway], "I thought they might kill me—some of the things they said scared me." He thought the visit helped him stay straight for a while; but asked why he got in trouble again, he said, "Some things just happen."[33]

MODIFYING DETERRENCE THEORY

The failure of these juvenile awareness projects and the limited success of other forms of deterrence do not necessarily mean that we must throw out the idea entirely. The ideas behind deterrence are theoretically valid. They work in psychology experiments, they work in housebreaking dogs, and no doubt they work for some crimes. Police crackdowns work, especially for offenses like drunk driving and illegal parking, that is, offenses committed by otherwise law-abiding citizens.[34]

On the other hand, some crimes and criminals will be unaffected by increases in the certainty and severity of official punishments. Most murders—even those committed during robberies or other felonies—are not planned in advance; they happen under stressful conditions that make cost-benefit calculation difficult if not impossible. Small wonder that the death penalty has proven an ineffective deterrent to murder.

Nor does the criminal justice system seem to be a deterrent to drug crimes. Here is one area where the severity and certainty of punishment have increased tremendously, with drastic, mandatory sentences even for first offenders and politicians calling for flogging and even execution for drug dealers. Between 1980 and 1992, the number of people sent to state prisons for drug offenses increased by more than 1,000 percent (from 8,900 to 102,000).[35] Yet these penalties seem to have had little influence on the amount of drugs sold and consumed in the United States. It's not hard to see why. As drug dealers are well aware, there is already a death penalty for drug dealing—a penalty meted out with much more swiftness and certainty than what even the most draconian legislators might devise. Of course, the penalty is imposed not by the state but by other drug dealers, a difference that is irrelevant to principles of deterrence. Risk is risk, and drug dealers risk their lives every day. No doubt the risks of robbery and murder deter many people from entering the field, yet when one dealer is killed, others are ready to take his place.

As for other street crimes like robbery and burglary—economically motivated but not quite a business like drugs—principles of deterrence may have some impact. Certainty and severity of punishment, however, are only two among several factors that influence crime, and it is unlikely that in reality the criminal justice system can increase these deterrent factors enough to offset the weight of other forces. If the criminal justice system could raise the real rates of punishment so that a criminal might commit only three or four crimes before being locked up, crime rates might fall significantly (though the cost for the additional courts and prison space would be very high). In any case, the system cannot approach such effectiveness.

Perhaps we expect too much of deterrence because we overestimate the long-term rationality of criminals. We mistakenly expect that criminals will calculate the long-term outcomes of their actions. But obviously they do not. As anyone who has tried to quit smoking or stay on a diet knows, temptations, opportunities, or group pressure in the immediate situation can force a person's attention away from long-range costs and benefits and focus it narrowly and irrationally on the present. Juvenile awareness projects fail probably because juveniles are especially vulnerable to group pressure. Even property crimes like auto theft and larceny may derive from psychological and social, expressive causes rather than from economic, instrumental causes. As for murder, it is much more likely to be affected by social pressures and available weaponry than by potential punishment. In the 1980s, many states changed their laws so that juveniles who commit serious crimes faced adult courts and punishments. Yet between 1983 and 1993, the rate of homi-

IN THE NEWS

Is prison a deterrent? In 1994, the New Jersey State Senate considered a bill that "would create a new prison that would force inmates to do hard labor ten hours a day and offer them few amenities.... It would offer no education programs, no vocational training, no gymnasium or other recreational areas, no televisions and no telephone privileges" (New York Times, September 28, 1994. The motive behind the bill was in part retribution—the idea that people who have committed crimes should suffer—but it was also in part deterrence. But as this article suggests, the deterrent value of prison depends not just on its level of discomfort inside but also on the way other people react to the ex-con (a term that itself now seems quaint and out of date).

WHERE PRISON IS A FACT OF LIFE

by Howard Manly and Zachary Dowdy

As owner of the Suffolk Pawn Shop, Ed Bean ... keeps small, inexpensive television sets with earphone jacks in stock at his shop.... "That's all some of my customers can have in jail," he says....

Keisha Bannister, 15, talks nonchalantly about many of her friends and their prison records, including her boyfriend, who recently spent a weekend in jail, busted for selling crack. "Prison is just a fact of life," she says.

Over at the nearby Roxbury Men's Club ... middle-aged men play checkers and pool and talk so casually about relatives and friends spending time behind bars that it's as if prison has become a common thread linking hard-working and decent people with thieves, murderers, and drug dealers.

The result is clear: In a neighborhood with one of the city's highest crime rates, the state's ultimate sanction has lost its stigmatizing effect, and, arguably, its deterrent value.

Many of the neighborhood's youths today see prison as a rite of passage, something to brag about, not as the great divide separating the civil from the lawless. Many emerge from prison heads held high, unashamed.

To many in this mostly poor and black ... neighborhood ... the people serving time are more than inmates.

They are fathers and brothers, mothers and sisters, uncles and cousins, customers and friends.

Even fashion has been influenced by what many call "the system," a pejorative reference to American criminal justice. The popular baggy jeans young men wear on street corners imitate the loose-fitting uniforms of prison.

"There is a generation of people growing up with no hope and they have no other way to survive but through crime," says Rev. Wesley Williams.... "Unfortunately, as a result, prison has become an extension of the black neighborhood."

Source: Boston Globe, July 7, 1993, pp. 1, 24.

---

cide among boys 13 to 17 nearly doubled among whites and nearly tripled among African-Americans.

The lives of adult criminals, too—except for the most professional—are not marked by a great deal of rational planning. Criminals generally feel that they have little control over their lives. They usually do not have the resources to leave the types of neighborhoods they know and feel comfortable in. They may try to stay out of trouble, but given the pressures of the moment and perhaps the effects of alcohol or drugs, they forget these long-range plans. They may drift to the opportunities offered by the world they live in, and sometimes those opportunities will be criminal. In their lives, too, as in that of the boy quoted above, "Some things just happen."

CRITICAL THINKING QUESTIONS

1. Deterrence theory maintains that criminals will be affected by the severity, certainty, and swiftness of punishment. Which of these variables has the most impact on behavior? Which is the one that the criminal justice system can most easily change?
2. Most available evidence gives very little support to the idea of criminal punishment as a specific deterrent. Why? Why does punishment not deter the person punished?
3. How can we find out if the death penalty deters crime? Nearly all research fails to find a deterrent effect. What criticisms might death penalty supporters make of this research? Why has this research not had any noticeable impact on public opinion in the United States about capital punishment?
4. Why have juvenile awareness programs been so popular, and how effective are they in deterring juveniles?
5. Getting tough on some crime usually means increasing the penalties for it. What effect do these changes have on the amount of crime?

KEY TERMS

certainty of
punishment

deterrence

displacement of crime

flat sentencing

general deterrence

mandatory sentences

presumptive
sentencing

recidivism

severity of
punishment

shock probation

simultaneity

specific deterrence

split sentences

swiftness of
punishment

CHAPTER SEVENTEEN

INCAPACITATION

CHAPTER OUTLINE

Why do we have prisons? So far we have looked at rehabilitation and deterrence as possible functions. Let us oversimplify for a moment and suppose that the evidence is clear—that prison does not deter people from crime, nor does it rehabilitate those who spend time there. Of course, the evidence does not speak quite so boldly, but it certainly should be enough to dampen both the liberal's enthusiasm for prison as rehabilitation and the conservative's enthusiasm for it as a deterrent. Even so, there is a third practical use for prison—to keep criminals off the streets. This purpose is known in criminology as *incapacitation*: literally, taking away the criminal's capacity to commit crimes.

In the 1970s, ideas about the purpose of prison were changing. This change in focus may have been a response to the discouraging evidence on rehabilitation and deterrence. It may also have been part of the disillusionment with efforts to get at the social causes of crime. In any case, incapacitation began to attract more attention, both from the public and from criminologists. The idea of incapacitation holds a great advantage over deterrence or rehabilitation: It is indisputable. You don't have to do fancy research to show that it works. As long as criminals are behind bars, they cannot be victimizing the public. Here was the basis for an effective policy: Put more criminals in prison and keep them there longer. It was the obvious solution to the problem of high crime rates. Or was it?

As with deterrence, we must distinguish between two types of effect—the effect on the individual and the more general effect on crime rates. Obviously prison keeps each individual inmate from victimizing the public. But will locking up more people for longer periods of time substantially reduce the overall crime rate? A lock-'em-up policy will undoubtedly prevent some crimes. The real question is how many crimes will it prevent and at what cost.

Human warehousing—keeping undesirable people away from the rest of society—has long been a function of institutions like prisons. Now it goes by the name of incapacitation—the principle that even if prisons cannot significantly deter or rehabilitate, they can at least keep criminals from victimizing the public. Measuring the amount of crime that didn't happen is one of the main tasks of incapacitation research.

COLLECTIVE INCAPACITATION—
LOCK 'EM ALL UP

Some rough evidence on incapacitation comes from policy changes that took place in the 1970s. As faith in rehabilitation faded, many states turned to policies based on incapacitation (and possibly retribution). Legislators passed laws requiring stiffer sentencing, and judges sentenced more criminals to prison. As a result, a greater proportion of criminals were going to prison. In 1971, state and federal prisons held about 200,000 people, an incarceration rate of 95 per 100,000; that is, for every 100,000 people in the country, 95 were in prison. (This number does not include those in county and municipal jails or juvenile detention centers.) Ten years later, the prison population and rate had risen by more than 60 percent.

Unfortunately, during the same decade, crime rates did not go down. Victimization surveys showed very little change in crime, and police statistics showed an increase. In the next twelve years (1981–1993), the number and rate more than doubled. The number of people in prison climbed from 353,000 to just under 1 million—a rate of 369 per 100,000, the highest of any country in the world. Still, taking an additional 600,000 criminals out of circulation did not bring consistent reduction in crime. Crime rates declined in the early 1980s but then rose again (see Figure 17–1). Why did crime rates remain high despite the great increase in imprisonment? Was the strategy of incapacitation a failure? And if so, is incapacitation a worthless idea?

Many other changes could have been affecting crime in the United States in those years, and had we not been sending so many people to prison, the crime rates might have increased even more. But how much more? Incapacitation research is a tricky business. It requires isolating the effects of incapacitation from other factors. But more crucially, when we ask, "How much crime can we prevent by increasing the prison time of people convicted of crime?" we are really asking, "How much crime would these criminals commit if we let them go?" The answer requires predicting the future. This is a difficult task at best, and often we have no way of finding out whether the prediction was correct.

A different way of asking the question is to look back and ask, "How much crime was committed by people who were arrested but not locked up?" This question is a bit easier to investigate. It also addresses the popular version of the incapacitation argument—that many crimes are committed by criminals who are arrested but not punished; that criminals walk out of court and go right back to committing crimes, crimes that could have been prevented had the criminals been sent to prison.

To test the accuracy of this popular view, one team of researchers looked just at violent crime (murder, rape, robbery, and assault) in a single year (1973) in a single county (Franklin County, Ohio, which includes the state capital, Columbus).[1] That year, roughly 3,000 violent crimes were reported to the police. The researchers asked, "How many of these crimes could have been prevented if the courts had been tougher on crime?" Suppose that beginning in 1968, every person convicted of a felony had been locked up for five years. How many

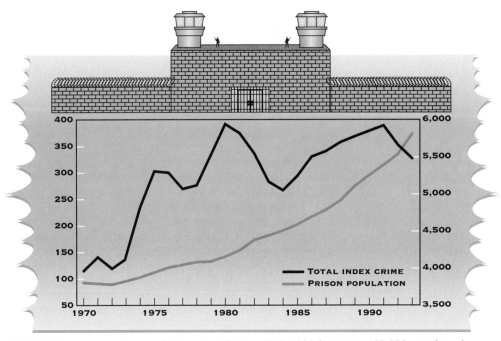

FIGURE 17–1   Index Crime and Prison Population, 1970–1993 (rates per 100,000 population)

Source: Kathleen Maguire and Ann L. Pastore, eds., *Sourcebook of Criminal Justice Statistics—1993* (Washington, DC: Bureau of Justice Statistics, 1994).

criminals would be affected, and how much crime would be prevented? Suppose that Criminal Smith had been convicted of a felony in 1970 but had served only one year, and that he had then committed a violent crime in 1973. Under the hypothetical five-year policy, he is a **preventable recidivist**; that is, his repeat offense could have been averted by a five-year sentence since he would still have been in prison in 1973. His violent offense was a preventable crime.

The researchers wanted to know how many of the 2,892 violent crimes in 1973 were preventable crimes. Unfortunately, they could not find out what they needed to know for all of these crimes. They could know only about the 638 for which someone was arrested (or in police terms, crimes that were cleared by arrest); 2,254 violent crimes remained unsolved. Not knowing who committed these crimes presents a serious problem in estimating incapacitation; but in criminology, researchers often must make do with the available information, even when it is incomplete, and make their best estimates about the rest. In this case, the information consisted of the records of the people—342 in all—arrested for these 638 violent crimes cleared by arrest. For purposes of estimating incapacitation, we are assuming that each person really did commit the crime for which he or she was arrested. Since some of the arrested criminals had confessed to more than one violent crime, these 342 people accounted for the 638 crimes cleared by arrest. How many of these criminals were preventable recidivists? That is, how many had convictions for any felony (violent or not) in the past five years?

It turns out that only 63 of those arrested (less than 20 percent) fell into this category. Therefore, a five-year sentence would have prevented the crimes of these 63 people. The violent crimes of the other 279 arrested criminals would have occurred anyway. Some of the 63 preventable recidivists committed more than one violent crime. In fact, they accounted for a total of 111 violent crimes. Since there were 2,892 violent crimes reported to the police, these 111 crimes constitute 4 percent of the total (see Figure 17–2). In other words, the five-year sentence that would have kept these 63 criminals off the streets would have reduced violent crime by at least 4 percent. I say "at least" 4 percent because we still do not know who committed three-fourths of the 2,892 violent crimes. Of the 638 crimes we do know about, 111 (17.4 percent) were preventable. So if we assume that the uncleared 2,254 crimes followed a similar pattern, the five-year incapacitation policy would have reduced violent crime by 17.4 percent. The researchers, using even more generous assumptions about who committed the uncleared crimes, estimated that if *everyone*, juvenile or adult, convicted of *any felony*, violent or nonviolent, had been locked up for five years, violent crime would have been reduced by 28 percent.

A 28 percent reduction in violent crime is good news. However, the question remains whether the five-year policy would be practical. Most states, for reasons of justice if nothing else, are unlikely to lock up most juveniles or nonviolent criminals for five years. In addition, the policy would be extremely wasteful and costly. To imprison those 63 people who later committed violent crimes, the state of Ohio would also have had to lock up many hundreds of people who did not do so. As a statewide policy, it would mean an increase of 500 percent in an already overcrowded prison system. Ohio would be spending quite a bit of money to lock up a lot of people to achieve a 28 percent reduction in violent crime. Also, even if all these people had been locked up

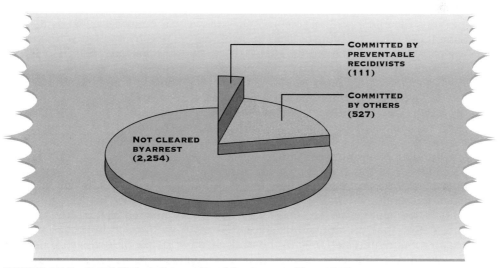

FIGURE 17–2   2,892 Violent Crimes (Franklin County, Ohio, 1973)

Source: Steve Van Dine, John P. Conrad, and Simon Dinitz, "The Incapacitation of the Chronic Thug," *Journal of Criminal Law & Criminology*, vol. 70, no. 1 (1979), 125–135.

beginning in 1968, about three-quarters of the violent offenses of 1973 would have occurred anyway.

In the collective incapacitation study, the researchers estimated that under their most stringent hypothetical policy—five years for any conviction, juvenile or adult—the prison population would increase by 500 percent. In the twenty years since, Ohio did increase its prison population by nearly 400 percent—from about 7,700 prisoners in 1973 to over 38,000 in 1992. The rate of imprisonment per 100,000 Ohioans showed a similar increase of nearly 400 percent. However, during this same period, violent crime in Ohio did not decrease by 28 percent or even by 4 percent. It increased from 292 per 100,000 to 526 per 100,000, an 80 percent increase.

This high percentage of unpreventable crime is not unique to Franklin County, Ohio. In New York State, for example, of all people convicted of felonies in 1982, 76 percent had no prior felony convictions, and the proportion was even higher for the more serious crimes. For A felonies, the most serious level in New York's five-category classification system, 94 percent of those convicted had no prior felony convictions; for B felonies, the number was 80 percent. Similarly in Maryland, incapacitation would have failed to prevent 77 percent of the major crimes. Of felons convicted in 1981 and 1982, 33 percent had only minor prior convictions, and 44 percent had no prior convictions of any sort.[2] A national study estimated that of all those admitted to prison, only about one-quarter were preventable recidivists (i.e., offenders on parole or probation). The others were either first offenders or recidivists who had served out their terms. Violent crimes were even less preventable than property crimes. Nearly half of the violent offenses were committed by first offenders; a third were committed by previous offenders who had served their full terms. Only one violent offense in five could have been prevented by keeping all offenders in prison till the expiration of their full sentences.[3]

Does all this mean that we should give up on incapacitation as a goal (perhaps the major goal) of prisons? One answer—the answer given by its proponents—is that doubling or even quintupling (as in the Ohio study) the number of prisoners is the wrong idea. The crucial part of incapacitation is not *how many* people go to prison; it's *who* goes to prison.

The Ohio study proposes an indiscriminate policy of putting all felons in prison—a policy called **collective incapacitation**. Usually this means putting people in prison, but most proposals for gun control are really a type of collective incapacitation: Make it harder (or in some proposals impossible) for *everyone* to get guns. If nobody has a gun, nobody can commit a crime with a gun. Opponents of gun control propose policies based on *deterrence*: Let people have all the guns they want but severely punish those who use them in crimes. With gun control, they argue, too many noncriminals will be incapacitated, and law-abiding sportsmen will be unnecessarily deprived of their guns. They make other arguments as well—that gun restrictions are unconstitutional, that criminals will get guns anyway—but for purposes of this chapter, I am interested only in the underlying principle of incapacitation, not the practical problems of putting policies into effect.

The same argument holds for imprisoning all offenders. And unlike restricting the sale of guns, imprisonment brings direct costs to the taxpayers. Parole, a less costly alternative to imprisonment, remains an unpopular

TABLE 17-1 •

PERCENT OF ALL INDEX CRIME ARRESTS IN 11 STATES,
REPRESENTED BY STATE PRISONERS RELEASED IN 1983,
BY TYPE OF REARREST CHARGE AND YEAR

REARREST CHARGE, 1983–1986	PERCENT
MURDER AND NONNEGLIGENT MANSLAUGHTER	2.3
RAPE	1.8
ROBBERY	5.0
AGGRAVATED ASSAULT	2.4
BURGLARY	4.8
LARCENY/THEFT	2.0
MOTOR VEHICLE THEFT	3.3

Source: Allen J. Beck, "Recidivism of Prisoners Released in 1983" (Washington, DC: Bureau of Justice Statistics, 1989).

policy, and no wonder. A follow-up for three and one-half years of parolees in eleven large states found that of the 108,580 prisoners paroled in 1983, about 68,000 (62.5 percent) were rearrested on a total of about 327,000 charges, including 2,282 homicides, 1,291 rapes, and 17,060 robberies. Twenty thousand of the parolees had 25 or more charges. However, preventing these 327,000 crimes by keeping everyone in prison would have cost, at today's prison costs, nearly $7 billion (108,500 prisoners at $50 a day for three and one-half years). And how much of a dent in crime would this costly incapacitation have made? Although the numbers of crimes seem very high, they represent a relatively small fraction of serious crime (see Table 17–1). Collective incapacitation may be emotionally appealing, but as a policy it is very expensive. However, there may be a more efficient use of our limited prison space.

SELECTIVE INCAPACITATION—LOCK SOME OF 'EM UP

We know that some offenders commit only a few crimes; others commit many crimes. It makes no sense, from the standpoint of incapacitation, to fill our prisons with infrequent offenders. Instead, we should reserve our limited prison space for those who commit the worst crimes and commit them most frequently. This strategy is known as **selective incapacitation**, and its proponents argue that the huge increases in the prison population in the 1970s were not a good test of incapacitation. If most of the additional prisoners were low-rate offenders, persistently high rates of crime should have come as no surprise.

Selective incapacitation seems like a more sensible basis for policy than does collective incapacitation. It promises reductions in crime without large increases in the prison population. Recall the relevant fact from the various cohort studies: A fairly small number of people commit a large proportion of the crime. In Wolfgang's study of all Philadelphia teenage boys born in 1945, the 627 classified as chronic offenders, constituted only 6 percent of the total cohort and 18 percent of all those who had ever been arrested. Yet this relative handful of boys accounted for over half of all arrests, including nearly two-thirds of all serious (Index) crimes and over four-fifths of all robberies.[4] The tempting conclusion is this: If somehow we could have incapacitated those 627 boys, we could have greatly reduced serious crime. Similarly, in the study of parolees, the 18.6 percent who ran up twenty-five or more criminal charges while on parole accounted for nearly half of all crimes committed by the entire group of 108,500 parolees.[5] As one police chief said, "If I could just get 200 guys off my streets ... I could cut the crime rate in half."[6] Criminal justice policymakers, using less blunt language, talk about focusing on the career criminal or habitual offender. They are all talking about selective incapacitation as a means of reducing crime.

SELECTING CAREER CRIMINALS

The crucial and difficult part of selective incapacitation is selection. Since we want to select those criminals who will commit the most crimes, we are once again in the prediction business. For selective incapacitation to work, we must be able to predict what a criminal would do if he or she were set free. In actual practice, people in the criminal justice system make this prediction every day. When a district attorney decides to charge an arrested person with a lesser crime or bargain for a lighter sentence, when a judge decides to sentence a criminal to a shorter term or to probation, and when a parole board decides to grant a prisoner early release, they are all predicting that the offender will not commit further crimes. Unfortunately, these predictions have, on the whole, been no more accurate than those made by flipping a coin.

Ever since Lombroso, criminologists studying individual criminals have tried to predict criminal behavior. Often, the prediction is disguised as a backward-looking explanation rather than a forward-looking prediction. But the implication is that if we had known about the important explanatory factors earlier—if we had seen the particular skull shape or the telltale signs of psychopathy or sociopathy—we could have predicted the criminality. As faith in rehabilitation receded, policy-oriented criminologists turned their attention toward devising more scientific and more accurate ways of predicting future criminal behavior, not just of children but of those already convicted of crimes. In 1982, researchers from the RAND Corporation published the results of a study claiming that selective incapacitation used as a basis for sentencing criminals could reduce robbery by 20 percent with no increase in the prison population.[7] A 20 percent reduction in robbery with no additional cost to the taxpayers is a rather attractive proposal. It even caught the attention of the popular press (e.g., *Newsweek*). Since this study was quite influential, I will discuss it in some detail here.

Peter Greenwood, who headed the study, and his colleagues interviewed men in jails and prisons in California, Texas, and Michigan. The researchers had information on the inmates' official criminal history (arrests, convictions, and imprisonment). But in the interview, they would ask an inmate not just about the crime he was locked up for but also about all the other crimes he had committed in the two years before he was caught.

On the basis of these self-reports, the researchers divided the inmates into three groups according to their recent amounts of crime. For example, among robbers, the low-rate group reported an average of two robberies per year; the high-rate robbers averaged thirty-one robberies per year (and hundreds of other crimes as well). Once the researchers discovered these ranges of criminal activity, they put this information out of sight and pretended they did not know the offense rate of any individual inmate. Instead, they made this information the fact they were trying to predict. In terms of statistics, this amount of crime—low, medium, or high—became the **dependent variable**, that is, the thing to be predicted. They especially wanted to be able to identify those whom they had classified as high-rate offenders—the worst 25 percent of the prisoners.

The researchers' problem, then, was to find some useful **independent variables**, that is, other information that would allow them to judge whether a person was a high, medium-, or low-rate offender. Therefore, Greenwood also asked inmates about their juvenile crime, their employment and marital histories, their use of drugs, their education, and other social factors. Information on race and age also was readily available. If a variable turned out to be correlated with an individual's rate of crime, using that variable would allow better prediction for sentencing purposes.

Greenwood and his colleagues discovered that by using seven items from their interviews, they could create a formula that improved the accuracy of predictions of how serious a criminal each inmate was. (That is, they could use this combination of independent variables to make a better prediction about the dependent variable.) The seven items are:

- Prior conviction for robbery or burglary
- Being incarcerated for more than half of the preceding two years
- Juvenile conviction prior to age 16
- Commitment to a state or federal juvenile institution
- Current heroin or barbiturate use
- Heroin or barbiturate use as a juvenile
- Employed less than half of the preceding two years (excluding jail time)

Does the scale really work? Could it really "reduce the robbery rate by 20 percent with no increase in the total number of robbers incarcerated?"[8] Yes and no. On the one hand, it is an improvement over random guessing; on the other, it still misclassifies a great many people. Whether these mistakes outweigh the benefits is a matter of debate, so let's see why some people object to Greenwood's seven-item scale.

BEWARE OF FALSE POSITIVES

No formula for predicting human behavior is perfect. In any prediction scheme, there will be two kinds of errors: false positives and false negatives. A diagnosis of positive means that the person has what we are looking for—in this case, a high rate of crime. But we could just as easily use pregnancy as an example. If you take a test for pregnancy and it is positive, it is predicting that you are pregnant. If you are in fact pregnant, the test result is valid—a **true positive**. But if you are not really pregnant, this prediction is a **false positive**. Similarly, if the test says that you are not pregnant, the prediction is negative. If you really are not pregnant, the test is a **true negative**. But if six months later you give birth, the test was a **false negative**. These scientific terms have become more familiar in recent years as a result of the increased concern over illegal drugs. As more businesses and agencies begin to test their workers for drugs, some people have raised the question of false positives: The test says the person is using illegal drugs, when in fact he or she has been taking a prescription drug or even nothing stronger than an over-the-counter cold medicine. (The drug-testing controversy involves much more important issues—questions of constitutional law, ethics, privacy, individual rights, and public safety. But for purposes of this chapter I am concerned only with the issue of false positives.)

Each type of error has its own costs. In predicting high-rate offenders, a false negative means that we predict someone to be a safe risk and release him or her from prison; the cost of our error is the further crimes that person commits. The cost of a false positive is all the money we spend to imprison a relatively harmless person.

How well did the RAND study do in avoiding these errors in classifying criminals? In Greenwood's seven-item test, anybody who had four or more of the seven characteristics was a positive (i.e., predicted to be a high-rate offender). Those who had only one or none of the seven characteristics were predicted to be low-rate offenders; those scoring two or three were predicted to be medium-rate offenders. Table 17–2 shows how well the predictions worked. (Correct predictions are in boldface type.)

The scale works fairly well in identifying the less serious criminals. Better than 75 percent of these predictions (159 out of 209) were correct, and fewer than 1 in 12 of the people diagnosed as good risks were actually high-rate offenders. These would have been false negatives since they were predicted, mistakenly, *not* to be high-rate offenders. But the scale is far less efficient in picking out the serious criminals. Of the 236 people predicted to be high-rate offenders, only 106 (45 percent) were actually in that category. The other 55 percent were false positives. If we were using this scale for actual sentencing, more than half the people receiving stiff sentences would be serving unnecessarily long terms.

TABLE 17-2 •
ACTUAL AND PREDICTED OFFENSE RATES FROM THE
GREENWOOD SCALE

		PREDICTED OFFENSE RATE			
		LOW (0–1)	MEDIUM (2–3)	HIGH (4–7)	TOTAL
ACTUAL	LOW	**159**	174	59	382
OFFENSE	MEDIUM	33	**89**	71	193
RATE	HIGH	17	73	**106**	196
	TOTAL	209	336	236	781

Since selective incapacitation requires accurate predictions, all those false positives weaken the argument for such a policy, even on its own terms. But in addition, there are other problems—technical, practical, legal, and ethical—that may undermine the use of this scale and others like it.

SELECTIVE INCAPACITATION
VERSUS DUE PROCESS

The technical problems, which challenge the accuracy of the results, involve statistical matters too complex for me to describe in detail here. But to give one example, it may not be accurate to use data from incarcerated criminals (presumably the most serious offenders) to make predictions about other criminals who will be coming through the courts. Also, the predictions were tested against the same group of people used in deriving the scale. When Greenwood tried his scale on two other samples of inmates, it was only half as accurate.[9] Other researchers have had a similar lack of success.[10] If the scale were actually used, the proportion of false positives would be greater than 55 percent, the reduction in robbery would probably be less than 20 percent, and the prison population would probably increase.

The legal and practical problems arise from the nature of the items in the scale. For the last three items, which involve drug use and employment, we must rely on the criminal's self-reports. Of the remaining four items, two deal with juvenile records. However, in many states, juvenile records are sealed; that is, they are unavailable to adult courts. If the scale were actually used for sentencing, it is unlikely that courts could require criminals to give this damaging information about their juvenile crimes. In fact, for most practical purposes, the only items readily available to the court will be the first two: prior convictions and prison time. Since judges already give these factors great weight in their sentencing decisions, the RAND scale could probably do little to change the real world of criminal justice.

Regardless of its practical effect, the RAND study raises an important question: Even if we could know all the information, should we use it to determine a criminal's sentence? A principle of our system of justice is that a person should be punished for what he has done, not for what he is and not for what someone predicts he will do. For example, a study of New York juveniles found that those most likely to become high-rate offenders were African-Americans and Hispanics who did poorly in school and who came from single-parent homes supported only by welfare.[11] Longer sentences on the basis of race or income might improve the incapacitation effects—that is, they might prevent more crimes—but they would violate some of our basic principles. So, too, with the Greenwood scale: Given two people convicted of the same crime, can we give a long term to one because he has been unemployed? Or because he used drugs when he was young? Such a policy seems to violate the constitutional principle of due process of law. The problem is especially troubling given the large percentage of false positives. Over half the people receiving long terms will have been sentenced on the basis of predictions that were incorrect.

Of course, under the current system, the same kinds of inequities exist. Individuals convicted of the same crime and with the same criminal history may receive quite different sentences. Judges, too, like the RAND scale, may take into account drug use and employment, as well as other factors like family status and perhaps even (unconsciously) race. Moreover, the current system—and this is the whole point of the RAND study—already imprisons many people who could safely be released. The study did not claim to make sentencing any fairer; it merely claimed to make it more efficient and more systematic.

WHY INCAPACITATION FAILS

Why has incapacitation not turned out to be the magic bullet that will stop crime? One answer is that even with the best scientific information (much of which would be legally excluded in court), we would still not be very good at identifying the worst criminals. To make sure that we catch most of the big fish, we have to cast a wide net and haul in a lot of smaller fish as well.

Of course these other criminals are not exactly small fry, and that's part of the problem. The courts already let the obviously good risks go with probation or perhaps a short jail term. The convicts in the RAND study were criminals who had committed enough serious crimes to wind up in state prisons. However, even within this group of convicts there was considerable variation. The worst 10 percent averaged eighty-seven robberies a year; the rest of the prisoners averaged only five a year. In other words, even among the prison population, it is still only a handful who have committed most of the violent crimes. Locking up one of these high-rate robbers would prevent as many robberies as locking up seventeen or eighteen of the others. Selective incapacitation would work if—and this is the big if—we could pick out this handful from the other convicts. The problem is not to separate the good guys from the bad guys—that would be easy—but to separate the moderately bad from the very bad. What selective incapacitation requires is an instrument sensitive enough to distinguish the worst criminals from those who commit "only" two or three robberies a year. Unfortunately, as matters now stand, it is unrealistic to expect the development of a simple set of questions that will allow us to identify the very worst 25 percent or so in this group of serious criminals.

If we are already incapacitating the most serious criminals, why do crime rates remain high? This question quickly brings us back to the different theoretical explanations for crime. For example, both liberals and conservatives may argue that incapacitation as a strategy does nothing to change the *causes* of crime. Liberal versions of this idea focus on unemployment, poverty, inadequate schools, violent families, and so on. Unfortunately, these theories do not explain why such causes should produce more criminals to replace those swept into prison.

INCAPACITATION VERSUS SUPPLY AND DEMAND

One conservative version does try to answer this question by taking a purely economic approach. Economists see the demand for crime as functioning in the same way as the demand for dentistry or accounting or any other service. This demand is clearest for crimes that provide illegal goods and services like drugs or prostitution. Between 1980 and 1992, the number of people imprisoned for drug offenses increased by more than 1,000 percent; by 1992, nearly one-third of the people entering prison were sentenced for drug crimes.[12] However, these increases had hardly any effect on drug dealing as a source of employment. As long as drug users were creating the demand, other sellers were willing to come into the market.

Can there be a similar demand for robbery or burglary? We usually don't think of anyone demanding crime in the way people with complicated finances demand accounting services. But anything that raises income or lowers cost contributes to the demand. If you or I buy stolen merchandise, we are obviously contributing to the overall demand for theft by bidding up the profit. In a less obvious way, we may lower the costs of crime by making ourselves more attractive as targets—by not locking doors, by putting stereos in our cars and not just in our homes, or by stocking our houses with easily resold consumer goods.[13] In this way, too, we are contributing to the demand for crime.

There is another fact to consider, one that incapacitation studies often seem to ignore: Many criminals work in groups of two or three or even more. Suppose that we catch a robber who, along with two others, has been committing fifty robberies a year. If we lock him up, will next year's robberies decrease by fifty? Or will his two uncaught friends continue their work in his absence, perhaps recruiting someone to take his place? In this example as well, incapacitation cannot decrease the supply or demand for robbery.

INCAPACITATION AND EXPRESSIVE CRIME

It would seem that incapacitation should work well for, say, the crime of rape. Locking up a rapist will prevent him from committing further rapes; in addition, it is hard to imagine a demand for rape that would lead others to take

ABOUT CRIME & CRIMINOLOGY

This is an example of one of the more question-able assumptions of incapacitation. In 1986, when Police Director Greenleaf made the follow-ing observations, Newark had almost 13,000 car thefts. According to Greenleaf's logic, locking up two dozen car thieves would have completely eliminated auto theft from Newark.

NEWARK LEADERS URGE ACTION ON CAR THEFTS

by Frederick W. Byrd

The Newark City Council yesterday urged increased efforts to combat car theft in the city, with Councilman Earl Harris commenting, "The story is getting around that it is not safe to drive your car into our city."

During hearings on the municipal police budget yesterday, Police Director Louis Greenleaf said the problem is not the number of arrests being made but the fact that many of the offenders captured are not incarcerated.... "The trouble is there is no strong enforcement after we arrest people," he said.... "A juvenile may be arrested 10 times in six months, steal three or four cars a day, and in court he gets probation, proba-tion, probation."

"If they would put one kid away, that would mean 600 less stolen cars," the director asserted.

Source: Newark Star Ledger, March 15, 1988, p. 1.

his place. But despite this logic, the evidence on the incapacitation of rapists is disappointing. Jacqueline Cohen, in her study of criminals in Washington, D.C., estimated that if every man convicted of rape were imprisoned for life, the rate of rape in Washington would decrease by only 3.6 percent. Life sentences for other noneconomic, expressive crimes would bring greater reductions—7.9 percent for murder, 13.7 percent for aggravated assault. Of course, no judge can hand down a life sentence on a first conviction for aggravated assault. Cohen therefore also estimated the reduction for repeat offenses. She concluded that if the life sentence were imposed after only a second assault conviction (also unlikely in the real world), aggravated assault would decrease by 3.3 percent.[14]

A life sentence for first offenders is unlikely, although as the recent history of drug laws shows, not impossible. And given the popularity of three-strikes laws, life sentences for third offenders will almost certainly become more common. So suppose for a minute that courts could and did hand down life sentences for first offenders. What would happen? According to research like Cohen's, crime would decrease—but only modestly. If every conviction for an Index offense brought a life term, the reduction might be as great as 25 percent. But this policy would also create a much larger prison population, and a much older one. After a while, newly arrived teenage convicts would be jostling grandfathers for elbow room.

In their career trajectories, criminals resemble ball players. Few stay active in the game past their thirties. Locking up a young man at the peak of his career may prevent many crimes. Keeping him in prison—perhaps by a three-strike law—when he is well past forty will prevent far fewer crimes, while the cost will be the same or even higher.

A FINAL WORD

The problems with incapacitation are not theoretical. They are practical and technical. Deterrence and rehabilitation each have central theoretical questions that are still unresolved: Under what conditions—if any—can prisons be a deterrent to crime? What kinds of programs—if any—can rehabilitate prisoners? But incapacitation is a fact: Locking up people prevents them from committing crimes.

The technical problems are of two types: estimating the amount of crime criminals commit when they are not locked up and constructing schemes to identify high-rate and low-rate offenders. The practical problems involve money.

HOW MUCH DOES IT COST?

As with other questions, we might best begin our answer with another question: compared to what? Keeping an offender in prison costs between $15,000 and $30,000 per year, depending on the state. Building new prisons costs roughly $75,000 per cell, with regional variations. Is this a good investment? That is, how much would it cost not to lock up criminals? Conservatives, of

ABOUT CRIME & CRIMINOLOGY

THE ULTIMATE FALSE POSITIVE

In incapacitation research, false positives usually refer to those who are incorrectly identified as high-rate offenders. In research on the death penalty, the term may refer to people who are incorrectly identified as likely to kill again. To most supporters of capital punishment, it is irrelevant whether a convicted murderer would kill again. Even once is enough. But what of the truly false positive—the execution of a factually innocent person? Perhaps as many as 200 innocent people have been executed in the twentieth century. Most of these occurred in the earlier part of the century, partly because that was when executions were much more common. But once again, as prosecutors respond to public pressure for more executions and as new laws and court decisions speed up the process, the number of these mistakes will probably increase. That the state is taking an innocent life will probably have little impact on the popularity of capital punishment.

In this article, supporters of the death penalty invoke three arguments: incapacitation (the executed cannot kill again); deterrence (even though there is no evidence that capital punishment has a general deterrent effect on crime in the way that a vaccine might have a deterrent effect on some disease); retribution (the idea that the overall rightness of the death penalty justifies the occasional execution of the innocent).

Speaking to the jurors who would sentence Jesse Dewayne Jacobs to death, Montgomery County District Attorney Peter Speers declared: "The simple fact of the matter is that Jesse Jacobs and Jesse Jacobs alone killed Etta Ann Urdiles." Actually, another prosecutor said a few months earlier, at the trial of Mr. Jacobs's sister, Bobbie Jean Hogan, in the same 1986 killing, it didn't happen that way at all: the sister pulled the trigger; Mr. Jacobs didn't even know she had a gun.

No matter.

course, estimate that cost as very high. Here, for example, is a prominent conservative politician, Senator Phil Gramm of Texas:

> Can we really afford to sentence more criminals to jail for lengthier periods of time?
>
> Of course we can.... A Rand Corporation study calculated that the active street criminal imposes a financial cost of $430,000 a year on the general public—not to mention such immeasurable but very real costs as grief, fear and anger.... Spending $30,000 a year to save $430,000 is a brilliant allocation of resources.[15]

The RAND study cited by Sen. Gramm arrived at this incredibly high number by adding *all* costs of crime—not just the loss to victims but also spending on police, prisons, courts, private security, and so on. The author of the study, Edwin Zedlewski, divided this dollar amount by the total number of crimes to get a cost of $2,300 per crime. Then he made an estimate, based on interviews with prisoners, that the typical inmate commits 187 crimes each year.[16]

While the arithmetic may be accurate, the logic is not—especially when extrapolated to the conclusion that spending $30,000 to lock up a

The state of Texas went ahead last week with the lethal injection of Mr. Jacobs.... No court ever sorted out the differing versions of events presented at the two trials. And death-penalty opponents and a Vatican theologian were left expressing horror that an innocent man had just been killed....

The Jacobs case raises a complex question for death penalty proponents. Is the risk of executing an innocent person worth the benefits they see in capital punishment?

The answer, at least that suggested in several interviews with such proponents, all of whom conceded that wrongful executions occur, is a surprisingly vigorous yes. One likened the death penalty to a childhood vaccine approved by the government with full knowledge that at least one child, somewhere, would die from an adverse reaction....

Dale M. Voler ... who is a leader of the effort to return the death penalty to New York ... cited the case of Lemuel Smith, a New York murderer who strangled a guard while he was in prison. "If he had been executed, that corrections officer would be alive today," he said.

Laurin A. Wollan, Jr., an associate professor in the School of Criminology and criminal Justice at Florida State University, who studies and supports the death penalty, says the risks are unquestionable. "Innocent people have been executed," he said. "The value of the death penalty is its rightness vis-à-vis the wrongness of the crime, and that is so valuable that the possibility of the conviction of the innocent, though rare, has to be accepted."

Source: Sam Howe Verhovek, "When Justice Shows Its Darker Side," *New York Times*, January 8, 1995, Sec. 4, p. 6.

criminal for a year will save the country $430,000, a net saving of $400,000. To see why, consider that the total cost of crime in 1983, according to Zedlewski's estimate, was just under $100 billion, of which $40 billion was accounted for by the criminal justice system. That year, the United States held 420,000 people in prison. Two years later, in 1986, the prison population had grown by 100,000. By Senator Gramm's logic, this increase should have netted the country a savings of $40 billion (100,000 more prisoners × $400,000 per imprisoned criminal). That is, by 1986, the cost of crime in the United States should have been cut from $100 billion to $60 billion. Unfortunately, in that year, criminal justice expenditures alone rose to $53 billion.[17]

This kind of reasoning, though, dies hard. In 1994, the chief economist of the Governor's Office of Planning and Research in California claimed that each incarcerated offender saved the state about $200,000 annually.[18] So the one-year increase of 4,500 prisoners in 1992 (the last year for which I have figures) should have saved the state nearly a billion dollars. Extending this logic, subsequent increases in the prison population (caused in part by California's strict three-strikes law) should mean that by the time you are reading this, California's crime costs will have shrunk to nothing.

John DiIulio, a more moderate advocate of incarceration, kept Zedlewski's $2,300 per crime figure, but he estimated that the typical criminal commits not 187 crimes annually but 12. "The social benefit of imprisoning the typical felon is ... $27,600. Even at $25,000 a year, therefore, paying to keep a typical felon behind bars is a positive social investment."[19] More recently, DiIulio upped his estimate: "it costs society about twice as much to let a criminal roam the streets as it does to keep him behind bars."[20] Of course, the question remains whether nonincarcerative sentences like probation and parole, house arrest, and community-based corrections—all much less costly than prison—offer no better protection than letting offenders roam the streets.

A GLANCE TOWARD THE FUTURE

Concerns over cost spurred the research on selective incapacitation, and researchers tried to discover ways of using valuable prison space most efficiently. Efficiency, in this case, means using the space to prevent the greatest amount of crime and thus requires predictions about what a criminal will do if released. Unfortunately, some prediction schemes require information that courts would exclude; and even when this information is allowed, many of these predictions turn out to be false positives.

However, in the current political climate, policymakers seem to have abandoned their worries about false positives and even about money. Collective incapacitation, regardless of cost, is the order of the day. As of this writing (early 1995), a Congress that was elected largely on promises to cut spending is in the process of voting $10.5 billion for prison construction, increasing the amount set in the 1994 crime bill by roughly 30 percent. Nor will states be allowed to reduce prison costs by paroling prisoners as they do now. To get the prison construction money, a state will have to ensure that inmates serve at least 85 percent of their sentences. No doubt, the resulting increases in the numbers of people behind bars (numbers that have doubled in each of the last two decades even without such laws) will have some impact on crime. Burglary rates have fallen steadily since 1980 and may continue to decline. If rates of robbery and motor vehicle theft, which decreased in 1992 and 1993, continue the downward trend, proponents of incapacitation will claim victory for their theories and their policies. The question of whether similar results might have been achieved at less cost in dollars and in wasted human lives will be largely unheard.

However, if crime rates increase or merely remain stable rather than falling, the conservative ideology may lose its attractiveness to policymakers and perhaps the general public—just as the crime rates and riots of the 1960s, despite the war on poverty, foretold the decline of the traditional liberal ideology. Some prominent conservative criminologists, notably James Q. Wilson, seem to be losing their enthusiasm for prison as a useful force for either deterrence or incapacitation. In fact, the terms *liberal* and *conservative* may start to lose their meaning. There seems to be increasing agreement that attacking root causes is more important than trying to lower crime by reacting to individuals who have already blossomed into criminality. There is even some consensus about these root causes. Where children grow up in neighborhoods with high concentrations of impoverished and female-headed households and low rates of employment, especially male employment; where people feel disaffected and alienated from the dominant institutions and values of society because those institutions and values are ineffective guides to life as it is lived in their world— there crime will flourish. As we approach the year 2000, the debate, already begun, about the causes of these conditions and the policies that can change them will move to center stage in discussions of crime, especially if the public feels no safer even after the current round of punitive laws.

CRITICAL THINKING QUESTIONS

1. In the last two decades, the number of criminals in U.S. jails has quadrupled, yet crime remains a critical political and social issue and the public wants even greater levels of incarceration. Why did the increases in prison population not reduce crime?
2. Why have the public and politicians not given up on incapacitation as a way to reduce crime? What kinds of evidence can serve as a rational basis for more incarceration?
3. How might researchers, if asked to advise a state considering a three-strikes law, estimate its crime-reduction effects?
4. What is the promise of selective incapacitation, and why has it failed to achieve that promise?
5. Many people think that incapacitation policies should be more effective for expressive crimes than for instrumental crimes motivated purely by economic consideration. Why? What is the evidence on the incapacitation of expressive crime? Can you think of any reason why these results have been so disappointing?

KEY TERMS

collective incapacitation	false positive	selective incapacitation
dependent variable	independent variables	true negative
false negative	preventable recidivist	true positive

administrative model   model of the courts that sees their chief goal as the efficient, bureaucratic processing of a large number of cases

adversarial model (or system)   a court system that conceives of the process as combat between two parties

anecdotal evidence   evidence from a very small number of cases (often one); such evidence is not necessarily representative; it illustrates, but does not prove, a more general proposition

anomie   condition of normlessness arising when legitimate means do not allow people to reach legitimate goals

Apalachin conference   a meeting in a small New York State town, attended by men from all over the United States who fled at the approach of a local police car; it led to the idea that there was a nationwide Mafia organization

atavism   an evolutionary throwback

attitudes   propensities to act or behave in a particular way toward something

authority   power that is recognized as legitimate by those whose behavior is affected by it

baby boom   the period of high birthrates in the United States, roughly from 1947 to 1958

beliefs   shared ideas among members of a group about the way things are, about what *is*; often distinguished from *values* (shared ideas about what is *better*)

birth cohort   all people born in the same year

booster   opportunistic shoplifter

broken windows   the hypothesis that where disorder is left uncorrected, predatory crime will soon increase; the phrase is taken from the title of an article by James Q. Wilson and George Kelling

bureaucratic model (of organized crime)   model that sees organized crime as operating like any other large-scale business, with formal offices, titles, duties, rules, and so on

buy and bust   frequent method of drug arrests in which an undercover officer buys illegal drugs and then other officers arrest the seller

carnival mirror   an explanation of the differences in the demographic profiles of offenders found by studies based on arrest data and those based on self-report data; it holds that the criminal justice system selects on the basis

of legally irrelevant variables like social class, race, and sex

certainty of punishment   the probability that a crime will result in punishment, often thought to be the most important element in deterrence

chop shop   automobile fencing operation where stolen cars are disassembled and the parts sold

classical theory   utilitarian theory of crime, forerunner of modern ideas of deterrence

clearance rate   the percentage of crimes known to the police for which someone was arrested

coarse net   an explanation of the differences in the demographic profiles of offenders found by studies based on arrest data and those based on self-report data; it holds that the criminal justice system selects on the basis of legally relevant variables like the seriousness of the crime and the frequency of offending (cf. carnival mirror)

collective incapacitation   reducing crime by incarcerating all those who commit crimes

common law   body of legal principles and precedents built up over centuries in England

community policing   style of policing in which the police, rather than being primarily an outside agency responding to individual criminal incidents, cooperate with citizens to solve underlying problems that create patterns of crime

concern with crime   reaction to crime as a policy or political issue (cf. fear of crime)

concordance   a measure of similarity, often used in twin studies, for example, to see if identical twins are more similar in behavior than are fraternal twins

Conflict Tactics Scale   questionnaire-based scale developed by Strauss and Gelles to measure family violence

conflict theories   theories that hold that laws and norms are the outcome of conflict between social groups, especially social classes

consensus theories   theories that hold that laws and norms are matters of wide consensus in a society

consent decree   agreement by a defendant to stop some practice in return for which the government ceases prosecution; often used in white-collar cases

consent defense defense in rape cases in which the accused claims that the complainant consented to sex; used most frequently in cases involving acquaintances

conservative view of crime a view that emphasizes punishment as a way to achieve crime reduction through deterrence and incapacitation and as a way to achieve justice; it usually favors the powers of government and desires of the majority over individual liberties (except on the issue of gun control)

control group in research, a group of subjects who resemble the experimental group but who do not undergo the experimental treatment

controlling for a variable removing the effects of an independent variable by using only one category of that variable

corporal punishment punishment inflicted on the body (whipping, branding, etc.)

corporate crime crime committed by employees for the benefit of the organization

corporate culture the ideas and ethics that are widely shared within a corporation

courtroom work group the judge, prosecutor, and defense attorney working together to dispose of cases

crime control model model of the courts that emphasizes the punishment of criminals through the speedy handling of court cases

crime rate a fraction measuring the amount of crime; the numerator is almost always the number of crimes; the denominator may be persons, households, or objects at risk. The UCR uses population as the denominator for all crime rates and converts the fraction to a base of 100,000

cultural explanations explanations that focus on the variance in shared ideas (values, norms, beliefs) as a source of the variance in crime rates

cultural factors learned qualities that vary among groups (e.g., language)

dark figure of crime the number of unreported or unrecorded crimes (called "dark" because prior to victimization surveys, it was unknowable)

date rape rape committed by an acquaintance on some social occasion (date, party, etc.)

deadbang cases cases in which the evidence is so overwhelming that the defendant has almost no choice but to plead guilty

delinquent subculture subculture based on rejection of conventional ideas and values

demographic overload the sudden change in the ratio of young people to adults; a result of the baby boom

dependent variable variable whose variation is to be explained

determinate sentence a sentence fixed by law, with no variability

deterrence preventing crime by making people fear the consequences

differential association theory that sees crime as arising from socially learned definitions favorable to crime

discretion the power to decide; in the criminal justice system, many decisions, rather than being narrowly prescribed by law, are left to the individual discretion of the police, prosecutors, judges, and others

disorder, incivility, signs of crime three terms for the same thing: visible conditions or behavior in the social environment that suggest that everyday social rules are not in force.

displacement of crime in response to efforts at deterrence, the shift to other locations or types of crime rather than complete desistance from crime

drift state of being uncommitted to either conventional or delinquent norms but moving easily between the two

due process model model of the courts that emphasizes protecting the rights of the accused

Easterlin hypothesis theory that the economic well-being and rate of social problems experienced by the members of a birth cohort depend on the size of that cohort relative to the size of those that precede and follow it (named for Richard Easterlin, author of *Birth and Fortune*)

empirical based on evidence or subject to analysis by evidence

ethic of self-expression a set of values that emphasizes the priority of the individual and his or her desires and feelings over conformity to norms of restraint; said to have become dominant in twentieth-century America

ethic of self-restraint a set of values that emphasizes conformity to social norms of propriety; said to have been dominant in nineteenth-century America

evil-causes-evil assumption   the assumption that leads people, once they have defined some behavior as deviant, to focus on its negative causes and consequences

exclusionary rule   rule stating that illegally obtained evidence may not be used in court

expressive   motivated by emotional, psychological, and social needs (cf. instrumental)

factual guilt   being guilty of committing a crime (cf. legal guilt)

false negative   in criminology, an incorrect prediction of noncriminality, nonviolence, and so on

false positive   in criminology, an incorrect prediction of criminality, violence, and so on

fear of crime   reaction to crime in terms of one's own personal safety (cf. concern with crime)

felony homicide   homicide committed during the course of a felony such as robbery or rape

fence   person who buys and sells stolen merchandise

flat sentences   determinate sentences, not subject to reduction by judges or parole boards

focal concerns   term coined by Walter Miller to denote important categories of thought characteristic of different cultures

frontier mentality   a way of thinking associated with life on the American frontier; it stressed violence and self-reliance rather than dependence on law and government as a way of dealing with crime

general deterrence   the effect of punishment on the general population

going rate   the standard sentence that goes with a guilty plea for a given typical crime

good burglar   a professional criminal (qv.) who specializes in burglary

good faith exception   exception to the exclusionary rule that allows illegally seized evidence to be used if the police were acting in good faith (i.e., were not deliberately trying to violate the rules of search and seizure)

grass-eaters   term used by New York City police in the 1960s to designate officers who took routine payoffs but did not actively seek opportunities for corruption

immigration   the influx of people from other countries; often thought, probably erroneously, to be a source of crime

incapacitation   taking away the capacity to commit crime, usually by incarceration

independent variable   variable used to explain variation in a dependent variable

indeterminate sentence   a sentence whose length is dependent on the discretion of the judge and parole board

Index crimes   crimes counted under the UCR Index to Serious Crime, so called because they are an indicator of serious crime; they are murder, rape, robbery, aggravated assault, burglary, larceny, motor vehicle theft, and arson

industrialization   the change from small-scale craft production to large-scale factory production

inquisitorial model (or system)   a court system that conceives of the process as a cooperative search for the truth led by an agent or panel of the government

instrumental   motivated by rational, usually economic, goals (cf. expressive)

intensive supervision   supervision in which probation officers or parole officers follow cases more closely than is usual

interactionist explanations   explanations that focus on the sequence of actions and thoughts that lead up to a crime (especially homicide)

interracial crime   crime in which the offender and victim are of different races

intraracial crime   crime in which the offender and victim are of the same race

journeyman burglar   term used by Cromwell and others to describe those who regularly commit residential burglaries, sometimes alone, sometimes with others

just deserts   retribution; punishment that the offender deserves according to some idea of justice

Kefauver Committee   U.S. Senate Committee that in 1950 held televised hearings on organized crime

law-and-order politician   a phrase often used in the 1960s and 1970s to denote a candidate for office who stressed crime as a public issue; these candidates took typically conservative positions on crime and other issues, especially race and civil rights

legal guilt   guilt established in court (cf. factual guilt)

liberal view of crime   a view that emphasizes rehabilitation as the primary goal of prison, social inequality and economic need as root causes of crime, and social reform as the best way of reducing crime; it also usually favors a broad application of the Bill of Rights to protect individuals against the desires of the government and the majority (except on gun control)

Mafia myth the argument that the idea of the Mafia—its existence, cohesiveness, and power—is exaggerated

mandatory sentences sentences in which the law stipulates incarceration, regardless of the inclinations of the judge

marginal effects effects of each additional unit

marital rape exemption a law that excludes from its definition of rape forced sex between husband and wife

market concentration the degree to which a small number of firms accounts for a large fraction of sales

meat-eaters term used by New York City police in the 1960s to designate officers who actively sought opportunities for large-scale corruption

media crime waves sudden increases in the coverage of crime or some particular form of crime in the news media; seldom related to changes in the actual amount of crime

MMPI Minnesota Multiphasic Personality Inventory, the most widely used personality test, based on patterns of responses to 555 agree/disagree statements

moral entrepreneurs term coined by Howard Becker designating those who create and enforce laws

mugging robbery of a person in the street or other public setting

National Crime Victimization Survey (NCVS) a victimization survey conducted each six months by the U.S. Department of Justice

neurotransmitters chemical substances that enable the flow of nerve impulses in the brain

neutralizations ideas that allow people to violate norms they believe in, so that general norms are held not to apply in some specific situation

nolle prosequi a formal statement by the prosecutor dropping charges against the defendant

nonpredatory crime, victimless crime crime in which nobody feels directly victimized (e.g., prostitution, drug sales)

normal crimes as used by Sudnow, criminal acts that are typical of some category constructed by DAs and public defenders for purposes of quick plea bargains. Many of the factors that make a crime "normal" may have less to do with the criminal statutes than with demographic qualities of the offender, victim, location, and so on

norms rules, mostly unwritten, of everyday interaction

occupational crime crime committed by people in their occupations, acting as individuals and usually victimizing the employer

opportunist criminal one who is less skilled and who often selects targets impulsively on the basis of convenience rather than payoff

parole release from prison in which the parolee is subject to supervision and certain restrictive conditions

particularism decision-making principle based on considering each individual or situation unique without recourse to specific rules

positivism the application of scientific methods to crime that emphasizes the search for the psychological and social causes of criminal behavior

predatory crime crime involving a direct victim (e.g., shoplifting, car theft)

prescriptive norms norms that specify which acts are preferred, that is, what people *should* do

presumptive sentencing sentences set by the state, usually according to some formula combining seriousness of the crime and prior record of the offender; judges may increase or decrease the sentence length by small amounts

preventable recidivist a recidivist whose crime could have been prevented had he or she not been paroled

primary homicide homicide resulting from an argument between acquaintances or intimates

probability a number (between 0 and 1) that tells us how often we can expect a particular outcome if we repeat a procedure a large number of times

probation a nonincarcerative sentence in which the probationer must meet certain conditions (usually regarding employment, drug and alcohol use, supervision, etc.)

procedural law law that specifies the procedures the government must follow in prosecuting people accused of crime

professional criminal one who is skilled, selects targets on the basis of payoff rather than difficulty, and is committed to crime as a way of life and source of income

property crimes crimes involving property without personal confrontation of the victim; in the UCR Index, burglary, larceny, motor vehicle theft, and arson

proscriptive norms norms that specify which acts are *not* permissible, that is, what people *should not* do

psychopathy a relatively permanent set of mental characteristics that result in antisocial behavior

qualitative data data derived from observation and description; useful for describing processes or how the important variables fit together

quantitative data data derived from measuring and counting; useful for answering questions about "how much?" and for testing hypotheses statistically

racial factors unchangeable, genetically transmitted qualities that vary among groups (e.g., skin color)

rape culture widely held ideas about sex and gender that support the idea of forced sex as legitimate under certain circumstances

rape myths widely believed yet questionable ideas about rape, for example, that rape victims are at fault for leading men on

recidivism repeating crime after release from jail or prison

rehabilitation providing elements that may have been lacking (education, psychological insight, etc.) in order to keep criminals from repeating their crimes

relative deprivation the idea that people feel deprived or satisfied depending on the others they choose to compare themselves with

retribution punishment in order to achieve what the offender deserves (cf. just deserts)

reward system method capturing criminals by having the state offer rewards; it flourished in England and elsewhere before the creation of modern, patrolling police forces

RICO Racketeer Influenced Corrupt Organizations Act; federal law passed in 1970 that, among other provisions allows heavy penalties for a "pattern" of crime; chief weapon in prosecuting organized crime but also used in civil and corporate cases

sample a proportion, comparatively small, of some population used for making estimates about an entire population

selective incapacitation reducing crime by incarcerating only the most frequent offenders

self-control basis of a recent theory by Michael Gottfredson and Travis Hirschi that holds that lack of control over egoistic impulses underlies all criminal behavior

self-report study research based on information people give about the crimes they themselves have committed

sell and bust method of arresting fences in which undercover officers pretend to be thieves and sell their loot; officers then arrest the buyer

serotonin a neurotransmitter, low levels of which are associated with impulsive and violent behavior

severity of punishment one element of deterrence

shock probation a short period of incarceration followed by probation

simultaneity a problem in assessing causality arising when variable A affects variable B but variable B also affects variable A

snitch professional shoplifter

social bond term used by Travis Hirschi to denote the link—based on feelings, beliefs, rationality, and behavior—that ties the individual to conventional social norms

social class category of people based largely on their economic position in society

social disorganization approach that sees society as organized around norms; crime will occur where the organization and norms are weakest

social ecology approach that sees crime as a function of land use and population patterns in a city's zones

social learning theory that emphasizes social reinforcement of criminal behavior

social pathology approach that sees society as an organism and crime and other forms of deviance as illnesses detrimental to the health of that organism

socioeconomic status (SES) position in society based largely on the prestige accorded to one's income, education, and occupation

sociopathy a condition of unwillingness or inability to conform to social norms

somatotype categorization of the body along three dimensions—ectomorphic, endomorphic, and mesomorphic—with associated personality traits

specific deterrence   the effect of punishment on the person punished

split sentences   a short period of incarceration followed by probation

stake in conformity   the social and economic value a person would lose if he or she were caught committing crimes

sting   law-enforcement method in which undercover officers offer suspects criminal opportunities

strain theories   theories that emphasize the strain between people's culturally induced aspirations and socially distributed means of achieving their goals

structural explanations   explanations that focus on elements of the social structure (poverty, inequality) as sources of the variance in crime rates

subculture of violence   an explanation for the uneven distribution of violent crime that emphasizes differences between groups in their typical ideas about the acceptability of violence

substantive law   law that specifies the things individuals may not do

superego   in Freudian theory, the largely unconscious part of the psyche that keeps antisocial thoughts out of consciousness or makes the person feel guilty for having such thoughts

suspended sentence   a sentence not actually imposed; less restrictive than probation

swiftness of punishment   time between the commission of a crime and the imposition of punishment

systematic evidence   evidence gathered in such a way that anyone using the same method would arrive at similar results

temperance   abstinence from alcohol

testosterone   male hormone possibly correlated with aggression

thief-taker   one who made his living by catching felons and turning them in for the reward (see reward system)

threshold   a minimum level required in order for some effect to become noticeable

underclass   those who live more or less permanently outside of the dominant institutions of society (e.g., traditional work and family) and the values that go with those institutions

Uniform Crime Reports (UCR)   a volume published annually by the FBI based on information from all police departments; it contains information on crimes reported, persons arrested, and police personnel

universalism   decision-making principle based on the application of rules to a limited number of facts about the individual or situation

urbanization   the shift of the population from rural and small-town areas to cities and the consequent growth of cities; often thought, probably erroneously, to be a source of crime

utilitarianism   the idea that people act with free will in order to maximize pleasure and minimize pain

variables   factors that can have more than one value or category; when something is not a variable, it is said to be a *constant*

victimization survey   research in which people are asked about their own experiences as victims of crime

violent crime   crimes in which the criminal directly confronts the victim; the violent crimes in the UCR Index are murder, rape, robbery, and aggravated assault (also known as crimes against the person)

watch system   a method for maintaining public order prior to the creation of patrolling police forces; a voluntary, unpaid, untrained person who walked the town watching for trouble

white backlash   a phrase from the 1960s indicating a reaction among whites to changes in the laws and public policy, which they saw as favoring African-Americans

working personality   a set of mental characteristics (attitudes and assumptions) acquired on the job that help the individual make sense of experiences in that job

writs of assistance   court orders that allowed English officials to require people to assist them in any search

XYY syndrome   the theory that males with an extra Y chromosome will be more violent; not supported by currently available data

REFERENCES

CHAPTER ONE

1 William C. Bailey and Ruth D. Peterson, "Police Killings and Capital Punishment: The Post-Furman Period," *Criminology*, vol. 25, no. 1 (1987) 1–25.

CHAPTER TWO

1 U.S. Bureau of the Census, *Statistical Abstract of the United States: 1993* (Washington, D.C., 1993).
2 *New York Times*, January 2, 1977, sec. 3, p. 15.
3 Marshall Clinard and Peter Yeager, *Corporate Crime* (New York: Free Press, 1980), p. 8.
4 *New York Times*, June 1, 1986, p. A16.
5 Federal Bureau of Investigation, *Crime in the United States, 1992: Uniform Crime Reports* (Washington, DC: U.S. Government Printing Office, 1993).
6 *New York Times*, October 19, 1975, p. 6. Annette Kornblum, "Some Customers Are always Wrong," *New York Times Magazine*, Part 2, *The Business World*, June 10, 1990, p. 56.
7 Jeffrey Reiman, *The Rich Get Rich and the Poor Get Prison*, 2nd ed. (New York: Wiley, 1984), p. 55.
8 Paul Brodeur, "Annals of Law: The Asbestos Industry on Trial," *The New Yorker*, June 10, 1985, p. 79. Morton Mintz, *At Any Cost: Corporate Greed, Women and the Dalkon Shield* (New York: Pantheon, 1985).
9 William C. Cunningham, John J. Strauchs, and Clifford W. Van Meter, "Private Security: Patterns and Trends" (Washington, DC: National Institute of Justice, 1991).
10 John Crothers Polloc and Arney Ellen Rosenblat, "Fear of Crime: Sources and Responses," *USA Today*, January 1982.

11 Charles Silberman, *Criminal Violence, Criminal Justice* (New York: Random House, 1979), p. 12.
12 Research & Forecasts, Inc., with Andy Friedberg, *America Afraid: How Fear of Crime Changes the Way We Live (The Figgie Report)* (New York: New American Library, 1983). Frank A. Bennack, Jr., *The American Public's Hopes and Fears for the Decade of the 1990s* (New York: Hearst Corporation, 1989).
13 Timothy J. Flanagan and Maureen McLeod, eds., *Sourcebook of Criminal Justice Statistics—1982*. U.S. Department of Justice, Bureau of Justice Statistics (Washington, DC: U.S. Government Printing Office, 1983), p. 212. Timothy J. Flanagan and Maureen McLeod, eds., *Sourcebook of Criminal Justice Statistics—1987*. U.S. Department of Justice, Bureau of Justice Statistics (Washington, DC: U.S. Government Printing Office, 1988), p. 139. Timothy J. Flanagan and Kathleen Maguire, eds., *Sourcebook of Criminal Justice Statistics—1989*. U.S. Department of Justice, Bureau of Justice Statistics (Washington, DC: U.S. Government Printing Office, 1990), pp. 152–153.
14 Gallup poll data reprinted in Flanagan and McLeod, *Sourcebook—1982* and Maguire and Pastore, *Sourcebook—1993*.
15 Flanagan and McLeod, *Sourcebook—1982*, pp. 220–222. *The Gallup Poll Monthly*, December 1993, p. 25.
16 The President's Commission on Law Enforcement and Administration of Justice, *The Challenge of Crime in a Free Society* (Washington, DC: U.S. Government Printing Office, 1968), pp. 164–165.
17 Wesley G. Skogan and Michael G. Maxfield, *Coping with Crime* (Beverly Hills, CA: Sage, 1981), p. 62.
18 The President's Commission, *The Challenge of Crime*.

19 The phrase comes from Arthur L. Stinchcombe, Rebecca Adams, Carole A. Heimer, Kim Land Scheppele, Tim W. Smith, and D. Garth Taylor, *Crime and Punishment—Changing Attitudes in America* (San Francisco: Jossey-Bass, 1980).
20 Dan A. Lewis and Michael G. Maxfield, "Fear in the Neighborhoods: An Investigation of the Impact of Crime," *Journal of Research in Crime and Delinquency*, vol. 17, no. 2 (1980), 160–189.
21 Research by Susan Estrich, cited in James Q. Wilson and George L. Kelling, "Broken Windows," *The Atlantic Monthly*, March 1982, p. 32.
22 Paul Theroux, "Subway Odyssey," *New York Times Magazine*, January 31, 1982, p. 71.
23 Wesley Skogan, *Disorder and Decline: Crime and the Spiral of Decay in American Neighborhoods* (New York: Free Press, 1990), pp. 111–113.
24 Wilson and Kelling, "Broken Windows," p. 29.
25 Ibid., p. 32.
26 Ibid., p. 29.
27 Wesley Skogan, personal communication.
28 Tim Hope and Michael Hough, "Area, Crime, and Incivility: A Profile from the British Crime Survey," in T. Hope and M. Shaw, eds., *Communities and Crime Reduction* (London: Her Majesty's Stationery Office, 1988), pp. 30–47, cited in Skogan, *Disorder and Decline*, p. 77.
29 Harold Takooshian and Herzel Bodinger, "Street Crime in 18 American Cities: A National Field Experiment," paper delivered at the American Sociological Association, 1979, Boston. Christopher Wellisz, "Bronx Neighborhood: One Big Family," *New York Times*, September 14, 1983, p. B1.

30 *New York Newsday*, July 30, 1986, p. 23.

31 Sally Engle Merry, *Urban Danger* (Philadelphia: Temple University Press, 1981).

32 Ibid., pp. 28–29.

33 Roper Organization, *Trends in Attitudes Toward Television and Other Media: A Twenty-four Year Review* (New York: Television Information Office, 1983).

34 Michael J. Robinson and Andrew Kohut, "Believability and the Press," *Public Opinion Quarterly*, vol. 52, no. 2 (1988), 174–189.

35 Jennifer Davis, "The London Garrotting Panic of 1862: A Moral Panic and the Creation of a Criminal Class in Mid-Victorian England," in V. A. C. Gatrell, Bruce Lenman, and Geoffrey Parker, eds., *Crime and the Law: The Social History of Crime in Western Europe Since 1500* (London: Europa Publications 1980), pp. 190–213.

36 Mary Holland Baker, Barbara C. Nienstedt, Ronald S. Everett, and Richard McCleary, "The Impact of a Crime Wave: Perceptions, Fear, and Confidence in the Police," *Law and Society Review*, vol. 17, no. 2 (1983), 319–353.

37 Mark Fishman, "Crime Waves as Ideology," *Social Problems*, vol. 25, no. 5 (1978).

38 Research by S. Robert and Linda S. Lichter, reported in "Who Breaks the Law on TV?" by Richard Lacayo, *New York Times*, March 6, 1983, sec. 2, p. 35.

39 The literature on this topic is quite large and controversial. See Garofalo, "Crime and the Mass Media."

40 Ibid., pp. 336–338. Julian V. Roberts, "Public Opinion, Crime, and Criminal Justice," in Michael Tonry, ed., *Crime and Justice: A Review of Research*, vol. 16 (Chicago: University of Chicago Press, 1992), pp. 99–180.

41 *New York Times*, August 9, 1968, p. 1.

42 Presidential Commission, *Challenge of Crime*, p. 52.

43 Quoted in Jerome H. Skolnick and James J. Fyfe, *Above the Law: Police and the Excessive Use of Force* (New York: Free Press, 1993), p. xiii.

44 Quoted in the *New York Times*, May 20, 1992, p. A20.

45 *The Gallup Poll Monthly*, December 1993. Flanagan and McLeod, *Sourcebook—1992*.

46 Frank Furstenberg, "Public Reaction to Crime in the Streets," *American Scholar*, vol. 40, no. 4 (1971), 601–610.

47 Flanagan and McLeod, *Sourcebook—1987*, p. 143.

48 D. Garth Taylor, Kim Land Scheppele, and Arthur L. Stinchcombe, "Salience of Crime and Support for Harsher Criminal Sanctions," *Social Problems*, vol. 26, no. 4 (1979), 413–424.

49 Furstenberg, "Public Reaction."

50 Flanagan and McLeod, *Sourcebook—1987*, pp. 143, 161, 340. Kathleen Maguire and Ann L. Pastore, eds., *Sourcebook of Criminal Justice Statistics—1993* (Washington, DC: Bureau of Justice Statistics, 1994).

51 James Q. Wilson, *New York Times*, July 17, 1983, sec. 4, p. 6.

52 Ibid.

CHAPTER THREE

1 Victoria W. Scheider and Brian Wiersema, "Limits and Use of the Uniform Crime Reports," in Doris Layton MacKenzie, Phyllis Jo Baunach, and Roy R. Roberg, eds., *Measuring Crime: Large-Scale, Long-Range Efforts* (Albany: State University of New York Press, 1990), pp. 21–48.

2 Bureau of Justice Statistics, *Report to the Nation on Crime and Justice: The Data* (Washington, DC: U.S. Department of Justice, 1983), pp. 4–5.

3 Interview with "Jerry," a house burglar, in Paul Cromwell, James N. Olson, and D'Aunn Wester Avary, *Breaking and Entering: An Ethnographic Analysis of Burglary* (Newbury Park, CA: Sage, 1991), p. 116.

4 Lawrence E. Cohen, Marcus Felson, and Kenneth C. Land, "Property Crime Rates in the United States: A Macrodynamic Analysis, 1947–1977; With Ex-Ante Forecasts for the Mid-1980s," *American Journal of Sociology*, vol. 86 (1980), 588–607.

5 Philip H. Ennis, *Criminal Victimization in the United States: A Report of a National Survey*, President's Commission of Law Enforcement and the Administration of Justice, Field Surveys II (Washington, DC: U.S. Government Printing Office, 1967).

6 Donald J. Black, "The Production of Crime Rates," *American Sociological Review*, vol. 35 (1970), 733–748.

7 Institute of Public Management, *Crime Records in Police Management: New York City*, excerpted in Marvin E. Wolfgang, Leonard Savitz, and Norman Johnson, *The Sociology of Crime and Delinquency*, 2nd ed. (New York: Wiley, 1970), pp. 114–116.

8 *New York Times*, May 2, 1983, p. A20. R. Block and C. R. Block, "Decisions and Data: The Transformation of Robbery Incidents Into Official Robbery Statistics," *Journal of Criminal Law and Criminology*, vol. 71 (1980), 622–636.

9 For a comparison of Philadelphia, San Francisco, and Chicago on this matter, see Wesley G. Skogan and Michael G. Maxfield, *Coping with Crime: Individual and Neighborhood Reactions* (Beverly Hills, CA: Sage, 1981), p. 29. For a British comparison, see Richard F. Sparks, Hazel G. Genn, and David J. Dodd, *Surveying Victims: A Study of the Measurement of Criminal Victimization, Perceptions of Crime, and Attitudes to Criminal Justice* (London: Wiley, 1977), p. 157.

10 Harold Pepinsky, "The Growth of Crime in the United States," *Annals of the American*

Academy of Political and Social Science, vol. 432 (1976), 23–30.

11 Derived from Lawrence Davidoff and Mark Greenhorn, "Violent Crime," paper presented at the American Society of Criminology, 1991.

12 Bureau of Justice Statistics, *Criminal Victimization in the United States*, 1976, 1992 (Washington, DC: 1978, 1994) and UCR, 1976, 1992.

13 Ennis, *Criminal Victimization.*

14 Richard F. Sparks, "Surveys of Victimization—An Optimistic Assessment," *Crime and Justice: An Annual Review of Research*, vol. 3 (1981), 26.

15 Ibid., p. 33. NCVS, 1992.

16 Walter R. Gove, Michael Hughes, and Michael Gerken, "Are Uniform Crime Reports a Valid Indicator of the Index Crimes? An Affirmative Answer with Minor Qualifications," *Criminology*, vol. 23, no. 3 (1985), 451–502.

17 John Braithwaite and David Biles, "Victims and Offenders: The Australian Experience," in Richard Block, ed., *Victimization and Fear of Crime: World Perspectives* (Washington, DC: U.S. Government Printing Office, 1984), pp. 3–10.

18 Ennis, *Criminal Victimization.* Edmund F. McGarrel and Timothy J. Flanagan, eds., *Sourcebook of Criminal Justice Statistics—1984*, U.S. Department of Justice, Bureau of Justice Statistics (Washington, DC: U.S. Government Printing Office, 1985), pp. 288, 380.

19 Charles Silberman, *Criminal Violence, Criminal Justice* (New York: Random House, 1974), p. 28.

20 Richard Hofstadter and Michael Wallace, eds., *American Violence* (New York: Random House, 1970), p. 212.

21 Silberman, *Criminal Violence*, pp. 21–47.

22 Roger McGrath, *Gunfighters, Highwaymen, and Vigilantes: Violence on the Frontier* (Berkeley: Regents of the University of California, 1984).

23 Marvin Wolfgang and Franco Ferracuti, *The Subculture of Violence: Towards an Integrated Theory in Criminology* (London: Tavistock, 1976).

24 Ray Ginger, *America, People on the Move* (Boston: Allyn & Bacon, 1975), p. 282.

25 Roger Lane, "Police and Crime in Nineteenth-Century America," in Michael Tonry and Norval Morris, eds., *Crime and Justice: An Annual Review*, vol. 2 (Chicago: University of Chicago Press, 1980), pp. 1–52.

26 David Ward, *Cities and Immigrants* (New York: Oxford University Press, 1971), p. 76.

27 Jeffrey S. Adler, "The Dynamite, Wreckage, and Scum in Our Cities: The Social Construction of Deviance in Industrial America," *Justice Quarterly*, vol. 11, no. 1 (1994), 37.

28 Dane Archer and Rosemary Gartner, *Violence and Crime in Cross-national Perspective* (New Haven, CT: Yale University Press, 1984).

29 Lane, "Police and Crime."

30 Wilbur E. Miller, *Cops and Bobbies* (Chicago: University of Chicago Press, 1977), p. 6.

31 Jeffrey S. Adler, "The Dynamite, Wreckage, and Scum in Our Cities."

32 David R. Johnson, *Policing the Urban Underworld* (Philadelphia: Temple University Press, 1979), pp. 30, 87.

33 James Q. Wilson, *Thinking About Crime*, 2nd ed. (New York: Vintage Press, 1985), p. 229.

34 Joseph N. Gusfield, *Symbolic Crusade* (Urbana: University of Illinois Press, 1963).

35 Martha Wolfenstein, "The Emergence of Fun Morality," *Journal of Social Issues*, vol. 7 (1951), 15–25.

36 Wilson, *Thinking About Crime*, p. 237.

37 Bureau of Justice Statistics, *Report to the Nation*, p. 10.

38 Lane, "Police and Crime."

39 Ted Robert Gurr, Peter N. Grabosky, and Richard C. Hula, *The Politics of Crime and Conflict: A Comparative History of Four Cities* (Beverly Hills, CA: Sage, 1977).

40 Laurie, "Fire Companies and Gangs in Southwark," quoted in Lane, "Police and Crime," p. 182.

41 W. E. B. DuBois, *The Philadelphia Negro, A Social Study*, cited in Roger Lane, *Violent Death in the City: Suicide, Accident, and Murder in Nineteenth-Century Philadelphia* (Cambridge, MA: Harvard University Press, 1979), p. 132.

42 Lane, *Violent Death* (emphasis added).

43 Roger Lane, "Urban Police and Crime in Nineteenth-Century America," in Michael Tonry and Norval Morris, eds., *Modern Policing* (Chicago: University of Chicago Press, 1992), p. 35.

CHAPTER FOUR

1 Gail Armstrong, "Females Under the Law—'Protected' but Unequal," *Crime and Delinquency*, vol. 23 (1977), 109–120. Meda Chesney-Lind, "Judicial Paternalism and the Female Status Offender," *Crime and Delinquency*, vol. 23 (1977), 121–130.

2 U.S. Bureau of Justice Statistics, *Criminal Victimization in the United States, 1992* (Washington, D.C.: U.S. Department of Justice, (1993), pp. 59, 63.

3 James Wallerstein and Clement J. Wyle, "Our Law-Abiding Lawbreakers," *National Probation*, March 1947, pp. 107–112.

4 Stephen A. Cernkovich and Peggy C. Giordano, "A Comparative Analysis of Male and Female Delinquency," *The Sociological Quarterly*, vol. 20, no. 1 (1979), 131–145.

5 Jeffrey Reiman, *The Rich Get Richer and the Poor Get Prison*, 2nd ed. (New York: Wiley, 1984).

6 Elizabeth Moulds, "Chivalry and Paternalism: Disparities of Treatment in the Criminal Justice System," in Susan K. Datesman and Frank R. Scarpitti, eds., *Women, Crime,* *and Justice* (New York: Oxford University Press, 1980), pp. 277–299.

7 Walter Reckless and Barbara Kay, *The Female Offender: Report to the U.S. President's Commission on Law Enforcement and the Administration of Justice*, quoted ibid., p. 279.

8 Michael J. Hindelang, Travis Hirschi, and Joseph G. Weis, "Correlates of Delinquency: The Illusion of Discrepancy Between Self-Report and Official Measures," *American Sociological Review*, vol. 44 (1979), pp. 995–1014.

9 Delbert S. Elliott, "1993 Presidential Address, Serious Violent Offenders: Onset, Developmental Course, and Termination," *Criminology*, vol. 32, no. 1 (1994), 1–22.

10 Anthony R. Harris, "Sex and Theories of Deviance," *American Sociological Review*, vol. 42 (1977), 3–16.

11 Freda Adler, *Sisters in Crime: The Rise of the New Female Criminal* (New York: McGraw-Hill, 1975), p. 1.

12 Ibid., pp. 13–14.

13 Rita J. Simon, *Women and Crime* (Lexington, MA: Lexington Books, 1975).

14 Leon E. Pettiway, "Participation in Crime Partnerships by Female Drug Users: The Effects of Domestic Arrangements, Drug Use, and Criminal Involvement," *Criminology*, vol. 25, no. 3 (1987), 741–766.

15 Rita J. Simon and Sandra Baxter, "Gender and Violent Crime," in Neil Alan Weiner and Marvin Wolfgang, eds., *Violent Crime and Violent Criminals* (Newbury Park, CA: Sage, 1989), pp. 170–197.

16 R. W. Hodge and D. J. Treiman, "Class Identification in the United States," *American Journal of Sociology*, vol. 73, no. 5 (1968).

17 Richard P. Coleman and Lee Rainwater with Kent A. McClelland, *Social Standing in America: New Dimensions of Class* (New York: Basic Books, 1978), p. 29.

18 Terence P. Thornberry and R. L. Christenson, "Unemployment and Criminal Involvement: An Investigation of Reciprocal Causal Structure," *American Sociological Review*, vol. 49 (1984), 398–411.

19 Paul E. Tracy, Marvin E. Wolfgang, and Robert M. Figlio, *Delinquency in Two Birth Cohorts— Executive Summary* (Washington, D.C.: U.S. Department of Justice, 1985), p. 7.

20 For a review and listing of this literature, see John Braithwaite, *Inequality, Crime, and Public Policy* (London: Routledge & Kegan Paul, 1979), pp. 23–63.

21 Irving Piliavin and Scott Briar, "Police Encounters with Juveniles," *American Journal of Sociology*, vol. 70 (1964), 206–214.

22 Charles Tittle, Wayne Villemez, and Douglas Smith, "The Myth of Social Class and Criminality: An Empirical Assessment of the Empirical Evidence," *American Sociological Review*, vol. 43 (1978), 643–656.

23 Stephen A. Cernkovich, Peggy C. Giordano, and Meredith Pugh, "Chronic Offenders: The Missing Cases in Self-Reported Delinquency Research," paper presented at the American Society of Criminology, 1983.

24 Delbert S. Elliott, Franklyn W. Dunford, and David Huizinga, "The Identification and Prediction of Career Offenders Utilizing Self-Reported and Official Data," unpublished manuscript.

25 Cernkovich, Giordano, and Pugh, "Chronic Offenders."

26 Delbert S. Elliott and Suzanne S. Ageton, "Reconciling Race and Class Differences in Self-reported and Official Estimates of Delinquency," *American Sociological Review*, vol. 45, no. 1 (1980), 95–110.

27 Charles R. Tittle and Robert F. Meier, "Specifying the SES/Delinquency Relationship," *Criminology*, vol. 28, no. 2 (1990), 271–299.

28 Donald Clelland and Timothy J. Carter, "The New Myth of Class and Crime," *Criminology*, vol. 18 (1980), 319–336.

29 Ken Auletta, "A Reporter at Large: The Underclass," *The New Yorker*, November 16, 1981, p. 95.

30 William Julius Wilson, "The Black Community in the 1980's: Questions of Race, Class, and Public Policy," *The Annals of the American Academy of Political and Social Science*, vol. 454 (1981).

31 David Brownfield, "Social Class and Violent Behavior," *Criminology*, vol. 24, no. 3 (1986), 421–438.

32 Delbert S. Elliott, David Huizinga, and Suzanne S. Ageton, *Explaining Delinquency and Drug Use* (Beverly Hills, CA: Sage, 1982), pp. 88–89.

33 George S. Bridges and Joseph G. Weis, "Measuring Violent Behavior," in Neil Alan Weiner and Marvin Wolfgang, eds., *Violent Crime and Violent Criminals* (Newbury Park, CA: Sage, 1989), pp. 14–34. E. Britt Patterson, "Poverty, Income Inequality, and Community Crime Rates," *Criminology*, vol. 29, no. 4 (1991), 755–776.

34 John Braithwaite, *Inequality*, p. 51. Brownfield, "Social Class and Violent Behavior," pp. 434–435.

35 Joseph G. Weis, "Social Class and Crime," in Michael R. Gottfredson and Travis Hirschi, eds., *Positive Criminology* (Newbury Park, CA: Sage, 1987), pp. 71–90.

36 Charles Silberman, *Criminal Justice, Criminal Violence* (New York: Random House, 1978), pp. 117–118.

37 James Q. Wilson and Richard J. Herrnstein, *Crime and Human Nature* (New York: Simon & Schuster, 1985), p. 468.

38 Ibid. Travis Hirschi and Michael J. Hindelang, "Intelligence and Delinquency: A Revisionist Review," *American Journal of Sociology*, vol. 42 (1977), 571–587.

39 Wilson and Herrnstein, *Crime and Human Nature*, pp. 459–486.

40 Dane Archer and Rosemary Gartner, *Violence and Crime in*

Cross-national Perspective (New Haven, CT: Yale University Press, 1984).

41 Herbert Gutman, "As for the '02 Kosher Food Rioters," *New York Times*, July 21, 1977, p. A23.

42 Ibid.

43 Wilson and Herrnstein, *Crime and Human Nature*, p. 459.

44 S. Shoham, *Crime and Social Deviation* (Chicago: Henry Regery, 1966), cited in ibid.

45 Andrew Hacker, *U/S: A Statistical Portrait of the American People*, (New York: Penguin Books, 1983).

46 U.S. Bureau of Justice Statistics, *Criminal Victimization*, pp. 60, 64.

47 Michael J. Hindelang, "Race and Involvement in Common Law Personal Crimes," *American Journal of Sociology*, vol. 43 (1978), 93–109. Elliott and Ageton, "Reconciling Race and Class Differences," pp. 95–110.

48 Cernkovich and Giordano, "A Comparative Analysis."

49 See Reiman, *The Rich Get Richer*, p. 79.

50 Marvin E. Wolfgang and Franco Ferracuti, *The Subculture of Violence: Towards an Integrated Theory in Criminology* (Beverly Hills, CA: Sage, 1967).

51 Daniel Patrick Moynihan, "Defining Deviancy Down," *The American Scholar*, vol. 62, no. 1, 1993.

52 John H. Laub and Robert J. Sampson, "Unraveling Families and Delinquency: A Reanalysis of the Glueck's Data," *Criminology*, vol. 26, no. 3 (1988), 355–380.

53 Wilson and Herrnstein, *Crime and Human Nature*, p. 261.

54 Laub and Sampson, "Unraveling Families."

55 Wilson and Herrnstein, *Crime and Human Nature*, p. 479.

56 Jeffery Fagan and Sandra Wexler, "Family Origins of Violent Delinquents," *Criminology*, vol. 25, no. 3 (1987), 643–669.

57 Robert J. Sampson, "Crime in Cities: The Effects of Formal and Informal Social Control," in Albert J. Reiss, Jr., and Michael Tonry, eds., *Communities and*

Crime, special issue of *Crime and Justice, an Annual Review*, vol. 8 (1986), 271–311.

58 Robert J. Sampson, "Urban Black Violence: The Effect of Male Joblessness and Family Disruption," *American Journal of Sociology*, vol. 93, no. 2 (1984), 348–382. Mercer Sullivan, "Youth Crime: New York's Two Varieties," *New York Affairs*, vol. 8 (1983), 31–48. Also see David Greenberg, "Delinquency and the Age Structure of Society," *Contemporary Crises*, vol. 1, no. 2 (1977), 189–223, which makes a similar argument.

59 William Julius Wilson, *The Truly Disadvantaged* (Chicago: University of Chicago Press, 1987).

60 Elliot Liebow, *Tally's Corner* (Boston: Little, Brown, 1967).

61 Silberman, *Criminal Justice*, pp. 117–165.

62 Ibid., pp. 129, 133.

63 Gary LaFree, Kriss A. Drass, and Patrick O'Day, "Race and Crime in Postwar America: Determinants of African-American and White Rates, 1957–1988," *Criminology*, vol. 30, no. 2 (1991), 157–188.

64 Silberman, *Criminal Justice*, p. 157. Nicholas Lemann, "The Origins of the Underclass," *The Atlantic Monthly*, June, 1986, pp. 31–55; July, 1986, pp. 54–68.

65 The National Advisory Commission on Civil Disorders, *Report of the National Advisory Commission on Civil Disorders (The Kerner Commission Report)* (New York: Bantam, 1968), p. 1.

66 Michael J. Hindelang, "Variations in Sex-Race-Age–Specific Incidence Rates of Offending," *American Sociological Review*, vol. 46 (1981), 461–474. Robert M. O'Brien, *Crime and Victimization Data* (Beverly Hills, CA: Sage, 1985), pp. 92–96.

67 Travis Hirschi and Michael R. Gottfredson, "Age and the Explanation of Crime," *American Journal of Sociology*, vol. 89 (1983), 552–584.

68 James Q. Wilson, *Thinking About Crime* (New York: Basic Books, 1975), p. 235.

69 Charles Murray, *Losing*

Ground: American Social Policy, 1950–1980 (New York: Basic Books, 1981), pp. 166–172.

70 Darrel Steffensmeier, Cathy Streifel, and Miles D. Harer, "Relative Size and Youth Crime in the United States, 1953–1984," *American Sociological Review*, vol. 2 (1987), 702–710.

71 Archer and Gartner, *Violence and Crime*.

72 Brandon S. Centerwall, "Television and Violent Crime," *The Public Interest*, no. 111 (1993), 56–71.

73 Marie Winn, letter to the *New York Times*, August 9, 1992, sec. 4, p. 10.

74 Quoted in Wilson, *Thinking About Crime*, pp. 13–14.

75 David Matza, "Subterranean Traditions of Youths," *Annals of the American Academy of Political and Social Science*, vol. 378 (1961), 116.

76 Richard A. Easterlin, *Birth and Fortune: The Impact of Numbers on Personal Welfare* (New York: Basic Books, 1980).

77 Steffensmeier, Streifel, and Harer, "Relative Size and Youth Crime."

78 Alfred Blumstein, Jacqueline Cohen, and Richard Rosenfeld, "Effects of Demography and Criminality on Crime Rates," paper given at the American Sociological Association, 1986.

79 I am grateful to James Alan Fox for providing these data from the UCR *Supplementary Homicide Reports*.

80 Janet Lauritsen, Robert J. Sampson, and John H. Laub, "The Link Between Offending and Victimization Among Adolescents," *Criminology*, vol. 29, no. 2 (1991), 265–292.

CHAPTER FIVE

1 Marvin Wolfgang, *Patterns in Criminal Homicide* (Philadelphia: University of Pennsylvania Press, 1958).

2 David F. Luckenbill, "Criminal Homicide as a Situated Transaction," *Social Problems*, vol. 25, no. 2 (1977), 180 (emphasis added).

3 Wolfgang, *Patterns in Criminal Homicide*.

4 Ibid.

5 Luckenbill, "Criminal Homicide."

6 Ibid.

7 Richard B. Felson, Stephen A. Ribner, and Meryl S. Siegel, "Age and the Effect of Third Parties During Criminal Violence," *Sociology and Social Research*, vol. 86, no. 4 (1984), 452–462.

8 Luckenbill, "Criminal Homicide."

9 Jack Katz, *Seductions of Crime: Moral and Sensual Attractions in Doing Evil* (New York: Basic Books, 1988), pp. 12–51.

10 Donald J. Black, "Crime as Social Control," *American Sociological Review*, vol. 48, no. 1 (1983), 34–45 (quote on p. 36).

11 Katz, *Seductions of Crime*.

12 The data are from 1987, the National Center for Health Statistics, cited in Elisabeth Rosenthal, "U.S. is by Far the Homicide Capital of the Industrialized Nations," *New York Times*, June 27, 1990, p. A10.

13 Christopher Jencks, "Genes & Crime," *The New York Review of Books*, vol. 34, no. 2, 33–40.

14 Marvin E. Wolfgang and Franco Ferracuti, *The Subculture of Violence: Towards an Integrated Theory in Criminology* (New York: Barnes & Noble, 1967).

15 Raymond D. Gastil, "Homicide and a Regional Culture of Violence," *American Sociological Review*, vol. 36 (1971), 412–427.

16 Ibid.

17 G. McWhiney, *Cracker Culture: Celtic Ways in the Old South* (Tuscaloosa: University of Alabama Press, 1988), p. xxxiv; quoted in Richard E. Nisbett, "Violence and U.S. Regional Culture," *American Psychologist*, vol. 48, no. 4 (1993), 441–449.

18 Ibid., p. 442.

19 Larry Baron and Murray A. Strauss, "Cultural and Economic Sources of Homicide in the United States," *Sociological Quarterly*, vol. 29, no. 3 (1988), 371–390.

20 Marvin E. Wolfgang, Robert M. Figlio, Paul E. Tracy, and Simon I. Singer, *The National Survey of Crime Severity* (Washington, D.C.: U.S. Government Printing Office, 1985), pp. 52–73.

21 Sandra J. Ball-Rokeach, "Values and Violence: A Test of the Subculture of Violence Thesis," *American Sociological Review*, vol. 38, no. 6 (1975), 736–749. Howard Erlanger, "The Empirical Status of the Subculture of Violence Thesis," *Social Problems*, vol. 22, no. 2 (1974), pp. 280–292.

22 F. Frederick Hawley and Steven F. Messner, "The Southern Violence Construct: A Review of Arguments, Evidence, and the Normative Context," *Justice Quarterly*, vol. 6, no. 4 (1989), 481–511.

23 Colin Loftin and Robert Nash Parker, "An Errors-in-Variable Model of the Effect of Poverty on Urban Homicide Rates," *Criminology*, vol. 23, no. 2 (1985), 269–287. Colin Loftin and Robert H. Hill, "Regional Subculture and Homicide: An Empirical Examination of the Gastil-Hackney Thesis," *American Sociological Review*, vol. 39 (1974), 714–724.

24 Judith R. Blau and Peter M. Blau, "The Cost of Inequality: Metropolitan Structure and Violent Crime," *American Sociological Review*, vol. 47 (1982), 114–129. Steven F. Messner and Reid M. Golden, "Racial Inequality and Racially Disaggregated Homicide Rates: An Assessment of Alternative Theoretical Explanations," *Criminology*, vol. 30, no. 3 (1992), 421–447.

25 Roger Lane, *Roots of Violence in Black Philadelphia* (Cambridge, MA: Harvard University Press, 1986).

26 Blau and Blau, "Cost of Inequality." Messner and Golden, "Racial Inequality."

27 See Carol Gilligan, *In a Different Voice: Psychological Theory and Women's Development* (Cambridge, MA: Harvard University Press, 1982).

28 Richard J. Gelles, *The Violent Home: A Study of Physical Aggression Between Husbands and Wives* (Beverly Hills, CA: Sage, 1972).

29 Ruth Horowitz, *Honor and the American Dream: Culture and Identity in a Chicano Community* (New Brunswick, NJ: Rutgers University Press, 1983).

30 Wolfgang, *Patterns in Criminal Homicides*. See also James D. Wright, Peter H. Rossi, and Kathleen Daly, *Under the Gun: Weapons, Crime, and Violence in America* (New York: Aldine, 1983).

31 William G. Doerner and John C. Speir, "Stitch and Sew: The Impact of Medial Resources Upon Lethality," *Criminology*, vol. 24 (1986), 319–30.

32 UCR, 1987.

33 Katz, *Seductions of Crime*, p. 182.

34 Mary Lorenz Dietz, *Killing for Profit: The Social Organization of Felony Homicide* (Chicago: Nelson-Hall, 1983), pp. 69–70.

35 Philip J. Cook, "The Influence of Gun Availability on Violent Crime Patterns," in Michael Tonry and Norval Morris, eds., *Crime and Justice: An Annual Review* (Chicago: University of Chicago Press, 1983), pp. 49–90.

36 Ibid., p. 212.

37 Peter Letkeman, *Crime as Work*, (Englewood Cliffs, NJ: Prentice-Hall, 1973).

38 Katz, *Seductions of Crime*, p. 183.

39 Dietz, *Killing for Profit*, pp. 157–59.

40 Cook, "Influence of Gun Availability," p. 73.

41 Dietz, *Killing for Profit*, p. 65.

42 William Wilbanks, *Murder in Miami: An Analysis of Homicide Patterns and Trends in Dade County (Miami) Florida, 1917–1983* (Lanham, MD: University Press of America, 1984).

43 Dietz, *Killing for Profit*, p. 175.

44 Ibid.

45 Jack Levin and James Alan Fox, *Mass Murder: America's Growing Menace* (New York: Plenum, 1985), pp. 123–138.

46 Ibid., p. 100.

47 Shervert H. Frazier, "Violence and Social Impact," cited ibid., p. 100.

48 *New York Times*, December 10, 1985, I, 18.

49 Levin and Fox, *Mass Murder*, pp. 16, 63.

50 Ibid., p. 143.

51 John F. Wallerstedt, "Returning to Prison," *Bureau of Justice Statistics Special Report* (Washington, D.C.: U.S. Department of Justice, 1984).

52 UCR, 1993.

53 Letkeman, *Crime as Work*, p. 96.

54 Ibid., p. 112.

55 Ibid., p. 125.

56 Nicholas Pileggi, *Wiseguy: Life in a Mafia Family* (New York: Simon & Schuster, 1985).

57 John Allen, *Assault with a Deadly Weapon: The Autobiography of a Street Criminal* (New York: McGraw-Hill, 1977), p. 52.

58 George B. Vold, *Theoretical Criminology*, 2nd ed. (prepared by Thomas J. Bernard) (New York: Oxford, 1979), p. 345. Letkeman, *Crime as Work*, p. 28. W. J. Einstadter, "The Social Organization of Armed Robbery," *Social Problems*, vol. 17, no. 1 (1969), 64–83.

59 Sylvie Bellot, "Les Auteurs de Vols à Main Armée à Montréal: Une Typologie Empirique," *Criminologie*, vol. 18, no. 2 (1985), 35–45.

60 For an excellent example, see Allen, *Assault with a Deadly Weapon*.

61 See John E. Conklin, *Robbery and the Criminal Justice System* (Philadelphia: J. B. Lippincott, 1972), pp. 65, 97.

62 Laurie Taylor, *In the Underworld* (London: Unwin Paperbacks, 1985), p. 39; quoted in Katz, *Seductions of Crime*, p. 204, note 9.

63 John E. Conklin, *Robbery and the Criminal Justice System*

(Philadelphia, PA: J. B. Lippincott), p. 82.

64 Nicholas Pileggi, "Meet the Muggers," *New York*, March 9, 1981, p. 32.

65 Caroline Wolf Harlow, "Robbery Victims," *Bureau of Justice Statistics Special Report* (Washington, D.C.: U.S. Department of Justice, 1987). Also *Criminal Victimization in the United States, 1992* (Washington, DC: U.S. Department of Justice, 1994), p. 83.

66 Robert Lejeune, "The Management of a Mugging," *Urban Life*, vol. 6, no. 2 (1977), 135.

67 Ibid., p. 136.

68 Einstadter, "Social Organization of Armed Robbery."

69 James Carr, *Bad* (New York: Herman Graf Associates, 1975), p. 38; quoted in Katz, *Seductions of Crime*, p. 216.

70 Bruce Jackson, *Outside the Law: A Thief's Primer* (New Brunswick, NJ: Transaction Books, 1972), p. 114.

71 Wayne H. Thomas, *Bail Reform in America* (Berkeley: University of California Press, 1976), chap. 20.

72 Jan M. Chaiken and Marcia R. Chaiken, *Varieties of Criminal Behavior* (Santa Monica, CA: Rand, 1982).

73 Harlow, "Robbery Victims," table 14.

74 Cook, "Gun Availability," p. 73.

75 Ibid. Chaiken and Chaiken, *Varieties of Criminal Behavior*, p. 27. Allen, *Assault with a Deadly Weapon*.

76 Cook, "Gun Availability."

77 Everett DeBaun, "The Heist: The Theory and Practice of Armed Robbery," *Harper's Magazine*, February 1950.

78 Letkeman, *Crime as Work*, p. 110.

79 Ibid., p. 105.

80 Lejeune, "Management of a Mugging," p. 144.

81 Pileggi, "Meet the Muggers," p. 32.

82 Lejeune, "Management of a Mugging," p. 142.

83 Einstadter, "Social Organization of Armed Robbery."

84 Lejeune, "Management of a Mugging." p. 145.

85 Ibid., p. 133.

86 See "Fraternity Bans Hazing," *New York Times*, July 30, 1987, p. A20.

87 Lejeune, "Management of a Mugging," p. 129.

88 Ibid., p. 144.

89 Katz, *Seductions of Crime*, p. 225.

90 Ibid., pp. 187, 193.

91 William Manchester, *The Glory and the Dream: A Narrative History of America* (New York: Bantam, 1973), pp. 72–73.

92 Letkeman, *Crime as Work*, p. 94.

93 Jennifer Davis, "The London Garroting Panic of 1862: A Moral Panic and the Creation of a Criminal Class in Mid-Victorian England," in V. A. C. Gatrell, Bruce Lenman, and Geoffrey Parker, eds., *Crime and the Law: The Social History of Crime in Western Europe Since 1500* (London: Europa Publications, 1980), pp. 190–213. Pileggi, "Meet the Muggers."

94 Eric Hobsbawm, *Bandits* (New York: Dell, 1969), p. 15.

CHAPTER SIX

1 Marvin E. Wolfgang, Robert M. Figlio, Paul E. Tracy, and Simon I. Singer, *The National Survey of Crime Severity*, U.S. Department of Justice, Bureau of Justice Statistics (Washington, DC: U.S. Government Printing Office, 1985), p. vii.

2 Edmund F. McGarrel and Timothy J. Flanagan, eds., *Sourcebook of Criminal Justice Statistics—1984*, U.S. Department of Justice, Bureau of Justice Statistics (Washington, DC: U.S. Government Printing Office, 1985), p. 693.

3 State Senator Bob Wilson, quoted in Diana E. H. Russell, *Rape in Marriage* (New York: Macmillan, 1982), p. 18.

4 Ann Wolbert Burgess and Lynda Lytle Holmstrom, "Rape

Trauma Syndrome and Post-traumatic Stress Response," in Ann Wolbert Burgess, ed., *Rape and Sexual Assault: A Research Handbook* (New York: Garland, 1985), pp. 46–61.

5 Ibid. Also, Joyce E. Williams and Karen A. Holmes, *The Second Assault: Rape and Public Attitudes* (Westport, CT: Greenwood Press, 1981).

6 Gail Wisan, "The Treatment of Rape in Criminology Textbooks," *Victimology*, vol. 4, no. 1 (1979), 86–99.

7 Mary P. Koss, "The Underdetection of Rape: Methodological Choices Influence Incidence Estimates," *Journal of Social Issues*, vol. 48, no. 1 (1992), 61–75. Ronet Bachman, "Violence Against Women" (Washington, DC: U.S. Bureau of Justice, 1994).

8 Mary P. Koss, T. E. Dinero, C. A. Seibel, and S. L. Cox, "Stranger and Acquaintance Rape: Are There Differences in the Victim's Experience?" *Psychology of Women Quarterly*, vol. 12 (1988), 1–23.

9 "Marital Rape Exemption" (New York: National Center on Women and Family Law, 1987).

10 Mary Koss survey for the National Women's Study reported in David Johnson, "Survey Shows Number of Rapes Far Higher Than Official Figures," *New York Times*, April 24, 1992.

11 Mary Koss, W. J. Woodruff, and Paul G. Koss, "Criminal Victimization Among Primary Care Medical Patients: Prevalence, Incidence, and Physician Usage," *Behavioral Sciences and the Law*, vol. 9 (1991), 85–96.

12 D. G. Kilpatrick and C. B. Best, "Violence as a Precursor of Women's Substance Abuse: The Rest of the Drugs-Violence Story," paper presented at the American Psychological Association, 1990, cited ibid.

13 Mary Koss survey in Johnson, "Survey Shows Number of Rapes."

14 Gary F. Jensen and Mary Altani Karpos, "Managing Rape: Exploratory Research on the Behavior of Rape Statistics," *Criminology*, vol. 31, no. 3 (1993), 363–375.

15 Randy Thornhill and Nancy Wilmsen Thornhill, "Human Rape: An Evolutionary Analysis," *Ethology and Sociobiology*, vol. 4 (1983), 137–173.

16 Suzanne R. Sunday and Ethel Tobach, eds., *Violence Against Women: A Critique of the Sociobiology of Rape* (New York: Gordian Press, 1985).

17 Peggy Reeves Sanday, "Rape and the Silencing of the Feminine," in Sylvana Tomaselli and Roy Porter, eds., *Rape* (Oxford, UK: Basil Blackwell, 1986), pp. 84–101.

18 Raymond A. Knight, Ruth Rosenberg, and Beth A. Schneider, "Classification of Sexual Offenders: Perspectives, Methods and Validation," in Ann Wolbert Burgess, ed., *Rape and Sexual Assault: A Research Handbook* (New York: Garland, 1985), pp. 222–293.

19 Susan Brownmiller, *Against Our Will: Men, Women, and Rape* (New York: Simon & Schuster, 1975).

20 A Nicholas Groth, *Men Who Rape: The Psychology of the Offender* (New York: Plenum, 1979).

21 Diana Scully and Joseph Marolla, "'Riding the Bull at Gilley's': Convicted Rapists Describe the Rewards of Rape," *Social Problems*, vol. 32, no. 3 (1985), 251–263, quote on p. 259. See also Gary D. LaFree, "Male Power and Female Victimization: Toward a Theory of Interracial Rape," *American Journal of Sociology*, vol. 88 (1982), 311–328.

22 Groth, *Men Who Rape*. For a summary, see Knight, Rosenberg, and Schneider, "Classification of Sexual Offenders."

23 Scully and Marolla, "'Riding the Bull.'"

24 Richard T. Rada, *Clinical Aspects of the Rapist* (New York: Grune & Stratton, 1978). For other references, see Neil Malamuth, "Rape Proclivity Among Males," in Arnie Cann, Lawrence G. Calhoun, James W. Selby, and H. Elizabeth King, eds., "Rape: A Contemporary Overview and Analysis," *Journal of Social Issues*, vol. 37, no. 4 (1981), 138–157.

25 Larry Baron and Murray A. Strauss, "Four Theories of Rape: A Macrosociological Analysis," *Social Problems*, vol. 34, no. 5 (1987), 467–489. Judith R. Blau and Peter M. Blau, "The Cost of Inequality: Metropolitan Structure and Violent Crime," *American Sociological Review*, vol. 47 (1982), 114–129.

26 Peggy Reeves Sanday, "The Socio-Cultural Context of Rape: A Cross-cultural Study," in Annie Cann et al., eds., "Rape: A Contemporary Overview and Analysis," *Journal of Social Issues*, vol. 37, no. 4 (1981), pp. 5–27.

27 Brownmiller, *Against Our Will*, pp. 31–113.

28 Ibid., p. 111.

29 Ibid., pp. 153–173.

30 Larry Baron and Murray A. Strauss, "Sexual Stratification, Pornography, and Rape," in Neil M. Malamuth and Edward Donnerstein, eds., *Pornography and Sexual Aggression* (Orlando, FL: Academic Press, 1984), pp. 185–209 (which found no correlation). Baron and Strauss, "Four Theories of Rape" (which found a correlation of 0.23).

31 Scully and Marolla, "'Riding the Bull,'" p. 260.

32 Martha R. Bart, "Cultural Myths and Supports for Rape," *Journal of Personality and Social Psychology*, vol. 38 (1980), 217–230.

33 Neil M. Malamuth, S. Haber, and Seymour Feshbach, "Testing Hypotheses Regarding Rape: Exposure to Violence, Sex Differences, and the 'Normality' of Rapists," *Journal of Research in Personality*, vol. 14 (1980), 121–137.

34 Lee Sussman and Sally Bordwell, *The Rapist File* (New York: Chelsea House, 1981), p. 198.

35 *New York Times*, June 15, 1977, p. A17.

36 *Boston Globe*, March 24, 1984, p. 18; cited in Valerie P.

Hans and Neil Vidmar, *Judging the Jury* (New York: Plenum, 1986), p. 203.

37 Robin Morgan, *Going Too Far* (New York: Vintage Books, 1978).

38 President's Commission on Obscenity and Pornography, *The Report of the Commission on Obscenity and Pornography* (New York: Bantam, 1970), p. 169.

39 Charles Keating, quoted in Clive Barnes, "Special Introduction," ibid., p. ix.

40 Daniel Linz, Barbara J. Wilson, and Edward Donnerstein, "Sexual Violence in the Mass Media: Legal Solutions, Warnings, and Mitigation Through Education," *Journal of Social Issues*, vol. 48, no. 1 (1992), 145–171.

41 Attorney General's Commission on Pornography, *Final Report*; quoted in Larry Baron, "Immoral, Inviolate or Inconclusive?" *Society*, vol. 24, no. 5 (1987), 6–12.

42 Richard Ben-Veniste, "Pornography and Sex-Crime: The Danish Experience," in *Technical Report of the Commission on Obscenity and Pornography, Vol. VII—Erotica and Antisocial Behavior* (Washington, DC: U.S. Government Printing Office, 1970), pp. 245–262.

43 Ibid. Also Berl Kutchinsky, "Deception and Propaganda," *Society*, vol. 24, no. 5 (1987), 21–24.

44 John H. Court, "Sex and Violence: A Ripple Effect," in Neil Malamuth and Edward Donnerstein, eds., *Pornography and Sexual Aggression* (Orlando, FL: Academic Press, 1984), pp. 143–172.

45 James Fallows, "The Japanese Are Different from You and Me," *The Atlantic*, vol. 258, no. 3 (September 1986), 35–41.

46 Paul R. Abramson and Haruo Hayashi, "Pornography in Japan," in Neil M. Malamuth and Edward Donnerstein, eds., *Pornography and Sexual Aggression* (Orlando, FL: Academic Press, 1984), pp. 173–183.

47 Rafael Patai, *Sex and Family in the Bible and the Middle East* (Garden City, NY: Doubleday, 1959), p. 133.

48 Linda Gordon, *Heroes of Their Own Lives: The Politics and History of Family Violence* (New York: Viking, 1988), p. 254.

49 Ibid., p. 255.

50 Bachman, "Violence Against Women."

51 Murray A. Strauss, Richard J. Gelles, and Suzanne K. Steinmetz, *Behind Closed Doors: Violence in American Families* (New York: Doubleday, 1980).

52 Murray A. Strauss and Richard Gelles, "Societal Change and Changes in Family Violence from 1975 to 1985 as Revealed by Two National Surveys," *Journal of Marriage and the Family*, vol. 48 (1986), 465–479.

53 Evan Stark and Anne Flitcraft, "Violence Among Intimates: An Epidemiological Review," in B. B. Van Hasselt, R. L. Morrison, A. S. Bellack, and M. Strauss, eds., *Handbook of Family Violence* (New York: Plenum, 1987), pp. 293–317.

54 Russel P. Dobash, R. Emerson Dobash, Margo Wilson, and Martin Daly, "The Myth of Sexual Symmetry in Marital Violence," *Social Problems*, vol. 39, no. 1 (1992), 71–91.

55 Gelles, and Steinmetz, *Behind Closed Doors.*

56 Stark and Flitcraft, "Violence Among Intimates," p. 308.

57 Lenore E. A. Walker, "Psychological Causes of Family Violence," in Mary Lystad, ed., *Violence in the Home: Interdisciplinary Perspectives* (New York: Brunner/Mazel, 1986), pp. 71–97.

58 Martin Daly and Margo Wilson, *Homicide* (Hawthorne, NY: Aldine de Gruyter, 1988), pp. 196–213.

59 Walker, "Psychological Causes," p. 85.

60 Strauss, Gelles, and Steinmetz, *Behind Closed Doors.*

61 Patrick A. Langan and Christopher A. Innes, "Preventing Domestic Violence Against Women" (Washington, DC: Bureau of Justice Statistics Special Report, 1986).

62 Martin D. Schwartz, "Age and Spousal Assault Victimization," paper presented at the American Sociological Association, 1986.

63 Kathleen Ferraro and John Johnson, "How Women Experience Battering: The Process of Victimization," *Social Problems*, vol. 30, no. 3 (1983), pp. 325–339.

64 Walker, "Psychological Causes," p. 85.

65 Ferraro and Johnson, "How Women Experience Battering."

66 Richard J. Gelles and Murray A. Strauss, *Intimate Violence* (New York: Simon & Schuster, 1988), p. 180.

67 Gordon, *Heroes of Their Own Lives*, p. 180.

68 Suzanne K. Steinmetz, "The Violent Family," in Mary Lystad, ed., *Violence in the Home: Interdisciplinary Perspectives* (New York: Brunner/Mazel, 1986), pp. 51–67.

69 Richard Bourne, "Family Violence: Legal and Ethical Issues," in Eli H. Newberger and Richard Bourne, eds., *Unhappy Families* (Littleton, MA: PSG, 1985), pp. 93–146.

70 Research by A. Sedlak, cited in Douglas J. Besharov (1993), "Overreporting and Underreporting Are Twin Problems," in Richard J. Gelles and Donileen R. Loseke, *Current Controversies on Family Violence* (Newbury Park, CA: Sage, 1993), pp. 257–272.

71 Strauss, Gelles, and Steinmetz, *Behind Closed Doors.*

72 Robert Hampton and Eli Newberger, "Child Abuse Incidence and Reporting by Hospitals: Significance of Severity, Class, and Race," *American Journal of Public Health*, vol. 75, no. 1 (1985), 56–60. Patrick Turbett and Richard O'Toole, "Physicians' Recognition of Child Abuse," paper delivered at the American Sociological Association, 1980. Also Richard J. Gelles, "Family Violence: What We Know and Can Do," in Newberger and Bourne, eds., op. cit., pp. 1–8.

73 Gelles and Strauss, *Intimate Violence*, p. 86. See also Carol Stack, *All Our Kin: Strategies for Survival in a Black Community* (New York: Harper & Row, 1974).

74 David Gil, "Sociocultural Aspects of Domestic Violence," in Mary Lystad, ed., *Violence in the Home: Interdisciplinary Perspectives* (New York: Brunner/Mazel, 1986), pp. 124–149.

75 Carolyn M. Newberger, "Parents and Practitioners as Developmental Theorists," in Newberger and Bourne, eds., pp. 131–144, quote on p. 133.

76 Ibid.

77 Gelles, "Family Violence," p. 6.

78 U.S. Department of Health and Human Services, National Center on Child Abuse and Neglect, *National Study on Child Neglect and Abuse Reporting* (Denver: American Humane Association, 1984).

79 David Finkelhor, "The Main Problem Is Still Underreporting, Not Overreporting," in Richard J. Gelles and Donileen R. Loseke, *Current Controversies on Family Violence* (Newbury Park, CA: Sage, 1993), pp. 273–287.

80 Gordon, *Heroes of Their Own Lives*, p. 210.

81 Diana E. H. Russell, *The Secret Trauma: Incest in the Lives of Girls and Women* (New York: Basic Books, 1986), pp. 96–99.

82 David Finkelhor, "Sexual Abuse and Physical Abuse: Some Critical Differences," in Newberger and Bourne, eds., pp. 21–30.

83 Daly and Wilson, *Homicide*, chap. 6–9.

CHAPTER SEVEN

1 Georges Duby, ed., *A History of Private Life, Vol. II: Revelations of the Medieval World*, Arthur Goldhammer, trans. (Cambridge, MA: Belknap Press, 1988).

2 J. W. Cecil Turner, ed., *Kenny's Outline of Criminal Law* (Cambridge, UK: Cambridge University Press, 1962), pp. 244–248.

3 Bureau of Justice Statistics, *Criminal Victimization in the United States, 1992,* (Washington, DC: U.S. Department of Justice, 1992).

4 Bureau of Justice Statistics, *Report to the Nation on Crime and Justice* (2nd ed.) (Washington, D.C: U.S. Department of Justice, 1988), p. 3.

5 Nicholas Pileggi, "1968 Has Been the Year of the Burglar," *New York Times Magazine*, November 17, 1968, p. 79.

6 Bureau of Justice Statistics, *Criminal Victimization in the United States, 1991* (Washington, DC: U.S. Department of Justice, 1991), pp. 94, 108.

7 Carl E. Pope, *Crime-specific Analysis: An Empirical Examination of Burglary Offender Characteristics* (Washington, DC: Department of Justice, 1977).

8 Dermot Walsh, *Heavy Business: Commercial Burglary and Robbery* (London: Routledge & Kegan Paul, 1986), p. 45.

9 Paul Cromwell, James N. Olson, and D'Aunn Wester Avary, *Breaking and Entering: An Ethnographic Analysis of Burglary* (Newbury Park, CA: Sage, 1991), pp. 33, 56.

10 Peter Letkeman, *Crime as Work* (Englewood Cliffs, NJ: Prentice-Hall, 1973), p. 52.

11 Paul Cromwell et al., *Breaking and Entering*, p. 26.

12 Pope, *Crime-specific Analysis*.

13 Neal Shover, "Structures and Careers in Burglary," *Journal of Criminal Law, Criminology, and Police Science*, vol. 63, no. 4 (1972), 540–549.

14 Darrell J. Steffensmeier, *The Fence: In the Shadow of Two Worlds* (Totowa, NJ: Rowman & Littlefield 1986), 48–49n, 57–58n.

15 Ibid., p. 26.

16 Shover, "Structures and Careers in Burglary." Also Bruce Jackson, *Outside the Law: A Thief's Primer* (New York: Macmillan, 1969), pp. 121–122, 138.

17 Steffensmeier, *The Fence*, p. 47.

18 Ibid., pp. 154–156. Jackson, *Outside the Law*, p. 133.

19 Steffensmeier, *The Fence*, p. 56n.

20 Walsh, *Heavy Business*, p. 17.

21 Shover, "Structures and Careers in Burglary." Also Richard A. Cloward and Lloyd E. Ohlin, *Delinquency and Opportunity: A Theory of Delinquent Gangs* (New York: Free Press, 1960).

22 Steffensmeier, *The Fence*, p. 43.

23 Cromwell et al., *Breaking and Entering*, p. 50.

24 Mercer Sullivan, "Youth Crime: New York's Two Varieties," *New York Affairs*, vol. 8 (1983), 31–48.

25 Walsh, *Heavy Business*, p. 26.

26 Ibid., p. 42.

27 Ibid.

28 Letkeman, *Crime as Work*, p. 56.

29 Ibid., pp. 77–78.

30 Steffensmeier, *The Fence*, p. 49.

31 Letkeman, *Crime as Work*, pp. 49–89.

32 Ibid., p. 60.

33 Ibid., p. 72.

34 Steffensmeier, *The Fence*, pp. 148–151.

35 Letkeman, *Crime as Work*, p. 84.

36 Ibid., p. 86.

37 Cromwell et al., *Breaking and Entering*, p. 24.

38 Ibid., p. 25.

39 G. Rengert and J. Wasilchick, *Suburban Burglary: A Time and a Place for Everything* (Springfield, IL: Thomas, 1985), p. 90; cited in Cromwell et al., *Breaking and Entering*, p. 31.

40 Pileggi, "1968," p. 80.

41 Pope, *Crime-specific Analysis*, p. 74.

42 Dan A. Lewis, Jane A. Grant, and Dennis P. Rosenbaum, *Social Construction of Reform: Crime Prevention and Community Organization* (New Brunswick, NJ: Transaction Books, 1988).

43 Pope, *Crime-specific Analysis*, p. 74. Peter W. Greenwood, *An Analysis of the Apprehension Activities of the*

New York City Police Department (New York: Rand Institute, 1970).

44 *National Judicial Reporting Program, 1990* (Washington, DC: U.S. Department of Justice, 1993), pp. 45, 46. *National Corrections Reporting Program, 1991* (Washington, DC: U.S. Department of Justice, 1994), pp. 26, 29.

45 Bureau of Justice Statistics, *Criminal Victimization in the United States, 1987* (Washington, DC: U.S. Department of Justice, 1989).

46 Sam Roberts, "Parked Car, No Radio: Where the City Is Losing Control," *New York Times*, July 3, 1989, sec. 4, p. 14.

47 *The New Yorker*, December 21, 1981, p. 34.

48 Mary Owen Cameron, *The Booster and the Snitch* (New York: Free Press, 1964).

49 Gresham M. Sykes and David Matza, "Techniques of Neutralization: A Theory of Delinquency," *American Sociological Review*, vol. 22 (1957), 664–670.

50 Jack Katz, *Seductions of Crime: Moral and Sensual Attractions in Doing Evil* (New York: Basic Books, 1988).

51 Timothy J. Flanagan and Katherine M. Jamieson, eds., *Sourcebook of Criminal Justice Statistics—1987*, U.S. Department of Justice, Bureau of Justice Statistics (Washington, DC: U.S. Government Printing Office, 1987), p. 265.

52 Federal Bureau of Investigation, *Crime in the United States: Uniform Crime Reports 1987* (Washington, DC: U.S. Government Printing Office, 1988).

53 UCR data, in Flanagan and Jamieson, *Sourcebook—1987*, p. 344.

54 Ibid.

55 Cameron, *Booster and the Snitch*, p. 164.

56 Marilyn E. Walsh, *The Fence: A New Look at the World of Property Theft* (Westport, CT: Greenwood Press, 1977).

57 Henry Fielding, *An Enquiry Into the Causes of the Late Increase of Robbers, &c* (New York: AMS Press, 1975, original date, 1751).

58 Cromwell et al., *Breaking and Entering*, p. 79.

59 S. Pennell, "Fencing Activity and Police Strategy," *Police Chief*, September, 1979, pp. 71–75.

60 Klockars, *Professional Fence*.

61 Ibid., p. 73.

62 Ibid., p. 79.

63 Steffensmeier, *The Fence*, p. 147.

64 Ibid., p. 149.

65 Klockars, *Professional Fence*, p. 80.

66 Ibid., p. 82.

67 Ibid., p. 99.

68 Gary Marx, *Under Cover: Police Surveillance in America* (Berkeley, CA: University of California Press, 1988), pp. 108–128.

69 Ibid., p. 126.

70 *Annual Report* (Palos Hills, IL: National Automobile Theft Bureau, 1988), p. 9.

71 U.S. Bureau of the Census, *Statistical Abstract of the United States: 1987*, table 710; cited in Caroline Wolf Harlow, "Motor Vehicle Theft," *Bureau of Justice Statistics Special Report* (Washington, DC: U.S. Government Printing Office, 1988).

72 *Annual Report* (Palos Hills, IL: National Auto Theft Bureau, 1987), pp. 9–12.

73 Bureau of Justice Statistics, *Criminal Victimization in the United States, 1992*, (Washington, DC: U.S. Department of Justice, 1994).

74 Charles H. McGaghy, Peggy C. Giordano, and Trudy Knicely Henson, "Auto Theft: Offender and Offense Characteristics," *Criminology*, vol. 15, no. 3 (1977), 367–385, quote on p. 379.

75 Harlow, "Motor Vehicle Theft," p. 3.

76 *Annual Report*, 1988, p. 5.

77 *Annual Report*, 1987, p. 24.

78 Ibid., p. 16.

79 Ibid., p. 24.

80 *Spotlight on Insurance Crime*, vol. 2, no. 3, p. 2.

81 Ibid., p. 24.

82 Ibid., p. 44.

83 Ibid., p. 29.

84 Ibid.

CHAPTER EIGHT

1 Russell Mokhiber, "Triple Damages," *New York Times*, September 14, 1985, p. 23. Paul Moses, "Suit II: Nancy Capasso Asks $70M," *New York Newsday*, January 18, 1990, p. 3.

2 Henry N. Pontell and Kitty Calavita, "The Savings and Loan Industry," in Michael Tonry and Albert J. Reiss, Jr., *Beyond the Law* (Chicago: University of Chicago Press, 1993), pp. 203–246.

3 Peter Reuter, *Racketeering in Legitimate Industries: A Study in the Economics of Intimidation* (Santa Monica, CA: RAND, 1987).

4 John M. Blair, *The Control of Oil* (New York: Random House, 1976). James William Coleman, *The Criminal Elite: The Sociology of White Collar Crime*, 2nd ed. (New York: St. Martin's Press, 1989), pp. 22–30.

5 *New York Times*, August 11, 1989, p. B1.

6 Jack Newfield, "The Myth of Godfather Journalism," *The Village Voice*, July 23, 1979, pp. 1, 11–12. Peter Reuter and Jonathan B. Rubinstein, "Fact, Fancy, and Organized Crime," *The Public Interest*, vol. 53 (1978), 45–67.

7 Tom Buckley, "The Mafia Tries a New Tune," *Harper's Magazine*, August 1971.

8 Humbert S. Nelli, *The Business of Crime: Italians and Syndicate Crime in the United States* (New York: Oxford Press, 1976), pp. 47–69.

9 Donald R. Cressey, *Theft of a Nation: The Structure and Operations of Organized Crime in America* (New York: Harper & Row, 1969).

10 Dwight Smith, *The Mafia Mystique* (New York: Basic Books, 1975).

11 Irving A. Spergel, "Youth Gangs: Continuity and Change," in Michael Tonry and Norval Morris, eds., *Crime and Justice: A Review of Research* (Chicago: University of Chicago Press, 1990), pp. 171–275.

12 Edward Crapsey, *The Nether Side of New York: or Vice, Crime and Poverty of the Great Metropolis*, excerpted in Wayne Molquin with Charles Van Doren, eds., *The American Way of Crime: A Documentary History* (New York: Praeger, 1976), pp. 17–21.

13 *New York Times*, November 11, 1987.

14 *New York Times*, August 24, 1986, sec. 4, p. 6.

15 Nelli, *Business of Crime*, p. 3.

16 Ibid., p. 13.

17 Ibid., pp. 14–23, 136.

18 Ibid., p. 136.

19 Ibid., p. 80.

20 Ibid., pp. 69–100.

21 Howard Abadinsky, *Organized Crime*, 2nd ed. (Chicago: Nelson Hall, 1985), p. 89.

22 *Kefauver Crime Report* (1951), p. 2. Quoted in ibid., p. 312.

23 Nelli, *Business of Crime*, pp. 199–210.

24 Ibid., p. 261.

25 Nicholas Pileggi, "The Lying, Thieving, Murdering, Upper-Middle-Class, Respectable Clerk," *Esquire*, January 1966.

26 Abadinsky, *Organized Crime*.

27 Ibid., p. 20.

28 President's Commission on Law Enforcement and the Administration of Justice, *Task Force Report: Organized Crime* (Washington, DC: U.S. Government Printing Office, 1967), p. 1; quoted in Peter Reuter, *Disorganized Crime: The Economics of the Visible Hand* (Cambridge, MA: MIT Press, 1983), p. 3.

29 U.S. Congress, Senate Permanent Subcommittee on Investigations of the Committee on Government Operations, 92nd Cong., 1st Sess., (1971), part III, pp. 772–838; reprinted as "Vincent Teresa on a Life in Crime," in Wayne Molquin with Charles Van Doren, eds., *The American Way of Crime: A Documentary History* (New York: Praeger, 1976), pp. 332–341.

30 Cressey, *Theft of a Nation*, p. 75.

31 Reuter, *Disorganized Crime*, pp. 43–44.

32 Ibid., p. 42.

33 Gerald O'Neill and Dick Lehr, *The Underboss: The Rise and Fall of a Mafia Family* (New York: St. Martin's Press, 1989).

34 For information on New York, see Reuter, *Disorganized Crime*. For Philadelphia, see Gary N. Potter and Philip Jenkins, *The City and the Syndicate: Organizing Crime in Philadelphia* (Lexington, MA: Ginn Press, 1985).

35 Nelli, *Business of Crime*, p. 228.

36 Reuter, *Disorganized Crime*, pp. 62–67.

37 "470 Betting Places Raided," *New York Times*, February 1, 1986.

38 Reuter, *Disorganized Crime*, p. 98.

39 Jay Livingston, *Compulsive Gamblers: Observations on Action and Abstinence* (New York: Harper & Row, 1974).

40 Reuter, *Disorganized Crime*, p. 100.

41 Ibid., p. 149.

42 Potter and Jenkins, *City and Syndicate*, p. 78.

43 Peter Maas, *The Valachi Papers* (New York: Bantam Books, 1968), pp. 245–246.

44 Patricia A. Adler, *Wheeling and Dealing* (New York: Columbia University Press, 1985).

45 Peter Reuter and John Haaga, *The Organization of High-Level Drug Markets: An Exploratory Study* (Santa Monica, CA: RAND, 1989), pp. 35–39.

46 Joseph B. Treaster, "More Drugs in Ship Containers Flood Ports," *New York Times*, April 29, 1990, p. 1.

47 Adler, *Wheeling and Dealing*.

48 Alfred W. McCoy, *The Politics of Heroin in Southeast Asia* (New York: Harper & Row, 1973).

49 Alan A. Block and Frank R. Scarpitti, *Poisoning for Profit: The Mafia and Toxic Waste in America* (New York: William Morrow, 1985).

50 Jonathan Kwitny, *Vicious Circles: The Mafia in the Marketplace* (New York: Norton, 1979), pp. 1–46, quote on p. 18.

51 Ibid., pp. 274–276.

52 Ibid.

53 The phrase comes from Henry Hill, the informant in

Nicholas Pileggi, *Wiseguy: A Life in the Mafia* (New York: Simon & Schuster, 1985).

54 Robert P. Rhodes, *Organized Crime: Crime Control vs. Civil Liberties* (New York: Random House, 1984), p. 7. Also, Joseph Albini, *American Mafia: Genesis of a Legend* (New York: Appleton-Century-Crofts, 1971).

55 Reuter, *Disorganized Crime*, p. 105.

56 Ibid., pp. 163–164.

CHAPTER NINE

1 John Braithwaite, "White-collar Crime," *Annual Review of Sociology*, vol. 11 (1985), 3.

2 Edwin Sutherland, "White-Collar Criminality," reprinted in Gilbert Geis and Robert F. Meier, *White-collar Crime: Offenses in Business, Politics, and the Professions* (New York: Free Press, 1977), pp. 38–49.

3 Ibid., p. 45.

4 Louis Harris, *The Harris Survey* (Orlando, FL: Media Services, Inc., 1988).

5 Edwin Sutherland, *White-collar Crime* (New York: Dryden, 1949), p. 9.

6 Marlys Harris, "You May Already Be a Victim of Investment Fraud," *Money*, vol. 18, no. 8 (August 1989), pp. 74–91.

7 Marshall Clinard and Richard Quinney, eds., *Criminal Behavior Systems: A Typology* (New York: Holt, Rinehart, & Winston, 1973), pp. 206–223. Herbert Edelhertz, *The Nature, Impact, and Prosecution of White-collar Crime*, U.S. Department of Justice, Law Enforcement Assistance Administration (Washington, DC: U.S. Government Printing Office, 1970).

8 Richard W. Stevenson, "Many Are Caught but Few Suffer for U.S. Military Contract Fraud," *New York Times*, November 12, 1990, pp. A1, B8.

9 Franklin E. Zimring and Gordon Hawkins, "Crime, Justice, and the Savings and

Loan Crisis," in Michael Tonry and Albert J. Reiss, Jr., eds., *Beyond the Law: Crime in Complex Organizations* (Chicago: University of Chicago Press, 1993), pp. 247–292.

10 Hirschi and Gottfredson, "Causes of White-collar Crime."

11 Darrel J. Steffensmeier, "On the Causes of 'White-collar' Crime: An Assessment of Hirschi and Gottfredson's Claims," *Criminology*, vol. 27 (1989), 345–358. Kathleen Daly, "Gender Varieties of White-Collar Crime," *Criminology*, vol. 27, no. 4 (1989), pp. 769–793.

12 Braithwaite, "White-collar Crime," pp. 1–25.

13 Edwin Sutherland, "Crime of Corporations," in Albert Cohen, Albert Lindesmith, and Karl Schuessler, eds., *The Sutherland Papers* (Bloomington: Indiana University Press, 1956), pp. 78–96.

14 Marshall B. Clinard and Peter C. Yeager, *Corporate Crime* (New York: Free Press, 1980), p. 118.

15 Ibid., pp. 118–120.

16 Quoted in Zimring and Hawkins, "Crime, Justice, and the Savings and Loan Crisis," p. 265.

17 James William Coleman, *The Criminal Elite: The Sociology of White Collar Crime* (New York: St. Martin's Press, 1989), pp. 200–204.

18 Robert Merton, "Social Structure and Anomie," *American Sociological Review*, vol. 3 (1938), 672–682.

19 Coleman, *Criminal Elite*, pp. 230–231.

20 Clinard and Yeager, *Corporate Crime*, pp. 31–34.

21 Harvey Farberman, "A Criminogenic Market Structure: The Automobile Industry," *Sociological Quarterly*, vol. 16 (1975), 438–457. William N. Leonard and Marvin Glenn Weber, "Automakers and Dealers: A Study of Criminogenic Market Forces," *Law and Society Review*, vol. 4, no. 3 (1970), 407–424.

22 Peter F. Drucker, *Concept of the Corporation* (New York: John Day, 1972).

23 Braithwaite, "White-collar Crime," pp. 1–25. John Conklin,

"Illegal but Not Criminal," *Business Crime in America* (Englewood Cliffs, NJ: Prentice-Hall, 1977), chap. 5.

24 John Braithwaite, *Corporate Crime in the Pharmaceutical Industry* (London: Routledge & Kegan Paul, 1985), p. 308.

25 Jack Katz, "The Social Movement Against White-collar Crime," in Egon Bittner and Sheldon Messinger, eds., *Criminology Review Yearbook*, vol. 2 (Beverly Hills, CA: Sage, 1980).

26 Francis T. Cullen, Bruce G. Link, and Craig W. Planzi, "The Seriousness of Crime Revisited: Have Attitudes Toward White-collar Crime Changed?" *Criminology*, vol. 20 (1982), 83–102.

27 Donald W. Scott, "Policing Corporate Collusion," *Criminology*, vol. 27, no. 3 (1989), 559–587.

28 John Braithwaite and Gilbert Geis, "On Theory and Action for Corporate Crime," *Crime and Delinquency*, vol. 28 (1982), 292–314.

29 Mark Dowie, "Pinto Madness," *Mother Jones*, September/October, 1977, pp. 18–32.

30 *New York Times*, April 29, 1990, p. 23.

31 Howell Raines, "Alabama Bound," *New York Times Magazine*, June 3, 1990, p. 42.

32 Mokhiber, *Corporate Crime and Violence*, pp. 196–203.

33 Braithwaite, *Corporate Crime in the Pharmaceutical Industry*, p. 291.

34 Stuart L. Hills, ed., *Corporate Violence: Injury for Death and Profit* (Savage, MD: Rowman & Littlefield, 1987), pp. 41–46.

CHAPTER TEN

1 David Harris Willson, *A History of England* (New York: Holt, Rinehart & Winston, 1967), p. 93.

2 Barbara W. Tuchman, *A Distant Mirror: The Calamitous*

14th Century (New York: Knopf, 1978), p. 141.

3 Graeme Newman, *The Punishment Response* (New York: J. B. Lippincott, 1978), pp. 89–94.

4 Ibid., pp. 126, 138.

5 Cesare Beccaria, *On Crimes and Punishments*, with an introduction by Henry Paolucci, trans. (Indianapolis, IN: Bobbs-Merritt, [1764] 1963).

6 Ibid., p. 12.

7 Ibid., p. xxii.

8 George B. Vold, *Theoretical Criminology* (New York: Oxford University Press, 1979), pp. 53–55.

9 Cesare Lombroso, *Criminal Man* (Montclair, NJ: Patterson Smith, 1911, reprinted 1972), pp. 6–7.

10 Cesare Lombroso, *Crime: Its Causes and Remedies* (Montclair, NJ: Patterson Smith, 1911, reprinted 1968), pp. 365–666.

11 Vold, *Theoretical Criminology*, p. 37.

12 Charles Goring, *The English Convict: A Statistical Study*, quoted ibid., p. 61. James Q. Wilson and Richard J. Herrnstein, *Crime and Human Nature* (New York: Simon & Schuster, 1985), p. 76.

13 Ibid.

14 E. A. Hooton, *Crime and the Man*, quoted ibid., p. 78. Vold, *Theoretical Criminology*, pp. 62–65.

15 Ibid., p. 62.

16 William H. Sheldon, *Varieties of Delinquent Youth* (New York: Harper, 1949).

17 Ibid., p. 752.

18 Sarnoff A. Mednick and Jan Volavka, "Biology and Crime," in Norval Morris and Michael Tonry, eds., *Crime and Justice: An Annual Review of Research* (Chicago: University of Chicago Press, 1980), pp. 85–158.

19 Melvin Konner, "The Aggressors," *New York Times Magazine*, August 14, 1988, pp. 3–34.

20 Leo E. Kreuz and Robert M. Rose, "Assessment of Aggressive Behavior and Plasma Testosterone in a Young Criminal Population," *Psychosomatic Medicine*, vol. 34 (1972), 321–332.

21 Daniel Goleman, "Aggression in Men: Hormone Levels Are a Key," *The New York Times*, July 17, 1990, pp. C1, 6, reporting on research by Richard Udry and others. Alan Booth and D. Wayne Osgood, "The Influence of Testosterone on Deviance in Adulthood: Assessing and Explaining the Relationship," *Criminology*, vol. 31, no. 1 (1993), 93–117.

22 Diana H. Fishbein, "Biological Perspectives in Criminology," *Criminology*, vol. 28, no. 1 (1990), 27–72.

23 Michael R. Gottfredson and Travis Hirschi, *A General Theory of Crime* (New York: Basic Books, 1990).

24 K. O. Christiansen, "A Preliminary Study of Criminality Among Twins," in Sarnoff A. Mednick and K. O. Christiansen, eds., *Biological Bases of Criminal Behavior* (New York: Gardner Press, 1977).

25 Gottfredson and Hirschi, *General Theory of Crime*, pp. 53–60.

26 Quoted in *The Trenton Times*, August 9, 1982, p. C1.

27 Hans J. Eysenck, *Crime and Personality* (London: Routledge & Kegan Paul, 1977).

28 Gwynn Nettler, *Explaining Crime*, 3rd ed. (New York: McGraw-Hill, 1984), p. 302. See also A. Petri, *Individuality in Pain and Suffering* (Chicago: University of Chicago Press, 1967).

29 For a review of these studies, see Mednick and Volavka, "Biology and Crime," pp. 119–122.

30 Lee N. Robins, *Deviant Children Grown Up: A Sociological and Psychiatric Study of Sociopathic Personality* (Baltimore: Williams & Wilkins, 1966), p. 16.

31 Lee N. Robins and K. S. Ratcliff, "Risk Factors in the Continuation of Childhood Antisocial Behavior into Adulthood," *International Journal of Mental Health*, vol. 7 (1979), 96–116. Also, Mark Peterson, Harriet Braiker, and Sue Polich, *Doing Crime: A Survey of California Inmates* (Santa Monica, CA: RAND Corporation, 1980).

32 Jennifer L. White, Terrie E. Moffitt, Felton Earls, Lee Robins, and Paul A. Silva, "How Early Can We Tell?: Predictors of Childhood Conduct Disorder and Adolescent Delinquency," *Criminology*, vol. 28, no. 4 (1990), 507–533.

33 Robert C. Colligan, David Osborne, Wendell M. Swenson, and Kenneth P. Gifford, *The MMPI: A Contemporary Normative Study* (New York: Praeger, 1983).

34 Arthur Volkman, "A Matched Group Personality Comparison of Delinquents and Non-Delinquent Juveniles," *Social Problems*, vol. 6 (1959), 238–245.

35 Donald J. West and D. P. Farrington, *The Delinquent Way of Life* (London: Heinemann, 1977).

36 Richard Herrnstein, "Some Criminogenic Traits of Offenders," in James Q. Wilson, ed., *Crime and Public Policy* (San Francisco: ICS Press, 1983), pp. 31–49, quote on p. 40.

37 Samuel Yochelson and Stanton Samenow, *The Criminal Personality* (New York: J. Aronson, 1976).

38 Philip G. Zimbardo, "A Pirandellian Prison," *New York Times Magazine*, April 8, 1973, pp. 38–60.

39 Goleman, "Aggression in Men."

40 Terrie E. Moffitt, "Neuropsychology of Juvenile Delinquency: A Critical Review," in Michael Tonry and Norval Morris, eds., *Crime and Justice: An Annual Review* (Chicago: University of Chicago Press, 1990), 99–169.

41 *New York Times*, April 11, 1970, p. 15.

CHAPTER ELEVEN

1 Lambert Adolphe Jacques Quetelet, *A Treatise on Man and the Development of His Faculties* (New York: B. Franklin, [1842], 1968).

2 Kai Erikson, *Wayward Puritans* (New York: Wiley, 1966). Emile Durkheim, *The Rules of Sociological Method*, S. A. Solovay and J. H. Mueller, trans. (Glencoe, IL: Free Press, [1895], 1957).

3 Robert Merton, "Social Structure and Anomie," in *Social Theory and Social Structure* (New York: Free Press, 1968), pp. 185–214.

4 Stephen Cole, "The Growth of Scientific Knowledge," in Lewis A. Coser, ed., *The Idea of Social Structure* (New York: Harcourt Brace Jovanovich, 1975), p. 175.

5 Jack Katz, *Seductions of Crime: Moral and Sensual Attractions in Doing Evil* (New York: Basic Books, 1988), esp. pp. 313–317.

6 Richard A. Coleman and Lee Rainwater, *Social Standing in America: New Dimensions of Class* (New York: Basic Books, 1978).

7 Peter M. Blau and Otis Dudley Duncan, *The American Occupational Structure* (New York: Wiley, 1967). Robert Hauser and David L. Featherman, *Opportunity and Change* (New York: Academic Press, 1978). Christopher M. Jencks et al., *Who Gets Ahead? The Determinants of Income and Success in America* (New York: Basic Books, 1979).

8 Howard S. Becker, *Outsiders: Studies in the Sociology of Deviance* (New York: Macmillan, 1973), p. 191.

9 C. Wright Mills, "The Professional Ideology of Social Pathologists," *American Journal of Sociology*, vol. 69 (1943), 165–180.

10 Robert E. Park, Ernest N. Burgess, and Roderick D. McKenzie, eds., *The City* (Chicago: University of Chicago Press, 1967).

11 Edwin H. Sutherland and Donald R. Cressey, *Principles of Criminology*, 7th ed. (Philadelphia, PA: Lippincott, 1934, 1966).

12 Sheldon Glueck, "Theory and Fact in Criminology: A Criticism of Differential Association," *British Journal of Delinquency*, vol. 9 (1956), 92–109.

13 Edwin H. Sutherland and Donald R. Cressey, *Principles of Criminology* (Philadelphia: J. P. Lippincott, 1978).

14 Robert LeJeune, "The Management of a Mugging," *Urban Life*, vol. 6 (1977), 123–148.

15 Daniel Glaser, "Criminality Theories and Behavioral Images," *American Journal of Sociology*, vol. 61 (1956), 433–444.

16 Jack P. Gibbs, "The State of Criminological Theory," *Criminology*, vol. 25, no. 4 (1987), 821–840, esp. p. 835.

17 Ronald L. Akers, *Deviant Behavior: A Social Learning Approach* (Belmont, CA: Wadsworth, 1973).

18 Ronald L. Akers, *Criminological Theories: Introduction and Evaluation* (Los Angeles: Roxbury Publishing, 1994), p. 104.

19 Ibid., p. 103.

20 All quotations are from Albert K. Cohen, *Delinquent Boys: The Culture of the Gang* (New York: Free Press, 1955).

21 Walter B. Miller, "Lower-class Culture as a Generation Milieu of Gang Delinquency," *Journal of Social Issues*, vol. 19 (1958), 5–19.

22 Ibid., p. 8.

23 All quotes in this section are from Richard A. Cloward and Lloyd E. Ohlin, *Delinquency and Opportunity: A Theory of Delinquent Gangs* (New York: Free Press, 1960).

24 Lamar Empey, *American Delinquency: Its Meaning and Construction* (Homewood, IL: Dorsey Press, 1978), pp. 294–300.

CHAPTER TWELVE

1 David Matza, *Delinquency and Drift* (New York: Wiley, 1964).

2 Gresham M. Sykes and David Matza, "Techniques of Neutralization: A Theory of Delinquency," *American Sociological Review*, vol. 22 (1957), 664–670.

3 John E. Conklin, *Criminology*, 2nd ed. (New York: Macmillan, 1986), pp. 191–192. James F. Short, Jr., and Fred L. Strodtbeck, *Group Process and Gang Delinquency* (Chicago: University of Chicago Press, 1965).

4 Hyman Rodman, "The Lower-class Value Stretch," *Social Problems*, vol. 42, no. 2 (1963), 205–215.

5 Elliot Liebow, *Tally's Corner: A Study of Negro Streetcorner Men* (Boston: Little, Brown, 1967).

6 Howard Becker, *Outsiders: Studies in the Sociology of Deviance* (New York: Free Press, 1973).

7 David Matza, *Becoming Deviant* (Englewood Cliffs, NJ: Prentice-Hall, 1969).

8 For example, see Richard D. Schwartz and Jerome H. Skolnick, "Two Studies of Legal Stigma," *Social Problems*, vol. 10 (1962), 133–142. For a variety of studies in the labeling tradition, see Earl Rubington and Martin S. Weinberg, *Deviance: The Interactionist Perspective* (New York: Macmillan, 1987).

9 Egon Bittner, "The Police on Skid-Row: A Study of Peace Keeping," *American Sociological Review*, vol. 32 (1967), 699–715.

10 Joseph R. Gusfield, *Symbolic Crusade* (Urbana: University of Illinois Press, 1963). Kristin Luker, *Abortion and the Politics of Motherhood* (Berkeley: University of California Press, 1984).

11 Ian Taylor, Paul Walton, and Jock Young, eds., *Critical Criminology* (London: Routledge & Kegan Paul, 1975), p. 44.

12 William J. Chambliss, "A Sociological Analysis of the Law of Vagrancy," *Social Problems*, vol. 12 (1964), 67–77.

13 Douglas Hay, Peter Linebaugh, John G. Rule, E. P. Thompson, and Cal Winslow, *Albion's Fatal Tree* (London: Allen Lane, 1975).

14 John Helmer, *Drugs and Minority Oppression* (New York: Seabury Press, 1975).

15 John E. Conklin, *Illegal but Not Criminal* (Englewood Cliffs, NJ: Prentice-Hall, 1977), pp. 99–129.

16 Jeffrey Reiman, *The Rich Get Richer and the Poor Get Prison*, 2nd ed. (New York: Wiley, 1984).

17 David F. Greenberg, ed., *Crime and Capitalism: Readings in Marxist Criminology* (Palo Alto, CA: Mayfield, 1981), p. 193.

18 Ibid., p. 20.

19 C. Wright Mills, *The Power Elite* (New York: Oxford University Press, 1956). G. William Domhoff, *Who Rules America Now?* (Englewood Cliffs, NJ: Prentice-Hall, 1983). Michael Useem, *The Inner Circle: Large Corporations and the Rise of Business Political Activities in the U.S. and U.K.* (New York: Oxford University Press, 1983).

20 Terence P. Thornberry, "Race, Socioeconomic Status, and Sentencing in the Juvenile Justice System," *Journal of Criminal Law, Criminology and Police Science*, vol. 64 (1973), 90–98. Dale Dannefer and Russel K. Schutt, "Race and Juvenile Justice Processing in Court and Police Agencies," *American Journal of Sociology*, vol. 87 (1982), 113–132. For a review, see Allen E. Liska, *Perspectives on Deviance*, 2nd ed. (Englewood Cliffs, NJ: Prentice-Hall, 1987), pp. 175–210.

21 David F. Greenberg, "Delinquency and the Age Structure of Society," *Contemporary Crisis*, vol. 1 (1977), 189–223.

22 Richard Quinney, *Class State and Crime: On the Theory and Practice of Criminal Justice* (New York: David McKay, 1977), p. 144.

23 Travis Hirschi, *Causes of Delinquency* (Berkeley, CA: University of California Press, 1969).

24 Delbert S. Elliott, David Huizinga, and Suzanne Ageton, *Explaining Delinquency and Drug Use* (Beverly Hills, CA: Sage, 1985). Terence P. Thornberry, Alan Lizotte, Marvin D. Krohn, Margaret Farnworth, and Sung Joon Jang, "Delinquent Peers, Beliefs, and Delinquent Behavior: A Longitudinal Test of Interactional Theory," *Criminology*, vol. 32, no. 1 (1994), 47–83.

25 Irving A. Spergel, "Youth Gangs: Continuity and Change," in Michael Tonry and Norval Morris, *Crime and Justice: An Annual Review*, vol. 12 (Chicago: University of Chicago Press, 1990), pp. 171–276, esp. pp. 199–208.

26 Lewis Yablonsky, "The Delinquent Gang as a Near-group," *Social Problems*, vol. 7 (1959). Walter B. Miller, "American Youth Gangs: Past and Present," in Abraham S. Blumberg, ed., *Current Perspective on Criminal Behavior* (New York: Knopf, 1974), pp. 210–238.

27 Ellen Greenberger and Lawrence Steinberg, *When Teenagers Work: The Psychological and Social Cost of Adolescent Employment* (New York: Basic Books, 1987).

28 Michael Gottfredson and Travis Hirschi, *A General Theory of Crime* (Stanford, CA: Stanford University Press, 1990).

29 Ibid., p. 22.

30 Ibid., p. 74 (emphasis in original).

31 Ibid., p. 158.

32 Ibid., p. 75.

33 Ibid., p. 97.

34 Ibid., pp. 101–102.

35 Elliott, Huizinga, and Ageton, *Explaining Delinquency*.

36 Lawrence E. Cohen and Marcus Felson, "Social Change and Crime Rate Trends: A Routine Activities Approach," *American Sociological Review*, vol. 44 (1979), 588–608.

37 Rodney Stark, "Deviant Places: A Theory of the Ecology of Crime," *Criminology*, vol. 25, no. 4 (1987), 893–909.

38 James Q. Wilson, *Thinking About Crime* (New York: Random House, 1965), p. 53.

CHAPTER THIRTEEN

1 John A. Webster, "Police Task and Time Study," *Journal of Criminal Law, Criminology, and Police Science*, vol. 61, no. 1 (1970), 94–100.

2 Ruben G. Rumbaut and Egon Bittner, "Changing Conceptions of the Police Role: A Sociological Review," in Norval Morris and Michael Tonry, eds., *Crime and Justice: An Annual Review*, vol. 1 (Chicago: University of Chicago Press, 1979), pp. 239–288.

3 John Van Maanen, "Working the Street: A Developmental View of Police Behavior," reprinted as "Kinsmen in Repose," in Peter K. Manning and John Van Maanen, eds., *Policing: A View from the Street* (Santa Monica, CA: Goodyear, 1978), pp. 115–128, esp. p. 116.

4 Carl B. Klockars, *The Idea of Police* (Beverly Hills, CA: Sage, 1985).

5 Ibid., pp. 7–12.

6 Egon Bittner, "The Functions of the Police in Modern Society," reprinted in Peter K. Manning and John Van Maanen, eds., *Policing: A View from the Street* (Santa Monica, CA: Goodyear, 1978), pp. 32–50.

7 Quoted in Klockars, *Idea of Police*, p. 16.

8 George L. Kelling, Tony Pate, Duane Dieckman, and Charles Brown, *The Kansas City Preventive Patrol Experiment* (Washington, DC: Police Foundation, 1974).

9 See evidence summarized in James Q. Wilson, *Thinking About Crime* (New York: Basic Books, 1975), chap. 5; in Samuel Walker, *Sense and Nonsense About Crime: A Policy Guide* (Monterey, CA: Brooks/Cole, 1985), chap. 7.

10 Lawrence W. Sherman, "Police Crackdowns: Initial and Residual Deterrence," in Michael Tonry and Norval Morris, eds., *Crime and Justice: A Review of Research* (Chicago: University of Chicago Press, 1990), pp. 1–48.

11 Ibid. Wilson, *Thinking About Crime*, p. 83.

12 Jan M. Chaiken, Michael W. Lawless, and Keith A. Stevenson, "The Impact of Police Activity on Subway Crime," *Urban Analysis*, vol. 3 (1975), 173–205.

13 Robert J. diGrazia, "Police Leadership: Challenging Old Assumptions," *Washington Post*, November 10, 1976.

14 Walker, *Sense and Nonsense*, p. 113.

15 Susan E. Martin, "Policing Career Criminals: An Examination of an Innovative Crime-Control Program," *Journal of Criminal Law and Criminology*, vol. 77, no. 4 (1986), 1159–1182.

16 Tony Pate and Robert A. Bowers, *Three Approaches to Criminal Apprehension in Kansas City* (Washington, DC: Police Foundation, 1976).

17 Charles Silberman, *Criminal Violence, Criminal Justice* (New York: Random House, 1978), p. 207.

18 I am grateful to Jennifer Hunt (personal communication) for this insight.

19 Mark Baker, *Cops: Their Lives in Their Own Words* (New York: Simon & Schuster, 1985), p. 249.

20 John Boydstun, "San Diego Field Interrogation Report" (Washington, DC: Police Foundation, 1975). James Q. Wilson and Barbara Boland, "The Effect of the Police on Crime," *Law and Society Review*, vol. 12 (1978), 367–390. Lawrence Sherman, "Attacking Crime: Policing and Crime Control," in Michael Tonry and Norval Morris, eds., *Modern Policing* (Chicago: University of Chicago Press, 1992), pp. 159, 230.

21 Federal Bureau of Investigation, *Crime in the United States: The Uniform Crime Reports 1993* (Washington, DC: 1994), pp. 206, 217.

22 Jan Chaiken, Peter Greenwood, and Joan Petersilia, "The Criminal Investigation Process: A Summary Report," *Policy Analysis*, vol. 3, no. 2 (1977), 187–217.

23 UCR, 1993, p. 20.

24 *Felony Arrests: Their Prosecution and Disposition in New York City's Courts* (New York: Vera Institute of Justice, 1977).

25 Donald Black, "Crime as Social Control," *American Sociological Review*, vol. 48, no. 1 (February 1983), 34–45.

26 John Allen, *Assault with a Deadly Weapon: The Autobiography of a Street Criminal*, Diane Hall Kelly and

Philip Heymann, eds. (New York: McGraw-Hill, 1977), p. 38.

27 Silberman, *Criminal Violence*, p. 220.

28 Webster, "Police Task."

29 Chaiken, Greenwood, and Petersilia, "The Criminal Investigation Process."

30 Walker, *Sense and Nonsense*, p. 112.

31 Jim Gomez, "Computerized Mug Shots Help Nab Suspects," *Boston Globe*, August 17, 1987.

32 Chaiken, Greenwood, and Petersilia, "The Criminal Investigation Process."

33 Jerrold K. Footlick, "Police Myths," *Newsweek*, February 6, 1978, p. 71.

34 Data from Louis Harris and Associates reported in Kathleen Maguire, Ann L. Pastore, and Timothy J. Flannegan, eds., *Sourcebook of Criminal Justice Statistics—1992* (Washington, DC: Bureau of Justice Statistics, 1993), pp. 169–170.

35 Eric H. Monkkonen, *Police in Urban America, 1860–1920* (Cambridge, U.K.: Cambridge University Press, 1981), p. 54.

36 Klockars, *Idea of Police*, p. 26.

37 Walter Besant, *London in the Eighteenth Century*, cited in Jonathan Rubinstein, *City Police* (New York: Farrar, Strauss & Giroux, 1973), p. 5.

38 Roger Lane, *Policing the City: Boston 1822–1885* (Cambridge, MA: Harvard University Press, 1967), pp. 10–12.

39 See Peter K. Manning, *Police Work: The Social Organization of Policing* (Cambridge, MA: MIT Press, 1977), p. 44.

40 Rubinstein, *City Police*, pp. 5–7.

41 George Rude, *Paris and London in the Eighteenth Century: Studies in Popular Protest* (New York: Viking, 1973), pp. 31–32, 268–318.

42 Wilbur Miller, *Cops and Bobbies* (Chicago: University of Chicago Press, 1977), p. 4.

43 David Harris Wilson, *A History of England* (New York: Holt, Rinehart & Winston, 1967), p. 629.

44 Klockars, *Idea of Police*.

45 Miller, *Cops and Bobbies*, p. 29. Mark Haller, "Historical Roots of Police Behavior, Chicago 1890–1925," *Law and Society Review*, vol. 10, no. 2 (1976), 303–323.

46 Miller, *Cops and Bobbies*, p. 43.

47 Monkkonen, *Police in Urban America*, pp. 86–128.

48 Roger Lane, "Urban Police and Crime in Nineteenth-century America," in Michael Tonry and Norval Morris, eds., *Modern Policing* (Chicago: University of Chicago Press, 1992), pp. 1–50.

49 Quoted in Haller, "Historical Roots of Police Behavior."

50 Frank Moss, "National Danger from Police Corruption," *North American Review*, vol. 173 (1901), 470–480.

51 National Advisory Commission on Civil Disorders, *Report of the National Advisory Commission on Civil Disorders* (New York: Bantam Books, 1968), pp. 6, 149, et passim.

52 Albert Reiss, Jr., "Police Brutality—Answers to Key Questions," *Trans-action*, vol. 5 (1968), 10–19.

53 Jennifer Hunt, "Police Accounts of Normal Force," *Urban Life*, vol. 13, no. 4 (1985), 315–341.

54 For some graphic examples, see ibid., p. 332; also Baker, *Cops*, pp. 233–236; Rubinstein, *City Police*, p. 183.

55 Reiss, "Police Brutality."

56 Hunt, "Police Accounts of Normal Force," p. 317.

57 Ibid., p. 321. Also Rubinstein, *City Police*, p. 319.

58 Reiss, "Police Brutality." Paul Chevigny, *Police Power: Police Abuses in New York City* (New York: Pantheon, 1969), p. 70.

59 John Van Maanen, "The Asshole," in Peter K. Manning and John Van Maanen, eds., *Policing: A View from the Street* (Santa Monica, CA: Goodyear, 1978), pp. 221–238.

60 Baker, *Cops*, p. 81.

61 William A. Westley, "Violence and the Police," *American Journal of Sociology*, vol. 59 (1953), 34–41. Katherine Jamieson and Timothy

J. Flanagan, eds., *Sourcebook of Criminal Justice Statistics—1988* (Washington, DC: Bureau of Justice Statistics, 1989).

62 Rubinstein, *City Police*, p. 420.

63 Baker, *Cops*, p. 252.

64 Rubinstein, *City Police*, p. 411.

65 *The Knapp Commission Report on Police Corruption* (New York: Braziller, 1972).

66 Ellwyn R. Stoddard, "The Informal 'Code' of Police Deviancy: A Group Approach to Blue-Coat Crime," *Journal of Criminal Law, Criminology and Police Science*, vol. 59 (1968), 201–213.

67 *Knapp Commission Report*.

68 See Peter K. Manning and Lawrence J. Redlinger, "Invitational Edges of Corruption: Some Consequences of Narcotic Law Enforcement," in Peter K. Manning and John Van Maanen, eds., *Policing: A View from the Streets* (Santa Monica, CA: Goodyear, 1978), pp. 147–166.

69 Jerome H. Skolnick, *Justice Without Trial: Law Enforcement in a Democratic Society* (New York: Wiley, 1966).

70 Baker, *Cops*, p. 244.

71 Skolnick, *Justice Without Trial.*

72 Elizabeth Reuss-Ianni, *Two Cultures of Policing* (New Brunswick, NJ: Trans-action Books, 1983), p. 14.

73 Van Maanen, "Working the Street," p. 119.

74 Baker, *Cops*, p. 243.

75 Junius Henri Browne, *The Great Metropolis: A Mirror of New York*, quoted in Miller, *Cops and Bobbies*, p. 43.

76 Peter K. Manning, *Police Work: The Social Organization of Policing* (Cambridge, MA: MIT Press, 1977), pp. 89–126.

77 James Q. Wilson, *Varieties of Police Behavior: The Management of Law and Order in Eight Communities* (New York: Atheneum, 1968), pp. 200–226.

78 Ibid., pp. 140–171.

79 Mark H. Moore and George L. Kelling, "'To Serve and Protect': Learning from Police History," *The Public Interest* no. 70 (1983), 49–65.

80 David R. Johnson, *American Law Enforcement: A History*, excerpted as "The Triumph of Reform: Police Professionalism 1920–1965," in Abraham S. Blumberg and Elaine Niederhoffer, *The Ambivalent Force: Perspectives on the Police*, 3rd ed. (New York: Holt, Rinehart & Winston, 1985), pp. 27–36.

81 Ibid., pp. 172–200.

82 See Chapter Two of this book.

83 Moore and Kelling, "'To Serve and Protect.'"

84 Rubinstein, *City Police*, pp. 129–148.

85 Reuss-Ianni, *Two Cultures*, p. 121.

86 Ibid., p. 100.

87 Stephen D. Matrofski, "Community Policing as Reform: A Cautionary Tale," reprinted in Carl B. Klockars and Stephen D. Mastrofski, eds., *Thinking About Police: Contemporary Readings*, 2nd ed. (New York: McGraw-Hill, 1993), pp. 515–530.

88 George Kelling, "Acquiring a Taste for Order: the Community and Police," *Crime and Delinquency*, vol. 33 (1987), 90–102. James Q. Wilson and George Kelling, "Broken Windows," *The Atlantic Monthly*, March, 1982.

CHAPTER FOURTEEN

1 Jacqueline P. Wiseman, *Stations of the Lost: The Treatment of Skid Row Alcoholics* (Chicago: University of Chicago Press, 1979), p. 47. Also Malcolm M. Feeley, *The Process Is the Punishment: Handling Cases in a Lower Criminal Court* (New York: Russell Sage, 1979), p. 11.

2 Theodore F. T. Plucknett, *A Concise History of the Common Law*, 5th ed. (Boston: Little, Brown, 1956), pp. 116–117.

3 Thomas Weigend, "Criminal Procedure: Comparative Aspects," in Sanford Kadish, ed., *Encyclopedia of Crime and Justice*, vol. 2 (New York: Macmillan, 1983), pp. 537–546.

4 Roger Brown, *Social Psychology: The Second Edition* (New York: Free Press, 1986), p. 282. ("It is even possible to argue that, as a social institution, trial by jury is more diagnostic of the real state of freedom and justice in a nation than is democratic election of political leaders.")

5 Edward Jay Epstein, *Agency of Fear* (New York: Putnam, 1977). pp. 18–19.

6 James Inciardi, *Criminal Justice* (New York: Harcourt Brace Jovanovich, 1987), p. 237.

7 *Weeks* v. *United States*, 232 U.S. 383 (1914).

8 *Prudential Insurance Co.* v. *Cheek*, 259 U.S. 530 (1922), which refused to extend First Amendment protections; *Gitlow* v. *New York*, 268 U.S. 652 (1925); *Near* v. *Minnesota* and *Stromberg* v. *California*; cited in Anthony Lewis, *Gideon's Trumpet* (New York: Vintage Books, 1964), p. 244.

9 *Rochin* v. *California*, 343 U.S. 165 (1952).

10 Lewis, *Gideon's Trumpet*, p. 163.

11 Michael Kent Curtis, *No State Shall Abridge: The Fourteenth Amendment and the Bill of Rights* (Durham, NC: Duke University Press, 1986).

12 "Any legal proceeding ... in furtherance of the general public good which regards and preserves those principles of liberty and justice, must be held to be due process of law." Justice Matthews in *Hurtado*, 110 U.S. 535 (1884).

13 Susan H. Herman, "Crime Control and Civil Liberties," in Joseph F. Sheley, ed., *Criminology: A Contemporary Handbook*, 2nd ed. (Belmont, CA: Wadsworth, 1995), p. 545.

14 *Judicial Review of Police Methods in Law Enforcement: The Problem of Compliance by Police Departments*, 44 Tex. L. Rev. 939, 941 (1966), quoted in ibid.

15 Joe Sexton, "Types of Perjury Common Among Police Officers Are Detailed," *New York Times*, April 23, 1994, p. 27.

16 Barbara Boland, Catherine H. Conly, Paul Mahanna, Lynn Warner, and Ronald Sones, *The Prosecution of Felony Arrests, 1987* (Washington, DC: Abt Associates. Federal Bureau of Investigation, *Crime in the United States: The Uniform Crime Reports, 1987* (Washington, DC: 1988).

17 Sheldon Krantz, Bernard Gilman, Charles G. Benda, Carol Rogoff Hallstrom, and Gail J. Nadworny, *Police Policymaking* (Lexington, MA: Lexington Books, 1979). "Crime Control and Civil Liberties," p. 543.

18 *Massachusetts* v. *Sheppard*, U.S. SupCt 35 CrL 3296 (1984).

19 *Maryland* v. *Garrison*, in the *New York Times*, February 25, 1987, p. B6.

20 *U.S.* v. *Leon* U.S. SupCt 35 CrL 3273 (1984), in the *New York Times*, July 6, 1984, p. B6.

21 Peter Reuter and Mark A. R. Kleiman, "Risks and Prices: An Economic Analysis of Drug Enforcement," in Michael Tonry and Norval Morris, eds., *Crime and Justice: An Annual Review* (Chicago: University of Chicago Press, 1986), pp. 289–340.

22 *Johnson* v. *Zerbst*, 304 U.S. 458 (1938).

23 Quoted in Lewis, *Gideon's Trumpet*, p. 158.

24 Samuel Walker, *Sense and Nonsense About Crime: A Policy Guide*, 2nd ed. (Pacific Grove, CA: Brooks/Cole, 1989), p. 30.

25 Quoted in Lewis, *Gideon's Trumpet*, p. 138.

26 Ibid., p. 133.

27 Boland, Conly, Mahanna, Werner, and Sones, *The Prosecution of Felony Arrests, 1987*.

28 Lynn A. Mather, "Some Determinants of the Method of Case Disposition: Decision-making by Public Defenders in Los Angeles," *Law and Society Review*, vol. 8 (1973), 187–216.

29 Boland, Conly, Mahanna, Werner, and Sones, *The Prosecution of Felony Arrests, 1987*.

30 Ibid.

31 Milton Heumann, *Plea Bargaining* (Chicago: University of Chicago Press, 1978).

32 Barbara Boland and Brian Forst, "Prosecutors Don't Always

Aim to Pleas," *Federal Probation*, vol. 49 (1985), 10–15.

33 Thomas M. Uhlman and N. Darlene Walker, "He Takes Some of My Time; I Take Some of His: An Analysis of Sentencing Patterns in Jury Cases," *Law and Society Review*, vol. 14, no. 2 (1980).

34 Howard Senzel, *Cases* (New York: Viking Press, 1982), p. 66.

35 David Sudnow, "Normal Crimes: Sociological Features of the Penal Code in a Public Defender Office," *Social Problems*, vol. 12 (1965), 255–276.

36 Ibid., p. 245.

37 Heumann, *Plea Bargaining*.

38 Ibid.

39 James W. Meeker and Henry N. Pontell, "Court Caseloads, Plea Bargains, and Criminal Sanctions: The Effects of Section 17 P.C. in California," *Criminology*, vol. 23 (1985), 119–143.

40 Abraham S. Blumberg, "The Practice of Law as a Confidence Game: Organizational Cooptation of a Profession," *Law and Society Review*, vol. 1 (1967), 15–39.

41 Herbert S. Miller, William F. McDonald, and James A. Cramer, *Plea Bargaining in the United States*, National Institute of Law Enforcement and Criminal Justice (Washington, DC: U.S. Government Printing Office, 1978), p. 177.

42 David Harris Willson, *A History of England* (New York: Holt, Rinehart & Winston, 1967), p. 228.

43 *Brown* v. *Mississippi*, 297 U.S. 278 (1936).

44 *Malloy* v. *Hogan*, 378 U.S. 1 (1964).

45 *New York* v. *Quarles*, U.S. SupCt 35 CrL 3135 (1984). *Nix* v. *Williams*, U.S. SupCt 35 CrL 3192 (1984).

46 *Escobedo* v. *Illinois*, 378 U.S. 478 (1964). Alexander B. Smith and Harriet Pollack, *Criminal Justice: An Overview* (New York: Holt, Rinehart & Winston, 1980), pp. 176–177.

47 *Miranda* v. *Arizona*, 384 U.S. 436 (1966).

48 *Brewer* v. *Williams*, 430 U.S. 387 (1977).

49 Michael L. Rubinstein, Stevens H. Clarke, and Teresa J.

White, *Alaska Bans Plea Bargaining* (Washington, DC: U.S. Government Printing Office, 1980). Walker, *Sense and Nonsense*, p. 155.

50 Senzel, *Cases*, pp. 64–66.

CHAPTER FIFTEEN

1 Kathleen Maguire and Ann L. Pastore, eds., *Sourcebook of Criminal Justice Statistics—1993* (Washington, DC: U.S. Department of Justice, 1994).

2 David J. Rothman, *The Discovery of the Asylum: Social Order and Disorder in the New Republic* (Boston: Little, Brown, 1971), p. 81.

3 Alice M. Earle, *Curious Punishments of Bygone Days* (1792); quoted in Graeme Newman, *The Punishment Response* (New York: Lippincott, 1978), p. 118.

4 Ibid.

5 Rothman, *Discovery of the Asylum*, p. 52.

6 Newman, *Punishment Response*, p. 145.

7 Ibid., p. 141.

8 Ibid., p. 114. Kai Erikson, *Wayward Puritans: A Study in the Sociology of Deviance* (New York: Wiley, 1966).

9 Newman, *Punishment Response*, p. 117.

10 Michael Zuckerman, *Peaceable Kingdoms: New England Towns in the Eighteenth Century* (New York: Knopf, 1970).

11 Ray Ginger, *People on the Move: A United States History* (Boston: Allyn & Bacon, 1975).

12 Samuel Walker, *Popular Justice: A History of American Criminal Justice* (New York: Oxford University Press, 1980), p. 113.

13 Rothman, *Discovery of the Asylum*, p. 59.

14 Walker, *Popular Justice*, pp. 32–33.

15 Rothman, *Discovery of the Asylum*, p. 56.

16 Ibid., pp. 53–56. James A. Inciardi, *Criminal Justice*, 2nd

ed. (New York: Harcourt Brace Jovanovich, 1987), p. 529.

17 Rothman, *Discovery of the Asylum*, pp. 82–88.

18 Inciardi, *Criminal Justice*, p. 517.

19 Robert Hughes, *The Fatal Shore* (New York: Knopf, 1987).

20 George Underwood, "Report of the Committee Appointed to Examine the Several State Prisons" (1852); quoted in Rothman, *Discovery of the Asylum*.

21 Zebulon R. Brockway, "The Ideal of a True Prison for a State," in *Transactions of the National Congress on Penitentiary and Reformatory Discipline* (Washington, DC: American Correctional Association, [1870] 1970).

22 *In the Matter of the Charges Preferred Against the Managers of the New York State Reformatory at Elmira*; quoted in David Rothman, *Conscience and Convenience: The Asylum and Its Alternatives in Progressive America* (Boston: Little, Brown, [1894] 1980), p. 36.

23 Ibid., pp. 135–143.

24 *The Harris Survey*, reprinted in Edmund F. McGarrell and Timothy J. Flanagan, eds., *Sourcebook of Criminal Justice Statistics—1984*, U.S. Department of Justice, Bureau of Justice Statistics (Washington, DC: U.S. Government Printing Office, 1985), p. 233.

25 John Wallerstedt, "Returning to Prison," Bureau of Justice Statistics Special Report (Washington, DC: U.S. Government Printing Office, 1984).

26 Robert Martinson, "What Works? Questions and Answers About Prison Reform," *The Public Interest*, no. 35 (1974), 22–54.

27 Robert Martinson, "New Findings, New Views: A Note of Caution Regarding Sentencing Reform," *Hofstra Law Review*, vol. 7 (1979), 244.

28 Gresham Sykes, *The Society of Captives* (Princeton, NJ: Princeton University Press, 1958). John Irwin and Donald Cressey, "Thieves, Convicts, and the

Inmate Culture," *Social Problems*, vol. 10 (1962), 142–155.

29 Gallup poll data, reported in McGarrell and Flanagan, *Sourcebook—1994*.

30 Maguire and Pastore, eds., *Sourcebook—1993*, p. 649.

31 George M. Camp and Camille Graham Camp, *Corrections Yearbook* (South Salem, NY: Criminal Justice Institute, 1993).

32 Don M. Gottfredson, Mark G. Neithercutt, Joan Nuffield, and Vincent O'Leary, *Four Thousand Lifetimes: A Study of Time Served and Parole Outcome* (Hackensack, NJ: National Council on Crime and Delinquency, 1973).

33 Lawrence Greenfeld, "Examining Recidivism," Bureau of Justice Statistics (Washington, DC: U.S. Government Printing Office, 1985).

34 Andrew von Hirsch and Kathleen Hanrahan, *Abolish Parole?* (Washington, DC: U.S. Government Printing Office, 1978).

35 Andrew von Hirsch and Kathleen Hanrahan, *The Question of Parole: Retention, Reform, and Abolition* (Cambridge, MA: Ballinger, 1978).

36 Joan Petersilia and Susan Turner, "Intensive Probation and Parole," in Michael Tonry, ed., *Crime and Justice: A Review of Research*, vol. 17 (Chicago: University of Chicago Press, 1993), pp. 281–335.

CHAPTER SIXTEEN

1 Lawrence Greenfield, "Examining Recidivism," *Bureau of Justice Statistics Special Report* (Washington, DC: U.S. Government Printing Office, 1985).

2 Allen J. Beck and Bernard Shipley, "Recidivism of Young Parolees," *Bureau of Justice Statistics Special Report* (Washington, DC: U.S. Government Printing Office, 1987).

3 For a more complete review of this research, see Philip J. Cook,

"Research in Criminal Deterrence: Laying the Groundwork for the Second Decade," in Norval Morris and Michael Tonry, eds., *Crime and Justice: An Annual Review of Research*, vol. 2 (Chicago: University of Chicago Press, 1980), pp. 211–268.

4 David Greenberg, "The Incapacitative Effects of Imprisonment: Some Estimates," *Law and Society Review*, vol. 9 (1975), 541–580.

5 Lyle Shannon, "Reassessing the Relationship of Adult Criminal Careers to Juvenile Careers: A Summary," *Report for U.S. Department of Justice* (Washington, DC: U.S. Government Printing Office, 1982).

6 Don M. Gottfredson, Mark G. Neithercutt, Joan Nuffield, and Vincent O'Leary, *Four Thousand Lifetimes: A Study of Time Served and Parole Outcome* (Hackensack, NJ: National Council on Crime and Delinquency, 1973).

7 Charles A. Murray and Louis A. Cox, *Beyond Probation: Juvenile Corrections and the Chronic Offender* (Beverly Hills, CA: Sage, 1979).

8 Elliott Currie, *Confronting Crime: An American Challenge* (New York: Pantheon Books, 1985), p. 74.

9 Thorsten Sellin, *The Death Penalty* (Philadelphia: American Law Institute, 1959).

10 *Furman* v. *Georgia* 408 U.S. 238 (1972).

11 Isaac Ehrlich, "The Deterrent Effect of Capital Punishment: A Question of Life and Death," *American Economic Review*, vol. 81, no. 3 (1975), 521–565.

12 Hans Zeisel, "The Deterrent Effect of the Death Penalty: Facts vs. Faith," in Adam Bedau, ed., *The Death Penalty in America* (New York: Oxford University Press, 1982), pp. 116–138. See also Lawrence R. Klein, Brian Forst, and Victor Filatov, "The Deterrent Effect of Capital Punishment: An Assessment of the Estimates," in Alfred Blumstein, Jacqueline Cohen,

and Daniel Nagin, eds., *Deterrence and Incapacitation: Estimating the Effects of Sanctions on Crime Rates* (Washington, DC: National Academy of Sciences, 1978), pp. 336–360.

13 Kenneth L. Avis, *Capital Punishment in Canada: A Time Series Analysis of the Deterrent Hypothesis*, cited in Zeisel, "Deterrent Effect of the Death Penalty," p. 129. J. Walker, "Homicides and the Death Penalty in Australia—1915–1975," *Criminology Australia*, vol. 3, no. 3 (1992), 19–25.

14 U.S. Department of Justice, Bureau of Justice Statistics, *Report to the Nation on Crime and Justice—the Data* (Washington, DC: U.S. Government Printing Office, 1983).

15 George L. Kelling, Tony Pate, Duane Dieckman, and Charles E. Brown, *The Kansas City Preventive Patrol Experiment: A Summary Report* (Washington, DC: Police Foundation, 1974). Richard C. Larson, "What Happened to Patrol Operations in Kansas City? A Review of the Kansas City Preventive Experiment," *Journal of Criminal Justice*, vol. 3 (1975), 267–297.

16 Jan Chaiken, "What's Known About the Deterrent Effects of Police Activities" (Santa Monica, CA: RAND, 1975).

17 James Q. Wilson, *Thinking About Crime* (New York: Basic Books, 1975), p. 96.

18 Cook, "Research in Criminal Deterrence," p. 234. Simon A. Hakim and George F. Rengert, *Crime Spillover* (Beverly Hills, CA: Sage, 1981).

19 Lawrence W. Sherman, "Police Crackdowns: Initial and Residual Deterrence," in Michael Tonry and Norval Morris, eds., *Crime and Justice: A Review of Research* (Chicago: University of Chicago Press, 1990), pp. 1–48.

20 David F. Greenberg and Ronald C. Kessler, "The Effect of Arrests on Crime: A Multivariate Panel Analysis," *Social Forces*, vol. 60, no. 3 (1982), pp. 771–790. Scott H. Decker and Carol W. Kohfeld, "Crimes, Crime

Rates, Arrests, and Arrest Ratios: Implications for Deterrence Theory," *Criminology*, vol. 23, no. 3 (1985), 437–450.

21 Blumstein, Cohen, and Nagin, *Deterrence and Incapacitation*, pp. 42–44.

22 James P. Lynch, "Imprisonment in Four Countries," *Bureau of Justice Statistics Special Report* (Washington, DC: Bureau of Justice Statistics, 1987).

23 Glenn Pierce and William Bowers, *The Impact of the Bartley-Fox Gun Law on Crime in Massachusetts* (Boston: Center for Applied Social Research, Northeastern University, 1979).

24 W. Gordon West, "The Short-term Careers of Serious Thieves," *Canadian Journal of Criminology*, vol. 20, no. 2 (1978), 169–190.

25 Mark Peterson and Harriet Braiker, *Who Commits Crimes: A Survey of Prison Inmates* (Cambridge, MA: Oelschlager, Gunn, and Hain, 1981), p. 113.

26 Ibid.

27 Charles Silberman, *Criminal Violence, Criminal Justice* (New York: Random House, 1978), pp. 75–76.

28 Robert LeJeune, "The Management of a Mugging," *Urban Life*, vol. 6, no. 2 (1977), 123–148.

29 Cook, "Research in Criminal Deterrence," p. 225.

30 Douglas A. Smith and Patrick R. Gartin, "Specifying Specific Deterrence: The Influence of Arrest on Future Criminal Activity," *American Sociological Review*, vol. 54, no. 1 (1989), 94–106.

31 Nicolette Parisi, "A Taste of the Bars," *Journal of Criminal Law and Criminology*, vol. 72, no. 3 (1981), 1109–1123.

32 James A. Finckenauer, *SCARED STRAIGHT! and the Panacea Phenomenon* (Englewood Cliffs, NJ: Prentice-Hall, 1982), pp. 137, 152.

33 Ibid., p. 52.

34 Sherman, "Police Crackdowns."

35 Darrell K. Gilliard and Allen J. Beck, "Prisoners in 1993" (Washington, DC: Bureau of Justice Statistics, 1994).

CHAPTER SEVENTEEN

1 Steve Van Dine, John P. Conrad, and Simon Dinitz, "The Incapacitation of the Chronic Thug," *Journal of Criminal Law and Criminology*, vol. 70, no. 1 (1979), 125–135.

2 Herbert Koppel, "Sentencing Practices in 13 States," *Bureau of Justice Statistics Special Report* (Washington, DC: U.S. Government Printing Office, 1984).

3 Lawrence Greenfeld, "Examining Recidivism," *Bureau of Justice Statistics Special Report* (Washington, DC: U.S. Government Printing Office, 1985).

4 Marvin E. Wolfgang, Robert M. Figlio, and Thorsten Sellin, *Delinquency in a Birth Cohort* (Chicago: University of Chicago Press, 1972).

5 Allan Beck, "Recidivism of Prisoners Released in 1983" (Washington, DC: Bureau of Justice Statistics, 1989).

6 Van Dine, Conrad, and Dinitz, "Incapacitation of the Chronic Thug."

7 Peter W. Greenwood, with Allan Abrahamse, *Selective Incapacitation* (Santa Monica, CA: RAND, 1982).

8 Peter W. Greenwood, "Selective Incapacitation: A Method of Using Our Prisons More Effectively," *NIJ Reports*, no. 183 (1984), 6.

9 Peter W. Greenwood and S. Turner, "Selective Incapacitation Revisited: Why the High-Rate Offenders Are Hard to Predict" (Santa Monica, CA: RAND, 1987).

10 Scott H. Decker and B. Salert, "Predicting the Career Criminal—An Empirical Test of the Greenwood Scale," *Journal of Criminal Law and Criminology*, vol. 77, no. 1 (1986), 215–236.

11 Laura A. Winterfield, "Criminal Careers of Juveniles in New York City" (Washington, DC: U.S. Department of Justice, NIJ Publications, 1986).

12 Darrell K. Gilliard and Allen J. Beck, "Prisoners in 1993" (Washington, DC: Bureau of Justice Statistics, 1944).

13 Philip J. Cook, "The Demand and Supply of Criminal Opportunities," in Michael Tonry and Norval Morris, eds., *Crime and Justice: An Annual Review of Research* (Chicago: University of Chicago Press, 1986), pp. 1–27.

14 Jacqueline Cohen, "Incapacitation as a Strategy for Crime Control: Possibilities and Pitfalls," in Michael Tonry and Norval Morris, eds., *Crime and Justice: An Annual Review of Research*, vol. 5 (1983), 67.

15 Phil Gramm, "Don't Let Judges Set Crooks Free," *New York Times*, July 8, 1993, p. A19.

16 Edwin W. Zedlewski, "Making Confinement Decisions" (Washington, DC: National Institute of Justice, 1987).

17 Katherine Jamieson and Timothy J. Flanagan, eds., *Sourcebook of Criminal Justice Statistics—1988* (Washington, DC: Bureau of Justice Statistics, 1989).

18 Philip J. Romero, "How Incarcerating More Felons Will Benefit California's Economy"; cited in Jerome H. Skolnick, "1994 Presidential Address: What Not to Do About Crime," *Criminology*, vol. 33, no. 1 (1995), 1–15.

19 John J. DiIulio, Jr., "The Value of Prisons," *Wall Street Journal*, May 13, 1992.

20 John J. DiIulio, Jr., "Let 'em Rot," *Wall Street Journal*, January 26, 1994, p. A14. (The title was the work of the *Journal*'s editors, not DiIulio, who in a published letter to the editor vigorously objected to it.)

PHOTO CREDITS